My House Has Two Doors

HAN SUYIN

My House Has Two Doors

*

CHINA
AUTOBIOGRAPHY
HISTORY

JONATHAN CAPE
THIRTY BEDFORD SQUARE
LONDON

First Published 1980
© 1980 by Han Suyin
Jonathan Cape Ltd, 30 Bedford Square, London WC1

British Library Cataloguing in Publication Data
Han Suyin
My house has two doors.
1. China – History – 1949–1979
I. Title
951.05′092′4   DS777.55

ISBN 0–224–01702–0

Printed in Great Britain by Billing & Sons Limited,
Guildford, London and Worcester

CONTENTS

LIST OF ILLUSTRATIONS

Between pages 176 and 177

With Papa

With my sister Marianne

Vincent driving Mrs Gandhi

With Françoise Sagan (*Marc Riboud/Magnum, Paris*)

With the Sultan of Selangor

With President Sukarno

Malcolm MacDonald and Prince Sihanouk

With Prince Sihanouk

Between pages 336 and 337

Yungmei

With Dorothea and Anthony Head

Chairman Mao Tsetung and Premier Chou Enlai
  during the Cultural Revolution

A street scene during the Cultural Revolution

Chou Enlai and Chen Yi with their wives (*Marc
  Riboud/Magnum, Paris*)

Students at work on a commune

With a peasant family in north China

Visiting the Sinkiang nomads with Vincent

Between pages 496 and 497

In the desert: at Tunhuang

With Chou Enlai

With Teng Yingchao, Chou Enlai's wife

Part One
My House Has Two Doors
(1949-1965)

One

December 1948 to September 1950

IN THAT MONTH of grizzled distemper I tossed away the marooning clutch of a career in England, despite the anxious admonitory chorus of friends predicting disaster, and by Christmas of 1948 departed with Yungmei for Hongkong. In my ears still linger their expostulations: 'crazy to cast a child into all this chaos', 'At least leave Yungmei behind', 'There's a revolution, Hongkong may fall at any moment'. But I was ensconced in seeming recklessness; so inwardly certain that it was right to go that outwardly I could afford to look hesitant until the last goodbye.

I could not explain that even if I could not live in the New China that the Revolution would bring forth, phoenix reborn and the sound of its beauteous wings filling the air for me, at the same time I could not bear to stay, for to stay in England would be to renounce China. The New China might be my executioner, but still I had to go, at least to stand on the threshold, and be both reckless and prudent, and survive. In Hongkong I would breathe the dust, smell the shift of air from China; if I did not go I would shrivel, inelastic living mummy; and this not because I was positively unhappy in England – I was not – but precisely because I had lost the faculty of happiness or unhappiness – I wrestled only with a numb mantling which magnified small events into major preoccupations and swallowed all sensation into a coma-like unreality. I longed for the absent forest where the new-born phoenix would sing, and I would hear its wings beat the air.

'I don't want flimsy non-events keeping me awake and that vague pettiness of ease gnawing at my days.' On a viscous grey afternoon of November 1948 I had called on Professor Gordon King. He was Director of the Department of Obstetrics and Gynaecology at the University of Hongkong. Briefly in London for a visit, he had agreed to see me.

The meeting with Gordon King had been arranged by my friends Francis and Cecilia Pan, whom I had known in Chungking,* and who turned up, in that fateful November of 1948, in London. Manchuria was being won by the Red Armies of Mao Tsetung; and while Chiang Kaishek

* See *Birdless Summer*.

proclaimed victory just in sight, he was transferring 400 million dollars' worth of gold to Taiwan. Francis Pan was in the Finance Ministry of the Kuomintang government and in London probably on yet another money-raising mission, but I did not inquire and he did not tell me. We had not met since January 1942 when, carrying Yungmei in a big wool blanket, I had flown over the Himalayas to Calcutta and thence proceeded via the Cape and Trinidad and New York to England, because Pao, my first and Chinese husband, had been promoted Military Attaché to the Chinese Embassy in London.*

Unchanging in their friendship, the Pans had tried to find me as soon as they reached London in October 1948; but the Chinese Embassy did not know my whereabouts; I had dropped all connection with them and my at one time numerous diplomatic friends. 'I reflected,' said Cecilia, miming reflection with one lovely hand to her brow, 'then I thought, "Isobel Cripps must know where she is."'

She did not ask me why I had thus vanished; she guessed that I had locked out that part of my life; out of the person I had become since March 1945, when Pao had left London by train, waving his stick at me in farewell, to return to China, and to die in bitterness upon a battlefield not of his own choosing, killed by his own soldiers; realizing at last that his life had been given to a dictator he now despised, Chiang Kaishek. Shivering in the cold morning, I had gone back to the Royal Free Hospital to start my entrance examination, my new life as a medical student, after having been a member of the Diplomatic Corps.

'Things are a bit unsettled at the moment,' said Francis agreeably. Chiang Kaishek's high officials were moving wealth and families to Hong-kong; the Pans had also rented a house there, 'just in case things get a bit out of hand'. Through the next three decades, Francis and Cecilia would live in Hongkong; Cecilia giving piano lessons and Francis teaching at the University and for a while doing some stockbroking. They would hold, intact, a certain vision of China, even when it became spectral, non-substance. They would not skimp their loyalty or withhold friendship from people such as myself, even when we no longer felt or thought alike. And in their courteous fortitude, they never blamed my headlong explorations, or my discovery of a reality which, in the end, would infuse with validity and hope both the past and the future of China and her people.

'We must wait for the dust to settle,' said Cecilia. We agreed. We sipped tea; theirs was a very luxurious hotel, all felted purple velvet. But we

* Ibid.

preferred to wait for the dust to settle in Hongkong rather than in London. Cecilia sprang to action when I told her I wanted to go back. 'I'll ring up Gordon King; he's here now on a visit; if anyone can fix a job for you in Hongkong, he can.'

I remember the impact of Gordon King's startling blue eyes, shaded by strong eyebrows, his rather disconcerting grin, due to ill-fitting dentures. In those years, Australians were prone to wearing artificial dentures, and Gordon King was Australian. He understood perfectly my need to be near China. 'So many Chinese feel like you ... they can't do without China, but they're also worried about communism, what it might do to them ...' I spoke about Yungmei: 'She is Chinese, she must get the feel of her own country.' 'We'll manage to find you a job in Hongkong,' said Gordon King, clenching his jaw in an encouraging grin.

In those days aeroplanes dawdled; halted at sundown. There was dinner, a stroll, hotel beds and breakfast before the morning take off. We spent agreeable nights in Cairo, Karachi, Calcutta, and stepped down in Bangkok, where I was to stay a week, until the next aeroplane to Hongkong, with John Coast. 'You can't miss Thailand, a most gorgeously civilized country,' John had written. 'Before you immolate yourself in that raging inferno further east, why not have a look at an enchanting country?'

Bangkok then was not today's nightmare of concrete gone amok, of packed raucous streets choking with the exhaust of jammed cars. It was a green and nonchalant huddle of bungalows interspersed with mosaic-dappled temples ringing little bells in the breeze. Banana and palm trees elegantly signalled pathways to entrances, grenadier-bright rows of cannas delineated tranquil mud roads with bullock carts and an occasional car. Rain trees along a magnificent mud avenue flung immense arms between sky and earth, and I have never forgiven the Thais for cutting them down.

Mango and champak trees adorned John's typical Siamese chalet. It was indeed enchanting, except that I had little time for enchantment. But the sun and the warmth worked their wonders; and within three days I had recovered acuity of perception and delight of eye and nose. John and other white men went, clad in pale seersucker, free floating like oil droplets upon water among the golden tranquil Siamese stepping gracefully about them. Here was, apparently, no friction or hostility—John and his friends all commented on it: 'So different from other countries where now they spit at a white man!' Almost, here, they could claim to have become partly melded within what they called 'the soul of Asia', a grandiloquent, subjugating phrase. I went to temples, the flower market, the *klongs*;*

* *Klongs:* water canals webbing part of Bangkok.

John explained South East Asia to me. He had resigned from the Foreign Office to devote himself to Indonesian independence. In November and December of 1948 the Dutch had started a military campaign to retake Indonesia; a return of Western colonial power in military guise in Asia still appeared possible to some Western politicians. It was, however, too late, and John knew it. He was buying guns and flying gold bullion for the Republic of Indonesia and Sukarno, commuting between Manila, Singapore, Djakarta and Bangkok.

In the late afternoon of January 5th, Yungmei and I watched through the aeroplane window our somewhat perilous landing in Hongkong; for the diminutive airport lay in a narrow gorge between cliffs; the aeroplane circled and then thrust itself at the ground. Hongkong was golden islands and cobalt water, and the sky was like an opal above the Nine Dragon Hills of Kowloon. 'Why, it's beautiful, beautiful,' I cried. 'Only in the winter,' said the English businessman who sat next to us. 'It's pretty awful in the summer.' He went on to explain that the Peak was wrapped in fog for a good part of the year, that Chinese New Year was hell because of the firecrackers, 'and all the boys and amahs go away', and to tell me that I must 'sign the book' at Government House as soon as possible.

We came down the gangway and there it was. I said to stolid Yungmei, clutching her small travelling case, 'You're home, Yungmei, almost. Look, everyone here looks like you.'

Francis Pan took us by taxi to Church Guest House, where Cecilia had booked (requisitioned is more apt) 'living space' in a Hongkong awash with the exodus of missionaries and businessmen from China. Church Guest House was a small grey building at mid-level on Hongkong Island; pitched just below the public park, where giant ferns like weird umbrellas dripped gentle seed upon the loiterers. Church Guest House has disappeared; I can no longer find it in the massive array of dinosaurian skyscrapers, the treeless and gardenless canyons crowded with frantic speeding cars like pursuing felines which is Hongkong today.

Already in 1949, Hongkong's metamorphosis into its Manhattan shape had begun; never has a city torn and built itself with such ferocity; nor has it stopped tearing and building throughout these thirty years. Hongkong is always bulldozers and cranes; always higher buildings, now on precarious ground, since the granite ridges of the hillfolds are built up and room must be made for yet taller constructions. Bays are filled to make building space until the sea itself becomes an extension of abode for Hongkong's architectural sprawl.

The first week we shared a room with a forever-knitting English missionary, unemphatic about China. 'It had to be, my dear, the people were just too miserable,' she murmured as she poked and clicked. We then moved to the basement to share a room with Ada Chung, her two children and her wolf-hound, Soossee. Ada was Cantonese, a widow, a Christian, energetic and discreet, hardworking and respectable. Soossee took up more space than the other five of us. We arranged ourselves and our luggage around her. She compelled us to become a courteous community.

Hongkong was a delight; the piercing blue sky; the reflecting, crystal, merry sea we crossed and recrossed by ferry to Kowloon to hear the gurgle and suck of water under the boat and feel the mild, cool wind upon our faces. We went to Cameron Road, where the Pans had their house, on the Kowloon side. I walked the slopes of Victoria Island, up Conduit Road. Poinsettias in pots spread their carmine explosions atop the stone walls which banked old and graceful villas. The ladder streets escalating the slopes, the innumerable tiny shops open day and night, and the food, the food! Everything was bliss of flesh, and Yungmei and I grew fat, almost, in that short respite. I found the Fung Ping Shan library, took a subscription, and started voraciously reading Lu Hsun.* I discovered the Peak, not only as a geographical promontory with a magnificent view of the Bay, but as a token of Hongkong's ladder hierarchy. Here the great merchant-princes — Jardine Matheson and others — lived in lofty summitry. Most of these *taipans*† were Scots, and the eating of haggis on a certain day of the year was the most solemn of Hongkong's functions. An invitation to Jardine's was more fraught with social significance than a 'do' at Government House.

Government House was at mid-level; it had white unobtrusive pillars and looked like a modest wedding cake when seen from the Peak. I signed the visitors' book and was duly asked to lunch.

Alexander Grantham (H.E. in Hongkong's parlance) was very tall; his American wife, diminutive, deaf and charming, wore Shirley Temple curls which never altered. I admired her flawless skin; it never changed either. 'I do hope you'll like it here,' said Alex Grantham. Somehow the Granthams and I got on famously; and from then on I was often — at least four times a year — invited to Government House, and even, later, to H.E.'s box at the races.

* Lu Hsun is the Gorky of China. Controversy raged round his role in the Chinese Revolution during the last ten years and became an issue of which Madame Mao (Chiang Ching) and her clique made much use to seize power. See *The Morning Deluge* and *Wind in the Tower*.
† *Taipans*: name given to the merchants of the East India Company in the nineteenth century.

Alexander Grantham had an eminent gift which he strenuously concealed. He understood history; felt it in his bones. He saw the time in which he lived as I did; in all its impermanence. And so I like to think that his liking for me was part of an extra-sensory, unvoiced recognition. We were both, in our dissimilar ways, pioneers, bridge builders between the old and the new. For him Hongkong, product of British colonialism and Chinese labour and want, would hold one day a special place in a new scheme of things. And he was right.

The blight of colonialism is that it produces in the colonized, when they accept its order, a willing and eager self-stunting of creative passion. This sensation of a lost identity not only pervaded a good many of the Chinese 'upper class' in Hongkong, it also infected the British; who laboriously revived, in order to feel non-alien, the habits of their homeland, and ascribed to the weather their curious indolence in the arts. And how the niceties of social distinction, long in abeyance in England, here survived to redeem the hierarchy and make it feel worthy of itself! How much effort went into the minutiae of a decrepit pomp and how violent and enduring the hostility towards those who disturbed the almost Victorian prudishness of Hongkong society!

In the 1950s, intermarriage between an Englishman (or should I say Scotsman?) and a Chinese girl was regarded with animadversion, certainly in the business houses; where it led to swift demotion. The students of Hongkong University (English-speaking) were educated to be docile and subdued, trained not to think, and to avoid offending 'authority' by word or deed. They became doctors and lawyers, to fit into that wedge of society which their wealth (most of them came from wealthy families) entitled them to occupy, and where money made money.

And yet in that year of 1949, all this was already beginning to change, and the change was due to the change in China; although at first unperceived in Hongkong. Today, Hongkong is no longer the Hongkong of meticulous distinction of race and colour and emolument. It is now an asset for a promising young Englishman not only to speak Chinese but to marry a Chinese girl (of good family, of course). Hongkong University has become bilingual; its professors (many of them Chinese) take their students to China on trips, and come back to make glowing speeches on China, duly reported in the flourishing 'communist' and non-communist newspapers of the Colony. Today there are painters and musicians, sculptors and even writers in Hongkong; many of them Chinese, catering, in Chinese, to an ever-growing appreciative public, but also appreciated by the Westerners living there. Amiably, the Hongkong government cooperates with the People's Republic of China, and rumour has it that Hongkong actually has two H.E.s; the British one (Scots, of course), still functioning in Government House, and an occult, unknown Chinese one, who drops occasional wise hints so that there should not be the slightest disturbance in Hongkong's prowess of prosperity, either now or when the time is ripe for Hongkong's return to China, an event which no longer spells dismay.

In February I began my assistantship in Gordon King's Obstetrics and Gynaecology Department at the Queen Mary Hospital. Gordon's house surgeon, a nice girl called Sophie Bard, a white Russian from Shanghai, was leaving to get married in April, when I would take her place. Meanwhile, I went every day to the Queen Mary, and on Sophie's day off I occupied her room. To my consternation, the first thing I did was to break her lamp by leaving the windows open, forgetting the sudden gusts from the sea which invaded the hospital rooms.

My salary was around 700 Hongkong dollars per month; ample for one person, but a little tight because of Yungmei to feed, to clothe, to put to school. Where would Yungmei stay when I was permanently on call, save for one day a week, at the Queen Mary? Once again Cecilia rescued me: she would house Yungmei, who would share a room with Cecilia's daughter, Shirley. But it would become increasingly difficult for the Pans when their own relatives and friends descended upon them from China, all through the summer of 1949, when the great offensives of the Red armies, begun in April, conquered Nanking and Wuhan and Shanghai so swiftly in fantastic campaigns. Yungmei then boarded at school, St Stephen's, and her upkeep took more than half of my stipend. Nevertheless I managed. I trained myself to eat a solid meal but once, in the evening, and five cents' worth of peanuts at lunch.

At first all went well. I worked hard; I was fervent and eager, although here too was hierarchy. The professors were English, the students Chinese. The upper nurses and matrons were English, the amahs and lower staff were Chinese. I had little to say to the other housemen; they were typically 'Hongkong'; they read only the comics, and only on Sunday. They were very keen to 'get on'; what was happening in China was, for them, unmentionable. They feared 'the Reds' even more than their masters, the British. However, time the devourer has also digested their mediocrity. Since then a good many have changed their views, although in 1949, the fact that I subscribed to the *Takungpao*, the pro-communist daily, led to ostracism by some of my colleagues. But then refugees from China who came here also remained apart from the Hongkong-born. My friends were the 'China Chinese' like the Pans. 'The Hongkong-born are not like us,' Cecilia would say. 'Their minds don't work the same way.'

Again this is no longer true, and even then, I would, in the end, make good friends among real Hongkong women like the almoners, and Ada Chung, and Teresa Kwa. The Hongkong group was resentful and fearful of being pushed aside by people from Shanghai or 'Shanghai more far', that is, north China. Their colonial training enhanced their dread of rivalry. Already, in a few instances, excellent doctors from 'Shanghai more far' had come to Hongkong and had been hired in the hospitals. The British colonial service did not have enough British staff, especially in the lower ranks; such recruitment of Asian personnel was also much cheaper. Within six months students from China would be enrolling at Hongkong University. Within two years some of them would pass examinations and compete for government service with the Hongkong doctors. Within three years a Chinese university would be set up. Along with the refugees, money poured into Hongkong and transformed it from a sleepy port into a massive metropolis of wealth.

I was busy. Operations and ward rounds and outpatients' clinic at Saiyinpun Hospital in downtown Hongkong. But after some weeks of an avalanche of wombs and vaginas, vaginas and wombs, I realized that this was not my vocation. Hysterectomies and more hysterectomies interspersed with ovariotomies were not filling me with enthusiasm. In fact, I craved no more pelvises to dig into, although the obstetrics part, the child's cry as it emerges into life, would always move me. But at the hospital few births were 'normal' cases, except those of the first-class private patients. I began to realize that it takes a special kind of person to like this speciality; and Gordon King was that special person. My talent lay in diagnosis, in smelling out disease; a perception about skin and flesh and what lay within, and this I have kept until now. But I have no deftness of finger and I was slow in operating, and clumsy with a needle. I could detect a faint heart murmur where no one else did; tap a dull tone in a chest when others passed it by; but I could not easily stitch up an ordinary appendectomy; and this awkwardness did not improve with time, although Gordon was extremely patient. And after a while, another assistant, who did not like me, would show me up. 'Forceps ... cut ... tie ...' she would murmur behind her white mask, always a little ahead of my gesture, and she was always right. Who could prevent this upwomanship? She wanted my job. She would get it in the end.

Of course, I also had my small victories; discovering a bleeding uterus, sent in for operation as fibroids, to be a leukaemia; or an ovarian tumour, diagnosed so even by a great white consultant, to be a pregnancy; but the patient was a widow of seven years' standing, and so deeply Confucian were my colleagues, and even my superiors, that they could not imagine that a Chinese widow would become pregnant ...

However, in surgery and gynaecology, a talent for cutting and stitching is needed, and this I did not possess. Gordon was in love with his profession and would rear extremely good gynaecologists, such as the small and wonderful Daphne Chun. Daphne's hands were a marvel; tiny and so able, so nimble! She was quite happy operating all day, and I both envied and resented her enthusiasm, the beam upon her face when yet another belly had to be opened ...

But the main reason why I became unsatisfactory was that I fell in love, into a sargasso churn of emotion, a torrid and absolute passion which, like a Hongkong typhoon, carried all my resolutions before it and left me racked and changed.

By April, Hongkong's dazzling winter had turned to spring, and Stanley Smith surfaced. I had met him in Chungking, so he said, though I do not remember how or where; but he had lived in a house belonging to my Third Uncle. We met at tea at the Gloucester Hotel, and he invited me and Yungmei to his beautiful house on Deep Water Bay. There, on my free days, I could swim with Yungmei, and it did the child a great deal of good.

Stanley was Australian; amassing a fortune from iron ore mines in Malaya. Tall, whipcord tough, with a bulging forehead and a thin mouth, he was a gifted wealth-maker, and his big house contained many valuable trophies. In his drawing room, prominent among other antiques, was a startling Chinese painting of a beggar in all his verminous degradation, extending, with a leer of disquiet and insolence upon his face, a twisted hand cupped in front of him. That hand seemed to thrust into the room, to pick and pluck at my very flesh; I hated it, but Stanley revelled in describing how he had acquired it from a painter in Shanghai 'in the good old days' before the Communist armies had swept all away and made it impossible to have any more such bargains. I felt the beggar explained some obscure yearning in him. 'There, but for my wits and my ruthless energy, go I,' Stanley seemed to say as he gazed upon his painting with singular joy. May, his wife, was Chinese, round and pretty, and we spent many happy hours together sunning on Stanley's beach while Yungmei swam and ran and ate enormously. I revelled in her health, as I did in mine.

Stanley warned me: 'People are saying that you are a communist.' I laughed. 'Of course I'm not, but I'm not against this revolution. I'm for it if it does any good for the Chinese people.' I thought my attitude logical; no one else appeared to think so. Only one attitude was allowed, and that was vehement anti-communism, horror at the revolution in China. Anything else classified one as 'communist'. Already the Special Branch in Hongkong was opening a file on me, entirely based on my emitted opinions. I explained to Stanley my dilemma, which was that of so many Chinese intellectuals. I would wait and see, wait until the dust settled. But inevitably I must go back to China one day. Stanley shook his head and told me I was crazy.

One day in the street I met Kung Peng. She had been my classmate at Yenching University in Peking. And now she had worked for many years under Chou Enlai. I had not seen her since 1941, when on the street in Chungking I had begun to sob because of the massacre by Chiang Kaishek of the New Fourth Army medical teams.* Now here she was, climbing a ladder street while I pelted down it. 'Kung Peng' I cried, and she lifted her head, and recognized me. She was unchanged, beautiful as ever, in a black dress. I talked first, volubly, telling her why I was there. She listened coldly. 'Where are you staying?' she asked. I told her. 'I'll write to you,' said Kung Peng, and walked on. A little perturbed, I went home, but two days later had a letter giving me her address and asking me to come to see her. I was so politically naïve that only with her address did I realize that she was at Hsinhua, the communist news agency, which had a branch in Hongkong. Despite the anti-communist stance and the shouting, the government of the Colony allowed not only communist newspapers and organizations but also leading communists into Hongkong. This was political wisdom and foresight; and it would last urbanely, despite America's pressures on the British government, throughout the next two decades.

Kung Peng and her husband, Chiao Kuanhua, had arrived in Hongkong the year before with the staff of the Hsinhua news agency. The offices of Hsinhua were small and cramped, in a nondescript building in the populous Wanchai district. I sat with Kung Peng and Chiao, drinking tea; I asked them about returning to China and Kung Peng turned to her

* See *Birdless Summer*.

husband. '*If* you want to do so, don't put it off for too long,' said Chiao lightly. When I left them, I was discouraged. I was glad that Kung Peng still spoke to me, but I sensed hesitancy; an aloofness, and I understood it well.

Of course, many hundreds of intellectuals were going back; but few had achieved my strange inconsistencies; managing to marry a Blueshirt, a Tai Lee man, a Chiang Kaishek addict, a general in Chiang's armies who had died in the war, on the wrong side. I knew in my bones, not with my brain, that a revolution starts by 'cleaning up', and in the 'cleaning up' process many people get killed or jailed; and I could not see these tough guerrillas who had slogged it for so many years, and suffered so much, able to understand and accept easily that I was *not* a spy, not a secret agent. Even before the campaign for 'remoulding intellectuals' had begun, I sensed that each and every intellectual would be thoroughly scrutinized. I could not see Kung Peng, with the best will in the world, able to vouch for me, merely because of my protestations of innocence ...

In 1938 I had not hesitated to plunge into the maelstrom of war; but then it was different. No one asked me my political inclinations, and at the time I did not have Yungmei. Now I had Yungmei, and if something happened to me, what would happen to Yungmei?

'I'll finish this year in Hongkong, then I shall see'. So resolved, I went on to live through the spring.

Conduit Road was at mid-level on Victoria Island; lined with those graceful stone houses with deep verandas and high ceilings dating to the early 1920s (alas, all gone today). There, among camelfoot trees and hibiscus, was the house of Dr James Anderson, known as Andy, a successful surgeon. Andy and his wife Sheila were friends of Molly and Terence Millin in London. Terence Millin, himself a famous surgeon and the originator of a new technique for prostate operations, was Irish; Molly and I had met in Regent's Park, where we promenaded our respective children (she had two daughters). We had become excellent friends, and when I left for Hongkong, Molly wrote to Sheila, and now Sheila asked me to dinner.

So in the late pink and gold afternoon, I climbed the winding path up the sloped garden to their porticoed veranda, and was violently greeted by Tattybogle, the Russian greyhound, and Dainty, the Dalmatian. We sat in the living room, and Sheila and I liked each other immediately. There were some guests, and then in came a man with an auburn shock of hair and a Shan bag, not very tall, but who walked like a Siamese cat, with prehensile feet, and he was introduced to me as Ian Morrison of *The Times* (in those days, the word Times was enough to denote the London *Times*, but I committed the gross discourtesy of asking which *Times*!).

I remember still with a catch of heart the topaz shimmer of that bright afternoon dissolving so reluctantly into night, the trees with great swathing movements of immobility gathering the night as we went to dinner. It is now thirty years ago; thirty years since I watched Ian come across the room on soft cat feet, and still my foolish heart leaps at the memory, although content that things should be as they are. Does one ever get cured of memory? How does one bury memory irrevocably? For after that, for a short while in time, but for ever for me, each day was to be sunflower splendour, time no more, and here again it rises, unbearable almost.

We talked, and left when Tattybogle, whose private sofa had been usurped by an agile and vociferous woman, started to bark, signalling the time for departure. Sheila would confirm to me that she had nearly trained him thus to get rid tactfully of her guests. For in Hongkong, as in Malaya, white people tended to cling to each other through the balmy hours of parties, unwilling to return home. Not so the Chinese, who always get up and leave fifteen minutes after the meal is over.

There was a letter from Ian the next day, asking me to dinner on my day off, Wednesday. I hesitated, even went to seek the advice of a friend, Anne Doyle, an American journalist whom I had met in that easy way of meeting people which has always been mine. And so it began.

Words have their nostalgia; their whisper challenges time and death. Words, the wind in motion of living. And that spring and summer words were oasis, marvel and privilege which my ears have not ceased hearing. I then discovered again the birds; the song and the sight of wagtail and laughing thrush, and the chorus of francolin and golden oriole at dawn. We met seldom, but Ian wrote to me, wrote to me, wrote, every day, twice a day, even when we were in the same city, and I grew very distraught for I had not wanted this, I had not wished this disturbance, this frightening potency of trouble. And tenderness. How difficult, how impossible when once it has begun is this strange thing now disfigured with the name of love.

Oh, what is going to happen to me, I cried, watching the moon rock the sea gently in her shining summer arms. It was not until August and four months later that we entered the great country of love and its power, and felt ourselves immortal, transcendent inhabitants of that mirage land where is no time or space. We walked, for a while, in the golden extravagance of a summer which dazzled the sea, and upon us was bestowed the stintless grace of that enormous illusion which moves the world.

And so of course my work began to suffer; delving into pelvises I could not burrow away from the shimmer of each of my body's cells. The heat of summer spread its grey haze upon Hongkong; but our bedlam season unhinged us and I only remember coolness; the breath of the moon rocking the sea; the troubled stolen minutes spent in silence, between two cases, just outside the hospital gates. And now that all this has been resurrected with words, what shall my busy heart do?

In January 1949 I had written from Hongkong to my father in Peking. Peking had been liberated by the Red armies that month. In August came his answer. The miraculous Chinese post office, which had functioned throughout the Sino-Japanese war, forwarded mail across battle lines reckoned unpassable and seldom lost a letter, continued to do so. By that August the waters around Hongkong bristled with ominous grey battleships, American men-of-war and a couple of British ones 'to defend Hongkong from the Red menace', so the newspapers wrote. Meanwhile Hongkong made a great deal of money out of China, out of the refugees. These came out with solid gold, in bars, in ingots, in rings, hidden within their body cavities. The colossal inflation in China (more than a twelve-million multiplication in the last five years) had made almost everyone turn to gold, but the entry of gold into the Colony was 'illegal'. Special plain-clothes police stood at all points of arrival; one of them told me how good he was at detecting gold carried by a woman in her vagina. 'It's the way she walks when it is in.' At night the sky was aglow with the beacons of work crews, building and levelling hills for mansions; a fungoid growth of slums crept upon the granite rock and the Secret Societies of Shanghai, complete with their top bosses, moved in. One of these God-fathers, Tu Yusen, was to die of old age on the Island and be buried with much pomp as a great philanthropist in a prime cemetery of Hongkong.

My father wrote that he had recovered from his illness; that the present government was kind to him and had asked for his co-operation in rebuilding the coalmines. 'I think for the time being you should help your mother and sister; they are now in Chungking with your Third Uncle.' The next week brought a letter from Chungking. It was Tiza's. Twelve pages, fairly incoherent but definitely demanding help.

Tiza had been cheated by her Chinese husband; he had made money as a black marketeer with the Americans, 'yet I had to pay him to get a divorce'. Wherever the Americans went there flourished corruption; miles and miles of barbed wire, cans of all kinds of food, chocolate bars, cheap fountain pens and engine spare parts and nylon stockings and oh, so much clothing, shirts and shoes and jackets, and when they left, they left all the stuff behind and the black marketeers scavenged mightily. Tiza's husband had sold American throwaways and had been arrested by the Communists. Mama and Tiza and Tiza's baby were now in Chungking. 'But we moved out of Third Uncle's house because Mama found it too noisy.' I was to write to her care of the British Consul in Chungking; I was to go to the Hongkong police and sign an affidavit to guarantee her and Mama residence in Hongkong; I was to do all this very quickly, before the Communists came, otherwise all would be lost. I was to send money.

The postscript infuriated me. 'Papa was ill when we left, but he's all right now. I think he had some sort of stroke.' I could see Papa lying in bed, saying in his low, spent voice, a little breathless, 'Don't worry, I'll be all right.' And Mama did not worry, of course not, not for him, but thudded about, hauling her luggage and making last minute recommendations to Papa and to the servant, Hsueh Mah. Mama had left Papa and gone with Tiza. It would always be Tiza ... I wrote back to Tiza that I was in no position to guarantee her stay and that of Mama in Hongkong; I had visions of both of them, and the baby, trying to live on my small salary; of Mama stirring up trouble (how good she was at it) between me and Tiza ...

When the letter had gone, anger subsided and compunction arose. Perhaps I should try to get them out. Perhaps I should sign affidavits. Then came Third Uncle's letter, in his beautiful calligraphy. 'Your mother is healthy. However, the food does not suit her.' This meant that they must leave. Szechuan province was still under Chiang Kaishek, who swore that he would win the ultimate victory or commit suicide. And everyone knew he would do neither, but simply run away. Third Uncle of course did not mention the war, although he too must have known that it was only a matter of a few months, a few weeks, before the People's Liberation Army came in, like a great tide, into Szechuan, into all the hinterland. Nothing could stop the Chinese conquest of China.

In early September I asked Gordon for a week's leave, to go to Szechuan and see my family. He said yes immediately. Off I went, and took with me Cherry, my friend from England. Cherry had now arrived in Hongkong. Although she had called it madness on my part to leave England, she had decided to come and have a look. She had obtained a position at the Queen Mary Hospital, in the Department of Internal Medicine. Being

English, she was paid about three times my stipend, and also had the benefit of a flat, which she shared with another English girl, a physiotherapist.

Ian came to see us off at the airport; the milky dawn had dispersed and rough light mottled the sea. 'I must know it is not only the sun and summer in Hongkong,' I told him. Even then, even in that ecstasy there were other stirrings within me, waiting to be born ... which one of those many mes would be the forever me? And once that fixed star of self-completion was reached, would my bones at last become resigned?

I have described the journey to Chungking;* arrival; the remembered landscape jolting me, bringing me home; the leaden heat, the dirt, the disintegration of everything, the smells, the beauty of the hills, their sinuous disarray and the fuzziness of their slopes across the heat-bleached sky; the sharp rock of the city like a ship's prow riding between the Yangtse River and the Chialing River, and the immense and terrifying misery, and the hope ...

Seven straggly hours by bus to reach Chungking; Third Uncle's house up the cliff of Koloshan just outside the city, and there they were in the light of lamps fitfully dotting the night, Third Aunt all smiles, and my cousins, and Third Uncle, loud and happy and trying not to show his joy, and a bustle of teacups and hot towels and talk, amiable, glad shouts, and always avoidance of even the nuance of impending threat. Cherry and I shared a room, a vast ornate Szechuan bed wrapped in a huge silk mosquito net, and also a large blue ceramic pot thoughtfully placed in a corner and regularly emptied, morning and evening, but maintaining in its rotund depths a permanent odour of excreta.

I went to see Tiza that very night, since the British Consul's residence was just down the pebbled road and belonged to the Meifeng Bank; and Third Uncle was on its Board of Directors. Into the English-style drawing room with its over-stuffed settee came Tiza, holding a candle (electricity had stopped functioning) and I could hear in the bedroom beyond Mama hovering, the faint dry rasp of her hands on the bedsheets, her voice whispering, 'Tiza, the baby is waking up...' She did not come out to meet me. And because of that rustle of hers, the suffocating, acrid tide of childhood resentment rose between Tiza and myself; Mama knew so well how to deal me a shadow blow; simply with a cough and a smoothing of the baby's bedclothes.

* See *A Many-Splendoured Thing*.

It was only when Mama died in 1966 that Tiza and I began to like each other. She then took lessons in square dancing, married again and became a charming, humorous person whose company was a delight.

Tiza had fallen in love with an American officer in the U.S. Marines' contingent sent to help Chiang Kaishek. Tiza had wanted to marry, but suddenly had come the order: 'No fraternization'. The officer had been moved and Tiza was pregnant; she had the baby and was proud of it. 'We'll manage,' she said. And now Tiza thought, 'If the Communists come, they will kill me and my baby.'

I went back and lay in the large bed, and Cherry complained of the smell of our toilet. I told her she would get used to it; 'everyone does in Szechuan'.

The next day I went back to the British Consulate. Like three judges upon the sofa sat Tiza and Mama (holding the baby) and the British Consul, frowning heavily. He was a portly, decent man who immediately upbraided me for my heartlessness in *not* sending a guarantee for my mother and sister to live in Hongkong. I told him that I myself was not secure. 'You are the British Consul, you can get them a guarantee any time you wish. Why don't you do it?' This stopped further argument, and in fact within the next two months he had done what was necessary, and all three would come together to Hongkong. Later Tiza and Mama went to Italy, and then to America in 1956.

When Tiza and Mama arrived in America, they stayed with my other sister, Marianne, who had married an American and had two children. Marianne's husband died suddenly of a heart attack while having breakfast, in June 1956. Marianne was at first overjoyed when Tiza and Mama came to live with her that year. And of course, pretty soon there was trouble, and again it was because of Mama. Poor Marianne, who hungered for love withheld, from Mama! Poor Marianne, whose childhood had been warped by Mama's indifference to her, the last of the brood! Mama and Tiza moved into a small house of their own; Marianne was not invited, and then she cracked. 'If I'm crazy, it all started there, right in Mama's lap,' she cried to me one night over the telephone, from Arizona to Singapore. And yet, despite all this, her two children turned out beautiful, sensible and gifted; both made successful marriages and happy lives, unaided, and both look after Marianne, and so do I, but none of us can give her back the love she never had.

The next few days with the family were happy. And of course the Kangs, the Tengs, and other families related to ours by marriage ties and ties of commerce and banking, all held little dinners, and we enjoyed ourselves as if nothing was to change. I walked about Chungking; I wrote to Papa in Peking. Third Uncle quietly let drop that 'Szechuan is talking', meaning that negotiations were going on for the peaceful takeover by the Communists of the province. When this happened, the streets of Chungking would be a stream of red flags and joy. Third Uncle was staying put, and so were the other families. The Kangs, like ourselves, had younger members who had joined the Communist Party.

One afternoon Third Uncle opened Pao's many suitcases of clothes, so many clothes. 'The person is no more, the clothes remain,' he said, and we distributed them to the servants.

I flew back to Hongkong with Cherry, and the ginger smell of autumn was about. Yungmei was now exactly like her Hongkong schoolmates, chewing gum and reading comics and wanting to go to the cinema and to swim at Repulse Bay. There was a press of patients, and too little sleep for me; I told Ian about Chungking and about Third Uncle, but not about Tiza and Mama. 'It's fascinating. You must write it down,' he said. 'I will, one day,' I replied. And so I would, when I came to write of the love between me and Ian Morrison.

Of that brief autumn, when time and space were a crystal sphere seemingly suspended for ever in a happy heaven, there was so much to remember, remembrance both pain and fearsome pleasure. Ian's talk about himself and about his father; small driblets of his life kept coming up between long silences while we paced the hills or sat on rocks hot with sun, in the company of lizards. How miserable he had been at Winchester, because he was an Australian. How he and his brothers were frightened of their father, a man of great severity, who believed in discipline and toughening, and thought Ian weak.

Dr George Morrison, the famous Morrison of *The Times*, had revelled in his white man's burden; he was, of necessity, an absolute Victorian, but his son was assailed by doubts about the same burden. George Morrison had paced the Chinese earth as if it was an unkempt property of his, treated all natives with a contempt fortified by his unflinching belief in a Divine Purpose (though he was virulently anti-missionary). His dispatches had earned him great fame. But now times had changed, and Ian knew it, and refused to get intemperately emotional over the Chinese Revolution. When a British gunboat, the *Amethyst*, mistaking 1949 for 1909, tried to sail up the Yangtse right in the middle of the civil war between Mao Tsetung and Chiang Kaishek and had been fired upon by the Red Army

(*Fired upon*! Furore in Hongkong; a stampede of correspondents) Ian went swimming with Yungmei and me and said, quoting Molière, '*Mais que diable allait-il faire dans cette galère?*'

Ian gave me his father's book, *An Australian in China*, describing a journey in 1894: 'Simply ... 1,500 miles up the Yangtse River, followed by a quiet though extended excursion of another 1,500 miles along the great overland highway into Burma.' 'The Burma Road before it existed,' said Ian. Under the casual modesty there was such arrogant assertion of George Morrison's capacity, as an Australian, for walkabouts! Perhaps that was his way of getting his own back on the English, who must at first have jeered at his accent. Ian also went on walkabouts. Thus in 1948 he had gone to north-west China and covered well over 1,500 miles, meeting the legendary New Zealander, Rewi Alley, in Kansu province, where Rewi ran co-operatives, and trekking with him. They had gone together to the famous Buddhist grottoes of Tun Huang, explored the caves and seen their extraordinary Buddhist frescoes, dating back to the fifth century A.D., and spent an afternoon at the Crescent Moon Lake, near Tun Huang. Nothing ever tarnished the lake's sapphire; round it the sand humped in hillocks, and broke into musical sound when one trod upon it. 'The singing sands ... *The Times* expected me to report on the civil war in China, but I'm afraid Rewi's conversation entranced me. He really explained to me why the Chinese Revolution was inevitable; and so I came up with something which my newspaper found slightly disappointing.'

Twenty-three years later, in the summer of 1972, I would also go to Tun Huang, on the edge of the Gobi Desert, to see the Buddhist caves. The man who took me round was the great scholar, painter and archaeologist, Professor Tsang. He had spent already more than three decades in Tun Huang, maintaining and restoring the frescoes, and during the first years of the Cultural Revolution in 1966, and until 1968, had had a very hard time preserving them from destruction. 'But Premier Chou Enlai gave orders that all should be preserved.'

After his father's death, Ian had become in his turn correspondent for *The Times*. But he was not made of the same stern stuff as his father. He was in what he called 'a state of permanent confusion'. His not the steel-shine of absolute conviction; for him the world was not simple, divided between the 'Reds' who represented Evil, and Good, which was the Western democracies. He no longer knew, and said so candidly, what role the white man had to play in Asia. 'I doubt that we have any role at all,' he wrote. This befuddlement he bore cheerfully. It was not, however, shared by his Anglo-Saxon colleagues in Hongkong. A very righteous, rabid hate-the-Reds lot, it was fascinating to hear them argue with the French correspondents who, however averse to communism, were not afraid to argue about its merits in Asia. They did not, like the Americans, feel polluted when producing neat intellectual arguments in its favour—this mental exercise, for them, had nothing to do with the practice of anti-communism. But the Americans had to scream, strenuously, of their hatred and horror of communism in order to function against it, and this made conversation with them rather boring—except with one man, a geographer-journalist, Norton Ginsberg.

'How can we ask the peasants of Asia to be anti-communist when communism is the only hope they have for a decent *human* living?' said Ginsberg.

On October 1st, 1949 the People's Republic of China was proclaimed, and Mao Tsetung stood at the Gate of Heavenly Peace of the Forbidden City in Peking, facing the south, the sun, and said, 'The Chinese people have stood up ... no one will insult us again.'

And I was happy, as also were some of my Chinese friends (the almoners, some of the lower nurses at the Queen Mary Hospital, but not, of course, the doctors). I procured in a small, obscure street in Wanchai a beautiful picture of San Mao dancing the Yangko. San Mao—Three Hairs—is the Tintin, the Peanuts of China; his creator, Chang Loping, an artist of talent, is still alive in Shanghai, though he suffered very much during the Cultural Revolution when San Mao was suppressed as 'insulting to the Party'. This poster of San Mao, the cherubic little boy dancing the seed-planting, a folk dance which the Communists had adopted and popularized in Yenan, hung above my desk in my room at the hospital. It would later bring me a good deal of trouble.

In October Ian went back to Singapore. 'There are so many material and mechanical difficulties we have to contend with,' he wrote, 'that more than anything else, our love is comical.' Ah, but how we clung to its hilarious, almost farcical untowardness. Now he had been told that news of his liaison had reached his wife. Like all men, he hated scenes; but there had to be one, and he was away for three weeks, telling me, 'I will not let you go by default.' When he returned it took him six days to tell me that his wife had refused a divorce; no surprise to me. How could Ian ever think that he would get a divorce so easily? 'But I want to marry you,' he said simply.

My only concern was *not* to turn this hitch into a tragedy. And my calm impressed Ian. But then he refused to accept what I kept on saying, that there could not really be for us a future together. In his quiet obduracy he was determined to marry me, to take me away from 'that monstrous god-like structure where you spend your days and nights'. That was the hospital.

Yet it was more than the hospital he would have to wrest me from; it was this vision and hope and unreachable within reach monster phoenix stirring just beyond the hills of Kowloon. Perhaps that was precisely why Ian persisted. 'You are so many women – who are you?' ... 'You are not a demanding woman,' he said, merely because I kept silent. 'I am more demanding than any woman you will ever know,' I replied.

The end of November, and he was off again. On a great walk, to test himself; for he was now afraid of his own emotions, and also there was Christmas and that meant going back to Singapore, to become the other Ian, father and husband, round the Christmas tree ... 'There will be parties, and they are a must.'

During the next eleven weeks he wrote not a single word.

'He's dropped you.' That was Cherry.

'He's got a girlfriend in Vietnam.' News through some fellow correspondents, kindly relayed to me.

Christmas, New Year, and Chinese New Year.* Now I had a small host of Chinese friends. The Chou sisters (three of them) from Peking, with snatches of children; Ada Chung, Miss Ku and Miss Lu, the hospital almoners; the Pans; European and American friends. The Andersons, and among Ian's colleagues the Liebermans (*New York Times*), who threw a large party for Chinese New Year, at which Hank Lieberman wept over China. He had been in China, had interviewed some of the Communist leaders; had been captured by their logic, their reasonableness and charm. 'Those people were friends ... we spoke heart to heart off the record ... now they've betrayed us ... They're dishonest and I can't bear dishonesty,' said Hank, sweating profusely. In what way had the 'Reds' been dishonest, I asked. It was the United States which had suddenly been seized with phobia. Hank, an excellent newsman, responded to America's current anti-Red obsession, which was to blossom with Senator Joseph McCarthy.

Among the Chinese newsmen were Eric Chou and Liu Pengju, both of the newspaper *Takungpao*. Liu Pengju came from Szechuan; he was a lineal descendant of Liu Pei, emperor of the Western Han dynasty and hero of that fabulous tale, 'The Three Kingdoms',† known almost by heart by everyone in China (including the Szechuan coolies, who sang of

---

* The Chinese New Year, or lunar first day of the first month, falls three to five weeks later than January 1st.
† A.D. 220–80.

Liu Pei and the great strategist his adviser, Chuke Liang, as they staggered under their inhuman loads up the steps of Chungking).

Liu Pengju had the oblong face, the widow's peak, the long-lobed ears of Liu Pei; and he wrote marvellous Chinese (he was a poet) as well as excellent English. We called each other cousin.

Pengju understood me well. 'Wait until the dust settles – your case *might* be complicated.' He was steeped in Chinese history.

Eric Chou was a heavily built northerner, witty and unctuous. He had openly declared himself for the People's Republic. He played bridge and mahjong ably, pointedly told me that, with my past, I would have 'complicated problems' should I return to China. I could not quite make him out until, in 1959, he absconded and 'went over' to the Americans. Perhaps he had a good reason; he had been suspected of playing a double game and was jailed in China for around eighteen months and then released. Eric did a great deal to discourage me. 'People in China don't know you except as the wife of a Kuomintang general.' So did a Mrs Poong, who held tremendously emotional 'born again' meetings condemning atheist China (I attended one of them, and was not enlightened). 'They are investigating everyone. Every intellectual. Many are being killed.' The Communist cadres, said Mrs Poong, were guerrillas from the villages; they did not understand city people, they did not understand the intelligentsia. Everything they could not understand they killed.

Perhaps I should mention here the campaign conducted at the time in Hongkong to gather 'Red atrocity stories'. Atrocity stories were concocted in Hongkong. The great shake-ups, which did lead to some true gruesomeness, would come much later, in 1951–2. 'Any atrocities?' was the standard question that newsmen poised at Lowu, the border station on the railway to China, asked of every refugee and Westerner coming out. And an amiable young American had a famous line, used by every reporter when a refugee denied having suffered 'atrocities'. 'You information is incorrect. I have got quite different info from my sources in Taiwan. And these people wouldn't lie to me. They know who I am. They trust me. You have been tortured.'

In February, my year with Gordon King was almost up; I did not wish to renew it, and neither did he. By now my reputation as a 'Red' was all too forcibly brought into prominence; and the poster of San Mao, seen by my colleagues, had a great deal to do with it. But there was also the fact that Yungmei was losing weight and her appetite, always capricious, was now very poor. I must find a job which had fixed hours; which enabled me to have her out of boarding school and with me, where I could give her more time and care.

To make my departure more certain, a very tragic accident occurred; I was called one night at four in the morning by a British government gynaecologist, who asked me to help him in a delivery. I hurried to the operating room to find an appalling situation. The British doctor was reeling about; it was clear that he was drunk; and the woman was dying, with the baby's head still high up, and the doctor had tried forceps. Within two minutes of my arrival the woman was dead. There was nothing to do. The rumour was spread that it was I who had applied the forceps. It was not true. But then the nurse in attendance did not dare to report a British doctor ...

Gordon, I think, believed me. By then he knew how many pinpricks, small sabotages of my work, I had had to endure from some of my 'colleagues'. I got a job in the Department of Pathology, under Professor Hou Paochang; undoubtedly with the help of Gordon King.

This job pleased me. It was from nine to five, and I could now find a room and have Yungmei with me, at least at weekends. I already had friends in the Pathology Department, for with the number of cancer cases in the gynaecology wards, I made frequent trips there. There was Dr Lim from Penang, a gifted young man whose hobby was goldfish and passion was beautiful pathology slides. 'Look,' he would whisper, entranced, allowing me to peer through his microscope at the most fascinating landscape of uterine sarcoma or oat-cell carcinoma of lung, or giant-cell cancer of marrow. These monster cells gone amok were there, irridescent in all their magnificent horror. Lim spent hours and days trying the best of various stains upon them and would shout with happiness when he had discovered a particularly effective dye. He would ring me late at night, to come and see a beautiful slide. 'That was your multiple myeloma woman —look at those cells, A-one, man!' As for Professor Hou Paochang, there was ecstasy upon his face as he plunged his hands into a corpse and palpated an unsuspected cancer: 'Ha ... I've got the bag!' he would say. Bag was his prudish abbreviation of bugger.

Professor Hou Paochang had come from China, which made understanding of our similar hesitancies, dilemmas, and self-questioning immediate, and our relations excellent. He too was waiting for the dust to settle. Educated by missionaries, he was fiercely nationalist, in love with Chinese culture, and deplored its destruction in Hongkong. 'A great and necessary earthquake', he called the Revolution, but he did not exhibit his opinions, being prudent. He had escaped the mindlessness of some of the more praised English-educated Hongkong-born, hovering in the no man's land left to them by colonialism. (However, so many of the Hongkong-born, within the next twenty years, and because of China, were to get out of that state of coma and assume self-assurance and identification with their Chinese roots.) Hou Paochang had seen so much change in so short a time that he needed a space to reflect in, and that was the Pathology Department of Hongkong University. We both hated colonial subjection, but we were also products of this subjection, and in this duality became supple, flexible, knowing our quandary not havoc; since behind us were many centuries of dilemmas surmounted, upheavals lived through; and fortunately neither he nor I were guilt-complex ridden, despite our respective Christian upbringings. We accepted ourselves, tolerating well the perpetual discomfort of being never entirely right, never entirely true, but in our imperfect way entire and flawless in our faith to our only religion, China.

Hou Paochang and I talked by hints and indirectnesses and stray sentences and long silences left suspended in air; and the silences were the most fruitful part of our dialogue. In the end the Chinese Revolution would make us whole; the new world coming so painfully into being would bring us to assimilate our own internal contradictions. We shambled after its comet process through the years, but also took our time. 'When I go back I shall go with clean hands and a clean heart,' said Hou Paochang one day. And he did.

After some failed attempts on my part to get a room, Ada Chung invited me to stay with her; she had a small flat in the university compound, where she looked after a students' dormitory. I was gratefully with her for some weeks; and then Sheila Anderson came to see me. 'We have a guest room,' she told me, and for a minute sum here was a superb room, with breakfast, and Yungmei could stay at weekends. Such tolerance, generosity, astounded me. For in Hongkong this was simply not done. Apartheid flourished and was the normal state of society, and Sheila was kicking in the teeth every white woman in Hongkong by having me (me, a Eurasian, and a woman openly flaunting a liaison with the *Times* correspondent) in her house! 'My dear, aren't you afraid that ... ' said her friends to her, and Sheila, knowing what they meant, would look at the speaker with faint contempt in her soft brown eyes and reply, 'Oh, but Andy and I do enjoy her conversation so much.'

So here we were, in luxury, and Yungmei with me, at least two days a week; and eating better. Professor Hou set me on a study of liver pathology, as well as my keeping all the records of the Pathology Department, and the stipend was a little more than what I had received before, so I could buy Yungmei and myself some new clothes.

Daily I chopped or sliced livers in the morgue, a quiet and businesslike concrete barn with concrete slabs, and there at times would come a young English homosexual much fascinated by death. He would some years later die in a sailors' brawl in Cyprus; but meanwhile he did very good work among the slum children of Hongkong. The livers we examined were very often gorged with flukes. 'The Cantonese eat raw prawns and raw fish,' said Professor Hou, who liked only northern Chinese food, well-cooked. Like a stream of swimmers the grey-brown parasites came lizarding down when we opened gall bladders and bile ducts and Hou would wade in joyfully with gloved hands shouting, 'Ha, ha'. He was looking for possible cancerous or pre-cancerous changes due to the flukes, since liver cancer was also very prevalent in the fluke-infested regions of south China.

Professor Hou took me walking with him during the lunch hour up and down the ladder streets of Hongkong; he hovered round Cat Street, tirelessly going from dim shop to dimmer, peering for old pottery and books and painted scrolls. So much, so much of value and beauty was coming out of China and being sold for almost nothing in Hongkong ... Hou bought and bought. One day he found a small beige pot and exclaimed, 'Shang ware! So even archaeological finds are coming out!' Into the backs of shops redolent with incense, amber and garlic he and I would go; the owners would materialize in the twilight of an inner room, we would sip tea in sumptuous and fragile porcelain; from smooth-running drawers would be extracted rare paintings; out of fragile silk paper deft hands unpacked statuettes and snuff bottles. We would sigh with happy surfeit of eye and heart at the sight of it all. Hou knew the name and story of every famous Chinese painter and their works, way back to the seventh century. Haloed with happiness, and laden, we would go back to the Pathology Department, and me to chopping livers.

From these jaunts I acquired a love and an understanding of Chinese painting, a shiver and gooseflesh when I saw a good piece. Hou communicated to me his passion and a little of his knowledge. The strength of a brush stroke now came to me, as did the quiver of jade when shape was coaxed out of its gathered light. Calligraphy entranced me now, and I understood why, to strengthen wrist and finger, calligraphers plunged their hands in sand and untiringly, back and forth, pushed their fingers through the gravelly substance. Knowing the great hunger within Hou

Paochang for his own country, I was not surprised when, upon his retirement, he took his family and the treasures he had accumulated in Hongkong and went back to China. I met him there in 1963. He was teaching at the Higher Medical Institute in Peking. 'God damn it, they're way behind in slide technique,' he muttered. 'Ah, if only little Lim were here, he'd show them how to prepare slides properly.'

Hou Paochang was given a very fine old-style house in the western district of Peking. Alas, in 1966 the Cultural Revolution started and I did not see Hou again. I heard that his house had been ransacked by some of the more violent Red Guards. I heard ... but through those extraordinary years from 1966 to 1976, when nothing was really what it seemed, one heard so many things later proved to be untrue. I asked to see him, but was not allowed to do so. And then I realized that the time was not a good one for inquiry. Merely a letter of mine, addressed to a friend who had begged me to write to him, had caused his death. I protected many of my friends by ignoring them.

So I burrowed, and waited, and tried to find out without placing in physical danger my friends and my relatives. And it was in 1978 that I was finally able to visit the family of my old friend, Professor Hou Paochang.

I went down the lane in Peking to the same beautiful house in which he had lived in 1963. Mrs Hou was there, and though now eighty-six she was still strong and vibrant, and clasped me in her arms, and told me the whole story. 'At last I can tell you. If you had come a year ago, I would still have been too afraid to tell you anything. Nothing was done to us when the Cultural Revolution began because we were protected by the Prime Minister, Chou Enlai. He tried to protect all the scientists, and he knew there were four eminent pathologists in China, of whom my husband was one.

'But in 1967 Premier Chou was himself being attacked, and it was then that Chiang Ching, that wicked woman, sent a band of the youngsters she controlled to "turn up hidden goods" in my son's wing of our house.'

Like all old-fashioned families, Hou Paochang's three sons, and their wives and children, lived with him in the same large house. His eldest son was a scientist of renown, who had spent many years abroad, in America and England. He was, therefore, an ideal target for attack.

'My husband watched his son's quarters being ransacked, his son hauled away to jail ... he could not understand why all this was happening. And one day he heard that of the other three pathologists he knew, two had committed suicide. His heart gave way and he died of a heart attack.'

The bulk of Hou Paochang's collection was saved, however, by being donated to Peking's national museum. By order of Chou Enlai the museum was closed, and a good many art objects were thus saved.

Another episode; seemingly pointless, but for me fraught with importance: my meeting with Lao Sheh in Hongkong in November 1950. It was Hou Paochang who arranged this. He asked me to dinner, and he also asked Ian. The only other guest was a short man with glasses and a quiet, smooth, clever face. It was Lao Sheh, China's greatest modern writer.

Born in 1897 of a poor Manchu family in Peking, Lao Sheh showed talent early; but his poverty forced him to become a teacher. He studied English, and in 1924 he was teaching Chinese at the School of Oriental Studies in London, which was then run by a Mr J. F. Johnston, who had been the tutor of the ex-Emperor of China, Puyi.

Lao Sheh became acquainted with many English writers, including Arthur Waley, whom he helped in his translations. By 1958 Lao Sheh had written more than 150 plays, short stories and novels, including the famous *Rickshaw Boy*, which was a best-seller in the United States when it was translated.

In 1949 Lao Sheh was travelling and lecturing in the United States. It was then that Chou Enlai, in Peking, sent him a message through his friend, the playwright Tsao Yu, asking him to return to China. And Lao Sheh immediately set sail, and he was now in Hongkong, on his way back to China.

I watched Lao Sheh, entranced. I had read him; his style and wit was of Peking, and he was both funny and tender when he evoked the people of the *hutungs*, the small dust lanes that wind entrail-like through the city. His voice was beautiful, a light tenor, and only a Manchu could handle the Chinese language so elegantly. Such pure Pekinese! Almost I forgot Ian, almost said to Lao Sheh, 'I'll go with you, and all the way I shall listen to your voice, and all my childhood is in the sound of the syllables that cast a spell upon me.' Lao Sheh and Hou Paochang talked of Sung dynasty glazes and the perils of translation from English, and the next day Lao Sheh went back to Peking, by a devious route, via Tokyo.

In Peking he was greatly honoured; and unlike some other writers, who suffered from mental block, he went on being creative and prolific, writing plays, and short stories, and essays, and he was at work on a major novel when he died. I would meet him fairly often, when I went back to China, and he would always say something striking and definite, which would remain, like a vermilion seal, upon the year of our meeting.

'History goes too fast nowadays; it is hard for a writer to have both the solace of distance and the attention of an audience perpetually distracted by new events.' ... 'I know the past well, the present not so well, but I am still teachable ... ' Always there was a tinge of irony within his gravest pronouncements. The grace of faint sarcasm was his; and his face remained unperturbed behind its large myopic lenses as he said things which, in Chinese, were perfectly outrageous.

It was from his wife, a talented painter that, at last, and only in 1978, I would hear the story of how Lao Sheh died. 'But had you come to me before today, I would not have told you. I would not have opened my mouth. Now, I can speak.' She knew how much pain his death had caused me; and how I had expressed, in China, my strong indignation at the manner of his death.

'It was August 23rd, 1966, and the Cultural Revolution was on; and Lao Sheh wanted to participate. He was always taking part in all the political campaigns. So he went to the Ministry of Culture as usual. But that day was the day that the devil-woman Chiang Ching had picked for an assault upon the Ministry, and Lao Sheh and about thirty other writers and Ministry officials* were made to kneel while in front of them were burnt all the embroidered robes and accoutrements of the Peking opera; a mountain of such apparel was burnt. And the hooligans who were burning them also beat the kneeling people, among them my husband.'

It was not true, she said, that the Red Guards had made Lao Sheh wear an old Manchu robe and crawl round and round. Neither had his house been ransacked. 'Other Red Guards, the good ones, protected our house.' But Lao Sheh was beaten so badly that his wife had to go to fetch him home from the Ministry that night. 'I found a trishaw to bring him home, at two in the morning.' The next morning, however, although he was bruised all over, Lao Sheh insisted on going out. Two days later his body was found, in the Taiping lake. 'But I do not believe that he killed himself, though everyone says he did. I believe that he was killed,' said his wife to me. 'And now I am demanding justice.'

If I write this today, it is not to justify myself in not going back. There is no justification for pusillanimity, for a certain art of calculating one's chance of survival. I did not have the courage of Hou Paochang and Lao Sheh; yet I too loved China and its people. But I had suffered too much already in Old China,† from the feudalism, the intolerance which was

---

* In China many writers, painters and artists also hold administrative and political posts. Lao Sheh held about half a dozen such posts.
† See *Birdless Summer*.

also part of that wonderful people, the other face of its tolerance, humanity and greatness. I did not believe that there would not be recurrences of savagery as I had seen – and endured – in the past. Today in China everyone reads Lao Sheh and speaks with sorrow of his death. At least it has served a purpose; never again must shocking things like that happen in China. Never again. This is the cry of all the people, and that is why I have told here what is no secret. But in my spirit there will always be, like a cigarette burn, a small blackness when I think of Lao Sheh; and I shall always remember the way he looked at me in Hongkong, bowed and then turned away, as I stared at his sure and certain back, so eager, so young ...

In early March, with the spring drizzle, came Ian's first letter since late November, and from Saigon. 'My dear, this is to tell you that I love you.' I took the letter with me and climbed the hill and looked at the grey sea with a baleful cloud raining upon it.

'I can never go back to emptiness ... there is nothing but the happiness of loving you.'

Now that I had won, I did not know what to do with this gift of life, and my hands and arms and body were sore from having clasped so long the black stone of solitude.

I went back to the Andersons and sat in the living room, in the invading darkness.

'Why are you sitting in the dark?' asked Sheila, coming in with a happy crowd of dogs, Dainty and the Bassenjee, Lotus of the Nile (Sheila had begun rearing Bassenjees, the first to do so in Hongkong).

'Ian has written. He's coming back.'

'Oh good!' Sheila said emphatically. 'You *must* ask him round as soon as he's here.'

I went out again in the immense night and said to the night the only thing I could say: 'I have survived.'

Spring came with honeyed fingers, cloyed us with sweetness; again the magic of resurrection in that fraudulent and so true marvel, the word, adding weight and colour to unreal substance. Lovely spring, seamed with delight, a dazzle we contrived to think perpetual.

And perhaps the abrupt destruction in that year's end was its final immortality, saving it for ever from disenchantment and corruption. For now, knowing myself slightly better than thirty years ago, I know a weary half-bitterness would inevitably have consumed our passion. I never said we had a future together, only a present.

May was burst of blossom and the swamp of body's juices; the wide sea and the wonder of being so childishly young, Ian at thirty-seven and me at thirty-three. And of course the letters, the letters, twice a day. Never had bird been so bird, nor rose so luminous. Sheathed in clearness, the racing midnight moon cloaked our walks; shifting dawn candled the itinerant seller of beancurd milk with the glance of discovery.

And at the end of May, Ian went back to Singapore, to that Emergency in Malaya which had started in 1948, which was getting worse, which was proof of 'Red aggression' in South East Asia, and was used to justify colonial reoccupation. Hongkong talked panic talk but went on making money and building, building frenziedly. It was not threatened, and knew it.

In May the post of Casualty Officer at the Queen Mary Hospital fell vacant, and I applied for it. Firstly in order to get back to medical work, and secondly because, as I had been told by my almoner friends (how staunchly these anonymous, cheerful, vital and hardworking women of the Social Welfare Department stuck by me), the job came with a government flat attached to it. A flat. Yungmei to be permanently with me ... I applied and was accepted. But alas, I was a woman and therefore not eligible for a flat before completing a probationary period of six months; and if I married I forfeited a permanency and the government pension, and possibly also the flat.

I could not stay with Sheila and Andy; they were leaving Hongkong to retire in Canada. As Casualty Officer, I would have a salary slightly higher than the one I had enjoyed so far, with a regular yearly increase if I went on the 'permanent' list by staying unmarried. I took the job.

June and a Sunday. Balmy weather and Yungmei and I went swimming at Repulse Bay and then had lunch at the Repulse Bay Hotel with Julia and Roy Gabbott. Roy Gabbott was one of my first cases in Casualty. He had come in during the lunch hour while I was munching my luncheon peanuts. 'I've been bitten by a rat,' he said. At the time there was rabies in Hongkong and Roy wondered whether he should have the injections. We had had accidents with anti-rabies injections, notably with a policeman, who after the third injection had become totally paralysed from the neck down. 'Have a peanut,' I said to Roy. 'You won't get rabies.' Julia was Chinese, an able painter, and we got on well. She had by then two children, and a third was expected.

The beach was littered with orange peel and plastic and families arrayed for the usual snapshot fusillade. As we sat at a table overlooking the bay, eating American fried chicken, someone from the next table bent over: 'Korea, they've started shooting. It's war.'

'Oh no, it can't be,' said Roy mildly.

'Oh yes it is, it's the end of the world. Armageddon.'

If there was a war Ian would have to go. He always went. War wouldn't be war without its correspondents writing it up, in fact *creating* the war for their newspapers, its profile and shape and dimension and reasons or unreasons. Within six days Ian's cable came from Singapore: I am going to Korea.

And so to the airport again, to see him emerge with a few of his colleagues, all in a nonchalant bustle of preoccupied people. Ian detached himself from the crowd, looked at me. 'You're smaller than I remembered.' 'I'm an illusion.' Lame. And then on to his small, cheap, Chinese hotel. 'I could wait for you for five years instead of two,' he said. His wife, apparently, had now fixed a limit of two years. As he told me this his face glowed, he was happy, with a set goal, conquest of time. 'The pillows stink,' I replied, sniffing. 'You'd better lie the other way round.' 'But that's where people put their feet,' said Ian, shocked. 'But they change sheets between two lots of people,' I replied, and he found this so funny he could not stop laughing.

Then it was time to go to Al's place (Al was the most important correspondent of a prestigious American newspaper), where a party for newsmen going to Korea the next day was being held; and it had all the lineaments of a heavy State Department briefing but I did not say so, not knowing the words, only the feel of something ponderous and contrived, I was reading the Chinese *Takungpao* newspaper as well as the English paper, and the enormous difference between the two versions of what went on made me understand why the correspondents now elucubrated and hypothesized and surmised and juggled facts like puzzle pieces. There was an exchange of 'hard' and 'soft' facts and unfacts, and Ian said, 'I simply wag my big long funny ears.' Al spoke heavily of the dangers of complacency. We returned and a cloud thick as beancurd came to wrap up the evening and it rained a little, and Ian fell asleep suddenly and inexorably; he had not slept much for a week. And then it was dawn.

Dawn, and I thought of Ronsard: 'In the midst of war, in a century without faith, and among a thousand troubles, is it not great folly to write of love?'

Dawn still star-faint, and the airport, and Ian once again turning to smile his bright, diffident, heartrending smile: 'Take care.'

'You take care. If something happens to you they might turn you into a hero.'

He laughed again and then was gone, and my astonished heart said, 'Well now, that's that. I don't think I'll see him again.'

And for a moment I simply hated him for making me suffer, whether in presence or absence. There would always be a war, I thought, for Ian to go to and me to wait for, and nothing really but this for him, and I would have my paper universe, letters and letters, a verbal crust upon my cake of life.

The prices of gold and rubber soared; fortunes were made. Some wealthy families left Hongkong for Brazil, Canada or California. Taiwan was protected by the American Seventh Fleet; Hongkong harbour bristled with men-of-war, grey in the grey heat, embodiment of heat. Contingents of British Tommies, later to go to Korea, arrived to reinforce the Colony's defences. Women were enrolled to make bandages and to practise first aid. Sheila persuaded me and I learnt to drive a truck.

I dreamt of Ian laughing, it was a bird, and someone said, 'You must cage it', but I could not.

In the evening the sun peacocked and pecked at the windows; I took Yungmei out for swims and walks. Two American senators came to dinner with Sheila and spoke with great dash of throwing atom bombs on Peking. Why on Peking? 'Because it's all coming from there.' 'If Korea goes, the whole of the free world will be under the communist boot.' I winced at the jargon, but shadows grew grim and immensely tall, and I was afraid.

So I filled notebooks with recollections; desultorily, not knowing that one day I would use them. I wrote to Ian in my notebooks since I did not have any address; where would one write: care of Korean War? Would we really have a life together? More than ever, I thought it could not be; but that was unfathomed sea, grievous love; and I would always turn away from tragedy, to watch the lilac evening begin a storm.

Casualty work was exactly what I could do. Though looked down upon by the more snobbish housemen in medicine and surgery (because casualty did not lead to better jobs, it was a dead end), it was for me occasion for my talent in diagnosis. Everything came to Casualty. Rare cases of leprosy, lupus, tetanus, enlarged spleens from long-term malarias, syphilitics, tuberculous meningitis (mostly children, and very common in Hongkong), accidents and suicides, homicides, fishermen blown up by the dynamite they used for fishing, early cancers and late cancers, pneumonias and jaundices and brain abscesses and the insane. A suicide who had swallowed 180 sewing needles came, was operated on, and then convalesced in the Casualty jail (there were four cells in which would-be suicides were placed, since suicide was a crime in Hongkong). I had an advanced leukaemia presenting as a swollen knee; a woman of sixty-five without any fever but with a board-hard stomach; I diagnosed her as peritonitis, and though I was jeered at, she was an aseptic peritonitis. She had swallowed an aspirin which had gone through her stomach and lodged outside her intestines. I had a ruptured oesophagus and several ruptured livers and spleens, and a fulminating cancer of the retina (the patient came in with a story of two days of blurred sight; he died nine days later). Everything uncanny, impossible and fantastic came to Casualty. The dressers of Casualty were seasoned men with tremendous experience. We got on splendidly; they knew far more than many young doctors, and they also knew how to save lives. Lysol swallowing, however, was their bugbear: 'If you wash them out, you never know if you're going through the stomach,' they said, and wielded the stomach pump with extreme care. They were cheerful, devoted and immensely courteous to the patients. They *liked* people; and in Casualty we truly did what we could to get the bad cases accepted in the wards.

Each time I filled a sheet with the results of my examination and with a tentative diagnosis. Casualty also set simple fractures and was empowered to take X-rays in cases of suspected tuberculosis or suspected bone and head injuries. I also had 'waiting' beds, for doubtful cases, but using these was at times difficult. It depended on the houseman or the medical assistant. At the beginning the houseman deliberately challenged my diagnosis and threw people out whom I had sent in. I sent up to Surgery an acute appendicitis, very typical; the assistant in charge sent the man home with a laxative. The patient died that night. I became very angry and rang up the assistant. He complained to the professor of Surgery, who made a rule that there would be no admissions of patients to the Surgery wards unless the Casualty Officer's diagnosis was checked, in Casualty, by his house surgeon. But this measure, intended to humiliate me, filled me with joy; twenty, thirty times a day I would call for the house surgeon to come down to 'diagnose a case for surgery'; and if he did not come down I filled the corridors of the surgical ward with patients 'waiting for the house surgeon'. Within a week, very quietly, that rule was done away with, and from then onwards, and as I proceeded to discover some very nice cases, I was increasingly accepted. Even Cherry came down one day from the heights of her Department of Internal Medicine to tell me, 'That was clever of you, diagnosing that leukaemia ...' Within three months my reputation was as 'a medical officer right on the top of the job'.

The Casualty matron was a splendid woman, Mrs Reynolds, from South Africa. I have never seen anyone less apartheid-minded. She invited the dressers and me to tea at her house, and she was heroically patient with the sick crowding in (up to ninety a day).

In another encounter with some department professor known for his bullying methods (my predecessor had resigned from Casualty because of him) I lost my temper, and seizing my pen, wrote a blistering letter, *in red ink*, to the said professor – and was hauled up in front of the Medical Director (government service), who informed me of my crime. It wasn't having made the correct diagnosis, neither was it writing a letter, it was ... using red ink.

'Don't you realize that in Hongkong red ink is only to be used by His Excellency the Governor?' said he severely.

'Next time I see H.E. I'll ask him why,' I replied.

The Director sat back, and then we both laughed.

Summer blazed into August, and it was very hot; one evening I was asked to a small party. The radio was on, but indistinct, and someone turned it off. 'What was it?' 'Oh, something about Korea,' said the man casually. I had no premonition. But the next morning when I came down to breakfast with Yungmei, and Sheila opened the newspaper, she screamed, 'Oh, Suyin!' I took the paper from her and there was the banner headline saying that Ian had been killed; his jeep had blown up on a land-mine. He and two other newsmen had died immediately.

I went to work. Mrs Reynolds came and put her arm round my shoulders and the dressers were very subdued. And then, after a while, I did not feel well at all; quietly a young Chinese houseman came down and did my work for me that day, and I went home. Mrs Reynolds gave me a brew of something with opium in it; useful, for I had nervous diarrhoea. I walked back across the heat-dimmed upland, along the stone path we had so often walked together, Ian and I, and the sea was glaucous with indifference. I was back at work the next day. And then Ian's letters started coming from Korea. One by one they came, and though I knew him dead, this protracted counterfeit of his presence blunted my perception of his death. How could he be dead when that most vital paper reality, his writing, the words that were his, were there under my hand? For three weeks they kept on coming, one by one, and by the date I knew when it was the last. And when the last had come and I knew there would be no more, I took my typewriter, put a sheet of paper in it, and began to write *A Many-Splendoured Thing*.

Two

Hongkong: September 1950 to February 1952

DURING THE WEEKS and months which followed, while the actual event was still a wound and a blindness, both kindness and cruelty were dealt out to me. Both fed my typewriter; since all I presented to such injury was transient silence, or inept retort, not the significance of precious earth in which my tree of words would grow. Foreign correspondents came back from Korea and took me to lunch, being decent, kind men. And a woman said in a restaurant, 'Too bad some of them won't come back.' Her luminous eyes watched for my wince.

Kindness — heaped and running over or unobtrusive, always healing, came from Sheila, Andy, the Pans, the dressers, the almoners, the Chous; but also from people like Professor Ryde, Chancellor of the University, and Gordon King, who clenched his teeth and came down to Casualty to ask how I was and teetered like a nice clumsy bear and crushed my hand. Cherry came to tell me that she had heard (from her very British friends) that Ian's family had cabled for his body to be disinterred from Korea and sent to Singapore for burial. With the war raging in Korea, this could not be done, and Ian was cremated locally, his ashes then sent southwards.

In my mind an imaginary dialogue: 'Oh, Ian, you so hated aeroplane trips. They could not spare you a posthumous one.'

Ian's reply: 'The Happy Hunting Ground. Your little Ian is in Heaven tonight, wagging his ears and thinking of you.'

'Oh stop it, it's you they're trundling and you know it.' I could not stop laughing. Cherry went away.

Sheila and Andy now left Hongkong for Canada, and in October sold their house, which had been my asylum, blessed home for many months.

Ada Chung surfaced once again and suggested my becoming the living-in matron of a small dormitory for female students of Hongkong University. The girls were all from Malaya; Malaya did not yet have a medical school, and so the Malayan Chinese sent their children to Hongkong to study medicine. No salary, but free residence; the only condition: looking after the moral welfare of the inmates. Ada was pious and a widow, and under the double burden of Confucianism and Christianity she stressed how important it was to see that no male hovered around the dormitory after ten at night.

I was matron until March 1951; the absurdity of my position seemed so evident, yet no one commented openly. As keeper of the girls' morals, I was provided with a long list of forbidding regulations. But from the start I assumed that there was no point in making sure that my twelve girls were *virgines intactae*, for the simple reason that they all came from good, conservative Chinese families; that they had their own very sound sense of self-preservation and a great pride; a shrewd lot, collectively supervising each other. They would make quite sure that until their weddings there would be no gossip about them. They knew only too well what disgrace would attend a moment's faltering. And if by chance there was default, there were quiet and discreet ways of becoming a virgin again ... So what was the use of supervision?

The English matron of the far larger, fatuously luxurious dormitory for women students up the road had a much harder task because she chose to snoop. In addition to the rules which I blissfully ignored, she had a further set of restrictions. She told me how 'rebellious' were her charges, and of the troubles she had.

'How do you keep order, my dear?'

'I treat my students as ladies and they behave as ladies.'

She then reported me to the Chancellor. Ryde asked me to 'drop in', but within minutes we were both laughing.

In February 1951, I became a 'permanent' employee in government service and was allotted, in March, a government flat, to share with another doctor. And as usual hazard, chance – or God – provided me with a sharer in the person of Mary Mostyn, my other friend from the Royal Free Hospital besides Cherry. I had made many entrancing bicycle excursions through the English countryside with Mary; her mother was a Yorkshire woman and fed me most wonderfully. Mary Mostyn, Cherry Heath. Both had decided to come East. I like to think there was, in both of them, a fundamental English romanticism, a spirit of adventure. But I think it was also my being in Hongkong which decided them. Mary had

45

become a Quaker, and was posted to China in 1949. And she had landed, of all places, in my own province of Szechuan, in Chengtu! But she arrived there only four months before Szechuan was liberated by the Communists. In January 1951 she became part of the exodus of missionaries from China. 'Any atrocities?' was the first question she was asked (as were all other missionaries) when they reached Lowu. But Mary had no atrocities to relate; she described to me the liberation of Chengtu, which she had seen. Like a maelstrom with a notch, it started with jubilation in the streets, millions of people streaming forth, and red flags; narrowing down to her filling in forms in order to get out; and being treated very kindly, for Mary had no racism and was liked by her Chinese colleagues at the hospital where she worked.

Mary had of course met Marian Manly during her stay in Chengtu. Marian Manly continued to run her small midwifery school and hospital where I had worked in 1939 and 1940-1. She and Mary had watched together the rice come in in bags from the countryside to feed the starved city after Liberation, the hoarders compelled to unload their stores at fixed prices; the city dirt cleared, the relief and exhilaration of the populace, the excellent behaviour of the People's Liberation Army.

Liberation was, for Mary, a real and solid thing; but not so for Marian Manly. She looked upon it with anger, with frustration, since it had all happened outside Western missionary effort, and dedicated missionaries like her found themselves suddenly aimless, unwanted. Some of the missionaries like Earl Wilmot, who had very quietly conducted seminars for pro-communist sympathizers under the bland title of studying the Bible, rejoiced, even when they knew they would have to leave. But Marian had put her heart into the small hospital, it was her life, she knew no other ...

Marian was irritated by the great noise, day and night, the singing, the marching, the drums, and the dancing and the flags. She saw the people she had helped, because they seemed so incapable of anything but disorder, suddenly orderly, with astonishing capacity for discipline and organization and running things themselves. One morning as she came into her class, there, above her desk, on the wall, hung a large picture of Chairman Mao Tsetung. Had she been wise, she would have realized that this was the way her students, who liked her, were complimenting her, identifying her and her teaching with the Revolution. But she did not understand. 'What is this? We don't want any politics here,' she shouted and tore the picture down.

There was, of course, an uproar. There was a meeting; the students, the midwives, the cook, the amahs and even the patients, all collected to discuss the case, and since Marian refused to put up the picture again, they had to call the public security bureau, newly installed. Marian behaved badly, so she had her hands tied with a rope as she was led to the bureau, where she was incarcerated for nearly a week. She then apologized and was released; and she was given an exit visa.

Mary and Marian reached Hongkong at the same time. I went to see Marian at her hotel; she wept a great deal. 'They're morbid, they're fanatic … it's no longer the China I knew.' I felt she had been treated with fairness, considering the insult she had so thoughtlessly dispensed — but she would not agree.

'Look, what would happen to me if I tore down the American flag in an American school or the picture of Jesus in *your* church?'

'That's quite different,' she said.

'No, they've discovered national dignity through Mao,' I replied.

She stared at me and the tears rolled down. 'I've kept all your letters, all of them,' she said. She could not forget that we had collaborated on *Destination Chungking*; and now she felt that I was far from her. I did not speak to her about *A Many-Splendoured Thing*.

Marian wanted to be a writer, assiduously typing short stories, poems, even beginning a novel. But the simplified ghosts she dealt with were declined by publishers, except for one short story, exceedingly romantic, of which I only remember that the heroine was built like a lotus with crimson lips. But Marian had discovered my talent for writing, and we had laboured together on *Destination Chungking*. In the end it had become almost her book, in that she read it out to people, she had elaborated and softened and embroidered the writing until it became a beautiful veil drawn over events too appalling in their reality and in my first draft. I think she did her best, and the times were not for brash-tongued horrors minutely described; America still expected coy and bashful female writing; coyness being regarded as exotic authenticity.

Marian Manly is still alive, and in America, where I saw her in 1965 when I went on my first lecture tour to talk about China. She still will not accept the Chinese Revolution. 'They are pagans … nothing they do can be any good.'

But history, whether we like it or not, shrugs off the notions of Good and Evil. Only enduring and success count, alas, for history; and good work well done has an immortality of its own.

Today, in 1978, in my province of Szechuan, in the city of Chengtu, the quality of the teaching which went on there, given by American and other missionaries, is recognized. The midwives trained by Marian Manly hold her memory in affection. I would like to say to her, 'You see, Marian, one must wait. And wait. One cannot compel gratitude, but gratitude and love will come. If only one can wait.'

Mary, Yungmei and I moved into the flat, which was luxurious, with three bedrooms and two bathrooms, a living room and a verandah. Mary Mostyn was provided with a job in the Medical Department. Yungmei now went to day school. I typed at night and worked in Casualty by day. We were going towards summer and the season of suicides (summer by drowning, Lysol swallowing in the winter) and of hatchet wielding. August was the month when they reached the year's high; tempers ran short in the heat and the Cantonese took their choppers to each other. I remember one woman brought in almost exsanguinate, her scalp criss-crossed with dozens of gashes; I gave her a drip and stitched frantically, catching spouting arteries, while two dressers close-cropped her long hair. She did well, and complained bitterly that we had disfigured her by scissoring away her tresses.

Writing was now a frenzy; not solace or opiate, but compulsion, insidious mastery of the white page waiting. As the book grew, I could not bear to be away from it. It became a great joke with all my friends. 'Let her get on with it, at least it makes her happy.' Mary Mostyn, to whom I showed a few pages, thought the style clumsy; Cherry was not interested. Someone else called it verbal diarrhoea. I eschewed all parties. Only the Pulitzer Prize winner, Keyes Beech, back from Korea said, 'The lady can write.'

The book was taking shape. I sent a few pages to Jonathan Cape in London. 'If it's no good, just put it in a drawer and forget it.' I got a contract by return mail and a letter from Jonathan, 'If you can keep it up, I think you have a splendid book.' I got piles from too much sitting on a hard chair, and had to be operated on; it was most painful, but I sat up in the hospital bed on a rubber tyre and went on typing ... and then, one night in late July, it was done. The next day I was down with 'flu; I ached all over and I was very feverish. But my body had waited until the word END. I thus got further acquainted with its potential, its capacity for slogging. I was very sick for four days and very miserable; and then I was cured.

During these months of work-glut I was not without other troubles. Yungmei caught a cold, was feverish for some two weeks, and then spat blood. I was frantic. For I always remembered that time in England when she had had a primary tuberculous complex; and though I had been assured that she would get over it, I was now frightened that there was a recurrence and a deepening of that initial tuberculous infection. Dr Hsu, the hospital paediatrician – who happened to have been a classmate of mine at Yenching University in Peking in 1933 – examined Yungmei carefully. Nothing untoward appeared on the X-ray. We put Yungmei to rest and on Rimifon, and for almost a year Yungmei, though going to school half a day, was under his care. He pronounced her clear in September, but I remained on watch, uneasy. I would never be free from anxiety about her health. I kept her as much at rest as possible; and at meals stood over her, pushing food into her. She did not have to walk to school but took a bus from door to door. She was entirely off gym or sports, and she grew well, and put on weight. 'Don't worry,' said Dr Hsu, 'she is well, she will get over it.' But I would have Yungmei examined every six months and I weighed her every fortnight.

'What the child needs is stability.' Thus, with pursed lips, some friends. 'But this is what I am working for, dammit, for Yungmei's stability,' I said.

Regularly, and even red-eyed with lack of sleep, I took her on Saturday afternoons to children's parties; with a round of families whom we now frequented. Yungmei was well-adapted to Hongkong and has kept friends of those days, and still visits them when in Hongkong. But I think one is inclined to feel more responsible and guilt-ridden if things go wrong with an adopted child than with one's own offspring.

I was also worried about my family in China. I had had no news of my father or of Third Uncle since the summer of 1950, the beginning of the Korean war. Scare stories about China were prolific in Hongkong. I met a Mrs Yu, a great friend of a friend; Mrs Yu was from Szechuan and had just escaped to Hongkong, or so I was told. Mrs Yu came to see me one night, greatly agitated, her hair all frizzed and awry, to tell me that Third Uncle was in jail as a counter-revolutionary and would no doubt be executed. She had the news, she said, from her brother, who had a friend who had just escaped from Szechuan. 'And my father?' The corners of her mouth turned down, her hands dropped. Who could tell? 'He must also be in grave danger, I think ... the Communists are killing *all* those who have some property.' She put her hand on her chest, breathing asthmatically with self-induced excitement, and told me of people being beaten to death. When she left (I still remember those short hurrying legs, the buttocks planted so extremely low), I was thoroughly miserable. I wrote to Jonathan to tell him what had happened ...

Reports of purges in China. They were true, and there were purges; the campaign for the suppression of counter-revolutionaries started in December 1950 and it went on through 1951. Certainly nearly a million people must have been either executed or condemned to lifelong jail. There were so many Blueshirts, Kuomintang spies, dope pushers, pimps, bandits, assassins, Secret Society gangsters, black marketeers, heroin dealers ... And then came Land Reform, and gruesome pictures were published in Hongkong of executions of landlords. I was very disturbed, thinking about my family. The Pans were also worried. 'I have a brother in Peking,' said Francis.

Casualty was a haunt of the British police investigating cases of assault, battery and murder. The Casualty doctors had to give evidence in court. This my predecessors shunned, and for good reason. The doctor's evidence was meant to conform to the police's opinion of the malefactor's crime. I remember one particularly burly British police officer who came in one day dragging a dwarfed, shrunken Chinese man with a face like driftwood from the sea, and insisting that the almost skeletal prisoner had aimed a heavy blow at the policeman's private parts. I was so stupefied that I looked at him open-mouthed; he insisted on my inspecting his genitals for evidence of 'contusion'. In court several days later I denied having found any trace of violence. All such cases made my dressers uneasy. On the one hand, to give evidence against another Chinese, and in a foreign court, was not done; if the man charged was a Secret Society man and the doctor's evidence sent him to jail, the doctor would be 'marked down'. On the other hand, not doing what the British police demanded also brought trouble.

It was with a local police officer that Leonard came to Casualty. Leonard Comber was an Assistant Superintendent in the Special Branch in Malaya, on leave in Hongkong. The case brought by his colleague in the Hongkong police was a man with his forehead sliced and an eyelid hanging by just a thread of flesh. I stitched him up; he swore that the wound was due to his inadvertently having fallen out of bed (it was certainly the result of a Secret Society gang fight). Leonard remained when his friend went away with the prisoner, and told me he had just returned from a police course in the United States. The Americans were studying the Emergency in Malaya, and the special methods the British used in preventing the population from helping the jungle guerrillas.

Leonard asked me to dinner at the Peninsula Hotel. He told me about himself. He came from the East End of London. His father was a type-setter; his mother, during the Depression in 1929, had scrubbed floors; they had saved and skimped to give Leonard an education. The war had come and Leonard, while soldiering in India as a non-commissioned officer, had learnt Urdu and Hindi; now he studied Cantonese and was learning Mandarin. He had a great talent for languages, and enormous obstinacy. He had joined the Malayan police after the war because he did not wish to return to England; but he wanted, above all, to study languages, to go to university. He wanted to escape the throttling class distinction from which he must have suffered very acutely in England.

I told him very little. What was there to tell? I felt sympathy for him. He had been hurt by the condition of his birth, had struggled and would fight on. I admired that. What could I say? That for so many years, due to Pao, I had been like one dead, and that Ian had come, and I was now alive, and now I would never die in myself again, never again? I don't think he would have understood that I had remained alone and without a man for so many years, until Ian ... that it had been impossible for me to have sex relations with a man until Ian.

What I did not know then was that this condition of mine, total repugnance for sex, would recur and recur, again and again. Sex would always be impossible unless there was love, a climate of love, a whole world of feeling and tenderness in which the body's act was submerged, necessary and evident. I did not think that Leonard was built that way; for him sex was very definite, a necessity, apart from love. I suppose this is what people call 'normal'.

I listened to Leonard because he did not give me the usual 'we must fight communism' clichés, but spoke intelligently about the Emergency and its injustices. 'We'd really no business to come back to Asia. It will all be over, sooner or later.' His words were flat, but his mind was lucid. 'We promise them independence, then we break our word and try to mess things up so that we have an excuse to stay.' He had seen Partition in India, and its horrors. He was definitely a strong character; everyone, including Mrs Reynolds, liked him. Yungmei liked him very much, and he set out to conquer her. He was at his best, delightful, with children. I think an unplotted, well-meaning conspiracy to make me marry Leonard began then, and among the conspirators I must rank an eminent Jesuit, Father Ladany, of Hongkong.

It was a few days after Ian's death that Father Ladany had come, tall and dignified and admirably versed in Chinese. In an hour the scholar had entranced me. Owner of uncommon intellect, Ladany spoke with eloquence and restraint. He had humour, zest and knowledge. He suggested a Mass for Ian's soul, and I agreed. Sheila and I attended. Through the months of Yungmei's illness, Ladany had come to see her. 'She is a charming girl, but she has no imagination at all,' he said. 'You, on the contrary have too much.' It was pleasant to relax by having an argument or creating one with him.

'Father, I was in my bath and I *think* I've solved the problem of the Assumption.'

'How, my dear Doctor?'

'Oh no, I haven't, there's a snag.'

'Perhaps another bath,' said Father Ladany, pretending to sound hopeful.

With him came Father John Turner, a delightful Irishman, a mystic and poet. I never showed them anything I wrote, neither did they ask to see; they gave me charm, good conversation. They were priests and they only wanted my soul for the Lord God.

When debate on the Fathers of the Church or the mysteries became wearying, there was Father Turner's Irish voice, liquid with poetry. But it was Mary Mostyn who entered the Catholic Church, and then Ladany set out to convert Yungmei. My turn came indirectly. A reconversion; yet it was not entire because of that abstemious demon in me, wary of absolutes, even when I would hunger for the unshaken bliss of perfect belief. But I could put on a good show of trying, not for faith, which I never understood, but for conformity, which I can deal with. And the occasion for exhibiting conformity would be my marriage with Leonard.

Leonard went back to Malaya and wrote to me: could I come to Malaya for a few days? This brought up the matter of my passport, which would expire in January 1952.

I had already worried about its expiry in April 1951. It would have been easy for me to have it renewed. It was a diplomatic passport, and through Francis Pan I could have had renewal by the Kuomintang for another ten years.

But I did not want to go to the Kuomintang. I wanted nothing to do with Chiang Kaishek. Whatever my misgivings about what was happening in China, I was not going back to Chiang Kaishek. And the People's Republic of China did not issue passports — not to people in Hongkong, nor even to Chinese in China. The only way out was to apply for a British Hongkong passport; for which I was eligible, having been more than six years in England and Hongkong. But here my reputation as a 'Red' (that communist dance poster — my heedless talk!) went against me. I was interrogated at Special Branch by a friendly young man, who asked me many questions, to which I replied candidly. I told him I wanted nothing to do with Chiang Kaishek, and he nodded understandingly.

The weeks went by and then one day I went to lunch again with the Granthams, and Alex bent towards me.

'How is your application for a passport getting on?'

'I don't know, I haven't heard.'

'I'll see to it.'

The next thing was that I had tea with Austin Coates, the son of Eriç Coates, who was also a 'government servant' in Hongkong, in charge of the New Territories. Austin was an art connoisseur, a collector of antiques, and would later write some most enjoyable books.

'My dear, you should have seen the files on you!' His hands curved up and down a pyramid of files. 'A Red, a pro-communist, a fellow traveller! The Special Branch was just going to turn you down when they got a little note, a little note, my dear, from H.E. himself! About you. What is happening about Dr Han's naturalization? I would like to see it dealt with quickly ... My dear, Special Branch almost *collapsed* ...' Austin giggled.

I was again called to Special Branch, and was interviewed by a short, competent man radiating reluctant appreciation.

'Tell me, what do you think of the Chinese communist leadership?'

'I think they are honest, I think the people of China want honesty ... I think this revolution had to be ... '

'That is all, thank you.'

I now saw myself stateless, perhaps thrown out of Hongkong, clutching Yungmei (Yungmei by now stateless as well, since she was not yet twelve, and still on my passport) and getting on a boat to nowhere. One such stateless person had commuted for forty-two days on the boat between Hongkong and Macao, denied landing at either end ... Two weeks later I heard that my application had been approved. All due to Alex Grantham's use of red ink.

Now I could go to Malaya for ten days, on a Hongkong travel document, because the passport would not come for some time. 'I'll look after Yungmei' said Mary, so off I went. Whisked through customs, driven to Johore Bahru across the Straits from Singapore to Malaya, I was at once overwhelmed by the intensity, the effulgence of Malaya's plant life; every leaf colossal, succulent; a passion of growth, and no bare rocks anywhere.

I went to Penang and stayed with the parents of one of the girls who had inhabited my dormitory. The Teo family was of the wealthiest; but to preserve his good luck Mr Teo had never moved from the old and rather dilapidated house where he had begun to make money. There was no bathroom, and I had to use chamber pots or piss on the flagstones of the toilet, which slanted to a small runnel. But there were six enormous cars, Mercedes Benz, Rolls-Royce and Cadillac, for the family's use, crowding the front courtyard.

Mrs Teo was absolutely delightful. She had a porcelain complexion because she kept out of the sun, under a parasol; and she had only one hand. The right one had been severed by her Indian cook in a fit of anger as she stood over him and criticized his cooking. He had wielded the hatchet and slammed it down upon her wrist. Mrs Teo was a typical *Nonya*, a felicitous product of centuries of intermarriage between Chinese and Malay; she wore a *sarong kebaya*, and spoke Malay, Chinese Techew dialect and English. Her glazed artificial hand was covered with a white glove. She was always afraid I had not enough to eat; so whenever I came in or went out, two maids in the kitchen served me some delicacy to consume.

Leonard asked me to marry him. I told him that I did not love him. And that I would marry him because everyone said Yungmei needed stability, and because it might work out, but if it did not work out he must let me go.

'Are you still thinking of going to China?' he asked.

'Yes, of course. I'll never give up. But at the moment I might become an error of the Revolution, and there is no point in becoming just a mistake.'

So now I put away those months of love, saffron glory, waking every morning with the taste of hope and joy, sunflower to the sun. Perhaps I felt that I must sober down; in me always contradiction, ambivalence, and of course necessary compromise. How much enchantment can one create? Perhaps it was true I wanted too much ...

The surprising thing was that I did not think of myself as a writer, even though I had written a book and it was being printed. Both Leonard and I were agreed that I would continue as a doctor in Malaya. I think I did not mention my book to him until after we were married; not subterfuge; I simply did not think of it.

Everyone was elated; Father Ladany, Mary and Cherry, and as for my Chinese friends, the Chous and the Pans, they said, 'If you are sure you will be happy, then of course we are happy.'

Cecilia said, 'Leonard is nice but he is not your type. Ian was your type.' I left quickly, not to break down.

In December I began to plan my wedding, and Mrs Reynolds gave me a beautiful piece of white Chinese satin. Father Turner and Father Ladany would officiate at the ceremony. This time I would have a proper Catholic marriage ceremony and I chose the spot, Our Lady of Lourdes at Pokfulum, a small chapel hidden away, and miles from the city. And since I invited the Granthams, the Public Works Department was busy for days building a road to the chapel so that Their Excellencies' car could drive up.

'There'll only be a few friends,' I told everyone. By the time I had finished inviting my few friends I had 150 persons on the list, and another 100 came along anyway. Now everyone was nice to me, and I basked in this solacing popularity.

Father Ladany insisted that I go to confession, to start clean. So I did; and after a few days of trying to pray (rather unsuccessfully) I went to an Italian priest. 'Come on, speak up,' said the priest a bit impatiently. But so much had happened since I last was kneeling in that little grotto of a confessional, way back in Peking when I was twelve or thirteen years old and angry because neither animals nor unbaptized babies were allowed in Paradise. I told him I had had lovers.

'Yes, yes,' he said, bending his ear towards me.

'I also got married.'

'Married in church?'

'No, a Chinese civil ceremony ... it was during the war in China.'

The priest exploded. This was wrong, extremely wrong. How could I marry without the Church? It was a heinous sin.

'Well, I'm getting married again, in Church,' I said and almost added, 'just for the kick of it.'

'You have greatly sinned, so you'll say a whole rosary for penance,' he told me, and muttered absolution.

I rose, and then I knew I was only play-acting, fascinated by the outcome of a few almost theatrical gestures ... but that's life, when one makes things happen.

We were married on February 1st, 1952, at four in the afternoon. I was given away by the Chancellor of the University, Dr Ryde, sprightly and handsome in a marvellous grey suit. Father John Turner officiated but no one heard a word of his; because a Chinese friend who was a singer had volunteered herself and another friend to sing, and they sang so loudly, their voices filling the church, that Father Turner started shouting, but in vain.

Father Ladany stood quietly on one side, looking powerful and benign. The Granthams came, and almost everyone who was anyone; I had arranged a reception at the Hongkong Hotel and I spent all the two thousand dollars which I had saved in the last few months, and had seven dollars left in the world. But two days later Yungmei and Leonard and I were on board ship for Singapore.

On the ship, in that porous sleep pricked by the restless stammer of the sea, I dreamt about Ian for the first time since he had died.

He was alive; he had not died, but he was in a faraway, inaccessible country; a movable Antarctica (distinctly, there was ice, ice that reached inside my chest and fingered my heart); or perhaps it was an unreachable African kingdom with no roads and only high mountains. I did not know how to reach him, and he, he had forgotten me. 'Oh, why then did you pretend to be dead?' I cried at him as an immense emptiness swallowed me whole and I woke sobbing and sore with the bruising inside my chest.

Several times, at intervals of three or four years or so, the dream has recurred. It is always the same and always it hurts because I can never remember that it is a repetition of a dream. I know that whatever I did to exorcise Ian was futile. But did I really try to exorcise him? Through writing a book about him? Was this not too a kind of resurrection, trying to wrest him from the grave in Korea? I do not know the answer to these questions.

One comes to the end of people, to the end of things. There is an end, somewhere. It is when life goes on, opening new doors, new avenues. Even if, in the end, they lead back to that porous sleep which the trains of my childhood, the ships of my youth, sieved with the restless rumour of an onward march.

Three

Malaya: 1952-1954

AT THE END OF MARCH 1952 I knew that I was pregnant and that I was going to have another ectopic rupturing, requiring surgery. That sudden unbearable jab in the belly, that heaviness in the loins, the rhythmic throb above the pubis ... My second Fallopian tube had burst, and it was just as it had been in 1943 in London, when I had been married to Pao and had my first tubal pregnancy.

By that March I had already started working at the Johore Bahru General Hospital. There was a great dearth of doctors because Johore State was reckoned the most dangerous of all the states of Malaya in the number of ambushes and attacks by jungle guerrillas.

Johore Bahru hospital was immense, spread within acres of rather unkempt shrubland. Its mile-long corridors always saw the few doctors and nurses jogging at a fast clip along their emptiness. They all acquired sore feet, and little supervision was possible through the enormous wards, where voices echoed and the light was cathedral dim. Patients sauntered in and out; families brought baskets of spicy foods to typhoid cases. It killed them off, but it was hopeless to try to forestall the relatives. One ward had become, by night, a gambling hall. I acquired seventy-odd beds to look after, in which lay children with diphtheria, meningitis, beriberi and pneumonia, almost side by side. I also cared for an annexe in which on my first day a woman, bright auburn and screaming with cancer of the pancreas, held hands with a snow-pale girl dying of aplastic anaemia.

Besides the wards there were about a hundred cases to see every morning in outpatients, from eight to twelve. No proper examination was possible. Sometimes the dead remained quietly in bed for a long time before their trespass was accidentally noticed by a nurse on the gallop.

Heroic nurses! Chinese, Indian, Eurasian and some European (at the top of course!). All of them with extraordinary devotion. There were no Malay doctors at the hospital; only six Malay doctors (mostly in private practice) in the whole of Malaya. Nursing was not allowed for Malay women. No woman was allowed to 'touch' a man or to be in his proximity; this was *khalwat*, the law of Islam.

57

The Malay patient was also a rarity at the hospital. The ordinary Malay lived in the rural areas, the *kampongs*; he did not come to town; he stuck to the *bomo* (magician); the bulk of our patients were, therefore, Chinese and Indian, with an occasional Malay official. Each doctor was on call one night a week for emergencies; pretty soon two of my colleagues left (one from exhaustion, the other felt he was going crazy) and I was on call two nights a week.

Now my belly clanged its alarm. I rang up Dr Pink, the hospital gynaecologist. It was six in the evening and the sun crumpled its gleaming aluminium foil into the Straits of Johore, and suddenly dusk and the sea breeze were there with cool, enchanted fingers. Dr Pink, bespectacled and enthusiastic, rushed in. 'Lass, how do you know?' 'Second time running. I want you to operate.' Pink blushed with pleasure. Mary Mostyn drove back from Singapore. Mary had come with Leonard and me to Malaya, and obtained a job at SATA, the Singapore Anti-Tuberculosis Association. She lived with us, and went across the Causeway to the city every day. I telephoned Leonard, who rushed back and started making us all tense. We went to the hospital, where a Tamil nurse fragrant with smiles prepared me for operation.

I recovered swiftly, and enjoyed as usual the enhanced perception of convalescence, when all small and daily things become unexpected pleasure, gifts of wonder. In the garden of my days those recoveries are like passing a bush of roses, a swoop of fragrance, sudden delight.

As Assistant Superintendent, Special Branch, Johore, Leonard was assigned the top floor of a rather splendid Spanish-type house. It made me aware of Malaya's chequered history of invasion: the Spaniards and the Portuguese had come here. A village near Malacca sheltered the descendants of the conquistadores, speaking old Spanish, living in abject poverty as fishermen, intermarrying into total decay ... The Chinese had come when their large commercial junks sailed across the Indian Ocean to Africa, to Zanzibar and to Mauritius, trading in rhinoceros horn and elephant tusks, porcelain and silks. The rise of the Spaniards had driven both the Chinese and the Arab merchants from the oceans of Asia; and later the Dutch, the French, the British occupied South East Asia.

Our house had walls of ochre, a red-tiled roof, a patio with a fountain, much gracious ironwork and an enormous living room with hand-painted beams. The windows were large, glassless apertures hewn out of the thick walls, with wooden shutters. On all sides the evening breeze, and at times a storm wind, poured in. The trees of the unhesitant forest advanced upon us in a massive sovereignty of leaf. I never tired of the terrifying ferocity of growth, exacerbation of the living cell, a shout of green in the hum of silence. Jacaranda and banyan and tulip tree, peepul and flame of the forest and so many others, they helped me to recover as I lay reading the history of South East Asia, of the extraordinary old kingdoms, of Singhapura, the Lion City, Singapore. I walked, tasting grass with my feet; hostile, sharp, no velvet sward but an emerald swamp set with a million small vicious spears, and beneath it the bulbous termite mothers, breeding and breeding the white soldier ants that devoured the wood and the books, and reduced houses to a quiet fall of dust.

The Emergency. We lived and breathed it; it penetrated our pores, we chewed it with every mouthful of food. Its formless pervasive threat held gaunt shape in my unquiet mind.

Leonard fed me chicken essence, which came in crates of twelve times twelve jars; gifts, from the local Malayan Chinese shopkeepers, as was the magnificent rattan furniture we had in our living room and sundry other 'gifts'. 'Every Chinese feels insecure; he can become suspect at any time; he placates with proffering ... it's traditional.' Not bribery, of course, just tradition. Special Branch was The Power in the Emergency. Feasts, by the local Malayan Chinese Association members to Special Branch; much jollity (what better way to hide one's fear than under chortling laughter), enormous quantities of brandy-ginger ale and stengahs★ consumed from sundown to four in the morning.

And yet so quickly, behind the back of the *orang puteh*, the white man, bitterness, rancour would surface. 'Emergency ... no British, no reoccupation, no emergency ... ' The 'reoccupation', a word used not only by the Malayan Chinese but also by the Malays. They uttered it nonchalantly; threw it with scarce breath upon the intimate air.

To our house came a stream of people; a small party would mean at least a hundred guests, if not two hundred. Singapore University historians and professors and economists; Malayan Civil Service officials brimming with Brahminic condescension; Chinese scholars, Chinese businessmen; and later students and school children.

I remember such parties, introduction to the land, as a blur of lights, a hum of talk, the gurgle of drink from an enormous punch bowl into which I would keep pouring bottles of gin or brandy, in which floated fresh

★ Stengah: whisky and soda on ice.

pineapple in chunks, and mangosteens and rambutan. And the talk, so much of it sieved, sifted, discarded, search for the bright nugget, a sudden illumination.

Parties. With the University of Singapore élite; the professors, the lecturers; British expatriates, and some with great talent. Echoes of England, and good music, the classics streaming out incongruously under the jacaranda, and Chinese ayahs distributing plates of cold cuts and salad, and the perfume of frangipani which went unheeded among the talk of new books and shows in London; and then all of a sudden of course the Emergency, and raised voices and arguments, and bad temper almost surfacing until talk turned to Siamese cats and their ways ...

Parties. With Special Branch. Much bonhomie, and here there was fried rice and other dishes dubbed Malayan (in reality Chinese), and oh, how smoothly the liquor flowed, and how efficient once again the services of those silent white-clad ones, the Chinese servants (and many of them the ears of the jungle, perhaps). And here again the Emergency, a theme repeated strenuously, unendingly, the speakers wishing to convince themselves, almost, or perhaps they were convinced and this was their effort at converting me? 'The Malay is a good chap ... he's happy and loyal, and he's satisfied with what he's got ... the Chinese ... they're untrustworthy and treacherous ... ' Round these words glided the Chinese servants. Special Branch was there, was necessary, to protect the good people against the bad ones, to stop South East Asia being overrun by communism. It was so simple.

Somerset Maugham nights, sensuous, velvet, tropical, with that small stir of darkness and silence; and the human voices, pathetic for all their assertiveness. And lurking in the darkness beyond the gardens the Malay police, on guard, watching, lest the silence turn suddenly into dangerous ambush and the liquor into blood.

In those years in Malaya I was to learn all the Malayas, the British, the Chinese and the Malay, and this through the Emergency. I read, and I travelled, and above all I met people. People, people, a never-ending procession of people. I went up to Kuala Lumpur, the capital of Malaya, to see the man whose reputation in South East Asia then equalled that of General MacArthur before President Truman fired him. General Gerald Templar was a professional military man, doing a job in the only way he knew; and of course for him the Emergency had to be simply the Goodies versus the Baddies; but he knew better, knew that the social order must change, and said so.

I went down to Malacca to visit the *Baba* Chinese, for here the Chinese had established themselves since the fifteenth century, and had inter-married with the Malays. I saw the venerable Tan Chenlock, older states-man, descendant of many generations of Chinese settled in Malaya; who spoke Malay and no Chinese but was proud of his Chinese ancestry and kept his old and lovely house filled with Ming furniture and priceless porcelain. I heard his mellow bitterness regarding the 'reoccupation by the British' and the unfairness of what was now being done to the Chinese in Malaya.

I went down to the Malay *kampongs* to visit Hajji Ma,* a Chinese Muslim. 'The only way is intermarriage,' he said. I would sally forth whenever I could along the tarmac roads which gashed the broccoli jungles. Large cars with protruding guns would whizz by, for it was considered unsafe to dawdle; and no rubber planter or Special Branch officer went at less than seventy miles per hour.

It was the Japanese conquest of Malaya in 1942 which spurred national independence. The white man's myth of invincibility was shattered by the Japanese victories.

The Japanese favoured the Malays, recruiting them for police and militia work in order to suppress the restive Chinese population of Malaya and of Singapore. The Malay sultans, the aristocracy, and the Malay bureaucracy, which had been created in the 1930s by the British, col-laborated with the Japanese. It was the Chinese who formed the battalions and fought rearguard actions and died while the British made a getaway from Singapore; who would organize jungle guerrillas and jungle bases, swooping on Japanese garrisons, ambushing convoys.† A Malayan People's Liberation Army, which was communist-inspired (as were many groups of resistance both in Asia and Europe during the Second World War), was created; the bulk of its members were Chinese, although there were some Malays and Indians and Eurasians among them. When Japan was defeated the contingents of this army paraded in Singapore's victory march, and their leader, Chen Ping, received the O.B.E. in 1945.

But the British military administration which took over in 1946 at the end of the war had orders to restore the colonial status quo, albeit in another form. 'They did a great deal to wipe out the first enthusiasm with which they were greeted,' a historian commented. It was inevitable that

---

* *Hajji*: honorific title in Arabic denoting a man who has made the pilgrimage to Mecca.
† Spencer Chapman's splendid book, *The Jungle is Neutral* (Chatto and Windus, London, 1949) details the courage and heroism of the jungle guerrillas.

the returning British should do precisely what the Japanese had done: lean heavily on the Malay police and militia trained by the Japanese. Former jungle guerrilla leaders were systematically arrested and jailed.

A scheme called Malayan Union, which would have resulted in direct rule by the British, failed when massive demonstrations by the Malays took place, showing very clearly their desire for independence. Another scheme was now set up which was unfair to the Chinese element of the population, for by 1947 the West feared that not only China but also Indonesia and other South East Asian ex-colonies would become communist or communist-influenced. The spectre of a Red China utilizing the Chinese in South East Asia as its advance guard for conquest was the catalyst in the creation of this new plan.

The scheme was based on two assumptions; the first that the Malays were the true 'sons of the soil' whereas the Chinese were 'outsiders'. The second was that in order to counterbalance the economic power of the Chinese, legal power must be given to the Malays; in other words, the administrative posts throughout Malaya would be reserved to Malays.

This caused great protest from the Chinese in Malaya; the Malays had come into Malaya — as they themselves averred — around the eleventh century, from Yunnan province in China; and the Chinese had made their first settlements three centuries later. But the bulk of the Chinese had come in the nineteenth and early twentieth centuries, with the development of tin and rubber in Malaya. They had become workers, rubber tappers and traders. Some of them had indeed accumulated vast wealth, but the majority remained smallholders, shopkeepers, repair-shop owners and small manufacturers. As for the Malays, apart from the aristocracy, the bulk of the population were farmers in the *kampongs*, their rice production at a primitive level.

According to the 'sons of the soil' theory, citizenship would be automatically granted to the Malay in a new Federation of Malaya, whereas this would not be automatic for the Chinese. Yet around 20 per cent of the Malays in Malaya had come from Indonesia or other Islamic or Arab countries within the last three decades, and were not born in Malaya. Thus the citizenship criteria became appurtenance to Islam and to the Malay culture rather than strictly the 'sons of the soil' theory. But, ran the argument, the Malay had 'no other home', whereas for the Chinese, their spiritual home would remain China. The counter-argument was: How do you want the Chinese to become loyal citizens of Malaya when you start by racially discriminating against them?

According to the citizenship regulations now drawn up, the Chinese could not become citizens unless they could give proof that both their parents were born in Malaya, that they were of 'good character' and intended to reside permanently in Malaya. In addition, they must have an adequate knowledge of Malay. No such adequate knowledge was asked of any British resident in Malaya, who acquired Malayan citizenship easily, and was even able to hold two passports, one British, the other Malayan, for a considerable time.

By 1950 the population composition of Malaya, together with Singapore, was 41 per cent Malays, 44 per cent Chinese, and 15 per cent Indians, Eurasians and others.

Without Singapore—with its almost 80 per cent Chinese—the percentages were 45 per cent Malays, 38 per cent Chinese, and 17 per cent 'others'. English administrators calculated loudly the results of such rigged citizenship. Of the one and a half million Chinese in Malaya, about 375,000 would be automatically eligible for citizenship were the rules stringently enforced; the others would have to show proof before being granted citizenship, and a good many would become suddenly stateless; in danger of being thrown out or placed in concentration camps, behind barbed wire.

The effectiveness of this scheme for debarring the Chinese from citizenship is all the more remarkable when one recollects that no identity cards had existed in colonial days; and that many of the Chinese in Malaya had mothers born in China. By custom the Chinese continued right up to the Japanese invasion of 1941 to send for brides from China, for until the mid-1930s, the British colonial policy admitted very few Chinese women to Malaya; only man-labour was wanted. Hence few Chinese could prove that both their parents were born in Malaya.

'If we left, there would be a bloodbath,' said the British. There had been racial clashes, in 1945 and 1946; in 1948, the Malayan Communist Party committed the grievous crime of executing some police officers in reprisal for mopping-up operations practised by the now British-led, erstwhile Japanese-trained Malay police, against former guerrilla leaders. And so the Emergency began. It would justify the suspending of all rights, giving the police (Special Branch) total power to arrest, search, detain anyone without trial and indefinitely, to disband all trade unions, arrest trade unionists, ban demonstrations, mete out the death sentence for 'possession of dangerous weapons', which included school penknives, to apply censorship in all its forms, to impose curfews, to shoot suspects on sight.

The division between the races was increased by the Emergency, becoming almost total through the 'resettlement of Chinese squatters', known as the Briggs Plan. This purported to remove Chinese 'squatters' (which meant smallholders cultivating vegetable plots and rearing pigs) from certain areas so that neither food nor recruits would be accessible to the guerrillas who had returned to the jungle. Whole villages, in some cases villages established for a century or more, in which Malays and Chinese had lived peacefully together, were now sundered, the Chinese taken away and put in 'new villages' behind barbed wire. Over half a million people were thus removed from their fields, market gardens and the vicinity of small towns.

I started my knowledge of Malaya with rubber. A pullulation of rubber; all the roads lined with rubber trees, a landscape of broccoli monotony displacing the jungle, soaked in perpetual shadow, buzzing with stinging insects, all the way up Malaya, rubber trees. There was a boom in rubber owing to the Korean war. Rubber was a big dollar earner, and this paid for the Emergency. With Chinese farmers removed from their fields and market gardens, the cost of food and meat had shot up; but the income from rubber allowed for purchasing food from outside. Luckily the trade unions were not operative and rubber tappers could not protest at their wages.

I visited the Dunlop Rubber Estates. The manager was personable and articulate, with a charming wife. They made me warmly welcome. I do not subscribe to stories of whisky-swilling rubber planters; most of them are sober, able, hardworking, and stengahs at sundown is an important ceremony, solemn like saluting the flag. The Dunlop manager did not conceal the fact that the whole point of the Emergency was 'to keep our vested interests in Malaya'. Independence would be handed to those who would protect and guarantee those interests. I watched the rubber tappers, stray ghosts and silent in the milky jungle of trees as they went from trunk to trunk, slicing the bark with their curved knives, and latex, the white blood, dripped into the tin cups.

Dunlop Estates built neat huts (behind barbed wire, to protect their tappers). They showed me a nursery for toddlers: an edentulous Tamil woman surrounded by about twenty small children sitting under a tree. 'The weather does not bother them; they're used to it.' There was even a small clinic, visited once a fortnight by a government nurse. Eighty per cent of the rubber tappers were Chinese, twenty per cent Tamil (southern) Indian. 'The Malay is lazy ... when he's been paid he just disappears until he's spent his money ... The Chinese are the best workers ...' The

Rubber Institute issued a pamphlet; with more efficient planting, double the latex could be produced, and the years needed for the maturing of rubber trees could also be shortened. Rubber was King, was Romance, was Wealth.

Dunlop was a good firm, thorough and treating the tappers well. Though there were patrols of Malay police, they were not allowed to ill-treat and to rob the rubber tappers, as happened in other plantations I saw, where the tappers' huts were appalling; where there was no clean water to drink.

I stayed for a short time with a Chinese rubber tapper, a patient of mine, on a small plantation near Johore Bahru. The family rose at three in the morning; three of the five children went with their parents into the darkness of rubber, their heads shrouded in black cloth to ward off the myriad stinging mosquitoes. They ran from tree to tree; two hundred, three hundred trees ... the tapper was paid by the load of latex he tapped; and there was a rush to bring it round to the factory in pails; rain spoilt it, as did too much lingering; he had to use his children and his wife to help him. After that the children went to school, 'but they don't learn very much'. Of course not; they were tired out. I had so many exhausted children to see in those years. 'Give him an injection, Doctor, so that he can work tomorrow,' implored the mothers.

Up to Kuala Lumpur to listen to the aristocratic Unku Aziz, a Malay economist trained in England. 'Eighty per cent of the rubber in Malaya belongs to the British, not to the Chinese; 10 per cent is in small plantations belonging to individual Malay tappers, whose trees are old, and who have no means of replacing them.' Unku Aziz had taken up the cause of the rural Malay. 'The economic power of Malaya is in the hands of the British. But the Chinese hold the web of retail trade; the fabric of the cities. The Malayan Communist Party has not analysed the Malayan revolution properly. It cannot be achieved without the Malay peasantry.'

Tin. Mined in Malaya for almost four hundred years, and first by the Chinese, Malay's tin is the purest in the world, 99·9 per cent pure after furnacing. In the nineteenth century, when the British first came, two-thirds of the tin mines then open were in Chinese hands; the profits were shared with the Malay sultans. By 1950, 80 per cent of the tin produced was from British mines.

I walked round tin mines; saw the gravelly hills of an excoriated land, dropping to a lake in its middle; buckets hauling out the soil, dredges working with great raucous screams. I visited the small, derelict mines of private owners for sale ... they could not compete against the big companies. Here again all workers were Chinese, some Indian; no Malay workers in the tin mines.

I was taken to see a 'new village' by no less a person than the man in charge of resettlement. Mr Winslow was tall, imbued with the importance of his task. At first there had been a bit of trouble in Johore because people had been dumped in cleared jungle spots without food, shelter, clothing ... but now everything was provided for them, said he. It took us four hours by jeep to get to the new settlement. The dirt road was a new red gash across jungle. There, at the edge of a fetid mangrove swamp, between the thrusting mangrove spikes like a field of spears for miles, the jungle rearing its sombre menace behind and the barbed wire manned by a police post, was the 'new village', spreading itself into the swamp. Four hundred beings, including children, huddled there; foot-deep in brackish mud. There were some atap★ huts with rusty zinc roofs, obviously brought from elsewhere. I shall never forget the pale and puffy faces: beriberi, or the ulcers on their legs. Their skin had the hue of the swamp. They stank. There was no clean water anywhere. Mr Winslow, standing on a box (brought with him in the jeep to keep his shoes from slithering in the mud during the talk), admonished them sternly in Malay; a Chinese interpreter translated in Techew dialect. The villagers had been guilty of passing food to 'bandits' and so they had been transported here. Now they must work hard to redeem themselves. 'What will they work at?' I asked. Expansively Mr Winslow gestured, showing the swamp and the jungle. 'They'll find something, they always do ... ' I tormented him on the way back with questions of food supplies, medical care for the four hundred grovelling on that lick of mud ... I drove to other 'new villages' and after a while I established a weekly medical visit to one village, behind barbed wire, not too far away from Johore Bahru.

'Do go and see how happy the Malays are ... they may be poor but look at their smiles!' A pair of nice British liberals; young civil servant with good taste, young wife doing tie and dye work, collecting Malay silverware. I went off in my miniature Fiat to Kelantan, to the north, where the population is almost totally Malay. I walked along the Beach of Passionate Love in Kota Bahru, nicknamed locally the Beach of Passionate Flies because of their enormous numbers. Here the Japanese had landed in Malaya

★ Atap: palm leaf used in making local huts.

in 1942 and had been welcomed most enthusiastically by the Malay population.

Now I was not driving through the infernal monotony of rubber plantations but through the Malay *kampongs* with their unkempt rice fields and limp, dying rubber trees and patches of jungle, and I was appalled. Appalled at the beautiful big-eyed children and their lassitude, their thin legs and the ulcers; the pallor of listless women, the obvious evidence of tuberculosis and hookworm and malnutrition ... True, they smiled; true they were charming, and hospitable, and infinitely courteous. I fell in love, in love with the Malay people, but I was ashamed because I knew they distilled pathetic helplessness, and it is so easy to love pathetic, helpless people. I could have wished them less lovable, more vigorous; self-centred and busy and uncaring, like the Chinese. This clutching at the compassionate heart ... how shaming for the compassionate. Beguiling, mild and half-starved ... and within them the converse fury, ferocity, fuelled by religion – Holy War.

Indeed, the Malay peasant was much worse off than the Chinese; even the Chinese behind the barbed wire of the 'new villages', for by dint of extraordinary courage and survival techniques, and also that efficient collective help of Chinese communities in which every person in times of stress is looked after, within a few years, a good few – not all – of the 'new villages' had become livable. With shops and markets; better off than the hopeless, charming, rural *kampongs* I went through with their markets at night selling such few, poor things. I saw the Malay fishermen in their bowed *prahus*, and the catch they brought back, sold for so pitifully little, grabbed by peremptory middle men, and those middle men Chinese. No wonder, no wonder it could be said that the Chinese exploited the Malays, as in Africa the Indian middle men were resented for exploiting the Africans. But the real overlord, the Great Beneficiary, his face was not seen.

I called on Dr Burhanuddin. He was an Arab, a Koranic scholar, and astonishingly influential because all of Islam was astir with a new definition of religion from Cairo. And in Cairo was the El-Hazar University, perhaps one of the oldest universities in the world, the legitimate fountainhead of Islamic thought and the mainstay of the creed.

Dr Burhanuddin was not only preoccupied with religious concepts. He was also very aware of the social and economic problems of Malaya. 'There is nothing more strenuous or less rewarding than the growing of rice paddi.' The Malay peasants had been 'protected', their land being reserved for them for paddi planting by the British colonial power. 'They were not deprived of land, as happened in the industrial revolution of Europe, and driven to the factories. But nothing was done for them. They have no machinery, no fertilizers, no scientific know-how. The Malay peasant is imprisoned in his feudal village, under his landlord, in his deprivation … ' I had a good look at the Malay rice fields. How uneven, how stray the planting, how inefficient the cropping and harvesting; and in the end only enough for subsistence, not enough to enrich the peasant. 'But they don't want to grow more,' a British university lecturer in agronomics had told me loftily. 'The Malay doesn't know thrift, not like the Chinese. That's why he has to be protected.' And protection, said Burhanuddin, was the root cause of the inability of the *bumiputra* ('son of the soil') to compete in his own land.

Nik Kamil, handsome, intelligent, educated in England and then at the special college for aristocratic Malay administrators, invited me to a marvellous dinner in Kota Bahru. 'We have no racial feelings against the Chinese … if all Chinese became Muslims, there would be no problem in Malaya.' This I have come to believe was true. Islam barred intermarriage on religious, not racial grounds, and the only way out was intermarriage. I would meet so many Malay families who had adopted Chinese children, girls especially; so many Malays proud of having a Chinese mother. Not race, but religion was the barrier between the races. But the set-up of the Federation, based on racial discrimination, made even Islamic conversion well-nigh impossible for the Chinese.

The Federation of Malaya, today renamed Malaysia, is still based on the powers of Special Branch, on the Emergency. The Internal Security Act, which allows arbitrary imprisonment without trial, has been retained. But the fundamental problem of the *bumiputra* also remains. Despite many schemes devised to create a class of Malay urban entrepreneurs by forcing all business companies investing in Malaya to have Malay participation, to nominate Malay directors and managerial staff, the *bumiputra* in the rural *kampongs* do not get their fair share of the wealth, and the gap between city prosperity and countryside poverty still exists. Therefore a smouldering Emergency goes on. But the composition of the forces which oppose the present establishment has changed. It is now chiefly Malay. A rising of famished Malay peasants took place in 1975 and again in 1976. In one instance, when the Malay peasantry demonstrated in protest because they were starving, they were tear-gassed by the Malay police.

I am glad that, willy-nilly, I became involved so early in this complex story, not through any love of politics, but because this was the very stuff of the air which I breathed. For me it was an unshrouding, divesting me of thinking only in terms of China; making me aware of so many other cultures and peoples, and opening another door to bring me towards a certain universality.

Trivia also helped: Leonard had to resign from his English swimming club because I was not allowed to dip in the pool with him (colour bar). Other pinpricks; the hallmarks of an era now gone. But these small practices freed me totally into the new world of South East Asia. A world which enriched me with love and knowledge and indignation; with fury and delight.

The Emergency also affected my plans for Yungmei's schooling. There were Malay schools, Chinese schools and English schools in Malaya, and in Singapore. There were three times as many children in Chinese schools as in English schools; but the Chinese schools had many problems. They were regarded as the hotbeds of communist infiltration; and Special Branch swooped upon them regularly. In the years to come I was instrumental in saving a handful at least of young adolescents from arbitrary detention and three to five years in concentration camps. The Chinese schools were in general not government subsidized as were English and Malay schools, but funded by the Chinese community clubs, associations and chambers of commerce. The overseas Chinese of South East Asia also built and funded universities in China for their children's higher education. This pattern was accepted until, in 1949, China became 'Red', and all intercourse with China was considered a legal offence and a crime. Youngsters going to China were refused re-entry to Malaya. A witch-hunt began against graduates of Chinese universities who had become teachers in the Chinese-language primary and middle schools of Malaya and of Singapore. Many of them were deprived of a living for suspected sympathy with China. Anyone possessing books or magazines from China was liable to be automatically detained, without trial, under the Emergency regulations enforced, and for a minimum of two years. Regularly, during my eleven years in Malaya, I would have books seized and destroyed by Special Branch. Such books as *Red Star Over China*, by Edgar Snow, were considered subversive.

Malay schools catered only for Malay children, and all of them were religious schools, where the pupils chanted the Koran, in Arabic, and went on chanting it for many years. Most of the Malay *kampong* children never reached any higher educational level; but those who did came from aristocratic families and attended English schools. Some of the Malays who had strong Arab ties went to Cairo, to El-Hazar University, and others went to London to study, usually law.

Obviously, it was dangerous for Yungmei to go to a Chinese school, and impossible to go to a Malay school.

I sent her to an English convent school, but I provided, as I had done in Hongkong, a Chinese tutor three times a week. In the English schools eight out of ten of the teachers were Chinese (English-educated) and 80 per cent of the schoolchildren were Chinese, the rest Indian and Eurasian, with a sprinkling of Malay girls from the nobility. The teaching in these English schools at the time was colonial; it bore no relation to what really happened in Malaya, or in any other part of Asia. But at home there was constant and ardent argument, a stream of disputation, every problem was debated aloud, and I was giving Yungmei a double education. Yungmei's Chinese tutor was an excellent man, headmaster of a small Chinese school, who taught and spoke good standard Chinese. Of course this did not go without demur from Yungmei. 'It's too difficult ... others don't study Chinese.' 'People who only know one language are one-eyed,' I retorted, and told her how long, how bitterly I had striven to educate myself, and succeeded. If Yungmei today is not alienated when she goes back to China, it is due to the teaching she had in Malaya.

'I must tell her she is adopted.' The Singapore Anti-Tuberculosis Association, with its team of able doctors, pronounced her totally well. This was the right time ... but still I hesitated. It seemed to me that I loved her so much, that she *was* my daughter, no one else's ... our lives had been so unsettled, yet so much together ... was it right to disturb her now? And in China we did not tell children they were adopted; it was not supposed to be traumatic for the child not to know, on the contrary ... I gave myself reasons, and kept pushing away, day after day ... adoption meant more, not less loving, she must know that I cared.

Yungmei was converted to Catholicism and duly baptized. For a while our house was covered in religious pictures; they blossomed even in the bathrooms. But this fervour ended as suddenly as it had begun. One of the nuns at the school, speaking against the heinous sin of family planning in the catechism and morality course, argued that 'God will send a plague, or a war, if there are too many people'. This upset Yungmei. Another item which made her less fervent was the problem of babies. Yungmei came back one day to tell me that I had lied in telling her that babies came from their mothers' bellies. The Mother Superior had told her they were found at the foot of trees ... But abruptly a Malay schoolmate of Yungmei's age, thirteen, was withdrawn from school. 'Fatimah's gone to have a baby. She'll come back when the baby is born.' Fatimah was a high-born Malay, so the nuns did not say anything. Yungmei was convinced by Fatimah's rounded belly. But the fact that at twelve she had preferred authoritarian conviction to cold reasoning worried me. I realized she would always be far more trustful, and therefore vulnerable, than I had ever been.

A Many-Splendoured Thing would come out in England in May 1952. Jonathan Cape wrote to me; he seemed worried about the way it would be reviewed; and certainly a great deal of hostility was exhibited against it. Chief among the critics were *The Times*, of course, and the *Observer*. A correspondent of some fame who had been Ian's great friend felt my book destroyed a myth he had propagated about Ian; devoted to his family, happy with things as they were. He felt it bad for Ian's children. 'I have done what all writers do, write about their love and praise it,' I said. Of course it was 'bad', but I did not claim to be 'good'. Leonard was superb. He suggested that Jonathan ask Malcolm MacDonald, at the time High Commissioner for South East Asia, to write a foreword. Jonathan did write to Malcolm, and he accepted and sent a foreword to Cape's for the second edition. (The first had sold out much too rapidly ... 'Every third woman I see on the London buses is carrying your book under her arm,' wrote Jonathan. And this despite the adverse reviews.)

Copies now began to circulate in Singapore and a swell of protest arose. At least a dozen persons appealed to Malcolm. He must not write a foreword! It was an insult, not only to Ian, but to all the British in Singapore.

Malcolm wrote a little note asking me to go to see him. I drove to Bukit Serene, one of the Sultan of Johore's residences, where Malcolm lived. It was on a small hillock just outside town, sloped with green sward, seemingly true English sward, kept so by the feverish weeding of at least a score of women and the scythes of another score of men. For here the grass grew visibly, audibly, by the inch during the day.

Bukit Serene looked like a Walt Disney fantasy castle with turrets and cupolas and marble terraces and shimmering green-tiled roofs and pink-hued walls. Malcolm had redecorated its splendid marbled interior with glassed-in cabinets containing his collection of Chinese porcelain and ceramics. He would give away 430 priceless pieces to Durham University when he returned to England. I sat in the living room and Malcolm came in, an unassuming, short man with a nice smile and a soft voice. Perhaps wrongly, said he, he had been told that the book was about Ian Morrison.

'It is, it's about Ian and me.' He looked at me, and a smile began. I said, 'You can take back your foreword if you want to.'

'Not on your life,' said Malcolm, 'it's a splendid book. I wish someone would write a book like that about me.'

From that day onwards Malcolm and I were friends: having a deep and undemanding friendship and trust. As the years went by I appreciated his talents and his skill more and more, even when we were on opposite sides of an argument. Only Premier Chou Enlai, among the men I have known (and I have known many ambassadors, diplomats, politicians and statesmen), surpassed Malcolm in a certain winning patience and a quality of serene, cold thought in the midst of conflict and controversy. Like Chou Enlai Malcolm could grasp swiftly the small middle ground which could be enlarged into something like agreement. The two men were similar also in a reasonableness of exposition which rallied even the hostile; and in a certain gift for life, a liveliness and humour, a grin and dash about them, the illumination of an unforgotten, minute detail ignored by everyone else.

Malcolm certainly did not have Chou Enlai's immense stature or his ideological dedication to a cause; but he is the same kind of person in a different environment. Malcolm was committed to the England he knew, and served her well, and was not appreciated as he ought to have been, because he fought steadfastly against stupidity, pig-headedness, intolerance, but somehow these always prevail when it comes to distributing the rewards. Both Chou Enlai and Malcolm had an incredible capacity for work; Chou even more than Malcolm. Both made themselves instantly available to ordinary people; but Chou Enlai went on growing and his work is of great significance in history. Malcolm's task was to liquidate the British Empire with the least amount of trauma, keeping a British foothold, British interests and the Commonwealth. And this, too, has its importance.

Malcolm created liaison committees between the races in Malaya, worked against both British diehards and native diehards. 'You make even neo-colonialism palatable, Malcolm,' I would say, teasing him, and his eyes would be a little sad. He was staunchly anti-communist, but was accused of being soft on communism because he was not rabid. Special Branch hated him; the Malayan Civil Service diehards gossiped about him; later, in Kenya, Malcolm would again bring harmony and conciliation in an explosive situation. He would be the first to break down the colour bar, to invite Africans as equals to places reserved for whites only.

In Malaya Malcolm was accused of 'placation' and 'compromise' and 'selling-out', not only by rabid Englishmen, but by even more rabid Americans. One of them, a newspaper correspondent with some literary pretensions, even purported to see *my* influence in the 'disastrous' decisions Malcolm took to hasten independence in Malaya and in Singapore. And the fact that he had so many Chinese friends, that he turned somersaults in the streets, stood on his head at parties, was anathema to this 'serious' American (who was enthusiastically pro-McCarthy). 'If we can make it stick another ten, fifteen years here in Malaya we'll be all right,' said Malcolm. 'I don't want to see a mess of blood here, as at the Partition of India.' Where the mess of blood was concerned, Malcolm was, alas, quite right, and so, despite the injustice, I would understand and admire his views and actions.

By the end of summer 1952 *A Many-Splendoured Thing* was a best-seller in England. I was so involved in Malaya, in hospital work, in so many things, I did not even want to read the reviews. I received many most joyful fan letters. Young lovers wrote to thank me, old people too. A pair of crofters from the north of Scotland, seventy-four years old, wrote, 'That's still the way we feel about each other ... ' Lansdowne, who has become a most famous painter of birds, sent me his first kingfisher; others wrote music and sent it to me. Reminiscence is a jade; it has to be handled firmly. I let Jonathan run everything, ignored accounts and royalties for over two years. I was already planning another book, which I began in 1953; it would be on Malaya.

Locally the uproar over *A Many-Splendoured Thing* was fearful, although it only affected the British. But then they had so little to talk about! With dreadful repetitiveness they rehashed old gossip. In Hongkong no conversation was complete unless it contained some well-worn anecdote about Emily Hahn, the American writer (author of many novels, including *China To Me* and *Miss Jill*) who had fallen in love with an English officer and had had a child and written about it, and this twenty years after Emily Hahn had not only survived the affair but married her Englishman! It would be, I thought, the same with me. In twenty years, at their coffee clatches, the *mems*★ would be rehashing Han Suyin.

A reputation as a loose nymphomaniac was now established for me by

★ *Mem:* name given to English women in Malaya at the time. Abbreviation of the Indian *memsahib.*

some of the more indignant. I was told this by Lily Abegg, correspondent for the *Neuer Züricher Zeitung*, who came to Malaya and stayed with me. 'You are a knight, a *chevalier*, you are pure,' she said after some days with me. 'That is why these dirty people hate you.' But I had no time for introspection, for self-scrutiny.

Jonathan sent *A Many-Splendoured Thing* to Little, Brown, whose editor was Ted Weeks. He declined it. His reader had reported that 'nowhere does the heroine appear physically attractive', a somewhat puzzling literary judgment. Weeks had not bothered to read the book himself. It was the writer Nora Waln who persuaded Weeks to take it.

I had met Nora Waln in England in 1943. Her reputation as a writer on China, because of *The House of Exile*, stood high. *Reaching for the Stars*, her book on Germany, was for me much more true, even agonizing, but people had not reacted well to it. Nora was in 1952 still writing the book on China she told me she had started in 1943. 'Our great mutual friend', wrote Ted, meaning Nora, 'has a major book ... about China coming out ... ' But I knew she could no longer write about China. No one could without going to China, and Nora had not been for twenty years.

The waste of Nora Waln's talent brought me unwillingly to face a decision. Would I be a writer or a doctor? If Nora shredded her talent in the kitchen shredder, as I had seen her do, would I lose mine through the stethoscope round my neck? And did I really *have* any talent? All I knew was that I had not intended to be a writer; I still wanted to be a doctor. And sitting down to begin my next book, the words came, the images; but also I felt lost, bereft, without the contact of people, the children, the sick.

I discussed this with Emily Hahn, who now came to Malaya to write about the Emergency, and stayed with me. I had seen her once in 1951 in Hongkong when she passed through, and this was because Ian had been enamoured of her face, so I had wanted to see it. She quoted poetry, and had a roguish bounce to her; her soft luminous eyes belied the hardness within. For Emily was never life's victim; her adolescence had taught her to regard all women as her natural enemies.

On the day that she arrived the Grand Prix for motor car racing was going on in Johore Bahru. The Sultan of Johore and his son were car collectors and speed addicts. The Sultan had raced in his youth; and one day his car had been overtaken by the car of the Tiger Balm* king, Aw Boon Haw. The latter's vehicle, a splendid Rolls-Royce, was painted to

---

* A famous ointment made up with ephedrine and selling everywhere in South East Asia. The Aw family is one of the wealthiest in that region, owing to Tiger Balm.

resemble a tiger, and its protuberant lights were the tiger's eyes, fringed
with painted lashes. The Sultan was enraged. He speeded up, overtook,
rammed the Tiger Balm Rolls, took out his revolver and shot out the
tiger's eyes. Aw Boon Haw felt that his whole spirit, his tigerishness had
been destroyed ... On Grand Prix day the Sultan and his family were on
the grandstand when the racing began. The schools were on holiday and
Yungmei and her schoolfriends were rushing in and out of the house,
elated by an accident: 'There's blood all over the stones.' 'How blood-
thirsty children really are,' remarked Emily. She then advised me to give
up doctoring. I did not take her advice; it seemed to me a betrayal of my
twelve-year-old self. I had wanted then to be a doctor; and I had become
also a writer. But it seemed to me I would exhaust the child within me
and her freshness should I give up medicine. I went on doctoring by day
and writing by night.

This would have been impossible had I not had servants. Ah Lai, the
cook, came from Hainan Island, as did all cooks to Europeans in Malaya.
He had a large, uproarious family; his wife and his wife's sister did our
laundry. Ah Mui the maid was an s.e.p. (surrendered enemy personnel).
Daughter of a rubber tapper, she had been captured in armed action by a
Gurkha battalion and turned over to Special Branch. After much interrogation she had 'come clean', betrayed. Ah Mui was a most charming
girl, with a round face and large eyes and a fetching manner, given to
soft sighing and smiling in turns or together. She moved gently, with
grace, and regularly disappeared, going to the jail as a stool pigeon. Into
the movable array of servants I did not inquire too closely. How dis-
agreeable is accuracy when service is efficient; for never were we left
service-bereft.

Other s.e.p.s, male and female, came and went, visited, chatted, served
the meals, cut the grass, made the beds, ate and talked. I could hear them
through the open windows, and in the evening they caught the breeze
with jollity and a blaring radio. I paid the bills when presented, only
grumbling when they rose too high. Ah Lai managed parties for 150 with
ease, produced the required crockery and glasses. I never asked where they
came from. Ah Lai was Chinese, and therefore took full responsibility, and
inquiry was an insult. Our only real disagreement was over Australian
tinned butter. We never ate butter, but it appeared on all the bills and in
vast quantities. I do not know how much of it went to the jungle guerrillas
but I smelt the air and I knew; and one day I shouted, 'Not so much
butter!' The bills came down.

Ah Mui returned from her stool pigeon sessions in jail to tell me bits of her life as a rubber tapper, the bitterness of resettlement (her family was taken from their home near Klang and settled in another mangrove swamp. The resettlement officials seemed to favour mangrove swamps as sites for 'new villages'). She was nineteen years old, inhabited by a vague, unverbalized resentment; which she expanded by ineffectual sweeping and tapping of cushions into place. She sloughed off her small treacheries, but this was the condition of her life; and she was pampered because she was such an eminently good stool pigeon, extracting facts from the most obdurate communist sympathizer. There was no compounded deceit in her, but always she would be deceived by her own betrayal.

Through Ah Mui and all the others, through my travels in Malaya and the medical care I brought to the 'new village' I had adopted, I began to see Malaya. And I wrote of what I saw. My book smelt of the jungle and the swamp, the secretion of people's lives; the rubble and the waste. The book would come out in 1956 and I called it: ... *And the Rain My Drink*. It is still in print, and still today it is high on the list of certain American universities as the best book on Malaya, on what the Emergency was like.

Leonard reacted to my success with something like euphoria. He became less cautious. His enforced resignation from Special Branch could have been predicted the day he married me, I think, and he now hastened towards that conclusion. Two high-up people in Special Branch came to our house: Leonard received them in shirtless defiance, which I thought unnecessarily provocative. He was considered a 'security risk', and would be transferred to some out of the way place. 'You wanted to get out of Special Branch, now get out,' I said. After some hesitation he did. Within a week our telephone was ripped out; notice was given us to leave the house. I had to give up the job at the hospital; without a telephone, I could not function.

Suddenly the rent of the few houses available went up and up ... the usual squeeze. But we managed to find a small house in a hollow, hot and the neighbours abominable. The man beat his dog to death; regularly beat his wife and children; one child also died one night, amid great lament. 'We'll stick it here until we find another and better house.'

Leaving the hospital was necessary though sorrowful. I could not remain on call at night; it was too exhausting, especially with my writing. I then discovered how nice, friendly, unimpressed by the 'dishonour' of leaving Special Branch were my colleagues and the nurses. The Chinese nurses accompanied me to the annual Topekong ceremony. Johore Bahru was actually a great trading centre for the Hakka Chinese* and had been founded by them in the seventeenth century; the temple then being erected to honour their 'leader', who once a year was taken out in a palanquin into the streets of what had been his city. All the Hakkas of Singapore came for the ceremony of the Topekong to Johore Bahru.

Dr Pink, who had operated on me, came often to call and Dr Nayar, the pathologist, asked me to tea. Nayar was a Brahmin Indian and as such could not touch corpses. Yet he was in charge of post mortems, one of many such bizarre touches which made Johore Bahru General Hospital such a wondrous institution. He directed autopsies with a long wand, and two Chinese helpers did the slicing up. Then there was the affable, wistful Dr Holmes, a Welsh nationalist. One of the last cases I had to bring to his attention as head of my department, was a dead man, head neatly split in two by an axe. 'Heart failure,' said Holmes. As I protested, he explained. Such 'incidents' might lead to a Holy War; the man, a Chinese, might have been 'accidentally' hit by a Malay. No one wanted an unneeded pogrom. Dr Holmes came very often to our house, and inveighed against Special Branch and the Emergency. He would leave Malaya quite abruptly one day, and I never found out why.

I was approached to open my own practice by Mrs Wong, who had been a nurse at the Johore Bahru General Hospital. Mrs Wong fat, jolly and practical, offered to partner me in a venture on the main street of Johore Bahru: a pharmacy below and doctor's rooms above, my own practice. She would assist me, we would go halves on fees, and there would be, to pay her back, the profit on the drugs sold by her in the pharmacy. This was the usual arrangement for young doctors going into private practice.

Mrs Wong was very efficient; within a week she had a house along Jalan Ibrahim Sultan, a qualified pharmacist, a young boy to sweep, clean, fetch and carry. But there were still some snags, such as the repainting of the rooms and plumbing to be installed. 'All will be ready in three weeks,' said Mrs Wong. And suddenly I felt exhausted. I decided to go to Bali for a fortnight or three weeks.

Off by aeroplane to Djakarta, and then in another small, rickety hopper to Bali. It was surprisingly full of rather sweaty Dutch who kept up a running commentary on how terrible everything was. One woman sitting next to me told me I would find the Indonesians not quite human, and the Chinese far cleverer.

We landed in Den Pasar, and I made my way to Sanur on the motor-

---

* *Hakkas:* a particular minority among the Han Chinese. See *The Crippled Tree.*

cycle of a German sociologist who was on a world tour to study ancient customs. He was going, like myself, to stay with Le Mayeur, a Belgian painter who had lived in Bali for three decades. Malcolm, who knew him and regularly purchased some of his paintings ('because he's such a delightful fellow') had suggested my staying with him.

Le Mayeur came running out on the beach when he heard the motor-cycle; he loved visitors. His house was of stone, and great clumps of pink and red bougainvillaea in blossom dotted his sandy garden. He was still strong and healthy, though seventy, and around him his dogs leapt and barked. His wife, Polok, came out, hands in prayerful welcome. She was truly beautiful and had been, in her childhood, a great dancer.

Le Mayeur gave me a room full of splendid old carvings interspersed with some of his paintings; sun and sea and bougainvillaea and slim golden girls in light and shadow. 'My house is Bali and Bali is my house. You don't need to see anything else,' said Le Mayeur firmly. Every morning an indefinite number of lissom relatives of Polok glided about the sand paths of his garden, tenderly setting down offerings of flowers in coconut shells and cooked saffron rice for the gods. 'The Balinese don't like to live near the sea; they think the sea is evil, but they like me to stay here to protect them from sea demons.' We went swimming every morning; the beach was grey and silver sand, volcanic lava. We sluiced at the sweet water well in Le Mayeur's back courtyard. Every evening eight Indonesian soldiers came and sat with us while we ate, and played with their guns. They were detailed by the government to protect Le Mayeur, for President Sukarno (who liked his paintings) had decreed that he and his house were 'national monuments'. 'He got the idea about national monuments from the Japanese,' said Le Mayeur, who endured his protectors with equanimity.

Mr Vreelander and his wife came to the house. Mr Vreelander was Dutch and represented Shell. He was enamoured of Bali and the Balinese. He was stuporose all day, dreaming of night. At night he woke and lived to watch the Balinese dance. And now I wanted to join him in discovering Bali, much to the ire of Le Mayeur. 'Just look at my paintings, *there* is Bali.' Mr Vreelander's wife was a timorous Dutchwoman who went swimming with a large bunch of keys tied to her waist. She hated Bali, she hated the beach. 'Even the sand is black here. It makes me feel so dirty.' She brought plastic cushions to sit on. 'I have to lock up everything. They're such thieves.' Le Mayeur told me that he had heard from Polok, who had it from her relatives, that Mrs Vreelander counted the sugar cubes remaining after breakfast and tea every day, and then locked up the sugar bowl.

I went to call on Theo Mayer, a Dutch painter who lived beyond the first range of hills in a beautiful house overhung with white dove-orchids. He painted dark, large, gloomy canvases. From his terrace there was a fabulous view of the valley, bestarred with glistening water patches; and oh, the softness, the pastel tints over all; here was not the raucous green of Malaya but a gentle medley of hushed jades and browns and mellifluous beiges; along the paths would walk a daintiness of cows, delicate on slim legs with jet hooves and luminous brown eyes. Flotillas of ducks gathered round a bamboo pole with a tuft of white feathers at the top; how or why this tuft managed to keep the ducks from straying I shall never know.

On the third night we managed, Mr Vreelander and the German sociologist and I, to escape Le Mayeur. Thenceforth I too went stuporose by day, soaking in the sun and the sea and with a perpetual smile of sleepy enchantment upon me. We went to one village or another; on the German's motorcycle (with sidecar three could manage) or by Vreelander's jeep, and sometimes trudging on foot, until we heard the music of the *gamelan* coming through the trees and then we trod the night, walking in ecstasy of expectation towards the laughter spreading in the satin dark, the music and the lamps. Vreelander knew a great deal about Balinese dancing. The German sociologist took notes. The village would make us welcome and we would sit on the ground or on a flat beam above ground. The dancing proceeded. Perhaps I saw then the best dancers of Bali; little girls moving in rapture, in brocade, in ritual, all below puberty, for they would no longer dance when their periods came. We would return home very late, still enchanted and not sleepy; the dogs would bark and Le Mayeur, vigilant and unsleeping, would rush out, torch in hand. 'Ah, there you are at last.' He recuperated us. The next day he would say, 'Why go there? I can always ask the dancers to come here …'

In a great hush of smiles the Balinese walked, small-boned and beautiful. But then I came nearer; and I could see there were many sick children. I went into the compounds and always a child lay sick in the darkness within the hut, dying enormous-eyed, and always there would be *bomos* chanting, and the blood of cocks to ward off Evil. So many must have died in the silence and softness of the island.

One day Le Mayeur did give a feast, and dancers came. We sat on the beach and ate suckling pig, cooked on spits above the pewter sand. A *gamelan* orchestra performed and a famous male dancer danced the Kebiar; a wonderful, unforgettable Kebiar. But then Polok seized two carved wings of painted wood and danced; she had been a famous Legong dancer when a little girl; the Balinese were very polite and clapped and laughed gently but Vreelander was indignant: 'It's not done for a grown woman to dance.'

We went another night to a cleared space ringed with trees to watch the Monkey dance. But how poor, how very poor the villages were, more so as one went inland to higher, smaller valleys. My eyes picked out the sores, the mutilations. And there was the caste system; there were Untouchables here, in this archaic Hindu island, just as in India; and when we went to see the Chokoda Agung, the lord of the community, at Ubud, a famous centre of Balinese wood carving, he was as hefty and stout a landlord as one could wish for, waited on by many servants crawling in and out, bent to the ground.

I have not been back to Bali. Le Mayeur is dead, and the beautiful and wise Polok has married again. I am told, however, that Bali has not changed very much; although there are many tourists, the Balinese continue to live in another century. The painting and the carving for tourists has nothing to do with the temples, or with the worship of the gods. I could detect, even then, a hint of ironic artifice as the dancers strove to catch a pristine golden fervour which had once made their gestures grandiose, magic against evil. But even today their non-nubile children still dance themselves into immortal goddesses, casting most potent spells upon the land. Too well they know we come to watch; but they have sundered themselves from the acts they obligingly perform for visitors. What is delighted trance becomes routine gesture eliciting tourist money, but it does not corrupt them ... or does it? Perhaps Le Mayeur was right to create his Bali, for himself. 'Bali is Bali. Don't go and spoil it. Look at my paintings instead.'

I had been in Bali ten days when Mr Dean arrived. He was neatly dressed in a suit, walked on the beach in good leather shoes and was Vreelander's superior. Vreelander took him to see the dancing by night, but Mr Dean got cramp sitting on his heels listening to the *gamelan* orchestra.

Mr Dean spoke to me of oil. He was single-minded and romantic about oil. Creased with heat and sweat, he was impervious to discomfort when he talked of the vast underground wealth of Indonesia. Then he decided to leave. 'There is a ferry from Bali to Java, crossing the Straits,' said Mr Vreelander. We would take the ferry. I decided to leave with Mr Dean as my time was almost up and I wanted to see a little of Java. We said goodbye to Le Mayeur and Polok and set off at dawn by jeep for Gili-manuk, and saw from its promontory the sea amble its green and blue waves like tiles, sliding them one upon the other, and the sun burst out like a dancer upon them. Mr Dean perspired gently as we waited for the ferry; Mr Vreelander was then struck with a most wonderful and disastrous idea. Instead of waiting for the ferry (which might or might not come, one never knew), why not take a sailing boat? Then we would be sure to get to the other side.

I do not know why Mr Dean said yes to this scheme; perhaps the sun dancing the Kebiar, the growing heat and the enticing coolness of water. We embarked in a boat with six men. After about an hour we could still see the coast of Bali. We then saw the ferry boat advancing upon us, going to Gilimanuk. Its swell tossed our boat. Mr Dean clenched his teeth.

After another hour of vainly trying to catch the breeze we saw the ferry boat again; it had left Gilimanuk and was chuffing Java-wards. Its wake tossed us again. Mr Dean swore, volubly. 'That Vreelander … what a rotten idea …' I suggested that we might all do a little rowing; the Balinese laughed obligingly and while the sail hung limp, began to row … By late afternoon, when the ferry had crossed us twice again, the wind picked up. Mr Dean's choler had expressed itself several times, but now we sat hungry, thirsty, mute and red-eyed while the sea sparkled unruffled and the Balinese talked cheerfully, laughed and rowed. After the sudden sunset we went on and finally landed on the coast of Java in deep night. A European employee of Shell was waiting for Mr Dean on the dock. We were driven to a hotel, and I slept soundly in a vast bed under a large mosquito net, and came to breakfast to find a good many Dutchmen and Dutchwomen seated before blue and white willow pattern plates with cheese in large slabs on white bread, sugar on butter on white bread, honey and jam on butter on white bread … oh, those pounds of flesh which billowed under the thin dresses around me; all this white bread transformed into flabby motion.

Mr Dean appeared, still angry. 'That Vreelander … he'll hear from me.' The car would take Mr Dean across Java to Surabaya, and he gallantly offered me a lift. We went through green, green Java, the dense crowded villages, the splendour of the paddi fields, and of the trees, but Mr Dean's conversation was all about the evils of communism. How could one, he asked rhetorically, prevent the workers, say in an oil company, from becoming infected with the Red virus? He gave the answer. By establishing a system of social security. All stores, the canteens on every plantation or oil field, or in every factory, should be company owned, so that the workers need not leave their place of work at all; everything they needed would be there, including schools, hospitals, shops, recreational facilities.

All the needs of the workers would be directly satisfied by the companies employing them. There would be adequate protection against 'subversive tendencies', and that meant barbed wire and patrols, if needed, organized by the company. And a provident fund, docking a portion of the workers' earnings for security and health and for their old age and good behaviour, and to make sure they paid their debts and did not squander all they earned.

I do not know whether Mr Dean has been able to organize this concentrationary paradise, and sometimes I wonder what has happened to Mr Vreelander.

I started private medical practice in Johore Bahru in the summer of 1953. The Chinese merchant community sent me a large rectangular mirror engraved with the words HUA TO IS BORN AGAIN. Hua To was a most renowned surgeon and physician of the third century A.D. My first visitor was Dr Ismail, the sole Malay doctor in Johore, and also a politician. He would give up his doctoring when independence came in 1957 and become Minister of the Interior.

Dr Ismail looked at the shiny new autoclave I had bought. He said kindly, 'You won't have any patients. People don't like women doctors.' By the end of the first month, I had twenty patients a day and by the second forty to fifty a day, more than any other doctor in Johore Bahru.

Mrs Wong was happy. 'People have seen you work at the hospital; they know you came at night to see the babies.' I had indeed sat up one night because a baby had been admitted, who had died within six hours of heart failure; I had not diagnosed him properly; only afterwards did I realize that he had had acute beriberi, which seemed absurd, for his parents were well-off. The mother came again to the clinic, fat, apparently healthy, with a baby with a rigid neck—beriberi presenting as meningitis. This time I was not caught. I administered vitamin B and the effect was miraculous. Because of this, I gained a great reputation. I got another mirror, inscribed STAR OF SALVATION.

Now I had time to take histories, to examine the patients properly. This was not always easy. Just as in Hongkong, patients deployed great ingenuity in not telling the truth about themselves; it took much contriving to get beyond prevarication. But Mrs Wong and another nurse whom we soon acquired knew three languages and nine dialects between them. I charged only three Malayan dollars for complete examination, including urine and blood. Very soon my peculiarity (examining urine and blood; apparently none of my colleagues ever bothered) became well-known and I acquired a fascinated clientèle just for that. My colleagues, all men, charged ten to fifteen dollars when they gave an injection. I charged five. I went visiting patients at home for my usual three dollars. It taught me much about actual living conditions. Thus a baby eight months old, dying of anaemia ... it had hookworm; the mother, a rubber tapper, left it on a mat on the earth floor of the hut. My wealthy fat woman ate only boiled noodles, nothing else. Hence beriberi in the babies she bore. I discovered mild diabetes in a woman married fifteen years, and sterile. I put her on a diet and anti-diabetic pills and within three months she was pregnant. The child was a beautiful boy. After that lucky miracle, I could do no wrong.

Many of my patients were infected with modernism. Anything out of a tin was better than fresh food. They gave their children vast quantities of English biscuits and sweets and soft drinks. Rotten teeth and gum abscesses were extremely common. The children liked me because I was 'the doctor who does not give injections'. Some of my colleagues, pressed for time (an injection is mystically worth more in fees), would resort to the needle unnecessarily.

Now I had the later afternoon to myself, and I could write at nights. Sunday was my free day, except that I went to the 'new village' I had adopted, about fifty kilometres away. At the time there was still curfew at night outside town limits. The cars and jeeps of British planters and police whizzed by me, sometimes with guns sticking out of the back, the occupants giving horrified glances at my car. The pretence of 'terrorist attacks' still went on, but I knew I was safe. 'Only bad people get killed, Doctor,' Ah Mui, my stool pigeon maid, had told me on those occasions when she dreamt herself back in the guerrilla camp in the jungle. And now I became too successful a doctor. My patients increased phenomenally. Occasionally some rubber tappers from a distant village would get together and hire a small bus, collecting relatives and would-be patients on the way, and would arrive at my door. Especially on festival days, or at lunch time. 'We knew you would be at home, so we came.' And since there was curfew, and they had to be home before dark or would be in danger of being shot by the British or Malay soldiers on patrol, I had to see them.

Four

Malaya: 1954-1956

WE HAD SETTLED IN the small hot house in the hollow. Leonard did his best to find a job. We lived on my earnings as a doctor. I did not touch my royalties. We acquired a family of Siamese cats, bluepoints, and Binky, a perfect mongrel with a hyena-striped coat, which Yungmei had brought home. My love of cats, stifled since childhood, came back; for a short time almost a mania. When cat 'flu decimated our seventeen Siamese, we went round with kittens snuggled close to our chests, feeding them glucose water with droppers. All the kittens were born in Binky's large basket; and Binky tenderly cuddled them while the mother cat looked on, purring pleasantly.

One morning, when I went to Yungmei's room to wake her up, she said, 'Mummy, I coughed up some blood last night.' She showed me her toothmug. In it was a dark brown clot. She had not wakened me, but waited for the morning. Then all the worry and anxiety which I held within me about her health came up again; I knew her tuberculosis was not over, despite the X-rays and the tests.

'Don't worry yourself sick over her, she'll be all right,' said the specialist reassuringly. I said it was impossible not to worry. So back she went to bed, this time in a first-class room at the hospital; she had tutors to give her lessons while she rested, and further tests were made. This lasted some two months, while she was on an anti-tuberculous drug, as she had been in Hongkong. I was by then quite sure that there was something seriously wrong with her lungs. Everyone assured me that it was not serious; and Yungmei herself did not want to rest; but I saw how her cheeks went rosy in the evening, and was worried, and she hated me for worrying so much.

Not only was I concerned with my practice, and with writing and Yungmei (and also somewhat about Leonard's future), but I had also, in that year, 1954, become drawn into the educational problems of Malaya.

The University of Singapore was set up for the English-educated young of Malaya. It applied the government policy of graduating Malays, even if they did not reach the required standards. The bulk of the students were, of course, Chinese, since 85 per cent of Singapore's population was Chinese and only 6 per cent Malay, the rest Indian or European. The Chinese resented this favouritism, but endured it for fear of 'no job later'. Exclusivity to every job in the administration and all liberal professions went to the graduates of English-speaking schools. But since two-thirds of the children of Singapore attended Chinese-education schools, and for them no jobs were available in government offices, the medical profession, law, engineering or architecture, the injustice was flagrant. I lectured on this, but the English-educated were afraid, and the professors blandly countered with arguments about the low standard of Chinese education. This was inaccurate. For the most brilliant scholars were those who first attended Chinese schools then switched to the lower standard at English schools.

Not surprisingly, in 1953 the Chinese communities of Singapore and Malaya began to plan for a local university to cater for the Chinese-educated, since it was now impossible for them to go to universities in China without being jailed or deported. Nanyang (the Southern Seas) University was conceived by the Chinese Chamber of Commerce, led by the Hokkien Club (also called the Millionaires' Club). The Chamber had protested in 1951 at the law arbitrarily passed making English and Malay the only languages valid for official documents of any kind in Singapore and Malaya. In January the Hokkien Club held a meeting and decided that since an 'English' university of Singapore had been set up to cater for the English-speaking minority, there must be a Chinese university to cater for the Chinese-speaking majority – logical, but for months I saw staid Englishmen at the Cockpit Restaurant and other haunts of Singapore's whites foam at the mouth and gibber when the Chinese university was mentioned.

It was this plan which led to my being solicited to talk at Singapore University. 'Why on earth is a university for the Chinese-speaking necessary?' 'Why does the élite have to be English-speaking only?' I countered. 'Nanyang University is a typical exhibition of Chinese chauvinism,' said one choleric Englsihman. 'What about English chauvinism at Singapore University?' Of course the wrecking of Chinese culture was designed to 'counter communism', and to prevent the young from being indoctrinated through the language medium. The British staff of Singapore University and the government administrators seemed quite certain that an English education would preclude communistic ideas.

In February and March 1953, 270 Chinese associations and clubs throughout Malaya had joined in the scheme, and Nanyang University was born. Everyone gave money; the millionaires some millions, the pedlars of the Singapore food market a week's earnings every month. How many oyster omelettes, sliced crab, noodles of all kinds went into Nanyang University? The trishaw pedallers of Singapore and Malaya pedalled for three days and turned in all they earned for Nanyang University, and theirs was the greatest sacrifice, for they were so very poor. Rubber tappers flocked to give; they knew that their children would never have a chance to go to university; but it was a gesture of cultural identity. It was incredible and magnificent, and it must be remembered.

In Jurong on Singapore Island a site was bought and building began. I was, by then, researching into Malayan Chinese literature. My contacts with Chinese scholars in Malaya had made me discover that there existed an extensive body of essays, novels, criticism and poetry by Malayan Chinese authors, different in content and feeling from Chinese literature proper. There were two excellent Chinese newspapers in Malaya and Singapore with a wide coverage of world events. There were some very good journalists who spoke superb English and Malay as well as Chinese, and I had had some lively meetings with them.* An incessant cultural ferment within the Chinese community, and much creativity, but all of it totally ignored by the British, and of course thoroughly suppressed by the Emergency as 'subversive' … Some years later I would collect, and help to publish the first compendium in English on Malayan Chinese literature. Meanwhile, students would bring me slim volumes of verse and novelettes, all of them anti-colonial, full of verve and spirit, if not always technically perfect. I kept them carefully; their possession meant imprisonment. Some of the writers did go to jail.

And so the image of the Malayan Chinese who had come as an illiterate labourer to wield a spade and build the roads and plant the rubber and mine the tin, and had suddenly become a crass, cupid, still uncultured 'millionaire', was totally false. Indeed, many had come as labourers, and some had become millionaires. Such people as Tan Laksai, head of the Hokkien Club, and Lien Yingchow, who mimicked for me the way he had shovelled to build the roads, and Li Kungchiang, who had worked his way up from a clerkship in a rubber plantation to a vast ownership of newspapers and business enterprises. These millionaires funded scholarships, subsidized newspapers, schools, and welfare societies and libraries; and were intensely concerned with the education of the young. Many of

---

* Some of them went to jail for 'subversion' later.

them had painstakingly learnt to read and to write. Some, like Li Kung-chiang, managed to do so in three languages.

I supported the project of Nanyang University from the start, but after the first year, added a condition to my support. Nanyang should incorporate the Malay language in its curriculum and open its doors to Malays who wanted to study Chinese.

Today, hundreds of European students go to China to study Chinese; hundreds of Americans study Chinese in American universities. But at the time, the idea of Malays studying Chinese seemed ridiculous and incomprehensible to the British (though curiously not to the Malays themselves), and also to a good many overseas Chinese, including some of the millionaires of the Hokkien Club. It became very evident to me that the overseas Chinese were, because of the war with Japan, resentful and suspicious of the Malays, just as the latter were being harangued by some of their more fanatic religious leaders to kill the 'infidel' Chinese. Something must be done about it; and it seemed to me that the Malayan Communist Party, although it preached unity of the races, had failed to tackle the problem, and even denied that it existed.

My support gave rise to an invitation to the Hokkien Club in Singapore. I went up the steps of the unimposing building; upon them, waiting for me, stood some second-magnitude businessmen. The Club was spacious inside, and contained a swimming pool as large as a miniature lake crossed by a series of pavilions linked by a zigzag bridge; the zigzags possibly prevented the demons from following the millionaires when, to discuss big business, they repaired to the cool pavilions in the lake middle. The renowned Tan Laksai came out from an inner room to greet me. He was clad in simple, loose trousers, his loose top open upon his inner shirt— which was the same as that worn by any ordinary worker in Singapore— and on his naked feet he wore the kind of sandals that were to be had in Change Alley for a dollar. The other members of the Club were similarly at vestimental ease, thus flaunting their labour origins. Courtesy tea was served in minute cups, Hokkien fashion, while Tan Laksai fanned himself with a coolie palm-leaf fan and surveyed me obliquely. He had a massive bullet head with a crewcut, and a very extraordinary face; simple and shrewd, bulldoggish with massive jaw, and yet wistful. I liked him; he had great power, and honesty. And now he was angry. He had had enough of being bullied.

There were journalists and scholars and teachers there, as well as the likable Li Kungchiang, far more subtle than Tan Laksai, with more vision. He was thin and his hair stood up in a mop. We developed a great liking for each other, aided by the fact that shrewd Malcolm also had immense regard for him. We were to meet several times during the next few years, always with a large concourse of people so that Special Branch would not accuse us of conspiring. Li Kungchiang told me how puzzled he had been, when young, by the use of English words. Thus to find the inscription POST NO BILLS on a wall had nonplussed him. Post was to mail, bill was a bird's beak. Why should one be enjoined not to mail birds' beaks?

After an imposing banquet Tan Laksai led the way to the coolness of the middle pavilion in the lake, and there talked of the necessity of Nanyang University. I responded. The next day Special Branch had all the information and had approached Malcolm to try to curb my enthusiasm. 'They seemed quite upset,' said Malcolm. The Chinese newspapers published the exact version of our conversation the next day. Tan Laksai, and Li Kungchiang even more so, were denounced by an American correspondent as 'Red agents'. Tan Laksai had some connection, through his father-in-law, Tan Kahkee (a millionaire founder of universities in China who had returned to China to avoid detention), with his native province, but certainly none of these millionaires were communist-inclined. It was, however, the fashion of those days to confuse the urge for cultural identity with communism. For those were the days of witch-hunts and Joseph McCarthy, as manifest in Singapore as in Hollywood.

At the second or third dinner at the Hokkien Club, I ventured to touch upon the admission of Malays to Nanyang University, and felt the immediate drop in temperature. Lien Yingchow meaningfully shook the ice cubes in his brandy-ginger ale, and an alert young secretary asked me what I was writing at the moment. Tan Laksai fanned himself with his cheap coolie fan. After a decent pause he began to speak bitterly of the terrible things that Malays had done to the Chinese under Japanese rule: 'We fought for the British, we died, we were tortured ... We came here and we made things grow where nothing grew, and Malaya is wealthy because of us ...' I listened with profound respect on my face.

Now the Board of Directors of Nanyang University had to find a chancellor or university president who would pick out staff, professors, lecturers. Within the Board was a strong pro-Kuomintang wing, which had the blessing of the American Consulate. The Americans thought the British weak-kneed, and the important pro-Chiang Kaishek lobby in America also became interested in Nanyang University. An anti-communist Chinese university in Singapore might not be a bad thing. It might offset the appeal of the jungle guerrillas; it might also, in the long run, offset Malay 'leftist' tendencies influenced by the Communist Party of

Indonesia. For despite the sedulous repetition of the 'loyal Malay' theme (loyal to what?), none knew better than the British that the Malays were also nationalists, sharing a common culture, language and script with Indonesia; and that the Islamic world, from Algeria to the Philippines, was effervescent. There were fears of pan-Arab, pan-Islamic movements affecting Malaya. *Utusan Melayu*, the Malay newspaper, reported favourably on upsurges against colonial domination in Iraq, Syria and Algeria, and Egypt's Nasser was immensely popular.

The choice of an anti-communist chancellor for Nanyang University fell upon Lin Yutang, author of *My Country and My People*. Lin Yutang had lived in America for a little over two decades. A two weeks' trip to Chungking during the Sino-Japanese war had been his only wartime excursion in Asia, but he was in Taiwan in 1953, actively denouncing Communist China, and participating in the formation of an Anti-Communist League which had the backing of Chiang Kaishek, and of course the C.I.A.

Tan Laksai was none too pleased with the choice. Lin Yutang arrived in Singapore with his family; his daughters and son-in-law were also given jobs in Nanyang University. The Lins were provided with a bungalow by the sea and a Cadillac or two. Lin Yutang then started to recruit staff, and I received a little note from him, asking me to drop in for a talk.

There was a mat with WELCOME written on it at the front door and in the cool living room orchids hung from the ceiling in fenestrated pots. There was some extravagant carved furniture and jades, kindly loaned by the Tiger Balm king's daughter, Aw Hsiang. Her father, Aw Boon Haw, had mansions filled with priceless jades both in Singapore and in Hongkong, and I had visited them with proper clucking awe. Rotund and charmingly effusive, Mrs Lin greeted me; Lin Yutang had impish bespectacled eyes and in spite of his small size was truculent. 'Now I want you to tell me all about the situation here in twenty minutes,' he commanded. I began to speak, but Lin's attention span was short. That creeping glaze, that fixity of face which denotes a mind turned off, already astride another subject ... I cut my exposé down to five minutes, and he nodded sagely. 'Mummy,' said he, turning to his wife, 'we must get round to see something of Malaya.' 'If it's safe,' said Mrs Lin. I assured her it was, and mimicked Ah Mui, my former maid. 'Only bad people get killed, people like police officers.' They looked stunned. 'Will you have some cawfee?' said Mrs Lin.

We then talked of the book Dr Lin would write about South East Asia, of the bastion that Nanyang University would prove against communism

... Lin Yutang had already announced this as his intention. He then asked me to be Professor of English Literature at Nanyang. I shook my head. I did not know anything about English literature. 'But you write English,' he exclaimed. 'Not English literature.' I did not want to teach Dickens and Thackeray, worthy though they might be. 'I'd rather be the college health physician; all the students admitted to the University should have a medical examination.' He agreed, but when I had gone summoned a press conference and told them, 'Han Suyin has accepted the post of Professor of English Literature at Nanyang University.' This appeared in the *Straits Times* the next day. I wrote to the *Straits Times* to deny it, and to explain that all I could do at the moment was to offer my services as college health physician.

My denial led to another interview with Lin Yutang. He was a bit ruffled. 'Why don't you give up medicine?' As a professor I would have ample time to write. 'We'll see to it that you don't have more than six hours a week of teaching.' I tried to explain my idea of literature; that we must create an Asian type of literature; we needed something other than nineteenth-century English writers ... but his mind wandered again, and I left.

Throughout the rest of 1954, while Nanyang University was a-building, I did not approach him again. Lin Yutang made pronouncements, called press conferences, gave talks revealing a blithe unconsciousness of the situation in Malaya. He declared a university a place of leisure, with time to smoke a pipe and to browse. To the rickshaw pullers who had gone hungry, sacrificing three days of earnings to build Nanyang, this was fury-rousing. People began to dislike him intensely; and the students of the Chinese high schools mounted campaigns against him and called upon the Board of Directors to force him out. In this Lin helped them greatly. For his idea was to start with a budget of incommensurate dimension, more in keeping with the requirements of a wealthy American university than one funded by the people of Malaya. He offered his recruited professors transport by air for themselves and their families, and transport for their household goods. He demanded luxurious bungalows for them.

The Hokkien Club was holding meetings in great perturbation. They contemplated in baffled silence the bills which Lin Yutang kept sending in. They received protest delegations from the students. By December, Lin's relations with the Board were very strained. He then took action in ways considered un-Chinese, and above all discourteous. Thus he summoned a press conference of Western newsmen (Chinese journalists were absent) to make his disagreement known to the English newspapers; to them he complained that the financial outlays provided were insufficient. This was considered gross betrayal by the Chinese, who in Malaya as elsewhere prefer to settle all disputes within their own community, without resort to the press, especially a foreign press. When questioned by a journalist, Lin said that Malaya and Singapore were 'outposts of civilization', hardship areas calling for increased financial recompense. By publicizing the quarrel before the Board had finalized its meetings, Lin Yutang had made his sponsors, and in particular Tan Laksai, lose face. In early 1955 Lin Yutang and his family were quietly paid a very large indemnity by Tan Laksai personally, and returned to America.

In the summer of 1954, at last, a specialist in tuberculosis came to Malaya, Beryl Wilberforce-Smith, a tall attractive Englishwoman. It was due to her that Yungmei's tuberculosis was at last cured.

Beryl had worked in many parts of the world in her chosen field, and had great experience. Her arrival was due to Lady Templer, who was launching a campaign for the prevention and cure of the disease in Malaya. For it was indeed prevalent; it caused great mortality among the Malays, who had apparently no resistance to it. Lady Templer was behind a scheme to endow Malaya with a large tuberculosis hospital (forty beds to start with) about twenty-five kilometres outside Kuala Lumpur. Beryl was called to Kuala Lumpur, but after studying the scheme told Lady Templer that she thought this was not the best way to tackle the disease in Malaya. The building was miles from anywhere; the patients would feel isolated; their families could not shoulder the expense of travel from the *kampongs* ... much better have, all over Malaya, a series of small bungalow-type annexes to hospitals. Lady Templer was not too pleased with Beryl's suggestion, and the hospital, which cost a great deal, was built and opened with much pomp. I asked Beryl to take Yungmei in hand. She examined her most carefully, took X-rays from many angles, and finally discovered a small cavity at the back, well-hidden behind the clavicle. Meanwhile, at last, a big campaign to give B.C.G. to all schoolchildren and to extend this to the *kampongs* was being launched throughout Singapore and Malaya.

Yungmei was now on streptomycin, but Beryl advised that she should have an operation, a lobectomy (the cavity was in the upper lobe of the right lung). This radical removal held a good chance of total cure. I took her advice; Beryl wrote to Mr Cleland in London, one of the two surgeons renowned for lung operations. At the time lung operations were not yet very common but the mortality rate, high some years previously, was down to less than 4 per cent.

In these circumstances, I felt justified in selling the film rights of *A Many-Splendoured Thing*. Ted Weeks had written a few months earlier to Jonathan Cape of an offer by Twentieth Century-Fox for film rights. But I had turned down such demands. However, I was now to go with Yungmei to England; I did not know how long I would be away; meanwhile my clinic would have to be taken care of by another doctor.

Mrs Wong and I searched for a replacement and we found a very nice girl, Dr Low, who had been a student in Hongkong and was now a graduate doctor. She gladly took over while I was away. Malcolm, who came in frequently to see Yungmei, arranged for a passport for her; and in December 1954 we flew to London, arriving on a day so dreary, so cold, so foggy, so dark, that both of us began to weep. Oh, for the green eternal summer of Malaya!

Mr Cleland, the surgeon to whom Beryl had written, received us the day after we arrived. He wanted to operate almost immediately, but I insisted that Yungmei should have a few days' rest; I knew she was very tired by the cold. For the next four or five days we never saw the sun. Yungmei slept solidly, woke up and slept again. On the Sunday every food shop and restaurant was closed in the vicinity of the rooms we had in Kensington. I searched that morning for some hours for food and eventually took the Underground to Oxford Circus to buy some sandwiches; I could not take Yungmei out in the cold. I then realized that I had forgotten how difficult simple things were in England at weekends; in Malaya the Chinese shops and restaurants were open every day and late into the night. By Monday things were better; breakfast could be had at the restaurant downstairs. On the Monday, Yungmei entered hospital for her operation.

'We were in time,' said Cleland happily. 'The cavity was full of pus; had we waited, there might have been a generalized infection.' For the next few months Yungmei would be on streptomycin; for the next few years on regular check-ups. After she left hospital I administered the injections and she took them well; in fact her recovery was uneventful and swift, and apart from a neat scar which scarcely shows, she would now lead a normal life, swim and dance and travel and study and marry and have a child.

During these months Yungmei showed herself stoical and good humoured; with immense fortitude. I knew that, whatever happened, in the end all would be well with her; and though in the years to come we would have our usual share of disagreements, yet I think that she is built to surmount, to survive woes and hardships, as I am.

I sought out the friends I had known when I had been in England between 1942 and 1948, both as a diplomat's wife and afterwards as a medical student living in a basement and hard put to it to make ends meet, raising Yungmei and studying medicine. Isobel Cripps and I met frequently. Since the death of her husband, Stafford Cripps, she had become most active in promoting good race relations in the Commonwealth. Margaret Godley – who had stood by me so staunchly when I was running away from Pao – also helped very much. She sat with me throughout Yungmei's three-hour operation; and then moved us from inconvenient Kensington to a large room in a quiet hotel in Mayfair. The restaurant was just one floor below, there was Sunday breakfast, and I could bring up Yungmei's tray to her in bed.

John Coast and his charming Indonesian wife, Luce, came to see Yungmei, and soon she was walking, slowly, but a little more every day.

Suddenly in London, beneath all the activity, the bustle and tremor of success, Yungmei's convalescence, suddenly again there was China for me. What could I do about this obsession, my obsession, which I would not understand until, almost twenty years later, a Chinese intellectual would say to me, 'But this is what has always been: our only religion, our only love, is China, and that is why China has persisted, endured, survived, and is reborn again and again, throughout the millennia.'

But in London then I had no answer except torment, and then it was that in order to escape inner conflict I consciously began to move as two people, between two worlds, whose actions and thoughts need not have any link between them. Suddenly my life in Malaya, my doctoring, my marriage, became for me ferocious dismay. The more I appeared ensconced in my Malayan niche, the less I was substantial; the more dutifully involved with Yungmei's illness, the more dreaming like a rebellious refugee of going back, going back ...

Throughout these weeks I had also been working on my book on Malaya. The time had come to type it; my hand was sore with writing. At Cape's, Wren Howard now looked after me. Blue-eyed, diffident, humorous, he twinkled amiably all the time. My dearest Jonathan had had a bad stroke in the autumn of 1954, and had not yet recovered. Wren Howard was helpful. 'I'll get you someone.' And so, one morning, into my room at the Mayfair hotel came a beautiful sprightly girl with shining dark hair and dancing eyes. 'I am Menina Mesquita,' she said.

Menina had been Jonathan Cape's secretary. I do not think the word secretary applies; she was far more than that. She had enormous flair for books and writers; and she had typed *A Many-Splendoured Thing* for Cape's from my manuscript.

Now I began to dictate parts of … *And The Rain My Drink* to her. She responded with such delight to a good sentence that it stimulated me; she never wanted less than perfection. And so those bleak cold days of January and February were also days of happy endeavour, while Yungmei recovered strength and I put food down her four times a day and walked her round the park, and at night boiled needles in a saucepan over a small gas contraption which the British seemed to favour (it ran on shillings) and with tremulous hand gave her the streptomycin injection.

Meanwhile I also tried an approach to the Chinese Chargé d'Affaires in London for permission to go to China. But I was turned down. A meeting could not be arranged. Patience, I thought, the day will come. Nothing can stop me, neither the Special Branch, nor even the Chinese themselves. One day they will understand me. One day, and I also shall have understood the Revolution then, and then all will be good, rounded out harmony. But first, let me get Yungmei back to Malaya, healthy again.

In March, while Yungmei was with Isobel Cripps for a week of milk and cream in England's beautiful countryside, I went to Paris to see my brother, who lived in France. I met him at the railway station and we sat in the downstairs café of the Hotel Voltaire, which Cape's had recommended to me (none of my English friends seem to know anything about comfortable hotels; Hotel Voltaire was … well, perhaps Voltaire had lived there and nothing had been done to it since).

We talked a great deal, and I was sad for he had accepted his state, was satisfied with his ruined, peaceful life. My brother had had great trouble; his wife had become insane while he was still in China, teaching at the Jesuit college in Tientsin. 'I took her to Lourdes but it did no good.' Because of the sick woman whom he loved so tenderly he had given up everything, his career, further study; he had returned to Europe, where she foundered totally and died. He went on teaching, brought up his two sons, adopted a daughter, and insisted he was happy.

And then, of course, he started about my mother; and like Marianne, he was unquenchable. Again and again, and all over again, as the afternoon paced itself out of the sky and the windows of the Hotel Voltaire, and in the frosty twilight the people of Paris hurried and jostled. I saw two policemen drag a black man between them, and everyone turn away, and somehow it was also Mama out there …

Oh, what was this enormous pain that Mama had inflicted upon her children? How could it cripple my brother, so beautiful and intelligent, so much? I saw ourselves, he and I, doing geometry and algebra problems under the lamp in Peking, just for the fun of it; both bent over the table corner arguing about the solution and Mama suddenly riffling our books off the table. 'It's time to eat.' And his piles of science fiction magazines, called *Amazing Stories*, which he kept in a corner of his room; almost forty-five years later I would find again some of the stories such as 'The Moon Pool', reprinted, which I first read when I was twelve. My brother could not release himself in uproarious laughter, jeer at himself in defiance. 'I'm bad, okay I'm bad. So what?' I would say. But not he. No acceptance of wickedness for him. Always he had to have good reasons for what he did. There are no good reasons for anything, I thought, never entirely good reasons for anything, nor is evil entirely vicious. And so when in doubt laugh, and wait, and don't use words to corner reality. I suppose he had made happiness of a sort for himself, especially when he told me with so much satisfaction that he had burnt all Mama's letters, save one scrap ... which he proceeded to read to me and which twelve years later would be the start of my book, *The Crippled Tree*. And sitting there, in the soiled, greasy air of the hotel café, I knew we would be leaving each other, we were rapidly getting so far apart, receding from each other even as we promised to keep in touch, even though he said, 'I have loved you so much, Sister.' I gave him all my royalties from the first French edition of *A Many-Splendoured Thing*, I do not remember how much it was, and we spent two more days together, and I was fighting against a bone-melting compassion; for he sucked my hard-gained strength from me, and I had to discard pity and go on with tough bones.

André Bay of Editions Stock, my publisher in France, admired the Chinese Revolution; which was not the fashion then. The French Communist Party, I was told, had attacked me ... but I never found out (or tried to find out) what they wrote about me and my book. *Le Monde* published extracts of *A Many-Splendoured Thing*, and it was a great success.

And then it was mid-March and Yungmei could travel. We left London for Switzerland and a few days in the crisp, delightful spring. Helmut Kossodo, my German publisher who lived in Geneva, put us up at a delightful small hotel on the lake; the swans came gliding by under our window and Yungmei was transfixed by the sight. A Swiss businessman I had met at a diplomatic party in Singapore, Mr Egon, invited us to visit him; we went to Zurich, stayed at the Storchen and shopped in the beautiful shops of Limmatquai. How tidy, how honest and precise the Swiss! How fabulous the clothes! We revelled in the fastidious good work, the good food, the cleanliness of the rooms, the comfort ... Mr Egon took us to his house for dinner; and then invited us to spend a few days up in the Engadine, at his mountain chalet.

Mrs Egon wore no make-up, her hair was dragged into a thin bun on top of her head, and she shut her mouth grimly and looked at Yungmei with dislike. Her particular brand of racism was not overt but it was unrelenting. My Hongkong Jesuit friend, Father Ladany, was a rollicking sybarite compared to Mrs Egon, who was convinced Sin began just outside Zurich, and that the whole of Asia was one vast orgy. I learnt later of (and saw with my own eyes) postcards she sent to poor sweet Mr Egon with skeletons and death's heads and graves, inscribed SIN IS DEATH!, when Mr Egon was on business in Bangkok, Hongkong or Singapore.

Nevertheless, having planned to see the famous Swiss mountains, we decided to ignore Mrs Egon. 'I think she's just born that way,' said Yungmei wisely. We had dinner with the Zigglebecks, who lived in the quiet unostentatious way of the truly wealthy of Zurich; their house was all smoothness and dark polish and valuable furniture and antiques and old masters. Mrs Zigglebeck was in Moral Rearmament, and Mr Zigglebeck was simply in high precision armaments, including a new type of very lethal gun. Mrs Zigglebeck tried to get me to go to a Moral Rearmament meeting up in the mountains at Caux. It would be excellent, she said, if Yungmei and I attended, for we would meet people from all over the world, gathered there to save the world. Yungmei ate stolidly. I said no. 'You will feel inspired in your writing,' said Mrs Zigglebeck. 'My mother does not need inspiration, she just writes,' said Yungmei.

Up to the Engadine, and the first shock of genuine postcardy sky and snow, the health, health, health of skiers ... Mr Egon went skiing with a very nice Swiss couple. Mrs Egon pursed her mouth and told me that it was very difficult for men to remain without sin, but it was up to women to see they did not sin, and women who dragged men into sin should be punished publicly. 'You mean stoning?' I asked. We had a beautiful room and shared a huge bed, Yungmei and I, and a maid in starched apron and cap brought breakfast with a curtsy, but I could not find a bathroom to wash in. Every morning we were supplied with two large jugs of hot water. 'Ask HER,' said Yungmei. I tackled Mrs Egon. 'Oh,' she said, 'you want to use *our* bathroom?' 'In Malaya we bathe *at least* once a day.' Very reluctantly, she led me to the bathroom, and so Yungmei and I had a bath.

'We'd better not stay too long. I don't think we can have another bath,' said Yungmei.

On to Rome, and just in time for Easter. We hired a horse carriage because Yungmei enjoyed feeding sugar to the horse, and it was the best way to see Rome; every day now she was better, rounding out, firm and rosy. I wanted to give her a good time, to make up for the suffering she had endured.

To Naples to see Vesuvius; but Vesuvius had blown its top off and only some smoky holes glowed redly, and Yungmei was quite disappointed. We then boarded a Danish ship in Genoa for a leisurely return to Malaya. The sea air, the rest, would be good for Yungmei. When we docked at Penang a policeman was there, asking Yungmei, 'Are you back from China?' I explained we were back from London and showed the tickets, but the police officer obviously did not like Yungmei's Chinese face and would not let her land. I then had to invoke Leonard, Special Branch, Malcolm MacDonald. Finally we landed and took the train for Johore Bahru. It ran through the night and the jungle; the rain started; the heavy, insipid, noisy rain of Malaya, soaking the trees and erupting from the drains, and we were back, back in the heat and the green. 'I'll have a lot to tell my friends,' said Yungmei. She had maintained a steady correspondence with some of her schoolmates, sending dozens of postcards; hers was the age of passionate friendship. We came out of the train and there was Leonard, in shorts and shirt, wearing the half-assured, half-fearful expression which was his face to me. And immediately I knew that, alas, he would always remain a stranger, unloved, despite his very great devotion, despite his qualities. And that I could no longer live with him.

We now moved into a large, airy house on a hill slope, with a garden full of frangipani trees. I kept five cats, two marvellous amber Burmese with green-yellow eyes, and throughout South East Asia sold the kittens I bred. Everywhere I found cat addicts, and for years sustained correspondence about my cat progeny with people in Malaya, Thailand, Indonesia, even Ceylon. I got rid of Auntie Hsu, my servant, tactfully paying her three months' wages. She fried everything in coconut oil and had a very frizzy perm; but the worst thing was that she insisted on frying the cats' fish.

In her place came Lao Chieh, Big Sister Lao, and until I left Malaya nine years later my life was smooth and easy because of her.

Lao Chieh came one morning to my clinic with three of my patients, her friends, who had persuaded her to 'help the Doctor'. She had a lovely classical face, a long pigtail down to the back of her knees; she was slim and tall and straight and she belonged to the sisterhood of silk.

There is a famous district in the province of Kuangtung, in which all the nurseries where the silkworms are reared, and the mulberry trees which provide the leaves for their food, are owned by women. And so that this wealth of silk and its labour should not fall into the hands of men, who would exploit the labour of women and their adroit fingers and reap the profit, the women live in sororities, and form their own couples, vowing love and sisterhood to each other. They wear their hair long in a virgin pigtail all their lives. This lesbian society, which is also an economic system, is accepted and respected. But in order to perpetuate their numbers the women must breed girls; and for this a man is needed. The sisterhood has devised its own system to prevent marriage being used to enslave them.

When a girl is of marriageable age, a man from another district is recruited by the matchmaker; and the marriage ceremony is celebrated. But at night, in the bedroom, another girl, bought for the purpose, takes the place of the bride in the marriage bed. The next morning the sorority makes sure that the marriage has been consummated (by inspecting the sheets) and then the real bride, still *virgo intacta*, serves morning tea to her in-laws and goes away, never to return except when the man dies, when she will wear mourning and perform the funeral rites. All the girls born of the substitute woman are accounted hers, and she will take them away and rear them as her own in the sisterhood.

Lao Chieh had two 'sisters', who came and went in our house. One of them had married and had therefore cut her hair and wore a bun, but this did not seem to damage the sisterhood. The sisterhood was highly thought of in Johore Bahru. Most of the women owned some land, or shops, or houses, even if they were mere 'servants'.

Lao Chieh took charge of me and my house. When one is lucky enough to have a Big Sister, one does nothing, except pay the bills. Lao Chieh decided what food Yungmei and I should eat, and she was a superb cook. She told Leonard when and where he must drive her on her afternoon off. She told me everything that went on in Johore Bahru and gave me advice about my patients. On her first inspection of the house she had sniffed at the mattress on her prospective bed.

'It smells of coconut oil.'

'I'll buy you a new one, Big Sister Lao.'

'No, don't go to that expense for nothing. I don't know if I'll stay.'

After three months, she said one morning, as she put down the breakfast, 'I think you'd better buy a new mattress.' She dosed me with Chinese medicine when I was tired or unwell. 'Your body is a Chinese body, you don't take well to Western medicine.' She made strengthening chicken soup for Yungmei. She hired and fired gardeners and laundry women. Our first gardener was a Tamil; he turned one end of my garden into a sago plantation. 'I was wondering when you would find out,' said Lao Chieh, and fired him. She bred orchids and planted trees. The only time I needed to put my foot down was about Hamid. He was a young boy straight from the *kampong*, a Malay, recommended to me by one of my Malay women friends, Che Katijah, who was a member of the ultra-conservative Pan-Malay Islam Party. She was Hamid's aunt by adoption. Because of Che Katijah, whom I loved dearly, I stuck by him when Lao Chieh would have fired him. I paid for driving lessons for him, and after a while Lao Chieh got used to him, and he would take her in the car to market and to see her friends on her day off. 'He shows his teeth all the time,' Lao Chieh said of him. 'He is just happy,' I would reply, and so she hurled a great deal of invective at him in her atrocious Malay, but Hamid only laughed cheerfully, and all was well.

Of course Lao Chieh fell in love with Yungmei; she would contemplate her with ravishment when Yungmei picked nimbly the cheek of the fresh, delicious garoupa she had prepared. 'Your thousand gold pieces* knows the best part of the fish, not like you, always thinking. You don't know what's at the end of your chopsticks.' But she did care for me, deeply, though she never said it; and late at night, after I had typed myself sleepy, I would find my bedroom smelling of fresh jasmine; Lao Chieh had plucked the white flowers and placed them on my pillow, and I would sigh with pleasure and fall asleep so quickly, knowing all was safe because of Lao Chieh.

It was on Lao Chieh's advice that I purchased, cheaply, a piece of land on the same hill slope, just in front of the house we occupied, and built three small bungalows on it. There was a marvellous view of the Straits of Johore, and we were neighbours of the Sultan of Johore's eldest son; his peacocks came to parade in our garden every afternoon. My bungalows were designed by a Chinese architect friend, Kee Yeap, from Singapore. He was inspired by the graceful Malay houses on stilts, and created airy, beautiful structures. 'You very lucky, Doctor,' said Mrs Wong, 'Lao Chieh give you big face everywhere.' The houses were ready in 1957 and we would live in one of them and rent the other two to agreeable families, one Chinese and one English.

* Name given to girls in China.

Outwardly in that year of 1955 all was well. My clinic prospered, Leonard found a temporary job and went on studying for a London University course; Yungmei was a heroine in her school, with accounts of her operation and her European travels. I finished my book on Malaya and sent it off to Cape. Ted Weeks annoyed me again with suggestions for cuts, which I refused. But I was absolutely unable to sleep with Leonard. It was physically impossible.

Pretty soon I was informed by a charitable Englishwoman, and also by an anonymous letter, that Leonard had a 'mistress' — she was the buttock-cheeked salesgirl of a certain shop selling cosmetics. This relieved me greatly. I had now relapsed into that state of sexlessness which was mine before Ian; but Leonard, of course, was different. He was a normally constituted man, a healthy, well-sexed man. I had once inquired, out of curiosity, from a newsman how many times a week he found it necessary to perform. 'At least three times,' said he.

But the trouble was that Leonard really cared for me; that it was me he wanted, and my total indifference irked him. Our relations thus became extremely difficult and since he did not understand my complete block, he thought I was behaving in a way calculated to enlarge his inferiority complex. He tried jealousy scenes. 'Don't insult me,' I said. 'If and when there is someone else, I shall certainly tell you.' But this was not the kind of situation he could explain to himself, or that I could explain to him. How does one explain a total inability to function sexually? Of course I knew the cause. It was Pao. He had wounded me mortally in that respect; until the end of my life I would suffer from relapses.

Meanwhile I felt disagreeably restless. I had finished my book, I was working too hard, I did not sleep well, and I was afraid Leonard might try to make approaches. We had many short, sharp quarrels.

I received a letter from Cousin Pengju in Hongkong. He wrote about Premier Chou Enlai and Chou's invitation to all Chinese intellectuals to return, even if only to see what had been done in China since Liberation. I felt parched and withered with that inner drought which compels me to go to China as a thirsty beast goes to water. I had to go back.

Christmas Eve. I had decorated a small tree, placed presents for Yungmei and her friends below it; and asked Leonard to return early because this was Yungmei's first Christmas free of tuberculosis. There was also a present for him. Gestures. Routine, accomplished with compunction and no pleasure. All part of that façade self which I had conjured up, that brisk mother and wife self which I wrapped myself in as a magician in his cape. Meanwhile, I knew something would happen that Christmas Eve ... almost, I willed it to happen.

'Let us see if he will come back early.'

Leonard had tended to stay out late at night; and this could be expected. He would return and watch me as I looked asleep and did not stir. He would watch me at breakfast; and I would not give him a chance. I never even inquired why he was late. But now I had mentioned the fact, obliquely, by asking him to return early. What would he do?

Leonard did not return until one o'clock. 'Where have you been?' said I. 'That's my business,' he retorted, braced for the showdown. And so we went into our parts, as if rehearsed. 'You're not a woman, you're a thinking machine,' he said. The ritual of a quarrel. I think he hoped – most reasonably – for anger, tears, then reconciliation and catharsis to end, as normally as possible, in bed. But this would not be. I had not prepared the script that way.

One afternoon in early January 1956 I drove to the hairdresser in Singapore and had my hair cut short. Until that day I had kept my hair long. It was thick and fell to below my waist; everyone commented on my beautiful hair, and some men slavered when they saw it, when I unloosed it to go swimming. Now it was strewn on the linoleum floor of Miss Peck Poon, the hairdresser, in great sheaves. Miss Peck Poon giggled as she gathered it tenderly. 'I can make at least three wigs out of this, Doctor.'

She then cajoled me into having a perm; and since I was determined to do the worst, I acquiesced. I looked at the lamentable result, an Afro-American dandelion. Even Miss Peck Poon was worried. 'You look different,' she said.

Ignoring Leonard's perturbation, I took an aeroplane ticket to New Delhi. Malcolm had moved to India in late 1955 and had invited me to visit him. With Yungmei healthy, Lao Chieh better than me at looking after her, I could go away. I had by now a permanent assistant, because the clinic was too much for just one person. But patients fell in number drastically when I left. 'I've kept my disease for you to look at, Doctor,' some used to say to me reproachfully when I came back. Nevertheless, I was beginning to detach myself from medicine.

And so to Delhi, to be the guest of Malcolm and his Canadian wife, Fiona, in their house and splendid garden, in the superb winter of north India. Squadrons of parakeets in battle formation swooped across the lawns, the drongos were more cheeky than in Malaya; jackals screamed at night and came into the suburbs of the city. And oh, the beauty of India! A totally different beauty from the untiring loveliness of China. China is pastel and nuance and discovery, and India hits you in the eye, flaunts everything; India is show and riot and gaudiness, extravagance and surfeit of everything. Indian skin changes hue with anger or happiness; India is audible, visible, melodious and raucous and garish and monstrous in its open cruelties; tinsel and gold, horror and marvel all at once. Mind-jolting in its profligate splendour.

Malcolm entertained well and much; and to the British High Commission came the Prime Minister, Jawaharlal Nehru, in admirable pure white with a rose in his hand, looking with a pout on his lips and moving eyes both moody poet and disgruntled lover, and yet with a prick of asperity somewhere. He started immediately talking about *A Many-Splendoured Thing*, which Lady Mountbatten had given him to read. 'I think great loves should be kept private,' said he. Perhaps he had known Ian well, and felt too near the impact of his death. 'In that case literature would be much impoverished,' I replied. For about three seconds Nehru stopped twiddling the rose he held between his fingers. As a result of this brief passage of arms, our relations, though amiable and friendly, would always harbour a twinge of strain.

He then asked me what I thought of India, but answered it for me. 'It's full of tragedy and comedy, laughter and tears.' 'You are a poet, Your Excellency,' I said, courtier-polite. He expected some tribute and nodded. After dinner Lady Mountbatten sat next to him, and kept patting his hand to make a point. But it was the Maharaja of Patiala who won my heart that day. He was the tallest, most handsome man I had seen so far. Among the maharajahs and maharanees a-glitter with diamonds and rubies and emeralds whom I met then and was to meet at other dinners, he stood out not only for personal good looks, but also for a kind of simple common sense. I learnt of Patiala's woes; his father had left him encumbered with something like five score (or perhaps more) widows and ex-wives, all to be looked after by the present Maharajah, his son.

Vice-President Radhakrishnan had a most magnificent turban — I wondered how this confection was held together; invisible pins, he told me. His grandeur depended on this headgear as well as on his extraordinary gift for lengthy verbal jousting. He talked philosophy solidly for about two hours, and the next day a large case full of his books arrived for me to read.

In the garden the crows swooped down at tea to wrest sandwiches from our hands. 'I must learn about this country.' Everything has the same largeness of dimension as China; big, and bigness stretches. The largesse of great size ... I went wandering in Old Delhi and its oily, rancid misery. 'I must learn about this country.' How big Asia was, how little I knew about it! And not only me, but so many Asians like myself! We had been more cut off from each other by the Western colonial period than from Europe and America; and now the time had come to know each other. 'What a wealthy country you have!' I exclaimed when I had been there some days. 'You have so much of everything ... ' 'That is exactly what Chou Enlai said,' replied Indian friends happily. Yes, India was rich, rich, so much more wealthy than China in resources; but even then I could see its primal fault, squander, waste, everywhere, in everything. Even the poor wasted, they wasted effort, energy, they made so many unnecessary gestures. Then it always irritated me to see the women trailing their sarees in the dust; such beautiful sarees, so much work in them and all the hems in the dust; and the way things were not kept working, and above all, the inefficient tools of labour. It was only after going back to China that the full *meaning* of this neglect of implements of daily labour struck me as the unforgivable crime.

I had tea with the Health Minister, a prim and proper spinster in white homespun. We discussed family planning; she approved of continence, and the teaching of the safe period to women by means of beads. I felt these ploys for denatalization were somewhat precarious; but no, said she firmly, in India they could be effective.

I went to small parties thrown by the New Delhi intelligentsia because they had read my book; but they had also read *The Wasteland* and T. S. Eliot was almost a god. Among the younger diplomats I met Tikki Kaul, just back from Peking, where he had fallen in love with a Chinese girl. But members of India's diplomatic service are not allowed to marry foreign women. Tikki shook his head, sighed, and returned to Delhi. He was writing a book, but not about thwarted destinies. A very intelligent, able deft diplomat, he would have a brilliant career as Ambassador to Moscow and Washington, which only came to an end when Indira Gandhi was deposed in 1977.

I told Malcolm that I wanted to go to China; and that I had come to India for that purpose. I had had no news of my father, not even through Hongkong. 'Of course one must have patience, but I feel in my bones that it's time to go and have a look.' Malcolm agreed. 'I don't think China and Russia are really alike,' he said. He then invited the Chinese Ambassador to lunch. The Ambassador and his wife came; they were both portly, grizzled, and both had been guerrillas in their days of strength. The

Ambassador had been a Long Marcher. I talked to him about returning to China for a visit and he said, 'Of course, you should certainly go to see what has been done.' A polite formula, and noncommittal. Not all overseas Chinese were welcome to return, I knew. And as for myself... Nevertheless, I presented myself at the Chinese Embassy the next day. The Ambassador was not available. The secretary was a severe young man, less than helpful. What was the purpose of my visit to China? I told him I had read Premier Chou Enlai's call to Chinese abroad; anyone who wanted to return to the motherland could do so, even if only for a visit. The secretary's stiffness increased. What were my qualifications? I told him that I was a doctor. But the story of my life was so eminently complicated that he obviously could not grasp any of it, so after attempting a short biography I gave up. He handed me a form to fill in and said he would send it on to Peking. 'When shall I know?' 'Three to four weeks, perhaps more.' I did not tell him that I was Han Suyin, which is my writer's pseudonym. This would merely have upset him even more. I gave my real Chinese name, my father's address in Peking and his profession, and wrote on the form that I wanted to visit my family. Always I felt worried that my connection with Pao might have caused prejudice against Papa and Third Uncle, although Cousin Pengju assured me that this was 'improbable'.

The French Ambassador asked me to lunch; he was erudite, passionately devoted to Indian mysticism, and advised me to go to Kathmandu. I heard a golden bell ring in that word. Kathmandu, Nepal. Malcolm's office cabled the British Ambassador in Nepal, and four days later I flew to Kathmandu.

The airport was handkerchief-sized, but all the Himalayas stood watch on it, and there was the primrose smell of snow in the air. Men with plaited hair and turquoise and coral earrings hung over the rickety airport barrier to watch our aeroplane land. And there was Judith Tollington, the wife of the British Ambassador, Boyd Tollington, brown and nutmeggy and eager and affectionate, come to meet me.

The British Embassy was a rambling mansion of modest demeanour, in marked contrast to the imposing white stucco and stone Buckingham Palace-type palaces of the Ranas, the ruling caste. Boyd typed all his reports himself on a small old typewriter, for the Foreign Office was then in a crisis, enjoining its diplomats to economize. 'We're a bit forgotten here because nothing very nasty ever happens in Nepal.'

Judith gave a party and a treasure hunt; the European community of Kathmandu came, including Boris Lyssanovich of the Royal Hotel and his beautiful Scandinavian wife, Inge. Boris was a giant of gaiety and Rabelaisian humour, bestriding his world with imperishable joy. His career, first as a ballet dancer, later running clubs in Calcutta, now as a hotel manager in Kathmandu, was interspersed with unbelievable episodes; unbelievable unless one knew Boris, when everything became credible … anything could happen when Boris was there. He had just emerged from jail, where he had been placed for reasons bureaucratic and confused, and was very proud of the parties he had thrown while under duress.

Boris could arrange anything. He conjured up the best Moët et Chandon champagne on a Himalayan peak; organized a banquet with ostrich eggs, elephants' paws, Boston clams and caviar without batting an eye. 'Ask Boris,' said everyone, and Boris obliged. He had a scheme for installing a dairy farm; another to cut the transporting of beef on the hoof from India across the passes (the animals were skeletal when they arrived, from the long walk). He wanted to lay a golf course up at 3,000 metres; he wanted to build a chain of hotels in Nepal. Boris was not wrong in these schemes; today Nepal is very much part of the tourist circuit, and many of the impossible things he then planned now exist.

How poor Nepal was, at first glance: in the medieval way Europe of the tenth century must have been poor. Yet it was almost impossible to be gloomy there; altitude seemed to prevent it and the Newaris, the real inhabitants of Nepal (as distinct from their masters, the Ranas, who had conquered them and stayed a class apart), were such a gay and singing people and beautiful to look at. Addicted, like the Balinese to festivity and honouring the gods, they were superb carvers of wood, and in the past centuries Nepalese had come up to Szechuan and even up to Peking to carve wood-latticed windows and stone pillars and arches. The streets of Kathmandu were glossy mud, shining with offal and cow manure; the garbage was thrown from the windows of the sculptured wooden houses with their projecting balconies; hence the stout black umbrellas everyone carried, hooked on to the shoulder. So Europe must have been, even up to the seventeenth century.

Holiness was greatly about, in magnificent and somewhat decrepit temples, which abounded; every street corner had its holy place, its holy stones, lingam and shrines and perpetual conjuring of malefice. The rulers, the Ranas, looked physically different from the Newaris, who were more mongoloid in appearance. They built themselves replicas of English palaces and piled the rooms with Victoriana brought on the backs of porters across the passes. Like Tibet, Nepal wanted no wheels, for wheels brought change. Hence no roads until 1956.

But now a road was to run from Kathmandu through the foothills of the Himalayas, and on down to the plains of India. This road was being built by the Indian army, more specifically by the Madras Sappers. Another road was going to be built by the Americans, running lengthwise across Nepal, skirting the mountain ranges. And yet another one was contemplated, to be built by the Chinese, linking Kathmandu across the Himalayan passes to the Tibetan plateau and to Lhasa.

'King Mahendra of Nepal is a far-sighted man; he wants his country to come out of seclusion, to be modernized and play its role among the emergent nations of Asia,' said Boyd. He then added that, as a treat, he had arranged to take me on the Indian road.

'It's going to be rough. Much of it is still being bulldozed into shape,' said Boyd. 'I shall introduce you to the engineer in charge. I hope you don't mind, he's quite dark,' he added, a little nervously. Perhaps Boyd had met with a colour bias in other guests ... it was so prevalent at the time, and accounted so natural. Even in Singapore and Malaya, even among the overseas Chinese and the Eurasians, the colour bar held sway. Lao Chieh deplored the fact that I went out without a parasol. 'You'll get so black,' said she. Among the Eurasians it was even worse. I knew at least two families who kept their darker children locked up in the bedroom when there were visitors, only showing off the light-complexioned ones.

As for India, never have I seen such a colour-ridden society! From my first day in Delhi I was secretly appalled by the advertisements in the English newspapers for marriage partners, specifying that the complexion must be 'light'. Small wonder that Boyd feared that I too might nurse a colour complex.

In the sunny afternoon of my third day in Kathmandu I went with Boyd and Judith to a Rana's palace for a wedding festival. Avoiding cows, holy men in contemplation, holy stones, and sundry other sacred obstacles, Boyd manoeuvred the car past the gates into the palace grounds, basking in the joy of a small, light rain that laid the dust. 'Awfully lucky sign,' said Boyd. The palace had ceilings painted blue and pink and green, with holes gouged into them for ventilation. And by the grand piano in the middle of the largest of the three reception rooms stood a tall man in Indian army uniform, with a glass of whisky in his hand. 'Do let me introduce you to the Colonel,' said Boyd. 'He's taking us on the trip I told you about, along the road he's building.'

Oh, I thought, what a marvellous, marvellous looking man! How beautiful, how beautiful he is! He was indeed very dark, almost blue in the darkness of his skin. But it was the most gorgeous, sensuous, satin chocolate colour in the world for me. Then and there I fell out of frigidity into the most blazing need to put my hands on him, to hold him, to want him to make love to me. Heaven—how was this possible, and so swiftly? I stared at him and my legs were unsteady, and all the juices of my body started to pour.

We shook hands. He smiled, and then I knew that if I wanted to have him I must not be too eager. He was a diffident man, unspoilt, and probably many women threw themselves at his head and he avoided them. I do not know how I could tell this, but it all came, affirmation, certainty. So I put on a timid look, and went off immediately to speak to other guests. And of course, as I went from room to room, it was not very long before I found that he was following me, although he too, was very busily speaking to other guests ... How silly, I thought, how silly and yet it was not silly, that we should both behave like adolescents in love for the first time.

Boyd and Judith and I had a very early breakfast the next day, and then the Colonel arrived in his jeep, and the morning became a shining glory, and all the world was full of laughter. Boyd and I got into the jeep and the Colonel drove up the road, which soon lost its tarmac and became an earth road, then a meander of boulders and crevices as it began to zigzag, mounting the soft and treacherous foothills shifty with the rains of summer. The sun beat down hard and after some hours, pausing at a bend when we had soared some 1,500 metres higher than Kathmandu, we saw the whole chain of the Himalayas, the peaks of shining ice, and among them Everest. When night fell we reached the Indian army camp, some 3,000 metres up. It was now bitterly cold, but in the common room for the Madras Sapper officers there was a great log fire burning, and the Colonel kicked the logs, and then looked at me, and then went back to kicking logs with immense concentration. He was jittery; his colour had changed, he looked darker now in the light of the fire. And suddenly the tales of Krishna, the God of Love, so dark that he is blue, came welling up, and I felt that all my skin was glowing with life, and I had a thousand eyes and ears; I could hear the fire lick and swallow the wood logs and the tiny bursting noise of sparks. But still it was not possible to talk.

We slept in separate small tents and I was wretchedly cold; an icy wind swept through the camp and my face was covered with cold sand, but I did not dare get up and ask for more blankets, lest the Colonel think it forward of me, so I froze until morning.

Morning; and after breakfast we had to return to Kathmandu, and what I was waiting for then happened. 'Now you will drive the jeep,' said he, turning to me. 'Oh!' exclaimed Boyd, involuntarily, by no means undisturbed. I sat in the driver's seat and we lurched and bounced abominably, jumped rocks and dived into holes and rolled a mere few inches away from the precipice edge, only saved by the Colonel swiftly turning the steering wheel. 'That was close,' said Boyd in a faint voice. We were now both distraught with love, but still we had not said anything to each other except 'Oops, sorry', when I nearly overturned, and 'Better sound the horn round the bends', and 'Now we'll stop for tea,' when we thought Boyd had had enough of my driving.

Judith saw us return and immediately she knew. She came to hug me that night as I lay in bed.

'Oh, my dear, my dear … ' she said.

'He's nice,' I said.

'I sometimes feel our only responsibility towards ourselves is to be happy,' she said.

'His name is Vincent … ' I broke off lamely.

Vincent. Because he was not a Hindu but an Indian Catholic, and Catholicism in India is said to go back to the Apostle St Thomas, whose bones rest in the crypt of the cathedral in Madras. Vincent came from Madras.

He had asked me to dinner for the next evening. He had also invited Boyd and Judith, but they said that they had another engagement. We went to the Yak and Yeti, Boris's bar at the Royal Hotel; and Boris took one look and knew. 'Altitude sickness,' he announced to the ceiling as he served us solidly packed drinks.

'Are you really a writer?' Vincent said.

'Yes I am.'

'And you are leaving tomorrow?'

'Yes I am.'

'Shall I see you again?'

'I don't know.'

He kicked the logs in the hearth of the Yak and Yeti and Boris threw us one look and smiled ecstatically.

'All I know is that I want to be a woman again. It is very difficult for me to be a woman sometimes. Make me into a woman again.'

Many weeks later, Vincent would tell me of Boyd's consternation when he had received Malcolm's cable announcing the arrival of a 'Chinese writer, female' in Kathmandu, to be entertained.

'I'm sure she wears glasses and she's probably quite old,' Boyd had said gloomily. 'What does one do with a Chinese writer, female?'

'Let's take her on the road. Maybe she'll leave more quickly,' Vincent had said to him helpfully.

And that is how it had happened.

He was at the airport the next morning with Judith, seeing me off. We had made no plans; how could we? I only knew that there was ache and glow, and what did tomorrow mean in front of the Himalayas? He stood looking at me from outside the aeroplane, and then rushed in (the pilot was his friend, and went on revving to oblige, delaying the takeoff). 'I'll come to see you in Delhi,' said he.

Then I was back in Delhi, and Malcolm himself opened the door (Malcolm often answered the door chimes without bothering the servants). 'Suyin, you look absolutely glorious,' said he. 'I am in love,' I said. 'Oh, how happy I am for you, Suyin.'

I spent the next few days not quite knowing where I was, exuding radiance, since several men suddenly fell in love with me (I disengaged tactfully). I also went to the Chinese Embassy, but there was no news of a visa. I went to Agra to see the Taj Mahal, and along the road the vultures were feeding on carcasses of dead cattle. I nearly bought a very large emerald, then desisted. And on the sixth day the secretary brought me a telegram: 'The mountain is coming to Mahomed. Will be in Delhi. tomorrow. Vincent.' Which was enough to make me quite incoherent, dissolving into smiles as I walked on the street. By the afternoon of the next day there was no Vincent. At 5.30 I went to the prim secretary. She disapproved of the stream of 'natives' whom Malcolm invited; a stream which had swollen to a small flood by my being there.

'Has anyone called for me?'

'Oh, some *dark* native came a little while ago, but you were having tea with H.E., in the garden. I told him to ring up or call later.'

I could have strangled her. But before murder was done, the telephone rang.

'It's the same fellow, I think,' said the secretary.

'I'll take it.' It was the same fellow. 'Come, here and now,' I said.

And within half an hour he was there and I was out and we held hands in the taxi, and there was no future, no future, only the small fragment of time now, and that was a marvel like Everest. Vincent also trod on air, caught his finger in a taxi door the next day: he had himself closed the door on it. 'I'm going crazy,' he announced. I went back to the Chinese Embassy. No visa. We persisted in doing the usual things, knowing that everything was no longer what it was; there was no logic, no future, only this.

'What shall we do about it?'

'There is no need for plans, is there?'

'It just is.'

'Yes, it is.'

No visa. I rang up Tikki Kaul and explained to him that I wanted to go back to see my father in China. Tikki Kaul had been a diplomat in Peking and had excellent relations with the Chinese Embassy. Would he intercede for me. He did. At last I obtained a visa for one entry, valid for the end of May. 'Everything will be arranged when you get to Peking,' said the visa officer, less rigorous now, but still baffled. And now I had to get back to Malaya.

We went to Benares for two days. Benares, where dirt and fervour were conjoined, and the smell of ordure and sanctity indistinguishable. But there was the Ganges, ample magnificence, and the funeral pyres and their blankets of flowers, and death had no dominion over all. To Calcutta, for one day and one night at the Great Eastern Hotel, and then I was off, back to Malaya.

'When shall we meet again?'

'I'll manage something,' I promised.

'I'll wait for you,' he said. 'Even if it is ten years.'

'Only ten years?'

'Twenty then,' said he recklessly.

Never did he reproach me for going away. And yet how was it that I could, with my new love and all its enchantment beckoning, how could I still go away? But then perhaps there is no explanation, except that all my life I shall be running in two opposite directions at once; away from and towards love, away from and towards China. Forever sidetracking myself; and in the end garnering both sides of my coin of life.

Back to Johore Bahru, and immediately Leonard: 'Oh, what's happened to you? You've changed.'

'I am in love, Leonard.'

He laughed. 'What nonsense.'

'It is not nonsense.'

'It will pass,' said he confidently.

'Oh no, not with me,' I said, 'I set like concrete.'

'I know this kind of thing,' he began. 'It happens in every marriage, but it shouldn't affect marriage.'

'I'm not built that way, unfortunately. I want a divorce.'

He laughed again, then lost his temper and threw a little soup at me, but it was not very hot.

I went to a few parties, and said I was going to China at the end of May to see my family, and this created an enormous commotion in the press. Li Kungchiang asked me if I really intended to go. 'Of course.' 'I think that's the future,' he said. 'Come back and tell us about it.' Then there were dramatic banner headlines in the *Straits Times*, for no one dared to say: I'm going to China. My letters were opened by the Special Branch, and plain-clothes men followed me. 'I'm going with my eyes closed to the politics,' I said grandiloquently to an American who came to interview me, knowing that silly semantics reassure people.

I took precautions. If Malaya denied me re-entry, I might enter Singapore; I even put money down for a small bungalow in Singapore, which I could then claim as my house ... And then, when all was neatly in place, I felt I must see Vincent again. 'Perhaps it was the Himalayas, the sun and the snow. Perhaps I won't like him when I see him again.' So I flew to Kathmandu for a week, for King Mahendra's coronation in early May.

I remember that week, for it was the beginning of another book, *The Mountain is Young*. I remember the dawn like pink candy-floss and the thousands of little pink and white radishes being washed in the river, and side by side with them the ablutions of brown, gaunt, holy men; everything transparent, and the childish sun lording it over all and the earth laughing. I remember the painted elephants and the dust under their feet, the tawdry and the magnificent processions, and Vincent and I going to Pagan by jeep and up in the hills, and what words did we have when there were no words, only this exultation of the mountains and the sky?

After five days Leonard turned up. The encounter was unpleasant, though unavoidable. I had to leave anyway, so I left with Leonard. He thought he had won; but when we arrived in Calcutta, I told him that it was all very simple. I wanted to be free, Vincent or no Vincent. 'You promised to let me go if I wanted. I want to be free.' But at the same time, knowing that he had no funds, and no job, because of me, I arranged for a living allowance, and we still went on living in the same house.

'I'll wait for you, whether you come back from China or don't come back,' wrote Vincent. And he had said, 'You are always with me now, until I die.' And so I left him, and I went to China, carried also by this renewed strength and beauty bestowed by love.

Four days after leaving Calcutta I was in Hongkong, to cross the border to China. People came and entreated me not to go. It was too dangerous. I would be shot or jailed. Some others came to take photographs of me. I was pursued right up to Lowu, the border railway station between Hongkong and China, by a persistent American television reporter. 'We want to film you in case you never come back,' said he heartily as he pointed his apparatus at me.

Francis and Cecilia did not panic. Francis merely said, 'Well, you must go, of course, to see your father.' And he asked me to take a letter and a leg to his brother, who was in Peking. The brother only had one leg, having lost the other in an accident some years ago. Would I take an artificial leg, the latest model? I would. I also bought two bicycles, some watches and other gifts for my Family. And thus one morning in May I crossed the border between Hongkong and China, holding the artificial leg under my arm, returning home.

Five

China: 1956

THE BARBED WIRE at the border looked theatrical, for as I crossed the bridge leading to China, grass-cutting women in black, with grand-motherly cackle and bare feet, sauntered into Hongkong. They did not produce passports and were not checked. Daily they came and went between these two universes. 'Please enter,' the Chinese Liberation Army soldier on guard at the bridge said politely to me. He had tennis shoes on. The customs official was meticulous. No taxes to be paid on the artificial limb and he suggested that I should wear a watch and use a Parker pen. 'Then we shall only tax the remaining ones: you'll save some money.' As for the two bicycles, surely I was going to ride one? He need only tax one of them.

The China Travel Service young man who took care of me was eager to learn more English. How young everyone was! An overwhelming impression of youth; among the train attendants, the people who carried bags and hauled loads, the few police (unarmed). And then the familiar churn of wheels began, train lullaby cradling my childhood back to me as we ambled among the jade green fields of May, dotted with Hakka women with black-fringed hats and their feet absent in water. I remembered denuded mounds and hillocks, dilapidation and ruin. Now the villages were neat and the houses new; everywhere there were trees, all of a size, six-year-old trees flapping small, young leaves like children's hands ...

Canton, now renamed Kuangchow. Entry into the station to music and young men wearing white shirts and neat trousers. No rags, no beggars. I was taken to the Love the Masses Hotel; a Yugoslav youth representative and some overseas Chinese came with me. My room was on the fifth floor, looking down upon the translucent Pearl River. The hotel was clean, whereas I remembered it filthy when I had stayed there in 1938.* The breeze flowed in and threw itself upon my bed. All night I would hear the frolicking water slap its freight of small sampans. The fishing junks clacked their sails as they went out to sea; ferries hooted reassuringly above the gurgle of the peopled stream.

I walked about Kuangchow, met more overseas Chinese from the train. They had come back to stay; they were going to build themselves bungalows in areas where repatriated overseas were housed. Most of them came from Indonesia. In 1958, and up to 1960, many hundreds of thousands would leave Indonesia; the Chinese government sending ships for their repatriation. They would start rubber and coffee plantations in the south. 'If you go to Peking, go to the Hsinchiao Hotel. My uncle has put some money into the building,' said one of them to me.

I read the newspapers pasted on boards along the main street. Achievements and production. I went to a cinema and saw one-third of a Russian love story. I came out in the evening and the Cantonese strolled by, clicking wooden slippers, that incessant tap dance which vanished when they switched to rubber and plastic sandals by 1964. A health campaign was on, and slogans everywhere enjoined people to refrain from spitting. People went on spitting. Accustomed to dire threats of fines and punishment in other countries for refusing to obey orders, I asked the young China Travel Service man, 'Why don't you punish people who spit?' 'But that would be oppression,' he cried. 'We believe the masses can discipline themselves.'

Acrobats in the People's Park; an exhibition of Polish painting, children roller-skating, couples with young babies in the open-air restaurants ... such security, such tranquil enjoyment of the balmy warmth, I had never

---

* See *Birdless Summer* and *Destination Chungking*.

seen in China, never without being interrupted by clawing hands, diseased bodies, hungry faces ... 'Lady, lady, open your compassionate heart ... I have not eaten ... ' But now it was not so. I remembered the streets as dreadful corridors of want; now they were calm and safe.

At dawn the Pearl River was solid pink and the sun heaved itself out of its seabed and light seized all the earth. Then I was on the train to Peking, and again young trees were everywhere. The attendant went round with a fly swatter, trying to look murderous; there were no flies. Every station was clean, with flower pots, and among them always the nice young face of one unarmed policeman in white, standing to attention. And this was not for tourists, since at the time there were no tourists; few people from the West went to China then.

The loudspeaker on the train never stopped dispensing exhortation, encouragement, warnings at each station to leave no luggage behind, and achievements in production. A perpetual self-congratulation, a little boring after two days. My companions in the compartment, two men and a woman, were amiable. I said I came from Malaya, and they talked about production and achievements. They reeled off satisfactory statistics; they were well-informed. Never, I thought, had I seen such a network of information at all levels. Unanimity of effort, unanimity of explanation, explanation repeated in a hundred thousand places at once; including the running trains.

At Wuhan we crossed the river by ferry (the bridge would only be built three years later). A gnarled peasant sitting opposite me picked up the book on my lap, one of those I had purchased at the Hsinhua bookstore in Kuangchow. Entitled *Story From the Old Mulberry Tree*, it was about Land Reform: well-written and unsparing, noting the brutalities which had taken place when peasants had been aroused. The peasant leafed through it, read a sentence aloud and replaced it on my lap. He could read. That was the miracle which kept me entranced for the next hour. Suddenly I saw the immensity of what had been done ... peasants travelling in trains, who could read.

We rolled through the plains of Honan and I craned at Sinyang, my birthplace, but could not see the house on the hill where we had lived. Chengchow and the Yellow River, and the loudspeaker waxing excited, and the bridge, my father's pride and pain, and the car attendant going round locking the lavatories ... no excreta in the noble stream. All the familiar stations and their names, and I thought of my mother's children buried here, their bones in the yellow earth with so many, so many millions of other bones. I thought of the locust plagues, and the famines, and the floods, and the droughts I had seen. And now there were young people washing the train, and flower pots, and outside in the fields the peasants wore clean white T-shirts, and there was peace.

In the late afternoon, a greyness on the mauve horizon; the battlemented grey walls of Peking with their crouched monumental gates. By the wall's base pyramidal piles of coal balls, made of coal dust and clay, and donkeys laden with them in baskets trudging into the city. The loudspeaker now went berserk with joyful recommendations. 'Beloved passengers, we are approaching Peking ... leave nothing behind ... please be careful as you go down ... please take care of the children ...'

Music, and the train sliding to a stop and Third and Fourth Brothers running along the platform ... I came down and there in a small group, his eyes screwed up to see better, was Papa, Papa, oh so beloved, a little thinner but well, and everyone round him smiling as if something good had been achieved. We greeted each other, cousins and nephews and nieces and aunts by blood and by affection, using the correct and appropriate names of family relationship and courtesy. And Papa said with love, 'Your dress is so thin, you'll catch a cold.' And Aunt Ting exclaimed, 'Ah, how much your father has waited for this! Now his face is like spring!' She had a plug of paper in her left nostril; she was being treated for a cancer of the nose. She would live another fifteen years. Papa smiled and introduced me to two people in sober clothes standing diffidently behind the family group. 'These are Comrades Li and Wu, of my organization; they have come to greet you. The organization has sent a car to take us home, and then to bring you to your hostel.'

'We welcome all intellectuals from overseas who return to serve the country,' said Comrade Wu, a jovial man, pumping my hand.

'I came back to see my father,' I replied, smiling noncommittally. 'May I stay at home with him?'

'We made arrangements for a hostel,' said Comrade Wu, 'but we can study the problem.'

I did not protest; it was now arranged that I would first go home with Papa and then proceed to the hostel for the night.

Home was, of course, smaller; part of the veranda partitioned off since another family now lived in what had been our living and dining room. Papa had kept the two bedrooms and the bathroom for himself. The kitchen was now in the outhouse where our rickshaw puller had lived; the veranda, glassed in, was the congenial living room.

Hsueh Mah, our servant, beamed and screamed. Her front teeth protruded more than ever. 'Big Miss is back, Big Miss is back, oh what a happy day!' She stomped around, ineffectual, taking up a lot of space trying to pour tea. I went in to wash my hands and I saw mother's large trunk in Papa's bedroom. She had come with it from Belgium in 1913; it was the one she always packed with winter clothes when she threatened to leave. Now she had gone but the trunk remained; perhaps it was too old, perhaps left to remind father she was still there. Oh, the dreadful tenacity of things; memory traps to ambush us.

First Uncle's daughter Ping, Fourth Sister in our generation, arrived and shook hands with everyone. She was a Party cadre in charge of education in the eastern sector. In her teens she had run away from middle school to the Communist base at Yenan. It was a most hazardous journey, through the Kuomintang lines, with their concentration camps and tortures for the young like her going to Yenan. She had taken part in the guerrilla wars against Japan; she had married another guerrilla and borne five children and lost three – she did not know where they were – whom she had had to leave with peasants when the guerrillas moved camp. 'There were bad people who sold our children behind our backs,' she would tell me years later. Like so many, so many modest heroes, the core of the Chinese Communist Party, and the reason why it succeeded, she had no time for self-pity or for reminiscence, until twenty years later, in 1976, when at last she began to tell me a little of her life.

But now she came in, portly and self-assured, and I only saw a glossy, managerial woman. She assumed a stance of 'teacher' towards me. I was a responsibility. Educating and remoulding into correct thinking such people as myself, come from the capitalist world – with gentleness of course, but withal firmly, not giving up until the teaching penetrated – was quite a task. It took us time, Ping and I, to become fond of each other; to realize that, in a way, we were both as domineering; but that I managed it with less frankness. She had the greater moral courage, the unflinching dedication.

We ate some noodles and chicken that Papa had prepared, for he was a good cook with a light, swift hand. On the wall hung a picture of Chairman Mao, looking debonair; below it was my father's 'model engineer' certificate, framed and with a big red satin flower pinned to the frame. It was all untrue about his having been in jail or ill-treated. 'How is Third Uncle?' I asked of Third and Fourth Brothers (who are Third Uncle's sons, and technically my cousins in the Western style). 'He is well, but very busy.' All private companies, factories, shops, were being nationalized that year. Many were going 'semi-public' as joint companies with the state. Third Uncle had managed many companies. 'I intend to go to Szechuan to see him.' 'Our government always give intellectuals returned from abroad the opportunity to see the achievements of socialism,' said Comrade Li graciously. I understood that I had spoken out of turn.

We smiled and burped with satisfaction. Then I was taken to the hostel on Hatamen Street. I was greeted there by the man in charge, Comrade Liu, most affable and solicitous. 'Welcome, welcome,' he cried, and took me to a very nice room, where I slept, after having stared at the ceiling for a very long time.

The next morning I went down to breakfast at 7 a.m. The refectory (the word leapt out, for there was such a school ambiance to the hostel) held round brown tables with eight stools to each. Some people were finishing breakfast, others just beginning. There was white steamed bread and gruel and pickles and tea, copious and hot. At my table sat a couple, husband and wife. They smiled at me and we introduced ourselves. They had returned from America to serve China, they had read of me, seen my book and recognized me by the photograph on the cover. They belonged to an illustrious, scholarly family; I had known Mr C.'s uncle and his father, both professors in renowned Chinese universities; both were now in the United States.

'How long have you been here?'

'About four months ... we read Premier Chou Enlai's appeal to intellectuals to return, so we came back ... It was difficult to manage; the Americans are not letting people like us out of the States.'

'But no work has been assigned to us yet,' said Mrs C. 'We are being re-educated politically.'

Mr C. nodded towards three people sitting at another table. 'They've been here longer ... one is a sociologist, the other two are students who have not completed their studies abroad. Some people are snapped up very quickly, especially scientists, engineers, mathematicians ... but others have to wait.'

'It's also a question of class origin,' said Mrs C. ruefully.

'But that's getting better,' said her husband.

I swallowed the words with little sips of gruel. 'What is your general impression?'

'At first we felt strange ... we were not used to many things ... everything is so organized here ... perhaps too much, although they try hard to be kind.'

'We had a walk in the park last week. They took us marching four by four,' said Mrs C. laughing.

'Now, dear, you must remember, they don't know how people react to small things ... but they mean well, they're so anxious, they *want* to do well ... it's shaming to us, really, how painstaking they are ... And we came at a bad time. There was a big campaign on, against hidden counter-revolutionaries. Of course it hit the intellectuals. They were checked and rechecked. It was ... unpleasant,' Mr C. said.

'Do you regret having come back?' I asked.

'Oh no,' they said together. 'It's our country, for better, for worse. We sacrificed a great deal. We had good jobs in American universities; we threw them up to come here.'

They did not look at each other, but I felt them most conscious of each other then; their love wrapped round them close as one skin. They had done this together and would stand by each other, for better, for worse ... and suddenly I could not swallow any more.

I felt hemmed in and constricted, shrunken and curtailed; and this came as a sudden realization as I sat there at breakfast. 'I have difficulty in breathing,' I said.

'We felt the same at first. We're not used to what they call mass movements, we're used to a capitalist society ... It takes time to get accustomed' — said Mr C.

'To tutelage,' I cut in brutally. Mr C. winced. 'To being controlled and checked at every turn,' I added.

'That isn't the whole picture,' they said. 'The peasants, the workers, they don't feel choked; they've got oxygen now ... it's our class feelings ... they make us feel guilty.'

'Guilty!' I echoed. 'Choked with guilt.'

We sat there and knew it was so.

Class guilt; not for particular sins individually committed, but for what we had omitted to do for our people. A sense of turpitude. Possibly, I thought as I tried to swallow, only the Chinese intelligentsia would feel that way. Because they had been for 2,500-odd years the administration, the establishment, the possessors of knowledge, and knowledge was power. The Chinese intellectual felt more responsible than any Western intellectual would ever do towards his own history, his culture, his society. In the Revolution the Chinese intellectual was still the lynchpin of whatever China would become. But he also represented the past, with all its misdeeds, its arrogance, and in this dreadful ambivalence he would remain for a long time, until the New Dynasty was stabilized ...

All this went through my mind as the gruel slipped past my gullet. Since waking that morning I had felt choked. Not terror, fear or outrage as in the old days, but guilt. And in my case it was almost unbearable, and my reaction was physical, nausea, because suddenly it put me right back where Pao my husband had tried to root me: in an unnamed, incoherent, morass of guilt, abasement without respite.

I got up and it seemed to me that I would topple, lose my foothold, fall, because I could not feel the edges of myself. I had lost me.

Twenty-one years later, in the *People's Daily*, I would read that Mr C.'s old mother had come from America to stay with her son and daughter-in-law and their children. The old lady was received by Chou Enlai's wife, Teng Yingchao. Now they would be together, with children and grand-children. The C.s must have had their good years and their bad ones; their love for their country helped them to survive until at last all was well again.

There would be others, so many others; writers of renown, artists and teachers and scientists, greater in knowledge and dedication and dignity than I would ever be. I followed them through the years, and they never reproached me for not having joined their ranks. 'You were more vulnerable than we were,' they say gently. They talk of the bad years they survived, and of those who did not survive them. Some of them, it seems to me, enjoy the recollection of what they surmounted; as all hardship becomes, in memory, joyous adventure.

Perhaps the Chinese intellectual, conscious of his value as the knowledge bearer, transmitting the enduring civilization which he represents, has fashioned an extra dimension of fortitude, a larger limit of personal endurance. I am forever conscious that my friends traverse the centuries. Their conversation refers to what happened to some poet of the sixth century A.D. They quote a philosopher of the Han dynasty; refer aptly to a neat treachery performed twenty centuries ago; and all this in a way which does not occur in any other culture I know. Allusion to the classics gives them an amplitude of examples; the very names they give their children are references to lyrical lines from famous poets. Thus their own living is forever witness to a universe of multitudinous lives; in which they take their place and find serenity. Through their span of years their predecessors remain alive in the great ocean of time which rocks us all. They bear witness not to one era, but to many.

And now the Revolution has wrenched from the intelligentsia the power, which was exclusive education. They have had to remould them-selves, change their views on society and their role in it; and as Mao Tsetung had already said in 1942, thought-remoulding is a very long, very arduous and painful process. But their main and traditional concern remains towards that culture-nation which is China and her people; the transmission of knowledge to the new society to come. But this new society —how was it going to treat them?

Comrade Liu inquired how I had slept; told me there would be a meeting after lunch, and asked me to criticize him. 'I make a lot of mistakes. People like myself, not cultured, never saw an intellectual until now, when the Party gave me the task of looking after them ... Chairman Mao says we must unite with intellectuals, who are valuable and also re-educate them ...'

'There are a good many here.'

'Indeed, from many countries; they are different in their habits from us, but patriotic ...'

'They need readjustment.'

'Even so, even so,' said Comrade Liu, abashed, for I had spoken too quickly; and who was I to say that others needed readjustment? I wondered whether Comrade Liu was gauging the readjustments that I needed.

'You seemed to enjoy breakfast, you have many of our habits,' said he charitably, thus pushing me right back into my difference. If it was a task to cope with pure Chinese returning from abroad, how much more difficult would a Eurasian prove to be? What new problems would I place upon Comrade Liu and others, whose job would be to remould my thinking? And how would they know what I really felt? And what were my feelings really worth? Would I be able, as they were, to give up everything, literally life itself, to fight and to die so that human dignity should come to those who had none? The answer was no. I despised myself then, and this was unbearable and made me sick.

I walked out with gentle suffocation wrapped around me, feeling culpable and disobedient and guilty. And Peking was so beautiful and beloved and well-remembered. I loitered in the streets, peaceful and clean despite the dust of the spring wind. I went to my father's house and no one followed me.

Papa worked half a day only, and only because he wanted to. He was entitled to a full pension, and the leadership* in his organization offered him a car, and milk three times a week. Papa refused the car. 'Our country is still so poor, why waste petrol?' He took the bus to his office, a long ride of over forty minutes each way.

Papa had bought mooncakes for me, going to the Muslim shop in the western city that made the best and most flaky ones. When I was a baby

* The word leadership refers to the Party committee in charge at the level at which the individual is employed.

he had named me his little Moon Guest. I told Papa I did not want to be re-educated, my skin crawled at the thought. He said, 'You must not show temper.' 'But I don't like to be under tutelage.' 'One must be patient,' said Papa, plucking at his hairless chin. 'Things will be better now, I think. The last campaign was very harsh, but I was not criticized. It's mostly writers who get into trouble. And that is due to the Hu Feng case.'

I had read a little about the Hu Feng affair* in Hongkong, but there was so much exaggeration in the reports of the Western press, and the Chinese press itself so suddenly and so virulently started denouncing him that I could not understand why this 'counter-revolutionary writer', once a member of the Communist Party, had been so powerful as to compel the Party to a major drive to sift 'hidden counter-revolutionaries' throughout the administration and intellectual circles.

Papa gave me some old newspaper clippings about the Hu Feng case. I read while he cooked lunch and Hsueh Mah screamed and hovered and interrupted. Then I went to stand outside the front door of our house, to watch the peasant horsecarts returning to the countryside, empty. They came into the city by night; I would wake to hear the soft step of horse and mule and donkey hooves, and a great sweetness would come over me. The peasants brought fresh meat and vegetables and fruit to the markets of Peking every day. Now the animals were sleek, with shiny coats; some had a cloth stretched behind their back legs, fastened to the cart, to collect their dung. No more flogging and whipping, which had been my childhood agony. Did security also bring kindness? And the peasants sitting on the carts' arms nodding drowsily, they were well-dressed and well-fleshed.

Opposite our house there had been a well with a windlass of pear wood. The windlass made a special sound when the pails dropped down the well; *humph, humph*; and it sang *loo, loo* when the well man wound up the wet rope of the pails, and water would come spurting out, so icy pure and sweet; for beneath Peking was much underground water. Papa, in the 1930s, had drawn up a plan for tapping and using this water. 'It's not done properly at the moment,' he had said.

The wife of the well man had large, floating breasts, always exposed, and a child hung at the right nipple year after year. Mama hated her,

---

* Hu Feng was a Communist Party member and a writer. He began to challenge many of the official policies. This resulted in the general campaign against 'hidden counter-revolutionaries' in the Party, the administrative and intellectual circles, from July to November 1955.

Note that the word 'intellectual' in China denotes anyone who has some learning, and includes schoolteachers. It was reckoned that there were five million 'intellectuals' in China in 1956-7.

but I thought her very beautiful; she laughed and she had magnificent teeth and a clear ivory skin. How she laughed! Like the water.

But now the well was covered over. 'There are taps in every house in our road,' said Hsueh Mah. 'No need to fetch water in wooden pails any more.'

The door-bell rope which traversed the veranda shook; the bell tinkled; it was our neighbourhood policeman. He had come to pay his respects to Papa; he did this once a month. Now he welcomed me, accepted tea, and chatted with us. Hsueh Mah told him that I had looked for the well. 'It seems it was there only yesterday.' 'Ah, don't look at today with yesterday's eyes,' said the policeman. He was so young, with that great candour about him which many young people now had; so scrubbed, neat and clear-eyed that he looked like a brand new toy policeman. Papa said that he was a very good young man, respectful of his elders.

Papa now took a little time to explain a few things to me. But it was no swift, machine-gun explaining. He said a few words, let them sink in, like water into soil. 'They really have done so much, pulled the country out of squalor and chaos ... I can forget their pettiness and their suspicion when I see all that has been done. But they turn up everything; they want to know every single thing in one's life. They don't trust us.' Why should they trust us, I thought. Even Papa had been under so many administrations, had kept trains running under so many warlords; had worked (although he had also been jailed) under the Japanese when they had taken north China ... The new government had inherited more than three million bureaucrats from the Chiang Kaishek administration; they could not let them starve; they had been confirmed in their jobs. But of course the Kuomintang must have had agents among them. To ferret these agents out of their various and manifold burrows would be a long and unpleasant process.

'Some people cannot stand the incessant questioning, the meetings. They commit suicide,' Papa said. 'But I only had to write my autobiography twice more, because of your husband, Tang Paohuang.'

The Party had sent people to search for intellectuals, scientists, engineers and artists, as soon as Peking had been liberated. Papa had been taken to hospital and given the best of care, had recovered. The engineering bureau where he had been assigned to work (at a top salary) asked him to help. 'We need you, we need all those like you who can help us put the country together again. Is it not a shambles?'

'It was Marshal Yeh Chienying who was in charge at the time,' Papa said, 'and the first thing was to get the coal mines going. Without coal, no electricity, no locomotives, no heating and no industry ... But the Japanese and the Kuomintang had destroyed the coal mines. I was sent to Tatung, to the coal mines there.' Papa was not alone. His old engineer friend, Hua Nankuei, and our external uncle, Uncle Liu of the stentorian voice and huge frame, all three old men, shouldering knapsacks, went off to Tatung on the edge of Mongolia. They toiled like youngsters, ate *kaoliang* (rye) gruel, slept on the beaten earth. 'When we needed machinery the People's Liberation Army got it for us. Yeh Chienying himself came down to see our work; he provided us with army greatcoats against the cold. The soldiers worked with the miners, repairing the shafts. Truly, it was wonderful ... we were very enthusiastic,' said Papa, falling into newspaper stereotype. It was the new vocabulary, a phraseology of enthusiasm and struggle and achievement, which transformed one's expression of feeling and possibly the feeling itself, since the way people talk affects the way they think.

The coal mines began working again. Papa and Uncle Liu and Hua Nankuei were named 'model engineers' and officially congratulated. The railways started running, and a new railway was built within two years, 1950-2, between Chengtu and Chungking, in Szechuan. 'It's the railway that I came back to build in 1913,' Papa reminisced, laughing and creasing his eyes. In 1952, when the first locomotive, beflagged and all its loud-speakers singing, had rolled into the new station in Chengtu, where crowds danced and beat drums, an old engineer, overcome with emotion, had knelt and kissed the steel rails. He too had wanted, all his life, to build a railway for his country.

I went back to the hostel in Hatamen Street after lunch, and then it was time for the meeting. A bus took us to a large new brick building. We marched in two by two, regular as a school snake. We sat in rows of chairs. To one side were five or six chairs, similar to ours; there the officials would sit, not elevated on a platform, but in a friendly manner, by our side. I was next to Mr W. from Indonesia. 'This is my fifth meeting,' he said. 'There's one almost every month. The officials change, but it's always the same thing ... they are helping us to progress in our thought-remoulding.'

In filed four men, one of them with face clad in thick spectacles, which radiated benevolence. He reminded me of Father Ladany, especially the shrewd mouth. He welcomed us in quiet, measured tones; praised us for returning to join in the country's reconstruction; and said that if there was anything on our minds we must speak it without fear. The Party welcomed criticism. Chairman Mao repeatedly emphasized that the people must be listened to; he and his colleagues were there to help us in every way.

(Suddenly the word 'help' gave me a disquieting feeling. Had not my cousin Ping, Fourth Sister, the night before, held my arm and said, 'We must help you ... '? I was allergic to soul-fingering.)

One person spoke. He said he had many difficulties in understanding, but would strive hard to dispel his doubts. He realized he needed more help. Another said that despite a great deal of help he found it difficult to throw away past burdens and turn around,★ although he knew he would feel much better when he had done so. Several other people said more or less the same thing. The bespectacled official nodded encouragingly; he did not fidget, but sat upright, untired, letting each person talk as long as he liked while the afternoon lengthened drowsily, endlessly, and I listened to a magpie call in the camphor tree, and was filled with fury and that suffocation familiar since breakfast. Perhaps the index of boredom was the measure of successful remoulding, I thought wickedly. One man talked sheer nonsense for twenty minutes. 'He's mentally deranged, from Indonesia,' whispered Mr W. He could whisper without seeming to move his lips. The unhinged man was listened to with the same attention as others and then gently led away, sobbing, to the garden outside by Comrade Liu. Spectacles then looked around. Did anyone else wish to speak?

Had Papa been there, had I been in a normal state of mind, I would have kept quiet; even found it humorous. But I must speak or stifle; something in me would not keep still. I said that I felt suffocated. I did not like tutelage. I had come to learn facts and ask questions but I did not want to be thought-remoulded. I did not think it would work with me.

Not a muscle moved on the official's kind lower jaw; nor did his glasses glint more fiercely. Round us the silence settled like an implacable velvet smother. After what seemed a long pause but was probably not more than ten seconds, the official said that the meeting was ended, it had been productive, he wished us all 'good progress, perseverance and success' in our own efforts to alter our world point of view. He then shook hands with everyone as they filed past him, and when I came up he said with a kind and terrible gentleness, 'You are certainly of big landlord origin.'

★ The expression 'turn around', in Chinese *fanshen*, means to change one's attitude, behaviour and thinking. It is a process of rejecting the old self and acquiring a new personality. The words 'born again' now used so much in America, convey exactly the same idea of conversion.

Bad origin. Good origin. There were five 'bad origins', which meant that in any mass political campaign, anyone from one of the five bad was due for special attention: landlords, rich peasants, reactionaries (counter-revolutionaries), hooligans or asocial elements – thieves, pimps, dope pushers, for example – and 'bourgeois elements who refuse to be re-educated'. For the next twenty years, this classification of 'origin' would wreak a great deal of harm in China.

And of all bad origins the worst was to be of big landlord issue. On the bus I felt like a leper, and did not inflict myself upon anyone, although Mr C. heroically did not avoid me.

In the late afternoon I went home to Papa. Sitting with Papa was a tall, thin-faced young man, from Szechuan, Wang Wanchun. He was a journalist working on the *Peking Evening News*. He came from a wealthy family, but he had renounced all his property and was classified as 'enlightened intelligentsia'. He told me very humorously, as I mentioned a little about the meeting, that during the campaign for ferreting out hidden counter-revolutionaries in 1955 (which was the campaign Mr and Mrs C. had talked about at breakfast), he had been rigorously grilled. But in the end, after a great many accusations which he rejected, he had said, 'Com-rades, I do have many failings and defects; but I love my country.' And suddenly everyone had let go, and the Party cadres in charge had con-cluded the meeting and he had been left in peace ever since.

Wanchun and I were to become very good friends; and my friendship was perhaps the cause of his death eleven years later.

Pretty soon, in came Comrades Wu and Li from Papa's engineering institute; I think they had been told about my outburst because they were so solicitous, inquiring about my health, until I began to feel indeed grievously ill. Why, oh why did I buck like a wild pony instead of trying to find out what it was like to be remoulded? Was I certain that my thinking was so healthy and correct? Comrades Wu and Li assured me that Papa was *not* classified as a landlord; they smiled reassuringly. We sipped tea and they said that Papa was being given a full holiday, as long as he liked, to be more with me. I then said, 'I am sorry that I did not tell you this straightaway, but I know Madame Kung Peng; she is at the Department of Information of the Ministry of Foreign Affairs. I think she would like to know that I am here; we were at university together.' 'We shall certainly pass on your request,' said Comrade Li.

I went back to the hostel to sleep with a little jingle in my mind: 'They want you to be docile, but you happen to be hostile.' Hostile – of bad class origin – but on the streets people were laughing, and strolling, and there was palpable cheerfulness and ease, and the children, oh, how beautiful were the children now, so beautiful and healthy. No more infanticide, no more selling of little girls, no more baby corpses wrapped in newspaper on the streets. At last there was order and peace; and the people were no longer miserable; they were free of disease and famine ... there was no sense in a freedom which did not first assure the fundamental needs of man ... so what was the matter with me?

The next day was study day at the hostel. Everyone read books or sat at tables and wrote in notebooks. Comrade Liu suggested I have a rest. I went to the Eastern Peace Market, and rediscovered all the little shops of my childhood. They were all there, including those in the alley where carved jades of all kinds and colour were sold. After lunch with Papa, Comrade Wu came to the house to tell me that Kung Peng indeed remembered me, and asked me to go to see her at five o'clock.

I went back to the hostel to dress and Comrade Liu came in with a book on Peking for me. I said I knew Peking, I had grown up here. 'Ah, that is why you're *almost* like one of us,' he said delightedly. 'I shall try to be more like you, with your help,' I said. Comrade Liu blushed greatly, for he was most modest, and he wrung my hand with such affection that I felt I had been stupid and arrogant at the meeting.

The block of flats where officials of the Foreign Ministry lived, including ambassadors and vice-ministers, was in Paofang Hutung. Kung Peng's flat was very small. The higher Party officials did not dwell in luxury, although they went to official parties in large black Zis cars with drawn curtains (the cars were from an official pool). Kung Peng greeted me with genuine happiness. 'You used your own name, so we did not know that you had arrived, although I expected you.' She had seen the foreign newspapers, which had made a great stir about my going to China. I had not written to her, thinking she would be informed.

We talked a great deal, and I find in my early notes of that day (May 21st, 1956), that as usual when I was with Kung Peng I was over-exuberant. I talked about the need for new words and expressions for the adjustment of new ideas; I thought both the jargon of the West and that of Marxism as I had heard it stale and inadequate. At this time the West had nothing to offer China except hostility, the language of prurient enmity. 'As for the propaganda from here, it's appallingly childish and has no influence or impact.' 'Is it so bad?' replied Kung Peng. 'Perhaps for someone as sophisticated as you are, but we get letters from many people, praising us ...'

We strolled in the courtyard. Kung Peng's little daughter was there with her nurse. A doctor had told Kung Peng that the child was backward. 'Not at all, she's perfectly normal,' said I. The girl grew up beautiful and intelligent; and Kung Peng always felt grateful to me.

Kung Peng's mixture of honesty and detachment, genuine affection and care, patience for my many quirks ... how can I ever describe them without a wild sense of loss? For so many years I would need her, need her, while I made my way so painfully through the unknown universe of the Chinese Revolution; a world not as it was represented: unilinear, unidimensional, both in the West and in China's propaganda, but infinitely complex and multitudinous; a wholeness made up of a million contradictory aspects; subject to swings and crises, each of which overlapped its contrary; magnificent in its achievements and colossal in its errors and failures. I sought clearness and Kung Peng said, 'You yourself must think it out.' This was the greatest boon of all; her trust in my ultimate lucidity. Meanwhile, she gave me the gift of time and space and silence, and so many encounters; argued for me against the Party cadres who were infuriated by the unorthodox, non-conformist me. Thus was I privileged; and if I feel like a thief, having purloined so much from living, then I must thank the bounty of Kung Peng who gave me to hoard in such great measure knowledge to last me all my days.

The restaurant we went to was the Kang Lo, also known as the Three Tables; literally only three square tables, a small room, and most excellent food, renowned throughout the city. Alas, in 1959 the restaurant ceased to exist. Perhaps now, when restaurants are being resurrected, it will open again. The reason for its closure was that it encouraged a 'bourgeois' aspect of life.

Kung Peng's husband, Chiao Kuanhua, was relaxed and friendly. He had great charm, and with wine we talked (I talked too much) until very late at night. I said many things that I have now forgotten; and I found Chiao's mind so swift, so arrow to its mark, that it was necessary to ask him to slow down and explain himself. Perhaps it was this great skill and intelligence which lost him in the end. One day when I was visiting them, as I did several times in the course of the next few weeks, he pointed to a rather awkward Chinese picture on the wall. 'See that beautiful curve, how the willow bends?' I wondered why he thought I did not understand anything about Chinese painting. He was always aware of himself as brilliant.

But at the time they were a happy couple, and well-informed, since they both worked in the Foreign Ministry under Chou Enlai and read all the outside newspapers. Kung Peng accepted immediately that I had come for a visit; and actually at no time asked me to stay. I think she realized the many difficulties I would have; and it is even possible that, after due consideration, had I brought up the matter, she would have asked me gently to remain 'outside'. Many overseas Chinese who did apply to return were refused for one reason or another.

Kung Peng said that I should move to the Hsinchiao Hotel, which housed journalists and minor diplomats and was the centre of all the 'news' filtering through Peking's grapevine; and so I moved there. I managed to spend a great deal of time with Papa, who grew younger and smiled all day. Many people came to our house, relatives and friends, and Chinese journalists to interview me. At weekends, and sometimes late in the after-noon, Third and Fourth Brothers came with their wives, Jui and Shuan. Together we walked a great deal in the parks.

Third Brother had been in America for six years, studying at the University of Minnesota; he had graduated and been offered a job in research. Then the Korean war had started. The American government did not allow Chinese scientists to return to China. Third Brother pretended no interest in 'Red' China, abstained from correspondence and went for a holiday to Brazil. In Brazil he got in touch with a Szechuanese friend who had emigrated there in 1943. The friend helped him on a very roundabout journey to Scandinavia, to Finland, to Moscow and thence back to China. Being a physicist, he had been immediately welcomed to a position at Peking University. Third Uncle had married him off to Jui before his departure for the United States, and she waited for him all those years, staying in Chengtu with Third Uncle and Third Aunt. Jui was a very beautiful girl, with a delicate skin, and was working in the Chemistry Department of the University of Chengtu.

As to Fourth Brother, he had studied in England, and had straight-forwardly travelled back to China.* For the first few months he had been the government's guest, and had been taken to see many new achievements; but in one political campaign against bourgeois ideas among intellectuals, in 1953-4, he had been violently criticized because he wore English trousers (plus-fours). 'But I had no other clothes,' he said. Third Uncle arranged a marriage for him; and despite the new advocation of freedom in courtship and romance, the young in China still bowed to tradition, and preferred

*The U.K. government recognized the People's Republic of China promptly in 1950.

proper parental introduction. Fourth Brother married at his father's suggestion.

Shuan was an excellent choice for Fourth Brother. A calm girl with great courage; very devoted and clever, with a good brain. Owing to his work, which brought Fourth Brother to Manchuria in 1960, they were to be separated for almost seventeen of the next twenty years; and at the end were most deeply in love with each other.

Fourth Brother loved beautiful things; he collected a great deal of old furniture. In that summer of 1956, we spent happy hours buying furniture for Papa. I acquired some beautiful Ming chairs and a rosewood table as a present, and Papa was pleased. Alas, during the Cultural Revolution, all Fourth Brother's carved bookshelves and other antiques disappeared.

I asked my relatives, 'Did you feel strange when you were first back?'

'Yes,' they said, 'not accustomed ... '

'As if not enough oxygen?'

Third Brother laughed. He always laughs when he does not wish to show perturbation. When during the Cultural Revolution he was condemned as a 'bourgeois' intellectual to keep the stove of a cook going, he laughed.

After laughing he said, 'It's better at the University. We are all high-class intellectuals and the movement there is careful and easy; I think the Party people in charge do understand that they must not press us too hard ... '

'But it is not like this everywhere,' said Jui. 'In some places it was very bad. If you have a bad leadership, Party cadres who hate the sight of you, then it is not good at all.'

'But can't you tell them?'

They looked at each other. When does criticizing a Party cadre become criticizing the Party line and therefore the Party? How can one stand it if one is accused of being counter-revolutionary?

We talked and talked; and Papa said, 'Up on top, no trouble. Down below, the lower cadres are pretty hardworking. But it's the middle cadres.'

'Commandism, bureaucratism, sectarianism, sit down and give order-ism,' chanted Fourth Brother. The last campaign, from July to November 1955, against hidden counter-revolutionaries, had been extremely un-pleasant and strenuous. 'Meeting after meeting, no rest ... people became exhausted ... There are suicides each time there is a campaign. The cadres sometimes go on and on. It's gruelling for them and for us.'

But how could the middle cadre be anything but rigid and unbending? He was the transmission belt for orders and their implementation from the top to the bottom. Upon him rested much responsibility and far too much work. He could not take decisions easily; and especially when, at the top, there were divergences and crises. 'And then rectification in the Party. The cadres do not have a good time. And they don't get the salaries or the privileges which we, as intellectuals, are getting,' said Third Brother. There had been two major Party rectifications in six years, and every time the middle cadre had to go to study sessions and meetings, criticism and self-criticism.

I said that, with such political campaigns going on, there would be a tendency to focus on the odd man or woman, the slightly different individual, as a 'target'. Both Party cadres and the people in the organizations would look out for a potential black sheep in their midst; someone more isolated, more vulnerable, who could be attacked safely and could not retaliate easily. My family had not thought of it that way. 'It's true that sometimes they do pick on an overseas Chinese,' said Fourth Brother, 'but it's not the policy of the government. However, some overseas Chinese have such different habits, and they have more money too, and they spend it ... ' 'That's exactly what I'm talking about,' I said. Would I be able to stand being the natural target for criticism, a horrendous example of bourgeois tendencies and decadence? I knew in my bones it would happen. I was too exuberant, too impulsive, and also too striking in my looks. A natural target. And what good would it do to me, after I had been picked ragged by 'the masses' – who would easily find in my past life so many examples of immorality and other vices – what good would it do for the Party leadership to console me, and to say, 'Comrade, this is to educate the masses'?

There was the young overseas man doing translation work; held up as an example of bourgeois defect because one day, trooping out of collective enjoyment at a cinema, he had broken away from the group to buy an ice cream from a pedlar at the gate of the cinema house. Another person, taken for a group march in the park, four by four, had lingered behind and started taking snapshots: typical bourgeois individualism. There was a girl who kept flower pots on her balcony; she brought a pot to the office and set it on her desk ... small things, trivial things; and the smaller and more trivial, the safer to criticize and pick up in a campaign ...

There was also the danger of beauty, and its outlandishness. A beautiful person would draw the lightning. Not everywhere, but should it happen that one of the Party cadres in charge had a hatred of beauty ... This fear of loveliness, and the desire for its destruction, is very common everywhere in the world. I was told of one Party cadre who, in the movement for thought reform of 1953-4, said that 'all beautiful things must be abolished'. He was, however, unable to carry this out, for it was pointed out to him that his own wife was very pretty.

And all this had nothing to do with socialism. It was still Old China, still there; feudal, medieval, rigid Old China, as I had known it, but now it surfaced again, trying to survive by assuming righteous, moralistic 'anti-bourgeois' attitudes. And now it deployed massive political pressure; it crushed non-conformism more efficiently than ever. In the process, people did get hurt. Perhaps, with a sense of humour and enormous courage, one could get over this constant attrition. But I knew that I would be broken, very swiftly. I had suffered too much in the past with Pao. And the effluvium of past distress now came up. I was responding to it by feeling restricted and choked.

On May 22nd Third Brother gave me a report to read. It was a draft report on the Hundred Flowers, not yet in the newspapers but circulating for discussion in the universities and among the intelligentsia.

The words Hundred Flowers came from an old saying: 'Let a hundred flowers blossom, a hundred schools of thought contend'. Now Chairman Mao had resurrected this saying. It indicated a change in attitude towards the intellectuals. After the campaign to ferret out hidden counter-revolutionaries in 1955, Chou Enlai and Mao (but especially, it seemed to me, Chou Enlai) had become very much aware that the campaign had engendered such terror among the intelligentsia that many refused to function at all; nothing could be got out of them except total acquiescence. 'In my newspaper,' Wanchun told me, 'there is an old scholar in charge of the historical section. He was so harassed and criticized that now he won't say anything; he just nods his head and mutters "Good, good, very good", whatever is said to him.'

Chairman Mao had now condemned the sectarianism and high-handedness, the brutality of some of the Party cadres conducting the campaign. Premier Chou had been even more outspoken; and since November 1955 had held meetings with intellectuals and scholars, and also with the representatives of the eight non-communist parties which functioned in the Political Consultative Conference.* Most of the intelligentsia, the engineers, doctors, scholars and scientists, belonged to these parties; unless they

* Eight non-communist parties were admitted by the Communist Party in a 'United Front' in 1949. The Political Consultative Conference, a body distinct from the State or Communist Party is the instrument whereby they express themselves.

were, of course, Communist Party members. 'There are far too few intellectuals in the Party ... there's going to be a drive to get more of them in,' said Third Brother. 'Anyway, the Party leadership at my university has already told us that the intellectuals are no longer suspect. They are considered sufficiently well remoulded politically.'

'Does that mean no more thought-remoulding?'

'It means doing it much more ... softly ... ' said Fourth Brother. 'Though of course it all depends where one is.' In his organization, there was little pressure. 'It depends whether the leadership is intelligent or not. But so many of them are just good guerrillas; they've fought so many years, and they don't understand the minds of the trained, professional scientist, or scholar, or writer ... '

'And we are also very complicated!' said Wanchun.

Anyway, the Hundred Flowers was to promote freedom of expression in the academic disciplines and especially in science. Also in art and literature; but the more we pored over the draft, the less we understood what the limits to this freedom were. For there must be limits. 'Too much searching for counter-revolutionary thought has just paralysed so many brains; now they have to be defrozen,' said Wanchun. ' "Learn to listen more to the masses," that's what Chairman Mao has said.'

'But who are the masses? I hear a lot about mass movements; it means rousing the people to perform, to criticize, to condemn ... but who exactly are the people? Are you the people? Would I be the people, part of the masses?'

'Yes and no.' In every unit, there was the leadership or the Party committee in charge; they had to define the political line and watch over the carrying out of the work to be done. Then there were the authorities, professors, experts, engineers; who were part of the leadership in the technical sense, but not in the ideological sense. Then there was the ordinary rank and file of the employees, the workers. In a hospital, for instance, the man who cleaned the toilets was one of the employees, and therefore part of the masses, and would join in the mass movements of the hospital together with its authorities, the doctors, and the nurses and all other personnel. 'That is why the professional people who are experts are both part of the masses and not part of the masses. They are when they criticize others in campaigns to eradicate counter-revolutionary ideas; they are not when they are criticized themselves.' The Party leadership was supposed both to lead and to guide the masses, and at the same time accept the criticism and suggestions of the masses, and put themselves at the service of the masses.

'This is dialectics,' said Fourth Brother. I said that I thought the way it worked out was usually that someone, the Party secretary, for instance, just laid down the policy and everyone acquiesced. My relatives and Wanchun grinned, and said, 'You're learning very fast.'

The Hundred Flowers was to reinforce the rights of the intelligentsia to conduct their own research, and to do their work unhindered. 'It is for the good of socialism,' said Third Brother. 'But who decides what is good for socialism and what is not?' There were two trends in the Party; one for total arbitrariness, clamping down on everything; the other for the intelligent use of people, for moderation and listening to contrary advice and opinion. Mao was always enjoining Party members to listen to contrary opinions, to criticism; had for years tried to curb bureaucratic tyranny. 'But it recurs again and again. Premier Chou Enlai understands the problem well,' said Third Brother.

'But will there not be a tempest, a tornado rising from the hearts of the intellectuals, or some of them, when the pressure is released through the Hundred Flowers, and they start to speak up?'

'Third Sister, you open your mouth far too wide,' said Third Brother, laughing cheerfully and long.

Third Brother's wife, Jui, had had the worst time of all our Family. Land Reform in Szechuan had been particularly harsh and prolonged and bloody because Szechuan landlords were the most oppressive; Szechuan had been the last bastion of Chiang Kaishek's domination. The structures of the old society were still very strong there when the Communist armies came into the province in November-December 1949.

Cleaning up the opium-growing areas had taken three years; cleaning up the Chiang Kaishek gangs, who fled to the high mountains, and proceeding with Land Reform, had been very difficult because the peasants were at first so frightened that they would even protect the landlords. Jui saw it both from the side of the social revolution, for the poor peasant, and of course from the side of her own class, the owners. She described the panic, landlords knocking their heads on the ground, begging the investigation teams to take away their lands and houses, but not submit them to the judgment of the people; landlords offering their wives and daughters to Party cadres ... Despite the Party injunction not to beat or torture landlords, the poor peasants, when aroused, would do so, suspend a landlord by the thumbs and beat him to death. 'There was so much furniture, and silk and books and valuable things, littering the streets, that most of the city lanes became impassable.'

And then there were the Secret Societies, especially the Brothers of the Robe, very powerful in Szechuan. Sometimes they bribed the Party cadres; sometimes murdered them. So deeply implanted were the Secret Societies that years later, during the Cultural Revolution, they would make a return.

During Land Reform in 1950-1, Third Uncle was in Chungking, and Third Grandfather, the head of the clan, and responsible for land ownership committed suicide by jumping down a well, so terrified was he. No one was there to answer for the accounts and the clearing up of fields belonging to the ancestral hall of the Family in Pihsien, and to remove the Family graves, which took up good land, to another site. Jui then came forward, in place of Third Uncle and in place of his eldest son her husband, Third Brother, who was then in America. She would represent the Family two or three times a week at the people's court. The case took eight months to clear up. Jui was never harmed physically; but it was a great strain having to stand for hours in court and listen to the accusations launched by former tenants; and she became very nervous.

When Land Reform was over there was the movement against counter-revolutionaries; but the Family was not involved in it. Then there was the movement against the three evils in the Party (corruption, waste and bureaucracy) and the five evils among the national-capitalist class, tax evasion, theft of state property, cheating on government contracts and stealing of economic information. Third Uncle was a national-capitalist. His case lasted for months; Jui had to answer for a certain amount of rice which was unaccounted for. Was it hoarded rice? In Chungking, at the time, the businessmen had organized a 'Thursday Dinner Club', devoted entirely to ways and means of defrauding the government. Third Uncle, was, luckily, not of that club. Finally the Family was cleared.

Then in 1953-4 there had been the campaign to change the ideas of the intelligentsia. Jui was an intellectual since she held a position in the Chemistry Department at the University of Chengtu. Because her husband was in the United States, and there was at the time the Korean war, some silly colleagues of Jui (not the Party) tried to make her divorce her husband. She refused.

Then Third Brother came back, and Jui became pregnant, but remained in Chengtu while Third Brother went to Peking to join the Peking University staff. Unlucky Jui. During that year, 1955, the Hu Feng affair erupted, followed by the campaign to ferret out hidden counter-revolutionaries. And since Hu Feng had many adherents in Szechuan, the drive there was most drastic. And because Chairman Mao had made a casual remark that *probably* 10 per cent of the intelligentsia in the administration and the Party harboured counter-revolutionary feelings or thoughts, such was the literal-mindedness of the middle cadres (and can you blame them?) that some were determined to expose at least 10 per cent in each organization as counter-revolutionary, to show they were not slacking ...

Writing out one's biography. Again and again. Meetings. In thirty days, twenty-nine meetings. Accusation sessions. Struggle sessions. People encouraged 'boldly to accuse each other without leaving any face to anyone.' Everyone called to account for every minute event in his life; until at last condemnation would centre on the few, and then meetings to criticize and to struggle against these few.

Meanwhile, Jui's belly swelled, and one afternoon during a meeting she felt the pains come on. But the comrade in charge that day did not know that she was pregnant, for Jui was intensely modest, and concealed her bulk behind a desk (the meetings were held in a lecture hall of the University). She asked to leave as she had a 'headache'. 'We have a most important meeting ... no one can leave,' said the cadre firmly. The meeting went on, and Jui could no longer bear it and she began to groan, while round her some of her colleagues stirred uneasily. And finally one bolder than the rest tiptoed to the cadre and whispered in his ear. Upon which, thunderstruck, he rushed for an ambulance and Jui reached hospital just in time. And to make up for this, Jui was cleared totally and sent to Peking to join her husband. But now Jui would not believe that things would be better. 'If a Party cadre has it in for you, it's no use, he will pick and pick at you until you have no way out.'

'It's a class struggle,' said Fourth Brother. 'That's why we feel so helpless; it's a different class in power today.'

But now a new policy: 'Let a hundred flowers bloom, a hundred schools of thought contend ... ' Now things were going to change. 'Is it because of what has happened in the Soviet Union?' Khrushchev's denunciation of Stalin in January 1956 was known in China; it circulated 'within', in the Party and administration newspaper and in documents. Everyone in China knew of the speech denouncing Stalin. No, said my relatives. The speech against Stalin was in January 1956, but already in November 1955 Premier Chou Enlai had started discussing a new policy for the intelligentsia, holding meetings with the eight non-communist parties. It was probably Chou Enlai who had called a halt to the campaign. We surmised, speculated, argued. The Hundred Flowers called upon the intelligentsia to speak up; called on the Party to listen to criticism. How, how much, how soon, we did not know.

During most of my two month stay I felt as if I was careering full speed on an enormous roller coaster, going up and down artificial heights and canyons at dizzying speed, and with my insides not following suit. The alternation of exhilaration and depression which fragmented my days and nights; the almost ecstatic joy levitating me, followed by deep nausea and utter prostration; I cannot explain, even now, why my reactions were so violent, so physical, so inescapable. I needed Kung Peng very much; felt lost without her, sought her out and often missed her, for she was very busy. I could not describe to her what I felt, only say, 'There are many contradictions fighting in me.' The word 'contradiction' was not only acceptable but understood. It was a useful word in this new political shorthand I was beginning to acquire.

Kung Peng arranged for me to see everything I wanted. I had a nice chauffeur, Comrade Ku; a demobilized People's Liberation Army man who had driven a jeep in the Korean war and took me everywhere in a Czech car. When I felt too near vomiting I went to the Western Hills to watch the summer burgeon in splendour, the wanness of long winter vanish. I went to the Temple of Heaven and to the Peihai Park and to the Summer Palace, and also walked miles and miles, trying to get a grip upon my unhinged body.

I visited the tuberculosis sanatorium in the Western Hills; a palatial spread, where Russian methods of streptomycin inhalation were used. I saw the ordinary, and very crowded, tuberculous clinics, not show places, in the city itself. Tuberculosis was still rampant; it was impossible at the moment to care for everyone. The workers were treated at government expense, but 'We cannot do this for everyone in China,' said the directors. I visited the children's hospital, which filled me with joy. I went to the cancer hospital ... I think I visited all the hospitals in Peking. And it was for me, as a doctor, fabulous. Something had really been done, and most effectively, about all the main epidemics and scourges which had ravaged the population. The result was an unbelievable lowering of infant mortality and just as impressive a rise in the population growth rate. Until 1949 the growth rate had been around 4 per thousand; by 1956 it was over 32 per thousand. No more cholera, no more smallpox, and venereal disease being eradicated ... I visited the opium treatment centre for the rehabilitation of opium addicts. 'The biggest problems were the heroin and cocaine addicts under the Japanese,' said the doctors.

I went to the Yung Ho Kung, the old Tibetan lama temple in Peking, and just as when I was a child, the halls containing statues in erotic poses were locked. In the past, a bribe to the priest would open them; now bribery was impossible, and they remained closed.

I duly delivered to Dr Pan Kuangtan his prosthetic leg, going to his institute to meet him. He beamed fatly, had a throaty, false laugh. Pan Kuangtan had been very much criticized because he held pro-American views. His exuberance ill concealed lingering shock. However, he would live on, and his children are today employed as university staff in China. Pan Kuangtan declared he did not need the new leg, for the wooden stump he wore was enough. He looked very much like Francis Pan, his brother.

Professor Cheng Chento, Vice-Minister of Culture, invited me to dinner. At the table was Kung Peng and the writer Lao Sheh whom I had met in Hongkong, and also the writer Hsiao Chien, whom I had met in England, where he had studied for some years. Professor Cheng was no obsequious, terror-stricken man. He went right into the problems of writing. 'We had no life at all under Chiang Kaishek. Now we have security, official positions, good houses and good salaries. But too many things have happened too swiftly for our minds to grasp.' He thought re-education through thought-remoulding good. 'But some of it is excessive. We hope there will be more flexibility.' Many writers found it difficult to write, although they produced inspired journalism, adequate reportage. They felt frightened because this was a new society whose bearings they had not yet understood, whose motivations they could not fathom ... On and on went the Vice-Minister of Culture, who was not a communist but belonged to another party; and Kung Peng did not interrupt or protest. I felt greatly encouraged; if this was what the Hundred Flowers meant, there was hope.

Lao Sheh looked very fit, glossily happy. He had not suffered during the counter-revolutionary campaign; but then his class origin was good; he came from a very poor family. He told some delightful anecdotes about his time in England. He had produced an excellent play, and was now a People's Artist, honoured and respected. I would go to visit him in his very beautiful house; he collected antiques, ivories and priceless furniture. He also grew chrysanthemums of rare kinds, and his Japanese friends would give him some very exquisite plants. He was Vice-Chairman of the Union of Chinese Writers, but also held a dozen other positions in various friendship associations, besides being a delegate to the National People's Congress.

As for Hsiao Chien, he was also an official in the Union of Writers, and most enthusiastic about everything. He agreed with Professor Cheng that some writers found it difficult to create, but thought this was a question of time. 'We are all bourgeois intellectuals; we took certain things for granted.' I saw Hsiao Chien several times, in private talk, in the days that followed. He told me about his own remoulding. He had found it difficult, but not insuperably so. He had been greatly helped by a revelation during Land Reform when he went with many other intellectuals to the villages to help the peasants become aware of class struggle and denounce their landlords. Hsiao Chien found that a landlord who had been his friend, whose hospitality he had enjoyed, was an individual who owned six male and six female concubines, some of them mere children. 'I was appalled at myself. I had never inquired into his private life ... I called myself the friend of such a monster!'

Dear, amiable Hsiao Chien! With his round face and appealing eyes, eyes with that opaque anguish which I had seen emerge, like a creature rising from muddy water, in the eyes of Nora Waln. I thought his ardent conversion a little too swift to be true, and alas, in 1957, he seems to have made inapposite attacks upon the Union of Writers and sundry other political targets, and was labelled a 'rightist'. 'He got changed too quickly,' I would say later to Kung Peng. 'The colour didn't stick.' Hsiao Chien was unjustly labelled; he would be rehabilitated, but it would take a great many years.

There was a reception with many eminent writers at the Peking Hotel. I met Tsao Yu, China's Chekhov, shy, his thick spectacles a wall between himself and the world. But such talent, such perception behind that uneasy vitreousness! His plays had been for me major events, and he was writing another play. In 1969 I was told by a Party cadre that he, Lao Sheh, Pa Chin—the latter an author from Szechuan, whose wonderful Balzacian novels had been a revelation to me when I was a student—were counter-revolutionaries. But this was the summer of 1956, when the Hundred Flowers had just begun, and in that year all three of them were honoured, and under no stress.

Suddenly there was a stir of excitement. The fabulous and eminent Madame Soong Chingling, widow of Dr Sun Yatsen, had come to the reception. Soong Chingling exuded glamour; she had a flawless, creamy skin, and her hair was bright jet. The eldest of the three Soong sisters (the second none other than Madame Chiang Kaishek), Soong Chingling was,

I think, the most beautiful of the three. She had stuck with immense loyalty to her principles, and was a great and honoured personage, a symbol of the Communist Party's determination to carry out United Front policies with non-communists who were loyal in serving their country and its people. I had already met Madame Chiang Kaishek during the war, in Chungking.* Soong Chingling had exactly the same voice, a beautiful voice, with faultless and melodious diction. Both had been educated at Wellesley.

'Why don't you make up your mind to stay here?' she said to me straightaway. Round her the air shone with her vitality. I could not reply; I merely smiled.

Then I met Mao Tun, the Minister of Culture, the famous writer of *Midnight*, the launcher of so many literary magazines in the 1920s and 30s. He was a genial, simple person with great courtesy, a humble person with a slight nervous tic, which he would lose in the following years. We discussed the Hu Feng affair. Mao Tun said that Hu Feng's crime was that he *organized* cliques of intellectuals against the Communist Party. There were always contradictory tendencies in all human endeavour; writers had to struggle against themselves and depict these struggles, said Mao Tun. I asked him how it was possible to distinguish between genuine criticism, which was welcomed by the Party, and counter-revolutionary statements, which got one into trouble. Mao Tun smiled with great delicacy and replied, 'They are being distinguished now.'

Mao Tun ascribed to Chairman Mao and to Premier Chou Enlai the new policy of the Hundred Flowers. 'It's too early to draw conclusions, but I am in favour of it,' said he. He told me that of the 18,000 people employed in the Ministry of Culture, only 3 per cent, or 540, were doubtful. He then gave me his speech at the second conference of Chinese writers in 1954 to read. It was full of useful hints. 'Many authors are confused ideologically and their standpoint is unsteady ... there are objective reasons why literary work is lagging behind reality ... The heroes of our fiction are drab, colourless; there is monotony and crudeness of literary form, not taking pains with language and structure ... ' 'Perhaps this comes from being salaried officials,' I suggested as respectfully as I could, and the Minister of Culture threw back his head and laughed happily. 'True, too comfortable a life sometimes makes the writer lazy ... We have some writers who expend most of their effort considering whether a theme is proper or not.' He said the state paid for writers' travels; they had summer bungalows in the hills where they could retire to write. Mao Tun was

* See *Destination Chungking*.

scathing about 'political critics who drive writers to impotence by hurling political epithets at them.' He said these critics did not understand anything about writing. 'In the West, too, critics just say anything; but then they contradict each other,' I said. I added that some of the journalists I had met at the big reception for writers had the notion that in the West all writers were capitalists. It was not so; some of them were labourers; and others had gone into coal mining and other manual jobs to acquire the experience and feeling for a novel. Mao Tun knew all this; for he, like Tsao Yu, like Pa Chin, like Lao Sheh, was very well-acquainted with Western literature.

I asked Mao Tun about Ting Ling, the woman writer whose book *Sun on the Sankan River* had been awarded a Stalin prize, but who was now in political trouble. Mao Tun professed not to know all the details because the case was still being studied. In fact, Ting Ling would be officially excluded from the Party and dubbed a 'rightist' in 1957.

Then an interview with Kuo Mojo, the distinguished, erudite poet, critic, archaeologist and head of the Academy of Sciences (founded that year). Kuo Mojo was from my province of Szechuan. He had immense learning, knew German and French and had done a great many translations from Western literature. He was in Japan for many years, he told me and 'indeed I grieve that I did not participate fully in the liberation struggles of my country. But then I am politically very backward.' He was not a communist (neither were Tsao Yu, Mao Tun, Pa Chin, or Lao Sheh), but he would be admitted to the Party that year.

'One must see beyond the transient, the instant capture of events.' He was frank, and commented on the writer's difficulties. 'It is the propensity of the mind to resist tutelage,' said he, 'yet all history has been made by the contradiction between those in power and others. There are contradictions, of course, between the Party and other sectors of Chinese society. The important thing is to construct a strong, prosperous and socialist China.'

'The writer's business is the landscape of the human heart,' I said. Kuo smiled. 'The human heart ... such an indefinite and changeable affair ... ' He loved miniature gardens, and said they made him think of the human heart 'fashioned by drought and a drop of water; a tree clinging to the ridges of a rock ... '

Kuo went on talking of China's needs for modernization, of the impossibility of practising socialism unless there was also some measure of abundance through 'the release of the productive forces'. The sunlight through the window sculptured his cheekbones and ear with the hearing aid glued to it; his delicate hands occasionally moved to mould a sentence. I remembered that he too, like Lu Hsun, had been a doctor of medicine before becoming a writer. He gave me facts. In areas where there had been 'the wrong leadership', productivity had declined. 'It is also bad when people dare not speak up.' There had been an obsession which had seized some Party members about a counter-revolutionary insurrection among the intelligentsia. 'Two photographers belonging to a newspaper were arrested because the flash bulb of one of them exploded accidentally ... ' 'It's also ignorance,' I said. The Party had grown from four million to ten million in six years; many cadres were inexperienced, yet administrators were needed. In December 1955 Premier Chou Enlai had begun to fashion a twelve-year programme for China's advance. 'We need science, science ... a million technical scientists at least ... our most urgent need is to create more intellectuals, not less.' One should be careful that the levelling process would not become self-defeating. There were at least ten thousand Chinese scientists and other 'brains' abroad; in the past six years one thousand had come back; and this one thousand had made a great deal of difference and had contributed already very much to China. 'Our policy should be to learn from everybody, to open doors.'

He agreed that badly handled, the intelligentsia could not function, would sink into passivity. 'Some research workers were accused of sending secret messages because the Party cadres could not understand their scientific equipment.'

I was very grateful to Kuo Mojo for giving me so much time and speaking so openly. He was a man who understood his era, its great potential and its limitations. He knew the immense trajectory in time which Chinese writers had to perform, and how vulnerable they were. Far more so than scientists. Scientists were immediately useful. But writers dealt with human beings; they conveyed ideas; so they were also dangerous. 'Engineers of the soul', they were now called. Their task was to fashion a human spirit ardently loving socialism ... how could they do it unless they themselves were convinced?

Some weeks later, in Szechuan, I was to read in the local paper Kuo Mojo's speech on the Hundred Flowers. Kuo was Deputy for the province of Szechuan to the National People's Congress: his speech was the most concise and also the most accurate explanation of what the Hundred Flowers really meant to the scientific intelligentsia. It would help me a great deal not to fall into the error into which so many fell; of considering it an attempt at liberalization followed by a clampdown.

To Peking University, once known as Yenching, my own university.

Again the chic, elegant willows scrutinizing the narrow water at their feet. Twelve thousand students by 1958, instead of the mere eight hundred we had been. Two young and beautiful women professors took me round the campus and told me most remarkable things. Already the spirit of the Hundred Flowers was at work. Already articles in the newspapers, critical of bureaucracy; critical of insufficient care in the factories leading to accidents ... The professors told me that a system of 'progressive classes' utilizing criticism and collective study had been started in 1953, at the time of the great campaign for thought-remoulding among the intelligentsia. But it would now be given up. Students must have self-reliance; they lost it with too much collective study. Research was important and promising individuals should be recruited early in the various disciplines. Too many meetings were bad for study, injurious to the health of the students. They left no leisure even for rest. 'We have had breakdowns. We hope to change all this.'

'There is no need to carry on more intensive politicization. Our intellectuals are already changed, they have truly reformed themselves mentally,' said the professors. How astonishing, their blithe confidence that in six short years, 2,500 years of mandarinate, of élitism, should be changed! That was not possible, I thought. And even though I was *also* on the side of the élite (was I not one of them?), I could not forget what they had not done for the Chinese people.

To the Peking library: 4,200,000 books; chiefly on science, says the librarian. *How to Win Friends and Influence People* is banned because it teaches a typically opportunistic, bourgeois attitude. But now the library must be enlarged, books must be purchased 'from everywhere ... we must study even from our enemies'. The librarian is quoting Mao, but I do not know it; because Mao's particularly important speeches of that year would not be printed for over two decades.

A morning with the Minister of Justice, Madame Shih Liang. She is a diminutive, frail, small-boned person, so tiny that in her youth she failed to pass a physical examination during the selection for a magistracy. But she is a person of indomitable rectitude, and she went to jail, although not a communist, because of her stand against Chiang Kaishek's spineless compliance when the Japanese invaded China. Shih Liang was active in drafting the new laws, and especially co-operated with Teng Yingchao (the wife of Premier Chou Enlai) in the all-important Marriage Law of 1951, which is the chief document for women's liberation in China. For the abolition of infanticide, the protection of children, Shih Liang has laboured greatly. 'The Marriage Law and the Constitution of 1954 are enormous advances in women's liberation.'

Shih Liang tried not to be too technical. She explained that it was not easy to change feudal customs so deeply imbedded. 'The notion of law and legality is still quite fluid in our country.' The legal system must also promote the socialist revolution; it must therefore not follow the bourgeois codes. In short, a legal framework must be made for a reality which was in the process of transformation in the interests of the Revolution. The concept of law, as so many other concepts, needed to be defined and revised. 'Mistakes have certainly been made; but then Land Reform was like a hurricane, and so were the other campaigns ... We are going through every case, rehabilitating as many as possible.' Over 1,300,000 people unjustly labelled counter-revolutionary had already been rehabilitated. 'The emphasis is on not carrying out the death penalty immediately; it is held up for two years in case new evidence turns up; and it may be postponed indefinitely.' Mao Tsetung had said that 'heads are not leeks that can grow again ... ' But of course there had been executions, especially in the 1950-1 crushing of counter-revolutionaries. Papa had told me how the lorries with their loads of the condemned rolled by the house at night.

I asked how judgment could be correct when one referred to the masses, whose passions were aroused by the recital of a culprit's crimes; and when was a mass not a mob or a crowd? Shih Liang explained that the Party's function at those popular trials was both to educate in class struggle and to restrain from physical violence. There had been excesses because Party committees, in launching movements in a hurry, were not acquainted with the situation, not clear about differential treatment. But the use of physical violence was abhorrent and severely condemned. 'And precautions are taken to avoid the culprits committing suicide.' But there were suicides.

Shih Liang had arranged for me to see the trial of an ex-counter-revolutionary, now on the way to reform, at the Bureau of Public Security. There was one judge, looking very young, and two assessors, one a woman. Hunched, but healthy-looking and burly, the culprit stood, and agreed he had been guilty of black marketeering, hoarding and passing information to remnants of the Kuomintang organization for about three years after 1949. He had been re-educated through labour. The judge, who tried very hard to make his gentle, suave face look grim and stern, discharged him with 'two years' supervision by the masses.

On to Peking's model jail, which contained a factory for making socks, at which the prisoners worked. Here was reform through labour and political study. I saw no young people; the average age of the eight hundred or so prisoners was around forty. 'We do not jail very old people, we place them under mass supervision but leave them at home. Unless they have no home; then we take them in but do not make them work.'

When I told Wang Wanchun that I was greatly impressed by the drive for women's equality, and the Marriage Law, he said, 'But not all Party cadres like it. Some of them are still quite feudal in their treatment of women.' For instance, there had been great resistance to allowing widows to remarry. It was still considered dishonourable; and that very year a poor widow would be pushed to suicide by her family, without the Party cadre interfering. Afterwards the All-China Women's Federation had intervened, and a full inquiry was held; in fact, it was through the Federation that women dared to protest against ill-treatment. The government backed the women fully.

The drive for women's equality was spearheaded by the women of the Long March, that small group of indomitable females who had survived, among them Teng Yingchao, wife of Premier Chou Enlai and Kang Keching, wife of Marshal Chu Teh.*

An afternoon with Madame Li Tehchuan, Minister of Health. Not a communist, Madame Li was the widow of the Christian marshal, Feng Yuhsiang; I had a photograph of Papa and me taken with him when he came to ask my father for rolling stock for his troops.† Madame Li was a cheerful and amiable person with a smooth, unlined face.

She received me in her house, and spoke of the great campaigns against epidemics. 'We could never have done it without the people's backing.' Over 180 million people had been vaccinated against smallpox in the first two years after Liberation, and now there was no smallpox in China. We talked of family planning and Li Tehchuan waxed voluble. Unlike her prudish colleague in India, she launched into detailed descriptions of methods. 'We'll try all the methods, Chinese and Western, old and new.' The Western world was laughing at China because someone had advocated the swallowing of tadpoles as a contraceptive device. 'We've tried it, but it doesn't work.' However, the ancient books did describe oral contraceptives (at that time the pill had not yet been invented in the West), and Li Tehchuan would have them tried. There was also a rather heroic way of avoiding inseminating a woman, which was practised in China in the past.

---

* Chinese women retain their own names after marriage. This does not apply only to professional women but to all, including housewives.

† See *The Crippled Tree*.

It consisted in the male pinching off the vas at the moment of ejaculation. 'Of course it demands discipline,' said Li Tehchuan brightly.

Her grandson came in, a very beautiful child, and suddenly Li Tehchuan was a doting grandmother; she hugged him in open love. 'At one time we thought every child must be brought up the same way ... but we must let children develop their own personality, not turn them into robots.' The newspapers had just published a cartoon showing Chinese youngsters, differently clad, entering a big book spread like a tent, labelled MARXISM-LENINISM, and coming out the other end all looking alike.

'We think families must be kept together. We encourage mothers to keep their children with them at night – but we provide nurseries and kindergartens for day care. In this way the children are at home, but the mother can be liberated for work or study.' I was to see the development of nurseries and kindergartens through the years; and on this point of caring for children there was no doubt that China was ahead of many countries in the world. I wrote an article on my meeting with Li Tehchuan for the *Observer* in London, and it was published.

A few days later I saw men in Central Park queuing up for condoms at a booth. The charge was one cent (half an American cent) for a packet of ten. At night, in many parks, open-air films on childbirth and on contraception would be shown. This was really an assault on the Chinese tradition of prudery, and my Chinese friends in Hongkong would not believe me when I told them. Francis and Cecilia, a devoted couple, blushed when I told them that now a man called his wife 'my loved one', and so did the wife call her husband. 'Shocking,' commented Cecilia.

A visit to the ballet school of Peking to see Eileen Tai. Eileen Tai, or Tai Ailien, was the sister of my dear friend Phyllis. Phyllis and Eileen were overseas Chinese born of a wealthy family in Trinidad. Both girls were of strong character; Phyllis went to Singapore and Eileen to London, where she studied ballet under Madame Rambert, and Jacob Epstein was so taken with her face that he made a sculpture of her. Phyllis was one of the exceedingly few Chinese who got out of Singapore when the Japanese came; and only because of an English family with whom she was friendly and who warned her in time: 'We're going, Phyllis, drop everything and come.' Somehow the English family had managed to get her on the evacuation boat (for British whites only). All she carried was a towel in her hands and her diamonds in a paper bag. She loaned me those diamonds in London, when I had to go to Windsor Castle to be presented to the King. Back in Singapore, Phyllis had told me, 'Try to see my sister Eileen, she's in Peking.' Eileen was intensely patriotic and had gone to China during the war against Japan, and remained there at Liberation. She was now running the ballet school in Peking. She was a small woman, with a spirit like a flame. 'We now have fraternal Soviet experts to teach us ballet,' she told me.

Eileen would train ballet dancers until 1966. Then, like so many others, she was made to 'stand aside' as unfit to teach and as a 'bourgeois authority', when Chiang Ching started to manage art during the Cultural Revolution. Eileen was not harmed, though harassed and subjected to humiliation. She stayed at home and drew a diminished salary. When in October 1976 Chiang Ching and her acolytes were arrested, Eileen Tai heard about it from a painter friend of hers who lived in the same compound. She put on her ballet shoes and danced right down the main avenue of Peking.

Now Eileen Tai put on a small ballet rehearsal for me and some other visitors who had arrived. My chauffeur Ku, who had strolled in, was amazed. 'How can they dance on their toes? It must be very painful — as much suffering as bound feet in the old days.'

Dinner with an illustrious lady, Madame Ho Hsiangning. Madame Ho was the widow of Liao Chungkai, who had been a revolutionary of the first vintage, and a close friend of Sun Yatsen. Ho Hsiangning had an oval face and piercing, lively eyes. A painter and a poet, she was also Chairwoman of the Overseas Chinese Affairs Commission, and chairwoman of one of the eight non-communist parties. She was seventy-eight when we met, but looked fifty. We talked a great deal of the overseas Chinese and their problems, and the difficulties they experienced. The Kuomintang in Taiwan was trying to capture them, promising them 'protection'. A policy for the overseas must be very clearly laid down. Madame Ho said there had been cases when overseas Chinese returning to China had met with difficulties, for instance, payments made to old retired people by their offspring working abroad might sometimes be held up. 'This is due to ignorance of the conditions,' she said. We discussed *jus sanguis*, whereby Chinese born anywhere are Chinese if the father is Chinese. On the whole, concluded Madame Ho, overseas Chinese returning to China were given privileges in order to give them time to get used to conditions.

I would meet this sagacious woman again ten years later, in 1966, at the start of the Cultural Revolution. As I think of her, of Shih Liang, of Soong Chingling, of Li Tehchuan, of so many others and of the immense work they did for their people, I feel grateful that I had the luck to meet and speak with them, for each one of them gave me spirit to live by.

Dinner with Uncle Kang of Szechuan, who was in Peking for the National People's Congress due to open that June. Uncle Kang and others of the Kang family were big businessmen, Third Uncle's partners in banking and commercial enterprises.* Uncle Kang was now also some kind of financial adviser for the province of Szechuan and a representative at the Political Consultative Conference, which was holding a meeting at the same time as the Party Congress, (some delegates of the one held seats on the other body). He and the other national-capitalists with him talked at length about the Hundred Flowers. They were obviously hoping for a new start. 'A great deal of potential talent has not been employed for political reasons. It's time for it to be used,' said Uncle Kang. It was part of this extraordinary country that is China that Uncle Kang went on, in his new role, serving his country, and died peacefully of old age.

A visit to my dear friend Yeh, the editor of *Chinese Literature*, a monthly magazine. Yeh, a man full of humour, a gentle and learned man, had spent some years in England and had written a best-seller in English.† He did not shout about his convictions or lack of them; he just performed to the best of his ability. 'Of course we must extend the scope of writing. Until now we have not really begun to describe what has happened in recent years. There is no depth to what we write because we don't quite understand ourselves what has happened ... so it's just a formal description of outward events.' As for being remoulded, Yeh agreed that it took time, but said, 'The thing to do is to plunge into the new without reservations, without looking back over one's shoulder.' I admired and respected him for saying this. Truly, it was like diving into an unknown sea, never to return as one had been, but metamorphosed, having suffered a sea-change ... But what would this sea-change mean for me?

The peonies spread their splendour in the parks, acres of them languid in the fragrant air. So used had I been to rapine and decay and dirt that I could not get over the restoration of beauty and of temples and palaces. It was enchantment. But in me turmoil continued. Scarcely did I feel exalted by some noble human achievement than its antithesis, some stupid and brutal act, would again plunge me into distress. Thus I heard of a man and a woman working in the same organization who had had a love affair some twenty years before, but since had gone their separate ways and married happily. However, in the course of a campaign this ancient love story had been raked up; not by the Party, but by their own colleagues,

---

* See *Birdless Summer* for the Kang family.
† *The Ignorant and the Forgotten* (Sylvan Press, 1946). He published two more books in English, *The Mountain Village* (1947), and *They Fly South* (1948), both by the Sylvan Press.

other members of the organization. It was written up on posters hung in the main hall of the office where they worked. 'Boldly criticize each other, discarding the hypocritical politeness which tries to offend nobody' was the quotation (from the *People's Daily*) which prefaced this revelation of 'reprehensible bourgeois immorality'. The result was three suicides: the woman, her present husband (loss of face), and the former lover.

And yet so much cruelty was being inflicted upon so many people in the 'free' world. In America, with McCarthy, guilt by association was current, and there were suicides, and ruin for many artists and intellectuals; and in Malaya 500,000 stateless were behind barbed wire. But those cruelties did not affect me so much because I did not relate to them. They were 'outside', not within. Here in China I was all the time thinking of myself in the same situation. 'Supposing I do stay; I too shall have my love with Ian exposed and made ugly ... and perhaps, who knows, I shall be persuaded it was a dreadful thing, and revile it ... ' And this made me quite sick. I think it was actually the pivotal factor which made me decide to wait for more dust to settle. For I never gave up the intention of returning to China; but it was a question of the right time. This Hundred Flowers opening did seem the right time; but one had to see how it would turn out.

The argument that there *was* a private life, that not all personal matters were political and that sex relations especially must not be held up as examples of villainy—how often I would have angry debates over this! 'There is too much nitpicking,' I said to Kung Peng. But where lay the difference between political and non-political, between private offence and public guilt? This was a matter of legal definition, and a legal code was still being fashioned.

Meanwhile guilt lay upon me like a poisoned itch; the guilt of class. The realization that with all noble emotions to the fore, such people as I had thrived upon the prolonged and terrible misery of the Chinese people; and that with all their faults and pettiness, and the 'mistakes' and wrongs perpetrated by Party cadres, the Chinese Communist Party had undoubtedly done more, in six short years, to free, both mentally and physically, the enormous majority of the Chinese people from oppression and misery than we had ever dreamed of doing.

Yet there was also this stranglehold pressure to reveal one's naked soul, to become transparent like a clean glass window, to repudiate one's crimes or sins; to confess and to be redeemed, accepted, no speck of spirit opaque, no corner of the mind unturned; established in a bright new house of living.

I talked with some intellectuals who had been sifting through their own lives, punctiliously, and was suddenly gripped by the sensation that I was Alice going through the Looking Glass. A depersonalization, almost unbearable. 'I shall have a nervous breakdown if I don't control my imagination.' I got up at night to walk, walk in the streets, walk to the park in the quiet, safe night. No one could have walked so safely in the night in Old China. I saw romantic couples demurely walking in the alleys, and in the park, sitting on an artificial rock, above an artificial pool, a pretty girl singing to herself. She was a factory worker on night shift, and her face shone with that extraordinary innocence which was the hallmark of the young in New China. She came here to sing, she said, especially on moonlit nights, before going to work. 'Only six years ago my whole family were beggars; now I am going to night school and I work in the textile plant.'

The foreign guests at the Hsinchiao Hotel provided me with moments of amusement and even illumination. There was the Englishman who worried about getting his shoes properly polished. 'The only place where they're done just right is Calcutta. Nice city, Calcutta.' There was the Polish expert on porcelain who said, 'I'm not doing good work. The Chinese have far better patterns than we have.' He borrowed Cyril Connolly's *The Unquiet Grave* from me, and sighed: 'We have no such good books now.' When I asked him about Khrushchev and Stalin he paled and walked away.

Delegations from fraternal socialist countries marching in to breakfast made the words 'groaning board' a vivid reality. I watched with wonder the pyramids of cakes and bread, the hillocks of butter and jam, the battalions of plates with fried eggs (three each) laid out on the tables, which the delegates contrived to engulf.

There were the newsmen, some with the most bizarre hypotheses about China. They speculated and made up stories; they were either from fraternal countries, in which case they were privileged with travel and interviews, and described everything in paradisial terms, or they were the few, rare representatives of the Western press. Correspondents of Reuter's and Agence France-Presse were accredited to Peking and somehow managed to do sound work without much help. There was Claude Roy, at the time a leading communist, with a delegation from the French Party. 'Han Suyin, why do you not become a communist?' he asked me sternly. 'I'm like St Thomas, I have to see and to touch ... ' In the last two decades

Claude Roy has changed; he now spends a great deal of time excoriating what he has worshipped. Whereas I, having clung to honest doubt, have always felt my solitude shared by those who have no need foolishly to burn, who hold the privilege to change their minds, but not their love.

There were the embassies. The British Embassy asked me several times to lunch and dinner. I think the Chargé d'Affaires felt that I might be brainwashed. He gave me a series of horrifying articles by Robert Guillain of *Le Monde*, describing all China as one vast antheap of 'blue ants'. Since then Guillain has been back to China, and explained with inimitable French elegance that 'ants' are hardworking and praiseworthy insects ... Nevertheless, the articles influenced me; I rushed to Kung Peng with them, and asked her if these horrors were true. Then I read them again; and I was not so impressed.

To the Indian Embassy, to meet R. K. Nehru, the Ambassador, and his very able wife. Both admired China. R. K. Nehru was very happy about the Hundred Flowers. 'Unless this policy is implemented, advance will not be so fast.' Intellectuals were always much afraid of re-education, 'yet all life re-educates us constantly ... it appears tyrannical when it has to be done consciously instead of just happening by circumstance.' He laughed at his Western colleagues and their 'obsolete' ideas of freedom 'based on the affluence they derived from exploiting us, India, China ... ' He agreed with me that some of the Chinese intelligentsia were afraid that the Hundred Flowers was only a flash-in-the-pan contrivance. 'There is a great deal of resistance within the Party to it,' he remarked, 'but Chairman Mao is all for it ... In China there are not enough competent cadres to go round.' In India the British had left a framework of laws and had trained judges and lawyers to carry them out. But in China everything had to be created anew, including not only a legal system, but the very notion of law. 'There are not enough seasoned administrators ... Those that the Communist Party have who know anything about running cities are mostly ex-Kuomintang bureaucrats ... No one can be sure of their loyalty ... I have just written a fifty-page memorandum to my government on the present situation.' Matters of jurisprudence interested him greatly; and he had had many talks with Chinese officials about them. They had agreed that 'mass movements are necessary in the first years of a revolution, but out of them must be born laws and regulations ... to improve the people's democratic legal system.' A penal code, a civil code, the law of criminal procedure – all this was being studied, and the Indian Ambassador was immensely interested. He was sure that the Hundred Flowers were a step towards drawing up clearly the rights of the individual, and the creation of a legal system. There must be more intellectuals in the Party, to overcome 'that small peasant mentality ... so many in the Party are peasants ... wonderful people, but knowing little about running institutions.' Chairman Mao himself had told the Ambassador that it was essential to raise the educational and cultural level of Party cadres, 'which is pretty low, considering that they've come through decades of fighting...'

I had other good Indian friends in Peking; among them P. N. Sharma, the photographer, who was, at the time, exhibiting his photographs to crowds in Central Park, and Natwar Singh, a young Embassy secretary, a delightful companion for rambles, and a devotee of the English writer E. M. Forster.* He was learning Chinese, but appeared in no hurry to become an expert. Both were to help me a great deal during the subsequent years of tension between India and China.

I also enjoyed impressively stimulating conversation with Jacques Locquin, the French representative of Agence France-Presse. He was impeccably logical, and he manipulated theories so deftly that it dazzled me. A revolution, said he, was made with what is best and what is most vile in man. It devoured, decanted, sifted, churned and changed, and spared no one. 'In fact, our world has already changed; but our politicians are not aware of it.'

'Why don't you write down your shock, your alternance of happiness and dismay, when you get back to Hongkong?' suggested Jacques. 'I will,' said I. And I did, in an article entitled 'Peking Revisited', which I would produce for *Holiday* magazine in America. But I could not write a book on China. Only when everything had fallen into perspective would I write. At the moment I felt too flayed, too raw. 'I think that we are only seeing the beginning of the Chinese Revolution,' I told Jacques; 'I think China will have to invent a new pattern, all its own, for socialism. Meanwhile, it'll take at least twenty years to disentangle the Old from the New, the recurrent obscurantism disguised as revolutionary advance.' I did not know then how accurate these words of mine would prove. I would have forgotten them, but that they are in my notes of that time.

I went to see Kung Peng and she appeared angry with me. This was because in the course of my visits some remarks of mine, deemed 'unfriendly' by middle cadres, had come to her.

'You make statements attacking us,' she said.

'I don't attack, Kung Peng—I state what I think. If every time one says

* Author of *A Passage to India*.

something the cadres don't like one is dubbed reactionary, then no one will ever speak the truth.'

Kung Peng nodded: 'Some comrades at a lower level are not used to anything but acquiescence.' It was difficult for them to recognize 'constructive criticism'. She was not upbraiding me; she was trying to tell me to be careful.

How does one tell the truth and yet avoid offending susceptibilities? The problem is worse in China, with its long tradition of 'face', than perhaps anywhere else. Any official in China, whether communist or not, was simply not accustomed to being contradicted.

Kung Peng said, 'How could you marry such a feudalist as Tang Paohuang?'

'How did I know he was a feudalist? It was wartime, he had spent three years in England at Sandhurst, he sounded immensely patriotic, and I married him because of a common ideal: to fight to save the country ... '

Suddenly the terrible bitterness, the harrowing anger of the past came back. I had then plumbed, I thought, the ocean of China's feudalism. How profitable, how truly beneficial had been those years with Pao, though I would keep the scars of this great battle all my life! Now I did understand to the marrow the medieval mind, its total absence of cause-to-effect logic, its subjectivity, its intolerance, its emotional composition. That is what made me so cautious now, about New China, because in the air I could still sniff the mustiness.

I was back to that searing time, when I was just seventeen years old, in Yenching University, and had been denounced in the Students' Association newspaper because my sister was going out with her American fiancé and I had walked with both of them to the cinema one afternoon, and the fiancé, being American, had asked a friend of his to be my 'date' at the cinema ... Kung Peng, and others who were now officials of the government, had then been in Yenching, prominent leaders of the Students' Association. 'What did you do to me then?' I cried. It was twenty-three years later, but the wound they had inflicted upon me then would never go away. 'Did you try to find out? Did you come and talk to me? No. Arbitrarily you denounced me. On the walls of Yenching University I was denounced, when I was having such a hard time trying to save money to study, when I wanted so much to be Chinese, to be Chinese ... it was you who rejected me. You never gave me a chance, did you? What do you call that but feudalism?'

'We did not understand you then,' said Kung Peng.

'And how do I know that it won't be the same again? I *know* it will be just the same again. Someone will dredge up that story, and embellish it. Trust some man who was a student at that time, who is a middle cadre today, whom I possibly irked, or ignored, twenty, twenty-three years ago – trust him to use the next "mass movement campaign" and to paste it on wall posters all over the organization where I would be working, and to have me up, standing to defend myself, against all my co-workers ... '

And no one could protect me against this since every unit, every organization, ran its own meetings with its own cadres and its own 'masses', solved its own problems, condemned or cleared its own people. I had heard enough to know that malice, jealousy, pettiness, envy, vindictiveness had not disappeared. They were present, they were there. Only now they were daubed over with political jargon; the fuelling force for political condemnation; not always, but sometimes. And I was target enough, for I was so different, so different ... not only because I was a Eurasian, but because I wrote. And *A Many-Splendoured Thing* was, in China then, a bad book (for McCarthy and his ilk it was also a bad book).

'Believe me, Kung Peng, I love China, but China to me means the Chinese people. It will take at least twenty years before all these confusions of the mind are sorted out. Twenty years. I believe that in twenty years China will be democratic. But until then ... '

And Kung Peng did not contradict. She did not attempt to persuade me to stay. 'You must come back again next year,' she said, thus audibly promising me a visa. And so gently led me back to quietness, out of pain and anger. And later I was to know that Kung Peng would come out boldly for me, to address many people who were irate with me and wanted to throw me out, and would tell them to let be; tell them the story of my life. Not once, not only that year, but many, many times through the years, she would fight for me against the witch-hunters, the sectarians.

And now Kung Peng is dead; she too suffered, suffered greatly from the witch-hunters, the sectarians, all disguised as 'revolutionaries' ... But she was a staunch, a dedicated woman, and she never gave me a hint of what she endured because she was a very loyal Party member. To be able to manage one's sufferings and fears without inflicting even a suspicion of them upon others, is not that true courage?

So many of my friends, so many, have that courage, obstinate and valiant as heartbeat itself. And although I realized that I could not stay in China then without betraying things that mattered to me – including my love, my love, a many-splendoured thing – yet I would also not betray my friends, who had given everything they were, everything for China.

Six

China's Hundred Flowers: 1956

I TURNED IN MY BED, and staring at me was a dinosaur, smacking its jaws. But it was the Hsinchiao Hotel waiter knocking at my room door to wake me up. Papa and I were to leave early, for the seaside resort of Peitaiho, about five hours away by train from Peking. That is where Mama used to take us for a month in the summer, leaving Papa to swelter in Peking during the dog days of July and August.

In the train a policeman came up to me to ask for my papers, and Papa showed him our travel permit. Afterwards a group of suspicious young train workers (the Masses' Committee) came to chat with me. They were polite but thorough in their questioning. I told them I came from Malaya, and that I was a doctor, and had returned to China to see my family. It was not the clothes I wore but the fact that I spoke Chinese that had disconcerted these good people. Had I been a Westerner, people would have muttered 'Soviet expert'. Had I been speaking in French with Papa, I would have been a foreign traveller – but 'You look like us, you speak Chinese, but you're different'. Hence the questioning.

In Peitaiho, the local Party organizers insisted on taking me to beauty spots I knew well and telling me totally inaccurate stories of how the resort had been reserved 'only for imperialists and their running dogs'. That Papa had a house there placed us in a strange category. The Party man pointed to a beach: 'Chinese were not allowed to swim there'. It was true that few Chinese came to Peitaiho, but I had seen little boys from Chinese families swimming everywhere.

Papa's house had been taken over by the government with compensation paid to him. But Tiza's house had been confiscated since she had not claimed it. Here Papa felt more at ease to speak to me about Mama, and as we walked with small steps along the well-kept sand roads, he sighed a little. 'We are old now. Perhaps I should try to go outside, to see her again.' Because of the new policy of the Hundred Flowers, Papa had begun to hope that a demand to go abroad, to undertake a study tour, might now be accepted. But Mama was in America; and Papa could not go there from 'Red' China because the Americans would not allow him to enter unless he pretended to be a refugee and against the present government, and this Papa would of course not do. I had to arrange a midway place for Papa and Mama to meet. I said I would ask David Marshall, now the Chief Minister of Singapore, who was a friend of mine and an able lawyer, whether he would let Papa come to Singapore.

Actually, the day before leaving the seaside, I had sent a telegram to David Marshall. A young journalist had called, obviously on orders from a superior. He asked me whether I knew Marshall. 'I do.' 'Do you think he might like to come here for a visit?' 'I think he would.' I told the journalist that prior to becoming Chief Minister, David had asked me to be his Health Minister, and I had refused. The young man was nonplussed, but too polite to ask why; he looked at me steadily and I clearly got the message. 'I can send him a personal telegram, just from me, suggesting that he might like to see Peking.' And I cabled. David would come to Peking later that year, and greatly enjoy himself filming the yellow roofs of the Forbidden City. David could help Papa to stay in Singapore; I would try to get Mama out of the United States so that they could meet.

I visited in Peitaiho a hospital for mental cases. But everyone was reluctant to call it a mental hospital: it was 'for cadres who are overtired'. The only mental illness which was acceptable was neurasthenia, and throughout the years innumerable were the cases of neurasthenia, transient or permanent, that I would hear about. There is something very Victorian about this coyness; one thinks immediately of the word 'decline' which covered so many cases of tuberculosis and cancer in the nineteenth century.

But inside the hospital the doctors were brisk and modern. There were around 70 per cent of cases of schizophrenia, they said, and the majority of the two hundred patients were under forty years old. I asked about nervous breakdowns and psychoses. One of the Party cadres objected to the word breakdown. 'Our cadres do not get enough rest. Their health is affected,' he said.

I saw the deep sleep therapy rooms. They were very comfortable. One patient sat up; the blinds were drawn and he was happy in the semi-darkness, and he talked. He had worked too hard at the time of the big floods of 1954, which had threatened to submerge the city of Wuhan. He had not slept for many days, and in the end, while behind him his comrades toiled to raise the last foot of the earth dyke, to stop the surging waters, he had been swept away ... he had been rescued, but had become very panic-prone. And then there had been so many meetings, and sometimes his heart beat so fast and loud that he could hear nothing except its drumming. He had sharp, quick movements and needed, said the doctor, another three months of rest. 'We try all forms and modes of therapy, both Chinese and Western; also the Chinese breath control exercises.' On the terrace, some patients were shadow boxing. I asked about homosexuality and again the Party cadre stiffened.

'There is none in China.'

'But there is. It is mentioned in the old Chinese novels, for instance, in *The Dream of the Red Chamber*.'

'But it does not exist under socialism.'

The doctor kept quiet. It was, said the cadre, a perversion due to the social system. In fact, most mental diseases were ideological in nature. There would be no recognition of homosexuality as anything but a disease due to 'ideological causes'. But then everything was being re-defined, both in jurisdiction and in mental disease; new concepts of insanity and of delinquency were being worked out. Thus rape was not only a common law crime, it was also a political sin; asocial behaviour labelled 'bad habits inherited from the past society.'

When Papa went back to Peking, I went to Wuhan by train and from there by aeroplane to Chungking, to see again Szechuan and Third Uncle.

In the train, a most unusual sight: in one of the compartments, a Russian, drinking and hugging a Chinese girl. He came down at the stations, still hugging and fondling her. Round him were four 'companions', all Chinese. The whole train stared. Never, never would this have been possible, had it been anyone but a Russian ...

Some weeks later I was to hear from a friend the remark that the Chinese were getting very angry because the 'fraternal' experts raped interpreters or other women working in their offices. 'But no one can say anything: one man who complained was punished for indiscipline.'

I was met at Chungking airport by Comrade Kao, who was not a Szechuanese but a northerner and obviously hated the heat of Chungking. I was lodged in a fantastic new building, a Temple of Heaven grotesque, which functioned as hotel and assembly hall for meetings, and where the kitchen was a hundred metres away from the dining room. It was pretty grim for the waiters, who had to run up and down flights of stairs with the dishes. In Peking Uncle Kang had termed the building 'extravagant'; it had cost too much.

I would witness a big criticism meeting in the main hall; I was on the balcony, too far away to see or hear clearly, but a group of people seemed to be accused of some crime or other; they were standing with heads bowed, and people were getting up, pointing and talking at them. I asked

Comrade Kao about it and all he said was, 'You should not have been looking.'

Third Uncle, with his daughter, Third Sister, and her husband Lin Jugao, came to dinner; this had been arranged by Comrade Kao. 'They can come here, it is more convenient.' Comrade Kao did not wish me to walk about Chungking. Third Uncle was well, not a whit older, and seemed cheerful; but then he had good manners, and would appear cheerful even under duress. Lin Jugao was a representative of one of the non-communist parties. Comrade Kao (who insisted on being present) frowned at him, but no one cared.

'What do you think of this building?' asked Lin Jugao. I was just going to say how awful it was when he added, as Third Sister coyly tittered, 'She is one of the fifteen architects who designed it.' Third Sister said, 'Shut up', fondly. I said, 'How interesting ... ' She had, however, only designed the balconies and the concrete mouldings on the stairways.

The next morning, before Comrade Kao was astir, I went to see Third Uncle. I had asked Third Sister where he now stayed when we went together to the toilet. Third Uncle lived in a new small house not far from the enormous hall-hostel. He was dressed in a light gown of grey, he had summer slippers of woven fibre upon his feet, and at once he gave me a pair. 'You'll be more comfortable.' Then he moved towards the cupboard where he kept his tea boxes; he brewed and we sipped, as always, he discoursing on tea. But his mind was not on tea; he let it be known, in small hints, that there had been some 'inconsiderate' times, but that now things were moving 'appropriately', and 'anyway order and peace have been restored so that the future is limitless'. 'Of course, our Szechuan is a most important province; and it has to be managed properly.' He reminded me of the poem written in Chengtu on one of the pavilions in the Wu Hou Sze Shrine: 'Should you wish to rule Szechuan, think, think, and think again'.

'The new cadres come from other provinces. They do not always understand our character,' said Third Uncle. But luckily there were many Szechuanese among the commanders of the army: there was the great Chu Teh, and Chen Yi, and Teng Hsiaoping and Lo Juiching, and Nieh Jungchen, all of them Szechuanese, all of them veterans of the Long March and Mao's companions. 'Szechuan is the heart of China, China's treasure box,' said Third Uncle. Then abruptly he opened a drawer and took out a parcel, long and slim, wrapped in cloth. He unrolled the cloth; there were papers. 'These are the rubbings of our gravestones. We had to remove the graves.' He stopped. I think he was very sad. 'Take them. Keep them. And

157

also the book of our generations.' This book, which each family in China draws up, lists all the family members, generation by generation, but the one that Third Uncle gave me contained only the names of nine generations, albeit the names to be given to thirty generations to come were also listed. The reason was that it was nine generations from the time our Ancestor arrived in Szechuan from our original Hakka home in south China, Meihsien.*

I put the rubbings of the gravestones and the book of generations in my bag and Third Uncle inquired about Papa, and before I could say anything he was saying, loudly, 'Yes indeed, the government has given us all security in our old age', and in came Comrade Kao, puffing and a little irritated by my absconding.

'We have to visit many places,' he said crossly, 'we are late.'

He looked round enviously. The walls of the room had been covered with fine white paper. 'What a big house, and very expensive ... it's very big for just one person.'

'I am expecting my loved one, and my youngest son and his wife next month,' said Third Uncle.

We left, Comrade Kao and I, and on the way Comrade Kao said, 'We cadres have a very poor life; only thirty *yuan* a month, and too much responsibility and hard work ... ' One could see he felt life was a bit unfair; here was Third Uncle, an arrant bourgeois and a capitalist, with fine accommodation and fine silk garments, and possibly ten times the salary of Comrade Kao, not counting the interest on his investments, at $3\frac{1}{2}$ per cent. And Comrade Kao was from the north; his wife and five children had stayed there. He had come with the army in 1949 and had been in Szechuan for all of those seven years since Liberation, and, 'I am not used to the food or the climate. Sometimes I get quite unhealthy,' said he, and described the way his bowels let him down.

The steel works of Chungking, which had been a private company (set up to make the rails to build that railway planned way back in 1903), were now nationalized, and I spent a very happy day there with the director, a Szechuanese. I inquired about the workers' health and accommodation; was shown their new brick dormitories, up a small hill. 'It's gruelling, climbing up that hill in hot weather,' I said. 'But there's no other space. All of Chungking is ladder streets climbing the many hills,' said the director. In 1972, I would again visit the steel works of Chungking. And the same director would greet me, with much emotion. 'We remember your visit in 1956; you asked so much about the workers, their welfare ...

* See *The Crippled Tree*.

we circulated your remarks ... the workers were moved by your concern ... ' The director himself had been under duress during the Cultural Revolution; sent back to manual labour; but in 1972, with the return to prominence of Chou Enlai that year, he had been reinstalled, and the steel plant was working again. In Chungking, as in all Szechuan, there had been a lot of fighting, almost civil war, in the Cultural Revolution.

Comrade Kao complained, 'I couldn't understand what you were saying,' because he did not speak Szechuanese well. He then duly took me round many places I knew, but also to the house where Chou Enlai had lived when he was working in Chungking, keeping the United Front liaison going with Chiang Kaishek. Kung Peng had also stayed there; she was then working with Chou Enlai, and that is how we had met, in January 1941. I looked at the small, hot house, with its tiny rooms; the desk, the beds with their neatly rolled blankets. Another Party cadre in charge, also not a Szechuanese, tried to tell me all about the bombings of Chungking. 'I know, I was here, I was bombed.' But he went on giving me totally inaccurate figures.*

I went to see the jail hewn out of rock where the (American) O.S.S., together with Chiang's hateful security service under Tai Lee, subjected Communist prisoners to torture. Since I had personally seen someone repeatedly beaten and then walked round, I knew that it was true that torture was used. But once again there was some exaggeration in the dramatic way the Party cadre presented the facts, as if he had to force me to believe them.

Then by train to Chengtu, on the railway which had been completed in 1952. It was a night flooded with moonlight, and the small villages clustering under their bamboo fronds looked delightful in the silver radiance. We reached Neichiang, the sugar city, where I had spent some weeks with Tenth Sister, at the local branch of the Meifeng Bank. Now the Meifeng Bank had become the People's Bank, but the government had kept all my relatives in their jobs; so that Second Brother and his wife, Ninth and Tenth Sisters, and many cousins further removed continued to serve the bank.

Chengtu, and a clean railway station, and to greet me some Szechuanese cadres as well as northern cadres. I felt slightly guilty of provincial chauvinism because I was happy to see cadres of my own province. Of course, during the Long March the Red Army had replenished its numbers in Szechuan, hence the training of seasoned Party members from my province; but the bulk of the Red bases had been in the north, and that is

* See *Birdless Summer*.

why there were so many cadres from the northern provinces all over China. They were hardworking, honest, but occasionally no match for the agile-brained Szechuanese.

I went to the university, where I had so often been in 1940 and in 1941. On the way to the university we passed the site of Marian Manly's former midwifery hospital. It no longer existed. In place of the small wood and brick building rose a new block of flats for workers. Chengtu was now becoming industrialized, I was told, and 'many workers from Shanghai have come and more will be coming to start industrial projects'. As a result of the influx of young workers, the same phenomenon of population increase was happening here as in Chungking. 'The first thing workers do is get married and raise a baby or two. They have never had such a good life.'

I thought of Marian as we went past, her tears when we had met in Hongkong after she had been expelled from China, weeping her heart out because she was no longer wanted. 'I must write to her, tell her I have come here.'

At the university I met professors I had known in the 1940s: Dr Huang of the Dental Department had cared for an awkward wisdom tooth of mine, coming out late and impacted; and Dr Yu, the gynaecologist, I had seen when I was working as a midwife at Marian Manly's hospital. Both had humorous, harassed faces. They had obviously been through some gruelling criticism meetings, but now all was well, and they continued working. The university and the hospital and medical school were expanding. Many more thousands of students were expected in the years to come; they would provide the staff necessary for medical care in the whole of south-west China. Already medical teams from here went to Tibet and Tsinghai, out of the way regions. The enormous drive against venereal disease among the national minorities (very prevalent, especially in Tibet, where it was the cause of so much infecundity among women) had produced good results. 'We hope to eradicate both gonorrhoea and syphilis,' said Dr Yu. Of course, this also meant changing social behaviour, laxity in morals, prostitution. The custom in Szechuan of selling one's wife for 'temporary employment' to government officials from Nanking and Shanghai, during the last years of the Chiang Kaishek regime, had disappeared, and so had the selling of girl children to the brothels, which had been closed.

At dinner that night I found the doctors gentle but stubbornly forthright. 'Of course interference with scientific work is not good; the Party must learn to listen to the masses,' said Dr Huang. The Dental Department, and in fact much of the university, had been started by Canadian and American missionaries, and staffed by them for a considerable number of years. But no one could refer to this fact for the time being; there was a violent reaction towards acknowledging that 'colonial imperialism' had left a little knowledge and training behind. And of course, among the very nice Party officials at dinner, there was the usual intransigent bureaucrat who told me quite inaccurate stories about the hospital and how it had catered only for the wealthy. But he had such a narrow vocabulary, such a paucity of words, that I suddenly understood how difficult it was for him. He was a poor peasant's son, and in a drought had seen his sisters and mother die of hunger; he and his father had become beggars. 'Wealth' to him meant simply enough to eat.

I launched into birth and death rates. Already in Peking the response when I made inquiries about death had been 'Nobody dies now', or 'Very few people die now'. And here it was the same. Oh, my China, I thought, my throat suddenly seized with love and nostalgia, still so involved with the totem and taboo of words! The word death had always been taboo; now it had become almost anti-socialist! There was such a big hoard of ancient symbols and myths to dispel: a new metaphysics was in the offing; and how could the cadres be blamed for thinking that fervour was truth, as in pre-scientific Europe? China had not yet accomplished her industrial revolution, or developed the scientific logic that goes with industrialization.

Dinner with the intelligentsia of Chengtu; the writers, among them the famous Li Liuju, whose book *Sixty Stirring Years* would provide me with so much information for my own book, *The Crippled Tree*. I inquired about Pa Chin, another Szechuan author, but he now lived in Shanghai. Li Liuju spoke at length, because I asked him, of the Secret Society, the Brothers of the Robe, of their beneficent and then nefarious role in the province. I also met Szechuan opera artists and went to the Szechuan opera with my cousins, and to drink tea in teahouses with the writers, and to discuss gastronomy while eating at the old Kokochuan restaurant. 'All the good cooks are being taken away from Szechuan to serve in the hotels in Peking.' 'Then we must train many more.' 'But the young look down upon the art of cooking.'

Enchanted strolls through the Chengtu I loved so well; to find the busy street of silversmiths and craftsmen almost deserted. 'It is reorganization of small commerce ... they will now enter co-operatives.' But the temples were kept and repaired, as everywhere else, and the harvest was good. Szechuan was providing rice for other provinces in need of rice. 'We have a surplus this year.'

At that time it was possible for outside visitors to read the local press; something which was changed in 1960. I never found out why. In the *Szechuan Daily* I read complaints against commandism and corruption, against shoddy work (a report that 35,000 water carts were unusable in Shantung province, so badly had they been joined together). I read of Party cadres pushing the peasants to fulfil quotas irrespective of the quality of the harvest; giving wrong orders about planting. The Hundred Flowers spirit was certainly catching on in Szechuan. Clearly, it was not 'liberalization' in the sense of sharing or relinquishing power to another party; simply a demand for greater co-operation from the intelligentsia in accelerating progress by speaking the truth about the many problems impeding China's advance to modernity.

I visited the National Minorities' Institute; thirty-five million people, fifty-odd national minorities. 'We've found some new ones; so small, only a few hundred individuals, still in the Stone Age,' said the director. The problem was, how could one construct an artificial language for them? 'Some of them count no further than two.' But here in Chengtu the bulk of the students were from Tibet, being trained as cadres. A Tibetan typewriter had also been invented. 'We aim to have 2,000 Tibetan accountants for the co-operatives which will come to Tibet at Land Reform,' said the director.

Up to the mountains, beyond Pihsien, our ancestral home.* On the road back, I watched the human labour, the human labour of Szechuan, people pulling and tugging and carrying ... when would that stop? And there was a coffin being carted away on a small cart, pulled by two men roped to it. Of course funerals were now furtive affairs. No one ought to die in a country six years old. One-third of the population of Chungking city, I had been told, was under six years of age. At the steel mill, two hundred children were born each month. Ten thousand two hundred workmen, but with their families they numbered 70,000. There never were enough living quarters. The steel mill must expand to ten times its size in the next ten years but the area for dormitories only three times ... In the rural co-operatives there were children, children, children ... 'Szechuan is very prolific,' said the Szechuan cadres beatifically. 'No child dies of hunger now, everybody lives.' Obviously family planning here was going to be difficult – a difficulty made worse by the fact that in the villages every baby received a full adult ration in rice, meat and oil from the day he was born.

* See *The Crippled Tree* and *Birdless Summer*.

I returned to Peking, and at the Party for the British Queen's Birthday I saw Premier Chou Enlai.

Chou Enlai looked no older than when I had last seen him in Chungking in 1941, fifteen years ago. His eyes, the most startling feature about him, were lustrous and moved quickly; everyone found him irresistible. 'What a man,' sighed a matron near me. People were being introduced to him by the British Chargé d'Affaires. Chou himself walked up to shake hands with ambassadors, and then Kung Peng pushed me forward and Chou Enlai, who never forgot anything said, 'Ah yes, you applied from India.'

I said, 'Prime Minister, I heard you speak in Chungking in 1941.'

I saw him turn inwards, groping in his store of memories (I think he had total memory and total recall).

'You couldn't see me, there was such a huge crowd. You were talking to the people.'

'Ah yes,' he said, and then someone else came up and Chou went round the rest of the party, which ended with a toast to the Queen. His coming to the British Embassy was of great significance, the correspondents said. It meant that China might 'liberalize'.

Some days later was the opening of the third session of the First National People's Congress. It was held at the back of the beautiful Peihai Park, and I remember the Tibetan delegates, in sumptuous scarlet and saffron robes clicking their beads and walking round the lake; the Uighurs and the Yis and the Miaos and so many other representatives in their own colourful embroidered garments and ornamental headgear; the many temporary restaurants to suit each minority, with various kinds of food; no pork for the Huis (Muslims), but then one-third of the city of Peking was reckoned 'Muslim', and almost every street had a Muslim restaurant. Representatives of overseas Chinese in ties and Western suits, and delegates from factories, and intellectuals, all walked about, admiring the beautiful pomegranate trees in pots which lined the avenues.

I still have some of the speeches that were distributed at the Congress – one by the representative of the national minorities, mentioning 'shortcomings' and errors, but also lauding the fact that at last the minorities were no longer treated in a degrading manner as in the old days, and that health and education, besides economic benefits, were theirs. There is also a speech by the representative for the overseas Chinese praising the patriotism of those who returned to China. Most of them were labouring people, and the money thay had sent their old parents from abroad should not be interfered with ... The spirit of criticism promoted by the Hundred Flowers seemed to belong among the routine sentences of praise ...

The correspondents of Reuter and Agence France-Presse, and I, had received invitations to attend the opening session of the National People's Congress (not, of course, the committee debates). I am certain that this was at Chou Enlai's initiative. It showed that China had nothing to fear; it got rid of this bogus 'secrecy' which plagued all communication. It indicated that China would open herself to the world and its nations, and learn from all countries to accelerate her own progress. However, some Western experts persisted in regarding the whole Hundred Flowers in a romantically wishful manner: as a falling away from 'communism', and a 'thaw', a change of purpose. This was confusing goals and aims with methods. If I have stressed this, it is because today, in 1979, China is back in the spirit and exaltation of the Hundred Flowers and all the bright hopes of that year.

There is, however, a major difference. In 1956, the bulk of the Chinese people were still illiterate; the intelligentsia was reckoned at five million, or 1 per cent of the total population. But by 1979 a new intelligentsia has grown up, derived from the sons and daughters of peasants and workers. Even in the hamlets of faraway Szechuan, the young can read and write, hold meetings, and if these meetings were streamlined for acquiescence, there have been so many crises, so many abrupt reversals in the last twenty years, that now even the partly educated insist on thinking and arguing for themselves.

On that afternoon in June 1956 in Peking Chou Enlai climbed on the rostrum and spoke. He looked happy, his eyes shone. He had delivered the previous day a speech on external policy which contained all the elements of an 'opening' upon the world. Now Chou Enlai gave a speech on internal policy that was so contrary to all that was current and habitual in Western minds about China and China's system that it held me spellbound.

I sat with Jacques Locquin of Agence France-Presse, occasionally translating for him. But my attention was riveted to Chou and his words, and the translation I made was inadequate. Locquin, however, was so fired by what I told him that he immediately sent a cable to Paris; to which there was no response at all.

Plans for scientific and economic advance; a total reshaping of the economy, and above all, *decentralization*, the regions being given more power of their own, with less central rigidity. The adjustments to be made between the individual and the group, between the small group and the larger collectivity; between the Party power-holders and the people – all these Chou talked about. The need for the intelligentsia, for non-communist parties to continue in their useful work of providing through advice and criticism a necessary foil for the Communist Party; the need for destroying the bad habits of commandism and sectarian behaviour in the Party; the need to listen to criticism, even if it was unpalatable ... an electrifying speech, and the faces of the listeners showed their elation, their excitement. Chou managed to pack into that hour the sensation of a new set of policies, the search for a framework to broaden the basis of consultation.

As in 1941, when I had heard Chou Enlai speak in the streets of Chung-king, because the crowd was so large no hall could contain it, I was moved by some quality in him beyond eloquence or rhetoric. He was not gifted with oratory; but he was immensely impressive through his deep sincerity, the reasonableness and the simplicity of what he said, which everyone understood.

What Chou Enlai said implied a departure from the accepted theses of how to run a socialist state. And yet I was to discover that he was not its sole originator; it was a combined effort, with Mao Tsetung as the visionary behind it; for Chou's speech was an interpretation of a speech delivered by Mao in April of 1956 to Party secretaries and state ministers and leaders from all over China. Neither was Mao's speech an individual creation; it was based on work done, for more than two years, by Chinese economists and statisticians and social science researchers probing and studying to discover what was the best, the more effective way to *accelerate* development in such a backward and poor country as China.

But none of us, at the time, knew of Mao Tsetung's speech, or of the collective effort that had gone into gathering the material for it. In fact, Mao's speech, which was to be called 'The Ten Major Relationships' was not to be officially published until twenty-one years later, in April 1977!

I have always been puzzled by this extraordinary delay. I think it was a regrettable error; for had this speech of Mao been known earlier, many things which harmed China might not have happened. I was able to obtain an 'illegal' version of it in the mid 1960s.

Chou Enlai's speech was the foundation (so frail, so chancy at the time) of the democratization of China. Twenty years would go by before its meaning would take hold.

The next morning I was surprised to discover in the *People's Daily* only a terse half column of summing up. Perhaps I had missed the main speech? But I checked with Locquin, and he confirmed: 'It hasn't been printed yet ... But if Chou Enlai's speech means anything, it means a democratic, socialist China, along the pattern of Yugoslavia, refusing the Soviet yoke.' We were both elated, but also puzzled, because neither of us had enough solid material to go on. And when, later, I spoke to some Party cadres about it, I discovered frowning and tight mouths. Even Kung Peng was to say to me ten years later, 'We did not realize the importance of certain things said and done in 1956 and 1957.'

I suppose I could have guessed, by the very composition of the Party, that there would be strong and obscurantist opposition to those more generous, libertarian impulses. But I was not at the time as knowledgeable about the history of the Chinese Communist Party as I later became. And Western experts were of no help to me in analysing what was then going on.

Why was so little publicity given to Mao's most important discourse, 'The Ten Major Relations'? Why so little about Chou Enlai's major speech in that June? I would try to figure it out in the following months.

In his April 'Ten Major Relations', Mao Tsetung had criticized in mordant terms the methods used by Stalin in Soviet agriculture. At the time, Mao was also beginning to have doubts about Khrushchev; the way the latter had proceeded against Stalin did not appeal to Mao, although Mao and Stalin did not like each other. Perhaps Mao was already becoming suspicious—there is evidence to bolster this view—of Khrushchev's real intentions in promoting in Russia what looked like a 'liberalization' and was spoken of as a 'thaw'. The word used today is détente. But was the whole purpose merely a softening-up directed towards the United States, to make the U.S.S.R. acceptable to the U.S. as an 'equal partner' in the sharing of the world? After all, the episode of Yalta, where Roosevelt and Stalin had divided Europe, and even attempted to divide China, must have rankled very deeply with Mao Tsetung.

There might be another reason why these documents were withheld.

Ever since the early 1930s Mao Tsetung seems to have been concerned and perturbed with the problem of physical liquidation or purges within the Communist Party. He had almost been a victim, himself, of the sanguinary liquidations which had been practised by the then leader of the Party, Wang Ming, a man trained in the most rigid Stalinist orthodoxy. Mao realized that Soviet Russia had never made clear the distinction between acceptable 'contradictions', that is, differences of opinion but within the limits of promoting the good of the socialist system, and 'enemy contradictions', that is, through opposition and rejection which could not be treated otherwise than by physical force because they sought to overthrow the socialist system.

In 1956 and 1957, Mao Tsetung was to do what I consider to be his major work in illuminating this problem. He would make 'acceptable' 'contradictions among the people', which must not be dealt with by force, and many divergences of opinion. He hoped thus to avoid the massive Stalinist purges.

It was this issue which, in June 1956, all unknown to me then, I was hearing debated – and sometimes violently opposed – in Peking. It was on this foundation that Chou Enlai's speech rested.

Mao would also then aver that Stalin had been wrong in assuming that, once a communist party had taken power, the socialist state was established and class struggle would disappear.

Not so, said Mao. In a socialist state, the struggle for supremacy between the former ruling class – the bourgeoisie or the feudal aristocracy – and the toilers still goes on for decades, even for centuries. But the forms and shapes it takes are different.Even if former exploiters are deprived of power, the ideas they have engendered, the habits and behaviour which germinate within the environment they have created still continue, and they permeate *all* the classes, and new exploiters are born.

But in early 1956, Mao Tsetung was not yet quite sure of these theories that he was elaborating. Only in 1977, when I mentioned again this problem, did I acquire from a high Party member confirmation that this assumption was correct. Mao therefore hesitated, and his speeches were not published although they were circulated within the Party, and discussed. It seems, moreover, that a good many Party members did not agree with him. Some – how many we shall never know – thought the whole experiment of the Hundred Flowers extremely dangerous. And so did the Russians. The Russian Ambassador was very forthright about it. 'We don't have this kind of thing in our country,' said he.

I asked Kung Peng whether I might have an interview with Premier Chou Enlai, and handed her six pages of wide-ranging questions. I then waited about ten days. During that time, I went to see Popovic, the Yugoslav Ambassador. Popovic was tall and handsome and spoke excellent French. Was it possible, I asked him, that China, like Yugoslavia, would go her own way? Would there be an alteration in the apparently indissoluble bond with the U.S.S.R.? Popovic was too good a diplomat to reply in a direct manner to my astounding questions. He agreed that China was 'in a new tide of total experimentation' and that probably 'the Soviet model does not correspond to Chinese needs ... National independence is of great importance to China as it is to us ... a fact occasionally lost sight of by the Great Powers,' said he. He told me that a delegation of Yugoslav journalists was in China and was explaining the Yugoslav way to socialism to the Chinese; but so far nothing had come of it.

I also had an interview with Chinese newsmen, and one of them appeared surprised that I should be both a doctor and a writer. He had a cataloguing mind. 'It's quite impossible. You must be one or the other.' We discussed the duty of newspapers; and I said I thought their function was to expose wrongdoing on the part of the government or its officials. I approved of two instances of bad handling being reported in the papers recently. The first report was on the high rate of accidents in factories caused by the 'killing' of machinery by running it too fast in order to beat targets. The second was about pigs, my favourite topic in agriculture. I don't understand agriculture, but I know about pigs.

Pigs too hastily collectivized, I said, had died, and brought the amount of meat for consumers right down. I had noticed the poor condition of pigs in the collectives. And I had been happy to see in the report that in one co-operative the pig population had dramatically shrunk from around 370 to 50 ... The reception to my remarks was mixed.

I mentioned Yugoslavia. 'Should one not study what they are doing?' And then, suddenly, one journalist – a Party member, and in the committee leadership – lost his temper and started shouting at me. 'It is all very easy for people who have done nothing to criticize us ... but we have carried guns and fought and died to build all this,' he cried, and the others kept quiet.

I went to see my childhood friend, Simon Hua. He was the son of my father's dearest friend, Hua Nankuei, the engineer who had gone with my father to restore the Tatung coal mines to working order. Simon had studied in Paris, where he, of course, had become a communist – the French variety, in fashion among the intelligentsia in France after the Second World War. He had married a charming and intelligent Frenchwoman, Irène, and they had come to live in China in 1951. Irène worked at the radio broadcasting centre and Simon in architecture. I congratulated Simon on the children's hospital he had designed. What was he doing now? 'Housing for workers,' said he, and his face clouded. He felt his talent was not being used properly.

I also met Rewi Alley, the indomitable and fabulous New Zealander, who had arrived in China in 1927 and stayed on, and whose books and articles and poems are an extraordinary and massive compilation; a great treasure trove to help future historians understand the Chinese Revolution.

Rewi, ever since 1927, has been totally involved in that Revolution. Both in the early Gung Ho co-operatives – in which Americans played a part – and later. He owned a fabulous collection of books. He had greatly impressed Ian when both of them had travelled to the Buddhist caves of Tun Huang and the Crescent Moon Lake. He talked quietly, and he knew everything. Every pulse and heartbeat of China. And oh, how much he set me straight, and in so many ways, through the decades which followed.

With Rewi I met the American doctor, now a Chinese citizen, the legendary Ma Haiteh, George Hatem. A Lebanese American, he had been in Yenan in 1936–7, the physician of all China's leaders, including Mao Tsetung. After Liberation in 1949 he had been one of the main figures in the drive against venereal disease in China – a drive so successful that 'we're working ourselves out of work', he would say to me.

With Ma Haiteh I would spend some hours of one night walking up and down, down and up, in the dust road trodden by the village carts in front of Papa's house, talking, talking … To him I revealed all my distress, my trivial and yet important hesitations, and it was he who made my spirit whole and healed me, for after that talk I no longer suffered from suffocation. The tremendous epic of the Revolution now came clearly to me. 'Sister, nothing under Heaven comes easily, and certainly not building a new world,' said Ma Haiteh.

And Rewi Alley would say, 'Take it easy, lass, take it easy', when I imprudently exploded verbally. 'China has a long way to go, lass … sometimes it's best to keep silent and to trust.'

A small black car with an unassuming young man in it came to fetch me. We drove towards Chung Nanhai, where China's leaders resided; but the young man did not know the exact entrance, so we were ten minutes late.

I was going to see Chou Enlai in his own home.

Through the neat avenue bordered with oleanders to a modest pavilion, and there were Chou Enlai and his wife Teng Yingchao, and with them only Kung Peng.

It was like a visit to one's own family, so simple, with no protocol of any kind. In the living room, many books on shelves, but no antiques, no curios, no priceless furniture. Old worn sofas, rattan chairs, a worn and cheap carpet ... At one time during the next three hours I had to use the toilet, and went through their bedroom. Small wooden twin beds, old blankets, no carpet on the floor, a washbasin, a desk with a lamp ... Spartan. And this was no fake. Chou simply did not care for any material comfort.

'So you did not go to the Anshan steel works,' said Chou immediately. I had been offered a visit to the Anshan steel works; they were the pride of China then, set up by the U.S.S.R., but I had refused to go.

'I don't understand machines,' said I.

'I hear you do not go to the United States, although you are popular there through your novel,' said Chou Enlai.

'I don't go to the United States, Prime Minister,' I replied.

Chou glanced at me and that grin, which some newsmen described as utterly devastating, swept over his face. Appreciation, humour, understanding, and beyond that the very human touch of recognition ... recognition that in himself also existed those impulses, those dos and don'ts, unexplainable.

Kung Peng said that I was 'very determined'. 'See how well she talks Chinese, although she had to fight for a Chinese education, and she has been abroad so many years.'

'We talk Chinese in Malaya,' I said.

Chou then asked about Malaya, and Singapore, and David Marshall. David had by then accepted the invitation to come to Peking.

'Now,' said Chou, 'you've given me a long list of questions. A very long list.' I had questions about law, legal trials, people's courts and 'mass' judgments with the attendant risk of prejudice and passion; a question on the writer Hu Feng and the demarcation between expression of personal opinion and counter-revolutionary thought or behaviour; the ineptness of Chinese propaganda abroad, with its bombast and smugness; the low political level of criticism of individuals in the mass political campaigns (in so far as I had been able to find out). There were questions about the plethora of bureaucrats, all non-productive, and the rising élitism among the bureaucracy, as exemplified by priorities, perks, such as travel on trains. There were questions on hygiene, and on the fact that too many meetings after work interfered with normal rest and were injurious to health. I asked about birth control, and finally I tackled the question of 'socialist realism' in writing.

'I'm not going to answer all of them,' said Chou Enlai. He would delegate Marshal Chen Yi to continue the conversation with me another day. Meanwhile, he gave me almost three hours; with measured clarity and conciseness he covered a vast amount of ground. His main theme was the long Chinese Revolution, with its many turns and twists and crises. How many times in the past people had said 'It's all over'. But true revolutionaries went on, despite setbacks and failures. And there had to be setbacks and failures; for how otherwise could there be advance? The future was still uncharted ground ...

'But one thing is certain. We are going forward. There is no going back. The door to going back is closed.' Chou said this with great passion, with an almost lyrical rising of tone and an abrupt gesture, his eyes flaming. 'The power we have will not be lightly cast aside, not in the name of pseudo-liberalism, which will only lead to a tyranny like the one we have just emerged from.' For the future, and because of the needs of the country, 'we are prepared to go along even with people who disagree with us, provided they do not sabotage the socialist revolution.'

This was the United Front theory; a major concept of Mao Tsetung, and one which had been practised during the war with Japan, and which had been an indispensable factor in victory.*

'You think there is no dissent in the Party; this is a common subjective view in the West; that the Communist Party is a monolith ... ' It was not so, Chou said. 'If you only knew how much we debate, discuss, argue ... we often hold very different opinions ...' Again there was a note of passion in his voice. There was always, he said, a lot of talk about individualism in Western countries, but it was in China that with progress, prosperity and security there would come the full blossoming of the individual ... for how could there be 'individualism' when in so many nations of the world people still died of hunger, were exploited and had no security? The Constitution of 1954 had been a great step forward to ensure the rights of the Chinese people, rights which they had not had before. Had I not personally known what the situation was in Old China?

But the West (and I think here Chou meant chiefly the United States) found it 'difficult' to face what had been inevitable, the triumph of the Chinese Revolution. 'There is always a time lag in understanding the realities of history.' It might take a long time before the West accepted these realities, but 'We are patient. We shall never provoke a war. We want, above all, peace.' This did not mean knuckling under. He referred to his speech at Bandung in 1955 and how it had been welcomed by so many countries emerging from colonialist dependence. Bandung in 1955 and the Geneva Conference of 1954, which had seen the end of the war in Indo-China, had been landmarks for Asia, Africa and Latin America. But

* See *The Morning Deluge*.

the United States strove to ignore history, and was even contemplating the use of military force to maintain or perhaps extend her hold in Asia. 'This is wild dreaming,' said Chou with great composure.

As for Taiwan, it was China's territory, and 'No one on earth shall tell us what to do with our own territory ... that is infringement of sovereignty.'

The world of the enslaved had now risen; and there would be battles fought because national liberation never came except through struggles; but this did not mean provoking a war. Neither did it mean attacking others.

Some people thought that once socialism was established everything was like Paradise; others saw it as unredeemed Hell. Actually, 'we have no experience in socialist construction ... we shall have to find the way which best applies to our own background and concrete conditions ...'

I had heard through Peking's ever-busy grapevine that the Soviet Ambassador, Yudin, had reported to Moscow with great concern about the project of the Hundred Flowers and the new orientation. Chou did not reply to my hint about this. 'No one can stop the tide of history.' Then he went off at a tangent. What kind of life, what frustrations had the intelligentsia of China suffered in the past? 'Look at your own father, who came back to build a railway in 1913. He had to wait until 1952 to see it built. By us.'

Of course the remoulding of an intellectual was a very painful process, but had the Revolution been easy? 'Our intelligentsia is, however, progressing towards socialism.'

'Prime Minister, my rate of progress is exceptionally slow.'

Again that lightning grin, impish; Chou liked controversy, argument, spirit in others. He hated flattery, fawning, servility. Thirteen years later, one November night in 1969, he would tease me about my rate of progress. This was the night he introduced me, at my request, to the redoubtable wife of Mao, Chiang Ching.

Chou now described the composition of the National People's Congress, the highest organ of authority in China from the juridical point of view (but it would take many years until it would assume its proper authority, as it is beginning to do today). He showed me how the eight non-communist parties, which represented at most only 1 to 2 per cent of the population, held around 39 per cent of the seats. The policy was to retain the non-communist parties 'for a long time to come'. In the same way, urban votes, representing only 10 to 12 per cent of total votes in China, had been given for the time being eight times the weight of rural votes.

Otherwise there would be a complete swamping of the intelligentsia in the cities by the peasantry in the rural villages.

We then spoke of the 'mistakes and errors' by Party cadres. 'I understand you have been collecting examples of such mistakes,' said Chou, again with that flashing smile. 'We do try to avoid them ... and we always want to know about them ... sometimes the top level does not know what is really happening down below.' I told him then what Jui had suffered in Szechuan, and both he and his wife listened sympathetically. 'Yes, such things do happen. We do try to rectify and reappraise, however ... and we must not say a system is bad just because mistakes are made. How long has it taken democracy in the West really to function? And what is its true basis? I think you should study more deeply,' said Chou Enlai. 'I heartily agree, Prime Minister.'

Teng Yingchao then spoke to me. She was a small-boned woman, attractive in her youth and still intensely charming and deeply intelligent. As a student she had been a fiery and gifted orator. She and Chou Enlai had worked together since their student days; both had participated in the first cultural revolution of May 1919.* Teng Yingchao had been one of the pioneers to go among the women factory workers of Tientsin and Shanghai and to mobilize them in the massive demonstrations of the 1920s. She had also run night schools. She had done the Long March, although at the time ridden with tuberculosis. She had had a prize placed upon her capture by the Kuomintang; Edgar Snow has told, in one of his books, of how he helped to smuggle her out of a city and thus escape capture and probably execution.

Teng Yingchao inquired about Yungmei's illness and my life as a doctor. And then she gave me a great gift: she suddenly spoke about the Communist Party, but in such a poetic way, with such deep feeling, that her words would stay with me vividly until today. The Party, said she, was not something created in the abstract; it could be likened to the white spume on top of the ocean waves. The ocean was the people; the white foam seemed to lead, but it was water-borne and water-bred and could not exist without the water below. 'This is our experience, those of us who have worked all these years for the liberation of the Chinese people.'

When I took my leave, I felt enlarged, another dimension added to my thinking. 'China will be all right if there are such people as Chou Enlai and Teng Yingchao,' I thought. 'I indeed have a great deal to learn ... judgments about China are so superficial,' I told Kung Peng.

Back at the hotel, Locquin tried to extract something from me but I

* See *The Morning Deluge*.

was unable to convey the warmth, the intimate friendliness and concern which I had felt right through the afternoon with Chou Enlai. But the newsmen were all, anyway, favourably impressed by Chou. 'He is a formidable type, an extraordinary personality,' they would say, as did the diplomats. Chou did not suffer fools gladly. He would fall silent, his face would darken; he never shouted; but sometimes his hand shook a little with controlled anger. He overworked himself every day of his life; he stretched his mind and those of the people with him to the utmost. Always he would demand facts, clearness, accuracy. 'We must stop using only percentages, we must use tangible figures.' Alas, the bureaucracy was stronger; and percentages went on being used, for many more years.

Several days later, Chen Yi saw me. Corpulent and jocund, his presence was not electrifying, like Chou Enlai, but he gave out such humour, such humanity, so much natural good temper, that I liked him immediately. Besides, he was from my province of Szechuan, and like all Szechuanese, he loved laughter, and had a great sense of humour (which northerners in China do not seem to have to such an extent).

Chen Yi had just returned from Tibet, where he had officiated at the installation of a committee, headed by the Dalai Lama, for the autonomy of the region. 'I heard you were leaving soon so I came along,' said he. And indeed, it was he who had come to the hotel to see me, with utter simplicity and lack of pomp. Both he and Chou Enlai detested those immense coffin-like black Zis cars, with thick clouds of veiling, black and brown and white, shielding the passengers from being seen. Chou's car was a battered old one; he rushed in and out of it carrying his own brief-case. As for Chen Yi, he scowled at the curtains and took them down. 'I can't see a thing ... In the past, in the guerrilla bases, any poor peasant could stop any high official on the street and talk to him ... and now with those big cars, they don't even know who's inside.'

We started with laughter: Chen Yi made some jokes about football, the Szechuan opera, recited a line or two of poetry – he had been known to entertain whole companies of soldiers, when in the guerrilla bases, with his imitations of Chiang Kaishek. Now he made me laugh, imitating the bureaucratic officials. 'It's a style we've got to get rid of ... we were infected with it when we came to the cities.'

But he had come to talk about the problem of Taiwan: there could not be two Chinas, or one China and one Taiwan ... the United States was trying hard to make two Chinas, but 'we'll never accept that. And on this point Chiang Kaishek is not such a bad guy.' As I evinced surprise: 'One must always judge people dialectically; there is good in bad people, bad in good ones. Chiang is a turtle's egg, but he also insists there's only one China. The Americans cannot twist him round ... so Chiang and ourselves have the same policy, the unity of China. We merely differ as to who holds power in China.'

He almost hinted – but so lightly that I would not be sure – that should Chiang or other high officials in Taiwan become 'smart' they would be very welcome and be most amply rewarded ... but there was small evidence that Chiang was very farsighted. 'However, we are not worried. We are prepared to be patient. The United States makes a great uproar and her navy runs hither and thither to contain us; of course, we must be prepared in case sudden war is launched upon us, but I personally think that who goes against the wheel of history courts defeat.'

We talked a little about Tibet; and the thousands of kilometres of road which had to be constructed in order to make it accessible. 'We are preserving the language and culture of the national minorities; but this does not mean there cannot be social change. The people of the national minorities have been cruelly oppressed in the past; they want to change.'

I told Chen Yi about Singapore and Malaya, and the setting up of Nanyang University. Chen Yi said that the question of the overseas Chinese 'was a problem still to settle ... it is the cause of many headaches for us ... ' But China only wanted peace. It was clear that the last thing Chen Yi wanted was to interfere in South East Asia. 'However, when the overseas Chinese are persecuted, of course we must protest, and help them ... '

My last three days in Peking, and who should I see on Morrison Street (named so by the British after Ian Morrison's father – although the Chinese never used that name) but my old friend, Hualan.

We stopped; fell into each other's arms. My dear Hualan, who had stayed with me when she studied in London during the bombings in 1944, and whose courage was awesome. When the shrapnel fell around us and I took Yungmei down with me to the cellar (we lived on the top floor in Welbeck Street), Hualan refused to go down. She was washing her hair. It was three in the morning.

Hualan took me to her home in Soochow Street. It was a lovely old house with a courtyard and very good furniture, much better than Chou Enlai's. Hualan's Polish mother, blue-eyed and fair-haired, fussed around me and poured tea from a samovar, and put jam in it, Russian fashion. Hualan's father was an expert in international law in the Ministry of

Foreign Affairs. He was a great scholar, and had been an able diplomat, posted to Russia for many years; that is where Hualan had been born, and with her sister and brother had spent her adolescent years. 'But we were back in China when Liberation came, and the Party sent people to ask me, "Will you help us?" And I said, "Yes, yes, oh yes, take me, hands and feet and all, I give you everything ... everything." ' Hualan reverted to Slav syntax in describing the scene. She was devoted, utterly, to China, although a Eurasian. She was, in fact, very much like me, except that she was far less selfish ... perhaps because she was not a writer. But never for a moment, during the many years that followed, and the many hours I spent with her through those years, would she reprove me for my doubts and hesitations. Until, at last, in 1978, she would say, 'Well, my dear, in a way you were right ... if you had stayed, I think you would have died.'

'No, I am not a Party member,' said Hualan, pouring me some more tea. 'I was asked to apply, but I thought I was unworthy ... some people want to join the Party because it gives them power. But I don't want power. I only want to serve.'

I then told Hualan of my reactions; how happy I had been seeing the peace, the healthy children and all that was being done for the people. No more the long lines of gaunt and starving beggars everywhere; no more the terrible sight of half-skeletons with enormous loads climbing up those immense flights of steps, up from the river, in Chungking. Now there were conveyor belts. 'And yet I, who have always wanted this, have vomiting fits when I hear of some stupidity, some vileness, some brutality ... as if it was possible to make a paradisial state all at once. And I feel ... mortified, humiliated, diminished ... '

'Because you are honest,' said Hualan. 'And you have had no share in all this. It has all been done without you. I think a good many of the intelligentsia also feel that way.'

She said that was the true substance of so-called liberalism: a certain hypocrisy. 'Preaching equality, but when it really comes, it's hard to take.'

I said there was something else. The constant harping on thought-remoulding. The relentless feeling of being controlled. 'And in order to propitiate the future, we have to become transparent, every bit of one's life known and recorded.'

Hualan shook her head with great serenity. 'No other way of keeping track of people. Think of the millions of bureaucrats from the old days we had to take over ... we don't really know what's brewing inside their heads.'

With Papa in his house in Peking, 1956

With my sister Marianne at my house in Johore Bahru, 1961

Vincent driving Mrs Gandhi to inspect the Nepal road in 1955

With Françoise Sagan in Paris, 1958

With the Sultan of Selangor, Malaya, 1960

With President Sukarno, 1962

Malcolm MacDonald, *left*, and Prince Norodom Sihanouk, *centre right*

In Cambodia with Prince Norodom Sihanouk

I asked Hualan about Stalin, and about Khrushchev's speech denouncing Stalin. She was a little vague, or cautious. 'Yes, I've heard about this speech, but we're still studying it in my organization.' But she told me a great deal about Beria. 'Beria was a monster ... and Stalin listened to him. Stalin did good things, but in the end he went crazy, he trusted the wrong people, he was out of touch.'

At the time, to me, the U.S.S.R. was still Stalin, and I had been inoculated at the university in Belgium with a deep horror of Stalin and his deeds. What concerned me, however, was China. 'I was afraid we too might have a Stalin in China one day ... but now I think we shall not.' 'No,' said Hualan, 'we shall not make the same mistakes. In fact, Chairman Mao and other leaders have talked about it.' But she would not give details. She confirmed, however, that Russian experts in China were 'high-handed, and some comrades don't like the way they behave with Chinese women'.

We then talked about what Hualan called 'the housecleaning', which meant the political campaigns and mass movements. 'One must never take criticism personally,' said Hualan. 'It is meant as an educational process.' She herself had been vilified because 'when I went down to the rural areas with my organization I would clean up the place where we lived. The others left chicken bones and bits on the table. I would sweep up the mess.' This had been called 'bourgeois' and 'typically Western' by some of her colleagues. 'But the people who reviled me are spoilt city people, they have servants at home, they still treat their wives in the old-fashioned way. They are always the first, in any movement, to jump up and denounce, to write accusations against the others.' Hualan was used to this kind of give and take, and in the end nothing was done to her. But I said, 'I don't think I could put up with this constant harassment. Think of all the posters and juicy denunciations one could write about my life. I'd have a nervous breakdown.'

'Of course, that's just the point, there are nervous breakdowns,' said Hualan. She said it so casually that somehow it seemed part of the group therapy involved in these mass movements; there could be no remoulding of the person unless there was some kind of breakup of the previous personality.

'All of us have got something to hide ... "To look at my body and my heart without disgust" ... it's very difficult.' So many people tried to cover up. Then the masses had to be educated in political criticism. Sometimes they didn't really know what had to be criticized; they went round looking for subjects to talk about.

'When are masses only mobs? When do they become crowds? When is political criticism just nit-picking?' I asked rhetorically.

'The leadership of the Party pays attention, not to let things get out of hand,' she replied.

'What you are saying is that we are all each other's keepers now.'

'Yes,' said she.

At the time Hualan felt that the intelligentsia itself was responsible for emphasis on trivial personalia. 'You know the Chinese intellectuals have always loved gossip; now they turn and hit and denounce each other and fabricate fantastic stories ... some of it is quite shocking.' I could not believe that my friends could do this sort of thing. 'Not the good ones,' said Hualan, 'but there are cowards everywhere.' They did not have the shoulder feeling, she said, solidarity, as did the workers, 'And when they go into the factories, among the workers, or into the villages, among the peasants, it sticks out. They don't think the same way at all.'

Fourth Sister Ping and her husband invited me to dinner. And Ping strove then to make me stay. She had walked me round Peking's magnificent new zoo one afternoon, trying to talk me into staying.

'Since you admire what the Revolution has accomplished, why don't you stay?'

'Because, Ping, I would soon become a hindrance, then an embarrassment to you ... I have very little to contribute, except another problem. And there are enough problems in China.' Had I been only a doctor, I do not think there would have been any difficulty; at least, no large difficulty; not until 1966 and the Cultural Revolution. But I was a writer, whether I liked it or not, and it is a disease, a perverse disease. 'I'd give you a lot of trouble, Ping.'

And where would I fit? Which niche, category, organization, label, would be mine? Suppose I was classified as a 'Western expert' since I wrote in English and had a British Hongkong passport. In that case I would have a beautiful flat or house, and servants, and a high salary, and a car, and I would be given interviews and would go on trips ... but pretty soon, I felt, I would begin to write the propaganda of which I had been so critical (and would continue to criticize, in letters to Kung Peng and other friends, for the next twenty years).

Were I to be classified as 'overseas Chinese', then I would have some privileges, and be with the Chinese; but the possibility of being picked upon in the political campaigns was somewhat higher than average.

Or perhaps I would be given employment in a university, teaching English; or at the Foreign Language Press, doing translation work ...

It was selfish of me to choose myself and my daemon, but I did. I was afraid of losing whatever talent I had; and although I was certain that the time would come when I could write in China, and write freely, that time was not yet. 'I need time to remould myself, but nobody can do it for me. I have to do it myself,' I told Ping.

Then Ping gave up. Other friends, Party members, came in and we all talked about the Hundred Flowers. And some of them said, 'We fought for everything under Heaven; now others dream of sitting on everything under Heaven.' Very clearly, they were afraid that the intelligentsia would again make a bid for power, displacing the Party. And their feeling was quite understandable; for after all, they had sweated and slogged and fought and died ...

A final meeting with Kung Peng, to say goodbye, and that I would come back next year.

'We are thinking of giving six visas to American newsmen to come to China,' said she.

'I'll tell them in Hongkong. That will really make news,' I replied.

Kung Peng then gave me Mao Tsetung's latest book, *Socialist Upsurge in China's Countryside*, because I had said, 'The key is in the villages, isn't it? But I don't know enough about agriculture to say anything yet ... '

'Let me know how you are. We like to have impressions from people outside,' said Kung Peng.

One last coffee with Hualan at the small coffee club in the Eastern Peace Market. This coffee club was to disappear in 1957.

And there, sitting at a table, were two American G.I.s, of those who during the Korean war had come over to the communist side. One of them was very homesick and his friend said, 'You talk too much, Pete.' All of them but one were to go back to the United States. The one who remained in China is very happily married to a Chinese woman and has five children.

The last evening with Papa. 'Don't forget about Mama,' said Papa. He was going to apply for leave to go abroad 'on a scientific tour'. I did not think he had much chance because he was old and the unit he worked for would invoke health reasons. But I could get him out, perhaps, and look after him in Malaya. Papa gave me a small box of mooncakes to eat on the train. 'I'll be back next year, I promise,' said I.

Back to Kuangchow, and to the cicada-loud night, and suddenly at the border I wanted to turn back. 'I'm staying. I'm staying.' But already I was being waved across the bridge by a very neat, polite soldier, and it was too late.

I was going back to the world I knew; but it had changed. Its ferocity clawed at me. I knew that in Hongkong I would have trouble; for no one wanted the whole truth. Because the whole truth was a mass of contradictions. Everyone wanted a simple picture, in one world and in the other ...

'How many years can I function as a writer?' I thought. And what does a writer have in the belly and the brain to keep him going? 'Twenty years,' I said to the hot sky, 'give me twenty years ... in twenty years, I'll be ready.' Meanwhile, I would not cut the umbilical cord. I would grow, nurtured by China, by China. I would not give up.

And it was at that moment that I knew myself doomed. I would never be able to get China out of my brain, my cells, my bones. I would write in order not to die, trying to bring to birth things and beings in words. But it would be China all the time.

Back across the bridge, the barbed wire, I was assailed by waspish irritation and a sense of bafflement. A world fatuous and brutal, people cocooned in their preoccupations; and an alien sheen about objects, for now I looked at my Szechuan slippers, so comfortable, so beautiful in China, and in Hongkong they were shabby.

'Oh, you have changed, what has happened?' said Cousin Pengju, full of concern, as his eyes expressed shock. 'You look so much older.'

'It's too much thinking, Pengju. I was upset inside.'

Pengju did not reply; doubtless he knew what I felt.

Now I felt guilty when asking the hotel waiter for service or my laundry, seeing servility spring into action. I felt lost among the street throngs, an avalanche of hurrying, resentful people. How they rushed. In China no one seemed hurried. One layer of skin was missing; I was no longer predatory.

There were the newsmen, reporters, journalists. They flocked, they rang, they clamoured. They did not want reasoned facts. Or ideas. They wanted something fit to print, which meant unfit to say. Sensation. 'Sure your father is still alive? You got a picture to prove it?' They were disappointed. 'What do you mean, you didn't see anyone starving?'

And how wrong I had been about the American newsmen in Hongkong! The China-watchers who gathered at the Foreign Correspondents' Club preferred to exchange information among themselves and to build great edifices of assumptions based on the rumours that filtered from China into Hongkong. But above all they were afraid, and I would find out why.

When I mentioned the six visas for American correspondents, the response was derision, anger. 'That's the best joke of the year.' 'They're fooling you.' 'You've been brainwashed. I didn't think it would happen to you.' 'You're losing your reputation as an objective writer.' 'Go and tell your Red friends, I won't shake hands with bloody murderers.' 'Why the hell do they issue their most important statements at night so I have to keep awake to listen to the late news?' was perhaps the most amusing remark of the lot.

Oh no, no eagerness for visas to China. It was much more satisfying to accuse China of shutting the door and isolating herself. Much better to carry on this myth rather than remember that it was America which had put an embargo on China and which blacklisted anyone in Hongkong trading with China. America was powerful then, and made herself felt everywhere, and everyone was afraid of the big witch-hunt which was being conducted not only in America, but also abroad, wherever there were Americans. Two at least of the correspondents representing American news agencies and newspapers in Hongkong had been questioned by the Committee for Un-American Activities when it carried out an investigation of State Department officials who had been to China.

What I said was not reported as I said it; the six visas were not mentioned. However, I was asked by the London *Observer* for an article on contraception.

The American Consulate in Hongkong sent two people to lunch with me. I was frank with them but felt that we were not talking about the same things, though we used words which corresponded to some common meaning. In the end, they were not satisfied.

'Don't you think you ought to be more positive?'

'Positive about what?'

'About principles. You must take sides. You've got to choose. The fact that you're here shows you chose freedom.'

The word had a majestic roll about it, something like those sudden gongs in a Chinese opera announcing the entrance of a major personage on the stage.

The Americans were polite, but obviously puzzled. At that time they saw the world in such simple terms that my uncertain-footed pursuit of clarity appeared almost idiotic. How can the fisherman explain his passion for angling? I was the fisherman, sitting on the shore of the coiled and passionate and muscular torrent, the changing and shifting and undulating water, floating my life away. The substance I pursued was a shadow sometimes named Verity – Truth. I tried to read it, observe it ... But the Americans asked me to produce a neat, encapsulated tin of sardines, clearly labelled. I could only tell them that I too had to change in order to understand China and the Revolution.

Francis and Cecilia came to tea with me in my hotel room. Then there was a knock on the door, and in came Father Ladany.

It was a council of cardinals which bore down upon me with austere disapproval. Never had Father Ladany looked more imposing as he folded himself carefully into a chair. And suddenly I had the experience of total dissociation. One me was here, watching him; the other stood, feet in the soft silver-grey dust, under the new trees of Peking.

'I am not pleased with you,' said Father Ladany.

'Oh.'

'You have come back from China and you have stated that religion was free there. Do you know what our Catholic brothers suffer at the hands of the communist regime? Han Suyin, when God in Heaven and the angels ask you: What have you done, what will you then reply?' He rearranged himself, and then: 'You have a grave responsibility. You must now make a statement, that religion is persecuted in China today.'

'I will not.'

I had entirely forgotten, while in Peking, to ask about Catholics and the Catholic religion. I had not been to church. I had visited my old convent school and talked to a very suspicious nun there. The school would cater for the children of diplomats until 1966, when it would be closed and the remaining six nuns expelled. But I had inquired about the Muslim religion, paid a visit to Peking's grand mosque in Ox Street, seen the Muslim hierarchy. And that was because, living in Malaya, a Muslim country, it seemed to me relevant, and I was involved in studying the impact of religion upon race relations in Malaya. I had not even called on the bishop who had proclaimed a Chinese Catholic church, and severed it from the overlordship of Rome. Yet he was a member of the Political Consultative Conference and of the National People's Congress.

Francis now interposed to say, 'I think Suyin needs a rest.' I felt I was being pressured, pressured. Throughout the night I was awakened by angry telephone calls from Catholics (not Chinese Catholics). Voices mouthing insults. It was not Father Ladany's fault. He would never do this.

Permission to bring Papa out of China was granted swiftly by the

Singapore police. I wrote to Malcolm in India, giving him many details of my trip, and he asked me to come to see him in Delhi, which I would do in the spring of 1957.

Seven

Periples and Perspectives: 1956-1958

IN THE AUTUMN of 1956 Nanyang University started to function. Thousands of youths from the Chinese middle schools of the peninsula and the island sat for the three-day examination held in Singapore and the chief cities of Malaya. Loud jubilation and unsubdued publicity over the completion of Nanyang was exhibited by the Malayan Chinese Chamber of Commerce and other enterprises. The photographs of a British Labour M.P. or two, of the Governor of Singapore Island and other British high officials wearing chilling smiles while attending Nanyang University's opening ceremony, were prominently displayed. Tunku Abdul Rahman, who in 1957 would become the first Prime Minister of independent Malaya, declared that the setting up of Nanyang was a matter for the Chinese in Malaya to decide, but he hoped 'other races would be admitted' to the University.

As college health physician, I drove to Nanyang three times a week to make physical examinations of the students. That meant twenty-five kilometres on a new dirt road (later tarred) across jungle and brush, with here and there a small atap hut. Jurong, where Nanyang was sited, was almost unpeopled then; today it is the industrial heart of Singapore.

I had to discard my mini-Fiat and buy a stouter car for these trips to Nanyang. I acquired a Ford, low slung, which stalled in Singapore's torrential rains. As soon as my blue and white vehicle was sighted, bumper-deep in water, along the Bukit Timah Road, shopkeepers and trishaw pedallers would remove their slippers and come wading through the downpour with cheers to push my car on to the verge. 'Going to Nan Tah,* Doctor? What you need is a jeep.'

Since my return from China, I had become quite popular, for I had dared what was unimaginable. The film of *A Many-Splendoured Thing* was

---

* Nanyang University was abbreviated in Chinese to Nan Tah.

being shown in Singapore. That it was possible to be both a ferocious 'Red' (me!) and successful with a made-in-U.S.A. movie astonished and overawed; increased my prestige as someone for whom obstacles to hinder ordinary mortals did not exist. I did not go to the première of the film. In fact, I did not wish to see it. It proved a seven-handkerchief tear-jerker, and stayed on screen in Singapore for thirty-six weeks. I received an amazing post from all over South East Asia; from demands to trace relatives in China, to offers of investment in ocean tankers, to solving amorous tangles. It was thought that I had become immensely wealthy. Little did people know Hollywood, or that all the money had already gone into curing Yungmei.

Yungmei was angry with me. 'The nuns say you are a communist.' Yungmei would always be easily taken in by conformity. But her schoolmates went to the film and cried and cried, so she continued as the school heroine, despite the great burden upon her of such a controversial mother.

In Singapore 1956 was a turbulent year. David Marshall, Chief Minister for a transient twelve months (1955-6), resigned. He had refused to give a guarantee that he would jail trade unionists or teachers with 'leftist' leanings, and the Colonial Office in London felt he was too weak to carry out what was now being prepared, a wholesale purge of the trade unions and the Chinese schools.

David talked to me at his house by the sea. He was bitter, and tossed his great mane of hair, and thought he would make a comeback heading another party, but he was not oblique enough, he was too visible and too audible; a whale flapping in the shallow mud-swamp of colonial politics. I liked him more than ever in his defeat; for he took it very well, but 'You'll never be a politician, David,' I said. 'Good intentions will always be your downfall.'

A small, quiet man with a round face, Lim Yewhock, became Chief Minister of a 'Labour Front' coalition government. He was very conservative, a great favourite of the local British and Americans. But he did not know that his role would also be transitory; for he would serve to carry out the big purge that the British had in mind, as a prelude to independence, both in Malaya and in Singapore. Without this purge there could be no independence for Singapore, neither could Singapore be 'safely' joined to Malaya.

Meanwhile, the astute British were already grooming for the future their best bet, Lee Kuanyew or Harry Lee. Lee Kuanyew, whose subsequent career as Prime Minister of Singapore fully justified the long-term and shrewd assessment of British officials, was English-educated. As his untiring hagiographer, the journalist Alex Josey, never ceased to write, Lee Kuanyew had been brilliant at Cambridge, where he studied law. In 1956 Lee appeared extremely progressive. His party, the People's Action Party or PAP, had come up very swiftly since 1954, and was now a force to be reckoned with. The PAP owned a left wing which comprised Chinese school-educated trade unionists and former Singapore Chinese middle school student leaders; people whom the Special Branch had jailed before, and would jail again, as communists or communist sympathizers. It also had a right wing which comprised most of the English-educated like Lee himself, who today continue to represent, as he does, the government of Singapore.

Because of its slogan, 'Socialism in Singapore', the PAP was massively supported by the workers, the trades union, Chinese school students, in short, a good majority of Singapore's people. Any party in Asia then that wanted to get on *had* to use two isms, socialism and anti-colonialism.

The Special Branch clampdown on Singapore's trades union and student unions began in September 1956, with daily arrests. The Chinese Middle School Students' Union was banned. The students barricaded themselves in the Chinese high school on the Bukit Timah Road, and were assaulted with tear gas and night sticks by the police. This led to the imposition of a twenty-two-hour curfew, which was maintained for four days. I drove just before the curfew, by night, along the Bukit Timah Road, returning from work. I saw the police charge. Two cars were overturned and burnt, not by the students but by Secret Society hooligans (who had come out to join the fray). Tear gas made us all weep, and a student offered me his handkerchief. 'Go away, Doctor, the police beat up anyone.'

Members of the left wing of the PAP were arrested, among them Lim Chingsiong, a young trade unionist, and the idol of the students of the Chinese high school (where he had been a student leader). Harry Lee was not in Singapore during the purge but resting in the Cameron Highlands of Malaya,* about six hours away by car. He came back when it was all over to demand Lim Yewhock's resignation and to make an excellent speech in the Legislative Assembly (November 5th, 1956), calling this a planned purge concocted between the British and Lim Yewhock. He thus enlisted enormous popular support while Lim Yewhock became the detested emblem of a 'colonial lackey'.

I attended a public PAP meeting held at the end of that year; I wanted to listen to Harry Lee speak. Cards for joining the PAP were being distributed

* A cool, high mountain resort frequented by British high officials and wealthy Malays and Chinese.

at the entrance to the hall, and I took one, signing my name and paying two dollars. This thoughtless gesture would cause me much trouble later on.

Lee spoke very well, and I agreed with his thesis that 'In order to get independence, and unity between Malaya and Singapore, between the Malays and the Chinese, the Malay government in Malaya must be convinced that the Chinese in Singapore are loyal to Malaya and not to China; that they have no intention of exploiting the Malays, but that on the contrary they wish to live and work equally and peacefully in Malaya as Malayans.' The myth of an overseas Chinese fifth column in Singapore was to be broken.

I asked Alex Josey whether I might meet Harry Lee, and it was agreed we should do so at the house of Rajaratnam, a Ceylonese Tamil, who is now the Foreign Minister of Singapore. He had just published another short story of mine in a magazine of his which promptly folded up, and he was trying hard to hold down his job as newspaperman at the conservative *Straits Times* while also publishing and editing *Petir*, the PAP newspaper.

Alex and Harry arrived late, in ebullient mood. Alex was never drunk, though he could put down vast quantities of Tiger beer and remain beautifully vertical. Harry was not a drinker; even two beers would make him flush. He was now flushed, and took refuge behind a newspaper which he held up at arm's length so that nothing of him was visible except his legs.

I waited politely, making small talk, but the paper would not come down. Harry did not wish to talk to me. Perhaps because I had been to China, and he did not wish Special Branch to suspect him of *talking* with someone from China ... After fifteen minutes in which he continued to prop up the paper Great Wall between us, by sheer muscle power and will, I got up without saying goodbye to the invisible Mr Lee, and went home. It had not been an unprofitable quarter hour. I had smelled the smell of single-minded devotion to power. No one would be allowed to stand in Harry Lee's way.

But my young Chinese students at Nanyang at the time idolized him and believed him a genuine 'socialist'. 'He is even learning Chinese now,' they said. Later, having endured beatings and torture in jail in Singapore under the PAP government, one of those students who got out would tell me, 'It was on our shoulders that Lee Kuanyew climbed to power.'

I started a medical clinic in Singapore, in Tangjong Pagar, the busiest part of the hardworking, restless city. My clinic in Johore Bahru was sold to a medical couple, man and wife, who did very well with it. I still occasionally saw patients at home at weekends, for some would not let me go, but I no longer went to the 'new villages' along the Johore road. Some of them had even prospered, owing to the all-conquering capacity of the Chinese for work, which could transform even a concentration camp, after a while, into a fertile market-garden! Even the mangrove swamps began to yield food through this endless labour of theirs. I used to stop and look at them, those work-obsessed people who created a new world out of the wasteland. A little help from the government went a very long way with them. Despite barbed wire, arrests, harassment, the rapacity of the Malay police, they did not stop making the land yield food.

The backers of my new clinic, which was called the Coral Drug House, were a Mr and Mrs Loke. Mr Loke was small, portly, round-eyed and disastrously optimistic. During the Japanese occupation he had made money selling vitamin B injections, and was paid in the existing paper currency. But the money became worthless when the Japanese were beaten and Mr Loke could only repaper a room in his house with the bank notes. 'What to do, Doctor, no luck is no luck.' He bounced back, however, and regularly came up with grandiose projects. One was to buy sugar, a lot of sugar, because the Suez Canal was closed and sugar was sure to climb in price. It didn't. Another one was to form a political party. Mr Loke got fifty votes, no more ... Mrs Loke was the strength and soul and mainstay of the Loke family. She had five children. She was beautiful, sweet, hardworking, thrifty, frugal, and infinitely jealous when Mr Loke wandered to the Great World or the Happy World dance halls or came home with brandy-ginger-ale-laden breath (the Chinese drank brandy, the whites drank stengahs). Mrs Loke knew nine languages and dialects and besides attending to the clinic and pharmacy she employed herself as a hairdresser at night, to make ends meet, for Mr Loke was prone to impecuniosity.

I hired a nurse and a pharmacist, and all four of us women were photographed in front of our new clinic, and no one thought it strange that four women should run a clinic right in the heart of the working class district of Singapore. We were protected. The two 'benevolent' Secret Societies which dominated the area would never lift a finger against a woman doctor, a midwife, a nurse (or for that matter a child). Compared to what happens in Europe today, their behaviour was honourable and trustworthy. I knew my life, my car and my belongings were safe in 'oui' district. However, having one day parked my car with my typewriter in it on a 'respectable' lane near the Legislative Assembly, I returned to find the top ripped and the typewriter gone. I was stupid enough to call the police. The police arrived; surrounded me and the area, blew white dust all over the car for fingerprints, delayed me for two hours, and of course the typewriter was never found. When Mr Loke heard of it, he exploded. 'Doctor, why call the police? Why not ask me? I would have asked a friend ... he would have found your typewriter for you in twenty-four hours. Now it is impossible, no more face ...'

I said I was very, very sorry, and would never again call the police. Never.

Of course the clinic prospered right from the first day. I had many cases, some of them, as in Johore Bahru, of great interest; and I had the services of an excellent laboratory which had been set up by an Englishman – one of those who had truly made Singapore his home. I had also the usual run of delicate problems. Homosexuality among the British troops quartered in Singapore; a couple of those cases came to me through my lawyer, Anthony Hills, who greatly pitied one he brought me, a beautiful and tongue-tied boy. At the time the punishment meted out by the British to homosexuals was extremely harsh and the youth, sad and withdrawn, was almost inarticulate. Cases of virginity, or the lack of it. The usual mother-in-law irate because the morning after her son's wedding there was no blood upon the sheets she had inspected. Cases of forcible deflowering. Two 'aunties' bringing a young girl, shaking from head to foot, to certify she had indeed been penetrated; they wanted money from the businessman who had been presented with this virgin. I only hoped he had not infected her with gonorrhoea; for it was still believed that one could cure gonorrhoea by using a virgin.

The usual Secret Society fights. A man came in with his face slashed right across by a razor blade. I stitched up, we all worked very hard. He uttered not a word while we repaired him. I should have reported him to the police. This was the law, but he said he had accidentally cut himself and I left it that way. Why send him to jail? Why get Mr and Mrs Loke into trouble? Why? I was not all that convinced that the representatives of law and order were less corrupt than the representatives of wrongdoing.

Leonard persisted in refusing to divorce. He could not believe that I loved Vincent. And why, if I loved him, had I not joined him in India, but remained in Singapore and ran a clinic and wrote books, and went to Nanyang University to give lectures?

We no longer quarrelled; civility prevailed. Leonard would continue living at home until 1957. But at that time (only twenty years ago) it was not done *not* to quarrel, not to accumulate grievances. English law on divorce made it an offence to practise 'collusion' – divorce by mutual consent did not exist. My lawyer, Anthony, pointed this out to me. 'As long as you live with Leonard, you won't get a divorce.'

Leonard obtained a job as Adult Education Officer in Singapore. It suited him well; not only had he a remarkable knowledge (far surpassing mine) of Chinese dialects, but also kindness, real good-heartedness with ordinary people. The Chinese and the Malays, faced with an *orang puteh* who spoke their language and understood them, confided in him.

Meanwhile, plans for building my new house went ahead. The architect, Kee Yeap, decided that instead of building one large house, I should build three bungalows, staged on the slope of the hill I had bought, all with a remarkable view of Singapore and the arm of sea called the Straits, which separated the island from Malaya. The houses had modern uncluttered lines, wide window space, the use of black marble on the floors to cut out the eye-paining reflection of the sun, and pastel colours. People came from all over Malaya to look, to photograph and to copy. One enterprising travel agency ran buses for tourists to Johore Bahru to come to see me and my houses.

I kept an enormous rain tree, so heavy and tall that it was a landmark, in the middle of the garden. It was far from the house because rain tree roots run shallow, and in a wind the tree can overturn. We had a special roadway inside the garden for the three houses, and the whole thing only cost 100,000 Malayan dollars (30,000 U.S. dollars). It was worth five million in 1978. But more to the point, the design has been reproduced (sometimes with unhappy additions) all over Malaya.

I managed to free-float myself away for ten days with Vincent in Nepal. I had started my new book, *The Mountain is Young*, writing in the cool night, when a bliss of darkness or moonlight makes words emerge smoothly, like quiet fish. Vincent never asked me about China. I just said briefly, 'There is more dust to settle before I make up my mind.' He was less cluttered with formulae, being an inarticulate man, than most people. He could accept raw facts even when put into untoward words, or not worded. He guessed that I would keep China to myself until the proper time came to smear words upon a page or in the air. 'I hope you did not come back just for me.' 'No, I did not.' And so he gave me breathing space without words, in which I could fashion new words for new things. No one else ever left me alone about China; everyone wanted an arbitrary, total judgment; phrases, clichés; they could not understand that verbalizing was castration.

'You are my good earth, in which I can grow,' I told Vincent. Always this total easiness, and silence. 'Comfort me with silence, feed me with silence.' And so I grew well and young and beautiful and I said, 'I am going back to China next year, and the next, and the next, until ... ' Meanwhile I would wait and wander all over the earth, and always live in that crystal sphere of clear doubt because doubt is the most blessed thing alive. And the earthbound presence of Vincent would keep my feet on earth, and make dreams move and shape words; his absence as potent (even more so) than his presence, but unthinkable if not interspersed with presence. For only in absence is presence totally realized; but total presence, like total absence is also somewhat a death.

Vincent's work in Nepal was almost completed. He would be given a prestigious medal by King Mahendra for finishing the road between Nepal and India in record time, but also threatened with court martial by his own government for having finished the work so quickly and within the budget allotted. Efficiency is always suspect to an Establishment, and one of Vincent's predecessors had distinguished himself by invariably reporting loss of equipment through white ant action, until some pernickety accountant, looking up termites, discovered they could not devour the steel of bulldozers.

On the verge of the nineteenth century, at the time of his great-grandfather, Vincent's family had been fishermen in Tamil Nadu, a state of south India. I could visualize Vincent's ancestors in their catamarans skimming the terrible shark-infested waters for food. Of course they had become boat-owners in time, but they were certainly not considered high caste, like the Brahmins; and just as in China only 2 per cent of poor peasants could, within fifty years, become rich peasants, so in India a small minority of fishermen, by dint of frightful exertion, thrift and good luck, became boat-owners.

Vincent's family came from the fishing settlement of Royapuram, very near Madras. The Portuguese who landed there in the sixteenth century had converted most of Royapuram to Christianity. Today Royapuram is no longer by the sea, but inland; the sea had withdrawn, leaving its sand behind; and upon this sand is built the big church with its thirty-nine crosses (why thirty-nine I shall never know), its roof like the waves of the sea, its windows down to the floor, and—oh, how strong the caste system was—its place, within the Catholic church, for Catholic 'untouchables'.

Vincent's great-grandfather went to school; and after the Portuguese came the British, and his grandfather and then his father were educated; his father going to Cambridge, becoming a lawyer, and later chancellor of a university in Madras state. The whole family took up education; even his sisters went to university. And Vincent's father became President of the Catholic Association of India; the Catholics being six million, the second largest religious minority after the Muslims (sixty million).

From Kathmandu we flew to Delhi; Malcolm invited us and Prime Minister Nehru to tea. 'You will find Nehru disquieted about China,' warned Malcolm. As soon as he saw me, Nehru glowered in that skin-colour-change way which Indians have when they glower.

His chiselled features became dusky marble and I thought: What a broody Brahmin. Malcolm strove to make me speak of China but Nehru would not listen and changed the subject immediately. That night there was a dinner, and Nehru was there. I asked him in the meekest voice I could muster, 'Your Excellency, I've been reading up on the Hindu religion. Tell me, why is Krishna blue?' Nehru glared at me and replied, 'He is blue because he is blue.' I think Krishna was Dravidian,* as is Vincent, and Dravidians do turn blue under certain conditions of the weather and sentiment.

Instead of thinking about blue Krishna, the God of Love, I should have paid attention to Nehru's bad temper and Malcolm's hints; but I could not believe a quarrel was brewing between India and China.

In August of 1957 independence came to Malaya. In Johore Bahru a rumour spread that the Malays would come out with their krisses† and kill everyone. Some shops closed; some shopkeepers keft for Singapore. A good many of the British in the town also went away to Singapore for that day. Johore Bahru was aglow with colour; the Malays came from the surrounding *kampongs* and their children were gorgeous, gaudy butterflies arrayed in silk and satin, pink and purple and green and blue, with trimmings of gold lace, the boys with small *songkoks*‡ of black velvet, the little girls with enormous kohl-rimmed eyes and their hair plastered with coconut oil. How beautiful they were, and always with that grace and softness which I had come to associate with the Malay people. There was music everywhere, and the mosque was full of men rendering prayers of thanks to Allah. It was a brave and splendid sight, and I went to see my Malay friends and enjoyed multi-coloured sweets and being sprayed with

---

* The original inhabitants of India, Dravidians are found chiefly in the south, especially in the state of Tamil Nadu.
† Krisses: Malay daggers.
‡ *Songkoks:* Malay velvet caps.

flower petals and perfume, and late at night under the soft trees that held the darkness the people strolled, carrying their children asleep in their arms back to the *kampongs*.

Meanwhile in China the Hundred Flowers had blossomed and faded.

I had a letter or two from Papa, relayed through Hongkong; Papa never mentioned in his letters anything except his own health. It was clear, however, that he would not apply to leave China in order to visit Mama. His organization thought him too old and frail to risk the journey.

I finished *The Mountain is Young* that summer of 1957 and an article on Nepal, and left for Peking in September, making the usual arrangement with a medical partner to take over during my absence. I stayed two days in Hongkong, reading the Chinese communist press and asking Pengju what was happening. 'Is it true what the Western press says that a total reversal of policy has taken place?' 'I think you had better find out for yourself.' We talked at length about mutual friends, writers, who had not been accused of being 'rightists', although one expected them to be, while on the contrary several others were denounced as 'rightists' who had appeared most revolutionary.

Papa was alone at the station to receive me, and this time I stayed in our house with him. This total lack of attention to me was a boon. I had no programme at all. How often in later years I would try my hardest to have no programme, nothing to visit or to see, no one to recite at me long-winded 'brief introductions', which for so many years were un-avoidable in factories, communes, everywhere.

I had left my Peking wardrobe, clothes bought in China, cotton shoes, with Papa. And in trousers and a shirt looked local and went unnoticed. So unnoticeable that when inadvertently I wandered into the lobby of the Peking Hotel, where I had arranged to meet Fourth Sister Ping, I was promptly thrown out. I was not an Honoured Guest. I did not look like an Honoured Guest. And one evening, at the theatre, standing in the aisle to look for my seat, I was suddenly shoved aside. 'Place for the Honoured Guests from Outside,' said the man, obviously an interpreter, who had shoved me. He exuded self-importance. In filed five very large Europeans, undoubtedly some delegation of a Party somewhere.

Papa was plucking at his hairless chin, in pensive turmoil. 'I don't under-stand it,' he said, handing me a thick folder, all the clippings he had collected about the Hundred Flowers from the start in May 1956 to its climax in May 1957 and its crash in June. He gave me brief notes he had taken at the meetings organized by his own bureau to discuss and to implement the Hundred Flowers. 'I was also asked to criticize, to say anything I wished … '

Papa shook his head, as if stunned. The stunned look was on many faces in that September when the campaign 'against the bourgeois rightists who attacked the Party and socialism' was in full spate. Third Brother was at Peking University, where the students had had no summer holiday that year, but meeting after meeting to 'uncover the ringleaders' of the 'rightists'. Fourth Brother was just as busy with meetings in his organization. Only Papa had time, and my friend Hualan, because her Polish mother was ill and Hualan herself was recovering from a nervous breakdown. And as for writers, major 'struggle' sessions were going on in the Culture Ministry, the Propaganda Ministry.

I went to the Hsinchiao Hotel to see Jacques Locquin of the Agence France-Presse. He was dramatic. 'The students are pulverized, atomized, annihilated.' With him was a young Swede, one of the several dozens of foreign students at Peking University studying Chinese.

Third Brother emerged in October from the 'struggle meetings' against the rightists: Wang Wanchun, my journalist friend, Fourth Sister Ping and others also resurfaced. Everyone had had to participate in meetings, including the rightists themselves; many of whom had repented and claimed they had been misled by 'reactionaries' in their midst.

Until early 1957, the Hundred Flowers had not blossomed fully, despite official encouragement. The memory of the 1955 counter-revolutionary purge was still vivid with the intelligentsia. Third Brother had cautiously confined himself to saying he thought there were too many lengthy political meetings and that it was difficult to get adequate rest.

During those months, however, a good many scientists, writers and scholars had been taken into the Communist Party. The treatment of the intelligentsia had improved. Political meetings were shortened, there was an abundance of books in the libraries and greater facilities for students. The curriculum was changed, became less rigid, many students began to work on their own, and by the winter of 1956 they were holding discussion forums, writing papers on subjects they had selected, and crowding the libraries to read everything. 'No more forbidden subjects. Never have I seen young people so concerned, so astonishingly willing to participate … of course they were naïve, they did not know very much, but they tried … ' Thus an old professor who dropped in to see Papa in October. Hundreds of literary and scientific magazines and periodicals, some of them with wildly heterodox views, came into print. 'There was even some pornography,' Wanchun told me. 'Handwritten, circulating under ground.' Wanchun was too proper to elaborate. After all, *A Many-Splendoured Thing* was considered pornographic ...

'My dear, one of the reasons why it all suddenly went wrong was the Hungarian revolt,' said Hualan. The Hungarian revolt of October 1956 had a great effect upon the Chinese students. 'At first it was a genuine mass expression against the Stalinist excesses,' said Hualan (whose job had been to translate all documentation on the subject). But later the revolt had fallen to 'unscrupulous counter-revolutionaries', who were 'agents of imperialism'. The ringleaders were the reactionary intelligentsia of the Petofi Club. The Petofi Club of Budapest was where the intellectuals gathered to drink coffee and apparently to plot against the socialist state.

The university students in China organized clubs and societies to hold debates, issue manifestos and assemble in open-air meetings. At first most of the meetings appeared innocuous but increasingly, as 1957 went into the spring, some 'began to do very bad things. They ran amok.'

'Even we were startled, alarmed at what began to take place ... ' said Third Brother. The students demanded total abolition of government, councils of students running all institutes of higher learning. They wanted to stay with their families and only have jobs in the big cities. 'There was anarchy ... ' The most active and outrageous demands came not from students in the arts but those in the sciences, particularly physics. Third Brother taught physics at Peking University. He could not explain why this was so.

On February 27th, 1957, Mao Tsetung made a most important speech at an enlarged session of the Supreme State Council. Unfortunately, once again, this speech was not published at the time; it would only be published in June, and with some modifications, and by that June the reversal of the Hundred Flowers' policy had taken place.

Because the speech was not published or tape recorded, the wildest surmises about what had really been said by Mao were current. Everyone heard what he wanted to hear. The 'small lane' gossip of Peking reported that some Party members present (top officials) were so hostile to the speech that they had walked out on it.

In April Mao Tsetung was to announce a rectification in the Party against the three 'evils' of bureaucratism, sectarianism and 'subjectivism'. This was a direct encouragement to the intelligentsia to criticize. It was specified that this rectification would not be harsh, but 'gentle as a mild rain, or a light breeze'. The eight non-communist parties were asked to help the Party rid itself of these evils by pointing out instances of errors and shortcomings.

A writer I knew said to me, 'What the intellectuals forgot is that the Party has increased sixfold since 1949, is full of new members who are badly trained and quickly corrupted ... being a Party member means to them power and privilege, and they'll fight to keep that. They cannot suffer anyone to criticize them.'

In March, to encourage more of the Hundred Flowers' criticism, the respected Tung Piwu, one of the founders of the Party,* made a speech at a meeting of military procurators and presidents of military courts. He expounded the need to abide by the law. 'We have conducted mass campaigns ... tempestuous revolutions relying on direct action by the masses rather than on law. But now the situation is different.' Tung called for a halt to illegal arrests 'without a warrant', and better control of juridical work. A system of laws must now be evolved, said he. Since Tung Piwu was President of the Supreme People's Court, Acting Chairman of the People's Republic of China, his pronouncements were weighty. But his speech of March 18th, 1957 was not published until October 19th, 1978!

By the time the month of May came round, the apprehensive leaders of the eight non-communist parties had plucked up courage and started a series of speeches, meetings and seminars. At least two leaders called for the Communist Party to share power and official positions with the other parties. The Communist Party was *not* the government; neither could it replace a government, they said. It acted arbitrarily and without consulting non-party administrative personnel in the government, who could only acquiesce.

Now followed, in the short space of eight days, a maelstrom of denunciations of the Communist Party and all its doings, by a great many intellectuals, including Party members themselves.

'The students went anti-Russian,' said Hualan. Since 1956 sporadic reports had appeared that some high-up party leaders had been critical of the U.S.S.R. The students denounced the inadequacy of the books and teaching on the Soviet model. Some Western-trained scientists complained of 'blind adoration' of the Soviet Union. Some traced the origin of the three evils in the Chinese Party to 'copying totally the Soviet Union'.

By mid-May there were not only student demonstrations throughout many cities in China but also a crescendo of attacks *against* Party cadres, both verbal and physical. In several places anyone who wanted to justify

* See *The Morning Deluge*.

what the Communist Party had done was shouted down or threatened. Students beat up teachers and when the police tried to protect the teachers, they beat up the police. And then Petofi clubs cropped up, whose avowed aim was to overthrow the government totally. Members of these clubs began to travel throughout the country for get-togethers with other universities. 'Marxism is outdated' ... 'The Communist Party has done nothing but evil' ... Posters called for the killing of obnoxious cadres and mass uprisings against the Party.

Of course the anti-Party stance was not a universal phenomenon. A small percentage of the students argued for the Party, another small group against it and the majority, as usual, was in between.

'What did the Party cadres do?' I asked Wanchun.

'They listened, they took notes, they kept silent,' he replied.

During those weeks, the Communist Party had allowed hundreds of explosive newspaper articles, banner headlines on the front pages condemning them. One headline asked Mao Tsetung and Chou Enlai to vacate their seats; another wrote that the Party consisted of 'uncultured laymen' and should give up office to 'experts' who would know how to run things.

Wanchun agreed with my cousins, that the students gradually lost the sympathy of the workers and of the general public; especially when one of the clubs demanded that the sons and daughters of peasants and workers should *no longer be admitted to the universities* from the short-term workers' schools which had been set up for them. 'Eighty per cent of our university students are still of landlord, rich peasant or city capitalist origin.'

On May 25th Mao warned publicly: 'All actions and speeches against socialism are wrong.' These words were propagated, within two days, among all university students. 'In our university the Party committee put up a prominent poster: "All actions and arguments which ignore socialism are wrong",' said Third Brother.

But it was too late for the groups which had called for a 'Hungarian situation' in China.

On June 8th an editorial in the *People's Daily* 'What Is This For?' marked the landslide reversal. On June 14th the magazine *China Youth* warned that even Communist Youth League members were 'unable to distinguish between two kinds of criticism'. One was well-meant, to help the Party and socialism; the other was counter-revolutionary, to attack the Party and to take power.

Then came the avalanche. Third and Fourth Brothers, using words sparingly, laughed and shivered at once as they spoke about it. Within three days, no more controversial posters. Instead a deluge of lavish praise and oaths of allegiance to the Party. 'The majority of the students turned round,' remembered Third Brother. And so did most of the members of the eight non-communist parties; and every organization, factory and institute. 'Then started the internal clean-up of each unit.' Each one searched among its own staff and employees for rightists. And then the confessions came pouring out. Within a day of each other, the four major rightists had come out with letters of self-accusation, apology, confessing their 'towering crimes'. The nationwide anti-rightist campaign was on.

'There were also rightists in the Party,' said Wanchun, detailing what had happened in his newspaper world. The 'three evils' rectification seemed laid aside; no more talk of gentle breeze and mild rain. From the end of August onwards every newspaper published excoriations of rightists, naming and labelling them; which meant that they had been condemned within their own organizations.

Papa said, 'A lot of innocent people will also be called rightists. That is bad.' Of course, he had also feared for himself; after all, he had written posters criticizing methods of work in his engineering bureau ...

In the great tempest, the Family gathered, counting its members. First of all, Szechuan. Szechuan was the province where everything that happened in China happened more ferociously, took on an extra girth and weight and amplitude.

But Third Uncle was fine. He had not been labelled a rightist. Sixth Uncle was not so happy. He had opened too wide a mouth. In 1956 there had been massive complaints in Szechuan about low pay and overwork of schoolteachers. Sixth Uncle was labelled a rightist; and he underwent eighteen months of re-education through labour, returning to work in 1959, and living another ten years. He died of cancer in 1967.

Pan Kuangtan, Francis Pan's brother, was not a rightist. Francis would be very happy to know it.

But my friend Simon Hua, who had always been so revolutionary, was a rightist. I could scarcely believe it. Papa and I went to the Hua house; only his old father, Hua Nankuei, was at home. Old Mr Hua was Papa's best friend. They had worked for forty years on the railways together; together had been to the Tatung coal mines. Now wrapped in a fur robe, attended by two devoted servants, and waiting for his French daughter-in-law to return from her work, he spoke with great dignity. 'Yes, my son is now examining his errors in his thinking ... ' But the Party had sent an official to reassure old Mr Hua that no physical harm would come to

Simon. 'Some foolish and irresponsible people went too far,' sighed old Mr Hua, 'and many will have to pay the price ... '

Irène, Simon's wife, went on working as usual, taking the situation with discipline and composure. Simon would do one year as an ordinary worker on a construction site.

Third and Fourth Brothers, Fourth Sister, everyone else in the Family was safe.

I still have the card on which Papa wrote down the names of the most prominent rightists. On the reverse is an invitation to Papa from the Vice-Chairman of the Academy of Sciences, to a scientific meeting in February 1957. It was at that meeting that the Hundred Flowers policy was discussed in the light of Chairman Mao's recent speech about it.

Now the speech had been published. I went out to the bookstore and purchased it. Its title was *On the correct handling of contradictions among the people*. It was Mao's famous February speech, only printed in mid-June, when the Hundred Flowers were already wilting with such precipitation. Was the printed version what Mao had really said, or were there additions? Jacques Locquin insisted there were additions, and that the whole thing was a trap.

Even today I remember my instant fascination, how gripped I was by this reading. I had tried, when I was a student in Belgium, to read some Marxist literature—my Belgian friends were so glib, so superior, so knowledgeable about politics, while I was so backward—and had found it insuperably dull and difficult. But not Mao's article. It became for me the key to coherence; coherence within the Chinese cultural pattern, of course. Mao was dealing with a situation which I not only understood but lived myself ... from that time, I began to read Mao Tsetung.

Was the whole exercise of the Hundred Flowers a trap? Just a cheap, mean trick? Somehow this appeared to me highly improbable.

As October wore on, my strongest impression was of the numbers of rightists named. Although the newspapers always called them 'a mere handful', everywhere I turned I bumped into rightists.

Again, here, I was confronted with that obtuse literal-mindedness of the middle cadres, implementing policy to the letter. Mao's casual remark made some years previously that 'probably 10 per cent' of the people in higher institutions of learning and other such organizations harboured counter-revolutionary leanings still held sway. Now the anti-rightist campaign would seek to discover its 10 per cent of rightists. Out of about nine thousand students at Peking University, a neat eight hundred were labelled 'rightists'. Since Mao had said in 1956 that there were five million intellectuals in China, that would mean around 400,000 to 500,000 rightists.

Actually, no less a person than the thoroughly outspoken Marshal Chen Yi, China's Foreign Minister, would tell me personally some years later that 430,000 rightists had been so labelled and he felt 'it was too many'. They comprised Party members, students, teachers, artists and writers.

The 'unlabelling' of rightists proceeded, with rehabilitations, from 1959 onwards. By 1966 there were still around 130,000 of them whose cases had not been cleared; but a thorough review was undertaken after the Cultural Revolution, and by 1978 all of them were cleared.

I went to the coffee shop in the Eastern Peace Market where Hualan and I had met the American G.I.s in 1956. It was closed. 'All clubs are closed. Clubs are bad things,' said the caretaker. Literal-mindedness again at work. The transcendent ideogram, weighty with meaning beyond reason. How often in the years to come I was to be told by Party cadres, reasoning in the feudal manner of analogy, categorizing not by reason but by resemblance, that the very word 'club' denoted something bourgeois and evil; that clubs were usually associations for conspiracy since there had been that Petofi Club in Budapest ...

In 1958 and 1959 an attempt to close all the teahouses, Chinese counterparts of the eighteenth-century English coffee houses, took place in my province of Szechuan, and was partly successful. Oh, shades of Boswell, and Li Po and Tu Fu, our great poets, and Verlaine too perhaps! I *needed* my teahouses; they reassured me that people could sit and talk and in companionship invent and create ... even if, as a woman, I would never go to a teahouse, since they were strictly for men.

Small, enchanting restaurants which I suppose were also capable of breeding jollity and letting the imagination run loose — and the tongue — they too would be closed ... It is possible that they were frequented assiduously by gourmet rightists, for as far as I know, all Chinese intellectuals are also gourmets.

A lengthy editorial appeared in the *People's Daily*, 'When a hundred flowers blossom, there are both fragrant products and poisonous weeds.' The 'poisonous weeds' were now being eradicated, leaving only 'fragrant products'. 'Pulling out too many weeds sometimes injures flowers,' said Papa.

The Minister of Culture, Mao Tun, had spoken against the indiscriminate labelling of the intelligentsia: 'Putting on them counter-revolutionary hats at will'. This was deemed acceptable. So were the criticisms of that great lady, Madame Ho Hsiangning, about the treatment of the overseas Chinese by some Party cadres – withholding remittances from abroad on the grounds that this was bourgeois funding. The Education Minister, Chang Hsijo, a charming man who spoke flawless literary English and could quote Shakespeare by the hour, deplored the neglect of historical and cultural factors. 'We apply foreign [meaning Soviet Russian] dogmas in dealing with everything ... Cadres tell people what to do, never why they have to do it ... dogma is their sole dictionary, their only support ... ' This was acceptable.

But to suggest giving positions of power to non-Party members, to members of other parties, to advocate rotation of rule among the parties, this was anathema. As Mao Tun would explain, the two slogans, 'Laymen cannot lead experts' and 'People other than Party cadres only have nominal posts', were not innocent verities. They were 'frontal assaults and side thrusts against the Party leadership'.

I went to see Kung Peng, but she was extremely busy. Two weeks later she invited me to lunch. By that time, Locquin had become slightly overpowering. He attempted to influence me in his fashion. 'It's a dirty trick that has been played on the intelligentsia, and you *must* proclaim it to the world.'

Kung Peng had bought small and delicious autumn crabs from Shanghai, only to be had at the time of harvest moon. She was wrestling with domestic problems, notably her bath which was old and losing its enamel; but she could not hope to get a new one, even though she and her husband were high officials. In the twelve years which followed she never got a new bath.

After lunch, she and her husband Chiao Kuanhua sat down with me. I referred to Mao's pamphlet, *On the correct handling of contradictions among the people*. 'It's really a most important work,' said I. Kung Peng appeared noncommittal. Two years later she would say, 'We did not realize how truly important this was at the time', thus indirectly confirming that there had been much opposition.

Neither had Kung Peng entirely liked my article 'Peking Revisited', published in America. Read collectively by some of her colleagues, it had been criticized because it was not all gush and praise. 'It's already difficult enough to have anything good about China printed ... one cannot write for a Western audience as one does for a Chinese one,' I told her. In my heart I hoped the time would come when both China and the West would accept what I wrote.

Kung Peng started peeling fruit for me to eat, and I knew that she and Chiao wanted to talk about the Hundred Flowers. But I did not want to be briefed. No official explanations for me. I did not wish to go back to Hongkong and have to say, 'This is what I have been told by such and such a high official'. I wanted to work everything out for myself, by myself, be responsible only to myself.

I left, saying I had another engagement.

I went to call on the Yangs. Yang Hsienyi and his wife Gladys, a beautiful, able Englishwoman, worked at the Foreign Language Press: both were scholars and superb translators. Their house was the meeting place for Chinese writers, painters, poets and also for many of the foreigners who came through Peking. But they did not wish to discuss the Hundred Flowers. Too many of their friends were being labelled rightists; among them a famous film director, some scriptwriters, a satirist or two, a few poets. However, they did see, as I did, the fundamental foolishness of challenging the Party in its holding of power, either directly or indirectly. 'Some party cadres are geniuses at detecting innuendoes in almost anything one utters, even remarks on the weather can become matter for political scrutiny,' said Yang Hsienyi in his bland, dead-pan manner.

I asked them: Was the Hundred Flowers nothing but a trap?

The words 'Yes, it was a trap' had appeared in a newspaper article, which explained that it was the rightists who had trapped themselves. The Yangs did not think it was a trick to catch whatever residual counter-revolutionary thought or sentiment might subsist in the souls of scholars. It was an openly baited, clearly signposted test for anyone who used common sense and was percipient.

Increasingly I began to feel that a very few people, ignoring or brushing aside wary common sense, had done a disservice, not only to the intelligentsia but also to the development of objective and academic discussion and the expansion of scientific reasoning. They had not distinguished between their present role, which was to help the socialist system, and the old role of the Chinese intelligentsia, which had been for two millennia *the* ruling bureacracy.

'All intellectuals always hanker for power,' said my Fourth Sister Ping, and many Party cadres.

I think that Mao and Chou Enlai (the latter especially) genuinely intended to use the recriminations of the intelligentsia to curb the evils of their own Party; to redress grievances and educate the cadres. But the repeated threats of bringing about a 'Hungarian incident' in China played into the hands of those in the Party (a silent but obvious majority) who did not want such an opening. The effervescence of the young was construed as the Party losing control of the educated youth, since even Communist Youth League members participated in some of the anti-Party demonstrations.

It was ludicrous to expect that a government like the present one in China, installed by a communist party which had fought its way to power through decades of agonizing suffering and two enormous wars, which had performed the extraordinary feats it had performed, including the Long March, would meekly allow itself to be displaced.

And from everything Mao had written and said, it was obvious that there was no intention of sharing *power* with the eight non-communist parties; they were invited to formulate suggestions to correct the flaws and defects of the ruling party, or as Mao had said, to become 'an opposition which would not oppose'.

There was also, most probable if not evident, pressure from the U.S.S.R. Right from the start, the U.S.S.R. had been against that 'feeling of early spring', as some Chinese scholars called the Hundred Flowers. And in that November of 1957, Mao Tsetung was due to go to Moscow, not only to patch up certain discrepancies in views between himself and Khrushchev, but also for negotiations of importance on sharing nuclear knowledge, indispensable to China's progress and defence.

The May climax of the Hundred Flowers had revealed, even among the Party hierarchy, criticism and hostility towards the Russians. It was all very well for Mao to harbour these (unpublished) feelings, but now, with the student posters and the newspapers, criticism of the Soviet Union, demands to follow the path of Yugoslavia were out in the open.

For all these reasons the wilting had to be. But the Hundred Flowers would be revived four years later.

Meanwhile, a campaign for 'socialist education' of the people started that October. Eight hours per week of political study in all universities and in all organizations. Which made everyone very tired.

In the countryside, the winter of 1957 saw very large water conservancy work being done, mobilizing tens of millions of peasants. The anti-rightist campaign went on among the collectives; for here too there had been trouble. Semi-terrorist bands led by ex-landlords and their sons (some of them university students) had burnt storage barns and executed Party cadres.

The unrest had been stimulated by the bad weather of the winter of

1956, in which twenty-three million *mus*★ of land, involving seventy million people, had been affected by drought. 'We think there will be a vast push for getting wells and reservoirs and canals constructed; and it will all have to be done by hand, since we have no machinery,' said the Yangs to me. 'We have plenty of redundant manpower.'

In one small factory in Peking there were 650 employees, of whom 200 were administrators, and 19 fully employed serving tea to the 200.

Chou Enlai had unofficially said there must be a cut-down in capital investment by at least 20 per cent, as the load was far too onerous and 'too many people were in non-productive employment'.

'The bureaucracy will have to do manual labour.' Yang Hsienyi thought that city cadres would be sent down in large numbers to help in the villages, thus relieving the strain upon the cities, and also curing, partly, the 'three evils'. 'I might be among them,' said he. I looked at his thin, aristocratic face; obviously he was not full of joy at the prospect, but he added, 'Of course I shall go. I'll serve wherever they put me.' 'You're too valuable to your organization,' I replied, and he allowed himself a bleak little smile, took a gulp of wine, and recited a poem to the moon.

Through the remaining weeks, articles in the Party newspapers inveighed against the 'frantic attacks by the bourgeoisie'. 'The old tail has not been lopped off,' I read one day.† 'They still think they're the lords of earth.' Arrogance was, according to the middle cadre, the hallmark of the intellectual; but arrogance was precisely what the intellectual complained was the outstanding feature of the Party cadre.

'Of course they were traitors, since that imperialist Dulles has called them openly "brave men" ... ' was another current opinion among cadres of the Party. Any praise from the outside was evidence of active collusion with imperialism, the enemy.

Another campaign, to reassure the intelligentsia, to dampen the irate feelings of the Party cadres. Mao was photographed speaking to non-Party writers and artists in Shanghai. Raucous demands for strict punishment of rightists were played down. By 1958 some rehabilitations were taking place.

In the literary circles, fierce 'struggle meetings' were under way; of such complex and convoluted nature that even today, twenty years later, I feel unable to disentangle the whys and wherefores of these condemnations. 'Some of these writers have been feuding against each other for

---

★ One *mu* is one-sixth of an acre and one-fifteenth of a hectare.
† To stick up one's tail: to be arrogant.

years ... there are long-standing grievances between Party writers who have come from the guerrilla bases and the writers who remained in the cities and only joined at Liberation. Some of the seasoned Party writers are asking of their new colleagues: "You haven't been through the re-moulding process — who knows what underhand games you were up to in the Chiang Kaishek controlled areas in the old days?" Writers have a natural disposition never to forget any little detail of the past histories of other writers ... '

The speaker was a writer friend of mine who ambled with me, speaking quietly. He asked me not to quote him. I would gather that a great deal of personal rancour between literary men (and how intense this becomes) must also have played a role in some of the accusations in literary circles that year.

I went to bid Kung Peng goodbye. She looked weary. The meetings against the rightists went on in her own department, and in the Ministry of Foreign Affairs. Twenty years later I would be told that at the time her own husband, Chiao Kuanhua, was under fire as a rightist, and that he was only saved by Chou Enlai's personal intervention.

'Whatever our enemies may say, we are not going to shed blood,' said she. 'The Chairman refuses to utilize violence, as was done in certain other countries. Heads are not leeks which can grown again.' We both knew to which other countries Kung Peng was alluding.

Vice-President Radhakrishnan of India came to Peking, and I went to a reception for him. I stood near the door and within a few inches of me Radhakrishnan walked in, and with him Mao Tsetung, and Liu Shaochi, and Chou Enlai and Teng Hsiaoping, and Chu Teh, and others. Everyone clapped, and they too were clapping themselves. Mao wore a pale grey suit. His presence seemed to abolish every other presence, for he conveyed power. He had a smooth, unwrinkled face and was taller than all the others, including Radhakrishnan, who did not wear a turban that day.

The Vice-President of India made an emotional speech in English; he spoke of the quality of mercy. Radhakrishnan had felt moved to utter a plea of compassion for the rightists ... Mao made a speech in reply, and so strong was his Hunan accent that I understood very little of what he said. But the drift seemed to be an emphasis on non-interference between different systems.

Papa took me to his bank and opened an account in my name. He would put all his savings into my account. He also gave me all his patriotic war bonds. During the Korean war, the government had issued war bonds, and all of them were redeemed by 1961, with a tax free interest of 3 per cent.

Papa would not leave China. 'My organization thinks I am too old to travel.' Comrade Wu had come to see him on his birthday, with a bouquet of carnations stiffly tied and a bottle of wine. 'They try to show your father that they value his criticism highly,' said Wanchun.

'I'll be back next spring,' I told Papa. 'Look after yourself well this winter. We'll see what happens next year.'

Hongkong. The usual barrage of newsmen. Jacques Locquin, perhaps because I had refused his advice, had sent an advance report, stating that 'Han Suyin alleges 99 per cent of the Chinese people are against the rightists.' I had said nothing so dogmatic.

I would repeat my view: there had been irresponsible and foolish statements made which had set back the cause of intellectual freedom in China; because the people who had made them had not kept in mind Chinese history and the traditional relationship of the intelligentsia to power. 'How do you want the workers and the peasants to approve them? They do not know them. They only know the Communist Party. And what have they done in the past to help the peasantry?' Allowing self-expression was never meant to be liberalization, I said; it was merely a method to help the Communist Party reinforce itself, not to challenge it, replace it or weaken it.

Of all the newsmen, it was two Americans, one the representative of the *Baltimore Sun*, who reported most scrupulously and exactly what I had said.

March 1958. Singapore's heat bleached skin and mind; our shadows vanished as the sun dissolved in a heat-drained sky. Only the abrupt evening sea breeze came to restore bodies driven by work through the day. There was an epidemic of influenza and I was extremely busy. There was also an epidemic of abortions, and some were ugly. Abortion was a crime then, but many doctors performed it.

One morning a cable came from Hollywood, signed Balaban, inviting me to a presentation at the Hollywood Bowl in April. I rang up the American Consulate and was assured there would be no problem about a visa. Just as I was drafting a suitable reply which our errand boy would take to the telegraph office, another cable came, this time from Peking. It said that my father had died on March 8th.

I prepared to go to Peking, and set off for Hongkong the next day. A cable from Walter Minton reached me in Hongkong. (By now I had left Ted Weeks and Little, Brown. Walter Minton of Putnam's was my new publisher.) *The Mountain is Young* was ready for publication, coming out both in London and in America that autumn. Could I come to America for the launching? I applied in Hongkong for the American visa, but left for Peking without waiting for the outcome. Francis Pan would ring up the Consulate and inquire when the visa would be ready.

China Travel Service surpassed itself. A death in the family – the visa to Peking was there within three hours of my calling them. An aeroplane seat to Peking had been booked for the morning after my arrival in Kuangchow.

In the very few hours I was in Kuangchow I noticed a change. A quality of exhilaration in the air. Effervescence. Posters, flamboyant on every wall. Red flags and banners and trucks with workers standing in them beating drums as they rolled through the streets, announcing achievements in production. Wall posters against rightists, a procession of chanting young children with wooden guns, older children with spades ...

And an explosion of women.

Women on posters, immense posters of women in factory clothes, in peasant clothes. 'We too can produce for the country.' Woman calling to women: Come out and work! Build our country! Women and men with that smile to the fore, looking starry-eyed into the sky. Women, large-sized, brawny, and on the radio in my room the voice of a woman: 'It is better for a woman to have big hands and big feet. Big feet are beautiful, big hands are capable hands. A white skin is sickly ... '

I was witnessing the beginning of the Great Leap Forward, which would take place that year.

Peking was still extremely cold when I arrived in mid-March, shivering, plunged into Arctic weather from the tropical moist heat of Singapore with the sun straight overhead. A shrieking sand wind from the Gobi Desert swooped upon the city and clawed at it, and tore the skin off my face. Yet even so, in the high wind, there were processions and marching, and drums, and exhilaration.

I went straight to Papa's house from the airport; noticing that there were more bicycles on the streets than the previous year. Hsueh Mah had shrunk upon herself, a dwarf bundled in Papa's cardigan, and she uttered long lament. Third and Fourth Brothers and Fourth Sister Ping came from work when night fell. They told me that it was on an afternoon with such a sandstorm, raging yellow, that Papa came home for lunch from the office. 'He insisted on taking part in the wall poster campaign.' The great campaign of wall posters which had been going on since 1956 had not stopped; on the contrary, there were many more of them, and now they were all directed towards the Leap Forward which was coming. How to produce more, more quickly, more thriftily; how to struggle for 'an upward stream' of achievement. Strangely enough, while some intellectuals had gone back into supine acquiescence, Papa had thrown himself into this campaign. 'How to do things better, it's my job to tell them how.' I do not know what wall posters he wrote. Only the organization and the Party committee in charge would know.

'Your father was very excited that day,' said Fourth Brother. Papa swallowed his food, then went to wait for the bus at the street corner to return to the office. The wind howled and threw great piles of sand in the air. It was difficult to breathe or even to see. Choking, covered with sand, Papa arrived back at the office, and spat out the sand in his mouth, and cleaned his nostrils.

A meeting took place. Papa rose to speak. He had just started to say, 'And we don't pay enough attention ... ' when he put his hand to his head: 'Oh, I'm unwell ... ' and then his face turned purple and he fell to the floor.

'The Party committee would like to tell you all about it. They have asked whether you can come tomorrow. They wish to offer you their condolences.' Of course I would go.

Fourth Brother came with me. He was, after all, almost Papa's adopted son. Rather than leave his brother without a male successor, Third Uncle had enjoined his son, Fourth Brother, to look after him, which he did most dutifully, giving up all his spare Sundays, as did his wife Shuan, to keep the old man company.

The Party committee head received me with utmost courtesy. He repeated what I had been told about the sandstorm: 'Very oppressive, your father could not breathe easily. We asked him to rest, not to take part in the meeting, but your father would not rest. He wrote so many wall posters, he participated in all the debates. Sometimes the criticisms he made were not apposite ... ' Here the Party leader tried hard not to frown a little. Undoubtedly Papa must, at times, have lashed out at the Party cadres, and it must have been hard to take. 'However, your father was a good man, most patriotic and devoted; we decided that he was an example for all of us in many ways, even if at times his world viewpoint was imperfect.'

The comrade then produced the doctor's certificate. A doctor had been there within ten minutes, but Papa had died instantly; a stroke had felled him. In view of his great merits, the Party committee had decided to bury him on Papaoshan, the hill where revolutionary heroes and people who have rendered great service to their country are buried. This was a signal honour, especially for a man like Papa, not a Party member, an old 'intellectual', and from a bourgeois background.

Ration tickets for a full set of funeral clothes had been obtained. Since 1954 cotton was rationed, as was oil and rice, pork and flour, to maintain stable prices. But for funerals, and also for marriages and for the birth of babies, extra cloth was always given. The clothes were made within twenty-four hours and Papa dressed in them, and photographs were duly taken, so that every step of the procedure should be shown to me and I could judge whether it had been carried out appropriately. There were many wreaths, and at Papaoshan a small ceremony, as friends and colleagues and the Party committee representative paid their respects. Papa was even mentioned in the *People's Daily*, a great honour for a non-communist.

'We wanted to delay the ceremony until you had arrived, but since you were so far, we did not know how long it would take.' I said they had done very well, and I was perfectly satisfied and very grateful. 'You have done more, far more than I ever expected. I thank you most deeply.'

Fourth Brother, Third Brother and Ping and I went to Papaoshan, and I saw the fresh grave. 'Should you wish a headstone, we can arrange for it,' said the keeper. We discussed the stone, its size, the words to be engraved upon it; it would cost a thousand *yuan*. 'We can afford it,' said Third and Fourth Brothers. As high-grade intellectuals, they had excellent salaries. I said, 'No, I will pay for everything.' By the summer the stone was laid upon the grave, Papa's name and a short biography engraved upon it.

Often in the years since then I have driven to Papaoshan, not only to sweep Papa's grave, but also to pay respects to other friends. I would stroll among the stone monuments on the slope of the hill where Papa was buried and stop in front of the grave of Agnes Smedley, just one row above that of Papa. 'Agnes Smedley, American revolutionary writer' and a hammer and sickle are engraved upon her stone, since she was an American Communist Party member.

Many times, too, besides visiting the outside slopes of Papaoshan, I would be allowed to penetrate the small rooms inside the modest building where lie the ashes of so many Party members.* Row upon row, upon shelves, they lie, nothing but the small casket, a name and a red star, and sometimes a photograph.

During the Cultural Revolution, a band of the May 16 group of Red Guards, the most virulent and savage of all the recruits of Lin Piao and Madame Mao, erupted into Papaoshan and started to destroy the 'graves of the bourgeoisie'. 'We shall scatter the bones of all those who have opposed Chairman Mao,' they chanted. The grave of a Communist leader of the 1930s† was broken up, but the family was able to take the coffin away with his bones and bury him privately elsewhere. This man had, indeed, been guilty of an error of 'line', way back in 1928–9, but this was no reason to throw him out of the Papaoshan cemetery. Some graves, like Papa's, of non-Party members, had the headstones smashed. But the keeper of Papaoshan arrived on the scene. 'I told them to stop. I stood there and would not allow them to continue. "This is not the way to fulfil Chairman Mao's injunction," I told them. There were about forty of them, but I was not afraid. And they went away.' Thus the damage was limited to the outside. The band had wanted to go inside the rooms where the caskets were stored. Since the rooms are of modest size and have no bars, no heavy doors, it would have been easy to rifle among the small urns. 'They wanted to check whether there were any "traitors'" ashes there, but I told them, "Go away, you are doing no useful work here among the dead." And so they did not enter.'

Another headstone, with Papa's face upon it, done by a sculptor who is a friend of Shuan, has replaced the old one. We continue to visit Papa, and in spring my cousins' children also come to sweep the grave, to read aloud his engraved biography, and to bow. The keeper comes forward with two flower pots which we reverently place and leave for Papa, who loved flowers so much.

I began to sort out Papa's books, papers and clothes. The bank transferred Papa's savings and bonds and cash to me. The housing committee made no difficulty about Papa's four houses. His clothes were remarkably few, and Hsueh Mah asked whether she could have them for her son. Since she was already wearing Papa's cardigan, I said yes. Ping said, 'Now Hsueh Mah must go back to her village. Her son can take care of her.'

Hsueh Mah wept heartrendingly. 'I have served Old Lady and Venerable Old Gentleman for so many years ... how can I go back?' She knelt

---

* Cremation is currently practised in China, especially for Party members.
† Chu Chiupai: see *The Morning Deluge*.

and knocked her head against the veranda's tiled floor. 'Do not send me away. I shall kill myself.'

When Liberation had come, Hsueh Mah had attended the meetings for equality between men and women. She went to the public security bureau and said, 'I want a divorce; I have been married against my will, and I was beaten all the time, and I have run away, and it is twenty-eight years ago. I don't want that old mule of a husband.' So Hsueh Mah wept, and clung to me, and said twenty-eight years, ah yes she had a son, but he would not look after her, and could she stay? And if I returned, she could serve me ...

And so I said, Yes, she could stay. I would pay her thirty *yuan* a month, which was the salary of a worker, and she would be caretaker of the rooms in the house where Papa had lived. 'You are making a mistake,' said Ping. 'Hsueh Mah is afraid of village life because she thinks of the past. But her village is now quite well off. It even has electricity.'

But I could not bring myself to send her back to her village. So Wang Wanchun and Uncle Ting, who lived in one of Papa's houses, arranged to pay Hsueh Mah out of the rent of the houses, and to bank the rest for me, except the 20 per cent which the housing committee took out of the rents in order to carry out repairs.

During the next six years, until 1964 when she died, I would see Hsueh Mah become more and more rapacious, greedy for money. All the instincts of the peasant came up in her, and every time I returned to the house something was missing, until all the furniture was gone, and when I asked for it Hsueh Mah wept and said there were bad people who had taken it away. No one of course would comment on my silliness in allowing her to stay. It was my fault, and I had no way now of getting rid of her. Then I found out through Uncle Ting that it was Hsueh Mah's son who was taking my furniture and selling it. Her son was a cadre in her village, a Party member.

'I'll complain,' I said hotly.

Uncle Ting and Wanchun, who was there, looked uneasy.

'Not possible,' said Wanchun.

Uncle Ting said, 'We must ponder this, ponder this.'

'But why?'

'To accuse a Party member is serious business, very serious ... '

But I went ahead, and Hsueh Mah's son was thrown out of the Party and punished. I said to Wanchun, 'The more scared you are, the more tyranny will grow. We must fight.'

Wanchun said, 'Big Sister, it is easier for you to fight than for me.'

Hsueh Mah dosed herself with a lot of medicines and forever wanted more money from me. She demanded a solemn promise that I would buy her a good wooden coffin and a new set of clothes, and that her coffined body would be sent back to her village, by train, for burial; she asked for the train ticket money in advance. 'I shall have it in my hand, and when I die, make sure that there is also some money for a horse cart to take the coffin from the railway station.' By the end she wanted a car, not a horse cart. Hsueh Mah was buried in common ground in Peking because the trains no longer took coffins to villages for burial. In 1963 she had placed her own picture, as large as my father's, by my father's picture, thus laying claim to having been Papa's wife. I took away Papa's picture, leaving Hsueh Mah alone on the wall.

During those days of April, I went to see some friends who lived near a village, and watched fields being made anew, wide and splendidly rectangular, and rows of people working together at planting, bowed over the furrows. Above them red flags shook in the wind with a noise like wings. Every day the newspapers would signal some achievement or new invention by a peasant or a worker. The people were mighty and invincible, an ocean of strength and wisdom. This was an immense attempt to mobilize one quarter of the earth's people to speed up the infra-structural work necessary, moving human energy, because it was in large supply, to modernize and industrialize China rapidly, and upon a sound agricultural basis. There must be an agricultural surplus before one could hope for enough funds for capital construction to proceed. The slogan of 'self-reliance' was heard everywhere. 'Pretty soon, perhaps we shall no longer need to rely on any aid,' said Wang Wanchun. But he would not say any more. Instead, he told me about the national minorities. 'We don't know enough about their customs, and sometimes we have inter-fered with them.' The Miaos of Szechuan at the autumn festival would erect a pole with knives sticking out of it; and a young girl, singing, would climb the pole barefooted, her feet scaling the blades like climbing stairs. 'But she never cuts herself. And when she reaches the top, she begins to sing, and then the young Miao girls each choose a man and go into the forest with him for a night of love. But our cadres felt that this was immoral, and we sent army men "to maintain order". The Miaos were very discontented with this interference.'

Now this was changed. Much more attention was being paid to the national minority customs. 'Some of our people still believe that we the

Hans are superior,' I said to Wanchun. 'But we are,' said he, surprised that I should doubt it.

A sparrow hunt started in Peking, part of a nationwide campaign to eliminate the four pests: flies, mosquitoes, rats and mice, and grain-eating birds. For three days the whole population turned out, banging gongs, beating drums, blowing whistles or just screaming; climbing on roofs and waving sticks and blowing small trumpets to keep the sparrows flying. Exhausted, the sparrows fell down and died, and were carted away in great mounds of feathers and beaks and diminutive clawed feet. On the city wall's remaining parapets (the massive Ming Wall was being torn down to make way for new buildings and new roads), on the watchtowers of the gates, in the high pavilions of the Forbidden City, people clambered to dislodge sparrows. An energetic young girl put her foot through the roof tiles of Papa's house in her pursuit of a bird. In distraught small clouds the sparrows flew and fell and flew and fell. Europeans from the embassies and Western journalists joined in the hunt.

I wrote a piece about the sparrow hunt for the *New Yorker*, in which it was printed.★ Roger Angell, the editor, wanted to cut out the end, but I did not let him do it. The piece as it stands displeased a good many people in China; but then I have always been sloppily sentimental about animals and birds.

The sparrow hunt was never repeated; for by the next year and for many years afterwards, owing to the dearth of birds, the trees of Peking would be assailed by insects. Caterpillars wrapped the foliage in great nets of silver strand, a lovely, lethal sight, and when all the foliage was eaten up the trees died. I saw fields of cabbages with their leaves peppered with holes as worms gorged. 'We must distinguish between good and nefarious birds,' the cadres would now say. But it was hard to get away from the first effulgent clamour of 'Get rid of pests'. In the 1970s I would still find, in Szechuan, people catching sparrows as 'bad birds'.

I went to see old Mr Hua Nankuei, to thank him for having come to Papa's funeral ceremony at Papaoshan, although he walked with great difficulty. While we were talking, his son Simon came in, exuberant. He had been working, together with many of the students and teaching staff of Peking University, at the new reservoir which was being built near the Ming tombs. Simon looked fit. He was doing his year of labour re-education and would return to architecture by 1959. 'It is the happiest

★ 'The Sparrow Shall Fall', *New Yorker*, October 10th, 1959.

time of my life. The workers are simply splendid. They treat me as one of them, joke and talk with me.' Never had Simon felt so full of joy and hope, and to remind him that this was 'punishment' seemed otiose.

'I've been five days at the reservoir. We sleep in tents, we eat *wotou**\
three times a day. Nothing else. But it's splendid ... ' He had a friend who had done a stint in the countryside. 'He never wanted to come back to the city. The peasants chose the heaviest and the dirtiest work for themselves — they left easy tasks to him. "You're not used to it, as we are." They were grateful whenever my friend did anything. The peasant he boarded with the first night put up a great barrier of blankets between himself and my friend on the *kang†* they shared. "Why do you do this?" "You see ... they ... jump," the peasant replied guiltily. My friend put his arms around the peasant. What delicacy of heart! He wanted to keep his fleas to himself.'

A small wind went prowling through Peking the day I left, but it was almost May, and warm. Third and Fourth Brothers came to see me off; soon Fourth Brother would go to Manchuria, to a research institute there. 'At present we're busy with the heart campaign.'

The heart campaign symbolized an exchange of hearts between the Party and the intelligentsia: 'You give us your heart and we give you ours ... our hearts are joined together in common endeavour.' It was meant as a pledge of the loyalty of the intellectuals to the Party, but also as a pledge that the Party would treat the intellectuals fairly, and trust them. There had been many meetings and much exhortation as each organization containing intellectuals overhauled itself for the coming Leap. Now parades with great hearts of satin or velvet carried in front of the processions signified a new and desirable harmony.

'Do you think it really helps to parade with a heart?' I asked Third Brother. 'Why not?' he replied. He was well, and happy in his work. Over a million office workers were going down to the countryside. Party and non-Party cadres. Third Brother was also going down for six weeks of labour. 'It will temper me,' said he, smiling confidently.

---

* *Wotou:* a coarse lumpy bread made of rye and millet.
† *Kang:* platform of stone or adobe which serves as the family bed in north China's peasant houses.

Eight

That Other Life, Outside China

BACK IN HONGKONG, I inquired of Francis Pan about my American visa. Francis looked uneasy. Yes, the American Consulate had rung up, saying, 'The visa is ready for Miss Han to collect.' 'She's in Peking at the moment,' Francis had replied unguardedly. There was a pause and then the telephone voice had said, 'Oh, that changes everything, doesn't it?' 'I explained you had gone for your father's funeral,' said Francis, who felt he might have bungled things. Then a message came through that 'on second thoughts' my case had to be studied. Two months later, in Singapore, I was advised that I was not eligible for a visa, because I had joined a 'communist' organization, that is, the PAP, Lee Kuanyew's party, in Singapore! Yet this information, that I had filled up a membership card for the PAP, had been on my first application, which had been approved. The change of mind after I returned from Peking was blatant.

I could have fought the case. I nearly went to the American Consulate to say, 'Look, I only filled in a card to hear Harry Lee talk; and I'm told that he's so upset at the idea of my joining his party that he's said to his colleagues, "I don't want that woman around." It's all a joke, really.' But Americans at that time were impervious to such joking. I felt I would gain nothing by fighting the case. I might be compelled to make a public anti-China statement, and this I would not do. I had to accept that freedom of opinion had its limits everywhere, and also in America at that time.

From then on until 1977, I would not enter America except on a waiver, which meant applying to the State Department each time. And each time I got my waiver, until it became a farce. 'Oh, it's you again,' the Consulate officials in Hongkong or Singapore would say wearily when I came in, all smiles, to tell them I *must* go to see my publisher, or I *must* go to fulfil my contract for lectures throughout the length and breadth of America ... 'It takes us five hours to go through the files about you,' one very nice official would tell me with a half grin (full grins were out of the question for people needing waivers to enter the U.S.A.).

How mighty, how feared was America then! I had brought some silk back from China, and given it to a tailor in Hongkong to make a dress, but he refused. 'This silk was made in China, Dr Han ... I cannot work on it or the American Consulate will put me on the black list and I shall lose all my American customers ... '

There was the matter of ducks' eggs. Since 1957, and for many years thereafter, each duck exported from Hongkong to the markets of South East Asia was to be accompanied by a certificate of origin. This was a stamp upon its webbed foot, vetted by the American Consulate and certifying the duck was born in Hongkong, from eggs laid in Hongkong by parent ducks resident in Hongkong. Certificates of origin were required for everything: furniture, silk, curios – they became an industry on their own. No antiques from China were to be purchased by Americans. No jade from China. An American friend of mine died of a heart attack because he had a magnificent jade collection, acquired before 1949. He intended to retire to California and sell his jade. But now he was ruined, for he could not take the jade with him, or sell it.

In these circumstances, to fight publicly would have inevitably strengthened the conviction that I was a communist. I preferred, therefore, to keep silent, to accept waivers, and to wait. Twenty years.

Meanwhile, I was selling the film rights of *The Mountain is Young* for a considerable sum of money to Paramount. *A Many-Splendoured Thing* had gone for a very small sum to Twentieth Century-Fox, and had proved an amazing success. It is still showing, a quarter of a century later, in many countries. Now I would ask a large figure for *The Mountain is Young* and not worry whether a film was made or not. Francis reminded me of that occasion. ' "I'm going to take a walk and decide on the money," you said. When you came back, you stuck out for six figures and would not be moved.'

The negotiations dragged on, and Singapore's multi-millionaire film magnate, Loke Wantho, who had become my friend, took over, relaying my demands to Paramount. Loke Wantho had inherited a fortune from his very famous father, Loke Yew. He was capable and shrewd, and although English-educated, intelligent enough to know that his was not the enduring cultural pattern in Malaya. He had remained profoundly attached to his Chinese roots, and though extremely conservative and afraid of communism, he would talk and argue with me, and try to inform himself. Wantho owned the Cathay film organization in Singapore, which had purchased *A Many-Splendoured Thing* for distribution throughout South East Asia. He hoped that *The Mountain is Young* would be a similar success. I was not sanguine, but I did not care. 'Whatever happens, now I shall have a sum of money set by, and money buys freedom, undoubtedly.' Like Bernard Shaw and Saul Bellow, I think the labourer is worthy of his hire, and if I have done many things for no money, only for love, I have also bargained doggedly when no feelings have been involved. Until 1958 I had spent and given, given and spent. Now I would become more choosy, but I would still give, more or less judiciously. I would tailor my life not to possess material things in great abundance, for they are hindrances, fetters, bad habits, but to be able to go as free as possible. Even my three small houses in Johore Bahru were not a burden. The rent of two of them paid for the upkeep of all three, and the servants' wages. With Lao Chieh there as general manager, I could be away and all would be looked after: the dogs and the cats and the garden and the tenants; and Yungmei was now eighteen years old, and healthy.

When *The Mountain is Young* came out as a book it was declared 'hot stuff', the equivalent of today's porn. Some reviewers were sorry that it was not a replica of *A Many-Splendoured Thing*. But I could never repeat myself, and all my books would be different, one from the other. I had written *The Mountain is Young* with irony and laughter, to please myself; and literature, after all, should not be all heaving and smoulder and wrung-out soul. It should also be fun for the writer. But the world of literature then was not attuned to that mixture of mockery and malice, tinsel and gold, drabness and glory, poetry and banality; and yet that was what Nepal, what India were like: tragedy is farce and the ingredients of drama the commonest in laughter. I was cast in the mould of a lovelorn and tragic person, talking and living Lo-oh-ove, when it was precisely the contrary, and love for me was a rare episode in a busy existence. The misunderstanding went very far. An earnest young Englishwoman, the wife of some British officer or other, volunteered to help me type some of my work, but after a fortnight burst out, 'All we ever do is work, work, work. And I thought I'd have such a glorious time.'

Yet *The Mountain is Young* was a success, and continues to be reprinted. Many women readers wrote to me: they felt it solaced their frustration. 'You've described my husband exactly', was the burden of letters I received, and one middle-aged person stopped me on the street: 'Han Suyin, where did you meet my husband?' I goggled. 'I never met your husband.' 'But you've described him to a tee. It's just like him, even the way he makes love ...'

Yungmei was now out of school, and idle, and rigorously conformist to the mores of her set. 'Everyone says you are a communist because you go to China so often'; 'Nobody likes your book on Malaya'; '*The Mountain is Young* is a dirty book ...' She sought a father image, and had taken to sleeping with Pao's sword hanging over her bed. Not knowing what to do with the unwieldy sabre, I had transported it with our luggage everywhere, even to Johore Bahru. Perhaps I should now have told her she was adopted. But in China, talking it over with friends, everyone had seemed to think it was no trauma not to know. 'I only knew it when my mother died, and I loved her all the more for loving me so much that she could not bear to tell me she had not borne me,' one of my Chinese friends had said. And so I did not tell Yungmei, alleging to myself that she would be more hurt by knowing than not knowing.

Yungmei was growing very beautiful, and I did not grudge her the pleasure she took in swimming, going to parties and dancing. Unlike the intense, hardworking, revolt-filled students of Chinese schools whom I met at Nanyang University, the products of the English schools could spend a whole day doing absolutely nothing except reading comics, giggling and looking fondly at the pictures of American film stars. However, compared with today's youth, they were an angelic choir. No sex. They drank only tea or fruit juice. No drugs. In the tropics, where the nights are more vital and awake than the drowsy, heat-stunted days, they went out all night, and yet chaperoned each other, so that the most that could happen was a hand-in-hand look at the moon. The main danger was car accidents, for some of the boys, from twelve-car owning families, would drive with show-off speed; and I often lay awake fearing a crash, reassured when I heard at last the giggles and the soft Malayan singsong of goodnights from the garden below.

Yungmei now decided to study in London because so many of her friends were going there. I thought it was a good idea. She would not be out of her depth as she still had many childhood friends in England. In September of 1958 I took her to London, where I was expected for the launching of *The Mountain is Young* and a Foyle's lunch in my honour at the Dorchester Hotel.

In 1953 I had semi-adopted another girl, Hueiying, of the same age as Yungmei. Hueiying's mother had died, and at twelve she had been taken out of school by her father and made to cook and clean and look after five other children in the family. Her father sold pottery and was poor. I put Hueiying through school, paying the fees, and helping a little besides, and she did well, as also did her younger brother, who became an art designer of outstanding quality, won scholarships to England, and has his own design centre now in Kuala Lumpur. Hueiying would marry a very nice young man, who has since built a solid fortune in the Chinese medicine business throughout South East Asia. Other protégés of mine would also turn out successes, but the point was that Yungmei resented greatly my concern for other young people. I tried to explain to her that all the world's children, in a sense, are one's own. 'Why can't you be like other mothers?' she said; meaning: 'Why can't you concentrate on me, on me alone?' And this also stopped me. I thought this jealousy of love part of that unconscious, deep-buried feeling of deprivation she must have suffered from, being unwanted, sold by her mother and sold not once but three times. No giving of love from me or anyone else would compensate entirely for this early absence of caring.

And then there was Ah Ping. Ah Ping was a waif adopted by Lao Chieh, and Lao Chieh, when she was angry with Ah Ping, would scream at her, 'I bought you and I'll sell you if you won't study properly.' She would also beat Ah Ping in the bad old Chinese way which maintains that it is wrong not to be strict with children. In Singapore society adopted girls were many, and were usually to be utilized, sooner or later, either as servants to the family or to be sold into prostitution. The defloration of a young virgin was the occasion for the 'mother' to regain her outlay, a large sum in return for her care of many years. I did not want Yungmei to think that this was going to happen to her; already she had mentioned to me one or two such cases.

All the time in London, this question beset me. Shall I tell her, shall I not? In the end I did not tell her, and that was wrong of me.

For in 1961 Yungmei, who was then studying in London, went to spend the Easter holiday with Joseph Hers and his family in Brussels. Joseph Hers had given me my scholarship to study in Belgium way back in 1935, when he headed a scholarship fund in China. He had returned to his native Belgium and married a very beautiful and vital woman, a sculptress, and Greek. She took to Yungmei and surrounded her with much mothering and affection. Did this make Hers jealous? He was almost forty years older than his wife, and extremely tyrannical in his old age. He was also carrying on a very acerbic quarrel by letter with me. About China.

Hers insisted that China had failed. He sent me cuttings from various newspapers to prove this failure. He gloated over the sufferings that would come to the Chinese people. He wrote, 'Why on earth should China provoke India?'; 'China has not one friend in the world today.' I wrote back, mordantly. Epistolary rage flourished. I said he was 'myopic ... deliberately unobservant ... thinking on such a small scale it made me laugh ... '

And then Hers told Yungmei that she was not my daughter, that she had been adopted. How did he know? I had not told him. Perhaps through missionary talk. The missionaries of Chengtu knew.

Yungmei took the knock. She did not write to me, and in fact she did not even say anything to me until six years later, when she had married and borne a child. What happened then? All I know is that she stopped studying. She then fell in love, but the outcome was not happy. However, as she said herself, 'I did not become a prostitute. I did not take drugs.' She not only survived; she recovered.

Of course there were difficult years between us; but never was there a complete break; always, somehow, we gravitated back towards each other. And there were good periods too. And now, I think, a great clearness has come in our relations, and they are good. I love her and I know she loves me, although at times she still reacts to the nightmares of her young days. But then, in this world, how many children have had far worse fates than hers? Going to China has helped her greatly to readjust, to understand, and to be enriched, not traumatized, by what has happened. For my Chinese friends all say to her, 'Oh, but there are so many like you ... '

But I do not think I can forgive Hers, even dead, for what he did. It was the action of a soured old man, jealous and destructive. I think it is because he still hungered for the China he had known, not the new China arising from the ashes of the past. For him there was no escape in the world except the world of China. He saw me go in and out, come closer to the heart of the change that was taking place. He then felt cast aside, unwanted. And that is why, I think, he did this to Yungmei.

That autumn of 1958 in London was the last time I would see Jonathan Cape alive. He threw a large party for me, and to it came Kossodo from Germany, Walter Minton of Putnam's, and Ragnar Svanstrom from Sweden. Walter Minton was a most impressive New Englander, and I was glad to see him in the flesh. I had liked his letters, and when I left Ted Weeks and Little, Brown, it was because I felt Ted and I had less and less to write to each other, despite Ted's effusiveness. I do not think it was his fault; perhaps we had started off with a misunderstanding, and it continued to grow.

A few English writers came to the party, including Peter and Ian Fleming, both published by Cape. Peter Fleming had been a friend of Ian's; they had bashed snakes in Burma together. The Flemings mono-polized the fireplace and stood there, with their wives (I think) as for an official photograph, and behaving as if the party were in their honour. At some point the Flemings ceased speaking to anyone else (they ignored me throughout the party) and quarrelled with beautiful manners among themselves.

Jonathan was recovering badly from the palsy due to his stroke; his face remained affected and at meals he dribbled. 'I did call you Sunflower, didn't I?' he said to me. 'Yes you did, Jonathan.' 'That's right. Sunflower.' Walter Minton came to dinner in the most elegant white hand-woven socks and with a delightful unknown whose Jayne Mansfield exposure reduced Cape's Wren Howard to feverish small talk. 'Do you write?' she asked me. As for Ragnar, he was very sweet and very English, in the way only Swedes can be. He said 'Hear, hear', but louder than I had heard it in the House of Commons. Walter and I carried on a friendly quarrel over *The Mountain is Young*. He asserted that I must tone down the swarthy hero because in the United States people were sensitive to the colour problem. Firmly and uncompromisingly, therefore, he had made a change. In the American edition the hero was 'burnished' or 'suntanned'.

On to Paris with Yungmei, to see my French publishers. The latter gave a luncheon and invited Françoise Sagan, who came with her husband of that year, Guy Schoeller. Guy was an explorer, a marvellous horseman and for a while one of the editors at Stock, my publishers. I had wanted to meet Françoise Sagan because she was then at the height of her popu-larity and in Malaya the young like Yungmei saw in her a cult figure for themselves. Her cool, precise, rather new-precious way of dealing with emotion fitted the adolescent dialect which I had heard Yungmei use. But as usual when writers meet, there was little that we could talk about. Sagan talked about cars and speed: 'I like *vitesse*.' I did not speak of Asia, of China, India, Malaya, Nanyang University—all of it suddenly was too large, too clumsy, sweaty and human, and ridiculous as an ocean is ridiculous, through sheer enormity.

That early November in Paris was also the Algerian war November. There was a fetor about the city, something bewildered under the beauty and the archness, the rank smell of unleashed violence filled one's nostrils. I met a small, middle-aged, plump woman, badly dressed, who at first sight made one think of ironing boards and returning from market with heavy-laden baskets and the violaceous varicose legs of overworked women with children and a husband who has long stopped talking. But how deceptive this appearance! For the woman was all fire and spirit, and she became beautiful as the minutes went by, and it was Germaine Tillon, writer, ethnologist, member of the Resistance, deported to Ravensbruck in 1943.

Algerian workers' bodies were found hanging on trees in the Bois de Boulogne, and the Seine even carried a cadaver or two. Those who spoke against the war in Algeria were quite often regarded as traitors. General de Gaulle was back as leader of France, but no one at the time could predict what he would do about Algeria.

From Paris I went to Geneva, for a reunion with Lily Abegg of the *Neue Züricher Zeitung*. Lily had come to Malaya to stay with me; we liked each other and she defended me when people called me names. She had an excellent grasp of Asian politics.

Walking into the Chat Botté restaurant for dinner, Lily and I fell upon P. N. Sharma, my Indian photographer friend. 'How shrunk the world is getting! One day Peking, the next Delhi, and now Geneva!' Sharma was in Geneva to ring up Moscow. 'My fiancée is in Moscow.' He had fallen in love with a Russian girl on his last trip to Russia, some months previously; and had been trying to get her out of Russia to marry her. 'Panditji* himself wrote a letter for me to Khrushchev,' he said. The telephone call came through, and Sharma bounded away. He returned, transfigured, and opened his shirt and began to ripple his belly muscles up and down and sideways, to make us laugh, while the Swiss waiters remained stone-faced. Sharma left with me an alarm watch (not a clock, a watch) and sundry items, altogether a suitcase of things, which he had purchased for his fiancée. He wanted them taken to India but knew he would be searched by the redoubtable Indian customs and would have to pay heavy duty on the watch and other things. Would I take it all to Delhi for him on my way back to Malaya? I would.

I note that in 1958 I also visited Cambodia, took up yoga, opened painting exhibitions in Singapore, started collecting antiques for the museum in Kuala Lumpur, and became associated with the Malaysian Sociological Research Institute.

---

* The Indian Prime Minister, Jawaharlal Nehru.

I had met Jean, a Eurasian lawyer whose mother was Vietnamese but who lived in Phnom Penh, during one of my sojourns in Hongkong. He had written, inviting me to Cambodia to lecture to the Rotary Club, of which he was President. Over a five-day holiday weekend in Singapore, I flew to Phnom Penh.

Sun-drenched, drowsy and pleasant, Phnom Penh was a small town of 200,000 souls with languid, unhurried streets and small buildings, peopled mostly by Vietnamese and Chinese. The native Khmer people were not only a minority, but the labourers and rickshaw pullers. Even the marketing of meat and vegetables was in Vietnamese hands. The Hotel Royal and its swimming pool were the centre, navel of the French resident community in Phnom Penh. Cambodia's tranquil countryside appeared to me to have an abundance of land and to be sparsely peopled; one did not feel that the country was on the verge of a revolution. Poverty and exploitation are not so stark when there is lush greenness and water; and yet exploitation there certainly was, for the rice crops and the fish trade were controlled by aristocrat landlords, and rice milling by mill owners, who again were either Chinese or Vietnamese.

Everything in Cambodia seemed stamped by the personality of Prince Norodom Sihanouk. Within three days I was received by the Prince, and I liked him very much. My affection for him and his wife, Princess Monique, would grow with the years and with the tribulations that they suffered.

Sihanouk was talkative, ebullient, extremely intelligent and still very much a Khmer king. He loved his country with a single-minded, fierce passion which was very moving. He was immensely concerned about preserving Cambodia's independence; and was most touchy on the subject. That he also maintained a feudal order, a class of privileged nobles who exploited and oppressed the people, was sad but inevitable. For Sihanouk, in a country handicapped by a lack of doctors, of engineers, of technicians and teachers, was prisoner of his class, of the aristocracy he belonged to. Personally, he was more enlightened and progressive than many another ruling head of state in Asia, and far more so than his neighbour, Ngo Dinh Diem, in South Vietnam. His personal charisma was very compelling. Sihanouk built schools and medical clinics and tried to improve the livelihood of the peasantry with canals for water and new houses. He tried to bring progress to Cambodia without a radical revolution. In his uncompromising neutrality, Sihanouk was regarded as perverse, erratic and dangerous by American State Department heads and officials. Among the British, his great friend was Malcolm MacDonald. Malcolm cultivated Sihanouk. 'He is of the utmost importance to us ... alas we don't know it.'

At our first meeting Sihanouk talked of his worry about the expanding war in Vietnam. The United States was getting more and more involved; and the Prince felt that Cambodia might be caught in a pincer movement between South Vietnam and Thailand, both countries basking in enormous influxes of American money. Cambodia had repeatedly been conquered and vassalized by both the Thais and the Vietnamese; the walls of her Angkor monuments bore in stone stories of heroic battles against invaders. 'I want my country at peace, my people secure, not dragged into the hideousness of war,' he said, and there were tears in his eyes. And Sihanouk did achieve for seventeen years that major feat: of keeping Cambodia out of conflicts, while all around war and devastation flourished.

In 1955 Norodom Sihanouk had divested himself of his kingship to become premier and *samdech*, or chief of state, of his country. His rule was perforce personal, authoritarian, but he contrived to keep the bulk of his people contented. Although fiercely anti-communist, he went to China, fashioning a policy combining old tradition with new vision. He had been impressed with Chou Enlai's wisdom and performance at the Geneva Conference of 1954, which had liquidated the French empire of Indo-China. 'The Chinese understand national independence, as we do,' said the Prince.

Sihanouk had a long conversation with Mao Tsetung. Mao was an excellent historian where China was concerned but not so well-informed on the history of South East Asia, that turbulent, prolific region with its multitudinous ethnic groups. When Mao commented favourably on Ho Chih Minh, on the socialist system in Vietnam, Sihanouk, it is said, blew up. 'Do you know that the Vietnamese, socialist or not socialist, tried to overrun us in 1953?' Mao listened attentively while Sihanouk gave him a historical account of the relations between Cambodia and Vietnam, Cambodia and Thailand.

Sihanouk loved Chou Enlai. 'He is the most far-sighted statesman in the world, and he understands history.' Towards Mao Tsetung, Sihanouk was reverent, but a little baffled by the size and scope of Mao's thinking, that cosmic touch which sometimes induces vertigo.

At that time, America had a truly obsessional view of politics. Anyone who did not toe the line of satellitism in the name of 'freedom and democracy' – however arbitrary, contemptuous of human rights the heads of state cherished by Washington were in practice – was an enemy.

Friendship with China was anathema. Sihanouk had to be brought down because he was too different. He was a friend of China; he was neutral; he would not be vassalized; he could not be bought.

Spasmodically, I did yoga. Whenever possible twice a week, with the yoga teacher, Mr Nayan, who lived in a small bungalow in Singapore.

Mr Nayan taught yoga free. He taught for love of people; he was fifty, but slim and youthful, small-boned, and he smelt sweet. A minor clerk in the government, he never thought of money and had no ambition. At the yoga classes we imbibed the peace he radiated. None of us ever inquired each other's names, or work. We just were; each one of us on his or her own mat, concentrating on the breathing, the positions, thinking of nothing else. And when I left, a surge of tranquil power and happiness would fill me, all tiredness gone. I often think of Mr Nayan; he seems to me immortal.

Suddenly, with independence, everyone in Malaya and Singapore became interested in art. Local painters, hitherto unknown, appeared as if born by spontaneous generation. Exhibitions were held. And yet, when I had arrived in 1952, it was said that there could be no writers or painters in Malaya because the climate was against them. I had discovered Malayan Chinese literature; I would go on to discover Chinese painters, calligraphers, Malay painters, sculptors, ceramic artists ... a generation of young artists afire with new endeavour.

And with this came, also very suddenly, an appreciation of antiques. People who had been breaking up their Ming plates to spike their wall tops against roving cats now brought them to the newly opened museum in Kuala Lumpur. The establishment of the museum was due to an Australian, Frank Sullivan, but now fully backed by the Prime Minister, Tunku Abdul Rahman.

Frank Sullivan had come to Malaya many years ago as a newsman, but he was now the Press Secretary for Tunku Abdul Rahman. Frank and I shared a fondness for Tunku (Frank was devoted to him) and now we shared the excitement over the painters and the museum.

This new enthusiasm for art went together with the beginning of a Malayan architecture. Architects like Kee Yeap, who had built my houses, were devising new styles for the houses of the wealthy. And whereas until then many a Chinese multi-millionaire holed up in an atap hut, even if he kept three cars outside it, his sons and daughters, university graduates, insisted on 'good taste' and Western comforts, bathroom, air-conditioner, refrigerator, and of course 'artistic' decorations on the walls. In the course of the next few years Singapore was to see many high-rise buildings, and Kuala Lumpur would prosper and adorn itself with some very stimulating architecture (part Arab, part everything else). English furniture, English styles, were out; everyone wanted to be Malayan; and batiks, once despised now became fashionable, as did paintings by local artists, some of whom used the batik techniques for their paintings.

In Nanyang University a splurge of amateur painting also occurred. I duly opened exhibitions, attended showings, wrote forewords, signed books and stated that 'the artist is trying to express the new, surging identity of Malaya', whatever that meant. I bought pictures, more to help the eager executants (most of them young and some very poor) than for art's sake.

My endeavour to make known Malayan Chinese literature had borne some fruit, and Nanyang University students came to my clinic to hand me short stories and poems, to confide their dreams of writing major novels, and sometimes to borrow money. Most of them returned the money scrupulously, even when the situation was very trying for them.

A consciousness that there were such things as novels, novellas, short stories, plays and poetry emerged as a manifestation of national identity and a book of Malayan Chinese short stories, with a preface by myself, emerged.

But Singapore became more, not less, prohibitively reactionary after 1960. The springs of writing and creation withered. So many magazines especially from Nanyang University, would be accounted 'subversive'. Nanyang University produced a high-standard economics magazine (in Chinese); an English-language magazine (of varying quality, but a brave attempt), and a magazine in Malay (of good standard). All this was done by the students. The pampered English-language media Singapore University only produced a rather mediocre English-language magazine. And yet there was an excellent teaching staff, including the brilliant and energetic Professor of English Literature, my friend the poet D. J. Enright, and the novelist Patrick Anderson.

The English-educated were perceptive, intelligent. I would meet so many earnest young men and women among them; and the one I remember best is the promising poet, Edwin Thumboo.* I had relieved his mother, a feckless and garrulous but attractive person, of a horrendous

* Author of *Rib of Earth* and *Gods Can Die*, published by Heinemann Far East.

debt she owed the egg-woman, who was a usurer. The egg-woman made small loans and sold trinkets to the housewives along the lanes where she peddled her eggs. She charged 'merely' 20 per cent per day interest, always pointing out it was so much less than the money-changing Sikhs who haunted Raffles' Place, waiting for penurious clerks outside the government buildings. They charged 50 per cent per day interest, nobly pointing out to their victims that in India it was customary to charge 100 per cent per day interest.

For an initial debt of fifty Singapore dollars, the total repayment due from Thumboo's mother was three thousand. Edwin struggled mightily to return the money; in this he was like so many of the Asian students that I would know. He had great compunction about owing anything to anyone.

Would that I could say the same about the only European student who came to my notice in those years! Pierre Ryckmans was Belgian, enamoured of Chinese culture, and had achieved the extraordinary feat of being admitted to Nanyang University, where he assiduously cultivated the more left-inclined students.

He had been to China in 1956 and now approached me, as he wanted to return to China and study there. I willingly wrote letters to China for him; but was not successful. Pierre then came to proffer a painting of his, a lion behind the bars of a cage. Not a work of art, but he wanted to indicate the spirit behind his slim, pale, scholarly exterior. I immediately, as a Chinese, made him a gift of five hundred dollars, which he graciously accepted.

Alas, perhaps naturally, Pierre Ryckmans repaid me as some other men whom I have helped have done. He has since become an eminent Sinologist, called Simon Leys. And he has written a highly fanciful account of meeting me, in 1972, to discuss the fate of some Chinese writers whom I knew, and whom he did not know.

I became involved with the Malaysian Sociological Research Institute in 1957 when a very infuriated Alex Josey came to me to complain about an American girl, Shirle Gordon. Besides being Lee Kuanyew's intimate friend, Alex Josey was also the South East Asia correspondent for *Eastern World*, a London based magazine run by a witty and mercurial Viennese called Hans Taussig.

I had met Hans in 1954 while I was in London waiting for Yungmei to recuperate from her lung operation. Hans and I got on very well; we exchanged many happy letters. Hans was always full of plans and *Eastern World* was a pioneer magazine, concentrating on news of Asia.

Eastern World was not prosperous; Hans asked me to help, which I did willingly, making loans of some few thousand pounds and in return acquiring a directorship and a say in the magazine. But my say was limited by the fact that I was in Singapore, too far away to attend board meetings in London.

One of the items on which we disagreed was the accrediting of correspondents to the magazine. Hans was generosity itself in distributing letters giving authority to people to write for *Eastern World*, since all its correspondents were unpaid volunteers. And now Hans, in a fit of good temper, had forgotten Alex Josey and given correspondent status to Shirle Gordon for South East Asia, India and the Middle East. Shirle Gordon had attended the independence celebrations in Kuala Lumpur in August 1957 as representative for *Eastern World* while Alex Josey, who for years had been *the* South East Asia correspondent for *Eastern World*, had been denied entrance. Understandably he was angry, and somehow or other thought it was my fault. I knew nothing of this switch, and Hans, questioned by letter, only said that 'we're all working for a good cause'.

Shirle Gordon was deemed eminently progressive; she had attended the Afro-Asian Writers' Conference in New Delhi in 1956. To this conference the Chinese had sent a prestigious posse of writers. The U.S.S.R. had also sent eminent authors to this conference, and so had the Indian Communist Party. I, being merely a 'bourgeois' scribbler of near-pornography, had of course been ignored.

As a director of the board of *Eastern World* I wrote asking Miss Gordon to come to see me. A most striking, most beautiful, big-boned girl appeared; with an astounding, radiant ripe-wheat wave of gold hair hanging almost to the waist. The effect of such a mass of golden hair in the tropics, where everyone is dark-haired, cannot be gauged by Westerners. It even hit me right in the stomach, and as for what it did to the men ... it drove them wild.

It was all a big mistake, said Shirle. She had been introduced by Clovis Maksoud of the Arab League, and also Arslan Humbaraci, a well-known Turkish-English correspondent, to Hans Taussig, and Hans had asked her to write for the magazine. I realized that susceptible Hans had once more been carried away by his endearing penchant for beautiful women; and who could resist that hair? Shirle told me that she was an Arab scholar, she had sojourned for ten years or more in several Arab countries, Lebanon and Iraq and then Egypt, researching into Islamic culture for an American university. She was a sociologist and interested in the study of Malaysian society. Malaysian, not Malayan, she specified. The term, according to her, applied to a large area encompassing the Philippines, Indonesia, Malaya, and extending right across the Indian Ocean (which President Sukarno of Indonesia always called the Indonesian Ocean) to Madagascar. All these lands, said Shirle, had similar ethnic groups and a fundamentally similar culture.

This theory of a 'greater Malaysia' had already been expounded, as I remembered reading in a magazine, by some American scholar named Pomeroy, resident in the Philippines. Pomeroy was reckoned a 'pro-communist', and there were floating rumours of a 'greater Malaysia' among left-wing circles in Indonesia too.

My curiosity was awakened. Shirle gave up being correspondent for *Eastern World* (but then so did Alex Josey), and settled instead to recruit adoring and willing men to help her establish the Malaysian Sociological Research Institute, and to run a newspaper called *The Seed*, with the motto 'Sow good seed into the sea, and an island will grow'. Later a magazine very handsome, called *Intisari*, a Malay word meaning essence, was to be published by the Institute.

The idea of the Institute appealed greatly to me. Its aim was to promote local research, to publish books describing and analysing conditions in 'Malaysia' by local scholars, for instance, on Islam and its impact on development in Malaya; on the many varied ethnic and cultural groups which here impinged upon each other; on the multitudinous aspects which made this mosaic of Malaya and Singapore so fascinating. There was indeed wide scope for sound scholarship and research; until then, beyond a very few British publications – not bad, but certainly colonial-oriented – there was nothing in the way of a serious team researching into the sociological problems of the area. And yet there were some excellent individuals such as Unku Aziz, the Malay economist who had taken up the cause of the Malay peasantry, and whose articles, books and speeches I followed with great attention, and Professor Fatimi, an Islamic scholar of renown.

Shirle was quickly surrounded by wealthy Arabs of Singapore's business community, and also by Malay religious teachers; for the core of the Institute's research was to be on Islam, and the relationship between Islam and the state, and Islam and the lives of the peoples of Malaysia. A grant from Prince Sadruddin, younger son of the Aga Khan, enabled the Institute to come into being.

I helped the Institute, both financially and in other ways. I had read the

Chinese chronicles of the sea voyages of the fifteenth century that had brought fleets from China to Zanzibar, to trade porcelain and silk and incense for ivory and rhinoceros horn and ebony. I had read everything about Malacca and the visit of the Chinese Admiral Cheng Ho, a eunuch and a convert to Islam. I offered, on my next trip to China, to write a series of articles on Islam in China, and Shirle sounded enthusiastic. A programme for the publication of books was to be launched; also for a symposium of local writers.

Then I heard some rumours about Shirle's political leanings, chiefly from her Arab friends. Nasser had expelled her from Egypt. Shirle maintained to me that it was because she was too progressive. As there was no coherence to the rumours, I decided that I would see how things worked out. Meanwhile, in order to facilitate the workings of the Institute I introduced Linda Chen to be a full-time translator there.

Linda Chen had been a student at the Chinese high school on Bukit Timah Road in Singapore, the one which had been twice assaulted by the police, and where many students and teachers had been arrested. Linda was among those arrested and detained by Special Branch in 1954, and again in 1956. Her husband had then come to me. Linda wanted to read my book on Malaya, ... *And the Rain My Drink*, but Special Branch had refused. I wrote a nice letter to the Police Commissioner, requesting permission to visit Linda in detention and to give her my book, and permission was given with great good nature.

I drove to the detention camp for women (the women's jail), and there were the wardresses, Indian and Eurasian, middle-aged and young, all lined up in beautifully pressed khaki uniforms and with autograph books in hand. They were happy to see me, and the head wardress said, 'You've come to see Linda, our prize detainee. She's no trouble at all.' She called out to Linda, who was sunning herself in the courtyard, and I spoke to her through the grille. Linda was thin, bespectacled, and knew English, Malay and three Chinese dialects. She made one point forcibly during our first talk.

'I am a Malayan of Chinese descent. This is my country, and I have never worked for China or Chinese supremacy.'

'I believe you, Linda, and I know it, but you know how our Chinese origin is used against us, under any pretext.'

The police had tried to deport her to China, but it could not be done because she was born in Malaya of parents born in Malaya, and her Malay was perfect.

I would go to see her several times in jail; then she came out and worked for the Institute for about a year and a half. I paid her salary, as I also paid for several other projects of the Institute. I seldom saw Linda, chiefly because I had nothing to say to her, partly because she was not allowed to cross the Straits and come to Johore Bahru. We never really became friends, although I did help her a little. Jail, I think, had made her suspicious and bewildered. The events that took place after 1960 were to increase her bewilderment. But I think that she also avoided me because, in 1960, I began to quarrel openly with the Malayan Communist Party on the subject of Nanyang University.

Vincent's job in Nepal had ended in February 1958. The road from Kathmandu across the foothills and the plains to India was built. Vincent left the Indian army a few weeks later. In 1958 he managed to come for the first time, for about a week, to Singapore.

His coming was due to Leonard. Leonard was going that summer to England, to take a course in adult education. He had done well, and seemed headed to become the Director of the Department for the whole of Singapore. However, in 1959, owing to the defeat of Lim Yewhock's government and the victory of Harry Lee's PAP, Leonard would lose his job, as the PAP now made a political appointment to the vacancy. I had again asked for a divorce. But Leonard, I think, felt that we might come together again. 'I'll never give you a divorce. Tell that bastard I'll smash his face in if I see him ... Tell the coward to come here and I'll smash his jaw.' Obviously Leonard was a bit irritable that day.

'Very well, I'll tell him.' I cabled Vincent: 'Come to Singapore.' And Vincent came to Singapore. I told him that Leonard wanted to smash his face in. 'I think the time has come for a showdown.'

Loke Wantho loaned us his luxurious penthouse flat so that we had total privacy. From the fifteenth floor of the Cathay building, we saw all of Singapore, its lights and the phosphorescent sea beyond the sequinned city. I drove Vincent early the next morning to the Adult Education Office and went as usual to my clinic. We were to meet for lunch at the Cockpit Restaurant. 'If I have any jaw left,' said Vincent. The Cockpit was the breeding ground and hothouse for all Singapore gossip; I felt the time had come to flaunt my wonderful new man. That would keep everyone in Singapore busy for a while.

I was at the Cockpit early and Vincent came in, pretending to hold his jaw when he saw me. 'You know, Leonard is not a bad chap at all,' said he, grinning hugely. As if I had ever said the contrary!

Vincent and Leonard had arranged to go to dinner that night. Together. They came back very late to Wantho's flat, both slightly drunk, and hoarsely cheerful. I was, of course, extremely mortified. Oh, that complicity, that solidarity of men! 'You're angry because he didn't hit me aren't you?' said Vincent. The next day we three lunched together, at the Adelphi, a widely popular restaurant. My lawyer, Anthony Hills, was appalled. 'You're messing up any chances of a divorce.' But I trusted Leonard and luck.

We then thought up a plan, together with Anthony. Leonard was to go to London in July for his course. There he was to commit adultery (or pretend to) and furnish me with the evidence. Then, said Anthony, the divorce would take place before a court in London, and all silliness and publicity in Singapore or Malaya would be avoided.

'But I don't know any women in London,' protested Leonard. I then decided that I would ask Hans to help in respect of procuring an eligible partner for the misdemeanor to be committed.

Hans had told me one day that he had probably slept with a thousand women. Considering that since then the estimable writer Simenon has claimed a score of ten thousand, Hans was being moderate.

Hans replied with exuberant alacrity. The main difficulty, he wrote, after due consultation with Leonard, was to find a suitable companion. Leonard seemed disinclined to do anything to help. Hans had to find someone more or less respectable, not a streetwalker, as this would not impress an English court and would smack of collusion. Hans had 'just what is needed ... a virtuous lady in Manchester ... ' Because Leonard showed continuing indolence in the matter, Hans promised money to the Mancunian lady, and I cabled him a hundred pounds for all incidentals.

In the course of time Leonard duly posted some hotel bills to me. I handed them to Anthony. The case began in London; not a word leaked into Singapore.

But alas, the lady had taken to Leonard, and refused to recognize him. The case fell through. 'There's only one other way. Leonard must divorce me,' I declared.

Anthony said this was highly dangerous. Leonard might ask for a vast sum of money, and he might get it. But I thought this would not happen. 'You don't understand Leonard; he's an honourable man.'

For the time being, however, as I was extremely busy with other matters, I decided not to press Leonard again. We three would often lunch together, to the puzzlement of all Singapore, and no bitterness or rancour, only good will and amity, were left in our relations.

Nine

The Leap in China: 1959-1960

In 1959 I BEGAN to teach in Nanyang University a three-month course entitled Contemporary Asian Literature. I taught at night, twice a week, for two hours. I was not paid, and at the end the Board, because some members were against my presence, declared that the course could not count towards graduation.

My intention was not only to open the minds of the students to what was happening elsewhere in Asia (colonialism had been only too successful in separating us from each other), but also to teach myself about other Asian countries. I wanted, besides, to have Malays admitted to Nanyang University and to make Malay one of the languages taught there.

But there was strong resentment, even among some progressive students, to admittance of Malays. The new set-up in independent Malaya privileged Malays so heavily that Nanyang University appeared to the Chinese students to be the last refuge for the Chinese-educated stream. Even if a Chinese student obtained the highest examination marks, he often was not granted admission to the new University at Kuala Lumpur, or to Singapore University; a Malay with lower marks would be given a place.

In 1959 the overseas Chinese situation exploded in Indonesia. Sukarno passed edicts to take all retail shops and all commerce out of Chinese hands. This led to pogroms, to racial strife, to the killing of many Chinese, but did not solve Indonesian economic problems; neither would it bring into being, suddenly, an Indonesian-manned web of trade and commerce. Consequently Indonesia would in the following years endure enormous inflation and countryside penury in consumer goods, which substantially eroded Sukarno's prestige and power. It is very risky to destroy one system of distribution and exchange and leave it to fate, heaven, chance suddenly to create the knowledge, the people and the capital, for another one.

This would not happen in Malaya, probably because of Prime Minister Tunku Abdul Rahman. It was due to his singular quality of tolerance (and a very shrewd sense of timing) that the extremists in his party,* who wanted to do the same thing as in Indonesia, were curbed.

* UMNO: the United Malay National Organization.

In March 1959 I was asked by Ed Morrow to participate in his television programme, Small World. I was to discuss China together with Joseph Alsop and Robert Boothby.

Alsop was in America, I was in Hongkong, Boothby in London. The hook-ups worked without a hitch and although I could not see his face, the heartening presence of Murrow filled the studio. I enjoyed the interview very much, expecially as, it seems, I won the debate. This is what the *Reporter* had to say about it on April 2nd, 1959: 'As for the clobbering of Joseph Alsop by Han Suyin, that was history ... The Asian writer caught the American columnist in statements about her China which were so sweeping in their assumptions and so dubious in their analogies that her indignation seemed amply justified. It was a great show.'

In 1974, reading Jo Alsop's columns and articles after he had (at last) visited China, I was glad to note that he seemed to have forgotten the gratuitous and startling assertions he was making in 1958. It takes courage (or amnesia) to contradict oneself so thoroughly.

Harry Sions, editor of *Holiday* magazine, had been delighted with my article, 'Peking Revisited', and now wanted one on Shanghai. He also discussed with me the possibility of a book on Mao. Inadvertently, after a public lecture of mine on China at Singapore University, the newspapers quite wrongly reported that I was going back to China to write a book on Mao Tsetung. I denied this, saying that I did not think I could even see Mao, but acknowledged that of course many people were tempted to write on a man of his stature. But the harm was done.

Apparently in China some middle cadre got hold of a garbled version of this and it was assumed that I had 'arrogantly' said I would interview Mao. And Chairman Mao was sacrosanct, to be mentioned only with the greatest reverence. But in that year of 1959, all was not well in China. There was irritability. Effluvia of this irritability seeped to me through Cousin Pengju in Hongkong, who was bewildered by the refusal of visas, the tone of certain articles. Even if he worked for a Communist newspaper, Pengju and others like him in Hongkong kept open their eyes and ears. They realized that the manner in which certain events were explained by China's propaganda organs was no explanation at all. An English friend of mine put it succinctly: 'China really needs peace, wants peace; the Chinese are honest, loyal and trustworthy, but the language that comes across makes them sound arrogant, boastful, conceited and bellicose.'

I had applied in March 1959, while in Hongkong for the Ed Murrow television programme, for a visa to China, not only because I had in mind writing the article on Shanghai, but also because I had been invited to attend, in Canada, the Twenty-Eighth Couchiching Conference, organized by Toronto University and the Institute of Public Affairs of Canada. The letter of invitation from the President of the Canadian Institute, Murray Ross, was most cordial. The topic of the conference was to be 'Changing Asia' and I was expected to comment on China, on the Leap, the communes. Horrifying tales were circulating (à la Alsop) about the communes. Millions of people, it was said, had died in them; the communes were concentration camps where husbands and wives were segregated, and so on.

It was obvious that the Canadian government regarded the Couchiching Conference as an important platform for soundings about China. Since 1950, the government of Canada had tried to recognize China. In 1956 it had tried again, and now in 1959.

I was refused a visa for China. Why was I turned down? Because of this silly report that I was supposed to write a book on Mao and interview him. Yet my denial had been printed too. I again wrote, asking for a visa. Pengju encouraged me. Every time I wanted to write a letter to Peking, I had to use ways and means to get it delivered through Hongkong, because of the censorship in Malaya. All this was rather nerve-fraying, and above all the growing feeling that perhaps, through the assessment of some cadre who put me down as 'unfriendly', I would never be allowed back to China.

Again I wrote, and cabled Kung Peng. No answer. The Couchiching Conference was taking place from August 8th to 16th; I suggested that I should visit China in July, as I had to be in Canada by August 6th and I needed some time to study and prepare my main speech, which was to be on social changes in China. I worried, worried. In March the Tibetan revolt had burst and the Dalai Lama had fled to India; the whole world was indignant at China's 'aggression', forgetting that Tibet was part of China. One of the best orchestrated propaganda campaigns occurred, at least five major Western countries co-operating, presswise, in this massive onslaught on China. And I would have to go to Canada without adequate preparation: without having seen the communes, which had only come to birth the previous summer; without being able to talk to Kung Peng in Peking about the events in Tibet.

I got a violent attack of psychosomatic colitis; and to cure myself flew to Calcutta. And there was Vincent, at the airport barrier, waiting. It was now June, and I had not seen him since the previous November. 'I am ill,' I said to him. 'I'll make you well,' he said. And just being with him cured me; my pain left me, and I fell asleep on his shoulder in the taxi taking us to the hotel. I slept twelve hours, my first good sleep in some weeks, and Vincent was there, by the bedside, when I woke up.

From Calcutta we took the train for Bhilai. Vincent was now working in a private concern belonging to Spitz, a very irascible Czech–Jew who had left Czechoslovakia for India when Hitler invaded his country. A small spare parts and equipment factory was being set up next to the Bhilai steel plant, which had been erected for the Indian government by the U.S.S.R., and there Vincent worked.

It was 130 degrees in the shade, the air like boiling glue; and I lay and sweated on a mat, sweating out the hours and my anxiety. And to Bhilai came a telegram from Cousin Pengju announcing that a visa had been granted for August, or after October. Pengju wrote: 'Kung Peng was away and then she was ill; her office did not see the necessity for an immediate visa.' 'Peking is a bit isolated emotionally,' I wrote back to Pengju. 'It has no sense of urgency.' Here was the Dalai Lama, giving press conferences and interviews and speaking of the near-annihilation of his country. And there was the Couchiching Conference due in August in Canada ... I had no time now to go to China and then to Canada, and my intestinal troubles returned. I was angry, and wrote directly to Premier Chou Enlai, and after having made the necessary arrangements for the clinic – hiring another medical assistant – I flew off to Toronto.

The Conference was held in a series of bungalows built on the edge of Lake Couchiching. The motto of the Conference was plain living and high thinking. High living and plain thinking would have been more agreeable. But, deliberately, the guests of the Conference lived in spartan conditions, and Murray Ross, looking like a boy scout, plunged into the cold lake water every morning.

The Conference was meant to represent all shades of opinion, and the Canadians had truly exerted themselves in that direction. But as one of them wryly said, 'We have got a Big Brother watching us', meaning America. And the time picked could not have been less propitious. Never had I known public opinion more hostile to China than in 1959, because of the 'invasion' of Tibet, and the 'atrocities' of the communes. I pointed out that there had been no 'invasion' or 'aggression' in Tibet, since Tibet had been recognized even by Nehru as an integral part of China. But so many people were impervious to reasoning, almost hysterical in their verbal violence against China.

The unease and worry I felt about what was happening in China itself increased. Then I suddenly remembered someone I should not have forgotten. Robert Godet.

Robert Godet was a French explorer who had spent some months in the Tibetan monasteries in Kalimpong, on the Indian side of the Himalayas. The Indian army became suspicious of his movements and he was asked to leave; India was at the time coping with a Naga revolt in Assam and did not like Westerners travelling around these territories. Godet had come to Singapore in February 1958, and told me, 'There is going to be war between India and China.' He also told me that the Americans were parachuting weapons, in connivance with the Indians, to Tibetan guerrillas, and training Tibetan 'resistance' fighters in India and in the United States. 'Tell your Chinese friends the whole of Tibet will blow up,' said Godet. I paid no attention; a rupture between India and China appeared to me incredible at the time; yet already in 1958, letters, increasingly abrupt and irritable, were being exchanged between the foreign ministries of India and China. And now, in Couchiching, the hostility of the Indian delegate greatly disturbed me.

The Americans had a galaxy of talent, including Reischauer, United States Ambassador to Japan, an expert on Asia, a pleasant person with a Japanese wife. The recurrent thesis of many participants was the consolidation of the rest of Asia against China, that China must be kept 'under threat ... until a change occurs in its system ... that China must be "compelled" to behave in a civilized (?) way.' This 'pressure', to be exerted on behalf of democracy was the line of the U.S. State Department, and the State Department was determined to win at Couchiching. But the Canadians did manage some opposition. The Americans were unable to get total condemnation of China, despite the help of the Indian representative. But the words 'invasion' and 'bellicose', 'aggressive madmen' and 'hideous massacres and atrocities' hovered like circling buzzards about Lake Couchiching. And I could not shoot them all down.

While I was in Toronto, my sister Marianne began to ring me up, night after night, pouring out her pitiful frenzies, breathing her paranoid phantasms at me like liquor, all the way from Arizona. It gave me insomnia, and again bad bouts of stomach ache which now combined with rather severe haemorrhages to depress me. I flew back via London to India, stopping in New Delhi for a few more days with Vincent. And there I was again comforted and made whole. Despite the growing friction, my friend Natwar Singh, with whom I had had so many delightful rambles when he was a diplomat studying Chinese in Peking, came to see me. I also met the blind writer Ved Mehta of the New Yorker, who was travelling with Dom Moraes, son of the editor of the *Indian Express*. Dom Moraes lived in England and was about to receive the Hawthornden Prize for his poetry. Both of them had called upon the Dalai Lama and interviewed him; Dom described the Dalai's youth, his bewildered, naïve air, short-sighted eyes and striped socks. I knew the socks; they were the kind I had seen woven by the prisoners in the Peking model jail; they were being sold all over China. 'He's brought a lot of gold out of Tibet,' said my friend, the photographer P. N. Sharma, who was still waiting for his Russian girlfriend to be processed out of Moscow and to join him in India.

There was at this time an uproar in the Indian parliament over the news that the Chinese had built a road through the Aksai Chin region, now suddenly considered 'sacred soil of India', although Indian maps printed in Britain before 1950 had the region labelled 'undefined', and not included within India.

Felix Greene landed in Delhi. Felix had been Malcolm MacDonald's secretary, and I had first met him with Malcolm in 1956, when Felix was trying to get to China. He had, so far, not succeeded, although I had introduced him to Pengju. An idealistic, thoroughly sincere man, Felix was greatly agitated by what had happened in Tibet. Although he got the Chinese publications in London, he was unable to understand them, so badly did they present the Chinese view. Felix went to call on the Dalai Lama, and also went to see Krishna Menon, India's Defence Minister, whom I think he had known in England when Krishna was a member of the British Labour Party. Krishna, who lived on strong tea and made immensely long speeches (seven hours was nothing to him), played a magnificent melodramatic scene for Felix, holding his head in his hands, body bowed in agony, and saying, 'Why, oh why are the Chinese doing this to us?' Felix was most impressed, although Vincent snorted gently, knowing his fellow-Indians and their genius for drama. So off Felix went to Burma, to see the Chinese Ambassador there. 'Read what we have published', he was told. Now he entreated me. 'Suyin, do tell them in Peking that they're not doing enough; the whole world is being turned against them.' 'I'll try.' I would also try (and succeed) in getting a visa for him; he would go to China in the summer of 1960.

I did not go to see the Dalai Lama (although I could easily have done so). I contented myself with listening to the Indian officials around me, and I realized how superior to the Chinese they were propaganda-wise. They had, of course, the advantage of writing directly in English, whereas all of the Chinese information was translated – and so badly translated.

I went back to Malaya. And then the border incidents between China and India, which had been multiplying, exploded into an armed clash, and there was an enormous outcry of 'betrayal' and 'invasion' by India and the rest of the world. China's 'expansionism' and 'aggression' were now blatant, according to every newspaper I saw.

I wrote two articles for the *Globe and Mail* of Canada, pointing out how the word 'aggression' was bandied about with little evidence to bolster it. My articles were necessarily limited, and certainly did not defend China. But they were meant to introduce some reason and common sense into the unmanageable hysteria which seemed to have seized so many intelligent people. And four days after writing them I left for China.

If in China in 1957 my doorstep had been 'cold' (which meant that I was officially ignored), it was Arctic Siberia now for me. From the moment I stepped down in Kuangchow it was obvious that I was in profound disfavour. The China Travel Service lady who took charge of me did not smile. She mentioned an interpreter, services to be paid by the day. Steady as a dripping tap, she aligned figures. I told her I did not need an interpreter. She said it was customary. I said I never had an interpreter ...

No aeroplane ticket to Peking was available to me. I would have to go by train. There was no free compartment, only a top berth, with three men. All the hotels in Peking were booked; I must apply for a hotel when I got there.

At breakfast in the train the next morning I saw some Europeans, obviously 'fraternal delegates', eating three eggs and bacon with mounds of toast and marmalade. I asked for two eggs.

The restaurant waiter said, 'Oh, not for you, comrade, it's only for honoured guests from abroad.'

'I'm also from abroad.'

He chuckled. 'I thought you were a Uighur, from Sinkiang. One of us.'

He himself was a Hui, a Chinese Muslim. We became very friendly and he quietly slipped me one egg. Suddenly I felt no longer lonely. We chatted. 'There is a shortage of eggs this year; we keep them for honoured guests.'

In the train corridor stood two fraternal comrades from a communist party of a Western country, surrounded by a respectful cohort of Chinese officials.

'My, oh my, isn't it wonderful?' said one.

'Yes,' said the other, 'now in our country, that factory out there would stink, we'd have a terrible smell for miles around, but here, not a smell.'

'That's socialism in action,' said the other.

The suet of flattery oozed thick from their mouths; the six Chinese who accompanied them (the more people in one's retinue, the higher one's rank) nodded and smiled happily. These were 'friendly' comrades. I recognized one of the two Anglo-Saxons. In fact, I had treated him for some eczematous eruption in Casualty in Hongkong some years ago.

I nudged one of the Chinese on the rim of the gathering. 'I know this honoured guest. I'd like to greet him.'

The Chinese comrade looked me up and down. 'On what grounds do you wish to speak to the honoured guest?'

'On the ground that I was the doctor who treated his illness some years ago.'

The matter was relayed echelon by echelon, until it reached the top Party comrade who then deferentially told the honoured guest who deigned to look at me, and recognized me. He shook hands heartily, but with a shade of condescension. After all, I was only a bourgeois and I had no retinue, so I couldn't be important in China.

'You're here too, good, good. Nice to see you.'

Five years later, the same honoured guest would distinguish himself by his vituperations against China, and especially on the miserable state of the factories during the Leap.

Arrival in Peking; there was no place at the Hsinchiao Hotel. I had to go to a much smaller hotel. No room with bath, of course. No one to carry my luggage. I dropped a note to Kung Peng at the Foreign Ministry. Then waited. During those days of waiting I went out with Wang Wanchun, went to Papa's house, went to see Hualan. Wanchun took me out to a good restaurant, and we drank *maotai*, a very potent spirit from my province.

'Wanchun, there are queues and shortages in the shops.'

'We'll talk about it some other time.'

'How was Khrushchev's visit?' Khrushchev had arrived for October 1st, straight from meeting President Eisenhower at Camp David in September.

'We'll talk about it some other time,' said Wanchun.

From other friends, more loquacious, and from the Western journalists at the Hsinchiao, my impression was confirmed. There was irascibility; tension. There were shortages. 'It's the Leap.' There were rumours also that 'something' had happened. A 'rift' with Russia was now openly discussed. The Western journalists at that time were all for Khrushchev. 'There he came, bouncing down from the plane like a rubber ball ... he'd just made a big scoop ... the Chinese stood like stone figures. Mao did not smile.'

I was received promptly, within four days, at the Foreign Ministry by Miss Chen. Miss Chen was Kung Peng's right hand, a quiet, hardworking girl, but our interview was at first unpleasant. It was obvious that I had done something wrong, unnerving, 'unfriendly'. Said Miss Chen: China was an *organized* country, there was a routine for visas and I had been given a visa. Why did I not come then? I was, by that time, quite ill, I told her. And afterwards it was too late. Miss Chen pointed out that the newspapers had referred to my writing about Chairman Mao. 'How can you believe every word you read in the outside newspapers? Do you believe what they write about you, and didn't you read my denial?' (So I was right in my guess. It was the reference to my possibly writing about Mao which had caused the refusal.) I mentioned Couchiching. 'We are not interested,' said Miss Chen. Neither were they interested in the Small World television show with Jo Alsop. 'Why are you people so arrogant?' I said abruptly. 'Why do you think you don't need people outside to put things straight?' Miss Chen, a very honest and shy person, opened her eyes wide with surprise. She had only done her duty as transmission belt for all the noes, and being a really nice girl, she immediately began, I think, to interrogate herself mutely. Had she, somehow, failed in courtesy? She looked at me, and did not reply. And suddenly the tone changed; she was no longer admonishing a child. We were talking. She took, even if unwillingly, the Small World tape which I gave her.

'Have a look at it. It will give you a better idea of what is being said about China abroad, and why Couchiching was necessary, even if you were not interested.'

'But what we publish—' began Miss Chen.

'It's no use, no use at all,' I said furiously, 'and anyway there is censorship in Malaya, and every time I want to read something I have to fly to Hongkong.'

I grew to admire and really like Miss Chen, who had a thankless job; she was the person who had to 'admonish' and 'guide' newsmen who went wrong; because China never did censor messages or cables sent out. Simply, after a while, the Ministry issued warnings to newsmen considered not to be reporting properly. This duty fell upon Miss Chen.

Three more days, and I now saw Kung Peng, together with Miss Chen. Kung Peng had been very ill and she had also done a stint of labour in the countryside. And now I tried to give them an idea of the kind of emotion that was being propagated against China abroad. They were aware, but not entirely, not of its enormous impact: 'The work of a few reactionaries ... the people are not fooled.' 'Oh yes they are.' But it is difficult to convey an atmosphere.'We have stated correctly all the facts,' Kung Peng kept saying. 'But when people get emotional they ignore facts: and newspapers give them emotion, not facts.'

We talked for a long time, and all was well. I went back to the small hotel quite happily. My doorstep might be cold and I was lonely and not courted, but this did not mean I could not see my friends. The next day there was a room vacant at the Hsinchiao Hotel.

Hualan, who had been ill with a nervous breakdown, was very much better, although her organization still entreated her to rest, and sent her work to her home so that she might not tire herself. I asked her straight-away about Russia. After all, Hualan had been many years in Russia, and her mother was Polish. 'I think if we quarrel I shall feel the world has come to a stop.' But a few days later she said, 'Well, we must go on. Even friends quarrel.'

There was also a rumour of a crisis within the Party involving Peng Tehuai, the Minister of Defence. But this was countered by another rumour that Peng was doing a very hush job somewhere. However, the number of articles condemning 'right-opportunist ideas' among 'some cadres' pointed to some very furious inner debate.

I went to see Anna-Louise Strong. Anna-Louise, an American, was housed in a flat just below Rewi Alley, in the compound of what had once been the Italian Embassy and was now the Peace Council. In 1959 strains were already showing in the Peace Council and its solemn meetings, but neither Rewi nor anyone else would discuss this with me.

Anna-Louise had been in China in the 1920s; she had chronicled the early Revolution in some excellent books. She had known Ho Chih Minh then, and Borodin, and when the massacres of the Communists by Chiang Kaishek started she left China via the Gobi Desert in a car driven by Percy Chen, the ebullient, always happy, unbeatable-at-tennis son of the erstwhile Foreign Minister of China, Eugène Chen, who had been an overseas Chinese and Sun Yatsen's great friend.

Anna-Louise scarcely remembered this epic journey through China, although it was no mean feat to drive right through China when heads were rolling in every city, right through Central Asia and the Gobi Desert, and on through the steppes, across Siberia to Moscow ... which is what Percy had done, bringing Anna-Louise to safety. 'It was unbear-ably hot,' was all Anna-Louise ever said to me about this Marco Polo-ish journey.

Anna-Louise stayed some years in Russia, but in the 1950s fell foul of Stalin and was denounced as a 'spy' and expelled. Immediately her own Party and many of her friends disowned her. 'No one asked my side of the story,' said Anna-Louise. She had been back in China in the 1940s during the war with Japan. She went to the Communist base at Yenan and was received by Mao Tsetung several times, notably in 1946, when she had a very famous interview with him, published as 'The atom bomb is a paper tiger'. And now she was back to live in China, since 1958 a guest of the government, and a most honoured one. Although seventy, she was incredibly active, pouring out articles and books, composing her 'Letter from China', which she sent to hundreds of Americans.

She loudly discounted all talk of a rift between China and Russia as absolute nonsense, and 'imperialist propaganda'. The old lady dreaded being left alone, and Rewi would say, 'Do go and chat with Anna-Louise', and all of us who could do so would drop in.

'I think people are very busy at the moment,' I said.

She asked me if I had heard about shortages.

'Yes, I have.'

'It's true then. But I had thought the harvests were terrific … '

I said, 'I've read Chou Enlai's report on China's 1959 economic plan. He mentions strains and problems and serious natural calamities.' In such a tremendous Leap Forward there were bound to be problems cropping up.

'When has anything new been easy or successful the first time? China is carving out a new road for mankind,' said Rewi Alley, who had come to join our talk.

The news of the poor harvest had by now solidified. It was 'quite bad', which meant rotten. There had been much drought in the north, floods in the south, and the cotton crop was affected. As for meat, it was becoming scarce. But one reason for its scarcity was that the peasants in the communes, in their delirious joy that 'communism has now come', had stuffed themselves with vast amounts of pork flesh, each peasant eating and carousing. 'Why save? The government will provide. This is communism.'

I visited the ten large public buildings erected in Peking to commemorate the tenth year of the People's Republic, 1959. Kung Peng told me she had worked on some of the marble tiles of the Great Hall of the People, polishing and polishing them, and 'Now I look at all that expanse of floor, and at the marble pillars, and I wonder which are the tiles I polished,' she said.

In railway sheds, in the courtyards of houses, in the basketball grounds of schools, I saw the relics of small brick furnaces; they had been used to make steel in the great steel drive of 1958. They were now partly ripped up, but black soot still encrusted their brick bases and a pipe or two lay forlorn athwart the ruin. It had been a truly fantastic endeavour: everyone had been making steel. 'There was soot all over the streets and all over the city; at night it was like a million fireflies. The masses now understood better the need for steel and for industrialization.' My friends said this but they also had reservations. Each of them had made steel; but what was the point of making it in these small, primitive, hand-built stoves? 'But even mistakes are necessary ... sometimes we learn more through making mistakes ... '

'It's to wrest our people, by the only methods at our command, out of feudalism and into the modern era,' said Third Brother. He too had made steel, and 'it was hard to get the soot out of my hair ... the city ran out of soap.'

Even the beautiful Madame Soong Chingling had made steel, setting an example. And millions of schoolchildren had made steel.

Looking at the ineffective small craters which littered the streets, I wondered. Were they, had they really been educative in their starkness? Well, perhaps. As I walked on and on, an immense warmth and protectiveness came upon me. 'It's fantastic, magnificent, appalling ... and also perhaps idiotic ... I don't know ... no one else would have the courage to try this ... you're trying to tell all of us that we must rely on ourselves, do everything the hard way because there is no other way, because we're going to be let down ... ' Thus I apostrophized my love, the faceless multi-millioned, whose courage and fortitude gripped my heart; and I both loved and of course feared, because its immensity would certainly swallow me. 'I'm with you, with you.' What could I do to speed up the process of maturation? I then had a brief, elusive vision of what it implied: one quarter of humanity, informed, intelligent, not submitting to fate and to the vagaries of tyrants ... was this too much to expect? 'Teach me to feel things correctly,' I said to the small brick base with its derelict pipe. The Westerners in the Hsinchiao Hotel had not stopped laughing at the steel drive and I could not bear their laughter. 'It may be silly, but at least you're trying, trying to make the sun and the moon shine in a new heaven. Silly or not, I'm with you.'

'Our tenth year is not too lucky a one,' said Hualan, brewing coffee (a strangely flavoured one, an early crop from Hainan Island) in her living room. Tibet, Indonesia, India, and of course the unspoken, indigestible morsel, the trouble with the U.S.S.R. In Indonesia almost two million Chinese had been deprived of a living, and several hundred thousand were being repatriated to China in Chinese-chartered vessels. Yet many of those leaving had been born in Indonesia. Chen Yi had greatly exerted himself, with skill and patience, finally settling the matter of the Chinese in Indonesia, but of course it had been an added burden and expense on China when resources were strained by the Leap.

Hualan denied the rumour that major insults had been exchanged behind closed doors between Khrushchev, when he had come to Peking from seeing President Eisenhower, and his Chinese hosts. 'These are bad people who tell such things.' On the contrary, at the ballet evening Khrushchev and Mao had exchanged pleasantries about the beauty of the dancers, pleasantries which had left the translators round-eyed with shock.

I walked the streets and noted the first faint signs of tension, lassitude. People were thinner, they bustled less. Rations were being cut. There was a lot of cabbage being sold, but little else. The waiter in a restaurant reproved me for leaving some grains of rice at the bottom of my rice bowl.

I tried to get a haircut at the Peking Hotel, but was turned out. 'Comrade, this is only for honoured guests from outside.' I telephoned my family. Fourth Brother was in Manchuria, Third Brother was busy ... I received a message, a certain Comrade Ku would see me; I was to go to his residence at five p.m. He seemed to be an important official, and would decide on a programme for me.

I duly arrived, around ten minutes to five; a woman servant opened the door. She seemed to recognize me when I murmured, 'Comrade Ku asked me to come', and showed me into a tiny study, where I sat. Next to the study were presumably Mr Ku's lodging quarters, for I could see another room with a narrow bed, a table and a chair. I sat and waited. And suddenly there was some commotion in the courtyard. I could hear the maid's voice: 'But she is waiting inside.'

Mr Ku erupted into the study. 'What are you doing in this room? You should never have come here.'

'Your servant put me here,' I said.

'It's a mistake,' he shouted. 'I have been waiting for you at the door.'

He ushered me across the courtyard into the living room, which was fairly large, with a big velvet-covered sofa and chairs. He was quite angry and our conversation was painful.

'I heard you want to go to Shanghai.'

'Yes, I do.'

'You must read our material on Shanghai. It is now a major industrial city. Can you do translations?'

'I don't think so ... people usually translate me.'

'Translations are important. You should train yourself to translate.'

For a moment I thought he was offering me a job at the Foreign Language Press. He then began to explain 'policy'. 'We distinguish between enemies and friends. Facts are facts. We always rely on facts.'

'But there is also compromise,' I began.

'Never,' he shouted, 'we shall never compromise on principles.' He thought I was pleading for 'compromise' with Soviet Russia. 'We have the policies of Chairman Mao. We shall never compromise on these.'

The reason for my use of the word 'compromise' was because that very afternoon, at Hsinchiao Hotel, I had met some foreign diplomats and all of them had talked of Chinese 'intransigence'. 'The Chinese are behaving like arrogant mandarins now that Khrushchev wants to come to an understanding with the U.S.' The 'irascibility' of many officials in Peking was commented on. 'The Chinese seems to have a bad case of nerves,' said an Englishman. Other newsmen complained: 'We can't make contact with anyone ... there's a sound barrier as well as an emotion barrier, no one gets through. The Great Leap has failed ... and because of the border trouble with India, China hasn't got a friend in the world today ... not even Russia. Some kind of compromise *must* be found to get out of the impasse.'

I had seized on the word 'compromise', used it with Mr Ku, and had greatly angered him. 'We shall never compromise on principles,' he repeated. 'You do not seem well-informed about our policies, you should read more, listen to our radio broadcasts.'

I forbore to tell him that radio or not, I could not *understand* what I read outside; only when I read the Chinese newspapers and was steeped in China's own atmosphere did it all begin to make excellent sense. It did not make sense to me abroad ... But Mr Ku now looked at his watch, and we shook hands and I left. It had rained and the lane was narrow. I walked close to the wall, but a large black car went by and sloshed me with mud. Mr Ku, going to his next appointment. I became furious. I rang up Wanchun and told him about it. 'Old Ku is a good guy really, he is just a little stuck in his ways,' said Wanchun, who had now done eight months of manual labour and had got over his fear of denouncing Party cadres. He cheered me with funny stories, then told me soberly that there was a terrible drought in the north: 'That's why I think the winter will be bad.' A day later I was on my way to Shanghai.

All along the railway to Shanghai, I saw the impetus of the Leap Forward. Electric pylons bestriding the land, and the new shape of the fields, straight-edged; horizon-reaching rectangles where I remembered curvaceous small plots; a new geometry, defined by tree-lined canals. And new brick buildings with chimneys, obviously factories; and in every station enormous piles of machinery, steel rods, pumps, steel rails, awaiting transport to inland destinations. This impression of a frenetic upsurge in industrial building was confirmed during my ten days in Shanghai. Despite the errors of the Leap, the shortages owing to the agricultural disasters (which would become tragic in 1960–1), the Leap did achieve its main goal, which was accelerated industrial development.

All along the way I could see that the reports of 'natural calamities' were not exaggerations. Within the next two years, almost 70 per cent of the land, both in the north and the south, and even in Szechuan, would suffer from the vagaries of the weather. I crossed the Yellow River that October and missed it, as I had missed it on my way to Peking. For it was no more than a sand waste, with a narrow trough of water in its midst. And no one in the train said, 'We are now crossing the Yellow River.'

It was on this trip that I began to tell myself that I must study economics; try to relate what I read to what I saw. 'It is an obligation to acquire knowledge,' I repeated to myself. Only then would I be able to speak with coherence and authority. I would begin to teach myself, tracing first the history of the Industrial Revolution in the West, comparing the dislocations and the sufferings it had imposed upon Europe (for it was undoubtedly an agonizing process, causing enormous suffering to the people when it took place) and what was happening in China. And what had taken so long in Europe was now being telescoped into a few years, two or three decades, in China. Hence the hurry, the frenzy and the setbacks, the failures. Yet unless we in China hurried, we would fail.

And so to Shanghai; and immediately the sensation that here was a city at the heart of the Leap itself, an industrial city producing, producing. Not only because of the posters and the slogans and the exhortations: 'Walk on two legs', 'Self-reliance', but because of an air of excitement and well-being. The stores were full of manufactured goods and peasants walked and bought in the large department stores. Shanghai would not suffer as much as the other areas from the agricultural disasters which would be heaped upon the land for the next two years; both because its own countryside and communes would be relatively unharmed by natural calamities, and because it was working full blast on industrialization, its own industrial expansion and that of many sites inland. Already many thousands of able Shanghai workers were to be found scattered over wide areas of China; whenever a new industry was coming up, there one could find the thin, clever faces of Shanghai and hear the soft sibilant atonal Shanghai dialect, in Manchuria and in Szechuan, in Shensi and in Sinkiang. They spread technical knowledge, helping to train the millions of technicians required for the second Five Year Plan. The second Five Year Plan to end in 1962, was by definition to be over-fulfilled before time. Everywhere in the factories of Shanghai I heard of the plan having been over-fulfilled.

The most impressive thing about Shanghai was the new suburbs, forming satellite cities around it; there would be ten of them, each housing 300,000 to 500,000 people. Where there had been slums and fetid ponds were now parks, avenues with central flower beds, lined with buildings of new grey and red brick, four storeys high, flats for workers and their families, schools and hospitals and department stores.

Food shortages here were not apparent, nor was there that vague stir of unease which had begun in the north. But there were some itinerant pedlars on the streets selling crab claws and small dumplings, and the cadres turned a blind eye on this individual enterprise. For the pleasure of the ambiance, I queued with others for crab claws. None were left when my turn came. But the restaurants were full and well-stocked. And remembering the rationing in England, during the war, when many old people, alone, quietly and gently starved to death on rations, I thought that perhaps we too in China would see this, unless the next harvest was good. When it began to drizzle I was happy, for an autumn drizzle is excellent for the crops. And all round me people were saying, yes, there is rain, it is good for the crops, so that their main preoccupation, which was the harvest, would surface and their faces light up with quiet joy, and we all knew we were thinking the same way, were apprehensive in the same manner. In the communes round Shanghai different kinds of hardy and more productive rice were being tried, and the weather and its vagaries were discussed with great abandon. And flocks of sparrows went undisturbed, and films were shown praising 'useful' birds.

I visited at least a dozen factories, large and small. I saw a small one where pumps and other equipment were being made by old workers who had come out of retirement to help in the Great Leap. Everywhere this had happened; people coming to volunteer. By dint of energy and handcraft and patience these old men were producing some machinery; they chiselled and planed with small, inadequate hand tools. Their faces, lined and tired, were beautiful with quiet faith. Truly they believed that soon, soon, want would be over for ever, and plenty would come, freedom from hardship and penury ... and they worked towards that new human freedom to come. 'We've been through the bad old times, we never want them again.' ABOLISH SUPERSTITION, UNFETTER THE MIND, shouted all the walls of the factories. DARE TO TEACH WATER TO CLIMB MOUNTAINS was carved on rock along roads we drove along. And everywhere in large characters was painted the motto of the Leap: TO DO THINGS FASTER, BETTER, MORE ECONOMICALLY BUT WITH GREATER RESULTS.

'Like ants,' said Comrade Liu, who took me around, 'gnawing a bone. We have to keep on gnawing at difficulties and obstacles, to make them disappear ... '

Poetry came out from the people. Everywhere, in the city and in the communes. Poems of the Leap. And there were the women, now so visible, everywhere, working in the small factories in each lane; almost every small factory had a big story to tell. One grandmother led all the grandmothers in her street to start a small repair shop; now they were producing electric spare parts. 'We all want to do something to build up our country.'

The eradication of prostitution in Shanghai had taken almost eight years, 'and we are still continuing with the movement,' said frail Miss Hu, who was in charge of the campaign. There had been altogether forty thousand registered prostitutes, and about the same number of unregistered, in the city of Shanghai before Liberation. 'There cannot truly be a women's liberation movement which does not also try to eradicate this most criminal and shameful blot upon womanhood,' said Miss Hu. Prostitution could only be eradicated through 'mass consciousness' of its evil. 'Some women, a very small percentage, like being prostitutes, or perhaps get used to it and see themselves as nothing else. Sometimes we talk to them all night, we do not let them go until we feel that an impression has been made.' Like water denting stone, the re-education programme went on and on, undiscouraged by temporary lapses. As for the pimps and the brothel keepers, 'They are the guilty ones. At first we talked to them, asking them to close the brothels voluntarily ... we gave them six months in which to reform, then in November 1951 we issued our last warning. As you know, we have a system of graduated warnings. Many pimps and brothel keepers thought we were weak because we spoke softly,' said prim Miss Hu. They were being re-educated through labour; and some of them, the worst, were shot.

But reforming a prostitute also meant setting up a social system in which prostitution would be almost impossible, and this meant that both men and women must be conscious of the degradation of the human being that prostitution implies. It also involved moving the prostitutes away from Shanghai, where they were known; finding them work, getting them into the normal circuit of normal women, even getting them married. 'The prostitute is fundamentally frightened, frightened of everything.' More than 90 per cent of them were girls from the countryside lured to the big city of Shanghai by promise of good jobs and money in factories, and then sold into prostitution; or little girls, sold because of family want, in times of famine. 'Most of them cannot read or write. They are very emotional, getting angry, screaming, kicking, breaking things ... but we never lose our tempers, we never shout, we are patient, always, always we exhort.' Miss Hu smiled like a small tired angel.

When the prostitutes begin to change mentally, they have crises and nervous breakdowns. 'When people go from one identity to another, they try to cling to what they think they are ... they feel they are losing themselves, when really all they lose is a state of mind and a few habits.' (I know exactly what Miss Hu is saying: have I not gone through this too? Only two years ago the threat of a change of identity was painful, unthinkable.) 'So we have to gauge when the breaking point comes. It is when they appear most violent, hostile, abusive, when outwardly it seems they will never change. That is the death agony of the old self. Then there is a period of semi-adaptation, a stuporous calm.' (Was I now in a stuporous calm?)

'They become interested in new things, conscious of having another function in society. They grope towards a new being. But which one? How, where do they fit in? Can they ever hope to be just like anyone else? There are vast terrors in them still ... most prostitutes have no sense of the future. And now, suddenly, they have to think ahead. That is when one has to be so cautious, so gentle, not to put them off ... We take them to parks, to enjoy flowers and birds and trees, and to films, and to people who do not know what they are and treat them like anyone else. We make them participate in public campaigns such as that for planting trees and flowers in the parks, or go to sewing and repair co-operatives with other women who treat them as equals, who think they are housewives...' The process at its shortest took two years, sometimes five or six. 'But we have patience and time, oh, plenty of time,' said Miss Hu. 'We never give up, even if it takes ten years or more.' And never, said she, must there be punishment or ostracism. 'They are victims. they need care, affection ... '

Linked to the eradication of prostitution was that of venereal disease. Once again, it had to be done by the most widespread propaganda, urging people to come to the clinics for cure. 'No one is punished; on the contrary, people are rewarded for coming up voluntarily.' Everyone suffering from venereal disease was treated free of charge, and then told to speak to others about it. This is what the Shanghai hospital doctors told me. As I knew already, the American doctor George Hatem – in Chinese Ma Haiteh – had been one of the chief medical experts in charge of this most successful drive.

Another clean-up was that of capitalists; and since Shanghai had been a great centre for business, it was appropriate that I should meet there efficient, handsome Mr Yung, who wore a Western suit and a very nice tie. He was now the manager of the factories he had once owned. He and his wife lived in their former house, a mansion with carpets, beautiful furniture and a large garden. The Cultural Revolution affected Mr Yung and his family, as it did every family in China. He had to leave the beautiful house he lived in and was reduced to a small worker's flat. But after two years of discomfort Mr Yung was given back his house. He is as neat and dapper today as when I saw him in that October of 1959. He is a member of the National People's Congress, a member of the People's Consultative Conference, a highly respected adviser on managerial matters, and represents one of the eight non-communist parties.

'It was difficult to adapt at first,' he said to me in October 1959, speaking of his first ten years under the communists. 'I wanted to resist, to burst out, sometimes to shout ... but always I would talk it over with someone. I thought: who comes first, my people and my country, or me? When I remembered the humiliations we endured when we were weak and semi-colonized, there was no doubt in my mind. However I may dislike certain things, the Communist Party is, by and large, creating a strong, prosperous New China. No one will insult us again. And so my private resentments, which appeared large and important at first, became trivial. I grew into a feeling of oneness with others; of sharing in everything, the good and the bad. I got peace of mind.'

That is what Mr Yung said twenty years ago, and having survived, he has proved his indestructibility.

One afternoon Comrade Liu came to say, 'You must now go back to Peking. Premier Chou Enlai wishes to see you.'

I was on the train that very evening; for with the small autumn rain soaking the land and fogging the fields, the aeroplane (which flew low and followed the markings of roads and railways) might not take off. I was in Peking by the end of the next day, and Comrade Ku was at the station, carrying a large fur coat. 'We were afraid you might be cold; you do not have enough clothes.' I was sorry that I had ever been angry with him. It was not his fault that his car had splashed mud on me. And I was such a maverick, not fitting into any pattern at all, no wonder I disconcerted Comrade Ku, and so many others.

Back at the Hsinchiao Hotel, I was told not to go out without leaving a message saying where I could be reached. The Premier was extremely busy, but would see me as soon as possible.

Kung Peng's friend Wu Chienta, a newsman who was also a student of foreign affairs, came to talk to me. I liked his company very much. He was a quiet, thoughtful young man with a steady intelligence; and we would entertain a lively correspondence in the course of the next twenty years. Wu was eminently reliable, had an astonishing memory and never misinterpreted any conversation or added any colour, weight or bias to anything I told him. In fact, he would correct me gently when I was inaccurate. We talked a great deal in the next few days, while I waited for Chou Enlai to be free, about foreign reactions to Chinese news coverage and information. 'It's most important to understand other people's psychological reactions,' said Wu. 'We don't have much opportunity to do so at present.'

The Hsinchiao Hotel was full of bad news about the harvests and the coming winter. 'There's going to be famine,' said one diplomat with a broad smile. I pored over the figures which had been published; the percentages. I could not understand them. I clung to Chou Enlai's casual words in his major report on the Chinese economy at the Leap: the *verified* figures, the *adjusted* plans ... conceding that there had been inflated, unreliable reports, and that goals and targets had to be cut down for the future.

'Please, Hualan, tell me, how bad are things?'

'I don't think they are so bad, but there is certainly something wrong with the statistics.'

'I heard from the diplomats that the bureau of statistics had simply stopped working in 1958.'

'They did not have the techniques or the ability to cope with the reports which came up from below, and which appeared phantasmagorical to some of them.'

Thus a coal mine had reported mining in one day as many thousand tonnes of coal as it had mined in the previous year, and one man had had great praise lavished upon him because he boasted he could grow ten tonnes of wheat on a piece of land the size of a small room ...

'People got carried away by their own enthusiasm,' said Hualan. 'They really believed that with three years of hard work they could magically transform the land. And many wonderful things have been done. But of course, temporarily, there was dislocation. No weighing machines in the new fields, and the fields were by then too large, so that no one really knew how much was produced. There were no bins to store the grain. The cadres just guessed at the harvest; much of it had not been harvested but left lying because the peasants had then been mobilized either into steel-making or into canal digging, and seventeen million people from the countryside had streamed into the new factories that were being built everywhere. In the south the banana trees were cut down in order to grow rice, and bananas were a staple crop producing ample income for many communes.

'We've also had an ultra-left wave,' said Hualan. Suddenly a rumour had spread: 'Communism is here.' And some communes had gone into an orgy of eating; killing pigs and ducks, and eating and eating. 'The government will give it back to you, this is communism.' Others had gone on a spree of buying, using all the funds they had been loaned by the government to purchase television sets, to erect cinemas. They had instituted free food, free clothes, free everything, including hair cuts. As a result, they had no reserves left.

And there had been a frenzy of work. 'Some cadres really had no common sense. They drove the work teams. Work, work, work.' A young man whom Hualan knew had worked around the clock, as a volunteer; and his heart had failed and he had died. 'Now we take death very seriously, as you know,' said Hualan. Within a week the most stringent orders had been given. Now everyone was guaranteed eight hours sleep.

There had been another anti-intellectual wave, when the peasants and the workers had been praised as 'the real heroes'. 'Of course they are heroic, but they don't know everything,' I said rashly. 'One must not pour cold water on the red hot fervour of the masses,' said Wanchun to me somewhat nervously. 'Does that mean no one can say: But it won't work?' He did not reply.

The engineers, the technical experts, the agricultural experts, knew that some of the claims made were sheer fantasy; they kept quiet. 'Because no rigorous scientific appraisal was made in time, there was no control over these massive projects ... and the leaders were given all the wrong figures for many weeks.' But none of my friends would vouchsafe an explanation for this.

Hualan was having a small argument with her department because she wanted to change the sentence in an article: 'People who see this monument will faint and swoon with pleasure.' 'People who read this sentence,' said Hualan, 'will die of laughter.' I do not know whether she succeeded in changing it. I do know that several efforts of mine to change such confections ended always in dismal failure.

Again I would press Hualan about the U.S.S.R.

'I can only say that my Polish cousin has written a letter. She says Polish youth is now demoralized. And that in Russia people are getting away from socialism; they have been infected with the devil of "immediate enjoyment". They want good clothes, good things.' And the Russian collectives were not working well.

'Do you think the communes will work in China?'

'They're bound to work. It's a different system, and we have so many more poor peasants than Russia has. To our peasants the commune is an unbreakable iron bowl of rice.'

At the theatre, all around me, men and women were falling asleep in their seats. Tired and cold. 'We've all been told to rest more, and this winter, many offices will only operate half a day,' said Hualan. This state of affairs was to become more pronounced in 1960 when food became scarce. Hualan, her relatives, and many others voluntarily cut down their own rations of rice by one or two kilogrammes a month.

'There won't be any intellectuals to labour in the communes this winter,' said Wanchun. He had enjoyed his months in a commune. 'I learnt to lead a buffalo to water and to plant rice ... when I came home, I realized how selfish I had been, letting my wife make up the fire, peel vegetables, cook, wash ... now I help her. I feel ashamed that I had no eyes to see her labour.' He had also accompanied Chairman Mao, who indefatigably had gone into the provinces to find out what was really happening. 'You should have seen the Chairman, the concern on his face. He sat in the house of a very old woman, listening to her complaints, as if she were his mother.'

Third Brother came to see me. He told me that because of the food situation 'undesirables', that is, people with no occupation, were having to leave the city and be resettled in villages. The villages ate much better; they ate what they produced. It was the surplus that fed the cities. 'There isn't much surplus this year,' said Third Brother.

'Did anyone try to give warning in good time, when things went a bit out of control?' I asked my friend Yu, a biologist. He was studying insect pests and had been away for months in the rural areas, training peasants in recognizing and dealing with pests.

Yu smiled, turning his head away from me, letting the words float like gossamer upon the cold air, as if they did not belong to him. 'People who tried to warn about excessive zeal would again be called rightists ... and you know that some cadres do not distinguish between bourgeois pessimism and sabotage ... '

Perhaps that was the reason for this new campaign I had read about in the newspapers, about 'right opportunists' spreading defeatism ...

This is what I thought at the time. I did not know that this new political campaign was due to the clash which had occurred in August 1959, at an important Party meeting when the Minister of Defence, Peng Tehuai, had written a 'letter of opinion' and circulated it, and spoken against the failings of the Leap. This was considered an attack upon the whole concept of the Great Leap Forward and the communes. But at the time no one in Peking told me anything about Peng Tehuai. It was a 'state secret'. It would be 1967 before what had occurred that August would be officially published.

Then Chou Enlai was free, and I was fetched to go to the Great Hall of the People. Kung Peng was there, and also some other officials, but I only saw Chou Enlai. He did not smile, and he looked a little tired, but he was as usual most courteous, though his brief look at me seemed to weigh me up to wonder whether I could ... what? Twice in the next fifteen years he would again look at me with that appraising glance. Each time there had been a crisis which was state secret, known only to the leadership, whispered among the middle cadres. Perhaps Chou Enlai thought: What does she know?

Such interviews have an unspoken protocol. From the moment one passes the welcoming screen with its painting of a pine tree, placed across the entrance and cutting the room from view, every gesture and word, from preamble to introduction to core of the matter to conclusion, seems almost, at least in my memory, like a ballet, whose choreography is well understood by host and guest. I recall today what Chou Enlai said in those many hours that he so generously gave me. Hours of such moment and reaching import; talk which went from policy to human speculation; no secret revelations; no directives or commands. He never departed, even when angry, from an equable, courteous exchange of views; and his words seemed casual and effortless, and were all the more to be pondered. He never assumed that irksome stance of a 'teacher', yet Chou was teaching me all the time. 'Perhaps you will think again about this point', was all he would say when I looked blank. He always took a subject to pieces, dissecting with precision its several component parts and tackling them one by one. He was never vague, never did he ramble. His brilliance resided precisely in that what he said sounded so simple, and yet he would always grasp the intricate details in a discussion and reassemble them in another pattern so that what appeared to be one argument would suddenly become quite different. Never did he raise his voice or become angry, except once, at a Frenchman who proved both arrogant and stupid, and then Chou, who had been held down over four hours by the Frenchman, finally did show a little temper, in his curt goodbye.

And his adversaries, those who had come to overwhelm him with their ingenious arguments and sought to bully or to trap him, would find themselves, suddenly, with their most perfect contraptions of thought collapsing sand castles half melted by the tide, unrecognizable.

Chou started equably, as we drank our tea, about my father's death, expressing condolences and asking me whether all arrangements had been appropriate. He then went on to say that he was sorry there had been so much delay in granting me a visa that summer. Kung Peng was absent and the office had not acted swiftly. 'Oh no, Prime Minister, it was I, I was far too impatient,' I replied. For now I knew what a year of torment and catastrophe it had been for China. The harvest failures; the drought and the floods and the insect plagues; the abrupt cancellation in June, by the Russians, of agreements to help China in nuclear and scientific research; the Tibetan revolt in March and the border clashes with India through the summer and the autumn; and attacks (the launching of parachute troops) by Chiang Kaishek from Taiwan — all this and more, which I would realize some months, some years later.

And all of it was upon the shoulders of Chou Enlai. Always, he would have to perform rescue operations; try to salvage, to patch up and to save; try to implement new policies and push China forward, forward in her development ... I wanted to say, 'It is you, Prime Minister, who carries the burden of it all. And you have to work to set aright all that has gone wrong. And none of it has been your fault. You have kept your head, but others lost theirs, and now you have to be careful to give them face ... ' For Chou Enlai had said, 'We, the leadership, shall take full responsibility for what has gone amiss.' And always he would be the one to apologize, and he was apologizing to me for what was the fault of some clerk in the Department of Information.

Neither was it altogether the fault of the literal-minded middle cadres, however much they irritated me with their blockheaded fear of taking responsibility. Upon them had fallen an avalanche of directives, sometimes totally contradictory ones. They had had to interpret and implement them 'correctly' and they had been told not to 'pour cold water upon the red hot enthusiasm of the masses', and so they had duly whipped up fervour and enthusiasm, and they had excoriated as rightists anyone who enjoined caution; and all this was also responsible for some of the chaos that had ensued. For instance, the fact that the big steel-making campaign had coincided with harvest time so that millions of peasants had gone off to make steel, and millions of tonnes of grain had been left to rot on the fields.

'Last time we met,' said Chou Enlai, 'you had many questions. Have you any questions now?'

'Yes, Prime Minister. Why did you let the Dalai Lama go? You could have stopped him at any time.'

Of course, said Chou Enlai. By deploying troops of the Lhasa garrison and other garrisons along the roads, the Dalai Lama and his suite could have been stopped. It was known that there was a plot to get the Dalai Lama away to India; in fact, a month or so before the event, an Indian newspaper had already announced such a possibility.* But any military action might have caused the Dalai Lama physical injury, and this would have seriously affected the Tibetan people. 'We gave him a chance to make up his mind.' The Dalai Lama was young. 'We have kept open his positions as Vice-Chairman of the National People's Congress, and as Chairman of the Committee for the Autonomy of Tibet. We have stated we believe he was ill-advised by his entourage.' The revolt had had only partial support from the population, and now there was peace and order in Lhasa.

We went on to the question of the border trouble with India, and to Nehru. Chou spoke in measured tones of map discrepancy, spreading map after map between us. All colonial privileges had come to an end with Liberation in 1949, and the British, who had 'manipulated' Tibet for a long time had had to give up. Nehru had understood this in 1954, 'but now, somehow, he chooses not to understand it,' said Chou Enlai. Should

* See *Lhasa, the Open City* by Han Suyin.

I consult Nehru's own autobiography, published in England, I would find, in the last edition of 1956, that the map tracing in the book showed the border where the Chinese said it was, and not where the Indian government now claimed it to be. Was it possible that Nehru had not checked his own book, and the map published inside it?

Chou Enlai was obviously puzzled by Nehru's character and his reactions. He assumed that Nehru would react in the way an Asian (meaning a Chinese) would react; and he debated whether Nehru himself was fully in control of what he was doing, or whether he was driven to it by the 'imperialists'. I think that the parliamentary flux and furore of the Indian Lok Sabha★ had escaped Chou Enlai.

The whole trouble, said Chou, was that Asians knew too little about each other. Whereas the West had a pool of 'China experts' and 'Indian experts', we had no such pool of experts in China. Despite geographical proximity, India and China had not had any direct contact during the many decades of colonial domination. This must be remedied, because India and China were the two great nations of Asia, twin pillars of Bandung, the hope of the Third World nations. Imperialism, said Chou Enlai (not calling it 'American' imperialism) wanted to provoke bad feeling between the two. 'But we are not frightened. We do not want war for a single day, but if we are attacked, we shall defend ourselves.'

Some people, said Chou Enlai, did not see clearly that 'imperialism does not change'. They put their hopes in what they called peace; in meetings which dangerously compromised socialism and the national independence of emergent nations. *Some* people even talked about a certain new spirit which would save the world ... 'On this point, *some* people have illusions,' said Chou Enlai.

Nothing could have been clearer. Chou was referring to Khrushchev; to Khrushchev's Camp David meeting with Eisenhower; to Khrushchev's speech, praising the 'new spirit' of Camp David. Khrushchev was even then proclaiming that this was the start of an era of peace 'for the whole world'.

In 1959 Mao Tsetung and Chou Enlai saw in this new spirit yet another attempt at a division of power and world supremacy between the two super powers. And it was plain that China might be the victim of such a strategy.

But at the time I too believed in the Camp David spirit. I too, because I detested Stalin's excesses, had been enthused by Khrushchev's glib words about peace. I thought there would be an end, for ever, to atomic war

★ The Indian lower house of Parliament.

257

threats ... 'I too believe that this Camp David meeting is a good thing for the world, Prime Minister,' I said to Chou Enlai.

The silence that followed was one of total immobility. The secretary who took notes froze with pen in air. Mr Ku stared at me with horror in his eyes. Chou Enlai's face looked suddenly more tired, a creeping of small wrinkles which began around the eyes. But there was no anger in his voice when he said, 'We do not think so.' Peace was concrete, not an abstract proposition, and there was no evidence that there would be disarmament; on the contrary. Compromise must have its limits, but it did not mean selling out the peoples of the Third World. 'If it does, then it is not peace, only submission and servility. We must decide now whether all the peoples of the world have a right to their national liberation or whether they will be slaves for a thousand years ... on this point we shall never compromise.'

Now I understood what the Western journalist had called 'Chinese intransigence'.

Chou Enlai had another engagement, and he saw me to my car, bowing formally, but without a smile, without that small repressed grin which lit up his face. Others climbed into the car with me, including Mr Ku. All were silent as we drove back to the hotel and I suddenly perceived with all my body's cells their tiredness, the strain under which they laboured. I said, 'I know what I'm going to do. I'm going to Delhi to see Nehru.'

I was back at the Hsinchiao, and one Western newsman had left an English newspaper for me; on the first page a large photograph of Nehru, a hunched and pacing man, the world a great weight on his shoulders. 'A sad and distraught man ... saddened by China's treachery', was the caption. And it mentioned that it was his birthday. I sent a cable to Nehru for his birthday; this would prepare the ground for a meeting. And I left the next day for Hongkong and for India.

Ten

Jawaharlal Nehru: 1959-1964

I FLEW TO Delhi on November 22nd, stopping only for two days in Malaya. Vincent was leaning on the airport barricade, watching me walk in the bright winter sun to the customs building. 'My life consists of hanging around airports, waiting for your plane to come in.'

Now I understood why Vincent had resigned. I realized the sacrifice that it had meant for a man who had been seventeen years an officer. He had done it for me. Even today I cannot quite understand why, why he gave up his career, because he did it so naturally, as if it was an easy thing to do. 'You've taken Nehru's blue-eyed boy away from him,' said an Indian diplomat to me. For Nehru had paid much attention to Vincent's road building, which was of strategic import. Vincent had built all the Himalayan highways in Kashmir, to secure the mountain bastions of India (ironically enough, also against a potential Chinese threat). He then had built the road from Nepal across the foothills to India, ensuring thus a semi-dependency for Nepal, the landlocked kingdom, upon Indian goodwill and Indian goods.

'Why the hell didn't you tell me that there was going to be trouble on the border?' I was furious now. He should have warned me. 'I *thought* there might be trouble,' he replied, 'and then someone would try to fix me because of you.' 'Fixing' people, getting them into difficulties with groundless accusations, is almost a habit, not only in India, but in all Asian countries. 'But you could have given me up,' I said, 'instead of giving up a seventeen-year career.' He might have become a brigadier, a full general; on retirement he might have become the director of a large company, with a big house and a motor car. All private businesses in India, and foreign businesses as well, always tried to recruit ex-army officers, the higher the better, as their top executives. The Indian army happens to be the best training ground for business management.

Vincent looked at me with his long-lashed eyes half-closed, and then he laughed. He laughed a long time, and the taxi driver turned round and also laughed. And I remain puzzled, and half angry, even now. Because anyone capable of such profligacy, of such extravagance, is for ever untamed, uncompelled, cannot be brought to any kind of servility. 'You don't understand my kind of love,' says Vincent cheerfully, as casually as noting the fact: 'Of course you have slanted eyes, you have Chinese eyes. And tiny eyelashes.' He accepts it. 'For you, it's China first, and that is your blessing and your curse. And after China, perhaps it's Yungmei. And after Yungmei, it's me. Perhaps. But for me, it's you.' That is how life is made and that is how Vincent takes it, and he sleeps soundly and is not tormented by love because he loves. And that is enough.

I too have a fixed pole star, magnet of my heart and brain. But it is not an easy thing, and perhaps it will be in the end unwholesome, an insanity to be scrutinized and categorized among the madnesses that besiege the mind. For how can one explain this obsession with an enormous mass called China, when I know so well that not one of the multi-millions will be either better or worse off, whatever I do or do not say?

'I am crazy, Vincent. Why do I do the things I do? Why did I decide to go to see Nehru?'

'Because that's the way you're made,' said Vincent.

So with strength in my voice and sureness of decision because of his arms around me, I told Vincent all that Chou Enlai had said. And how the idea of seeing Nehru was all my own. And Vincent said, 'I'll fix it,' and when we got to the Ashoka Hotel he rang up the Prime Minister's secretariat, and he got a very courteous secretary who said that he would relay the message and let us know, and then we sat waiting in the hotel room. And at that moment we were together half the world, the people of India and the people of China, knowing our future to be the same. 'Our people must never fight each other,' said Vincent. 'Some politicians in the West would like us to go to war with each other because then the whole of Asia would lapse into slavery again. And so it must not happen.' Of course when Vincent says 'the West' he does not mean only the United States and Europe; he includes Russia within the West, as I do; as so many Asians do. And that day in Delhi, we were not at all sure that, in the end, the U.S.S.R. would not be more eager to see India and China confronting each other than America — however open and vigorous at the time American encouragement to Nehru to carry on challenging China appeared to be.

Two days later, in the evening, Nehru received me at Rashtrapathi Bhavan. The large living room was cool and silent; beautiful with soft glowing alabaster lamps and roseate carpets. All was lived with, ungarish, not the usual over-ornate Indian living room. Nehru came in, so young in the diffuse light, a spring in his step, in white with a rose in his buttonhole. 'How beautiful you look,' he exclaimed, and smiled, a truly fascinating smile.

Our conversation started well, on a note of personal affection, as I told him I was back from Peking; but it worsened perceptibly as it proceeded. Very slowly the smile disappeared from Nehru's face. He did not scowl, he merely turned to bronze. At no single moment during the next forty minutes did our words or minds meet, effect a link. Not for a second was there any real exchange. I blame myself for this. Each culture has its own particular climate which the culture-bearers engender as they proceed in the art of conversation, which is the highest of all arts, and the most perilous, since it is exchange of thought and feeling through the dangerous manipulation of words. When two culture-bearers confront each other, then what is said by one is heard quite differently by the other; and this happened now, I think. I should have greatly lengthened the preamble, taken my time, coquetted, continued the softening up, all the more since I knew how susceptible Nehru was in a very personal way. I should have said, 'Oh, dearest Panditji, Panditji, how I have thought of you these days! My heart was in a turmoil because of you ... I could not eat nor could I sleep ... ' I should have intuitively, unashamedly fawned, with unctuous, Asian wit (I tried, subsequently in letters, but it was too late and unconvincing). I should have taken days, not less than an hour over my plea, and tried to see him again and again.

Alas, I was back from China. Which means that I was my Chinese self uppermost, logical and reasonable and quiet and calm, but not appealing enough to emotion; only convinced that 'the superior man listens quietly, and weighs himself and the universe'. I had with me maps of the frontier, copies of the documents exchanged, including Chou Enlai's letter of November 7th to Nehru. The letter was courteous and clear, and a radical departure from the somewhat unhappy epistolary exchanges which had previously taken place. 'Your Excellency, Panditji, you know all these things better than I do. I shall only talk of my own preoccupation, the overall effect of a misunderstanding between the two greatest nations in Asia; and the dangers of such a situation.'

I agreed that the Chinese had been untactful, I even conceded the word 'arrogant', for it was true that some of the truculence of their written word gave an ill impression (oh, those translators, how I wished I could do something about Chinese translations!). But in *deed*, I said, the Chinese were never anything but modest, prudent and careful. They had shown clearly that they were ready to negotiate and to compromise. Peking's English was not as excellent as that used in Delhi, but the point was not who talked well, who used the better rhetoric, but the facts, the actual situation and its historical development. And was it not a strange coincidence that in 1959 such a wholesale avalanche of hostility towards China, from 'various quarters', should coincide with the unhappy border clash with India? I went on; I drew examples from history; drew a picture of 'both our struggling nations' and their need for the least amount of interference.

'It seems to me from what you say that the Chinese do want to talk,' said Nehru, as if making a discovery.

'Panditji, this is far more than just some border question left over by

British colonialism. Only you can resolve it, for the sake of both our countries, for the sake of Asia.'

His face hardened imperceptibly here and I added quickly, 'I can see you have been hurt ... have you been hurt?'

'Yes, I have been hurt,' said Nehru.

I returned to the hotel, and wrote down what had taken place, and also my assessment of Nehru's present mood. Nehru would not, or could not, change his stance and negotiate. Meanwhile, he was doing a saraband of remarkable political dexterity. The conclusion was that it suited him well not to negotiate the border at all. It was a matter of choice, and also, possibly of personal vanity. After all, the Chinese had published articles which lectured Nehru on his political deviations ... and that had certainly not helped matters.

In the next months and years I would ponder over the roots of Nehru's decision. Obviously he had arrived at it gradually, reversing the stand he had taken in Bandung in April 1955, when he had gone out of his way to establish friendship with Chou Enlai and with China. When, and why, had he decided to change? I had been told by Malcolm in early 1957, when the slogan 'Hindi-Chini bhai bhai'* resounded everywhere still, that Nehru was unhappy with China. Something had happened. What precisely had happened in 1956 or 1957? All I could find out was that in 1956 Nehru had seemed to want to discuss the undemarcated border between the two countries with Chou Enlai, but that the Chinese were not ready for it; Chou Enlai had not been perceptive or alert enough at the time, and had pushed back the issue. Had the border problem been tackled then, and frontier delineation begun, the emotional fury unleashed in 1959 would not have happened. The Russian intention to utilize Sino-Indian border incidents in order to obtain leverage with the Indian government would not have worked. And had the border problem been settled before certain aspects of India's own developmental needs occurred to Nehru, history might have been somewhat different; at least for a couple of decades.

In December 1959, President Eisenhower came to Delhi. This meant a drastic change in American policy, which had been somewhat hostile towards India. Eisenhower praised 'this democratic country ... respected and revered ... throughout the councils of nations ... ' Nehru said contentedly, 'Yes ... it's true that people look up to us.' He was gratified, and the image of 'democratic India' was to last a very long time.

* 'India-China friends for ever'.

And now there was a sudden multiplication of aid; whereas in the previous twelve years India had scarcely obtained 1.4 billion dollars in aid, now she obtained four billions in the next four years from the U.S.A. Disapproval of India's 'neutralism' was over; her 'immorality' was as dead as Dulles. Nehru was the champion of Western values in Asia because of the border quarrel with 'Red' China. A special Help India lobby took shape in Washington, and functioned for many years. India needed immense funding for an industrial takeoff. And here, perhaps, is part of the answer to the puzzle of Nehru's change.

For Nehru was a master politician. He would not give up his great prestige with the other undeveloped nations of the Third World through too close an understanding with America. He preserved India's neutralist stance and became the Man of Peace, a role which he would play with superb aplomb at the first non-aligned conference in Belgrade in 1961.

Throughout those years, Nehru would exhibit pained bafflement at 'Chinese conduct' and 'treachery'. I cannot forbear to admire Nehru. What skill, what superb and ruthless use of the China bogey, to obtain from both the United States and the U.S.S.R. the most massive aid ever extended to any country at peace!

Close on the heels of President Eisenhower came Nikita Khrushchev, in February 1960.

By that time I had cultivated the acquaintance of some Indian intellectuals near to the Indian Communist Party, all of whom professed themselves distraught by the India-China quarrel. Among these I shall only mention one, my dear friend Mulk Raj Anand, versatile, prolific, and a humanist as well as a world-renowned writer. Mulk actually came to Singapore to see me; he was most concerned about India-China relations and we made many plans to dampen the fury in India, which eschewed cogent and reasonable debate, and to explain Indian reactions to China.

When Khrushchev came to Delhi, Mulk was overjoyed and wrote to me, 'I think he has come to restore friendship between India and China.' Mulk felt this was essential; because the border dispute also placed the Indian Communist Party (though not a member, Mulk was a sympathizer) in a very invidious position.

However, my photographer friend P. N. Sharma was less trusting. 'Perhaps K. will do some good, perhaps not,' he wrote to me.

Of course Khrushchev did nothing to ease the border dispute. He pledged lavish aid to India and deplored China's 'stubbornness' and 'inability to accept the realities of today's world'. Within the next two years, twice as much aid went to India from the U.S.S.R. as China had received; and Krushchev's visit laid the foundation of the friendship and alliance, which continues today, between the U.S.S.R. and India.

Nehru could afford now to show willingness to 'talk' with China. But 'negotiations' were refused. The opposition parties in parliament – notable among them the Swatantra Party – were vociferously against negotiations with China, which they considered to be a betrayal of India's cause; and an election was pending, and its results could be prejudiced by any inclination on the part of Nehru, suspected or real, to 'negotiate' with China.

Chou Enlai had not been inactive. In that year of 1960 he had successfully obtained two boundary agreements where hitherto no frontier had been demarcated, one with Burma and one with Nepal. With Burma Chou Enlai had accepted the 1913 McMahon alignment, which had been set up by the British. This was a very big concession. For no Chinese government had ever before accepted the 1913 McMahon Line. Chou Enlai let drop hints that China might accept the McMahon Line, in the eastern sector of the China-India border, in return for the much smaller knob of the Aksai Chin in the western sector. It was through the Aksai Chin that the Chinese had built a road in early 1954, linking Tibet with Sinkiang. The Indians only realized that a road had been built in 1956, when the Chinese held a celebration at its completion.

Nehru's opposition clamoured: 'Not an inch of soil must be given up.' The only people who kept cool were the Indian army officers. 'Nobody really knows whom this piece of land belongs to,' said one Indian military man to me. After all, if there was fighting and dying to do, dying in frozen wastes no one has ever mapped out is not a particularly delightful prospect. Unfortunately Indian politicians did not need to be cool-headed; only vocal.

Chou Enlai came to Delhi for 'talks' in April 1960. He stayed several days, trying to talk with Nehru. And he found that it was like trying to cut water. 'I could not move Nehru at all. I think he had made up his mind,' said Chou Enlai to me some years later. 'As we were leaving for the airport,' (Chou was flying from Delhi to Kathmandu) 'Nehru talked to me at great length about the evil, reactionary upper caste, the Ranas of Nepal, telling me to beware of them,' said Chou Enlai with an amused smile. 'One newsman at the airport said to me, "Your Excellency, have you noticed something? India has just received a great deal of wheat, a gift from the U.S.A." "Thank you for telling me," I replied, "then I understand fully the situation."'

I went on writing to Nehru, and he wrote back to me charming, affectionate, courteous replies. In none of them did he give anything away. I think he was amused, and perhaps a little scornful, of my obduracy and my idiocy. For it was, I confess, quite idiotic of me to think I could do anything to influence him. Nevertheless I persisted.

On my return from India to Malaya in December 1959 I had written a letter to the London *Times*, pointing out what Chou Enlai had mentioned about Nehru's own autobiography, which I had checked. The result, however, was merely some crushing correspondence from Peter Fleming, although he could not adequately explain why Nehru's own book showed on its map of India the borders where the Chinese said they were. Such, however, was the emotional pitch to which some Englishmen worked themselves that they managed to sound, and act, more irate than even the most hypersensitive Indian. Among those who succumbed to unchecked passion was, alas, my old friend Kingsley Martin of the prestigious *New Statesman*. I had flown back to Delhi in March 1960 for a few days with Vincent and in order to see Mulk Raj Anand, who had a 'plan' to approach Nehru and speak with him (nothing came of it), and there I found Kingsley and Dorothy Woodman. 'The Chinese have always been expansionist, it's in their blood,' roared Kingsley, staggering with pent-up rage.

'Our dear exalted friend [Nehru] is steadily moving to the right ... ' wrote Mulk, much distressed. He though that All-India Radio might be interested in getting both of us talking about the border in a series of broadcasts. This scheme went the way of all our other schemes to air the border dispute in a sensible way.

'Nehru sees hundreds of people. He thrives on being all things to all men,' said Mulk to me after one more fruitless attempt. He was then invited to Moscow — for Mulk was also a Stalin Peace Prize winner for his books — and remained there several weeks. I think that he was given the U.S.S.R. view, not only of the China-India border dispute, but, more importantly, of the Sino-Soviet dispute, which was now almost in the open. Under Moscow guidance the Indian Communist Party policy became to support Nehru 'at all costs'. 'Because', as Mulk wrote to me, 'the position of the Left is that all those who stand by the Prime Minister's basic policies have to push these policies and save him from himself, or rather from his so-called friends.' This meant that the Indian Communist Party would almost outdo the Swatantra Party in its anti-China stance.

Friendship with me became difficult for Mulk. But he courageously kept it up. By August 1960 he was in Europe, working for UNESCO and producing a most marvellous art magazine, *Marg*. He wrote to me that 'the mountains of bitterness and suspicion between India and China have now become higher even than the Himalayas ... ' This meant that our final scheme, which was to publish a book entitled *Across the Mountains*, containing our letters to each other about the India-China situation, was also to be given up.

Other Indian politicians, diplomats, also saw me; among them Jayaprakash Narayan. Unfortunately, Mr Narayan got a violent toothache within ten minutes of the start of our meeting.

I did not have so lethal an effect on army generals, friends of Vincent, with whom I continued to entertain the most courteous relations, despite the border dispute.

By 1961 I realized that there was no way in which the China–India border problem could be solved in the near future. Not only because Chou Enlai warned me of this, but because he had added, 'In the end we have to put our trust in the Indian people ... in the people of the sub-continent.'

The use of the word sub-continent was very important. Chou Enlai was thoroughly acquainted with the Partition of India into India and Pakistan. And although Pakistan was most friendly with China, Chou Enlai, who thought in terms of history and people rather than of political procedures, also realized that one day India's influence might again – should the religious problem of an Islamic Pakistan and a Hindu India be resolved – extend over Pakistan. He therefore kept the options open. He told me, 'We do not want a morsellization, a fragmentation of India. India has fourteen main languages, and it is really a mosaic of peoples and cultures. We do not wish to see it fall into separate pieces, each piece manipulated against the others. That has been the history of India in the past; and that is why it fell a prey to colonialism.' In China, the homogeneity of the culture kept China together. Although the colonial powers had tried to divide China, it always came together again.

In 1962 it was P. N. Sharma who stuck his neck out. Although he, like Mulk Raj Anand, was connected with the Indian Communist Party – so many people in the Ministry of Foreign Affairs would be thus connected, both in Nehru's time and in the time of Indira Gandhi – yet he was bold enough to revolt against the remarkable structure of unfacts that was being erected in New Delhi and duly and faithfully transmitted, without being checked, by most of the Western correspondents placed there.

In April 1962 P. N. Sharma turned up in Hongkong. I happened to be there, on my way to China. He had come especially to see me. Cousin

Pengju and I saw P. N. Sharma together in my hotel room. Pengju was now running a Hongkong monthly magazine called *Eastern Horizon*. It had published some of Sharma's photographs and wanted to publish some more. This gave Sharma an excuse for coming to Hongkong.

P. N. told us that India was preparing for war, 'all along the whole border'; and that in the western sector of the border, in Kashmir and in Ladakh, facing the Aksai Chin, the Russians were now obligingly providing helicopters and other army equipment to the Indian army. Meanwhile, the C.I.A. was just as obligingly providing means for dropping Tibetans trained in camps in the U.S.A. and sophisticated means of monitoring what was going on in China. (All this would be revealed as fact around 1974-5, when tempers and attitudes towards China had changed.)

P. N. Sharma also said that the Russian Ambassador in New Delhi had told a member of the Indian Foreign Affairs Ministry: 'Don't worry, we'll drop an atom bomb on Peking if they do anything.' At the time, Pengju and I could scarcely believe Sharma. But since then we have both realized that a tactic of Russian diplomacy is to make bombastic verbal pledges, which are not backed by the Kremlin but which overawe and influence the gullible in the Third World.

Sharma was unhappy. His Russian wife was proving 'extremely bourgeois'. She did not like Indian austerity. She did not like vegetarianism. (P. N. Sharma, being a high-caste Brahmin, was a strict vegetarian.) She wanted 'only to go out, to dance, to buy things'. Two years later, she would leave him and return to the U.S.S.R.

Pengju said, with Taoist wisdom, 'We must now go to lunch and eat well. One reflects better after digestion.' And so off we went to the best restaurant in Hongkong, while P. N. continued to be agitated about what was being concocted in New Delhi. There were also, he said, receiving sets and detecting devices installed by the C.I.A. 'somewhere in Kashmir', high up in the mountains. We managed to provide for him a totally vegetarian meal, even going to the extent of buying, on the way, a new set of crockery and implements, so that nothing he used would be contaminated by animal oil, and when P. N. said, in that enormously dramatic Indian way which I relish but do not share, 'I think there will be war', Pengju said sagely, 'War or no war, it is only the other face of peace. Now let us eat well, and toast our friendship.' He seemed totally unruffled by Sharma's revelations.

Pengju duly reported to his newspaper what P.N. had said. It elicited no surprise. 'We know there will have to be a show of force, sometime or other, do not worry', was the message relayed to me. So I did not worry. I told P.N. not to worry. 'The Chinese are in full control of the situation. They are prepared. Do not worry.' I relayed the total message to P.N.: 'Sometimes it is necessary to do a *little fighting* to unblock people's minds.'

In July 1962 the Soviet Union began hostilities on the Chinese borders, in Sinkiang province. About 60,000 Uighurs, of the national minority of Sinkiang, would be persuaded to flee to Soviet Russia.

I now think that this was the 'trigger', or signal for the Indians to proceed with what Nehru and his Defence Minister, Krishna Menon, had been preparing since 1961, and what was termed, in military language, a 'forward policy' on the border between India and China. The very fact that the Chinese did not seem to retaliate, had not even broadcast the Soviet incursions or their own losses, seemed to convince Nehru that the Chinese were pusillanimous, were frightened, and would not do or say anything if he pushed 'forward'.

I think he underestimated the Chinese. I think he did not listen to Sharma's warning, which was duly relayed to him: 'Be careful ... the Chinese are prepared.' Neither did his entourage translate for him the fairly numerous newspaper articles of that summer, in which very plainly the Chinese warned that they were 'fully prepared'. Nehru preferred to trust his friends in the Kremlin and his advisers, of whom at the time a good few were members of the Indian Communist Party, subservient to Moscow.

From 1960 to 1962 India's Ministry of Defence, under Krishna Menon, had worked out the 'forward policy'. It was designed to probe, to push, to infiltrate, to annoy and to provoke. The decision was made because of the very difficult internal situation in China. The shortages, the drought, the aftermath of the Leap Forward and its errors. It was predicted by 'experts' in Hongkong that China might now break up. And this was also the confident assessment (for the benefit of India) passed on by Moscow to New Delhi.

Nehru found himself confronted with reluctance, and even downright opposition, by his most tried and tested generals, who showed great hesitation towards the plans proposed by his Defence Minister. But then up came a General Kaul—no relation of my good friend Ambassador Tikki Kaul—and somehow he became in his turn Nehru's blue-eyed boy. In his interviews with Nehru he injected such jaunty confidence that the Prime Minister found any doubts he had swept away. A few highly placed commanders in the Indian army are on record as warning that they could not agree with Kaul's notions; that a large offensive, such as envisaged in the autumn of 1962, at a time when the passes were being blocked by snow, and with the unprepared state of the Indian battalions, was not only downright hazardous but a major onslaught on common sense. However, Nehru persisted, sustained by Krishna Menon, and on October 10th the final order was given, in Nehru's direct words: 'Drive the Chinese out'. The Indian army complied.

But of course, as was obvious, and known to everyone except perhaps to the Indians, the Chinese were prepared and waiting. After issuing the usual 'three solemn warnings' and imploring Nehru to 'withdraw from the brink of the precipice', the Chinese moved their border battalions on October 21st, eleven days after the Indian army took the offensive.

The Indian troops were not prepared for the winter. Many of them came from south India, and among them cases of frostbite, owing to inadequate clothing, would be numerous. They had not been supplied with adequate outfits for the high passes.

The Chinese came down the slopes and rolled the ill-clad Indian battalions right into the plains of India. And then the most surprising thing happened. The whole world, brainwashed by its press, forgot that eleven days previously Nehru had given the order to the Indian army to push forward, and saw only the spectacle of a Chinese army advancing like an avalanche into the plains of India. An enormous furore was created. This was once again proof of Chinese aggression. The cities of the plains even began to evacuate. The politicians who had been most raucous about 'not giving up an inch of India's sacred soil' were of course the first to flee.

In November, twenty-five days after the beginning of the Chinese military reprisal, the Chinese government announced a total and unilateral military withdrawal to ten kilometres behind the McMahon Line, on the eastern sector; stated that all weapons and ammunition captured, and all prisoners, would be returned without any compensation demanded; gave the lists of the prisoners captured – who had been treated, mainly for frostbite but also for wounds, in Chinese hospitals – and then sat down, waiting for Nehru to come to the negotiating table.

Many people in the world were puzzled; not least the newsmen and the agencies. How to explain what China had done? It did not fit into any known, recognized Western pattern of diplomacy ... and therefore reasons had to be invented. With fertile fantasy, they were. But all of a sudden the current talk of China's 'bellicose, mad aggressivity' somehow rang false. However, no new words had been coined in the Western vocabulary to describe what China was doing. Hence one 'expert' even tried to invent a 'Russian ultimatum' to China, forgetting that the Moscow press was just as surprised as those in London, Washington and Paris.

Ordinary people, here and there, wrote to me. I think they began to recognize that there was a Chinese way of doing things, of thinking, of acting, which need not refer to what they were told in the newspapers, and that the fascination of China resided precisely in this different way of handling situations, people, facts. 'For clarity of thought, look towards China,' one person wrote to me. And another. 'Well done, China!' I have never received so many letters from all over the world, asking me to explain what China was doing, as I did then.

But perhaps the most important result was that in the Third World, among the emergent nations, suddenly Nehru's prestige had entirely crumbled, and China's stood higher than it had ever done.*

In China itself the explanation for the handling of the conflict was simple because it was historical, it had precedent, and it was treated in the grand manner which the Chinese affect.

For in China in October 1962 the major issue, the greater danger, was not the 'inconvenience' of Nehru's 'forward policy'. It was the Cuba affair of that same month, and the resulting Kennedy–Krushchev shadow play of confrontation and collusion. Within the rivalry of the two super powers there always loomed, for China, the unwelcome spectre of an entente at the expense of China. This was not an imaginary threat; Stalin and Roosevelt had come very close at the Yalta talks to the division of China between the U.S. and the U.S.S.R.

As for the Indian episode, it was quite secondary, needing brisk local dealing but no more. History in China is replete with border incursions from all sides. And this one had a precedent: it was, as Chou Enlai would say, a repetition of the episode 'Seven times capture and release Meng Hou'.

In the time of the Three Kingdoms in China, A.D. 220–80, a famous Chinese strategist named Chuke Liang was holding together the Kingdom of Shou, whose King, Liu Pei, had died, leaving an infant son.

Since my cousin Liu Pengju was a direct descendant of King Liu Pei, I had ample opportunity to talk about this episode with him, and he gave me an abundance of details, almost enough to write a book on its own about the characters involved.

* See Neville Maxwell, *India's China War* (Cape, 1970).

The strategy of the military wizard Chuke Liang was to guard the Kingdom of Shou, which at the time extended from today's Szechuan down to today's frontier with Burma, against invasion from wayward tribal chieftains. These chieftains, mostly from the present-day Shan states of Burma, were often in league with other rival Chinese kingdoms, such as that of Wu, and received many gifts from Wu in order to attack Shou.

Such a tribal chieftain was Meng Hou, leader of the Yis; he had been recruited to become a constant marauder on the borders of the Kingdom of Shou. Chuke Liang personally led an armed expedition against Meng Hou. But since the aim of military action is not crude physical victory but a long-term peace, his tactics were to win over the whole tribe to allegiance, through their chieftain. Meng Hou must be captured alive and then released and challenged to a series of contests.

Every time Meng Hou was captured, he was released; although he refused to swear allegiance, and each time insisted that he had lost the battle not through inferiority to Chuke Liang but through fate, the weather or fewer men. Thus, seven times did battle occur; and seven times Chuke Liang released Meng Hou. The last time he let him go without a word, without even the usual admonition.

Then Meng Hou's heart was touched by the magnanimity of his foe; instead of walking away to rally his forces, his soul was changed and he swore friendship and eternal allegiance to Chuke Liang.

From A.D. 225 until today the Yis of south-west China have been included in the Chinese entity, as one of its fifty-odd national minorities. For 1,700 years the Yis and other tribal hosts of the border with Burma, have venerated Chuke Liang as a demigod. Cousin Pengju told me with much relish that when the Jesuits came to China and settled in Yunnan province (where all these encounters happened), they had been able to convert whole villages of Yis at a single stroke merely by telling them that Jesus Christ was the younger brother of Chuke Liang, and both of them sons of God.

Now, seventeen centuries later, Chou Enlai remembered the power of magnanimity and decided to treat Indian border incursions in the same way as the great strategist Chuke Liang had treated the border marauder Meng Hou.

None of this was reported in the Western press. But all the Chinese, whether in China, in Taiwan or in South East Asia, duly used the phrase, and overseas Chinese of all political blends would say to each other, 'Ah yes, seven times catch Meng Hou.' In Taiwan jubilation was apparent: even the head of the Taiwan intelligence in Hongkong would approach me a year later with that phrase on his lips.

This was also a judgment passed upon Nehru. It meant that whatever he or his government envisaged to provoke China, China would retaliate with magnanimity. One day the Indian people would understand, 'Because,' said Chou Enlai, 'after all, they are Asians, as we are. They too are heirs to a long culture.' But I doubted that Nehru would understand or appreciate the comparison. Would the story of Meng Hou induce in him the proper humility? He would not relish being compared to a wayward tribal chieftain who had to be re-'educated' into Chinese civility, whose soul was likely to be touched by forbearance.

The military débâcle of 1962 was the beginning of Nehru's death. For his self-esteem was now dealt a mortal blow. Krishna Menon resigned. For a while all was, once again, emotional fury in India. Emergency regulations were passed suspending all laws. Anyone found commenting unfavourably on the defeat was likely to be arrested for spreading unwholesome rumours ... the small Chinese colony in Calcutta, most of them laundrymen and shoemakers and petty shopkeepers, had a gruesome time; a good many landed in concentration camps for some years.

'Astonishment almost blots out relief at the sudden Chinese decision,' wrote the magisterial London *Times*, commenting on the Chinese withdrawal. And slowly, among the experts, the realization that Nehru did not want to negotiate began to be seen as a weakness. For Nehru still refused to negotiate. 'This weakens India's case' was the comment of Malcolm MacDonald. Malcolm MacDonald had been transferred from India to Kenya because of the Mau Mau insurrection there. He was giving his usual splendid performance, making the unacceptable seem obvious and even desirable to both sides. 'Of course Chou Enlai showed very clearly that the Chinese were ready to accept the McMahon Line in exchange for that bit of the Aksai Chin, and Nehru knew it. The whole thing could have been solved with face for everyone. But our friend Jawaharlal did not want to negotiate ... it's a great pity.'

But the status quo on the border would remain undisturbed, 'with no more deliberate encroachments or provocative sallies from the Indian side'.*

In India the famous, secret and constantly leaked Henderson-Brookes

---

* *India's China War*, op. cit.

Report on what really happened in that October–November 1962 was being prepared.

General Henderson-Brookes was a fiercely moustached and delightful Anglo-Indian, almost the living portrait of Colonel Blimp, and I often met him in Calcutta as he was Vincent's good friend. The report that bears his name remains 'top secret', although Indian newsmen and others have been able to get segments of it, and so has the Western press. In it the Indian army blamed its Minister of Defence, Krishna Menon, and General Kaul, Nehru's choice, for the defeat. The army had warned that with winter coming the Indian troops were not in a condition to fight in the high passes.

'Those civilians screaming: Fight the Chinese! should be parachute-dropped out there,' said Henderson-Brookes jovially. 'They haven't a clue what it's like.' Both he and Vincent agreed that the Chinese would never have been able to carry out an invasion because the passes would have been snow-blocked behind them and they would have been left stranded. From the beginning only a very limited action was planned.

Because of emergency regulations, anyone with Chinese ancestry (father or grandfather Chinese) was not to be given a visa to India. This affected me directly. But Vincent's web of connections worked well; of course I obtained a visa. And I used it to go to see Nehru in 1963.

I would see him twice. Once from afar, at a party, where we merely exchanged greetings. But another time Nehru received me in the late afternoon for a talk.

It was again pleasantly cool in his air-conditioned room; a contrast to the broiling temperature outside. Nehru had wizened, shrunk, as do old people whose bones begin to shorten. His face was thinner, but he was extremely affable, in a stony way. This time he did not volunteer anything, letting me speak, letting me ask the questions. And I did not ask him any questions about the border. I knew that this was a buried crypt within him; so deeply buried that he would not even refer to it. So I did not refer to it either. I had by then lived with the problem for some years.

We sat, Nehru and I, and had really nothing to say to each other. Nothing to say except: Well, here we are. And looking at him, old and tired, I felt old and tired too; as if we had been a warring couple, suddenly aware of the little time left to war or to love. So I talked of India. Not a word about China.

I told him that I was happy to see that India had made good progress. 'Yes,' he said, 'our peasants are quite comfortable now.' It was not so true, but I let it pass. By then I had become interested in India's Untouchables, another topic of long-term interest to me. But I knew that Nehru would say that the problem was being solved; whereas, as events have proved, it has not been solved at all, even now. I therefore avoided Untouchability. I was treating him carefully, like a sick person, a person who does not have a very long time to live. And indeed, he had only eight months more to live, though he and I did not know it as we faced each other with love and carefulness and kindness, and talked about India.

The expenditure of the Indian army had doubled. Aid was flowing in, abundantly, and from all sides. The myth of China's 'aggression' towards India was being ubiquitously sustained. Oh yes, said Nehru, life was more comfortable in India now for the common man. I avoided sudden jolts, and Nehru courteously responded in kind. He did not ask about Chou Enlai. I added a final sentence: 'Your Excellency, whatever may have happened, please be assured that Premier Chou Enlai's regard for you is entire.' 'Thank you. Please tell him I also regard him highly,' said Nehru.

Why, if there was nothing to say, did he receive me? Perhaps because, in a way, he needed contact of another kind.

In 1964 Nehru died. The Indian community in Malaya and Singapore held a ceremony and did me the honour of asking me to pronounce the funeral oration for Jawaharlal Nehru. I spoke only of Nehru's greatness, and how much I missed him personally. Which was true. I did miss him. I never reached him at all; in his presence all my emotions rang false, as did his to me. We evaded each other admirably, and this is also, perhaps, a kind of love.

Eleven

The Years of Want: 1960-1961

IN THE SUMMER of 1960, my health broke down.

I had been to Cambodia in February, and begun a new book, *The Four Faces*. I continued to worry about the Sino-Indian border dispute. My clinic was very busy and my sister Marianne had been placed in a mental hospital. I had also quarrelled bitterly and long with the leftist Students' Union of Nanyang University; allegedly infiltrated by the Malayan Communist Party. The reason was that I had publicly approved of a speech made by Prime Minister Lee Kuanyew at Nanyang University, and this had angered the leftists. They published a very rude letter against me in the papers. For a while I was ostracized; then 108 students rallied to support me, and in the end I met the student representatives at my home, and there was a reconciliation. It enhanced my position as an independent, but now drew upon me the anger of the PAP government, which had begun to demand 'obsequious compliance', as the poet D. J. Enright, at the time teaching at the University of Singapore, would remark.

But worry over China was the main cause of my illness, because 1960 was a terrible year for China, and I knew it, sitting in my clinic and doctoring my patients in Singapore. I was often aroused at night by spasms of anxiety. I grew thin. The spectre of want in China stalked me. The reports in the Western newspapers were all of dire distress: of floods and drought and insect plagues and failure and disaster. Every time I opened a paper it contributed to my body's defeatism.

I haemorrhaged almost continuously. I developed a nasty skin eruption after being stung by an unknown insect. I went on working, driving myself. Soon I could not sit anywhere in safety; I might leave a great smear of blood on the seat. I had a curettage, but nothing was found. Then Vincent arrived. 'You need me to look after you. I'm going to look after you.' Vincent abandoned his job with Spitz and Spitz was very angry. But Vincent was not helpless. Through an English friend, a delightful sturdy half-Scot named Workman, he had obtained an introduction which resulted swiftly in a job with Jardine Waugh, a branch of Jardine's in Singapore.

Throughout these years there had been the problem of Vincent's family. He never dreamed of letting them down. He would be able to provide for them as well as when he was in India.

The only snag was Lao Chieh. She had liked Leonard, who spoke perfect Cantonese. She strongly objected to Vincent, chiefly because of his colour. She would shout from the kitchen, 'A Kling devil! In this house! Who would have thought it possible!' Kling is a shortening of Kalinga, the ancient name of the Tamil kingdom, a word used throughout South East Asia for southern Indians.

Lao Chieh broke a number of my best plates and cups. She was so rude to Hamid, the Malay errand boy cum chauffeur, that he threatened to knife her. But my face was unmoved; my ears were deaf to shouts or crockery crashes, and the Siamese cats and the dogs climbed all over Vincent. The dogs now had someone they could wag tails at, bark at, who threw balls for them to catch ... my prize Burmese, Titi, went berserk with adoration of Vincent. He would sit on the veranda watching the road, and when he saw Vincent's car he would leap, tear across the garden screaming raucously with excitement, to greet Vincent at the garden gate. Hamid was also happy. There was at last a man in the house, one of his swarthiness, who taught him to back the car. For despite the lessons I had paid for, he had never learned to back.

Lao Chieh calmed down. And then one Sunday Leonard came to lunch, amiable, unruffled. Lao Chieh now decided that she would accept the unexplainable.

'Now that you've come to stay with me, I'm leaving you to go to China,' I told Vincent. He had cured me almost, his nearness and that golden glow of happy warmth he exuded, and all the many mes jostling each other in ceaseless activity came to rest like a watchful sea, a healthy sea between two tides. 'You are my good earth,' I kept on repeating. 'Without you I go into bewilderment.'

But my spirit was not at rest; it would not be until I went to China. Vincent cured me so that I could go. With everything well in hand, in September I went back to China.

In the train from Hongkong to the Chinese border a small Philippino who spoke in high-pitched singsong American talked to me unquenchably. He was a camera man and would take photographs of the Chinese travellers who came in and out of 'Red' China carrying unwieldy large packs on shoulder poles. 'I hear there's a terrible famine out there ... I want to take photographs of these people coming out, they're eating just anything. No more rats left in China, they've all been eaten up.' In the train to Kuang-chow some of the Westerners were craning their necks to catch glimpses of the 'famine' in China – or so they told me.

For me, this time was going home, a total feeling of return. No longer the seasick, topsy-turvy nausea, the mad roller-coaster careening. Growing in me was a fierce protectiveness for China. 'It's a failure, China has failed, the people are starving – rejoice, rejoice!' said the well-fed pink faces round me, and I hated them with savage fury.

I too craned, for I had to know. The trees were taller, green the fields which now lay in long rectangles with trim, straight borders. Never had there been such fields in China. The pattern of the countryside had changed. The hills bordering the faraway horizon were fuzzy with trees. Was there really a famine?

In Kuangchow the restaurants were full of foreigners and the food was lavish, for the bi-annual fair was on. I went to the fair before it was officially opened and was shown many new things, chiefly industrial machines, row upon row of them. From the window of my room at the Love the Masses Hotel I saw the grey, translucent Pearl River slide its flocks of junks and sampans; and I tramped the streets in a fine, small rain, and sat in a cinema to see a film on Nieh Erh, the musician of the old days in Yenan.

I visited Fo Shan, the town famous for ceramics. Fo Shan had won the national prize as the cleanest city in China that year. Its Ming dynasty temple, all its timbers so delicately dove-jointed that there was not a nail in the whole building, glowed with colour. I talked about Malaya with a poet and Miss Shen of the Friendship Association. We walked into shops. There were no apparent shortages, but then it was September, and because of the festival of October 1st there were always more consumer goods available at that time. The poet and I talked about Dostoevsky. He quoted Dostoevsky, that people are often irrational and do things against all sense and all reason and even their own benefit; this appeared preposterous to Miss Shen. 'Only imperialists are unreasonable,' she said.

On the train to Peking I shared a compartment with Comrade Li – very young and so pale that he looked exsanguinate, but he assured me that he was in perfect health – and a most exuberant and highly articulate Professor Chang. No cowed intellectual he. Long and loud and rumblingly he talked, scathingly he monologued. 'Too many administrative posts for intellectuals, too many meetings … not enough time for research … we've got to stick to research, expand it … we've got to have more time for academic pursuits.' He taught classical Chinese literature, and talked of the benefits and drawbacks to Chinese education should the Chinese language be romanized. It was an issue which we debated, my Chinese writer friends and I, almost every time we met. A topic inexhaustible, endless. In fact we are still debating it some twenty years later. Professor Chang did not want to give up the marvellous old classical language of China; 'yet China has to move into an industrial society: and language is a powerful brake upon invention unless it can become flexible, create new words and phrases.' He agreed with the simplification of the ideograms which was being achieved. 'Romanization versus simplification. I prefer the latter. Look at the Japanese. Ideograms haven't prevented their acquisition of science.'

Chang spoke enthusiastically of his investigations into Ming and Sung literature; and also of the literatures of the national minorities. 'We emphasize Han literature too much, spare and bony and moralistic, as a model to be imitated; but I hold that we must fertilize it with other modes

277

and moods, and the great beauty of other cultures accessible to us.' He shouted at dinner, 'Academic debate should not be turned into a political issue. This has been the trouble. Too many problems which are problems of research and scientific orientation are treated as political problems ... ' He thumped the table: 'I am not a communist; I do not believe in communism, but I love my country and I am willing to study Marxism; however, I maintain my own opinion ... ' Comrade Li read and slept, and never uttered a word. Only when we reached Peking would I discover that he had bone cancer and was being sent by his factory to the capital hospital for treatment.

'The Westerners say we have broken with our traditions. I tell you no government has ever paid so much attention to the total body of our heritage as this one,' said Professor Chang.

At each station we came down to do exercises; Comrade Li and I did some arm-waving, and bent at the waist and touched our toes; Professor Chang made a full exhibition of the art of shadow boxing, and did it very well. A team of athletes, girls about five foot eight inches and boys over six foot, who were in the next three compartments, also did exercises, and so did a team of Japanese businessmen. All the stations were beflowered; I plucked one small carnation, and then felt terribly guilty, pilfering public property. 'We're going to build many more railways,' shouted Professor Chang. 'We must. Have you seen the new bridge over the Yangtse River? You'll pass over it.' We did, and the loudspeaker on the train told us its length and size and how many tonnes of steel and concrete had gone into it, and we were of course impressed. We all manifested due reverence, and the lavatories were locked by the train attendant, a wonderfully chubby man with enormous dimples in his cheeks, who seemed to think that all life was laughter and who laughed all the time and washed the compartments and poured tea and entertained us indefatigably. 'Our new youth, they're magnificent,' bawled Professor Chang. 'It's adequate diet. Our children will be a head taller than we are.'

'How foolish you are to worry, to worry,' I thought. While the Professor slept, I looked at the beloved land through the window, and smiled to myself. 'How foolish you have been to worry so much.'

'Shortages, just shortages,' said Chang briskly when I broached the subject with him. Of course there were errors, and a lot of inexperience, and especially a lot of bombastic talk. 'But now everything will be taken in hand.' I would learn later that he was a member of one of the non-communist parties, and was going to Peking for important conferences. Once more the Chinese pendulum was swinging. The intelligentsia, rightist or not, was once again in demand for a needed economic re-adjustment. The next year, 1961, a New Hundred Flowers would be proclaimed ...

As Chang siestaed, I read a letter from Felix Greene, who at last had obtained a visa to China. It had not been easy to get him there; Felix had asked me and Pengju to help. But it was only in 1959, after seeing Chou Enlai, and when Kung Peng and I had been discussing several ancillary matters, that I could do something. The reason for his not being admitted was because he had an enemy in the British Communist Party who had spoken ill of him as a 'capitalist'. 'Felix is a very good man; of course, he's not a communist, but he is truly concerned about the future of the world,' I managed to say, also pointing out his usefulness and enthusiasm.

On September 20th, 1960, he succeeded in taping a television interview with Premier Chou Enlai, the first one Chou had ever done, and this was a major scoop. 'The China visit ... is the most significant thing that has ever happened to me,' wrote Felix. Felix had also met Edgar Snow in Peking. After much difficulty, Ed Snow finally had obtained U.S. State Department permission to go to China. At the time, any American who went to 'Red' China was considered a traitor, and was very likely to have his or her passport removed. Ed was commissioned to write articles on China for *Look* magazine, and would also complete a thick and exhaustive book entitled *The Other Side of the River*.*

Would we be able, Edgar Snow, Felix Greene, and myself, to establish better understanding between China and the Western world, so that China would no longer be considered a threatening, hostile planet on its own? When would China be seen as she really was, neither Heaven nor Hell, but simply a very large country with an enormous number of hard-working, poor people, frighteningly poor, but indomitable in their determination to achieve prosperity and social justice and to get swiftly into the twentieth century? After all, this was not a new dream; already in 1911 Sun Yatsen had proclaimed it when China's first revolution had taken place. China must take 'her rightful place in the sun ... equal among all the nations of the world.'

But there was the jargon. The exhortation, political and strenuous, sounding to Western ears a fanatic note. I understood the need to instil in the Chinese people conviction and faith, to exalt endeavour into significance and greatness, to strive to multiply effort, that human factor, by

* Edgar Snow, *The Other Side of the River* (Gollancz, 1963).

continuous preaching. After all, little else in the form of material benefit could be offered, at least for quite a time, to the Chinese masses. Only the emotional satisfaction of having surpassed themselves.

I had seen the almost mystic enthusiasm animating the people at the Great Leap Forward in the previous two years. What would I find in 1960? Had the exaltation been sustained? Was the British businessman right, when he told me, at lunch in Hongkong on his return from China, that 'their bigotry has waned – reality has now hit them and the people are tired and bitter and disillusioned'? Or was Felix Greene right, who had come back with stars shining in his eyes and written, 'People are high-spirited and inspired ... '?

There was fine rain at 7.30 in the morning, when we reached Peking, and soon it became bitterly cold. Professor Chang was met reverently by a big car and Party cadres and whisked away. Just before leaving he said, 'One day China will be the most democratic country in the world, but it will take time; we do not have a democratic tradition and feudalism is still heavy upon our backs.'

Wang Wanchun was at the station to meet me, his face glowing with pleasure; we drove to the Hsinchiao Hotel, where he had breakfast with me and told me about the new rationing.

'The harvest has been bad. We have had many natural calamities; a bad drought in the north.' There were shortages. Wanchun produced his ration tickets for the toast he ate, and then I noticed that he was thinner because his collar was too large for him when he turned his head. 'I have enough because I am an intellectual,' said he. Rations differed according to work done. Steel workers got the most in bulk and grain, but intellectuals got more meat, sugar and fats. 'Brain work needs meat and fats,' said he.

Deliberately eating less was, however, absolutely apparent as soon as I went out of the hotel. It was a feature of all the meals I would have with writers, relatives and friends. We simply fell into a natural constriction of appetite, each one urging others to eat more while restraining the self, and all of us saying to each other, 'I'm already full. I've eaten so much.' When I dined with Westerners I was immediately and almost shockingly aware of this absence of self-withholding; absence of awareness about the preciousness of food.

In the evening, Lin Lin of the Friendship Association, who had written me such a nice letter in July, came to see me. He had always been thin; he now had no cheeks, and it was difficult to judge. Only when I saw him again in 1962 did I realize how gaunt he had become in 1960. An elegant man with a sense of humour; a lover of painting and calligraphy, I enjoyed his verve, the way he overcame his Fukkien accent, above all his activity. At a glance he could tell my mood, whether there was temporary chaos within me or whether I had solved a problem to my satisfaction. Have I such a readable face? He noticed that I had not enough warm clothes for the winter. 'It's going to be cold,' he warned. The morning's drizzle had become an icicle-bearing wind, and it was freezing hard. The next day the wind grew in strength; its winged cohorts of sand and ice came howling down upon the city, flayed its walls and turned the ground to iron.

Lin Lin arranged for me to meet the heads of Islam in China, scholars and mosque imams; and also to visit Buddhist temples and priests, in order to bring back some material for the Malaysian Sociological Research Institute in Singapore. I spent many hours with Chinese Islamic scholars in Peking, in Kuangchow, in Sian. I visited the mosques everywhere; those which had not been closed. One-third of the East District of Peking was Muslim, with Muslim restaurants in almost every street.

It was in Sian, in the old and beautiful Ming mosque in Ox Street, that I found extensive documentation on Admiral Cheng Ho, the Islamic Chinese eunuch who had led seven great sea expeditions to South East Asia, to the African coasts and Zanzibar. There were stone stelae erected to him, one recording a voyage when he was accompanied by a Malay named Hassan. A storm arose and Hassan prayed to Allah, and the storm abated.

Islam's history in China is 1,300 years old. The 'pure and truthful' religion — for so the imperial edicts had proclaimed it to be — had come to China both by sea and by land: by sea, following the ships which the monsoon winds blew agreeably to Kuangchow. And from the minaret of the great mosque there, erected in the eighth century A.D., the merchants of Kuangchow watched for the return of the fleets. By land, it was brought by the Silk Road across the continent of Asia.

Prosperous Arab establishments had sprung up all along the south China coast; and Arab communities took Chinese names. Even today Arab blood can be discerned among the populations of coastal towns. Islam extended across north China in a large horizontal pale, from the confines of Turkestan to the frontiers of Korea. In 1960 there were twelve million Muslims in China, grouped as a national minority, the Huis. When I protested that the Huis were actually Chinese, the imam of the Sian mosque pointed to the Jews, who were not a race but a religious group. To make the Huis, believers of Islam, a national minority gave them privileges, explained the imam. Throughout the years of want, the Han Chinese would be on short rations but there would be adequate feeding for the national minorities. And family planning, which was gradually being enforced upon the Han people—93 per cent of China's total population—was not being enforced upon the fifty-odd national minorities.

I was amazed to find out that around six thousand pilgrims a year left China to go to Mecca, and much more so when I realized that a good many of them travelled via Hongkong and Singapore. Oh, the marvellous and strange subtleties of Special Branch! I wondered whether they had an extra posse of plain-clothes policemen watching when the pilgrim ships carrying passengers from 'Red' China anchored in Singapore.

The Muslim Huis had their own special representatives at the National Assembly; they had their own Party cadres. Now they acceded to education, to universities; they had autonomous rights as to custom, religion, and to studying the Koran in Arabic script. There had only been thirty doctors among them in 1949; there were now 262. They had 129 university professors instead of the eleven there had been in 1949. All meat consumed by Muslims was killed by Muslim butchers. The Muslim Cultural Association had members who had studied in Cairo's El-Hazar University.

But of course there were changes; such as Ramadan, the month of fasting. It was not proscribed, but 'We absolve people from fasting who work in offices, schools and factories,' the ulama of the Great Mosque in Peking told me. There were 130,000 Huis in Peking, and 30,000 worked in factories.

Unlike Malaya, where four wives per man were still permitted, here much effort was concentrated on trying to achieve monogamy. Whereas by 1958 monogamy became the rule among the Hans, in the Hui communities this would not occur until about 1965.

I wrote all this information down and prepared a report on it, and sent it to the Malaysian Sociological Research Institute in Singapore.

Noticing my interest, Kung Peng gave me a series of volumes: the records of transactions and exchanges—cultural, commercial, diplomatic—between China and other countries of the world, starting in the Roman times before Christ. This provided an invaluable perspective. My self-appointed task (one for which I was naturally fitted, as Kung Peng obliquely let me know very often) was to convey views and news, the aroma, savour, atmosphere, reactions of the outer world to the great 'within' of China; and to convey the sensation of China to the outer world.

How thin were my friends becoming, how thin! And how rude to refer to their loss of weight! One had to say, 'You look very fit.' Though some of them, in the evening, returning from work, staggered with fatigue and empty stomachs, they would reply with a big smile, 'Yes, we are very fit. We have all the food we need.'

Wu Chienta looked the ghost of himself as he took me to lunch. He refused my invitations. He ate reticently, and would only say in his low agreeable voice that there were temporary difficulties owing to natural calamities; that there had been great advances in industry although there were 'shortcomings owing to inexperience', but these were 'not more than the equivalent of one finger in ten'. He had worked for almost a year in a commune, and was now an expert in balancing burdens (he could carry eighty kilogrammes) at both ends of the flexible bamboo shoulder pole. He always looked neat and well-scrubbed, but now he had eschewed hair oil and wore a crew cut. There was no hair oil to be had in Peking, except for foreigners, in the hotels and at the Friendship Store.

I bumped into Edgar Snow in the lift of the Hsinchiao Hotel. I spent the evening freezing in his room before the heat came on at ten p.m. While Ed unburdened himself, talking of his travels through China, and the major questions, and the minor ones, which occurred to him. I gave him an aspirin because he was beginning a cold. Everyone caught colds in Peking. Ed was now waiting for some final important interviews: one with Chairman Mao himself; another one (his second or third) with Premier Chou Enlai. Ed did appear a little puzzled – as Felix Greene had written to me – because he suffered from a surfeit of information; and because, unlike me, he took down every word, being a meticulous and painstaking man who did not rush to conclusions. He could not make up his mind about the shortages. There were shortages, avowedly, yet everywhere he went he also saw enormous progress. How bad, how significant, were the shortages and the shortcomings of the Great Leap Forward?

Ed told me how gruelling had been his quarrel with the U.S. State Department. 'They treat anyone who wants to go to China as an incipient criminal.' The State Department did not think that Ed could be 'objective' about China, 'Which means that they don't think I'm going to write the things they want to hear.'

Another problem which bothered him a great deal was relations between China and Russia. How true were the reports of the Western press that these relations were getting worse? He was waiting to hear directly from Mao and Chou about them.

A reception was organized by the Foreign Ministry at the International Club; I think it was in honour of Ed Snow. There was a large spread of dishes, succulent in colour and taste. Kung Peng was there. She beamed at me. She was obviously much thinner. 'Come, I want to show you someone,' she said to me. And took me to a side table, where a tall gaunt man dressed in blue with a worker's cap on his head, which he removed in salute to everyone who came up to him, was cramming food into his mouth. I have never seen a man eat so fast or swallow such large mouthfuls making them disappear without chewing. He turned upon me heavily myopic glasses and removed his cap. His head was neatly shaved. It was Puyi, ex-Emperor of China.

Puyi had lost his throne when he was a mere infant, in 1911, at the first Chinese Revolution. He had been hauled out of private life and proclaimed 'Emperor of Manchuko' in 1931, when the Japanese invaded China and detached Manchuria's three provinces from her. He had been supplied with a Japanese wife and had become a puppet. In 1945 he had been abandoned by the Japanese in their precipitous retreat and captured by the Russians when they in turn invaded Manchuria.

Puyi was imprisoned in the U.S.S.R.; he was then recuperated by the Chinese Communists, re-educated, living with workers and peasants, doing manual labour, receiving political indoctrination and stitching his own clothes. Now he was free. He would begin a new life, and that is why he had been invited to the reception. He was taking a course in botany at the university. Within another year, he had married again, a hospital nurse. He lived quietly, in a comfortable house. He would write his autobiography, which I purchased in 1963.

Kung Peng thought I might be interested in seeing him. I was. Ed was also led up to him and did exchange some words with him.★ Back at the hotel, Ed said he was not attracted to Puyi. He had, after all, been a traitor. Some quislings in Europe had been executed at the end of the war; but in China Puyi was reintegrated in the new society, and would die of cancer in 1968.

In that winter of 1960, the gossip about divergences within the Communist

★ See *The Other Side of the River*, op. cit.

Party became widespread. There was, so Peking 'small lane' rumour had it, a rift between Mao Tsetung and some other, unnamed Party leaders. This had to do with the Great Leap Forward, with the agricultural disasters which had occurred, and also with the expanding quarrel with the Soviet Union.

I did not know what really went on. The 'within' *Reference News*, which is circulated round about 50 million cadres and Westerners living and working in China, was inaccessible to mere visitors like myself. Peking is an outrageously gossipy city; an inventive city where people have fertile imaginations and love to create sensational stories. How could one believe all that was being said?

Information in Peking has three levels: the first level for 'fraternal comrades', who are shown secret Party documents and told things that are not told to the unbaptized, non-Party, not living in China people. Then there is the level of the overseas Chinese who visit their families, hear ordinary talk and are confronted with the problems which their relatives encounter. Overseas Chinese are also allowed to read the local provincial newspapers; whereas from 1960 onwards, I was not allowed to see them, even if they lay on the tables before me.

The third level is the level for visitors. Increasingly, and especially during the Cultural Revolution, it would become the level where heavy mendacity prevailed. From 1960 onwards, so much became 'secret' that the middle cadre, the intepreter who was in contact with visitors, was often in a quandary. What could he do, when he was supposed to inform 'honoured guests', but lie, lie and lie again, since he could not reveal anything of what went on? The habit of absurd secrecy started to assume fantastic proportions: even an academic discussion on a medical pursuit would come under a ban, as 'state secret'.

In conversation with Chinese officials, with Kung Peng, I would stress that all provincial radio stations in China were monitored by the American Consulate in Hongkong; that a considerable number of local newspapers were almost daily smuggled out of China. 'The situation is that China's enemies know better what is going on in China than China's friends,' I would say again and again. But nothing could be done about it, such was the power of bureaucracy and its inertia. 'It is illegal for a friend of ours to know these things' was one of the prizewinning answers I received from an official. I thought then of all those eager, willing friends of China; for whom every word uttered by interpreters was the truth, the policy, the line, the very word of Mao himself. How many of them, in the years to come, would realize that they should have been, perhaps, a little more sceptical? And that even includes me, for I believed, by dint of hearing them, certain things which turned out later to be falsehoods.

But I was neither misled nor taken in that winter, nor for a good many subsequent years. My ear to the ground, my qualified criticisms, were not perturbing to Kung Peng. But they would be perturbing to others in the bureaucracy, and every year, therefore, I would have to do battle, not only outside China, but within China, in order to remain honest with myself.

As winter deepened and the days stretched a longer darkness, I saw the hunger grow, the queues at the food markets lengthen, the scarcity become more evident. I walked the streets; adopted the shuffle of those around me; a wordless eavesdropping when clothes obfuscated one's being: I had a wardrobe to look like an inhabitant. In the market, row upon row of small shops with nothing in them but a passive, seated salesman and empty shelves. No nails, no string, no shoes, no glasses, no ... everywhere people with their heads well within their shoulders and scarcely lifting their feet went from store to store. No buttons, no needles, no thread, no kettles, no saucepans, no ...

They stared at the bare shelves and went on to the next shop. Wearily and steadily.

But still it was not like Old China. And the difference was the Party cadres. They too shuffled, they too went hungry. They got thinner even more quickly than ordinary people did because they went on working; and so many of them, to give an example, had voluntarily cut their already scarce rations.

I got an idea of the scale of rations instituted that winter.

For the high intelligentsia, scientists, professors, researchers, writers and artists, more sugar, more fats and oils, more meat, an average of around 2,000 or more calories per day. 'The active brain needs a great deal more energy-giving food,' I was told again and again.

Less fat for the 'average intellectuals', the schoolteachers. This brought them to 1,800 calories or thereabouts.

For steelworkers and workers in heavy industries, thirty-five to forty catties (a cattie is half a kilogramme) of rice per month, but less fats, oils and sugar. They must have had an average of 2,500 calories per day.

For ordinary workers, round about thirty catties per month, depending on physical demand, and an average of 2,500 calories per day.

For students, possibly 2,000 calories per day; more protein than for the workers, but less carbohydrates. For lower office cadres and sedentary occupation workers, between twenty-six and thirty catties of grain per month; their calories worked out at 1,500 to 1,800 per day. Enough to live on. Not enough to keep them warm and active in the unheated houses and offices of that bitter winter.

The worst off, finally, were the city housewives, except when they were pregnant in a factory, in which case they got extra rations, equivalent to workers' rations. Otherwise, I realized, they would get 1,200 calories or less.

Of course each city, each region, each province differed in its allocation of rations. The north of China was possibly the worst off. There were some communes in north-west China where there would be no meat at all to eat throughout that winter and the next spring, only rough flour, maize mixed with rye and buckwheat, dumplings filled with seaweed, which were steamed. Seaweed, a great item of consumption in Japan, was at that time introduced in China and used as a filling; it proved important in sustaining the population until 1962.

North China was far too cold for winter vegetables except for cabbage. There were great mountains of cabbage to be seen everywhere along the streets of Peking; every lane had its cabbage hill. But sweet potatoes could not be had, nor was beancurd available, or beans of any kind.

However, in the kindergartens and nurseries in Peking and Shanghai, beancurd milk and peanuts were given to the children as extra food. The peanuts came from Szechuan; but in 1961 Szechuan would run out of peanuts.

Areas in south and west China did not at first suffer as badly as those in the north. In Szechuan, in 1960, there would be four vegetables a day available in all the communes; and milk for the sick and for the children in Chengtu. Then in 1961 Szechuan was badly hit by drought and by the fact that so much of the food it produced had been taken to feed other provinces.

I began to see in Peking and Sian and Taiyuan cases of beriberi on the street, in the queues waiting at the hospital gates. The swollen faces were obvious.

Before the Chinese New Year, which occurred at the end of January, the ration of pork meat would go up; it had been reduced to about half a cattie per person per month; it would double for the two months of January and February. And there was also a small rise in poultry available, and in fish. But it was difficult to get people in the north to eat fish. They were not accustomed to it.

Every institution, factory, school and university department, as well as the ministries, would grow their own vegetables. In Peking and Sian and

287

Lanchow and Taiyuan and Tientsin, hens and rabbits were bred indoors and quantities of edible vegetables would be grown in flower pots. Many of my friends would grow cabbages and tomatoes on their window sills or on shelves built near the windows.

The people swept up the falling leaves lining the roads in and out of the cities. The leaves made an infusion which was taken to prevent scurvy. The sweeping was a daily sight until there were no more leaves.

Resourcefully schools, factories, universities and administrative departments organized 'transport corps'. These teams went to the countryside communes to buy and bring back, sometimes on their backs, necessary food for the community. 'Some of these units are pretty smart; they have leased fields in the communes and entered directly into contracts with the communes to supply food and to raise pigs. Each unit has its own pigs,' Wanchun told me. This splendid ingenuity, ostensibly ignored, enabled the people to survive and to go on working. The bank in Chungking where Second Brother worked had a special 'transport team', and Second Brother became extremely adept at finding food.

'The Party keeps one eye open and one shut,' said Wang Wanchun, 'it knows what is going on, it ignores it.'

At first the villages ate better than the cities; peasants ate up the grain, the meat, everything that was available. But in some places requisition of grain and food left the peasants with almost nothing, and there were revolts. I saw evidence of such a one on the train going to Sian: about twenty people, some with chains on their feet. They were obviously peasants, and they were obviously being taken away as 'counter-revolutionaries'. These cases of arbitrariness would be denounced in 1961. A writer told me, 'Every small Party secretary at commune level can wield the power of a petty tyrant. It takes well-trained cadres, and disciplined ones, to resist corruption in times of hardship.'

In the communes I visited I was at times deluged with statistics proving how much more per *mu* of land was grown, all due to the Leap Forward, to close planting, to the water canals and reservoirs and wells. Of course these figures were correct for experimental plots; but I could not find full barns anywhere in 1960, although two years later a point was made of showing me the well-stored grain. The fundamental trouble was the hasty harvesting of 1958 and 1959, owing not only to the steel campaign in the first year of the Leap, but also to the drafting of so many millions for dam and canal building, and also of seventeen to twenty million peasants from the suburban communes to the cities and small towns to work in the thousands of new factories which had been erected.

More and more, as time went on, I heard about the 'communist wave' which had taken place in 1958. It had seized the land like a frenzy, had lasted about six months, and had done untold harm. With beating of drums, flag waving and dancing the peasants had celebrated the advent of communism. Money was abolished. Everything was free: clothes and haircuts, television sets were purchased with available funds and cinemas were built when electricity had not yet been installed. All private plots had been abolished; and privately owned trees felled as they were 'capitalist symbols'. Secondary occupations such as weaving and embroidery, basket making, making of noodles and curing of hams and of tobacco had all been abolished too. The slaughter of pigs was phenomenal. Eat, eat, eat. The state will provide. Then privately owned pigs and hens and ducks were collectivized, which meant that they were crammed together so that no one looked after them properly. How had this come about? Who had given the directives which led to this insanity? There were no directives, but a general permeation of overweening enthusiasm, brooking no reason or caution of any kind. The losses were enormous. In 1960, they were being felt everywhere.

I saw pig cholera in the north, as I took the new railway which had been built from Sian to Chengtu, across the Tsingling Mountains. All along the roads, by the rail track, the peasants carried dying pigs, pigs that could no longer walk, to market, to be killed. Impassive, the other train passengers looked on. There were no eggs to be had anywhere. No meat in the restaurant dining car; I got a little tinned ham with cabbage.

'How did this come about, Hualan?' I sat with her and her sister, a painter. Her sister was back from the countryside. She and other teachers and the students of her academy of art had 'gone down' to teach the peasants in the communes. Peasants were now learning to write and to paint. Hualan thrived on difficulty; she was energetic and hopeful and had voluntarily cut down her grain ration from twenty-six catties a month to twenty-two, and then she would cut it to eighteen. She and her sister, as high-class intellectuals, got more sugar and fats and meat. 'That's enough for us, so long as we have coffee.' Coffee was very hard to get, but Hualan could obtain a supply from the shop for foreigners because of her Polish mother.

Hualan's sister the painter was not well; she had worked too hard in the countryside. She had bad haemorrhages. 'We were building a dam and we worked sometimes fourteen or sixteen hours a day.' One of the young, enthusiastic art students with her died of exhaustion; he had not wanted to stop working and he worked and worked, and suddenly he fell down dead.

'Everything was done too quickly, far too quickly,' Hualan and her sister told me. Now everyone was looking forward to readjustment. 'Premier Chou Enlai will do it. He will find a way to clean up the mess. He always does.' Everyone, it seemed, was looking towards Chou Enlai to salvage the situation.

'It will be better in the spring,' said Hualan.

All my friends stuck strips of newspaper around every window and door in their homes, for insulation against cold draughts. There was not going to be any coal that winter. 'We have to work with our coats on,' said my friend the writer, Yeh, and so he did, writing and sometimes blowing on his fingers when they became too cold to hold the pen.

Winter crept on. In the streets people walked very slowly, saving strength. They bicycled slowly. But there were no complaints. There were no beggars either. Everywhere in the small lanes shops sprang up for mending and cobbling and making do: for repairing kettles and pans and the soles of shoes, and garments that were getting threadbare, and for carding cotton for padded coats, and for blankets. In the market a tailor had found a new way of cutting clothes which economized on cloth. This was publicized and crowds came to watch and to learn. The ration of cotton that year would be very small: three metres per person. Only new-born babies would get a good deal, up to fifteen metres. And of course there was an allowance for clothes for funerals.*

I bought shoelaces in place of string. I used them to tie books I had bought and was sending to myself in Hongkong. Shoelaces were suddenly plentiful, but they disappeared quickly. And there were no shoes, neither of leather (very expensive), nor of cloth.

Suddenly the market was invaded by African dates. They were all bought up in Peking within a day. But in Szechuan, where I went later, no one wanted them; because the consignment that reached Chengtu was full of worms.

Schools were closed part of the time to spare the strength of teachers and children. 'Everyone can take days off to sleep if they want to sleep.' No one exacted attendance. 'It is better to keep your strength and move as little as possible.' In the factories, too, the workers were on half time, to conserve their energy.

At the Hsinchiao Hotel and at the embassies to which I was invited, a polite game was going on. It was called 'counting the Chinese calories': estimating the calories the average Chinese man or woman consumed; evaluating how long the Chinese people could hold on with the rigorous

* Every dead person is buried in a new set of clothes.

diet they were on. 'It is quite impossible. They're getting less than 1,200 a day ... '

I was stiff with fury. I wish I could say that true concern, real goodwill, was dominant. It was certainly there, among some individuals; some diplomats, some newsmen. But on the whole there was gloating and satisfaction that the Great Leap had 'come a cropper'. 'China's setbacks may make her less inflexible,' said a European ambassador. Among people from Third World countries there was surprise and genuine concern. 'I thought the Chinese knew how to run things ... what's really happened?'

'We have enough, more than enough,' said my friends with thinning faces. Their smiles were pinched and a little haggard, but they carried on. Unfailingly courteous, they would invite me and ply me with food. To what incredible trouble had they gone to obtain this food; and perhaps, for this one meal, they had sacrificed a week's ration, or even the meat for a month ... 'Please let me have the pleasure of inviting you,' I would say to them. The restaurants were open and foreigners could eat in them, although they were expensive. But my friends would fall silent for a space, and then smile and say, 'Oh, but it is so much more pleasant to eat at home.'

Pride, Chinese pride. Dignity. They would not even accept a meal from me. Especially because times were so hard, food so difficult to come by. How could I then reveal to foreigners who were not friends what my friends ate? Outside China there was a campaign humiliating China, launched in America. 'Feed thine enemy' was the slogan; and food was offered. 'We practise self-reliance, we have enough,' everyone said to me. And to deny this, at the time, would have been to insult them.

Hualan lost four kilos that winter; and almost everyone I knew lost far more. Yet it was I who caught one cold after another, whose nose streamed, who would come down with bronchitis in January, when the air and the earth rubbed each other raw and the wind clawed at my skin and tore it.

'We have enough, more than enough.' A Canadian doctor had sent me a small bar of soap to give to a Chinese doctor whom she had known. 'Our newspapers tell us there is no soap in China.' It was quite true that soap was extremely scarce, but the Chinese doctor handed me back the soap with a smile. So I had to post it back to Canada.

'The shortages are temporary ... transient difficulties ... soon with the spring harvest ... natural calamities ... but in the spring ... ' So everyone round me said.

There were no political meetings held anywhere that winter. People were too tired.

Around the shop for foreigners on Hatamen Street, at dusk, sometimes small groups of people collected to watch those going in and coming out laden with food parcels. They would watch quietly, then slowly shuffle away.

Suddenly everyone began to talk about fertilizers, and the need for them. Simon Hua told me that 'the Russians don't know much about chemical fertilizer factories'. There were meetings held by scientists, engineers, agronomists, and fertilizer factories were a-building in many places. Just as suddenly people were talking of alkalinity in soil. 'It's due to upsetting the water level by hasty water conservancy projects ... one hundred million peasants have been building dams and reservoirs and there's a lot of improper building and inadequate drainage ... ' Simon's friend, a hydraulic engineer, had warned the cadres, but no one had paid heed.

I went to see Hsueh Mah; she now stayed in Papa's room. She had some coal. I brought her tins of food and she always asked for more. The Party cadre in charge of the street came in when I was with her. His face was swollen. Beriberi. 'I am ill, I am ill,' moaned Hsueh Mah. 'You are not well, your face is swollen,' I told the cadre, ignoring Hsueh Mah. I tried to give him a tin of ham but he refused politely. 'It is nothing. It comes from eating too much cabbage.'

One morning, through my hotel window, I watched an old woman with bound feet, a grandmother, come out on the street complaining that her hen had run away and very shortly several other old women, all with similarly bound feet, materialized on the street, out of the walls; they discussed with great civility the matter of the missing hen. 'Perhaps now she will come back,' said the first grandmother loudly, hobbling away cheerfully. I had no doubt that the street would look into the matter. Of course there must have been petty larceny. I think that after a certain point of hunger, inevitably, the social order does begin to be eroded.

However, the rationing was fairly well done and there was tight control so that prices did not go up; nevertheless, a small free market was allowed. 'One eye open, one eye shut,' said Wanchun. 'That's the wisdom of the Party. It allows certain things.' In fact, the Party was trying to stimulate free markets, and all private plots had been restored, and there would soon be another policy in agriculture, to undo the harm done by the 'communist wave'.

The hospitals were very busy caring for the sick, who were many. But the maternity hospital, which had been quite full in the previous year, was fairly empty. 'We do many abortions,' said the gynaecologist, a young woman, matter of factly. 'The women ask for it.' With food scarcity wombs were emptied speedily. There was also a great deal of both amenorrhoea and haemorrhage: amenorrhoea mostly among house-wives and female workers. 'No periods since the cold set in. Nature's way of preserving the body.' 'But some people I know have haemorrhages,' I said. The gynaecologist laughed gently. 'Usually high-class intellectuals. Because they get more proteins and fats perhaps ... '

How strange, I thought, woman's reaction to stress. There was I, well-fed in Malaya, suffering the same uterine troubles as women in Peking.

My overseas Chinese friend, Mr H., came to see me. He regularly returned to China, every two or three years. And now he was upset, for he had been back to his old village in Anhwei province to see his relatives. Things were not too good. Anhwei has always been a difficult province. And now it had no reserves; and a harsh winter, and the crazy, pushful cadres in Anhwei had liquidated the most gainful occupations of the peasants and left them only some rice and wheat, and then they had not been able to collect the harvest because of the steel campaign and the water conservancy projects ...

Mr H. had relations in the village. They now clung to him. Although they did not actually starve, they were very short of food, and panicky. 'You're so fat I'm going to eat and eat with you until I get as fat as you,' clamoured the head of the clan, who was Mr H.'s first cousin. He installed himself in Mr H.'s hotel for overseas Chinese and ate and ate at Mr H.'s expense. And Mr H., who from the age of twenty-four had been abroad in America, fed his cousin. 'It is the old, old fear of starvation which is coming up again; although the communes do provide subsistence,' said Mr H. when he told me his story. 'But in Anhwei the peasants have reverted to old times. The people who die are the old and the babies. The old women are simply not given any food; and as for girl babies, I think that infanticide has come back ... '

'The iron bowl. The communes are our unbreakable iron bowl.' So said the slogan, and it was also true. Never before had so many millions been provided for, even if they received only enough for survival. In the past landlords used to starve out fractious tenants by breaking their cook-ing utensils, which they could not replace because they were too poor even to buy a cooking pot. I thought back to England during the war years, the rationing, and the old people, the lonely, single individuals I had seen dying with sweet muteness of hunger ... Here in China the strong did survive; the weak had a chance, but a lean one ...

293

From 1960 onwards the communist government would buy grain abroad, in Canada, in Australia, for the cities, in order to allow the peasantry to keep what they had.

I offered a waiter at the Hsinchiao Hotel a bar of chocolate. He refused a little angrily. 'I have enough to eat,' said he.

I lay in bed; the heat came on. I coughed and sneezed; it was always too hot at night in the hotel. But out there, in the web of lanes, dust and cold harried; in the darkness there would be deaths from pneumonia.

I took Wang Wanchun out to a restaurant. Not being a Party member, he was not averse to an occasional meal, and so we ate Peking duck, and it cost 23 yuan, four times as much as the previous year. The restaurants were, of course, prohibitively expensive, except those for the ordinary people, which retained the same prices but demanded ration coupons. The expensive restaurants did not ask for ration coupons.

I went to eat with my friends, Gladys Yang and her husband. They offered me a well-laid table. Gladys, as an Englishwoman, a foreigner, could get food from the foreign shops inaccessible to the Chinese. But her three children, who sat with us at the table, absolutely refused to eat the food spread out before them; they ate only half a bowl of rice and some cabbage. 'I am not hungry,' said the boy, scowling at his mother. Neither would the two girls eat what was before them.

'It's the schools,' said Gladys. 'The children have been told that this is a very bad year and that one must economize every mouthful of food, if possible.' And so she and I felt guilty, guilty, with all the food staring at us on the neat round plates and the children not eating, deliberately. And I think Gladys was sad, but she was also a little awed and proud that her children were able to understand, to participate, to show such self-control. 'I think that is what makes the strength of this country. It reacts, at times as one single body, a biological unity.' 'No one is going to moan and groan,' said her husband. 'We'll see it through, as we have so many bad times and good times in our long history. We'll see the bad times through.'

There were twelve Latin American delegations in Peking that October, including one led by Che Guevara, from Cuba. The Latin Americans at the Hsinchiao Hotel occupied large tables; their whole faces worked when they talked; and also their bodies. Their eyebrows went up and down. I had never seen so many handlebar moustaches, even in the officers' clubs of the Indian army, where such moustaches are carefully cultivated. A smooth-faced person must appear sinister, inhuman, in Latin America, I told Ed. 'I wonder that they are not disconcerted by the wrinkleless placidity of Chinese features.' 'What's the Spanish word for inscrutable?' asked Ed.

I went to see Third Brother and Sister-in-Law Jui at Peking University and, diffidently, to bring some tins of food. Third Brother was thinner, his neck scrawny. He had three children now, and a fourth was on the way. 'We have everything we need,' he said automatically as I handed over the ham and the honey and the dried walnuts and other eatables. A Canadian man named Fitzgerald had left behind him at the Hsinchiao Hotel some food and also some medicines; somehow or other they had fallen to me and I now brought them to Third Brother in case the children needed them.

Jui, who was still tremulous, easily upset, had been told by the Party woman in charge of welfare: 'Comrade, you must really find a way not to have another child. Four is enough.' Jui stuck to four children after that. She told me, 'I never wanted four, it just happened.'

Third Brother agreed that all classes at the University had been cut to spare the strength of students and teachers. The following spring it was envisaged to send 46 per cent of the city cadres down to the rural areas to help with the spring sowing and planting and to ensure a plentiful harvest. 'It's also a way to get the city people fed at village level,' I said. Third Brother laughed his usual cheerful, noncommittal laugh.

I visited Simon Hua and his wife, Irène. They had extra rations since Irène was French and a foreign expert. Always, at home, throughout their almost three decades in China, they would eat French food, prepared by an old and faithful servant. Simon was no longer a 'rightist'. He had now been rehabilitated. And the house was warm and the food plentiful.

But Simon's father, Hua Nankuei, had died, and we talked about him for a long time, for he and my father had been inseparable friends. 'Both of them worked for China right up to the time they died,' said Simon. All these old engineers were forever afraid that something might go wrong with their beloved railways. Warlords and Japanese and new systems had come and gone, but all they cared for was to keep the railways running. 'They were indispensable, so they stayed on.'

'They were Chinese intellectuals, in love with China, in love with their people,' I said.

With the passing of Simon's father and the death of my father, only my Tibetan Uncle Liu remained of that batch of engineers trained in Belgium and France, who had humbly dreamed great dreams for China.

'China is the religion of every educated Chinese,' I insisted. 'It was so for your father, for mine. It must be so for us too.'

'You are so Chinese in a way,' said Simon. 'All your reactions and your feelings ... sometimes I feel that it is you who have never left China, and who live here, and that it is I, who came here in 1951, who is the foreigner.'

Where feeling was concerned, there was no doubt. Especially in that winter of 1960. Fiercely, wholeheartedly, I was defending China, even lying through my teeth (with a smile) to the diplomats and the newsmen who probed. Because only China was the heartbeat of my heart, the rise and fall of my blood, the substance of every cell of my body. I had not chosen this. It had chosen me. And all the more so when the wind howled like a wolf and winter fastened its iron will upon the land, and the whole world seemed to rise with glee to threaten China. Then, above all, I was Chinese.

It was Anna-Louise Strong who gave me the story about the Russians, which was only a wisp and a rumour until then.

In June 1960, both at the World Federation of the Trades Union Congress in Peking and at a meeting in Bucharest, there had been the most violent clashes between the Chinese and the Russians. In Bucharest Khrushchev had made a personal appearance, attacking Mao Tsetung as a dogmatist and a visionary. He had said, 'If the Chinese won't listen to us, there are ways and means of bringing them to heel.' He had called the Leap an exercise in waste and dogmatic extravagance.

Then in July, within a month, all Russian personnel, all experts and technicians, about twelve thousand of them, were abruptly withdrawn from China. In certain plants every blueprint and diagram was removed. Essential parts of machinery were also taken away. And no spare parts would be available. All construction work on many plants came to a standstill. Newly bought machinery was left to rust without shelter because the workers were inexperienced and there was no one to give orders; China did not have enough trained personnel to go round (and anyway, those who did give warning or say something cautionary were not listened to in those hectic days of the Leap Forward).

I went to the large Friendship Hostel, built a short distance out of the centre of Peking, in a park-like area. The hostel had housed several hundred Russian experts and their families. The buildings were imposing, Chinese style, with glazed green roof tiles, which must have cost an enormous amount. Inside the buildings were very large and beautiful flats with parquet floors, high ceilings, excellent furniture, bathrooms and the best plumbing in China. There were also two restaurants, one for Western food and one for Chinese food.

In that winter of 1960, the Friendship Hostel was sinister in its silent emptiness. Except for a few representatives of foreign communist parties who lived there, it was a ghostly, uninhabited city. The Canadian with whom I was going to lunch was a gloomily inarticulate man who spent the greater part of his time playing billiards. He had seen Edgar Snow, and Ed, fresh from major interviews, had implied to him—as to me—that the quarrel with the Russians would not become worse. 'I was worried sick. Ed's made my day,' said the Canadian. As many other communists from the West whom I would meet in Peking, he felt the earth would stop in its tracks if China and Russia fell out.

With us that day was a vivacious and garrulous woman, a foreign expert teaching in Peking. She was quite unable to utter a sentence without launching a couple of statistics. 'There's been a 29·4 per cent increase of wheat in the Ukraine in the last year ... there are 41·2 per cent more sheep in Azerbaidjan ...' She hugged and nursed and cradled and crooned statistics; they were her babies and she became upset if one questioned them. She and many others were easily irritated in those days of stress; and all of them were waiting, waiting to hear what was happening in Moscow.

For, ever since early November 1960, eighty-one communist parties of the world had been meeting in Moscow to thrash out differences; or rather, to argue, debate and come to a common declaration over the differences that had emerged between China and the U.S.S.R. There was no mention of anything material: of contracts, or economics, or joint ventures, or the demands from the Kremlin for immediate repayment ... it was all on a very high plane of theoretical argument. Hours and days and weeks of debate; which would continue in the following years. Millions of words. And so many, so many were waiting, their souls suspended to what was going on in Moscow.

After lunch I wandered round the palatial Friendship Hostel. Nothing could be more helpless-making than the stolid look of these massive grey piles, with their bright glazed tile roofs in the sunswept dust of a Siberian wind, which swirled thick armfuls of fallen leaves (here they were not gathered) round and round the paved courtyards. And that bleary old-man look of the uncleaned windows behind which no one peeped or stirred. Desolation. Or so it seemed. 'Let us wait until the north wind has stopped. Then we shall see.'

Ed had had a long interview with Mao Tsetung on October 22nd; then he had talked again with Chou Enlai. After he left, I kept him and Felix acquainted with all modifications, because so many policies were changed in that winter of 1960-1. They both found my news somewhat disturbing, because I was telling them things that were diametrically the reverse of what they had been told. This was our first, but not our last, experience of how quickly things change in China.

For instance, the urban communes, which had been instituted in the cities in the first flush of the 'communist wave': all three of us were to see them; but I was to watch their disappearance. What remained was a web of small factories which have lasted until today: make-do and mend shops, embroidery shops, spare parts shops, electric bulb factories, cobbling shops, tailoring shops, established in every street, and chiefly operated by women; four million of them having been recruited for these auxiliary but indispensable services, which allowed more women to go into the factories for productive work.

In the rural communes, the mess halls, instituted in 1958 in the flush of 'everything must be collectivized since communism has now come', were already disappearing when I left. They would only serve people who did not live too far away. And the main complaint of everyone who ate in them was about quality. The stolid, realistic peasants pointed out that the food dispensed was absurdly bad; whereas the cook got fat. I was told the truth, that commune cooks were in many cases ex-landlords or rich peasants. Why so? Because somehow the job of cooking is regarded as a 'low' occupation. And this in a country famous for its cuisine! Can anyone explain to me this illogicality? But then, it was also true that ex-landlords and rich peasants were the only people available for such jobs, since poor and middle peasants were supposed to work the land.

Kung Peng invited me to dinner. We talked at great length, and frankly, of the 'shortcomings' of the Leap. This was, I think, because Premier Chou Enlai had said that the truth about the difficult agricultural situation must be told. Chen Yi too, in interviews with visitors, would blurt out how he had been carried away by a wave of euphoria in 1958. 'I believed a lot of the nonsense that I was told by some people,' he said. Kung Peng also told me, 'We trusted too much secondhand reports and grossly inflated figures ... to tell the truth, the harvests were large, but they were guessed at.' There had been in some areas the determination to grow two crops where one had grown before; as a result, the peasants had harvested the first crop before it was ripe, and the grain had been unusable, but it had looked good to have so many sacks filled.

And then there were the producers of 'empty talk'. Some of them promised things that were totally impossible, but these were reported as if they had already been achieved, and then became hard fact—until they were exposed.

It was obviously painful for Kung Peng to go over the mistakes and the errors, the exuberance and the rashness; but this was only part of the story. She said not a word against the Russian sabotage, nor did she ascribe the evident industrial semi-collapse to anything but natural calamities and 'shortcomings in our way of doing things'. This, again, was due to Chou Enlai, who had said, 'It is up to us, the leadership, to take full responsibility for what has gone wrong.' Always, always, Chou Enlai would shoulder the total burden, when the mistakes were not of his doing; even when he, as well as Teng Hsiaoping, were warning, 'Stick to facts, and no boasting.' But what could this do when any sobering, waking up of people from the dream of immediate prosperity, was qualified as 'right-wing deviation' and 'pouring cold water on the people's fervour'?

'Kung Peng, I know all this', I said, 'but I have full faith, full faith in the Chinese people. And I tell you that I also think that only with the system of the communes, only with the Communist Party, can China weather this period of disaster. I'm not saying this to please you, but I think that's how things are.'

I could compare with what happened in Old China: in times of famine and want, hoarders and millionaires making money out of the people's misery; prices shooting up; skeletons on the road, people eating mud ... total social chaos. Here the centre held all things in place. And would hold.

A film was being shown in all the cinemas, and all over China. It was on Lenin during the great famine of the early years of the Soviet Revolution. It was not a very good film, but the point was obvious. The drawbacks, the shortfalls in food in China, were to be compared to that time in the U.S.S.R. At the same time, perhaps, it was a preparation for a new economic policy such as Lenin had carried out in those years.

The Chinese press was also full of articles on Lenin. But their aim was different. The articles were meant to point up the political correctness of the Chinese line. They were, I think, for the benefit of the great debate which was then going on in Moscow among the eighty-one communist parties and other affiliated parties of the world.

Lord Montgomery, hero of El Alamein, came to China on a private visit and was received by Mao Tsetung. Mao told Montgomery, 'We know something about fighting, about guerrilla war, about running villages. But we really do not know anything about economics. We shall have to learn it the hard way.' Montgomery predicted that China would prove a worthy friend and partner. He advocated making friends with China. He was politely ignored even in his own country.

I saw my first and only prostitute at dusk near the foreign bakery and cake shop in Hatamen Street. The cake shop had once been owned by a Greek family; and as a child I went there every Sunday with Mama, because on Sunday we were allowed a cake each. Later I gave private lessons in arithmetic to the daughter of the Greek cake shop owners and in return received a cup of chocolate and cakes to eat. Now the Greek owners had gone. The cake shop still functioned, however, and continues to do so today.

That evening I was bulkily clad, wore trousers; perhaps the would-be prostitute thought I was a man. She looked savagely at passers-by. She did not smile or speak. She wore a skirt and stockings and stretched one defiant, abrupt leg in front of me.

I told Rewi Alley about it that night, when I went to see him. 'Honey, there are bound to be such things in times of stress,' said he.

Twelve

Survival: 1960-1961

THE RAILWAY FROM Peking via Sian and the north-west to Szechuan province had been built after Liberation; many new railways were undertaken, opening regions never accessible before. How glad Papa would have been to ride on them with me, I thought, as the locomotive puffed painfully up the mountain slopes and I watched a land so primitive that it was like being in another country. This was the area through which the Red Army had walked its way in the Long March. The locomotive engine often stopped for hours in the night, as if to catch breath.

It was extremely dry and cold on the north side of the Tsingling range separating the north-west from Szechuan, and most of the time I played cards with my fellow travellers. At each small railway station there were one or two food sellers, and everyone came down to buy, queuing in orderly fashion for rough loaves of coarse bread, and sometimes dumplings filled with seaweed.

Suddenly the land changed. The train gathered speed: it was now going downhill. The air was soft and moisture-laden. There was still poverty, but we were now in a moist green world, Szechuan, where the swallow does not depart all winter. And all of us sighed with relief as our necks eased out of our shoulders, and stiffness out of our bones. We repeated to each other how Szechuan was China's great treasure house, rice basket, and someone recited Li Po's poem: Oh how difficult are the roads to Szechuan!

We came to Chengtu without fanfare. There were bamboo groves on both sides of the road, and the thatched houses were rickety and moss-grown. The Szechuan cadres who greeted me were as thin as string. Although Szechuan was not a calamity area, and the crops that autumn had been fair, yet it was on strict rationing because it was supplying five provinces with rice. And by the spring of 1961 Szechuan would be hit by a most terrible drought, the worst for over a century, which lasted 180 days. The black, life-giving soil which squeaked with a myriad lives in every handful would become dead and caked in that puzzle pattern which is seen in parched fields when all the water has been sucked out of the ground. But the real problem of Szechuan was that at the Leap close planting and other experiments and blanket application of directives ordered by ignorant cadres had brought the harvests right down, and there were no reserves.

Third Uncle and Third Aunt and their son, Sixth Brother, with his wife, and many cousins, gathered in Third Uncle's new house. It was almost like the old days, when the sun sparkled just before the New Year festival, and the Hall of the Ancestors was redolent with incense, while from the painted eaves hung parrots chained to pewter perches, squawking.

The government had moved Third Uncle because a school was to be erected on the site of his old house; and the new one was built according to his specification. 'The government is very kind to me now,' said Third Uncle contentedly. But, he added, I might have noticed, perhaps, some difficulties ... which he knew were transient, of course ... because certain people did not understand Szechuan or its agriculture ... now we should hope that in the spring all would come right. He would not say more, and we did not discuss agriculture again. Everyone in the family was thinner, though not ill. There was enough for them to eat, but not enough to acquire that smooth padding of underskin fat which keeps one warm during the cold season.

'Come and eat with me at the restaurant of the People's Palace Guest House,' I said. 'We shall,' said Third Uncle, and rose immediately, dusting his grey wool gown, and swinging his arms to unstiffen them. 'Let us go.' He trusted me entirely to know that this was not sponging, and he would not pretend that he did not want a good meal. I ordered all the dishes I could think of, and Third Uncle gave no advice, although I doubted that the composition of the banquet was up to his standards. I was as nervous as the first time I had cooked a meal for him in Chungking, and thereafter was for ever without face as a housewife because, as the lid of the soup tureen was lifted there, on the top of the liquid, floated a big bluebottle ... And Third Uncle, kindly, had said, 'It's only more meat in the soup,' and served himself, after spooning the fly out.

Third Uncle and Third Aunt and all my cousins ate with deliberate slowness, not hurrying. Good manners. At the end Third Aunt asked that all the food that was left be wrapped up, and she took it away with her, and the waiters nodded understandingly. But when I tried to have them to another meal, Third Uncle would not accept. 'Once is enough. It is too expensive,' said he. And this despite the fact that the Szechuan Party cadres who were taking me around urged him, saying, 'Your niece has come from so far on such a long journey ... of course you must see more of each other ... ' Rationing in Szechuan was stricter than in Peking, and Third Uncle and Third Aunt could not give me a meal at their house.

Before I left Chengtu, Sixth Brother procured for me an enormous ten-kilo caulked basket of pickled beancurd; that wonderful red beancurd made in Pihsien, the small town where our Family has lived for three centuries or more. How had be obtained it? Nowhere had I seen beancurd that year. 'From a farmer I know ... ' The countryside ate up its own beancurd, and also ate up the noodles produced there. Sixth Brother had cycled twenty-five kilometres back and forth, after his work, to get the beancurd for me. It had such a wonderfully beancurdy tang that my room in the hotel was redolent with it; and outside in the corridor I would find groups of curious people, standing still, breathing in the beancurd smell; and that was because it was in a woven basket daubed with clay, and then wrapped in oilskin, and the clay leaked slightly. The Family looked at the beancurd, and our mouths watered as we contemplated the paunchy container, but no one would share it with me. 'It's yours. It's yours.'

I walked about Chengtu, and of course I saw new factories, and was told about all the leaping advances, and duly recorded them, for much of it was real and true. The little cattle of Szechuan, shoed with grass shoes because of the eternal gooey black mud which ate into their hooves, did not look in bad shape. Small black pigs sauntered in the rutted mud lanes, and they did not have pig cholera — or so I hoped. There were hordes of young children about. 'There are too many children,' I said crisply. But the cadres smiled and said, 'But we have plenty.' Obviously they were not in agreement with the family planning policies I had heard about in Peking. 'Of course we *hope* each family won't have more than four children,' they said condescendingly. 'But it is difficult; we are still educating the masses.' The whole problem, it seemed to me, was that the propaganda for family planning was being done by one organization, the National Federation of Women, but that there was no co-ordination between them and the medical staff of hospitals and clinics. Only in the cities, and chiefly among the Party cadres, would there be family planning and also abortions; even then, the consent of the potential grandparents on both sides was first required. In the countryside, every baby born received a full adult ration of food from the very first day. And this militated against family planning. The quick-witted Szechuanese already had a jingle to sing that year: 'Oh, better produce a little meat ball than work for workpoints ... ' The meat ball means a baby.

Third Uncle continued to be active; this kept him cheerful. Inactivity made him morose and aged him. That winter he seemed to regain vital essence. He had kept his golden monkey fur, which covered his armchair and stopped arthritis. He filled many sheets with calligraphy, sitting at his beautiful Ming desk, which had been his father's and his grandfather's and even before that had served, and I coveted it greatly; but of course it disappeared at the Cultural Revolution.

Third Uncle talked in a leisurely but vague way of meetings which were being held; meetings of scholars, and intellectuals, convoked to put their heads together and readjust matters. 'It is not good to despise knowledge,' said he. He looked at all of us challengingly. 'Szechuan is still the treasure house of China,' he stated, with the pleasured assurance of a man well in his own country and his own skin. He asked me about Papa and about the funeral arrangements; he was glad there would be a stone with Papa's name engraved upon it, as well as his profession. 'Papa was never denounced as a rightist,' I asserted.

Third Uncle's prominent cheekbones stuck out a little more; his skin was smooth ivory over them, and he had small fits of silence; that was all that age and having less to eat imposed upon him. His vocabulary had

303

both extended and shrunk; he searched within today's political phrases for convenient words which would not recall the past too much, yet at the same time convey a hint of the consolations of memory. The fact that his son, Sixth Brother, could never be moved out of Chengtu was great solace. For the government had a ruling that in every family, one grown-up son or daughter must remain with the old parents, to look after them, and therefore must be provided with a job in the same city.

I went to Chungking, and called on Third Sister and her husband. Third Sister was ill; she had not lost weight at all, but because she had heart trouble and high blood pressure she was an invalid and received extra food. Of course, when one had a weak heart one was dispensed from work, meetings and political sessions as well. 'She is very sensitive, very easily shocked,' said her husband, who was most concerned, and hovered round her chair (he had lost a great deal of weight).

Sixth Brother was the opposite of Third Sister. He actually enjoyed meetings and political debate: 'I like to argue.' He was happy with his job, which had to do with communications, telephones and cables throughout the whole province.

I gave Third Sister my basket of beancurd; it really leaked too much; I did not think I could take it all the way back to Peking with me. She would share it with Second Brother, who was in Chungking and who described to me how the bank had organized teams of its employees to go to the neighbouring communes and bring food back. 'But we have not seen beancurd recently,' said he, and his mouth watered as he looked at the basket. In the streets of Chungking the shops were very bare. 'It's because the peasants from the communes came into the city and bought up everything they could lay hands on with the money which had been given to set up the communes.' All of a sudden there were no more socks or shoes or clothes, or satchels for schoolchildren or exercise books or paper. Because there were now schools in the communes and they needed paper and exercise books ...

I stood on the top terrace of the hippopotamic People's Palace, the ornate balconies of which had been designed by Third Sister, and I noted what I was to see in all the cities of China: the new tall chimneys. Factory chimneys. All built and waiting. But no smoke came out of them. And along the banks of the Great River, and at the railway station and on the streets and in courtyards, there would be piles, large and small, of machine parts: tubes and shafts, and whole machines too, and even dynamos without covers, and all this was for the factories that had been built. But now the factories were left, vacated, empty; some had no roofs or doors or windows. I hoped that the piles of machinery would be removed quickly, used elsewhere, would not rust ... it was such a waste, such a waste. But I would see the piles right up until 1963, and then they had rusted.

Along all the streets were pedlars, squatting in front of square pieces of cloth, selling screws for door jambs, and tape, and small scissors, and a thousand other disparate and wonder-making odds and ends; an empty bottle, a comb, two rusty nails and sometimes a piece of embroidery. Before them people squatted, choosing carefully, bargaining slowly. 'We have some shortage of consumer goods, the demand has been so great ... ' 'There's been too heavy an investment in capital construction. Our light industry has suffered somewhat ... ' 'Perhaps too many things have been attempted at once, too quickly ... ' Thus the cadres. But none of us would give birth to words that curse and alienate and bring on disaster by the power of invoking evil and calamity. We knew too well the power of words, the headlong precipitous thrust of words. For the strange alchemy whereby, with a casual and careless sentence, 'Communism is here', so much drama and want had come—was that not a lesson for us to be cautious? The only safe word, the one we all used, was 'readjustment'. And so at dinner we all agreed that the troubles were temporary and would be speedily over, and we beamed at each other and raised small thimble glasses of *maotai* wine, pledging our confidence in the future.

I went back to Peking, and the Foreign Minister, Chen Yi, received me. We talked pleasantly of many subjects, but not of the U.S.S.R. And this was because the conference in Moscow was still proceeding. Every day foreign diplomats anxiously scrutinized the Chinese newspapers (and their own) for hints of what was happening in Moscow among the eighty-one communist parties assembled there. The Chinese delegation was headed by Liu Shaochi, who in 1960 had become the Head of State; Mao had relinquished the chairmanship of the state, keeping the chairmanship of the Party. Rumour had it that Liu Shaochi favoured an accommodation or a compromise with the Russians, but that Teng Hsiaoping, the Secretary-General of the Chinese Communist Party, who was in Moscow with Liu, had upset the Russians with his bluntness ...

Chen Yi talked about the massive aid programme to the Third World which China was launching. 'Whatever our sacrifices, we shall not give it up.' He said America was getting very deeply involved in South East Asia, courting military adventure there in the name of 'containing Red China', and that this was dangerous for her. 'We want to untie knots, to smooth out difficulties ... they wish to *make* difficulties. Yet we need peace, only peace ... '

And then we talked about the internal situation. Yes, Chen Yi said, mistakes had been made. 'Look at me. I believed someone who told me: I can grow ten thousand catties of rice on twenty square metres of land ... ' There had been a breakdown in communication between the basic production level and the leadership. 'We did not really know what was happening below ... ' It was time, he said, to 'open up'.

Now this problem of 'opening up' rather than 'clamping down' was of course connected with the policy of the Hundred Flowers. 'There seems to be a tendency to fall for the loud mouths,' I said. 'Yes, there should be less big empty talk,' said Chen Yi. But how to get rid of the talkers and promote only the doers? Party members did not listen enough to the people; they behaved 'like tigers whose tails cannot be touched,'* and they took revenge on anyone who criticized them.

'We must stop putting caps on people,† hanging political labels round their necks whenever they open their mouths and we don't like what they say ... this is not helpful to our cause.' But the problem was there; and would recur, and assume fantastic proportions during the Cultural Revolution. Chen Yi himself was then called counter-revolutionary and brought before a kangaroo court to be grilled by young Red Guards.

Chen Yi then spoke of 'readjustment' and the need to enroll the efforts of the intellectuals 'to consolidate the gains of the Leap and eliminate the mistakes made'. This truly meant 'opening up', another Hundred Flowers; and in fact another Hundred Flowers would be launched, in early 1961, and both Chou Enlai and Chen Yi would be most active in promoting this new era of criticism and comparative freedom.‡ That meant another swing of the pendulum, that immense Chinese pendulum, going right-left, left-right, all through the history of the Revolution.

Kung Peng told me how Chen Yi had mislaid his ration book a few weeks previously and had been in dire distress for about a week; during which time he refused all privileges, including eating in a restaurant. His friends fed him until he could get a new ration book.

Chou Enlai also received me, later in December. He walked up and down, slowly, looking vaguely about the room. He was obviously under strain, But it was controlled strain. With him, passion and fury exteriorized as

---

* A saying by Mao Tsetung.   † Politically labelling them.
‡ Chou Enlai's major speech of 1961 on democracy would only be officially published in 1979.

lambent ice. His voice shook a little when he was very tired or upset, but it was always cold, restrained and low. How thin he was! I noticed that his collar was too large for his neck now. He had not slept the night before, Kung Peng told me. Too much work. Nor the night before that. He slept about two hours a day, after lunch; and not always then. But there was a diamond-cutting elegance in his voice when he spoke of 'those who think they can bring us to our knees', who thought that because of China's difficulties she could be threatened and subdued.

Who was he talking about, America or Russia? He did not specify. In fact, throughout that year and the next no Chinese would openly accuse the Russians of anything. Chou Enlai said that America was like 'a man balancing an armful of eggs. He cannot move or he will lose them all.' This did not sound altogether threatening to China. Or again, that the U.S. was like a man trying to catch ten fleas with ten fingers. This was actually citing Mao's jest: 'How difficult to put ten fingers on ten hopping fleas! The fleas hop at will, the fingers are bound to each other.' Obviously it was not, in Chou's mind, America that was the main 'threat' at this juncture.

Chou Enlai talked a long time of Lenin; of the hardships in the U.S.S.R. during the 1920s. 'Nothing is ever acquired without pain ... we shall overcome our present problems.' There was hardship, but there was no famine. 'You may go anywhere, you will meet problems and difficulties, but not the famines of the past ... the Leap has already brought us results that people do not know about ... those who think that China has failed, they will be surprised one day.'

As I watched his thin face with its beetling brows I thought, 'I am not going to give ammunition to those who rejoice when China is in dire straits.' Chou Enlai held China together with all the love and strength of his spirit and his body. And many they were, millions they were, who also, stoically, worked themselves to the bone, to death, and uncomplainingly gave up their lives for China ... and would I insult them, their self-respect, their dignity? I thought, 'When the bad days are over and the sun shines there will be time enough to tell the world how a whole nation gritted its teeth and so many pinned a smile upon their faces; how they refused to be degraded with gifts and charity; how their insides ached with hunger, and their bodies were so cold, so cold in their icy small houses ...'

Cold. All my friends were cold. Kung Peng did not light a fire; the heating only came on for two hours every night in the residential flats of the Foreign Ministry, just enough not to freeze entirely. When I went to my cousins', we all pretended not to notice the cold; but it was difficult to sit with one's legs and feet turning to ice.

And someone told me that Chou Enlai, too, did not light a fire, and in his office everyone was called upon to save coal and electricity. He sat in his overcoat and worked through the freezing night.

When I took my leave of Chou Enlai and returned to the hotel, I lay for a long time in bed with my head way down the side of the bed. I felt ashamed of myself, ashamed ... but at that moment I too could have died if Chou Enlai had asked me to die. He was China's hope, and all depended on him.

The Chinese delegation of the Communist Party was now back from Moscow. It arrived at Peking airport. Liu Shaochi with a fur hat on his head and a coat with a fur collar. The Politburo turned out to greet him. But Mao Tsetung was not there; whereas he would be there a year later to greet Chou Enlai returning from Moscow, where he had bluntly told off Khrushchev.*

And that absence, that glacial non-presence of Mao filled the winter air until every breath we took seemed to be a shudder through the cheers and the jollity and the smiles of those who jostled each other there, who crowded to clap.

'Hualan, why do you think Mao Tsetung was not there?'

'I think the Chairman may be travelling; or in the south. Anyway, everyone else was there ... '

Hualan would read the document brought back by the Chinese delegation, both in Russian and in Chinese; her organization would discuss it at meetings. It was of great length, and it was for study. But now because of the cold, 'we are enjoined to study it at home, we'll be more comfortable,' said Hualan. She and her sister poked fun at me as we sat companionably huddled in our coats, trying to pretend the stove was warm.

Hualan's brother came in. He was an engineer and worked on the aeroplanes at the airport. Most of them were Ilyushins, and quite old. There was an enormous dearth of spare parts and some aeroplanes were being cannibalized to keep the others running. Hualan's brother did not discuss his work. He was under great strain because he was a Eurasian and because the whole family had been in Soviet Russia for some years. But they were entirely Chinese in feeling, although they did not look Chinese.

* See *Wind in the Tower*.

We talked about the city cadres. Forty-six per cent of them were being sent to the countryside to help in the spring planting, which would take place right after Chinese New Year, in late January. 'If you went down to the countryside,' said Hualan, 'you would probably become the head of a brigade, or a model worker. Because you would not only fulfil quotas and beat norms, you would even crank up the shirkers.' Some of the cadres sent down to the countryside fell into an extraordinary passivity. They did not like manual labour; they did not say it, they just took so much time bending down, making a hole in the ground, planting seed … and they kept on asking for discussion meetings because 'that means they can screw their backsides to a chair', and perhaps they would then be elected to some sedentary job in the team or brigade, something cultural or administrative. They kept on repeating, 'We must not be hasty.'

I replied that had I been back in China and a cadre – which of course I would have become – and been sent to the countryside, I would probably have been accused of trying to show off by working too hard; of being élitist, of sticking my neck out. I would be criticized for setting impossible norms. Hualan said, 'I was able to do three times as much planting as one large, fat man, an "administrator" cadre, was doing. And so of course it was resented.' We laughed heartily, knowing these reflexes of the bureaucracy. Had we not all known and survived them in Old China? Bureaucracy was negativism, procrastination, inefficiency, an affliction which persevered and continued. And it would take a lot more than even the Chinese Revolution to change bureaucracy. 'Bureaucrats flourish all over Europe,' I told Hualan. 'The trouble isn't too much socialism but far too little, as if socialism and bureaucracy were interchangeable words,' said Hualan's sister.

Based on the treatment meted out to some Eurasians who had worked in the communes and had been used as targets in criticism meetings simply because they were of 'mixed blood', I put up a protest to Kung Peng. 'This looking down on Eurasians comes from Old China; it is chauvinism. Something must be done about it.' But Kung Peng was tired that day (there were so many meetings to discuss the Moscow document) and she said somewhat crossly, 'That's the fault of the people who do not integrate.' But how can one integrate one's looks? How can one become anonymous and merge totally when one's nose and eyes and hair are different? However, the next day Kung Peng had thought it over, and when I saw Chou Enlai again, he would talk at length against Han chauvinism and condemn its manifestations. And he would help Eurasians in China, right up to his death.

Now that the Chinese delegation was back from Moscow, Anna-Louise Strong was radiant. She read the joint statement and could find no fault with it. She exuberated. 'All difficulties will be ironed out. We'll show the imperialists what socialist solidarity means.' And her hope was that of so many people, so many of good will, of high ideals, who believed in communism, in socialism! I certainly did not rejoice at the subsequent disenchantment; the trail of nervous breakdowns, of divorces and rejections, the agonizing dilemmas in front of so many communist party members of many nations, when the dispute, at last, became a total rupture in 1963–4. I was preserved from this internal turmoil simply because I was not a communist, and therefore had no faith or creed to resift. As long as something was good for the Chinese people, however illogical, however opposed to theory it appeared, I was for it. Not for ever, but only for the time that it did any good. For me there was no eternity in policies or in methods or in people. And in this simplicity I had ample space for all vagaries, seasonal and political. I did not erect great logical structures divorced from the solid, concrete, and changing realities of China. I told Anna-Louise all this; I also told Simon Hua.

'You do not have principles then,' said Simon.

'Only when principles work,' I replied.

And Anna-Louise: 'Well, my dear, I suppose you keep a cool head … maybe we need cool heads.' But she too was baffled by someone who did not profess great and majestic reasons to live and die for. 'And yet you are so concerned, you must believe.'

'I believe in the Chinese people.'

'That's not a class analysis,' replied Anna-Louise.

I called on Prince Norodom Sihanouk, who had arrived by train from Moscow via Siberia, for he hated aeroplanes. The Western press had unleashed attacks on him, saying he visited the socialist countries 'too frequently'. Sihanouk, who was greatly concerned about the growing U.S.-fomented war in Laos and in Vietnam, had gone to Moscow to ask for the reopening of the Geneva Conference. 'The whole of Indo-China will go up in flames,' he said to me. All he wanted was to keep Cambodia neutral, out of the war.

The war in Laos was due to America. America was obsessed by the domino theory, had been caught in the trap of Indo-China since 1954, when Dulles saw every minor national liberation movement as a mighty enemy, communist-inspired.

A banquet was held in Peking for Prince Sihanouk, at the Great Hall of the People. I dressed up smartly, for Prince Sihanouk liked to have well-dressed people around him, and Sika, the Chinese wife of Charles Meyer, Sihanouk's private secretary, was covered in fabulous jewellery.

We assembled in the Great Hall of the People, trying to recognize the dignitaries, who kept to themselves in little knots. And then Liu Shaochi came in with Prince Sihanouk, and all the important people walking behind them. Liu had a great thick mop of beautiful white hair. I have never had any feeling for this man; yet I suppose he had his merits; how otherwise would he ascend so high? But he was impossibly colour-less although handsome, with a tall spare figure and a good profile. I do not know why he radiated dullness; perhaps it was our fault, since inevitably we compared him to Mao. And only Chou Enlai was not dimmed by Mao's formidable aura.

Mao Tsetung was not at the reception.

Anna-Louise, clad in a fabulous imperial embroidered gown (she collected them and owned a remarkable collection before she died), observed wistfully, 'I was told Mao would be here; I looked forward to seeing him again.' Mao's absence made the whole reception hollow, as if it had not really happened. But with beautiful American non-diffidence and spontaneity Anna-Louise rushed into the vacuum, went up to Liu Shaochi and wrung his hand repeatedly. 'You've done a great job, a great job in Moscow,' said she.

Liu Shaochi smiled a glabrous, modest smile. He shook hands with Anna-Louise, shook hands with all those who went up to shake hands with him.

The reception's organized cheer ended. Everyone left according to protocol, in big black cars. I rode back with Charles Meyer and Sika. Charles was exultant. Sihanouk had already had talks with Chou Enlai and it looked as if there would be a successful meeting in Geneva the next spring to thrash out the matter of the war in Laos.

Wu Chienta came to my hotel room, bringing with him two copies of the Moscow declaration of the eighty-one parties, one in English and one in Chinese. I laid the texts on the second bed; and read and read every evening until my eyes gave out.

Lin Lin came in a week later and saw the texts on my bed and my bleary eyes. 'You really do work hard,' said he. 'I'm trying to educate myself,' I replied weakly. 'Because I don't want to be re-educated by others.' And Lin Lin laughed uproariously. Then Chienta came again, to ask me what I thought of the Moscow text. I kept him to lunch; but he insisted in handing out his grain coupon when he had a slice of bread. 'Most of the text seems to me all right but I don't understand the phrase "by parliamentary means". It contradicts the rest.' I thought that to envisage a revolution by parliamentary means in the Third World, which has not known any such process, was really quite extraordinary. 'It's very European, the text ... it may work in Europe, perhaps.' 'Ah,' said Chienta beaming at me, 'your understanding has greatly improved.'

Only months later would I know that Mao Tsetung objected to the wording of the communiqué, and especially to that phrase. But at the time, and until 1963, this was not official. However, after Chienta had left me, I began to apprehend confusedly the possibility of a break between China and Russia. Unthinkable? Yes, it seeemed unthinkable then.

Russia was so much more powerful than China. Even among the intelligentsia in China, covertly debating the same unthinkable possibility, one would come across people saying, 'How can we quarrel with the U.S.S.R.? They have the atom bomb ... we shall be left without a friend in the world ... ' It was, in fact, hard to get away from the notion that China needed a nuclear umbrella to shield her from what then appeared as a ferocious, war-bent enemy, the United States.

I did not know, at the time, that China was devoting many of her scarce resources to catching up in atomic energy. How else could she accede to dignity and respect among nations, save through her own exertions in acquiring nuclear equipment? 'Even if we go trouserless, we must have atomic knowhow,' said the ebullient Chen Yi to me.

Power. Of course the reality of power could not be avoided. How wonderlandish of intellectuals to ignore the power-wielding machine of which they are, after all, also a component, in an equilibrium of strength which made up the system in which they thought and spoke; a duplicity of the social body since they also carried dissent and fission within them.

A new drive, to 'walk on two legs', that is, to employ both more sophisticated machinery and the traditional implements, was on in China. 'You too can break mental fetters, can think scientifically,' was the message. In the end it was science, the scientific spirit, which liberated man from the kingdom of necessity and of want.

'This is what we believed when we were young,' a famous professor,

Wu Wentsao said to me. Dr Wu was a very old friend, dating back to my Chungking days. His wife was the marvellous and renowned writer, Hsieh Pinhsin.

There would still be for a long time in China opposition to science, because it had come with the colonial powers; and the tendency to expunge everything 'foreign' would recur, disguised as revolutionary fervour. How could science become a homegrown product? A spontaneous function of the mind among the Chinese people? As we debated the process then, in 1960, it seemed to us that glorifying the names of the old Chinese inventors and making the people feel wise and creative might be a good beginning. 'During the Leap the masses were told that they could change heaven and earth,' said Dr Wu. But still 'foreign things' were identified politically with capitalism, and also with that small section of the intelligentsia which was both needed and suspect. 'The more science you learn from the West, the less revolutionary you become' was one of those unexplainable sayings which had sprung up during the Leap. And others were 'Rather be red than expert'; 'When one is revolutionary one does not need to study in a university'.

We were discovering these sayings with surprise; but we did not know that at the Cultural Revolution they would recur and be reinforced, until they became entirely identified with a so-called 'revolutionary line', which would cause great loss and suffering in China. Thus the claim, which I found in a newspaper of 1958, that a worker 'scientist' had proved Newton's law of gravity wrong. No evidence for this was given; it was simply published and spread all over China. Ten years later, during the Cultural Revolution, exactly the same claim, about the velocity of falling bodies, would reappear and be proclaimed as a 'discovery ... which breaks foreign models which have been used to restrict our thinking ... '

'Abolish superstition, unfetter the mind,' Mao Tsetung had said. 'Let foreign things serve China.' But this was turned into 'Abolish all rules and disciplines, and especially foreign ways of thinking which limit the mind.' And this would lead to machines being run at top speed and broken because all directives as to maintenance, method of running, were disregarded as foreign tricks to 'slow down' production.

'There's something wrong with the way we think,' said Hualan. 'It's feudal thinking,' I said. But that was no explanation. Her brother had been criticized because he had restricted the use of the aeroplane engines placed under his care. 'Only when we have more education shall we change ... we have many people who are just barely literate ... they want to know, but they don't know how to reason.'

'If we, the knowledge-bearers, give up this battle for science, then we shall have betrayed our people,' said Wu Wentsao to me.

Hualan was criticized in a meeting of her department for wearing skirts. 'It was the usual guy who finds fault with everyone,' she said. 'Comrades, if you wish me to go into trousers, I shall certainly leap into them with great pleasure, but will you please give me the necessary coupons to buy them? Unfortunately I only have skirts,' Hualan had replied. 'Everyone roared with laughter and it was all over,' said Hualan.

'Why not start a campaign of criticism against useless, idle, foolish, personal and non-political criticism?' I suggested to my writer friends. I nearly added, 'Do you think this would produce unemployment among certain Party committees?' 'I shall certainly criticize myself for uselessly criticizing myself,' replied one writer gravely. 'My performance is short of ideal, because things change so fast,' said another. Then someone told me about Pa Chin, the famous writer of *Family*, who had said that sometimes the campaigns to which writers were submitted made him think 'that we are all monkeys, made to jump through hoops'.

The great writer Lao Sheh was indefatigable in those years of stress. He produced and he produced, new plays and essays and a short novel and poems. He created twelve plays, arranged several Chinese opera scripts and wrote two novels between 1949 and 1962. And he also held eight official jobs. But now a new debate on literature was on, and the writers interrogated themselves. 'There is as yet no book which has truly described what has been done in China since Liberation,' said my old friend, Yeh.

READJUSTMENT began.

Wu Chienta came to tell me about it. 'We shall be giving all the policies to the people to carry out.' What this meant was that the Party cadres had been told, 'Hands off; give the people their heads.' Private plots restored; free markets; and encouragement for secondary occupations in rural areas. Above all, an enormous, wholesale campaign throughout all the rural areas, to 'speak bitterness', to complain of all that had gone wrong.

'How can one get the Chinese to grumble?' We had almost three thousand years of non-gruimbling behind us. And how to train the people to protest; how to make this protest legal and admissible without having, immediately, the Party cadres screaming 'counter-revolutionary!' and inflicting punishment? The Chinese word *fan*, which means to revolt and oppose and protest, has always implied armed opposition since verbal opposition was always suppressed. This was the frightful undemocratic tradition which China had inherited and it showed all the signs of being passed on into the Party, except that Mao Tsetung and Chou Enlai strenuously, continuously, repeatedly, fought against it. 'Words must be listened to ... Heaven won't fall, the earth won't stop turning,' Mao had said. But alas, the Party rank and file did not really understand what it meant to listen, to accept criticism and unpleasant opinions. 'How does one distinguish between valid criticism and malicious attack? Better stifle all protest.'

Perhaps in another generation some of these efforts at democracy would penetrate; but it all depends on how quickly China could achieve material security and a higher standard of living for her people. Democracy was inseparable from four factors: the industrial revolution, scientific thinking, some affluence, and universal education – and all four were the aims of Communist China, however awry things went.

I went to discuss this with the Yangs, and we argued about it for a long time. 'I hope that now there won't be any more thought-remoulding for the intelligentsia,' I said. 'It's been greatly softened down,' said Hsienyi. 'After all, our intelligentsia have had ten years of liberation and are adapting themselves ... ' Then Gladys would tell me how she had gone through the process. 'I was teaching in Nanking when Liberation came. I took part in the movement for thought-remoulding. It was extremely painful, but also fascinating. I wept, I broke down, I even became a little hysterical ... but at the same time, we were all in it together and there was a sustaining togetherness. I watched myself become other, sprout another me, a personality which no longer suffered alienation. I did, in a way, become someone else, but not altogether; in the end I chose what adapted me and I remained myself. I co-operated in the process, even if, at times, I was co-operating in humiliating myself. Now I am able to see things in several ways at once.'

We discussed what I would have done; and Hsienyi said, 'You would have remained yourself in the end, but I think you would have pretended a lot.'

'There was deliberate sabotage,' said Hualan.

It was Christmas Day and Hualan was up and about, cooking a big duck for her mother. 'It is quite impossible that the ultra-left communist wave of 1958 was not due to sabotage,' she repeated.

315

Within this campaign for 'speaking bitterness' and for exposing all that had gone wrong during the Leap, most of the offences had been committed during that 'communist' period, including the militarization of some communes, which were run like barracks and in which some people had died from overwork and exposure to the weather.

Now the production team, which was the original 'natural' village, would be an autonomous unit doing its own accounting, planning its own crops and production. It would own its implements and organize its manpower so that there would no longer be any forcible drafting of manpower away from the village or taking away of needed handcarts and poles and tools and draft animals.

'No more boasting of over-fulfilling quotas is allowed.' Hualan said there had been a total breakdown in communication between what was happening and the top Party leadership. 'Don't boast, speak the truth' was the new slogan.

The Central Committee had issued a directive that before the Chinese New Year of 1961 everything must be put in order and all errors rectified, and all people unjustly accused must be rehabilitated. All private belongings confiscated in the rash of 'communism is here' must be returned.

'Less empty talk, more real work,' said Teng Hsiaoping. Hualan repeated all this with relish. 'But someone has committed sabotage,' she persisted.

'How?'

'There are two kinds of sabotage, my dear. One is to go slow, to drag one's feet; that's more visible and easily corrected. The other is to manifest hectic enthusiasm, to exaggerate, to prove ultra-left, to drive people at an inhuman pace. Chairman Mao has said that ultra-left is as bad as right. But this second form of sabotage is more dangerous than the first because it all sounds so revolutionary.'

'But who did it?'

'I don't know,' said Hualan. 'We are trying to find out.'

'But didn't Chairman Mao himself suffer from ... a bit too much enthusiasm?'

Hualan bent over her duck. She was angry with me. 'The people love Chairman Mao, they love Premier Chou,' she replied. 'Chairman Mao never said that "communism was here".'

So, after the usual sifting and reappraisal, someone was going to be found guilty of sabotage during the Leap. I wondered who it would be.

I went to Tientsin to meet the writer Yang Mo, a portly round-faced mother of four who had just written a book called *Song of Youth*.

'You are a friend, so we tell you our difficulties,' said Yang Mo, 'but our enemies would like us to fail.'

How European Tientsin still looked in some of its streets, notably the erstwhile British Concession. The hotel where I stayed—formerly a British-run hotel—was opposite Gordon Hall, the Gordon Hall of my childhood, where I had endured my school-leaving examinations. In my imagination it remained a massive, imposing fortress; how it had dwindled to some ridiculous copy of a large pub in Edinburgh! It was now a government office.

Here, too, there was no smoke from the factory chimneys. Yang Mo tried to explain but I said, 'Never mind. The factories are there; the machinery is not yet come; the workers have been recruited and are being paid by the state, but they have nothing to do. But there will be readjustment and all will be well.' Yang Mo touched my arm and smiled. I then asked abruptly about the writer Ting Ling, who had been condemned as a rightist. But Yang Mo did not know anything about her fellow-writer.

I left Peking in mid-January by train for Wuhan, to see the new bridge across the Yangtse River, to visit the factories, to see the Wuhan steel plant. The Wuhan steel plant was not working. Embers glowed in one of the furnaces. That was all. Why the stoppage? 'We have fulfilled our quota for the year,' said the engineer in charge. That of course was not true. But what else could I expect? That the Party committee in charge would tell me, 'Comrade, we've been left in the lurch. This plant was built by the Russians and it is not completed. And there are a lot of snags. And we do not have enough coal for stoking, there is a coal shortage, and not enough iron ore, and some of the machinery is not functioning as yet.' The workers seemed well-fed, but the Party committee in charge looked like a bunch of cadavers. The engineer wrung my hand and said quietly, 'Come back next year; by then, we shall have solved *all* our problems.'

The hotel in Wuhan was of course not heated; neither was there any hot water. I wore my fur coat to bed.

By now I had adapted myself. I walked downstairs and upstairs rather than use the lift, I washed in cold water, just one degree above zero, and I turned off all the electric lights I met. And this habit of thrift, frugality, which then began I could not lose. For years I would 'save electricity, save power' by walking up and down stairs, turning off lights … no more would I waste a single moment, a single thread, a single sheet of paper.

In Wuhan workers stayed at home to rest one day in two. Market stalls were organized in every street to spare the strain on housewives. The Wuhan Women's Federation did very good work. 'The small urban factory is most important in keeping up the standard of living,' said a splendid woman, forty years old, a beggar until she was twenty, now a Party member. She had organized the women in her street into several such factories. 'We repair kettles and saucepans. We make small earthenware stoves. We cobble shoes. We mend clothes and make children's clothes. We also manufacture spare parts for bicycles, for electric fixtures. We have started a rope factory.' The schools were closed; not because it was holiday time but because of the cold, to spare the children. Hibernation. 'Wait until the spring comes.'

I watched the huge stretch of the Yangtse, rolling its khaki water under the new bridge, and the beautiful parallelograms of the new fields on both banks. Within the next eighteen years two dozen bridges would span the great river, from its source down to the ocean.

To trust the Chinese people and the present government to make mistakes, to find them out and work out their own solutions; or to run to 'denounce' these failings and errors, the tyrannies and the flaws? Run to whom? To those in the West, sitting on their three hundred years of industrial revolution, with its carnage and exploitation and tyranny? To those who had indeed evolved democracy, but at the cost of how many bloody repressions? To those who had contributed to China's downfall and misery in the past and to China's present difficulties? They were so immensely concerned with freedom and liberties ... but had we known these liberties when we were but their colonies? When China was a land of starving beggars, where was their beautiful indignation?

All I could do was trust. Trust the Chinese people.

In Hongkong the press was at the railway station. 'I am convinced that China will overcome her difficulties.' There is a photograph of me, looking almost like a missionary, saying this.

I was again reviled for not denouncing tyranny, for not speaking up for freedom. 'You've either been brainwashed or you've seen nothing,' said a very superior newsman to me.

Today I can still see the replete diplomats in Peking counting the calories of the average Chinese ...

'China will solve her own problems ... we lack nothing ... we shall not beg.' I would not betray my people.

Thirteen

The World Outside China: 1961-1962

THE DAY AFTER I reached Hongkong I went to see Pierre Mardulyn, director of the Belgian bank. Pierre had been a friend of our family for many years. Mama used to go to the Belgian bank, taking me (I was eight years old then) to cash money which her father sent because Papa, though working, was not getting any pay ... the warlords swallowed all the railway revenue.

'I want to send money to China, Pierre. How much cash is there in my account?' Pierre told me and I transferred it to the Bank of China in Hongkong. Pierre said, 'Putting money in China at present is a dead loss.' Then his banker's instinct took over. 'On the other hand, it might pay off as a long-term gamble.'

The Bank of China director, Mr Huang, was frail and bespectacled and did not look surprised. 'There is of course a company for investments by overseas Chinese ... we could transfer your money to it.'

My uselessness in China was now so obvious, so evident. For I had offered to stay, so involved had I become with the suffering and the dignity, the power of the people to absorb the suffering and to endure. But Kung Peng chided me. There was Vincent, she said. I had had the luck of finding a man who made me happy; it was not right to do things impetuously ... There was really nothing I could do which was not already being done by other people. And so the only thing I could do was to send some money. Foreign exchange. U.S. dollars. 'Bridges of understanding can be built, they must be built ... ' Chen Yi had said this. I could, perhaps, build a bridge. Between China and the rest of the world.

'I don't want this money, I want to give it to the Chinese government,' I said to Mr Huang. He smiled benignly. 'We have our policy. You will get 12 per cent per year interest, and after eight years the capital is returned to you. That is our policy.' I stressed I wanted neither capital nor interest.

319

Mr Huang continued to smile and repeated that this was the policy. Twelve per cent, and of course no income tax since there is no income tax on individuals in China. After eight years, should the money remain in China, then the interest would come down to 2 or 3 per cent, as for ordinary Chinese currency in China.

I would not touch any of the money for many years; in fact not until 1972, when the Bank of China got in touch with me. 'You have a great deal of money with us ... you must use it.'

Many thousands of overseas Chinese did what I did; put foreign exchange in China. Not with any intent to profit, but because at that time China needed foreign exchange. Several hundred millions of dollars must have thus gone into China in those bad years, 1960 to 1962. And a steady flood of parcels, food and clothing to help the families.

I flew back to Malaya. Many unsettled thoughts like feathered spring seeds flew in my brain. Because now, without any political indoctrination, or thought-remoulding, or compulsion, or persuasion, a transformation had taken place. Now it was in China that I felt at ease, secure, and it was when I crossed the border back into the world outside China that disquiet invaded me. Not a large disquiet; a nagging, small and constant one. It was a slight flapping around the heart, like the erratic wingbeat of a caged bird, a helplessness in the throat. Nothing that could be explained. How had this happened? Why had I changed?

Home. Vincent. I said to Vincent, 'I almost did not come back ... ' He replied, 'I thought you might not return.' Another me taking over, frogman swimming upwards from the sea floor. What had been important receded; what I had forgotten, concerns, worries, small pleasures and trivia, loomed larger now. Names which had lapsed from my memory in China returned to my tongue. And as I began once again to speak in English, my Chinese also went dormant. Anyone who manoeuvres in several languages has this experience; it takes a day or two, sometimes more, to go easily into the next medium.

In the next few weeks and months I was literally invaded by overseas Chinese, all of them anxious about one thing or another, all of them wanting something. They wanted to know whether parcels via Hongkong could be received in China. No parcels could be sent to China from Malaya and Singapore. And there were men who had left their wives and children in China for many years, but now suddenly wanted them out. Could I get them out? Could I write a letter making sure that Old Mrs Su, someone's grandmother, aged eighty-five, was getting adequate hospital care? Could I ... Someone else wanted to operate a ring for smuggling penicillin and vitamin B into China. Would I help, and make a lot of money?

The Secret Societies flexed their biceps and came in. A very nice man, whom I shall call Mr Liu, and who was 'protecting' the district where I practised, dropped into the clinic to have his smallpox vaccination and cholera shots before going to China. 'My brothers will look after me there,' said he. He went to China for three months, and came back. Would China ever get rid of her past when the past was waiting to pounce upon her future?

I wound up the clinic gradually, without haste. I had come to the end of my childhood longing. The medical me was being replaced by another me who fused medical diagnosis with social and historical perception. There were too many mes jostling, each one occupied with a single activity; I must merge them, and one or a few of them must be dismissed. It was impossible to continue doctoring all day, writing at night, and doing what I now wanted to do: document myself fully on China, the Chinese Revolution. There was simply not enough time in the day.

In that year of 1961 I began to be very uneasy about the Malaysian Sociological Research Institute.

The material I had brought back about the Islamic religion in China was not used. The policies of the Institute puzzled me. I would find its Secretary-General, who was Shirle Gordon, and who by the statutes of the Institute could never be fired or moved,—difficult. Shirle flung her beautiful blonde mane at me and hissed: So-and-so is a saboteur. No discussion was allowed; I was not called to general meetings; although my money remained welcome.

In 1962, a member of the Institute went, most mysteriously, on a trip to Moscow. By then, owing to my studies of Islam and my meetings with Arab scholars involved with the U.S.S.R., I was becoming suspicious. It seemed to me that research to illuminate the roles of the various peoples in South East Asia, that fantastic jumble of superposed and conflicting cultures and ethnic groups, was important, not pro-Russian or pro-Chinese propaganda.

Honest and truthful and sincere scholars of every kind were to be involved in the Institute; out of fascination for Shirle, or for the sake of knowledge, or Islam. In the 1970s the government in Kuala Lumpur would allegedly discover evidence that certain members of the Institute were colluding with a foreign embassy, engaging in intelligence activity. I do not know what became of Shirle Gordon, save that an item in a newspaper from Malaya reported that she had been expelled. I had left the Institute definitely by 1963.

I would also have a problem with the magazine in London, *Eastern World*, which I had subsidized. And for almost the same reasons: divergence of opinion as to how the magazine should be run. But I have always preserved a good memory of Hans Taussig and his capable and cheerful and competent assistant, Emma Leibovici. I wish, somehow, one could disentangle personal relationships from business and other decisions. But this seems difficult.

The struggle for power between the Prime Minister of Singapore, Harry Lee (Lee Kuanyew), and the left wing of his party (the PAP) became more acute in April 1961, when the PAP was defeated in a somewhat maverick by-election.

In that April the Prime Minister of Malaya, Tunku Abdul Rahman, proclaimed the intention of forming 'Malaysia'. The switch from Malaya to Malaysia sounds simple. Actually it was not. Malaysia was devised by the British to get over the problem of a direct merging of Singapore and Malaya, in which the Malays would have been swamped by a Chinese majority. Erstwhile colonies, protectorates and other territories loosely connected within the British Empire's multiplicity of domination in South East Asia were to be federated to Malaya. This meant the territories of North Borneo, Sarawak and Brunei, totalling altogether about a million people. This inclusion would 'balance out' the racial equation, the Chinese majority, because, so it was stated, all the people in these territories were 'Malay'.

I do not know by what sleight of language, glibness of image, the British were able to convince the Malays of Malaya, at least for a while, though only for a while, that the Dayaks of North Borneo, who were animists and head hunters, and the Kadazans, who were Christians, and other various tribes, were all good Muslim Malays.

Only in tiny, oil-rich Brunei (Shell worked the oilfields) with the largest mosque in South East Asia, because of oil, and a Malay Sultan, were there 63,000 bona fide Malays out of a population of 80,000 ... and in the end, the only territory to refuse to be included in the new Federation of Malaysia would be Brunei.

What no one talked about but everyone knew was that in order for Malaysia to be established a purge had to take place. And since the left wing of the PAP in Singapore now openly declared its opposition to Malaysia, of course they had to be purged. In August of 1961, this left wing would break away to form another party called the Socialist Front, or Barisan Socialis.

I watched the purge being prepared.

Firstly, there was a series of lurid articles in the *Straits Times* which beat any thriller in style, called 'The Open Conspiracy'. It purported to detail a plot by the Malayan Communist Party to take over Singapore. Secondly, Lee Kuanyew (he now refuted his English name of Harry) denounced the British, still the dominant influence in Singapore. He said they were trying to force him to jail his own left wing. 'The British government has tried to manipulate the PAP ... into a position where the Communist Party will be attacked not by British Imperialism which is the supreme power in Singapore, but by us, the locally elected government, with its limited powers.' Thirdly, in Malaya itself the Emergency regulations, promulgated during British times and practised by the British Special Branch, were refurbished as an Internal Security Act. Preventive detention without trial, arbitrary arrest, and other efficient inventions were retained, and are used today.

Lee Kuanyew denounced the 'diabolical cynicism' of the British High Commissioner, Lord Selkirk. Lord Selkirk now courted the left wing of the PAP. Nothing was funnier to me than the sight of the left-wing leaders, among them, prominently, Lim Chingsiong, later the acknowledged leader of the new Barisan Socialis Party, and his aides, all reputed members or sympathizers of the Malayan Communist Party, all people who had been jailed at least once, if not twice, by the British Special Branch, sipping cocktails at receptions given by Lord and Lady Selkirk. The left-wing Barisan leaders came in open shirts while Lord and Lady Selkirk wore their most starchy get-ups. I could not help applauding, so excellently did Lord Selkirk perform.

A Chinese politican from Malaya came to see me. Citizenship laws for the Chinese were being tightened up; the Malays, confronted with merger between Singapore and Malaysia, wanted to make quite sure that they would remain a legal majority, even if not a real majority by head count. There was a lot of talk about birthrate. The Chinese birthrate was higher than the Malay birthrate — the Malays had so many more diseases, especially venereal, which engendered sterility—and the Chinese infant mortality rate was lower than the Malay.

This Chinese politician wanted to know what the Chinese government policy on the overseas Chinese would be. The overseas Chinese had not given up the hope that China would protect them. The Chiang Kaishek government, after all, had always claimed to 'protect' them. 'I am afraid there are going to be massacres and pogroms of the Chinese in the new-founded Malaysia,' said this politician.

I told him that the policy in Peking was: the overseas Chinese were to be encouraged to take the nationality of the country they lived in; to become good and loyal citizens; there could not be any dual nationality, nothing like what the British operated in their remaining colonies and what the Jews of Israel and the United States were able to enjoy.

'But we shall be second-class citizens, almost slaves, kept only because of the wealth we bring, for ever and ever,' objected this politician.

I could offer him nothing but cold comfort.

Had this discrimination in all fields profited the Malay population at large, the 'sons of the soil', I think one might have seen the end of this situation in not too long a time. But the establishment of privileged bureaucrats, achieved by reserving three out of four jobs in the administration to Malays; by lowering university standards for them; by not admitting to university brilliant Chinese students proficient in Malay and in English; and by establishing company directors and managers who are Malay in each company, thus creating entrepreneurs, does not really change the fact that 80 per cent of Malay rural families still live below what is called the 'acceptable' poverty level.

The newly formed party, the Barisan Socialis, with Lim Chingsiong as its head, was against merger and Malaysia. It declared that Singapore could live on its own. This was denounced as a 'communist plot', even though it has since become a reality and Singapore is held up as a shining example of prosperity.

Of course, it could only become prosperous when its radicals were curbed, since it had to enter the orbit of capitalism, however much the PAP would continue to call itself 'socialist'.

I sought out Lim Chingsiong for an interview. He was the idol of the Chinese middle-school and university students. He spoke three Chinese dialects, English and Malay, all of them fluently. He was handsome, with regular features, but I was surprised to note how unaggressive he was. In contrast to Lee Kuanyew's forceful, abrasive personality, Lim appeared hesitant, diffident, almost wistful. And above all, somewhat naïve.

Lim Chingsiong gave me a short biography of himself; but he was far more interested in talking about the Sino-Soviet dispute. 'I do not understand it,' said he. I offered to lend him whatever documentation I had, and duly brought him the clippings I had smuggled through. But the file would never be returned to me because Lim Chingsiong would go to jail shortly after, and all his belongings would be taken over by Special Branch; and I did not ask for my clippings to be returned.

The Students' Union of Nanyang University came out against Malaysia. In the summer of 1961 an attempt was made to break it up; and I was cited as supporting those who were breaking it. Of course I had to refute this, as it was not true. What was my intense surprise when my moderate refutation – which, however, had led to the Students' Union not collapsing – drew on my head the wrath not only of British officials like Lord Selkirk but also of influential British administrators like the Chancellor of Singapore University?

Meanwhile, Prime Minister Lee Kuanyew of Singapore had collided somewhat with the more conservative Malays of Malaysia. This was not at all his fault. It was due to his over-ebullient and enthusiastic friend, Alex Josey, who had proclaimed him 'The leader of the overseas Chinese – heir to five thousand years of Chinese civilization'. And Lee himself, in one of his more abrupt moods, was quoted in the press as remarking that the Malays themselves had 'come from China in the eleventh century', and that the 'sons of the soil' theory might as well apply to the Chinese.

This infuriated Malay extremists ... a motion to jail Lee Kuanyew was even set afoot.

I went to see Prime Minister Tunku Abdul Rahman in April 1961, to confirm the matter of my giving scholarships both to Malay students to study Chinese at Nanyang University and to a Chinese to study Malay culture and literature. Tunku accepted the idea and the money,* and I would continue for five years providing for the one and only student – a Chinese – who elected to study Malay history, language and literature. No Malay student turned up.

I spoke with Tunku of the problem of the overseas Chinese; it was difficult for these hardy, industrious and thrifty people to understand the hostility towards them and the position they were in. 'But we built this country ... it was jungle before we came ... our work, our sweat, our

---

* I began with a $12,000 scholarship.

lives have gone into this soil,' they would say, incredulous that they should be discriminated against.

Tunku agreed that they suffered from the relics of a colonial situation and that now they must adapt or would be 'neither fish nor fowl'. He let me understand that it was not possible *not* to discriminate against them, at least for a generation ...

Malaysia would not adhere to the American edifice of SEATO, the South East Asia Treaty Organization, erected by Dulles in 1954 in order to counter the 'Red' threat in South East Asia. SEATO was aimed at China; but 'we Asians do not like SEATO, it bears a stigma,' said the wise Tunku. 'We shall ensure our own security ... I've always said there cannot be two Chinas,' he added, showing his independence of mind. It meant that, in due course, Malaysia would recognize China.

Three days after seeing Tunku in Kuala Lumpur, I flew to Geneva to attend the conference on Laos, which had indeed convened. I received a letter from Cousin Pengju telling me that he would be there, and also Kung Peng, and Prince Sihanouk, and Malcolm MacDonald and Marshal Chen Yi ... would I come and join the party? It would be great fun. I did.

There was a muddled, muddy war in Laos, which had already lasted three years; the United States were involved in the usual tense, emotional manner which characterized them in the 1950s and 1960s. There were three Laotian princes, all related to each other, and each backed by one or other of the powers. They squabbled and denounced and intrigued and knotted and unknotted alliances; and all this was taken most seriously by the Washington experts, who saw the dread hand of 'Red' China everywhere.

However important the Laos question appeared to be at the time, I am afraid that I could not contrive to work up a passion for it; neither would I ever get clear all the ramifications of the tangled situation. The Laos war, it seemed to me, was but an episode, a boil in that rash of abscesses of war which would erupt, pus from a plagued body, throughout the Third World; wars by proxy between the two superpowers, the U.S. and the U.S.S.R. But Sihanouk of Cambodia was perturbed, and had reason to be. For with war in Vietnam and war in Laos, when would war come to his beloved country, Cambodia, wedged between the two?

I never understood why Laos, with its two million people, was, in the eyes of America, so important, needed such a torrent of corruptive aid, and weapons, and why so much hysteria was involved in the process. As to my keeping track of Boum Oum, Souvanna Phouma, Quim Pholsema (whom Malcolm nicknamed quinine for short), Nai Champassak, Phoumi Nosavan, Vong Vichit, and others — it was more than I could do.

I lunched with Malcolm, who was staying at the Beau Rivage Hotel; I called several times on Prince Sihanouk, and listened to his exposés; and of course I went to see Marshal Chen Yi and had hours of relaxed, cheerful talk which romped from the colour of Lake Leman, to Rousseau's island in Switzerland, to the knots of war to be untied in Laos and Vietnam. Pengju did his newspaper work, but also prepared a whimsical delight for himself: interviews, not of political personages, but of residents in Switzerland such as Charlie Chaplin, Graham Greene, and Brigitte Bardot ... he also wanted to interview Françoise Sagan, going to Paris for the purpose, but she was not available.

Sihanouk had rented a magnificent villa; and the Chinese too had rented quite a large estate. 'The conference will last a long time,' was the prediction. 'Why are there so many Chinese in the delegation?' one journalist asked Pengju. 'Because there are a lot of people in China,' Pengju replied. 'The Americans want to isolate us, but we're very much here,' said Chen Yi at dinner. Despite all protocol, it was obvious that the Laos conference was also the opportunity for discreet, unofficial meetings, casual soundings. Ambassador Wang Pingnan, one of the best and ablest of Chinese diplomats, a man Chou Enlai trusted greatly, was also there. He was Ambassador to Poland, and in charge of the intermittent talks at ambassadorial level between the U.S. and China. These talks had begun, at Chou Enlai's suggestion, in 1955, and though given no publicity, were of major significance.

Every delegation was stuffed with important people. The American one, led by Averell Harriman; Ambassador Parsons, once holding the Laos post, was now Assistant Secretary of State, and perhaps that is why Laos loomed so large in the United States' preoccupations.

A remarkable arrangement whereby Harriman and Chen Yi could shake hands, and even, possibly, exchange a few remarks, was worked out. It was at a party thrown by a neutral country, and timing was so perfect that as Chen Yi hovered courteously in the entrance to the main hall, taking leave of his host, Harriman arrived and could shake hands with Chen Yi. This was History. Dulles in 1954 had refused to shake hands with Chou Enlai.

Of the tortuous course, the eddies and ripples and whirlpools; the treacherous undercurrents of the conference, I can say little; for I had no role in it, merely hovered on its outskirts. The only manifestation of my

327

presence was an article called 'Swans on Lake Leman: personal portraits of Chen Yi, Malcolm MacDonald and Prince Sihanouk at the Geneva Conference'. It was printed in *L'Express* of Paris.

There was a large garden party for the delegations. The weather was superb, Swiss-postcard bright, and I was sitting, I think with the French, when I noticed that the Western delegates mixed quite freely; but that no one came near the Chinese table. So I walked up to them and sat down with them. Chen Yi was there, and his wife Chang Tsien, a beautiful woman with a lovely smile. I could see, out of the corner of my eye, two Englishmen stare in my direction with great ire. Why were they so angry? But as the garden party began to move towards its end I saw Malcolm edging nearer. 'Malcolm, I want to introduce to you my dear friend Kung Peng.' Malcolm, as usual, was superb. He smiled with great charm, and shook hands and said, 'But of course, I've heard so much about you from Suyin.' And then he was chatting with Chen Yi and Chang Tsien. I shall never know whether or not Malcolm's proximity at that moment was a dexterous calculation of steps. A few days later Malcolm charmed Chen Yi at a dinner given by the latter; he stood on his head and then turned somersaults (Malcolm used to turn somersaults right down the street in Singapore). I told Malcolm how much we missed him; his successors in South East Asia were uniformly dour, celluloid-collared and impossible to talk to.

Malcolm went to China in 1962, at the end of the Laos conference. When he returned to Hongkong he gave an enthusiastic press conference, praising China. 'The Chinese are quite right and they are doing things which have never been done before by any other people on earth,' he said to me. 'If only I could get it into the heads of the Americans that China is not a danger to them, that the Chinese want peace above all, the whole world would be changed ... '

But within England, and from the Labour government, Malcolm would encounter frowning hostility. Because so many members of Britain's Labour government had a sentimental attachment to the U.S.S.R. Some of Malcolm's projected articles, due to be written for large circulated newspapers, never appeared.

On my return to Singapore from Geneva I was bodily searched at the airport. This meant that Special Branch – or someone – had decided to make life uncomfortable for me.

I have always suffered from the mountain of mail which awaits me, everywhere, when I return from a trip. This time it was from my sister Marianne. She had to be looked after. Tiza and Mama had come to stay with her, then moved out when Tiza had found a job; and then they would not open the door when Marianne rang the bell and thumped on the wood. 'Yet I know they are there, I can see the curtains move,' wrote Marianne to me. 'She disturbs Mama's sleep,' wrote Tiza. No one lied. Everyone said what they really believed, and upon this grew the great tree of Marianne's mental breakdown. In 1960 Tiza had written to say that Marianne had been committed to a mental hospital; Tiza had signed the papers committing her. I started corresponding with Marianne's doctors; and now, in 1961, she was discharged and came to Malaya: I had asked her to come.

She was much better; but convinced that her husband had been poisoned; that she had cancer. As the days went by her strangeness increased. She now refused to take the pills she had been provided with. 'They' had changed the colour of the pills behind her back, she explained. Vincent, accustomed to a wider panorama of erratic behaviour through his Indian culture, could see nothing wrong with her.

Menina Mesquita, who had helped me type my manuscripts ever since 1954, came to Malaya. She had brought her typewriter, and expected me to work as she had always seen me work. But she found me strangely disassembled. I was emptied and empty; I waffled. My book on Cambodia, *The Four Faces*, was ended. I was now toying with a film script set in Cambodia. A French producer, M. Coureau, wanted to shoot a picture there. I was half-hearted about the script. Menina's buoyancy also depressed me. Unconsciously, I was already abandoning South East Asia; but this underground germination of my books on China was not perceptible. I also filed and refiled my father's papers, and letters, and poetry ...

As a result of this in-between state, I would write a book called *Winter Love*, which was about a lesbian affair in England. It would be published in America and also in England as a novella, part of a volume entitled *Two Loves*; the other part, also a novella, being based on the film script I wrote for the film in Cambodia, entitled *Cast But One Shadow*.

Menina hated *Winter Love*. My French publisher was puzzled, and thought it an early novella written in my younger days, reminiscent of some adolescent effusions, like Colette. It was not so. *Winter Love* was based on some of the emotional links I had seen forged while I was in England during the war, when there were so few men about and it seemed absolutely normal that women should go two by two. But my main

329

reason for writing it had to do with reviews of *The Mountain is Young*. Its critics had complained that I had always dozens of characters and was unable to handle a taut, tense situation with only two or three persons. I thought: Let me try. And the result was *Winter Love*.

I would go again to Cambodia, accompanying the film crew shooting *Cast But One Shadow* in the ruins of Angkor. The whole enterprise was directed by a small, Spanish-looking Frenchman, full of fire, fun and talent, named Marzelle. The film was made, and shown in Singapore. Tunku Abdul Rahman came to the première and politely said, 'A very nice film.' It was disastrous; infected with slowness, turgid. The languor of Cambodia had crept into all of us, the jungle and the leprous magnificence of Angkor were timeless ... so was the picture.

I thereupon wrote the novella *Cast But One Shadow* in three weeks. It was very different from the film.

I had immensely enjoyed galloping around Cambodia with Prince Sihanouk, whose physical energy was astounding. '*Comment vous sentez-vous aujourd'hui, Madame?*' he would inquire, his face showing great concern. '*Monseigneur, je suis claquée.*' It delighted Sihanouk to know that I could not stand the pace of his excursions. After a whole day of travel, interviews, speech making, inspections, we danced all night until six in the morning, when regretfully Sihanouk, who had danced, sung several songs of his own composition, played the clarinet, conducted the orchestra, announced we would have two hours' rest ... before going off to the beach for a swim, followed by a banquet and dancing, and then off by jeep to open some hospital or school or to consecrate a canal, or to do some digging on the projected railroad from Sihanoukville Port to Phnom Penh ... After a week of following Sihanouk around, one was really *claquée*. 'I kill all my ministers,' said Sihanouk, thoroughly happy.

Leonard now fell into great jeopardy. Back from England, he had found a job which enabled him to live; and at the same time he was writing two books, one on Chinese Secret Societies, which was to become a standard text on the subject. He now lived in a small flat in Singapore. I think that since his job concerned social welfare, he met a good many people; among them an Irish priest who introduced to him a girl I shall call Helen, who appeared to be in difficulties.

With Leonard's help Helen acquired a job and a small flat not far from his. I think that Leonard used to visit her occasionally; and perhaps they had a liaison. Leonard liked to play squash and to jog, and one Sunday morning after his usual exercise he went to Helen's flat, as he was accustomed to do. He found the door open, but this did not disturb him, as it had happened before; Helen going round to the shop at the corner for some food for lunch. He went into the flat and decided to have a shower before her return. After washing himself he opened the door of Helen's bedroom and found Helen on the bed, quite dead. She had been strangled.

It seems that Leonard then went to the police in a state of great agitation; or so the newspapers wrote. I think it natural that he should be very perturbed. So perturbed and distressed, in fact, that he forgot entirely to tell the police that he had first had a shower and only afterwards discovered the body. The police, going through the flat, found Leonard's fresh prints in the bathroom, and immediately made him the number one suspect.

I read about it in the newspaper and rang up Leonard and my lawyer, Anthony, and asked him to defend Leonard. I was convinced Leonard had not murdered the girl. It simply was not in his character. The police tried to make up a case against him but it was dropped, thanks to Anthony, who was a very good lawyer and poked holes right through the police witnesses. The Irish priest turned up to explain that he had asked Leonard to look after Helen. Helen's previous 'troubles' were never explained; but I am convinced, from the police silence about them, that this was a Secret Society murder.

Vincent rallied to Leonard's side; the three of us went to lunch together, to Anthony's groaning despair. 'You'll never get a divorce,' said Anthony. But I did. Leonard, as soon as he was able, did take proceedings against me, and all it cost me was fifty pounds, and we remained very good friends.

Distressed students regularly poured in upon me. All kinds of distress: jail, no money, no job. One student with naso-pharyngeal cancer, to go to England for treatment. A student from Nanyang University questioned by Special Branch: he could no longer walk. For days he had been held in the vertical position with a beam between his legs and a weight upon his back; the sciatic nerves of both legs were injured. Others had been made to sit on blocks of ice for hours during the Emergency. Repressive measures and torture are never new. They seem to be passed on as precious heirlooms, handed down the centuries, and from one country to another.

In February 1962 I went to Cairo to attend the Second Afro-Asian Writers' Conference taking place there. I was curious to know what an Afro-Asian conference was like, and certainly I wanted to meet Asian writers, for my course on contemporary Asian literature at Nanyang University.

I flew to Delhi and there changed to an aeroplane for Cairo, which left around midnight. And who should I see at the airport but Mulk Raj Anand, surrounded by roughly 150 friends. Mulk was being garlanded; wreaths of champak and jasmine wrapped in cellophane were being placed around his neck; only his eyes and the top of his head protruded above the garlands. Mulk's friends alternatively sang hymns of praise to him or shouted slogans. Someone dived into the crowd holding a tray with a cup of coffee on it for Mulk. 'Mulk, Mulk,' I cried, but I was too far away. I wrestled my way to the departure door and caught up with Mulk, who greeted me with effusive disquiet. 'I've got to talk to you about some very important things, Suyin. We shall sit together,' said he.

During the rest of the night, in the aeroplane, Mulk talked to me. 'Suyin, the most important thing in the world is *peace*. We must have peace *at all costs*, otherwise the world will see a nuclear catastrophe. We shall all be dead unless there is *peace*. Think of Hiroshima; there will be ten thousand Hiroshimas. Think of the devastation! Humanity will cease to exist. Our Chinese comrades unfortunately don't see it that way. They're playing with fire. Now you can do an enormous amount of good at the conference. You can stand up for peace and the whole world will be grateful to you for it.'

On and on went Mulk, radiating honesty and horror, earnestness and supplication. He was extremely worried. 'The Americans are ready to destroy the whole world if they are challenged.' I protested. 'No, Mulk. As far as I know, the Americans on the contrary are preparing for brush-fire wars, for small wars erupting here and there, for what they call "counter-insurgency".'

What Mulk was really saying — but he did not know it himself — was that the Third World must *not* have liberation struggles; must not fight for independence, because any small, local conflict might bring about an atomic holocaust ... and this of course was utter nonsense, as has been amply proved since.

On arrival in Cairo, Mulk was wreathed and greeted by a small posse of people, including two Chinese delegates, and I by no one. For of course the Chinese had no idea that I was coming as an observer (I had arranged this directly with Youssef El-Sebai, the secretary, and the Egyptian government). The Chinese shook hands cordially with me, but were perplexed. What did I represent? Why had I come? And why with Mulk? 'Comrade Mao Tun is leading our delegation,' they said to me. 'I'll be so glad to see His Excellency the Minister of Culture, Mao Tun,' I replied. 'I shall ring him up tomorrow.'

Thomas Cook's of Singapore had reserved a room for me in a small hotel in Cairo. It was indeed small; but outside my door, in the corridor, lounged a huge six-foot-two Egyptian, Hamid. He slept there. He would stop everyone from coming to see me. I was at first puzzled, but later realized that he was anxious to guarantee my morality since I was a single, unaccompanied woman. I grew quite fond of Hamid in 1962; but when in 1965 Vincent came with me to Cairo, and we booked in at the same hotel (it had a certain ambiance), the situation became acute as Hamid burst in throughout the night, every hour or so, to make sure that we were not sleeping together. We moved to the Semiramis.

In the afternoon of my first day in Cairo, I went to Mulk's grandiose hotel (the delegates to the Afro-Asian Writers' Conference were lavishly lodged and fed). Mulk was in the lobby, conversing with a Chinese. I came closer, the man turned his head ... it was my dear, dear friend, Old Yeh!

'It's worth coming to Cairo just to see you again,' I said happily. We sat companionably while Mulk went on explaining with great force his point of view – which at the time was the Russian view – to Yeh. Since the whole of the Writers' Conference was a political gimmick, part of the struggle between the Russians and the Chinese on the ideological plane, there were from the start any number of people like Mulk going round putting their point of view to other writers, for all resolutions would finally be voted upon.

In the end all the writers, poets, artists, novelists, assembled (and some of them were great names) would be caught in the theoretical argument, which was also a power struggle. I do not blame them for 'wasting their time', as I am sure some Western writers would have said. For these writers in Cairo had consciences; and they knew that the future of the world did depend on this struggle.

For whereas Russia argued that there must be 'peace' and therefore that all countries must keep quiet and not indulge in 'national liberation struggles' which would simply end in a nuclear war, the Chinese argued that this was not so, that local liberation struggles would go on, and they would not lead to nuclear war. The Russians drew a dreadful picture of American imperialism stopping at nothing to exterminate mankind. Only the U.S.S.R. could stop American ferocity ... by what means it must be left to the Kremlin to decide, and therefore it was important to follow Russia's leadership.

Not so, said the Chinese. What the Russians and their satellites were proposing was blind obedience, 'the peace of slaves'. It was removing the sovereignty of the independent nations to decide for themselves whether they would or would not engage in a struggle for their own liberation. It was admitting that 'only two superpowers can make the rain fall or the sun shine' upon the world.

An Arab writer came to fetch Mulk, and Yeh and I walked out into the soft, balmy cooking-scented night. For it was Ramadan, the Muslim fasting month. Egypt fasted all day but ate enormously after sunset and before dawn. The night was uproarious with all the shops open and blazing fires to roast meat, and people laughed and strolled and children played.

I called on Mao Tun, whom I had met in Peking in 1956, and who looked very well. In the delegation was the Vice-Minister of Culture, Hsia Yen, a thin and wiry man bursting with nervous energy and talent and intelligence; also two poets I knew, and the frail, diminutive, brilliant writer, Hsieh Pinhsin, Heart of Ice. Pinhsin was sixteen years older than I, but looked beautiful and young. She had started writing in the early 1920s when she was still a student. She used a pseudonym, and in her literature class no one knew—and one day the professor arrived with her first book in his hand, which had been widely acclaimed, and started to teach from it the very class in which she sat as a student! Her English was mellifluous and perfect, for after Chinese university she had been to Wellesley. I had read Heart of Ice when I was a student at Yenching University; two generations, and now three generations of Chinese women read her love stories ...

Mao Tun wanted to know why I had come with Mulk. 'We happened to be on the same plane,' I said, and he looked relieved. 'I am not going to talk at all,' I added. 'But even if you do not talk, people will ascribe to you notions and opinions,' said Yeh.

The Cairo meeting was to last four days; and I do not recall a single speech in its entirety. Only long-drawn and somewhat dreary hours and plaudits or folded arms as delegates succeeded each other on the rostrum. The serried ranks of writers—I still have a photograph of them. How many countries were there? I think nineteen or so. Japanese and Indians, Chinese and Turks and Ceylonese, and Arab countries, and the Indonesians and some African countries, and the Russians in various delegations according to their several republics. The most outstanding person, where looks were concerned, was Kenneth Kaunda of Zambia, not yet head of state. He was magnificent, sweeping by in pure white robes. The one who caused the greatest uproar was Nazim Hikmet, the Turkish writer, a leonine-looking man who strode in a great fanfare of handclaps to do battle against Mao Tun: 'The tiger of American imperialism is not a paper tiger,' he roared. 'It has atomic teeth!' Mao Tun shook his head and smiled.

Algerians, Egyptians, other delegations tried to steer a middle course; taking neither one side of the argument nor the other. Malek Haddad, the Algerian poet, recited French poetry; came to drink coffee with me and talk of the Algerian war, which was coming to an end; the Evian Accords would be broached that month. The Japanese took notes and made few speeches, and invited me to Japan, where I would go that autumn.

The meeting itself merely consecrated the rift between China and Russia; from then onwards, at every conference, symposium, meeting, the battle would rage; and so many writers would be involved, some of them for years, in these skirmishes and alarums and excursions.

The embassies of various countries threw gargantuan dinners; after sundown everyone was extremely hungry. The men would crowd round the tables, and the food would disappear ... another batch of food would come up ... the men would crowd again. We, the women, could neither push nor shove and consequently never reached the table at all except towards the end of the reception, when a lot of the men were picking their teeth and exhaling small burps of fulfilment.

'I don't see what good all these speeches do,' I said to Yeh and Pinhsin at the end of the conference. 'Oh, my dear, that's the way the struggle has to be conducted,' said Pinhsin, while Yeh merely smiled. Pinhsin spent a great deal of her time with the Japanese writers, many of whom she knew personally, since she and her husband* had been teaching in Japan before returning to China in 1951.

On the last day, I think, Mulk came to me. It was the crucial day for a final communiqué to be issued. 'You're not going to talk, Suyin?' 'No, Mulk.' A shadow crossed his face but he smiled, kissed my cheek gently, and went. I wanted to tell Mulk that the core of the longwinded arguments, of that strenuous and somewhat futile battle of wits and phrases, was really *power*. Nothing but power, which creates, of course, its own reality. But Mulk was innocent, and full of idealism, and so I did not tell him.

---

* The eminent Dr Wu Wentsao. See pp. 312–13.

I explored Cairo, loving the tall-wheeled carts, so high-perched with their diminutive pulling donkeys or their majestic camels and their load of silent, black-clad women. I discovered Egypt's darker people, the Nubians, and their great beauty. For while the 'upper classes' were short, fairly white-skinned Levantines, the lower classes, the servants like my chaperone Hamid, and the market vegetable sellers and the carters, and the women who swung great loads and bales, all were like the Egyptians of old, the people of the ancient pharaonic cities sculpted in stone; and they had skins of burnished gold. How handsome, with their long, slim legs and that extraordinary acute angle between corner of eye, nostril and earlobe they were! I could never stop watching them walk, as long-legged birds walk, picking up their toes. They were all profile as they lifted their faces to the sun.

I went down the Nile to Luxor, taking the night train, and cursing Cook's all the way for its discomfort. In Luxor the hotel was splendidly English—with mostly German tourists. Afternoon tea was served by the handsome 'real' Egyptians (as I now called them to myself) in white gloves. I hired a guide (Cook's recommendation) and experienced the disadvantages of being a single woman touring ancient monuments. The guide, a young man, evidently thought that his services would include bed, since, he said, he had satisfied a few American and English women who had come to Luxor. And he produced letters to confirm it. I indicated that I was not interested and he did not insist, but came to see me off with a large bunch of yellow daisies and zinnias.

A farewell reception was given in Cairo by President Nasser for all the delegations. We massed into an immense hall with journalists and sundry diplomats. The marble floor was so highly polished that it not only glared but sent people spilling if they walked too fast. We stood and we stood. Not a chair in sight. We stood for two, three hours ... Nasser talked. And went on talking. I looked at him. He was a walking, moving, talking picture of himself; a picture one saw in every house, every shop, every cinema, every school, in every taxi, smiling that sun-burst smile, with radiantly white teeth, well-spaced. He had those teeth; and they were white. And he was tall, taller than the average, well-put-together and well-dressed. A clever man; a hardworking man. He appeared not to notice that after the first ninety minutes a woman had fallen to the floor and had had to be removed; in another thirty minutes two more slid to the horizontal. Heart of Ice and I stood; she untired, straight and slight

Yungmei in 1959

With Dorothea and Anthony
Head in Kuala Lumpur, 1965

Chairman Mao Tsetung and Premier Chou Enlai during the Cultural Revolution

A street scene during the Cultural Revolution, 1966

Chou Enlai, *centre right*, with Chen Yi in 1962; *left*, Chen Yi's wife, Chang Tsien, and *right*, Chou Enlai's wife, Teng Yingchao

Students at work on a commune, 1966

With a peasant family in north China, 1971

Visiting the Sinkiang nomads with Vincent in 1971

and unbreakable, me clutching at her, my shoes off, hopping from one collapsing arch to the other.

I also called upon the eminent Dr Khalid, the Head of El-Hazar University, and therefore the Pope of Islam, or its equivalent. He had a face whose chin and nose aspired to meet, and a most beautiful voice. It was important for an Islamic leader to have a fine voice; to chant from the minarets the daily prayer; to thunder and to expostulate and to inflame the roaring multitudes ...

'Allah will bless your work,' said he in melodious Arabic, with the sound of sunset prayer in it. A Copt journalist friend, who went with me everywhere, translated. I asked Dr Khalid about family planning. What was Islam's attitude to limitation of births, and birth control? There was nothing against it in the Koran, replied Dr Khalid, provided the laws of marriage were kept, the sanctity of the family ... he went on and on; it was a most beautiful speech, and my Copt friend translated, and I am still unclear as to what Islam really thinks of family planning.

Hassanein Heikal, the very able editor of the newspaper *Al Haram*, Egypt's *New York Times*, and Nasser's confidant and friend, invited me to lunch. Heikal would not pronounce as to Nasser's intentions, save to stress Egypt's important role among the non-aligned countries of the world. My Copt friend was more informative. 'For Nasser, it's the Soviet Union and America. He has to play between those two; only those two can really help. China ... not for thirty years ... China is poor, and she is not powerful ... maybe in thirty years ... '

The Pakistan Guild of Writers had invited me to visit Pakistan, and from Cairo I flew to Karachi. The Guild was lavish in its hospitality. From the moment I stepped down from the aeroplane in Karachi I was entertained most royally, with a warmth, a prodigality, a joy which has remained with me.

At the airport was a small and happy crowd of writers, H. Mottaher Husain and Jamiluddin Ali and also two women, Mumtaz Shirin and Mussarrat Temuri. Temuri was to be my companion on all the trips I made through Pakistan; and a most amusing, stalwart and lovable travelling partner she proved.

I duly toured monuments and museums and gardens and hospitals and universities and schools, duly went to dinners and receptions, and to private houses to meet writers and artists. The museums in Pakistan were prodigiously interesting, but handicapped by lack of money. Thus in

Peshawar there were some extraordinary pieces in the museum – invaluable relics of early Graeco-Indian art that had been exacavated in British times. But now the museum was only allotted twelve thousand rupees a year and archaeological diggings could not continue for lack of funds. The curator, enthusiastic, knowledgeable, was very thin. He looked starved. What can one do with only twelve thousand rupees a year on which to run such an immense and wonderful museum?

Neither was the Guild of Writers precisely affluent. Many writers worked very hard for what could be considered a pittance. Since the Guild was government-supported, it was obvious that dissenting writers would not be particularly helped; but was it not like this all over resurgent Asia? Except for Japan, and to a certain extent India, and until an affluent readership, picking and buying its own books, could make the writer financially independent ... I wondered whether in China, one day, when everyone would be able to read, the Federation of Writers would not be faced with a vast demand for 'more books, different books, better books.'* Readership was a function of literacy. Now in Pakistan there were five languages, Urdu was the main and official language, and I was very pleased with my visit to the compilers of the great Urdu dictionary. They had been working on it for some years, and it would soon be done. In Cairo I had discussed with writers the fact that the ordinary language that people spoke and classical Arabic, in which literature was written, were now wide apart. 'We have to keep on inventing a new written language, a new vocabulary,' said the writers. I told them that the same adaptation had been made in China in the 1920s.

Purdah still prevailed in Pakistan. In Lahore University each classroom was neatly divided in two by a large curtain; boys one side, girls the other. And yet in the beautiful hanging gardens and among the fountains, boys and girls, women and men, walked about, and some were veiled and some were not.

I would be invited to dinner by an official; would go into the house and be received by several women (the hostess and her friends or sisters, all bejewelled and made up). And when the men were announced, the women would disappear into inner rooms, and I would be left alone with the men. The further north I went, the more purdah. In one household in Peshawar, that of a writer, the women were behind hermetically shuttered windows on the first floor. One could only guess at their being there. I could sense them as my eyes travelled over the blind wood of the shutters. They must have peered down at me, at my naked face sitting in the main

* This is happening now.

room below with men. My host the writer had three wives. He told me that he had a hard time because he had to rent shelf space at the local all-purpose shop in order to be able to sell his books. He had found his books covered with dust. 'You only pay me to keep your books, not to clean them,' the shopkeeper had retorted.

Jamilia came to see me. Beautiful and young, she had twelve 24-carat gold bracelets studded with rubies coiled like red-eyed snakes upon her arms. She had written a best-seller, which had won a prize. 'But I used a man's name, otherwise no one would have published me.' Then it was found out that the writer was a woman. The prize had evaporated and she was blamed for doing such an unwomanly thing. Her husband, a landlord, was kind to her. 'All he wants is a son.' He let her do what she liked 'in the house, but I am not allowed to leave the house; coming to see you he allowed because you are well-loved everywhere ... Look, these are my chains,' she said, lifting her gold-laden arms. Jamilia had been married to breed, not to write; her in-laws were always around her; she produced a son who died at birth.

Temuri and I went by car up the Khyber Pass, and on the road met a small posse of fierce-looking horsemen all slung about with rifles and ammunition. 'Oh,' said Temuri a little nervously, 'I'm afraid they mean to rape us.' We had non-veiled faces, and the Khyber horsemen were not used to this and therefore had dared approach the car. But the driver talked to the men and I think he told them that the government would not like it if they raped us. Temuri and I gazed fixedly into space, unmoving as statues. The horsemen rode away, and after that Temuri, much shaken, told me about her family.

'My family lived in Lucknow, in India, but when Partition came and British India was split into India and Pakistan, my family decided to come to Pakistan.' Temuri was already in Karachi then. 'But there was madness upon the land; people went crazy, Hindus and Muslims killed each other for weeks ... two million people, perhaps more, died at Partition.' There were Hindu killer bands on all the roads to Pakistan. They stopped the carts and cars and trains and killed all the Muslims that they found.

'When the train with my family in it pulled into Karachi station I was waiting there, but the train carried only corpses ... there was a dreadful smell ... and fifty-five of the fifty-six members of my family on the train were dead; only my niece, six years old, was alive because she had buried herself under the bodies ... '

And so we talked of Partition, and looked down at the bleak grey-brown slopes of the bare Khyber Pass, and thought of so many of the massacres of history; history so abundant, so revelling in blood, everywhere, in every corner of the earth, and here at this grey duct between the cliffs too. We drove across the Pass and found a village. All the rooftops were flat, since there was little rain. We both needed to pee but there was no convenience except one of the rooftops; they were layered with clean sand. There we urinated, the whole village in the street staring at us and blinking against the sun to catch a view.

Up to the Kingdom of Swat, ensconced among the mountains between Pakistan and Afghanistan, and oh, the road, the locking cliffs and the ecstasy of stark and void, sudden realization that all life is exiguous, a narrow condemned valley. Swat was a narrow corridor hewn out of rock, and along the rockface of the cliffs were carvings of uncommonly Greek-looking buddhas. The inhabitants of Swat had the same noses coming straight down from the forehead as the Greeks, for Alexander of Macedon had been here; and Swat was a relic of the great ancient Graeco-Indian kingdoms. Prince Aurangzeb of Swat received me at dinner. He was tall and fair; he, his wife and his brother were all three patrician handsome. We had a very lively and somewhat heated dispute about China, but in 1966 Aurangzeb would write to me: 'I have changed my mind and joined your ranks about China.'

From West Pakistan I flew to Dacca in East Pakistan (now Bangladesh), and how depressing it was! Whereas I had found West Pakistan lively and sinewy and vital, and had enjoyed uproarious conversational tussles, here was furtive and clammy depression, a hothouse stillness. Physically a totally different people: Bengalis with enormous charcoal velvet eyes and pointed faces; fine bones, not burly. And Dacca was not prosperous. Therein lay the bitterness which surfaced among the writers. For the only link between East and West Pakistan was religion, Islam. It was frequently mentioned, but was it enough? The writers said, 'We are treated as second-rate citizens.' (Like the Chinese in Malaya, I thought.) East Pakistan grew the jute, and jute supplied so much of the money needed for the divided country (all the breadth of India between them – who had invented this absurdity? The British). 'We receive nothing in return for what we give. The money goes out, nothing is put back, we are drained of wealth.' And indeed the country looked to me unkempt, the standard of living much lower than in Peshawar, Lahore and Karachi.

I was entertained by a couple of famous writers (famous in the Bengali language) one evening. For me they had burnt incense and set little lights throughout their house; and I felt ashamed and uncomfortable, for they had worked so painstakingly, as if, because I had such access to the

Western world, I was superior ... yet how I longed to tell them it was a fluke, hazard, circumstance ... a love and a death; I longed to tell them: 'Actually, I am a cadaver-eater; my fame rests upon a corpse.' But would they understand such self-clarity? 'You must learn to be a little brutal with barbarians,' said I. 'I would not have had such material success without some brutality, both received and given. You must accept the existence of brutality.' They were shocked; for they strove so hard to be meek and likable, to live up to an ideal of goodness (but how precarious it was). I told them that babies came into life kicking and bawling, and sometimes one must kick and bawl one's way through, but trying to kick only the strong, not the weak. I do not think they understood.

Could I make these Asian writers confident when they were so penurious, so dependent on the government to subsidize them, when their reading public was so restricted? 'It will all change,' I said. But I could not promise that Western writers would care for fellow-authors in Dacca, or Peshawar, or even in China; I could not promise that women writers in London would think of Jamilia raising her gold-heavy arms. How few, how very few of them would ever be translated for readers in the West ...

On the way back from Dacca, I stopped over in Madras, for Vincent had a week's leave from Jardine Waugh in Singapore. Vincent and I spent four days in Colombo, at the Galle Face Hotel. We had a room perched on the rockface; and just below was the ocean, and its colour and sound and presence filled the room; the beat and roar of its power made love to us all night. We were always damp with spray, and the insane sea wind rushed in through all the open windows.

When we returned to Malaya, I prepared to go back to China. I left in mid-June, via Hongkong, and there I was to see Pengju once again. We never knew it would be the last time. In that July, a telegram came to me while I was in Peking. Pengju had been invited on the inaugural flight of some Arab airline; the aeroplane had gone into a mountain, and all aboard had been killed. I miss him terribly, even today.

Fourteen

China - 1962-1964: Resurgence

NEVER WAS CHINA twice the same; untiring as the ocean, there was always tumult and conflict beneath her outer placidity. Whenever I have the illusion of a tranquil China, I know it is the imprisoning eye of another storm.

In that summer of 1962 China was resurgent. The hunger and the want of the three bad years, 1959 to 1961, were going and in the air was promise of a good autumn harvest despite renewed accounts of droughts and floods and insect plagues. But now the words 'natural calamities' were automatic, on all lips; the merest cloud in the sky would be interpreted as a hailstorm ... 'We're a bit allergic to the weather because we've had such a bad time with it,' Yang Hsienyi, who had now put on weight, said to me. As so many people were putting on weight, eating more, eating audibly, visibly. 'The Old Man in Heaven has been unkind to us for three long years,' said the cadres, peering cautiously towards the sky. 'We still have many problems.'

Kuangchow burst with energy. New whitewash on the walls of the houses, new paint. And by the side of the usual human labour – men pulling carts, men carrying loads; and how long this would still go on, how long – there were new blue and white buses, new trucks and lorries. 'Diesel oil buses and trolley buses,' pointed out Comrade Chen, the poet, cryptic face hinting at a major change. The major change was that oil had been discovered during the Leap; in a region where the Russians had said there could be no oil. And the trolley buses showed that China could now make reactors and heavy water, which was a technological advance. 'Since the great Leap we have made our own trucks.' New wide avenues cut a swathe through the city; new flats were coming up 'for workers of the industrial complex'. There was a new sports stadium and a new park. 'We are beautifying the city.' And bicycles: a steady stream of bicycles, not only in the city but also in the countryside. 'We began to supply bicycles to the countryside communes last year. We make them ourselves.'

There were new areas with houses built by and for the overseas Chinese who had returned from Indonesia: neat tarred roads, and the houses looking exactly like the middle-class bungalows of Singapore; with electric light, running water, refrigerators. 'They must have what they are used to.' Between 1959 and 1961 almost a million overseas Chinese had returned and been resettled. They had started pineapple, rubber and coffee plantations in south China. 'We try to integrate them, but they have different habits ... ' The overseas Chinese indeed looked different; when they walked in the streets, with money in their pockets and jaunty suits and permed hair and make-up they were visible, too visible in the pastel subduedness of China's cities. There were special shops for them where they would buy tins of better cigarettes, and jade carvings, and clothes. How difficult for the government not to privilege them. 'It provokes subjective reactions if they feel deprived,' said the comrade from the Overseas Chinese Department. But at the Cultural Revolution in 1966 the overseas Chinese would pay dearly for these privileges.

I dallied in the south because the provinces are so much more creative and interesting than official, stiff Peking, where the ghosts of past emperors still reside, and the bureaucrats congregate. I needed to find my family origins for my book, *The Crippled Tree*. And the root was here, in this province, among the Hakkas of Meihsien district.

Comrade Chen was also a Hakka, and he gave me a book of his poems and an old novel, *Flowers in a Mirror*, which dated back to 1783. Together we went to Egret Island to see the dainty, snow-plumed birds in their sanctuary, and then by boat to the lychee fruit plantations. The heavy lychee clusters pulled the boughs of the squat, strong trees to the waiting mirror of the water; our boat glided among the branches. At one time during the Leap, said Comrade Chen, there had been 'precipitancy', and some ultra-leftists had advocated doing away with the lychee trees. Others had wanted to swell the figures of harvest for lychee fruit, and gathered it unripe. 'We have now corrected these errors ... the people gave us their opinion on these harmful things ... we must listen more to the people.' I remembered my previous visit, when I had been told that meetings were held everywhere to assess errors, to have the people 'speak up their bitterness'. Obviously this had been done. But I also remembered that, at the time, there was a search for the culprits of the 'ultra-left' communist wave which had hit the Leap in 1958. Had the culprits been found? Now there was total silence on that point ...

'When shall we truly obtain deliverance from the kingdom of necessity?' Thus Comrade Chen, quoting Mao Tsetung, but not telling me that it was Mao.

There were rumours that in January of 1962, five months previously,

Mao had made a most important speech to seven thousand of the prominent Party leaders, to intellectuals, provincial Party secretaries, on democracy. He had stressed the need for it; without it, there could be no real socialism, and no material progress either. But the speech was not made public, nor would it be 'official' or printed until the autumn of 1978, sixteen years later.

There are pages and pages in my notebooks of those years about the new projects, new canals, new improved rice breeds, new experiments — everywhere this spurt of strength, and everywhere too the demand for knowledge. Not a sickly world of listless shuffling; a strong clamour, and a thousand, a million demands. How would they be fulfilled?

A peasant woman in a flowered blouse perched on the back of a sturdy bicycle (the bicycles for rural communes were heavier than for city denizens), a child strapped to her back in the colourful embroidered carry-baby; another one between her and her husband riding the machine, and the eldest child in front, legs dangling over the handlebars ... A new food-canning factory, weaving factory, plastics factory, chemical fertilizer factory ... much talk about chemical fertilizers. 'Our peasants do not like chemicals. They say they burn the soil. But we must modernize agriculture, mechanize agriculture.'

I went to see Meihsien, a typical Hakka district. Not far from it is Hua Hsien, forty-eight kilometres from Kuangchow, the birthplace of the leader of the great Taiping peasant rebellion, a man named Hung Hsiuchuan. There had been so many peasant revolts in China, through the centuries. At least a major one per century, three thousand minor ones in the last two millennia. It was through peasant revolts that dynasties were changed and the imperial throne conquered.

I told Comrade Chen, since he too was a Hakka, how my family originally went to Szechuan from the district of Meihsien; because Szechuan had been laid waste and depopulated in forty years of war, in the seventeenth century, when the Manchus conquered China. And the Hakkas, always land hungry, always relegated to the worst land and to hilly slopes because they were really refugees, nomads,* hunted down from north China by the great invasions between the ninth and the twelfth centuries, had heard of available land in Szechuan and settled there. And that is how we were now identified with Szechuan, but also proud of our Hakka origin.

My grandmother was a Hung, from the same clan and village as the

---

* The word Hakka means 'the guest people', indicating their refugee status.

leader of the Taiping rebellion. When I went to see the house of Hung, the Taiping King of the Heavenly Kingdom, I discovered that over 90 per cent of the people in his village were still named Hung. But this is not strange. All Chinese villages are clan villages, even today. Always around 70 to 90 per cent of the village families have the same family name, and so village girls are always betrothed to boys from other villages because the Chinese have a horror of incest. Two people bearing the same family name, in the past, were not allowed to wed. Yet in all of China, because of the antiquity of its clan names, there are only 186 family names among the 900 million Chinese.

Peasant revolts ... the present communist revolution had also sprung from massive peasant uprisings. What else, in a country of over 400 million peasants, and only 2 to 3 million workers by 1949? But Mao Tsetung, himself a peasant, had gone beyond the usual pattern; he had utilized this great strength of the peasantry for a modern type of revolution. He was attempting to leap a stage in history; to go directly from feudalism — with very little capitalism superimposed upon it — into socialism. Theoretically it could not be done ... could it be done? It must be done. There was no other way if China wanted to catch up with the developed world by the year A.D. 2000. And so the Leap ... a phenomenal attempt to hurry, to catapult China into her own future. Was it crazy? Was it a failure?

For the next four years, until the Cultural Revolution began in 1966, I would travel my fill, going everywhere I could possibly go; far south and north and to Szechuan and Yunnan, to see the new and the old, the traditional and the revolutionary side by side; travel in and out of time and within China's time, which is her continuum of being. All that happened in the past was still so accessible, still argued about and discussed as if it were just familiar yesterday. China's Revolution of today was thus not a break, not a rejection, it was an integral part of China's many becomings, of her eternity. The Revolution would go through many metamorphoses, as an insect does, larva and caterpillar and butterfly, and yet is always the essential insect.

Through eight provinces and many major cities in 1962 and 1963, through communes and scattered villages, going by train and sometimes by car, deep away from towns, nowhere was there any sign of famine or of beriberi or even of gross malnutrition, as there had been in 1960–1. I wrote to Edgar Snow and to Felix Greene:

Everywhere the streets are full of vegetables and fruit in small mountains; pears and peaches and apples and raisins and four kinds of melon and ten different kinds of vegetables, including tomatoes and carrots, parsley and onions. In Sian, in Taiyuan, in the cities of the north ... in Peking too, except that in Peking much of the fruit seems to have been plucked too early. I am told it is to avoid the hailstorms in August.

All this produce was unbelievably cheap: four *fen* for a kilo of melon, three *fen* for a kilo of carrots, five *fen* for a kilo of onions, one or two *fen* for a bagful of spinach.* In Yunnan province sugar was off the ration. There were great mounds of cakes and sweets and almonds and peanuts, and such a surplus of pears that half the crop had to be given to the pigs to eat; because there was not enough transport to send it to markets outside the producing areas. In Szechuan delicious oranges littered the streets of Chengtu; a pound of sugar was given free to anyone who would buy a pint of milk. In the Leap new milch-cow farms had been established, but such was the rooted prejudice and horror for milk ('It smells bad, it tastes bad, it gives stomache ache, it's only good for very sick people'), that even with the gift, few people would take milk.

The oil ration in the provinces of the Yangtse Valley was twice that in Peking, and the meat ration in Wuhan was three times that in Peking. Everywhere people were eating, eating. A perceptible fattening process was on. And visible in all the streets of the cities, except in Peking, pedlars and small shops, free markets; very few queues.

In the courtyards of houses in north China, rabbit hutches under the eaves. But the price of rabbit meat had taken a steep fall. Where it had been a *yuan* or two for a month-old rabbit a year previously, it was now twenty *fen*. There were many delicious ways of preparing rabbit, and I often travelled with comrades carrying, in the plastic bags made in the new plastics factories (difficult to get a plastic bag, everyone wanted one!), rabbit steeped in soya sauce and ginger and then gently roasted.

Seaweed growing, which had been started in 1959, was not given up; seaweed continued to be used, mixed with maize, to make unleavened bread; and for animal fodder. But people were gradually abandoning it. By 1964 no one would use seaweed for food any more.

In that spring, according to doctors I saw in various hospitals, there had been an increase in mortality among young infants after measles. Otherwise no main epidemics had occurred. As for tuberculosis, I checked up

★ 100 *fen* = 1 *yuan*. In the 1960s 1 *yuan* was equivalent to half a U.S. dollar.

346

again on the figures I had acquired on the previous visit to the sanatorium in Tientsin, but could come to no conclusion.

Cotton was still extremely short. Still only an average of two metres per person per year; except of course for new born babies (10 metres) and also funeral clothes. Everyone, including the middle cadres, wore patched clothes, worn clothes. Cloth shoes were very difficult to get, but now there were factories making plastic sandals for summer and cloth shoes with plastic soles for the rest of the year. No one liked them; it would be quite a hard process to teach the Chinese to wear synthetic materials; they loved cotton so much, it was so comfortable. 'But in the end we must expand synthetics, we cannot go on planting enough cotton for everyone,' said an official in the cotton industry. That year the first nylon shirts were produced. They were called 'thoroughly cool'. Everyone promptly called them 'thoroughly stifling'.

Patching, contriving, retrieving clothing became a profession, an art. Patching factories manned by housewives were found in every small lane. In Chungking some pedlars were selling tanned and softened skins of rats, which were used for patches and for the uppers of shoes. The rats of Chungking had been notorious in the past; large, heavy creatures, they attacked cats and ate them up. They had been decimated in repeated 'get rid of pests' campaigns since 1949. They were said to have disappeared; but clever rat catchers still found them, and now they became useful at last.

The teahouses and restaurants which had been closed during the 'ultra-left' phase of the Leap were opened again. In Kuangchow they were pretty, adorned with flower pots; in Chengtu the teahouses in the park were full of people, and in Peking too there were teahouses and small restaurants. But it was still difficult to get chickens' eggs because the demand for hens was still very high. Every family owned at least one hen, if not more; hens were kept on balconies, in bedrooms, in coops suspended from windows ... A doctor friend of mine had an upstairs neighbour whose eight hens were conducted by him or by his wife, every morning, down five flights of stairs to the communal garden, there to pick and scratch. My medical friend was irritated because the clucking woke him and the excreta which were left upon the stairs were not cleared up. 'People are very ingenious when given their heads,' said he. On this gallinaceous enterprise the Party kept 'one eye open, one eye shut', allowing it because it was necessary; but by 1964, when it was no longer necessary to keep hens at home because eggs had come back on the market, the Health Ministry started a small 'health' campaign, and hens on balconies and in flats were not allowed. However, since there was no law against it, people went on keeping them for quite a long time.

There were also, here and there, faint reminders of the fact that not so welcome things were returning, in the wake of the relaxation which now existed. Thus in 1963 it was obvious to me that large clan houses, which had belonged to wealthy landlord families, were being repaired and re-painted in some areas. There was also the fact that despite the commune system some villages were being worked to the benefit of one person only. Was this a return of landlordism? Or was there a new class of landlords? In some communes the private plots flourished but communal fields of grain looked neglected. In others one could see along the road groups of peasants going off to work on house building or hiring themselves out for day work in city suburban factories because in that way they made a little more money. Grain planting, self-reliance in grain, was the official government policy; but peasants made more money from secondary crops, rape oil, tobacco, ginseng, pigs and chickens and ducks, and hiring manpower out to the cities.

Yet there was progress. I sat in a village where electric light had come at the Leap and the wonder of it had not ceased; the wonder of light at night, making it possible for people to look at each other in the new small sun of the single bulb hanging from the centre of a room. The school-master said proudly, 'Now we can have night schools for the peasants.' There were many villages which had thus the gift of light bestowed upon them. And with electric power came flour mills; so that the so-common sight of the past of a woman or a mule, or sometimes both, milling flour between two stones, pushing and pulling, disappeared totally in China.

It was hot in Peking; 39 to 40 degrees Centigrade (over 100 degrees Fahrenheit), and there had been in 1961 the worst drought ever seen, both in the north and also in Szechuan province.

'We are concentrating on producing water pumps,' said the engineers. In whatever city I was I would climb to the top floor of the tallest building and watch. I watched the tall chimneys of the factories. I watched for smoke, for that lazy elongated cloud, grey or black or yellow, which indicated industrial activity. As one watches a new born baby for breath. Because that would mean industry had picked up; and there were mach-ines and men working producing what was needful ... and no sight ever made me more glad than that of new electric pylons bestriding the fields to make the wheels turn, to feed the lathes.

'We are brimming with confidence,' said Wu Chienta, toughened by yet another spell in a commune, where 'there was enough to eat'. The peasants were now encouraged to store grain for themselves, whereas during the early part of the Leap this had been discouraged as 'capitalist enterprise'. Mao Tsetung himself had said that 'too much was requisitioned' from the peasantry then. 'It spoilt the relations between the Party and the masses,' said Chienta, soberly.

There was a faint, stray rumour in Peking that Mao criticized himself for 'rashness' and having had too much trust in inflated reports from below during the early part of the Leap.

Wanchun has learnt to lead water buffaloes to pasture, to reckon time by the burning of an incense stick. He has stopped asking me to bring him English cigarettes. He now smokes the ordinary Peony brand. 'When I saw the work that went into growing tobacco ... ' Three years ago, when he had seen me clean my hotel room (it was a windy day and within half an hour everything was filmed over with Peking's inexorable dust), he had cried, 'How can a high-class intellectual like you do such menial work?'

The slogan is: Consolidation, readjustment, filling in and elevation; which means to garner and salvage what lessons the Leap has taught (good ones and bad ones) and to improve the quality of production.

A new poem by Mao is also being quoted: 'On perilous high peaks dwells beauty in her infinite variety.' 'Of course we must reach for the sky,' says Hualan. She too brims with tough assurance. 'No one is going to help us, to lift us up; we shall have to do it all ourselves.'

Round Taiyuan, capital of Shansi province, the commune fields are green, though farther south, in Honan, they appear parched. This is because there are pumps, pumping underground water. The city is cool at dusk and there are many bicycles. The people do not look hungry; and the women wear flowered blouses.

The Confucian temple in Sian is a museum. Round the 1,095 stelae of stone, carved through the centuries, a forest of historical records, schoolchildren are gathered, listening intently to the guides. Everything is pink at sunset, the beautiful houses with their carved brick ornaments and eaves and their roofs with everted tiles convex to the sun. All the Buddhist monuments are well-preserved. 'Many delegations from Buddhist countries come here to worship,' say the cadres. Here in Sian, as in so many other Chinese cities, I see women with incense sticks bunched in their hands, praying in the temples and sanctuaries of the past. 'We allow religion, though of course we do not approve,' say the cadres tolerantly.

Professor Wu, historian, curator of the museum, is with me while I visit the old temples and the new factories.

In the streets of Sian are many pedlars, selling ribbons and summer hats, ladles and kettles and pots and wooden combs and nails ... private enterprise again; 'We allow these small things.' There are also free markets in the countryside with an abundance of food: 'We allow these small things.' By now I know the formula: the Party keeps one eye open one eye shut. I wonder whether both eyes will open and once more there will be an ultra-left wave, sweeping away these relics of private enterprise. Or can they be allowed and integrated in a socialist system?

I go to see a project, the tapping of subsurface water, twenty-five kilometres from Sian. It is obvious that this is the work of engineers and geologists, of intellectuals; but the cadres there insist that everything was done by the peasantry. They quote proudly from Mao: 'The people, only the people, are the locomotive of history ... ' As if the intelligentsia were not also the people.

But this shows that the problem has not yet been solved: the fusion of the intellectual and his acceptance by the majority of workers and peasants. Although since 1961 the intelligentsia has been back and is honoured again instead of being humiliated, and there have been many rehabilitations of 'rightists', there is also, there will be for a long time, resentment of intellectuals. 'Class struggle', it is called. And it is quite true that some of the intellectuals are quite insufferable, and that it is only too easy for an élite to form once more, another mandarin class.

Back to Szechuan again. Here the slogan is: Produce pigs. The target is: a pig for every person in Szechuan.

Pigs are my favourite topic, my favourite animal, the mainstay of China's fields, the reliable standard of rural prosperity. I see the pigs change their anatomy ... there are now far fewer of the small black Chinese pigs with lordosis of the spine. Most of them are mixed breeds, for large male pigs have been imported from England. The pig is bigger, the spine is straight ... 'But our peasants complain that the foreign-mixed pig is not so good to eat,' say the cadres. I look at these Eurasian pigs and I feel sympathy.

Here, as everywhere else in China, the pigs have been collectivized and decollectivized twice since 1956, and the result has been bad. They have been badly fed and badly looked after, and everyone now says it. In 1960 I was told in one place: 'Out of 170 pigs in 1957 in our village, only twenty-eight were left in 1959.' The team which achieved the worst records had only four pigs left out of two hundred. But the masses can never be blamed for anything. The Party has to blame itself, to take responsibility for anything that goes wrong: for its own obscurantism and authoritarianism and the wrong methods and policies it applies so literally, and indiscriminately always. Anything that goes right, however, is due to the 'correct leadership' of the Party.

'Last year we only had leaves and some wild grass to feed our pigs ... the drought was terrible in Szechuan. Even the bamboo split on its stem.' This is what the peasants say. They add, 'Now we have learnt ... '

'Learnt what?'

'To walk on two legs.'

'What does it mean?'

'It means that the pigs are partly collectivized and partly private.'

The big boar, the sows, are the common property of the production team (which is the village), but the piglets are sold to individual members to look after and to fatten. 'Then we buy back the grown pig when he has reached 220 catties and is ready for the market. The commune member is given meat coupons equivalent to one quarter the pig's weight, and a sum of money, and is also paid for the manure he contributed from the pig. Then he buys more piglets.' This judicious mixture seems to work.

Such excursions in rural areas cannot provide anyone with a total picture; they have to be supplemented with numerous tales by those of my friends who have lived and done their manual labour with the peasantry. Such a one is Danny, who is an overseas Chinese from Canada, and was two years in a commune. 'The peasants just watched me at first. They are so quick to perceive if one is disgusted by them; they are humble and they go away, but one can never be friendly ... to become real friends, one must adopt them as they are, dirt and all.' He was a tremendous success because he got up early on his first morning to sweep the courtyard.'Then they would tell me, slowly, their stories. About the cadres. They knew very well who were the good ones and who the bad ones.' Danny had seen both kinds during his two years. 'It's my impression that most of them are good, but then they are mostly the older type ... some of the young ones are pretty brutal, and they behave like landlords. They force the peasants to work for them, cut wood and draw water, and build them their new houses ... '

Once again I am in Chengtu; and I bring tinned food, a Yunnan ham, clothes and extra ration coupons to my family. The extra coupons are issued by the Bank of China in proportion to the interest paid on my capital; they empower my Family to shop at the overseas store in Chengtu. Of course I also have to provide some money, because the goods in that store are more expensive than in the usual shops for the Chinese population.

There are many ration coupons: 'You won't be able to use them all, not in ten years,' says the official who unwinds the long chain of tickets for grain, meat, oil and cotton. 'We shall use them soberly, only as we need something,' says Third Uncle matter of factly.

'I am in good health,' announces Third Uncle, but he walks painfully, with a cane; he has lost the lithe, soft step he had. And now he is worried by the idea of his own death. What worries him is the disposition of his body after death. He feels that a coffin made of the best lanmu wood should be his; lanmu keeps the body from the putrefaction of after-life. He talks a little about a coffin; but no one, not even me, ventures to say: I shall buy you a coffin. Because, somehow, we feel that this might draw upon the Family the attention of ill-wishers who would say, 'See these unrepentant bourgeois ... still wasting money on extravagant coffins.'

Our premonition turns out to be right. For during the Cultural Revolution, a friend of mine living in Hongkong came to me in great agitation. Her mother lived in Shanghai, and of course had provided for herself an excellent coffin, which she kept in her bedroom. But the young Red Guards had criticized her for being so old-fashioned, and had removed the coffin ... 'Can you find a way to get the coffin back to her? She cannot sleep well without having it by her bed,' said my friend to me.

I understand Third Uncle's worry, but still I keep silent. Sometimes I feel that I know what is prudent and what is careless better than the Family ... He and Third Aunt, and all the Family, have survived pretty well until now, and I intend that this should go on. In 1962 all the Family eats well, and now with the extra rations they will even have a little more.

Nostalgia; retracing my footsteps, checking on old places I knew ... with my younger cousins I go up to the Taoist temple among the Tsing Cheng mountains. These are the offshoots of the great staircase ranges which climb up and up to the Himalayan plateaus. I know the Taoist temple: I went there with Pao, my husband, in 1940.

At the time we were carried in bamboo chairs up the mountain, Pao and I. Men carried the chairs: skeletal men in rags, and at every halt they wanted a little money, to smoke opium. And Pao reviled and scolded them for doing so. But they gazed at him with hard faces and glazed eyes. Who was he, so well-nourished, to tell them not to smoke a few opium dregs to take away the pain of hunger, the pain of pitiless labour in their bones? Only with opium could they carry us up to the top ...

And so when we arrived at the beautiful temple Pao was in a bad temper, and after a long lecture on virtue, and how it was lack of virtue that had brought China to her miserable estate, he beat me in the bedroom. And I remember also that there were many bedbugs; all through the night I caught them, and killed them ...

But now there was no opium, not anywhere; everywhere I looked at the people carefully; looking for the yellow faces, the parchment skin, but I saw only young round faces, good bodies. The monastery was just as it had been but it had now become a production team. The monks grew vegetables and made their own incense. Around the temple grew gingko, maidenhair trees, one of them almost 1,700 years old, and a small fountain cascaded deliberately down rocks, pouring music as it went from trough to trough of stone.

All that region was famous; here was the great Ming River, tributary of the Yangtse, which had been divided by the engineer Li Ping over two thousand years ago; instead of being an angry turbulent stream rushing through the Szechuan plain, it had become a million rivulets, irrigating 400,000 hectares of rice fields; and this made Szechuan the richest land in all China. But now more work had to be done on the river; 800,000 hectares could be irrigated.

Szechuan opera is more fun, less stilted, nearer to folk art than Peking opera. The lyrics are far less official. Szechuan opera allows the singers to ad lib; and so, right in the middle of the most tragic scenes, there is a quip, and laughter, and comedy interrupts the tears. It is this mixture of ribald farce and classic tragedy that disconcerts the purists of the Peking opera. Then there is the chorus, singing from behind a screen, singing the unspoken thoughts of the actors on stage. It gives depth to the opera, and tension. And all Szechuan opera, somehow or other, contrives to make fun of bureaucrats, mandarins, authority. This is what has prevented it from having a more official appeal. Peking opera is far more 'establishment'.

I call on the opera actors and singers. They have returned from three months of manual labour, practising 'togetherness, new inspiration, creative fusion'; which means that they have lived, worked, eaten with the peasants, that this has led them to write new scripts and to revise some of their notions of opera, and finally that they have also compiled a new repertoire, based on stories and legends (which are innumerable) among the people. 'It is most enriching,' they say.

There are forty open and one hundred closed gestures in Szechuan opera. In the old courtyard of the temple which serves as the opera school, the actors and singers demonstrate their skill. There is much less 'warlike expression' in Szechuan opera than in Peking opera; themes about love, flirting and especially poking fun at bureaucrats and evil officials are in every repertoire. There are twenty-six walking gestures and most of them depict the human passions, love and evil, and they are satire, not acrobatics. Szechuan opera is over ten centuries old. 'It has no connection with Peking opera, which was Mongol influenced,' the chief star, who has been on stage since he was eight and is now thirty-two, tells me.

Before Liberation all provincial opera, just like Peking opera, was badly remunerated. Most artists were poverty stricken, save for one or two renowned singers. But now all of them are paid salaries, are given houses; and there is an institute of research into Szechuan opera, and four hundred students to train. The institute sends teams all over Szechuan for likely scripts and folk tales and old operas (many are now resurrected). It has accumulated 1,470 old scripts, and is studying them. The institute also sends teams to all the schools, to recruit new students from the children.

The artists show me the fan gestures and the walking gestures and how they combine; how the edge of a scholar's dress can be made to undulate slightly to indicate hurry, distress or love. 'The eyes are the most important feature,' says the famous woman singer, Chen Shoufang, one of the greatest and best-loved of Szechuan artists. 'There are eighteen eye expressions.' She demonstrates. 'In Peking opera the forehead of the woman actor is painted narrow and low; in Szechuan the forehead is painted large and noble, and the body is held much straighter.' The institute is printing books and textbooks, and photographing gestures, and the way faces are painted; there is a whole street devoted to embroidering the clothes that the actors and singers wear. 'We must train for posterity, to elevate and to enrich.'

Of all provincial operas, Szechuan opera was to suffer most from the wrath and fury of Chiang Ching, Madame Mao, who would allow only one kind of opera, the one she sanctioned.

But in 1962 and 1963, all is hope and advance in that domain. And of course, because the physical output of the singers is high, they have large rations of meat and oil. 'But our steel workers in Szechuan get more than in Peking; the ration here is forty or even forty-five catties of grain a month per man.' During the bad years, they tell me, 'our playing and singing did a lot to sustain morale'.

And what about mechanization of agriculture in Szechuan? There is much talk about it in 1963 and 1964. We walk through fields that are still garden patches, handmade and asymmetrical; and they will not change for a very long time; because to change their conformation will require altering the whole of the immense web of water canalicules through the plain. Each field is bordered by a neat hem of water; making bigger fields means blocking off these capillary vessels which irrigate the plain and turn it into one enormous liver. It means digging new and larger canals. Can this be done? And when mechanization comes, what will happen to all the redundant people in this prolific land?

Problems. Problems. But everyone tells me that the production team manages its own land, animals, tools and manpower, and its own workpoints, and is responsible for what it sells to the state. Now the private plot *cannot* be removed, they tell me (the fury of the 1958 'communist phase' is gone).

But mechanization will upset this pattern, which is stable but still a feudal, small producers' pattern, perhaps even more than any 'communist wave' ...

Chou Enlai's 'readjustment' is working.

In July 1961 Foreign Minister Chen Yi has made a most important speech, talking of the need to use intellectuals intelligently. He has made it to the graduates of the institutes and schools of higher learning in Peking. He says that 'intellectuals must primarily re-educate themselves ... coercion and compulsion will not work.' He says that 'class origin' must not be the main criterion by which to judge anyone. 'People can only be judged by their own behaviour, not by their association with a brother, father, mother, sister.' A bad tendency has grown up now in the Party to judge everyone by three generations of ancestors; and whatever his own merits, however zealous, politically conscious, enthusiastic, hardworking, he will *not* be trusted or usefully employed if his 'class origin' is bad. Nonsense, says Chen Yi.

He says also that 'Red and expert' does not mean that one can be judged solely on glib politicalese. Politics alone do not compensate for lack of knowledge; empty slogans 'are like the Buddhist prayers ... they don't achieve anything'. Expertise and knowledge are precious and valuable; and they must be cared for. 'Even if politically the intellectuals still have lingering bourgeois ideas and habits', they can be useful and must be used properly and taken care of.

All those once labelled 'rightists' and since rehabilitated should not be compelled, every time there is a campaign, to criticize themselves again and again, or hold themselves isolated from others, says Chen Yi.

Chou Enlai has made a speech deploring the lack of democracy, saying people are afraid to act, speak, think ... yet Mao had enjoined them to do so.* And Mao has made a major speech, in January 1962, which I cannot lay my hands on (not until 1978!), saying it is necessary and indispensable for China's progress to develop democracy, to safeguard legality, to create 'a vigorous and lively political situation in which there is both centralism and democracy, both discipline and freedom, both unity of will and personal ease of mind ... '

I am happy; especially as I hear that once again work on a legal code is being undertaken; that the framing of laws, interrupted during the Leap, is starting again.

Chungking is bustling with life. The fungoid-like sheds clinging to the steep cliffs above the river have gone. New brick settlements, uniformly dull but neat and with water and electric light, replace them. Chungking is now a large industrial city, with 4½ million people.

I visit the Seven Star Cliff Commune, 76,000 people in 18,000 families. Of these 76,000, 36,000 are children under sixteen, in thirteen primary schools and one middle school and one technical school. Nineteen thousand of the 36,000 children are under seven years old.

The labour force of the commune is 12,000; 80 per cent women. That is because the men work in factories adjacent to the commune and don't count as commune labour force; while the women work on the land.

There are 214 nurseries; mess halls have been kept because they are practical and necessary. There are twenty-six small factory repair shops and flour mills; beancurd and noodles and vegetable pickles are made and sold to the city. There are night schools for the illiterate women. 'The women came out to work in 1958 ... for the first three months not one of them even asked for a salary.' 'We started making ball-bearings by hand during the Leap,' say the women. 'We also made light bulbs ... the day the lights came on everyone beat drums and cymbals and danced.'

It is August and very hot, 42 degrees Centigrade by day and by night. But everywhere people move, work; at night they drag their beds outside and sleep in the streets for coolness. 'Once upon a time there was malaria

* This all-important speech addressed to the intelligentsia in 1961 would only be made public in 1979.

here, but all the mosquitoes are gone, and there is no longer malaria in Chungking.'

I go down the Yangtse Gorges from Chungking to Wuhan. The dreaded rocks in mid-stream have been blasted; the channel, though narrow, now allows steamboats. 'You are the first foreigner for years to take this trip,' says the captain of the small, old boat which takes me. (The larger boat will soon be ready. In fact Prince Sihanouk will inaugurate it in 1964, going down the Yangtse Gorges with Chou Enlai, sketching and singing all the way.)

I am given a tiny bunk ensconced just above the boilers – and it is August, and I boil gently. But I am almost all day on the bridge, to look up at the 1,000-metre-high sheer walls between which the Great River has carved its fortuitous channel, and to hear the mighty song the wind plays high above my head, among the crests. At night the boat anchors, and then it is very still, there is no breeze, and we suffocate in silence.

All along the river are landmarks of history; battles and kingdoms wrested and won. Here the ancestor of my dead cousin Pengju, King Liu Pei, and his genius strategist Chuke Liang, fought back and forth for the kingdom of Szechuan.

At Wanhsien in the evening, about twenty men are defecating on the slope, and our boat anchors in full sight of them. They defecate and fan themselves and exchange jokes. Downstream a junk is still being pulled up by a string of men, and I think of my mother in 1913, her boat being pulled up, up, up the great river, through these very gorges, for weeks and weeks ... and at the time the river was dangerous, full of treacherous rocks and whirlpools and the junks often broke up.

I visit the Wuhan steel works and they are going full blast. 'We have surmounted our difficulties,' says the same engineer whom I met in 1961. 'We even have a new, totally Chinese-designed blast furnace.' The words 'self reliance' hang heavy and proud in the resurrected city.

In Yunnan province are new factories, an industrial complex: in the capital city, Kunming, new roads. The Stillwell Road, built under the command of the well-remembered American General Stillwell during the Second World War, which linked up with the Burma Road, is well-kept.

On Saturday evenings a dance is held at the place where I am staying, which is the former palace of a former warlord of Yunnan. It is a dance for the cadres, and of course I cannot join in; I have been advised to rest as I 'look tired'. Meekly I withdraw, but later stroll down the terrace and peer through the lighted windows with their thin veiling. The cadres dance sedately, a foxtrot, a waltz; the tunes are very old-fashioned, they make me think of Victor Sylvester's orchestra during the Second World War.

In the communes of Kiangsu province I visit the silkworm farms; white and russet and yellow, the silkworms spread their cocoons in large flat baskets: three qualities of silk. 'Owing to inexperience and natural calamities', a hard time was had by the silkworms during the three bad years; and the mulberry trees too were afflicted. But now all is well and recovering. In the large sheds, kept at even warmth, the women come and go, the girls with deft hands and silent feet.

To Nanchang in Hunan province, to see the new industries, but also to see the hotel room where Chou Enlai in July 1927 planned the capture of the city; defied the orders of Stalin to 'give up weapons'. August 1st was the day of Nanchang's capture, and it remains Red Army Day, in commemoration of that historic event. Here are heroic oil paintings of Chou Enlai surrounded by famous generals. But in some of the photographs of those heroic years, one man is effaced, erased, blotted out.

That man is Peng Tehuai, former Minister of Defence, former Long Marcher. A prestigious man, a man well-loved by the soldiers, a simple and a very straightforward man, but not always, perhaps, very politic or wary.

What has happened to Peng Tehuai? No one talks about him. No one will answer me if I ask. Even Ed Snow does not know.

It is now Marshal Lin Piao who is in command of the Red Army. We all know it. But we also know that Peng Tehuai has not been denounced. Several times in the history of the Chinese Party, leaders who took 'the wrong line' have been castigated, openly denounced. Peng Tehuai has not been openly condemned. This means he has a hope of returning.

I go to Chingkangshan, the first Red base founded by Mao Tsetung in 1927. Here Mao came with seven hundred men after the terrible massacres by Chiang Kaishek in 1927. It is an eagle eyrie in the wild mountains. All the villages, tiny and very poor, are Hakka. The Hakkas knew the pathways up these mountains and down to the plains, and Mao Tsetung relied on them as guides and porters. Chingkangshan is a most important place in New China, for here the Revolution was born again.

At the time of my travels, before the Cultural Revolution of 1966, there were very few tourists and travellers, and nothing had been done to 'prettify' the holy places of the Revolution. In Chingkangshan there was no large hotel; neither was there in Yenan, only a guest house, with no running water and the latrines outside. Now the Confucian temple in

... ught,
...enan have
...a large hotel in

I we... ... g the crests. Just below this mountain... ... of a valley. Here it was that the fiery Szechua... ...ander, Chu Teh, led his ragged remnants of Communi... ...ns to unite with the mountain guerrillas of Mao Tsetung. And without this fusion, perhaps the Revolution would not have happened; fragmented, divided, those forces would have become terrorist bands of men running for their lives, and hunted everywhere ...

We stood to look at the monument, a plain one, commemorating this event. Chu Teh was a great hero, a most courageous man. During the Long March he accomplished great feats, unknown until after his death in 1976.

But Chu Teh, like so many other Long Marchers, was to be attacked, vilified, during the Cultural Revolution. Millions of Red Guards then went on long treks to the sacred places of the Chinese Revolution. Many went to Chingkangshan. But from 1966 to 1971 Chu Teh had become a non-person in Chingkangshan. A very large oil painting showing Mao Tsetung meeting Lin Piao, no one else, had taken the place of the former painting showing Chu Teh with Mao; and the monument had been removed (it was to be replaced when Lin Piao died in 1971). Millions of young Red Guards, ignorant of history, were told that it was Lin Piao who had operated this union with Mao, and that Chu Teh was only a vile, counter-revolutionary saboteur.

Back to Peking. Browsing in bookstores; seeing new and old plays. The New Hundred Flowers has taken on. The intelligentsia is very visible and audible. Some of the cadres are wearing most expensive suits ...

There are new plays conveying political lessons. One called *Comrade, You've Taken the Wrong Road* is obviously a warning to the U.S.S.R. But by 1963 there are also plays showing bribery and corruption among the Party cadres (young, naïve workers and Party cadres seduced, of course, by landlords who bestow their beautiful daughters upon them so as to infiltrate the Party). All plays point up political lessons, but some are well done. And there are also plays with no political lessons at all, which are just great fun.

Chou Enlai is busy encouraging the arts, music, the dance (as well as

managi...
October 19...
Twenty-Secon...
welcome him, carr...
that Chou was a stalw...

'Chou Enlai is more and ... A saying goes round in Peking: 'What is it that Cho... ot do? Three things: he does not sleep, does not look after himself, and does not stop working.'

Kung Peng takes me to see a comedy called *The Pressgang*. It is hilarious, based on the forcible recruiting of soldiers, such as I had seen myself, in old Kuomintang days. It eschews tragedy, everything ends well. 'We should write many more comedies,' says Kung Peng. 'People want to laugh … we're much too serious.'

But in 1966, *The Pressgang* is dubbed 'counter-revolutionary' and a 'poisonous weed'. So are many other plays and operas which I have enjoyed in those years.

'And I took you to it,' said Kung Peng when she saw me in 1966. She had been under fire and criticized all day. She had not eaten all day. But she smiled at me, and was kind.

'I did not see any harm in *The Pressgang*,' I said.

'Neither did I.' We did not say any more; she for my sake, and I for hers.

In 1962 it was obvious that the Communist Party was being subjected to another 'rectification'. 'Some … have become steeped in bureaucracy, exhibit feelings of insolence and self-satisfaction, forget realities … estrange themselves from the masses,' wrote the *People's Daily*.

'It's no fun being a Party member in China … constant rectifications and shake-ups,' said Simon Hua. 'Too much hard work, too little pay, and there's a new generation of youngsters who don't want to become Party members unless it means a cushy job in the cities.'

And then again, rumours, small-lane gossip, this time about Mao. 'Even the sun has black spots … we must not be frightened of mentioning defects and errors in the Party.' The sentence floated around Peking. Mao Tsetung was identified with the sun because of the song: 'The East is Red'

> The east is red, the sun has risen
> In China is born Mao Tsetung …

Is someone criticizing Mao?

students.' This
                                              talk of two levels of
educa....   wer education. The higher
education o..   ....ed 'teaching points', which are
really special schoo...   ....titutes of very high grade, with all the
best facilities. This is élit.... .. a kind, of course. And not everyone agrees
to these schemes.

My dearest friend and former boss, Professor Hou Paochang of the
Pathology Department of Hongkong University, with whom I chopped
up so many livers, is now back in China. For good. Hou has come back to
teach at the Higher Medical Institute. Medical studies have been cut down
to five years; some people even advocated three years as sufficient (and
during the Cultural Revolution in Manchuria some hospitals would turn
out two-year graduates!). But at the Institute there are eight years of
study; to form a solid nucleus of top-grade medical scientists and
researchers.

Hou gave me a wonderful dinner; for which he borrowed the cook of a
friend of his, General Fu Tsoyi. Fu Tsoyi was Chiang Kaishek's general;
a pragmatic man, he saw who was winning and in 1948 relinquished
Peking to the Communists, with much charm and little fighting. Since
then he has held any number of posts in Communist China, and led a
Ministry of Water Conservancy.

Fu Tsoyi's cook is one of the best in China, and a delegate at the National
Assembly. He kindly comes to cook dinner; Fu Tsoyi sends his ministerial
car to fetch him and to bring him back. I have never eaten such a dinner,
never in my whole life.

Hou tells me that modernization must be pushed ahead. 'It is nonsense
to debase intelligence in the name of socialism,' he says.

I tell Kung Peng I am going to write about China. 'I have waited six years.
Other people rush to pen a book after one visit.' And in the end, no book
can really convey anything but one's own experience, assumptions,
judgments ... I shall not try to do more.

'Whatever you know, you can only project one-tenth of it, like the tip
of an iceberg,' says Kung Peng's husband, Chiao Kuanhua.

We talk about history. I ask: why is there no history of the Chinese
Communist Party, of the Revolution, of recent history in China? A book

did appea[...]
until 1978, ag[...]
How can you teac[...]

But when history is [...] [...]
(and reinserted), it is very di[...] [...]ially for
teaching purposes. And in China a[...] [...]tten word carries
so much weight, where people who fa[...] [...]ce have their photographs effaced from magazines, their names expunged from books ... I
complain in 1962 and 1963 about this, to Hualan and also to Kung Peng.
'It was a Russian habit ... I don't think we should copy the Russians in this
instance.' But I have not had a reply, not even today. And the habit of
expunging, deleting, effacing, has been maintained.*

In June 1962 the Chinese press reported on preparations by Chiang
Kaishek to invade the coastal areas of China – with the assent of the
U.S.A. Parachute drops, agents going into China, surprise attacks, the
capture of documents by raids on coastal districts had occurred since 1949.

Chiang Kaishek's proclamation brought out in the rural areas of the
coastal provinces ex-landlords and rich peasants. I am always astonished at
the number of landlords and rich peasants who remain, and are seemingly
very active. As soon as they heard that Chiang Kaishek might return, the
landlords came to the peasant associations: 'Ha, now you will have to give
us back our lands. I have kept all the records of what you owe me. Every
penny must be paid back. We shall now settle accounts.' Landlord-formed
bands of hooligans seized villages, passing themselves off as Party members.
They pillaged grain stores. 'Sometimes they pretend to be the militia.
They have weapons parachuted from Taiwan,' said the cadres.

No one seemed exceptionally worried in 1962. But the trouble festered.

Marshal Chen Yi gave me lunch, to thank me for having written him up
in an article for the Paris L'Express. Chen Yi's cook was not as excellent as
Fu Tsoyi's, but the Marshal did not have the heart to admonish him, and
stoically endured tasteless meals.

We talked of Montesquieu and Voltaire, Machiavelli and Churchill, and
Rousseau of course; Chen Yi had gone especially on pilgrimage to
Rousseau's tomb while in Switzerland. Then he talked about the situation.
The harvest was short by several million tonnes (about five million) said

* It seems, however, that now it will be given up (author's note of 1980).

362

he; so 'We shall buy again from Canada and Australia, as we have done since 1960 ... we need to replenish our reserves; we also need to make up our stock of good seed. Of course, now the population has increased, we need 200 million tonnes a year; we are aiming to double it, and then we shall have a large surplus.' But whatever the difficulties, still things were better than in Old China. 'Everyone nowadays is employed. In my family there were thirty people and only my father worked for all of them ... some went into pawnshops to become apprentices, working for nothing but food for three years. My father was a clerk at twelve dollars a month in the salt gabelle. Today any little girl in a department store gets thirty *yuan* ... our young people do not know the hard times we've had ... '

Fish seemed to interest Chen Yi. He reminded me how in Szechuan a coloured wooden fish was placed on the table to close a meal; to symbolize plenty, but to take the place of unobtainable fish as well. In north China millions had never eaten fish in their lives. And breeding, preserving, cooking and even eating fish, all these steps required education, persuasion. In a village in Kansu province a child had choked on a fish bone. 'That village will never touch fish again, not for a hundred years,' said Chen Yi. To educate people into one food habit and out of another required almost a political campaign. 'Changing food habits changes the economy of a country,' said Chen Yi.

Chou Enlai was not in a good mood. He frowned; he was tired. There were many long drawn out debates and conferences that summer, and the foreign diplomats had noticed an unusual number of 'higher-ups' gathered at the seaside resort of Peitaiho. Obviously a major Party meeting was on. Dean Rusk had announced in Washington that the policy of the United States was 'containment of China'. China was *the* enemy.

Chou talked about South East Asia. It was obvious that he was anxious about the war in Vietnam, which was expanding. He gave me a broad hint not to go too 'left' in Malaya and Singapore; because 'there will not be socialism there for a considerable length of time'. Malaysia, said Chou, was a British, not an American invention. It was not, for China, a preoccupation. The British and the Americans were not in agreement on South East Asian policy. Therefore it was not a priority in his scheme of things. Chou also referred to the successful conclusion of the overseas Chinese problem in Indonesia. Indonesia was now a very good friend of China's. She would not enter into a 'containment belt' project against China.

I told him that I would be going to Japan, and to Indonesia, in the autumn. He nodded briefly, very preoccupied.

I would see him again, on happier occasions, when we talked of history, of many things. I had never seen him as exhausted as that summer of 1962. He must have had many things on his mind.

I met Nien again. I was eating by myself in the Hsinchiao Hotel on the sixth floor – the European floor, for there I could have small snacks – when she came in.

Nien was exquisitely dressed, in some sort of pale beige silk, with a touch of gold at the neck, and high-heeled shoes, also beige, on her feet. Her hair was carefully waved, and her face a perfection of make-up (even in Chungking, during the war years, she had worn the most marvellous make-up). I could not at first believe it was Nien, because I had seen all my other friends from Yenching University, and we all – including myself – kept scrubbed faces without make-up, and short clean hair without adornment, and wore very simple, faded clothes. I looked much like them in those years, not through deliberate concealment, but because it was so much more pleasant to merge. I was stopped on the streets, or even in the hotel, by people asking me the way or for information.

Nien was with an English couple, business people, obviously opulent, representatives of an oil company.

It was some years since our last meeting, in Chungking during the war.* She had been there with her husband, Cheng Kanghsi. At the time he was an important member of Chiang Kaishek's Foreign Ministry. He had even been sent, with Pao, on a mission to India during the war to negotiate having Chinese troops trained in India, under Stillwell.

'Oh, it's you,' said Nien. She was surprised, as I was; her eyes travelled over my clothes, my striped Chinese socks (shades of the Dalai Lama), my soft cotton Chinese shoes, my baggy Chinese trousers, my open-collared, comfortable, shabby shirt; all Peking made. And of course my face. No make-up. But then I seldom wore make-up.

'Nien, what are you doing here? Where do you come from?'

'I live here,' said she. 'I live in Shanghai. I've come up to Peking to see my friends.' She introduced the business couple.

I was even more astonished. I nearly said, 'But if you live here, how come you dress the way you do? I thought you had just arrived from Paris or London ... '

* See *Birdless Summer*, 1939-42.

We all sat together. Nien saw me staring at her clothes, and she smiled that dainty, tiptoe smile of hers which I had found so arrogant when we were together at the university. 'To look at us, of course one would think you were living here and I was living abroad ... you look exactly like ... an interpreter.'

'All writers are chameleons, Nien. I like it when people come up to me and say: Comrade, can you direct me to Goldfish Street? And I can.'

Nien had been a brilliant student at Yenching University. And she had copiously snubbed me. Repeatedly and thoroughly. Something which now I fully understood, of course. Her husband, Cheng Kanghsi, was from a wealthy family, and a graduate of the prestigious Tsinghua University. And he had become a high official under Chiang Kaishek.

Pao had told me that Kanghsi had made some nasty allusions to my lack of virginity in front of Pao and other members of the mission while they were in India. This was the greatest shame that any man in China could ever endure. It was horrible. Pao should have returned to kill me immediately, to wash his honour clean ... But since Pao was a fabulator, and since I am a person who likes to make friends out of enemies because it is a better revenge, I did nothing. However, on the street in Chungking one afternoon, Nien and Kanghsi cut me dead; but then so many people pushed me down because I was a Eurasian ... how many insults of all kinds I absorbed, digested, converted into cynical strength throughout the years ...

Two months after cutting me dead, Kanghsi and Nien had invited us to dinner. Pao and they talked of schemes and projects. Kanghsi needed Pao because Pao had just been picked as aide-de-camp to Chiang Kaishek; and Kanghsi was ambitious. No one talked to me at all. I just ate, drank tea, and sat waiting for the time to go, an illiterate peasant wife, ignored in a corner.

Kanghsi had become an ambassador under Chiang Kaishek. But when Liberation came in 1949, of course he 'saw the light' and gave up Chiang, and stayed on in Shanghai, and was classified, with his wife Nien, as a patriotic national-capitalist. He established connections with Shell Oil; and had not only possibly been instrumental in the Dutch recognizing China, but was also the Shell representative in China. And China, of course, needed oil, for oil had not then been discovered in abundance in China, not before the Leap of 1958–9.

Then Kanghsi had died of kidney cancer, and Nien took his place with Shell, and carried on as their representative, and brought up their only daughter, and lived comfortably in Shanghai. According to friends of hers whom I met later, she had a fabulously beautiful house, full of antiques and exquisite porcelain, and at least eight servants: in Shanghai, in communist China! She also had bank accounts in Switzerland and in London. Her shoes and clothes she bought in London and Paris, on her frequent trips abroad.

Nien was not alone in having such privileges, a life in China completely out of touch with the people of China. There were, after all, 90,000 or so national-capitalists in Shanghai, who continued to live in great luxury, on 3 to 5 per cent tax free interest paid on bonds, which were compensation for the factories and properties that had been nationalized by the government. All of them had servants, imported cars, refrigerators and television sets; and they had bred a new generation of golden youths, who went to university.

Can one wonder, then, at the resentment of the sons of workers and peasants, who had slogged and endured and died for the Revolution, at these small enclaves from the past, maintained by the government? Yet they *had* to be maintained. They too were necessary for China's grand scheme for the future.

The son of one of these national-capitalists, for instance, did nothing at all except breed goldfish. Others made friends with the offspring of high officials in the Party, and so rottenness came in ... One nationalist-capitalist I met had the rents of twenty-two houses and blocks of flats to spend; another had an income of two million *yuan* (one million U.S. dollars) a year. Tax free. All of it.

Nien said, 'The Party understands. They will not ask more of me than I can give. I cannot be anything but what I am. Meanwhile I am pretty useful. I am the agent between the Chinese Ministry of Trade and a foreign concern ... ' She held a lifeline in her hands, at the time. Until oil was discovered in China.

Nien gave me her address and telephone number in Shanghai. 'Do come to see me when next you come by,' said she. And rose, graceful on her high heels. Italian shoes.

But although I was briefly in Shanghai in the next few years, I did not go to see her. And now I feel guilty about it. Because when the Cultural Revolution came in 1966, then of course Nien was a target. Such an obvious one! Of course the Red Guards who were under the control of Mao's wife and her acolytes surged into Nien's house. Of course they smashed everything.

Nien went through a kangaroo court of youngsters. And these youngsters included her own daughter, who was a Red Guard, who participated in the condemnation of her mother ... Nien was sentenced to work manually, cleaning an office. This was not a very harsh thing, on the whole: my friend Kung Peng, who was a high Party official, had to do the same during the Cultural Revolution; and her husband, Chiao Kuanhua, was treated worse. But because Nien had never endured any hardship, had never had her image of herself smashed in the cauldron of revolution, she could not bear it. I think her daughter's condemnation of her was the last straw. She committed suicide.

So many of my friends, my whole family, were similarly scourged: Third Brother, Sixth Brother, Third Uncle and Third Aunt. But they endured.

I still feel that I should have made the effort to see Nien; to talk to her, although she might have shattered me again with her assurance.

Fifteen

Departure from Malaya: 1962-1964

WHEN I RETURNED from China to Singapore I was again body-searched, and my clothes and luggage jumbled mercilessly. 'Orders, Doctor, *lah*,' said the customs men regretfully; friendly in their deliberate harassment.

In that year and the next my two novellas, *Cast But One Shadow*, and *Winter Love*, were published, as well as stories in the *New Yorker* and articles in several magazines. Outwardly I continued to busy myself as usual; in my mind I was preparing to write my series of books on China describing the story of my Family and what had happened to them before and after the Chinese Revolution; intermingled with my own life story.

In late September 1962, I went to a Quaker-organized conference for diplomats, held in a resort called Puntjak Pas, in the mountains near Bogor, Java. The convenor was Russell-Johnston, a tall, frail-looking New Englander.

At Puntjak Pas many diplomats congregated, including Poles and Czechs, and the Russian Ambassador. India was also represented, by a likable person named Ghosh. Mr Ghosh and I were at cross purposes; he talked a great deal about China's 'traditional expansionism' and 'aggression', and was supported – none too well – by the British delegate. The American representative, a remarkable young man named Levine, was uncommonly non-hostile about China. He said to me one day, when we happened to be alone, 'I do hope that China's experiment does succeed, otherwise America and Russia may be at each other's throats on the plains of China.' Which put the geopolitics of our planet into a new perspective for me.

Puntjak Pas was high in the mountains and the rain cascaded coldly down the abundant foliage of the park in which our bungalows were erected. There were many speeches. I tried hard not to be aggressive to the U.S.S.R.; I thought the Russian delegate amiable and handsome.

After the conference I stayed with my Indonesian friend, Lasmijah Hardy, in Djakarta. Lasmijah's house was pretty, with a garden like a small trim jungle and a well for sweet water in its middle. She had almost a thousand sarongs, some hand-painted and very valuable. Two women sat all day unrolling and then rolling them up again; they were stacked row upon row on shelves, like scrolls.

There was hunger and want in the villages of Java. Djakarta was full of soldiers. The military seemed to occupy every institution I visited. Even the hospital and the university seemed to be run by the military. There was a total erosion of all public utilities; the post office, the telephones, the buses ... inflation was ugly and continuous and would become quite colossal.

In the villages, any manufactured object was of a price beyond the reach of most of the people. There was the usual subsistence economy: rice and bananas, and some vegetables. In the city, food was extremely expensive. The cashier of a bank only came once a month to her office, because her monthly salary only enabled her to pay one bus fare to and from her house to work.

Lasmijah, as other wealthy Indonesian women, gave asylum to many of her relatives, who of course cooked and washed and cleaned and rolled the sarongs. 'They come from my village,' Lasmijah would say. President Sukarno made many speeches; he would exhort his people to 'eat rats' if they had no other meat. The military and the wealthy seemed to have everything, including enormous new cars. They deplored the economic depression which was due, they said, to the influence of the Indonesian Communist Party, and Sukarno's kindness to them. Actually the catastrophic economic situation was the result of a number of causes, not the least being corruption; and the ousting of many small producers and merchants from the countryside (because they were overseas Chinese) had disrupted a whole level of production and commercial transactions. Now the army controlled almost every commodity: paper, rubber, sugar, medicines. Under the label of 'nationalization' it took over enterprises. Army generals (and navy and air force commanders too) shared the profits, and nothing went back to the people.

I met Subandrio, the Foreign Minister. He had just returned from a tour of Malaya and Singapore, and was very agitated about Malaysia. He felt that it was a threat to the structure of Indonesia, and especially he seemed afraid that Sumatra, so large and so unpeopled (only seventeen million at the time), might fall a prey to 'neo-colonial' Malaysia. 'We are very greatly helped by the Soviet Union,' said Subandrio. The U.S.S.R. supplied the equipment of the Indonesian army, navy and air force.

I could not say to him that Premier Chou Enlai had appeared to think that Malaysia, despite its reprehensible beginnings, was a better bargain than a very large confederation under one or the other of the superpowers. And it was, of course, useless to repeat to Subandrio the remark of my friend Rewi Alley, in Peking, who had said, 'How curious that the U.S.S.R. should help the Indonesian army, which is notoriously hostile to the Indonesian Communist Party.'

Subandrio seemed to believe that Lee Kuanyew was a true 'socialist'. At the time the word was one to pink the cheek of the anaemic, to brighten the eyes of all of us virgin children of Asia ... Since then, how often have we been raped with that word?

I did not tell Subandrio that I thought merger would not take place between Singapore and Malaya. At seven or eight in the morning when interviews are held, before the heat makes one drowsy, I am not at my most articulate.

The next day, also at seven in the morning, I saw Sukarno. Breakfast with Sukarno was almost obligatory in Djakarta for every V.I.P. I waited in the large living room; on the walls hung many large and bafflingly bad oil paintings of women (all very properly dressed). Sukarno came in. He was arrayed in a heavy cloth uniform (air force I think). He had a major fear of draughts, could not bear air conditioning, and so no fan could ever be turned on in his presence. I have seen him raise his collar, shiver and glare at a whirring fan. He had a *songkok* upon his head and he kept it on because it enhanced his looks and hid his baldness. He was a vital man, exuding lustrous vitality, and he now saw me, pulled in his stomach and straightened his *songkok* and advanced jauntily, carrying a short stick like a British army officer.

We sat and talked; about Malaysia. 'You know the British and the

Americans want to take Sumatra and Borneo from Indonesia, leaving Java with its sixty-two million people to stew,' said he. He did not care who ran Malaysia, but he was worried about its ultimate use as a confederation against Indonesia.

One was here in the presence of another kind of politics; Malay-Indonesian politics, in which there is always the possibility of *mushawaira*, consultation, entente, in the midst of much sound and fury and mutual imprecation. And this is what would happen. Within another eighteen months, Subandrio and Tunku Abdul Rahman would meet in Manila, and make up; and Tunku would even launch the idea of MAPHILINDO, a confederation of all the Malay races in Malaysia, the Philippines and Indonesia. But this would remain a stillborn idea because in such a troika of course it would be huge Indonesia which would dominate. Finally, some years later, the ASEAN, or Association of South East Asian Nations, would be promoted, and it would try to keep away from superpower military alliances and entanglements.

I walked on the streets of Djakarta. A depressing city; and such beautiful people ...

I saw tanks on the street. There was a police parade. The police, in tanks, rolled down the street. I watched, unbelieving. Why tanks?

I had met in Cairo, in February 1962, the Indonesian writers' delegation. I met the writers again. Of course a good many were communists or sympathizers. But the Indonesian Communist Party was supposed to be respectable: there were communist ministers in the government, including Aidit, the head of the Party. Everyone said the Party was immensely strong; the strongest in Asia after the Chinese Party: it had three million members.

I went to the seaside for a day with some of the Indonesian writers. It was a day surfeit with beauty and light; the sea was brittle sapphire, there was a wonderful small wind, and the fishermen sailed in, swinging their curved boats, a ballet on the glistening water. The silver fish came spilling out of the nets; we stood on the pale beach bargaining for the fish, and ate those we chose, grilled with chilli and citronella and fresh coconut and unripe mango. 'Oh, what a succulent country you have, a mouth-watering country,' I said. 'You must take great care of your country. It is a paradise.'

But the writers talked of the economic problems. There were too many people in Java and too few in Sumatra and the many other islands; Indonesia was large and communications between the several thousand islands were bad. Sukarno has started a programme of population transfer, which was called 'transmigration'.

'Have you seen the police tanks? I smell danger,' I said. But the writers laughed. 'The Party has three million members, we are well prepared ... and President Sukarno is good to us. We need not fear anything.'

The villages glowed ochre and emerald, laughing women and children stood under coconut palms and waved at us as we drove by. There was misery and want, but with the sun and the spiced air it did not appear loathsome. Yet some of the writers were so poor that they could not afford the paper on which to write their novels, or even a lengthy article ...

I went to see Aidit, the head of the Indonesian Communist Party. He was a small man, with a round head, large soft brown eyes, and a very gentle manner. He was with Lukman and Njoto, the two vice-chairmen of the Party. I thanked Aidit for granting me an interview; he had some weeks previously given an interview to Alex Josey. I wanted to verify a few statements that Josey had made. Aidit replied with great candour. He thought Alex Josey was a 'true socialist', he said.

'Have you seen the tanks on the streets?' I asked. 'Who supplies tanks to the police?'

'They are American tanks,' said Njoto. 'But the U.S.S.R. supplies the army; we have many friends among the military.'

'I'm sorry, but it just does not smell right to me. Don't you feel there may be a military coup?'

'Oh,' said Aidit, 'we are well prepared.' The communist militia in the villages numbered almost a million men, said he.

But it did not seem to me that the militia was well-weaponed; perhaps they had old rifles, and possibly bamboo spears, as had been used against the Japanese during the war.

'But we have the people with us,' said Aidit simply, as a crushing argument.

Aidit had led a life of great courage and self-sacrifice; he had much experience in insurrection. How could I say: I think you're going to be massacred, just as Chiang Kaishek massacred the Communists in China in 1927?

And why should I think so?

That winter, dropping into Peking briefly, I could not help telling Kung Peng that I was worried about Aidit. But I could not tell her why. And as usual when she did not wish to discuss something with me, she merely said, 'Comrade Aidit is a good comrade.' After all, he was the head of a three-million-strong party ...

I decided I would forget my foolish premonitions; I was overcautious, owing to my warlord experiences in childhood.

And yet, so many times, when I do what my mind tells me to do and my belly tells me is wrong, I end up wrong. When I take time to listen to that buried restlessness without a voice which lies in entrails, not heart, I am fairly often right.

On September 30th, 1965 there was a coup in Indonesia. No one even today knows exactly what took place to precipitate the blood bath. It seems that the army had planned a coup against the P.K.I.* which the Communists attempted to forestall by a coup of their own, entirely botched, under a certain army colonel who was a Communist.

The massacres that followed were truly horrible. 'The river was bright red with blood; and the bodies floated like dead fish,' some escapees, refugees in Holland would later tell me. The estimated number of killed varies from 300,000 to 600,000. No one will ever know.

I would meet a Party member, one writer, who had escaped. I asked him about Aidit, and Njoto, and Lukman. 'All dead,' he said simply. In the first days of October, 'Comrade Aidit was like a man lost, he did not know what to do ... that is why our losses were so heavy.'

But in those years before the coup, the 'left' indeed looked strong in Indonesia, especially at a big reception which I attended at Sukarno's palace. Sukarno came in, in army uniform, surrounded by his ministers; among them Aidit and Njoto. The press, the diplomats attended. Sukarno made a speech announcing 'confrontation' with Malaysia, which meant a cutting-off of trade. But the trade was chiefly smuggling through Singapore, so that did not amount to much of a threat for Malaysia. However, paradoxically, while the left-wing newspapers praised confrontation (*konfrontasi* in Indonesian), its existence allowed the military to remain in a position of dominance, with the key economic sectors in their hands; under the slogans of discipline and 'preparation against imperialism and neo-colonialism'.

Twice again before the coup of 1965 put an end to his prestigious career, I was to meet Sukarno, once in Cairo, and once in Cambodia. We never clicked. I never felt for him that immediacy and rapport which I felt with Chou Enlai, and Chen Yi, and Sihanouk, and Tunku Abdul Rahman –

* Indonesian Communist Party.

all so dissimilar persons, but persons I could talk to. With Sukarno, perhaps because of his over-abundant masculinity (and his awareness of it), I was always at a loss. A little as with Nehru; except that Nehru radiated self-satisfied intellect rather than conscious sexuality.

In Cairo Sukarno was too busy with a belly-dancer to pay much attention to the conversations he was having with Chou Enlai and Nasser; he baffled the earnest Chinese thoroughly. In Cambodia he was accompanied by a very beautiful American girl, so that even Prince Sihanouk became – despite his suave and impeccable courtesy – a little confused. How could Aidit ever have placed so much trust in the hands of this great, magnetic, popular, but rather erratic Sukarno?

In the summer of 1965 I received through the Indonesian Consulate in Hongkong an invitation from Sukarno to come and live in Indonesia ... a house was being given to me ... I declined politely.

And then came the coup of that September. Friends of mine died. Others are exiles. Still others are in jail, perhaps for the rest of their lives.

Back from Indonesia and on to Japan; invited by the Japanese Foreign Ministry for a fortnight's tour.

It was then October 1962, a month of crises. The Cuba crisis, the Sino-Indian border war ... I left Singapore for Tokyo on October 10th, the day Nehru ordered the Indian army to 'throw the Chinese out'.

As I landed in Tokyo, the Foreign Ministry representative met me. Mrs Oiwa was a lady diminutive and prim, but of delicate beauty; a widow. She would accompany me everywhere. Everything had been thought out, arranged; I was handed my programme. Everything was minuted, and when the programme said Mrs Oiwa would call at 8.15, she called at 8.15. At 8.25 we would arrive at the museum (factory, ministry, hospital), and at 8.25 and ten seconds I would descend from the car and be greeted by the director (manager, chief surgeon). At 8.34, after a talk, we would start the visit ... and so on, for two weeks.

It was most restful to be time-programmed, especially after Indonesia, where I had had gruelling experiences with the vagaries of my friends' idea of time. In fact, so exasperated had I become that I had said, 'You cannot make a revolution if you don't have a notion of time. Great battles have been lost because battalions arrived late.'

I knew very little of Japan until my visit, except that we had been at war, and there had been untold suffering in China because of that war; and even now it was difficult to make many Chinese, both in China and overseas, accept the idea of friendship with Japan. But I was, I confess, captivated, charmed, and remain reverent towards the enormous capacity of the Japanese always to learn – always on the alert to better themselves.

The variety and excellence of what I saw, the iron discipline of the conversations (led at a gallop), all fell into a hypnotic rhythm for me. I was a particle of some large, overall plan, and since I was tired, I let myself go. I had two hours with the writer Kawabata, who was to become a Nobel Prize winner; and here Japanese efficiency broke down, because we could not find his house in Tokyo, where houses are not properly numbered and one wanders round a *ku*, or district, asking for the person one seeks.

A weekend in a Japanese inn. Introduction to its pleasures, including a dip in the very hot pool. In the morning I saw the hotel maid wash the pebbles of the garden pond, rubbing them clean and putting them back into the clear sparkling water, one by one …

Visits to magnificent factories; shipyards and steel-making plants; a transistor factory: rows of young girls, all programmed; little red lights twinkling when one of them temporarily left her seat, away from the slowly rolling rubber ribbon in front of her. The girls were paid so much, they lived in dormitories, and at the age of twenty-three they left to get married because after that their eyes were no longer as sharp and accurate. The savings on their salaries were programmed to meet the required dowry for an eligible bride …

The enormous sense of belonging of every Japanese … a vast invisible mesh which seemed to hold all together, utilized to create 'company spirit'. The Honda spirit, the Toyota spirit … the company morning hymn; feudal loyalty metamorphosed, transformed into a technological bond … Japan was for me a revelation of how 'the past can be made to serve the present', a phrase which Mao Tsetung had used frequently. It was also an example of 'making things foreign serve Japan'. And Mao wanted China to do the same. But could it be done? Sun Yatsen's phrase, when he visited Japan in 1923, stuck in my mind: 'Japan and China … have a common destiny'. And had not China's first reform movements been stimulated by the example of Japan's Meiji reform?

Two things preoccupied many of the Japanese I met. The first was the Nobel Prize for Literature. Invariably I would be asked (an interval of ten seconds was left in conversations for this question) 'Do you think that Japan will win the Nobel Prize?' Of course, it was an oblique way of finding out if I read Japanese authors.

The second preoccupation was baseball. Two of my interviews had to be postponed because of important baseball matches. Everywhere on the streets, on the pavements, in front of the shops, one could see Japanese men making the gestures of wielding a bat and hitting a ball.

I had many pleasant meetings with writers, including some I had met in Cairo, among them the President of the Pen Club, Yoko Matsuoka, who arranged a party for me. But the party coincided with the Cuba crisis, and among the invited writers were some who felt the world was coming to an end. One of them discussed seriously with me his intention to die that very night. 'Perhaps tomorrow there will be nuclear war,' said he. He did not want to be a victim of nuclear war ... he had seen Hiroshima.

I strongly dissuaded him. 'Nothing will happen. The Cuba crisis is a "confrontation" [shades of Sukarno!] and there's something artificial about it ... ' 'Artificial!' exclaimed the writer with great indignation. 'It's a tragedy! A tragedy involving the whole world!'

I apologized for not being able to take it seriously. 'I just lack a sense of tragedy, even in my own personal life.'

The writer promised to wait. And of course he is still alive. So is the world.

Suicide was a national fascination, though waning. I went to see a Japanese film. The scene of *sepuku* (disembowelling) was so realistic that I fainted (it was also extremely hot and overcrowded in the small cinema). 'Oh,' said Mrs Oiwa, bending over me as I came to, 'you have a soft heart.'

'I thought it was ... so cruel to give the young boy a wooden dagger to disembowel with, Mrs Oiwa ... he had to try so many times ... '

(The process, filmed in detail, included the victim biting off his own tongue to stop himself from screaming.)

'Yes,' said dear Mrs Oiwa, shaking her head, 'so cruel to give him a *wooden* dagger. He should have been given a good sharp dagger, that would have been *so* kind.'

In the large stores on the Ginza, gentle, porcelain-faced girls stood white-gloved at the foot of the escalators, saluting and thanking everyone who went up or down; eight hours a day. I learnt about the special sex equipment provided for lonely women and widows; artificial objects they could use themselves. So practical. Abortions so calmly accepted and performed; no guilt feeling about them. 'You are really a very wonderful people, Mrs Oiwa,' I said.

The Foreign Ministry gave me a banquet at a renowned geisha house; the geishas plied me with drink; we talked politics, which meant, of course,

China. The Japanese view was then very much modelled on the American view: the domino theory in South East Asia. The Ministry officials felt that China was in the process of inner disruption. I said that countries like China are so huge and unmanageable, and yet have such a spring and bounce to them, such power of survival, that they cannot be crammed into any economic or political framework; but then I was no political expert.

On October 23rd, while I was still in Tokyo, Vincent rang up from Singapore. He was calling about the Sino-Indian border; for on the previous day the Chinese had started to push back the Indian troops and were coming down the passes into the plains. Vincent was worried because he could be recalled for military duty. I rushed to book the next aeroplane; cut my visit short by a day, and returned to Singapore.

The next few weeks were fairly tense for both of us. And then in November came relief, with China's unilateral withdrawal. Vincent and I hugged each other so tight, as if we would never let go. 'I told you not to worry,' said Vincent. But he had been very worried. But now there would not be war, not between India and China. And that meant that Asia had a chance to grow and to prosper.

In December 1962, Vincent and I met the representatives of the Chinese press of Singapore and Malaya, and members of the Nanyang University Graduates' Union. We were expected to give them a talk on the India-China border conflict.

I spoke moderately. For I would not, in any way, stress the Chinese case in such a way as to offend the Indian community of Singapore and Malaya. Racial hostility, communalism, riots and bloodshed are easily stirred up.

Vincent spoke after me. He, too, did not argue the rights or wrongs of the case. He said that border conflicts occurred between many countries throughout the world; they must not be exaggerated; and he felt sure that all would be settled peacefully through negotiation, one day. Meanwhile the Chinese and the Indian people would continue to be friends, as they had been for two thousand years.

Yet at the time, deep hysteria prevailed in India. Calcutta's 14,000-strong Chinese community was raided – laundrymen, tailors, shoemakers and shopkeepers were assaulted, their goods confiscated; many were interned and lost all their belongings. Emergency regulations, which allow the suspension of human rights and of all normal law procedures, were applied; they gave the police in India unlimited power. The Chinese in

Calcutta were Indian citizens, with Indian passports. They spoke Bengali or Hindi, and English; most of them were born in India, had never set foot in China ... they were condemned by their faces alone.

As for the Indian people, the Indian government had decreed that it was 'treason' to 'spread rumours' or 'doubt' about the official explanation of 'savage Chinese aggression'. The all-obliterating *unfact* acted very thoroughly.

At the time, in the United States, a general called Maxwell Taylor was making a report to Congress, telling the facts; but this report was not made public.

'Such is democracy,' I said to Vincent. The limits of freedom to tell the truth, in both worlds, were never more apparent to me than in 1962.

Vincent's courageous and modest action in speaking so wisely, to appease inflamed emotions, was to be utilized against him shortly thereafter.

In 1962 a referendum asking the people of Singapore to vote on 'merger and Malaysia' was set up. The English weekly, *The Economist*, called it 'calculated dishonesty'.

And so it was. For although the main issue was merger, whether the people of Singapore wanted or not to join in Malaysia, this was not a part of the referendum at all. The people were asked to vote only for the *terms* under which they would join Malaysia, and three choices were offered to them:

A. To join Malaysia with the Singapore government retaining its autonomy in labour and in education.
B. To join Malaysia on the same terms as Penang, Malacca or any other state of Malaya.
C. To join Malaysia on the same terms as would apply to North Borneo, Sarawak and Brunei. (The only hitch about C was that these terms had not yet been defined when the referendum took place, which meant that C did not exist, and so only the choice between A and B remained.)

What palpable fear over the referendum in Singapore! Dread and terror; an underground campaign of threats. 'We have been told to tell the children in our schools to tell their parents to vote A.' Schoolteachers I knew

377

said this to me. 'Although polling is supposed to be secret, every ticket is marked, and so the police will know who votes what.' Another rumour, but people are so easily scared ... It was hinted that vote B would lead to 300,000 Singaporeans losing their citizenship and becoming stateless ... the inevitability of voting for A became very clear.

The opposition party, Barisan Socialis, called on the people to cast blank 'protest' votes at the dishonesty of the referendum. But the PAP government let it be known that any blank vote would count as a B vote. Of course A won.

The anti-merger explosion occurred, of all places, in Brunei, the oil-rich little sultanate which was supposed to join Malaysia; which had 84,000 people of whom 63,000 were Malays ... almost the only Malays in the three territories, meant to 'balance out' the Chinese.

The Azahari rebellion, for such was its name, was led by a thin be-spectacled Malay, Azahari, whom one saw occasionally hanging around political meetings in Singapore. He was a bookseller by trade, and an important man in the running of the People's Party (Party Rakyat) in Brunei. It was, of course, vaguely 'socialist' in orientation.

Azahari was an opponent of the fusion proposed. But then, so was Brunei's Sultan (although this was an unsayable, unpublishable fact). On December 8th, Party Rakyat started an insurrection, led by what was called the North Borneo National Army. In Sarawak too a rebellion against the merger began. Strangely, Azahari himself was eight hundred miles away, in Manila, when the insurrection started.

British battalions, Gurkhas, and the Queen's Own Highlanders, were flown into Brunei. The 'rebellion' was held to be a 'communist plot'. It was of course crushed. The role of the Sultan of Brunei (whose support for Azahari was obvious) remained unstated. The role of the 'protective power', the United Kingdom, was very clear: to restore law and order through military action. It took several months to 'mop up' the so-called rebellion, which was a genuinely popular uprising, with 80 per cent of Brunei's male population between eighteen and forty taking part.

The Special Branch launched a crackdown (what else?). In Malaya, fifty persons were arrested for conspiracy. In Singapore, the Barisan Socialis came out openly on the side of the rebels. The head of the Barisan Socialis, Lim Chingsiong, and other leaders were arrested in February 1963. Linda Chen, the girl to whom I had given a job at the Malaysian Sociological Research Institute, was re-arrested.

And then came the turn of Nanyang University. A police raid, at night: 117 students rounded up. All university publications banned. Nanyang

University out of bounds to everyone except persons with special permits from the police.

In the course of 1963, I would help some students, not communists, but people implicated in writing for banned magazines, to make quiet exits from the green gulag of Singapore.

But I never went near Nanyang University again.

I went to Brunei in February 1963 to find out what had happened. Journalists returning from there spoke of savage pursuit of the rebels with dogs; of the Dayak head hunters of neighbouring Sarawak being mobilized to perform some large-scale massacres. Even English publications found the role of the British army 'distasteful' and the methods employed 'gruesome'.

Brunei's small capital looked like a spectral town, because most of its stilt-perched houses were shuttered, their doors closed. The rest of the town seemed to consist of one very large new mosque, the British Resident's mansion, the Sultan's palace, and the Yacht Club – the snob club of Brunei.

'I wish Azahari had succeeded,' a prominent British 'government servant' said to me. We were at the Yacht Club and not alone. Nervously, I looked around. One went to jail in Singapore for expressing such sentiments.

'We knew Azahari. He ran the only decent bookshop in town ... he only wanted to keep Brunei out of Malaysia,' continued this seasoned official. 'And so does the Sultan, who's now sitting on the fence ... '

Six months later people were still being processed in Brunei for their share in the rebellion.

'Half the male population of Kampong Ayer is under detention ... that's why the women and children stay locked up in their houses,' said the Englishman as he got up and left.

In Sarawak, next door to Brunei, the police patrolled the streets; they were police from Singapore.

The Chinese businessmen were rapturous about Lee Kuanyew. 'Wait until he starts running Malaysia. There'll be no trouble with the workers then.'

In North Borneo, Donald Stephens, later to become Prime Minister of the territory when it joined Malaysia, had lunch with me. He was then editor of the leading newspaper and the chief of the Kadazan, the natives of North Borneo. 'I am being cajoled and pressured and threatened and

379

bribed to get into Malaysia,' he said. 'Azahari was not a bum and a liar, as Alex Josey calls him. He just wanted Brunei to remain independent. And it will, you will see.' He was right. Brunei stayed out of Malaysia.

'We're scared of Singapore,' continued Stephens. 'Lee Kuanyew has sixty thousand unemployed Chinese, and we don't want them flooding us out here.' He did not wish for interference from Malaya either. 'We, the Kadazans, the Muruts, the Dayaks of North Borneo, we're only 450,000 people. We're not Malays. We are not Muslim. And now there are imams and Muslim preachers all over the place, trying to convert us.' He wondered aloud where Tunku had got the idea that these inclusions would 'balance out' the potential Chinese majority. 'If Tunku ever finds out how he's been fooled, he'll push Singapore out,' he prophesied. And again he was right.

In May of 1963, Vincent and I took our first holiday together in Europe. Vincent's contract with Jardine Waugh had expired, but he had signed a new one. The company wanted him to go to Sweden in order to study some new machinery to be sold in South East Asia. So off we went together, to Sweden, and then on holiday to Austria, to England and to France.

In England Vincent felt at home from the very first day; something which was never true about me. Because, although he had never been to England before (in fact he had not left India until he had come to Singapore for me), he had been so thoroughly impregnated by English manners and moods and ways of doing things that he found everything natural and uncomplicated.

On the return journey, Vincent remained for another fortnight with his family in India, while I, after calling on Nehru, returned to Singapore.

It was now August, and I was expecting Vincent back that very day, by the aeroplane from Calcutta; he was due back at work the following day. Another three hours and I would start driving across the Causeway, to Singapore airport, to meet him. The telephone rang. It was Vincent calling from Calcutta, and sounding puzzled. 'I am not allowed on any aeroplane to Singapore ... the airline company has just notified me. I am not allowed to land in Singapore. No reason given. Just orders.'

'But why?'

'No reason has been given.'

'Try flying to Kuala Lumpur,' I said.

'I've tried. But that's also impossible. Orders from Singapore.'

Although that August the two territories were still separate (Malaysia would be established in September), the police and the governments of Singapore and of Malaya had agreed on 'joint action' in control of travel and entry.

'Don't panic, I'll think of a way.'

I rang up Vincent's boss, Charles Letts. Charles was a solid, reliable man, and he liked Vincent. But he would never, of course, cross Authority. Not in an arbitrary state like Singapore. He said contritely, 'Well, if Vincent can't get back, I'm afraid his contract with us falls through.' Which meant that, automatically, Vincent had lost his job.

Lao Chieh came in to say, 'Someone is looking for you.' From the way she said it, I knew she was worried.

In the garden was a small car, and emerging from it was a Singapore trade unionist of the PAP whom I knew rather well. Let us call him K. Why had K. come to see me? He had never called before. He walked up the stairs to the veranda. 'What a nice house,' said he.

By this time my insides were beginning to pain me very much. Someone was trying to hurt Vincent, but it was only to get at me. 'The bloody cowards. They don't *dare* to attack me, so they do this to Vincent.' I became slowly very angry, and as K. sat down, I faced him with my anger.

'You haven't come to talk about my house, or Malaysia,' I said. 'Why have you come?'

'I was just passing by,' said K.

'What a coincidence,' I said. 'The very day, half an hour after I get the news that Vincent has been banned from landing in Singapore.'

K. raised his eyebrows, pretending surprised ignorance. But of course, that was precisely the reason why he had come.

It was so obvious. Someone wanted me to knuckle down, to pray for mercy, to let Vincent return. As the poet D. J. Enright had said, 'They'll only accept obsequiousness ... '

'There's been no banishment order. There's no reason given. You know Vincent has never been involved in any politics. Why pick on him? Why not pick on me? Because it's me you people want to hurt, don't you?'

'I don't know what you are talking about,' said K.

'Oh, you know. Anyway it's illegal; I'll sue.'

K. smiled. 'According to the Internal Security Act, the government can prevent anyone from landing, and no reasons need to be given. None at all.' So of course he knew. And he had come to offer a deal. 'Perhaps if you went to talk to some people ... '

'I won't. But you could talk to Rajaratnam.* He's your friend.'

'I don't think he had anything to do with it,' said K., giving up pretending.

He told me Special Branch didn't like some of my activities. But I knew that it was not Special Branch which had chosen this singular method. This was personal vindictiveness. I was registered in Malaya; could not be touched by the Singapore government; Vincent was only registered in Singapore, at his place of work, and could be affected by a local dictum.

'I'm going to fight this, you'd better tell your bosses,' I said to K. 'I'll fight it.'

K. smiled and his canines protruded a bit. 'You cannot. There's nothing in writing,' he said.

I telephoned David Marshall, my lawyer friend, the ex-Prime Minister of Singapore. He sized up the situation and said, 'Well, it is true that under our set-up there is little you can do.'

I went to see my film magnate millionaire friend, Loke Wantho. 'Wantho, only Tunku can help. Please, will you talk to him?' And Wantho said he would. 'You're asking me to stick my neck out, but I'll do it for you.'

While Wantho acted, I waited. I went to parties, more than usual, showing myself everywhere. Everyone knew what had happened; no one said anything. Everyone expected me to leave. I did not. I lost weight very rapidly, however, but apart from that even managed to go to see my dear Malay friend, Che Katijah, a member of the ultra-conservative Pan-Malayan Islamic Party. She represented the Malay rural people, which is why I liked her. I continued to take down from Che Katijah bits of her own life story, which I found quite fascinating, and they were published as a series of articles in the magazine *Eastern Horizon* which Cousin Pengju had started in Hongkong.†

But already the buzzards circled. One 'businessman', whose brother was in Special Branch, burst in upon me one afternoon.

'You're selling your houses, Doctor?'

'I'm not selling.'

'But you're going away?'

'I'm not going away.'

---

* Now Foreign Minister of Singapore.

† The life of Che Katijah binte Sidek, published under the title 'Arjasni' by *Eastern Horizon* magazine, Hongkong.

He looked at me, a little surprised. Then decided I was bluffing. 'I have good price for you,' he announced loudly. Then he tapped a wall, threw a derogatory look at the garden, and mentioned a ridiculous sum.

'Go away. I'm not selling. I'm not leaving Malaya.'

Lao Chieh was valiant. She went to the market as usual. She did not leave me (so many people would have been frightened, would have abandoned me).

I went to Kuala Lumpur to see the Indian High Commissioner: Vincent was an Indian citizen and the case should be taken up by the Indian authorities. But he was supercilious. 'I am not responsible if the Colonel has done something against the government ... '

'He has done nothing against the government, and you know it.' Where was the evidence? What was he accused of? The Indian High Commissioner kept silent.

Meanwhile, I had asked Vincent to fly to Hongkong. And to wait there. With the emergency regulations in India, I could not easily obtain a visa to India (because of my Chinese origin). In Hongkong he was safe and I could come to see him.

I now learned that there was indeed a charge against Vincent. He was said to have declared, in his speech of 1962 to the Nanyang University Graduates' Union, that 'India is wrong and China is right'. He had *not* said anything of the kind. But this had been reported, apparently, to the New Delhi government.

However, it was not the Indian government who had refused to allow Vincent to land in Singapore, or detained him in India. It was the Singapore authorities, who had nothing to do with the Sino-Indian conflict! In fact, when Vincent's father, who was a Senator, and the President of the ultra-conservative Swatantra Party, demanded a probe into the allegations, he was told that this was a 'semi-official' report, but 'it is not even in writing; only a verbal message'.

Presented with this impalpable accusation, the Indian government of course took no action at all. On the Singapore side, two lawyers told me that nothing could be done because the authorities they approached simply denied knowing anything about Vincent or his case. He had become a non-person! 'There's nothing in the files.'

After six weeks Tunku did find a temporary way out. He could not grant Vincent permanent residence in Malaya, but Vincent would be allowed multiple entries, at any time, each entry not to exceed three weeks. That was the best that could be done. 'Tunku is very fond of you,' said Loke Wantho, 'though certain members of his cabinet are not.'

Frank Sullivan, Tunku's personal secretary, was at Kuala Lumpur air-port with me when Vincent landed from Hongkong, for Christmas.

Vincent was back. Cheerful as usual, his hair curled as usual; radiating a natural happiness. Lao Chieh had a smile creasing all of her smooth face. The cats — who had been off their food, as I had — picked up; and suddenly the house was full of joy again.

'What shall we do now?' said Vincent. He had, of course, lost his job; and it would be difficult to get another one in Malaya or Singapore after what had happened. Police or government opprobrium was a black mark against being employed.

'We'll move to Hongkong,' I said. 'Anyway, I cannot write about China with half my files in London and the other half in Hongkong, and the censorship here.'

But we had to move slowly, without undue haste. I retained a suite in a new hotel being built in Hongkong, the President. This suite was to be our home for the next four to five years.

We began to pack and send our things to Hongkong. Meanwhile, there were the usual Chinese New Year parties, and we attended the one given by Loke Wantho; which was a way of showing ourselves to all of Singapore. Rajaratnam was of course there. 'I had nothing to do with Vincent's banning,' said he precipitately to me. I believed him. Rajaratnam is not a mean person.

We rented all three of my houses (I would sell them later), gave Lao Chieh a large sum of retirement money, and continued to visit Malaya two or three times a year, for three weeks at a time. In 1965 Tunku wrote to me, and I was offered permanent residence in Malaya, which was a wonderfully kind and trusting thing to do. But by then I felt that, to write about China, I could not profitably live in Malaya, so I had to decline very regretfully.

And in 1965, suddenly, Singapore was thrown out of the Federation of Malaysia, by the will, primarily, of Tunku Abdul Rahman. Singapore became a separate, independent state, and a most thriving one. And I wrote an article demanding why people in the past had been jailed and had suffered harassment, precisely for wanting an independent Singapore, when this was now accomplished and everyone seemed to think that it was all for the best. But no one paid heed, nor were the prisoners released.

Leaving Malaya and Singapore meant also losing sight, partly, of so many lives which had come into mine; and which had brought me so much of value. So many, so many now to be filed away. I shall only write about Lim Chingsiong, because when I meet again those students of Nanyang University whom I was able to rescue from jail (all of them happily employed in other countries now) we always, somehow, talk about Lim Chingsiong.

'Others can give up, but not Lim Chingsiong.' So often this was said in the years of his incarceration as, one by one, the detainees recanted and were freed. Linda Chen gave up, and went to England. The years passed. The prisons of Singapore and Malaya are not particularly nice places. The use of torture is not banned. Worst of all are the isolation cells; some of metal, and under the Equator sun metal does become very hot. The unfortunate prisoner is alone sometimes for weeks inside the metal cage.

The government of Lee Kuanyew prefers not to have too many people in jail for political opposition. Each prisoner is offered 'recantation'; and the promise not to indulge in politics again gives them the right to leave for England. Lim Chingsiong took eight years to give up. He was then allowed to go to England.

But his brain has gone. Some say it is because of what he suffered in jail in Singapore.

In 1977, walking down a certain street in London with a Chinese friend, I saw Lim Chingsiong. The street has many Chinese shops selling vegetables, spices, beancurd, fruit, soy sauce and tins from Hongkong and from China. My friend nudged me: 'Look, that man, that is Lim Chingsiong.'

Setting up the stalls for the fresh vegetables, helping to cart the garbage: a handyman in a vegetable shop in London. He was fatter. Or rather, he was no longer what he was because everything had gone out of him. The meaning of flabbiness came as I looked at his face. Lim Chingsiong.

'Sometimes people come and jeer at him, and all he does is to hold his head in his hands,' said my friend. 'We think that he is still afraid of being hit on the head. He was often hit on the head when he was in jail.'

But I remember Lim Chingsiong when he was handsome, a little indecisive, but with a certain shine about him, perhaps a little too much candour. I prefer to remember him that way.

Sixteen

Towards the Cultural Revolution 1964-1965

LIVING IN HONGKONG had many advantages. We occupied two suites at the President Hotel, and I had no household cares. Vincent found it difficult to get a job (he was forty-seven). He went to India to do temporary consultant engineering work while I was in China, but he would always drop everything to return to Hongkong when I was back. And for this total gift of his life there are no words which would not mutilate the perfection. In China I did not need him; and he knew it. But outside China I did. He blessed my heart with laughter. 'You keep me young. Without you I could not work.' He would smile that slightly quizzical smile, knowing he was feeding my absences from him, accepting to seek me beyond mere waiting: so we would live successfully for twenty-three years.

The years 1964-5 were years almost of abundance in China; people robust, well-fleshed; in the cities new buses – blue and white in Kuangchow, red in Peking – and hosts of bicycles; in the shops and markets, so many consumer goods, although not as great a variety as in 1957. A certain chic returning to women's clothes; hairdressers busy giving perms. Silk and brocade in the better stores, crowds jostling to buy. And the restaurants full, everywhere; but especially full of middle-ranking and fairly high-ranking officials. Ordinary people eat at home when food is plentiful; only when there is penury do they eat in restaurants.

Even the toys of my childhood were making a return after their disappearance in 1958. Glossy, gaudy paper windmills, painted lanterns and kites, and little tigers of soft cloth; and many new toys: dolls and trains and aeroplanes and boats, mechanical toys for a new generation of Chinese children oriented towards science, technical knowledge. My nephew wants a train.

The adolescents are tall, a head taller than their parents at thirteen or fourteen. 'It's the food,' says Jui. My nieces have beautiful straight legs. The children run and laugh and play and sing, in groups, always in large groups, like starlings. In the spring and summer, from all the offices people erupt, young and middle-aged, coming out twice a day to do the regulation twenty minutes' exercises to keep fit. In the numerous parks – the old and the new parks — under the trees there are games of Chinese chess, acrobats train, and old men do shadow boxing to keep their joints supple. Flower shops have reopened; they are crowded with people buying jasmine and camellias in pots.

The Hongkong newspapers and magazines comment on China's remarkable recovery. 'The industrial increase has been considerable ... ' Some conjecture that there will be another Leap Forward. But China still buys foreign wheat every year. Chen Yi tells me that this is in order to keep Western markets open to Chinese goods, to promote more active trade, and to replenish stocks in China.

There is renewed aestheticism; scholars browse in the old bookshops; old painting scrolls are highly prized; the art of calligraphy is back; there are many exhibitions: of stamps, of photographs, of woodcuts, of paintings, of carved jades, of embroidery. The romantic novel, *The Dream of the Red Chamber*, is reprinted and I do not know how many millions of copies it has sold. In a China with so many millions of new readers, in the villages, in the factories, any book will have a first printing of at least half a million copies.

Relaxation. Couples in love dawdle in the Summer Palace or boat among the lotus of the Peihai Park. Many questions are asked of me: about the West. Is it true that Western women have washing machines? That one presses a button and a meal comes out of the oven, all cooked?

I wrote an article for the *Daily Mail* noting this new concern for material comforts.

Agricultural mechanization. I fly over the loess region of north China, that one million square kilometres of gulch and gully, the product of erosion, of centuries of deforestation. I note among the yellow ocean of silt large, flat, verdant plains. State farms. They are mechanized. But elsewhere there is little mechanization: in several provinces I am shown footpowered threshers and some rice-planting machines (the latter do not function — they will never function properly).

Never have there been more symposia and reunions of scientists, engineers and medical men. Intellectuals show liveliness and vigour; there is argument and debate. Among the writers, too, there is a new spirit — almost defiance. Some writers have been talking about humanism, about the creative impulse and its needs ...

Never have there been so many Western businessmen in China. For the rupture with the Soviet Union is complete by the summer of 1964. Throughout a whole year and a month the ideological dispute has raged: brilliant and vituperative editorials have appeared; millions of words, a veritable avalanche of denunciation. 'We shall never trust them again ... they sold us shoddy old machines ... then they withheld the spare parts, to bring us to our knees.' Never again. China is repaying the aid the U.S.S.R. gave between 1953 and 1960. By 1965 all debts are cleared. Now, obviously, China is turning to the West for the industrial machines and the technology she needs. De Gaulle has recognized China. French businessmen are here to sell prefabricated houses. Simon Hua, the architect, is enchanted. 'We need to do a lot of rehousing.' Japanese businessmen swarm in many cities. Armed with notebooks and cameras, they interrogate hotel and restaurant waiters. 'What do you eat in the morning? What does it cost? What did you pay for your bicycle? How much cloth do you get a year?' British businessmen are holding an industrial exhibition, and hundreds of thousands of workers and technicians and engineers will come to it. Canadians are also here, and others. There is a West German businessman, and he speaks excellent Chinese, at the hotel.

In the Hsinchiao Hotel an old waiter from before Liberation is teaching the young. 'Muffins for tea,' he says. There are muffins. He shows the young waiters how to pour coffee for the guests.

'There is a change of policy ... an opening to the West ... people are relaxed. It is quite wonderful,' says Freddy Dahlmann, a Belgian businessman who has been my friend for many years and now heads Belgium's first trade delegation to Peking.

But within this sunny, peaceful, pleasant and impressive landscape there lurk intermittent, elusive hints of bad weather. From time to time one hears a small rumble, as of distant thunder. In the tranquil stillness a small seismic shock, as in my Peking childhood, when an earthquake would suddenly move our house and the lamp would sway, only to settle into immobility again.

In the early summer of 1964, the perturbation sensed still appears to me – because I want to be happy, I do not wish to go through the throes of worry again – merely a verbal campaign, something like those health drives which take place yearly, when prizes are given to the cleanest cities. But I cannot avoid being troubled by certain things. To begin with, the very obvious: the large, top-heavy and somewhat arrogant bureaucracy; the privileges now openly flaunted by some officials. They have suits of the finest cloth, superbly cut. They eat in the best restaurants, and black official cars chauffered by large, burly drivers carry their wives and children to the shops, to school, to the parks. And then, a perceptible number of privileged youngsters, belonging to the families of high officials, hold parties and dress as the young in Hongkong, and look like a new wealthy class. In fact, that year the words 'very Kong' come into the vocabulary of the young, to indicate this Hongkong style.

Wang Wanchun comes to lunch with me, and talks about 'the four cleans'.

'What is that?'

'It's part of the socialist education movement which began last year ... '

The socialist education movement, described as a 'deep-reaching, soul-searching' political campaign, is designed to alter attitudes and behaviour and conduct from bourgeois and capitalist modes. 'The relations between the Party and the people in some rural areas has not been too good ... it's designed to purify the Party.' Is this another rectification?

After the Leap, the Party allowed private production and black markets for a while; and then some Party cadres (the word some is so indefinite, but it is constantly used and always with a hasty additional clause: of course, extremely few in number) became corrupt profiteers and exploiters, as in the old feudal way. Then Chairman Mao issued 'Ten Points' for an overhaul of the rural areas – 'To check this general loosening of conduct, the squandering, the corruption,' said Wanchun. Mao called for a clean-up: the clean-up of granaries, of commune accounts, of the methods of giving workpoints, of commune property as distinct from private. He urged the cadres to participate in collective labour. Apparently public granaries occasionally became the 'private property' of Party cadres in the commune; accounts, and money coming in, were used for private purchases, and some cadres allotted themselves a very large number of workpoints for 'administrative work' – from five to ten times the average.

'Please may I read the Ten Points?' I asked a middle cadre.

'Sorry. Secret document. Not for outsiders.'

'But I can get them in Hongkong, I expect ... they are available there ... '

'Our friends *do not* read information stolen from China.'

It would be the same in January 1965, when I asked to see the Twenty-Three Points, also on the socialist education movement, and issued by Chairman Mao. The Twenty-Three Points are considered by some scholars the first tentative blueprint for the Cultural Revolution. I agree, for the preamble says: 'The key point ... is to rectify those people in positions of authority in the Party who take the capitalist road ... ' The Cultural Revolution grew out of the socialist education movement, and the twenty-three-point document bridged the two campaigns. There was always reticence in the cities about the socialist education movement.

There it was known as 'the four cleans', meaning anti-corruption, bribery, bureaucracy and arrogance among Party cadres.

Perhaps too much pushiness on my part led to my temporary 'demotion'. A good few receptions given to 'friends' and visitors passed me by. Neither would I be allowed to interview people I asked to see.

'But X. [a French writer on his first visit] has been invited ... he has had an interview.'

'Yes, but he is *very* famous,' is the retort.

Another reply I get is: 'Our leaders are too busy.' I take this as a 'rectification' of my by now notorious 'bad temper'. A middle cadre prefers a docile, even-tempered, unquestioning honoured guest, to be led about.

Anyway, neither Premier Chou Enlai nor Marshal Chen Yi refused to see me, and to me they were the people who mattered most. I was once vouchsafed an explanation for the 'lesson' I was getting. 'You are friendly towards our workers and peasants, but sometimes with our Party cadres you are quite rude.' 'I don't like meaningless lectures,' I replied; which did not help my case ('refractoriness'). Soon, however, I left for the provinces. And in the provinces no one had demoted me. In Szechuan I learnt a great deal about the socialist education movement.

At Tayee, some eighty kilometres from Chengtu, rose the palace once owned by the great landlord, Liu Wentsai. A medieval tyrant, he died during the Land Reform of 1951–2. His mansion was a museum of atrocities. The gruesome tortures he practised upon his serfs were represented by figures in clay, fashioned by local sculptors from the art academy in Chungking: ragged and stunted peasants, defenceless under the whips of the landlord's servants, their children wrested from them to be sold by the truculent mercenaries of Lord Liu; dungeons and jails, the cages into which the peasants were thrust, too small for a man to stand; the pool of water in which feet rotted ... all this, of course, was Old China. The sculptures were vividly realistic.

At the same time, another exhibition was held in the palace, on the socialist education movement. 'We don't usually show this to people from abroad,' said the Szechuan cadre taking me around. 'The four cleans started in this district last year. We checked up on corruption, theft, exploitation ... some cadres (very few, of course) were using grain from the stores to sell on the black market; they forced the peasants to build new houses for them, free of charge; they did not pay for their food ... '

There were four 'uncleans' among the Party cadres, 'class status, political history, ideology and work style. Bad elements, counter-revolutionaries, landlords, have in some places taken over Party organizations; have even killed good cadres ... all this has to be cleaned up.' The campaign would take a year in the district of Tayee.

If the Soviet Union had gone wrong, it was because Party degeneration had set in, unchecked. 'Stalin's methods were not the correct ones. The struggle is very sharp,' the cadre added, meaning that physical incidents, and bloody ones, occurred.

Twelve rooms housed the exhibition of the socialist education movement: walls were covered with pictures, drawn and painted, showing cases of embezzlement, corruption, bribery, theft, and even murder. 'We have uncovered 274 serious cases in the district. Schoolchildren are brought here, to see that making a revolution is not easy; that, even in our socialism, class struggle continues ... '

One case showed how a peasant, a low-level Party member, having protested at the extortions of the cadre in charge of his village, was beaten to death by order of the latter.

'When the clean-up is satisfactory, the commune members are happy, the peasants feel elated, and production goes up. The masses are not vindictive; they readily forgive cadres who clean themselves with self-criticism.'

In December 1964 Chou Enlai said, 'The overthrown landlords ... remain powerful ... new bourgeois elements ... new exploiters ... are being generated in the Party, in government organs, in cultural and educational sectors ... Revisionism as in the Soviet Union is the first step towards becoming another imperialism. China must not change colour; must not lose its revolution ... the revolution must continue ... '

The great problem is youth, the 'successors to the Revolution'. As summer proceeds, everyone talks about the younger generation, about training revolutionary successors. The papers are full of the subject. 'What is the next generation like? We don't know.' There have been cases of hooliganism in Peking, at night, in the streets ... something inconceivable in 1956.

Whereas at one time Kung Peng seemed absolutely sure that my difficulties with Yungmei stemmed merely from our being in a capitalist society, now she listens carefully as I talk of the generation gap, of the difficulty of transmitting experience, of continuing a tradition, a revolution, a culture, a spirit and a way of life. 'Only through the word ... but the word must be convincing, bolstered by action ... '

'We don't know our youth. They haven't been tried out,' she replies. Youth is everywhere, clean-limbed, healthy, uproariously joyful, candid-eyed, unsubdued, because now it is no longer done to beat and ill-treat children as in the past; because now the young dare to discuss with their parents, to argue against them, a thing they never did before; something which, in Vincent's Indian family, is still not done: his sons, aged twenty-five and twenty-eight, do not dare contradict him when he speaks. India is as patriarchal as Old China was. But now the father's rule is weakened in China. What will the father's role be in another twenty years?

The young whirr on their new bicycles; they fill the buses; great streams of children (healthy, healthy!) come out of the schools at midday, and every lane is crammed with babies, and on the great sunny Square of Heavenly Peace long queues of kindergarten toddlers in brightly coloured clothes, holding each other's neat apron strings, wait to view the monument to the Heroes of the Revolution, which bears an inscription by Chou Enlai.

'They have never eaten bitterness ... never known hunger or pain ... they do not know what the past was like, just one generation ago. They do not understand the long and dolorous Calvary, to the security of today ... they think that everything is *owed* them: education and health and a job and security and care ... everything. They are cocooned; they do not know what it really is like to fight in an enemy world, for dignity, for equality ... '

Chen Yi had already said to me in 1963, 'All that the young want is a bicycle and a transistor radio, a fountain pen in their pocket and a good life in the cities.'

The Communist Youth League, through its Chairman, Hu Yaopang, has voiced its concern: 'Brought up under conditions of peace and stability ... the young are lulled into a false sense of security ... they look for a life of ease ... '

There is a campaign on, to write history as lived by the people; the history of the peasantry who slaved for so many emperors of China; to educate young people who do not know history. Chou Enlai has asked people like the celebrated actors, Mei Lanfang and Chou Hsinfang, to write their own autobiographies, to tell the next generation how penurious, how precarious, was the life of an opera star in the past. He wants the young people to have a wide understanding of what Old China was like.

There is an undiscussed problem. Every year, many millions of young people are coming on the labour market.'Our industry is not developing swiftly enough to use them.' Chen Yi, always startling in frankness, has said this soberly to me. If not industry, the only other gateway to employment is agriculture ... and so the trek to the communes of young, educated people who can read and write, going to the backward villages where amenities are lacking. But how else to lift up the villages and their inhabitants?

In 1964 this is going on all over China. The young leave for faraway provinces, alien lands to them, so strong are provincialism and feudal family ties. They go, and will labour as peasants, but they are also to become book-keepers, tractor drivers, village school teachers, agro-technicians, health workers, veterinarians. In 1965 the barefoot doctors, young para-medical personnel, aged between seventeen and twenty-five, begin to serve the rural areas in primary health care. A million of them by 1974.

These educated young are counted upon to build and maintain small fertilizer plants, small methane gas plants, small electrical plants for flour mills, and improved agricultural tools workshops — all this lower level industrialization is the great need of Asian rural society. The communes will then become agro-industrial complexes with more processing of agricultural produce: canning factories, mushroom factories, seedling care, chicken, duck and pig raising — so much can be done to make life for the peasant prosperous and to achieve a high, diversified production.

The alternative is to have cities crammed full of half-baked 'educated youths'; unemployed mouths to feed. I cannot see any other way in which China can cope with the problem of the many millions of youths apart from a very strong family planning programme and this 'hsia fang', sending them down to the villages of rural China.

Old Yeh's two sons are studying: they are mentally prepared for manual labour. They hope to return from the communes in two or three years, and to enter a university. 'It is not demeaning to become a worker or a peasant,' says Old Yeh pleasantly, mildly, perhaps a little sad at the thought that his sons may not be high-class intellectuals as he is, but placing the common weal before his own wishes. So many of my friends face similar problems for their children; because there is not enough place in the universities, and there is an immense, overwhelming tide of workers' and peasants' children coming up, coming up, also going to the universities. 'We need two hundred more universities within the next ten years,' says Simon Hua to me. He has three children.

In education there is a campaign against 'revisionist' teaching. Much of Chinese education since 1949 has been on the Soviet pattern. Until 1958, it was the correct political stance to scorn the 'capitalist' pattern. But the Leap put an end to that. Since 1961 and the Sino-Soviet rift, Third Brother can freely say that sciences are just as advanced, if not more so, in the

Western world as in the Soviet Union. Fortunately many professors have gone on staunchly teaching their best, without falling into the aberrations of the Stalin era in Russia. Of course some of them were dubbed rightists in 1957, but now, in 1964, there is a strong demand to rehabilitate rightists.

Never have I seen the intelligentsia more academically free in its pursuits than in early 1964 (though by the end of the year unease is plain to see). Institutes of higher learning have been created. Fundamental research is back. It was very seriously interfered with: in 1956 Chou Enlai restored it, but again, during the Leap, it was derided as 'useless'. 'What is the use of looking at the wings of a fly?' said an article of the time, criticizing studies in genetics.

In the factories I witness a great struggle: in some the managers have regained a power of decision; they have restored a rigorous framework of rules; the workers are paid according to efficiency; there are bonuses for better work done; political meetings are pared to the bone. But in others it is not so.

Unquestionably, an anti-intelligentsia wave looms below the surface. The Western businessmen in Peking are joyful, thinking of much business to come, of an accelerated industrial pace for China. The Cultural Revolution will catch all of them, all of us, unawares. Already there are warnings. Youth 'must not become infected with the bad habits of some bourgeois intellectuals,' warns an article. The anti-intellectual wave calls for battle against Soviet 'revisionism'. I watch as a most terrifying misconception is built up: any expression of aesthetics, material ease, culture, intellect, is in danger of being labelled 'revisionist'. To collect old books, to like flowers, to sing, is revisionist. To want a good education is becoming revisionist. 'Progress and material ease are not revisionist ... they are the goals of the Revolution and of socialism ... ' I say feebly. But I am only a bourgeois. China's pendulum is swinging. It always overswings.

This anti-revisionist war takes on so many aspects that it involves every domain of action and thought; none as eclectic as the contest around the phrases: 'one divides into two' and 'two can combine into one'.

I am confronted with these postulates at a dinner party with writers, a most delightful and witty banquet, to which came even the famous Chou Yang, whom we all privately called, at the time, the Emperor of Literature, because he was in charge of the ideological correctness of literary creation. We drank a great deal and in the amiable banter Wan, the literary critic, asked me smilingly what I thought of the sentence 'Two can combine into one'.

I had seen articles condemning this phrase. But the hermeticism of intra-Party struggle escaped me – as it escaped the majority of the Chinese. I knew, though, that many crises in the Party were first presented as highly philosophical debates or couched in historical terms relating to situations in some previous century (B.C. or A.D.). It takes weeks, even months, to arrive at the final denouement, to know who is being aimed at, and by whom, and what it is all about.

'It reminds me of Taoism,' I said. 'At the Beginning was the Unique; then one divides into two, two becomes multitude ... but perhaps I'm remembering it all wrong.' Wan gave me a nice smile, almost as if to say, 'You've passed the test.' Only two weeks later, reading articles and documents, would I realize the divisive heretical significance of the phrase 'two can combine into one'.

'One divides into two.' Mao had said it; it was the Chinese formulation of dialectics, which recognizes that all phenomena, situations, events, persons, things, in the world, are dual, made up of separate, contradictory units or segments which 'struggle' against each other, and that this action/reaction state is the cause of all change processes. Nature knows not immobility. Its only constancy is the constancy of change; and also of reversal, for in the struggle one or other of the 'contradictions' ultimately wins, and a new being, situation, event, thing, is created with a new set of contradictory units or segments ... and so on *in aeternum*. This is dialectics, 'one divides into two', and dialectical thinking lies at the core of scientific thinking.

The phrase 'two combines into one', however, opened another realm of speculation, that opposites are not concrete, but symbolic; that the Unique, the One, has two aspects, but remains the only reality; that the very nature of things compels a seeking for reunion and fusion of apparent opposites.

This syllogistic view appeared, at the time, a plea to side with the Soviet Union in the fraternity of a 'socialist camp', monolithic and indivisible. Not surprisingly, it was fiercely denounced as 'revisionist'. But the 'one divides into two' dialectics implied that class struggle, contradictions in society, and therefore turmoil, was incessant, even within socialism; and in 1964 this posed an enormous problem. Should there be 'politics in command of everything', which meant that the very basis of all action would be class struggle? And should the class struggle in China be sharpened to bring about swifter change (for theory held that 'revolution stimulates production'), or should attempts at class conciliation, at concentrating on productivity, be made, in order to accelerate progress? The technologists, the managerial layers, and some of the Party leaders, held that China needed internal peace, a diminution of political emphasis, an end to the 'mass campaigns', which might educate the multitudes but which disrupted production, a dampening of class struggles, which always ended in the intellectuals getting mauled, pushed around, browbeaten. But this 'technological view' also meant *more* centralization, directives from above; less decision making processes in the hands of the common people and above all, élitism.

Which was the right way for China, taking into account its history, its feudal past, its present handicaps? The Leap had been one attempt to solve by crash methods the problems of progress. What other experiments would be tried?

Peking's small-lane rumour that year was that rehabilitations of 'rightists' were proceeding. In fact, I was to see two of the main 'rightists' of 1957 sitting, much at ease, attending a theatrical performance, surrounded by their families and by an aura of respect.

By 1964 it was well known (although never mentioned openly) that Peng Tehuai had been called a 'rightist opportunist' because he had greatly criticized the Leap and the communes. He had lost his post as Defence Minister, but not his Party membership or his freedom. Lin Piao, who abroad was reputed to be a military strategist because of his prowess during the anti-Japanese war, was now Defence Minister. In China Lin Piao was simply known to have Mao's trust.

So many plans, projects, schemes, which I first heard of in those two years of 1964 and 1965 are the ones which are being taken up now, in 1978 and 1979. Among the dozen or so schemes I call to mind is the development of hydro-electric power in Tibet and Szechuan. Some 70 per cent of China's hydro-electric power sources lie in Tibet and Kweichow, Szechuan and Yunnan provinces, along the upper reaches of the Yangtse and Brahmaputra rivers. In 1964 there were meetings and technical articles and discussions about building a major dam in the Yangtse's upper reaches; the industrialization of the area, which is immensely rich in minerals of all kinds, depended on this energy grid. Another scheme, whereby the surplus water of the voluminous Yangtse River would be directed northwards into the drought-afflicted areas of the Yellow River basin, was also first mooted in 1964.

In education, the invisible struggle was pursued through articles of dissimilar content and orientation closely following each other in the press. Thus the plan to erect 'special' schools for the specially talented (189 of them are being erected today) was lauded in one article, and in another it was castigated as deflecting youth from integration with the masses, the workers, the peasants, the soldiers. The Ministry of Education was to be split into two in 1965: one department for higher education, for an élite of researchers and top specialists in all fields, and one for lower education, to run the part-labour, part-study schools which had first been created during the Great Leap Forward of 1958. The latter were to be set up in rural areas. They ploughed their own fields, reared pigs, planted their own vegetables. Expenses were drastically cut, but the teachers sent to them were of inferior quality. Then, there were in 1964 some 120 million children aged from seven to twelve in primary school. How could China afford universal education? How could she, while dispensing literacy to all, train an élite corps of scientists in order to reach, very rapidly, international standards in all scientific and technological sectors? Yet Mao Tsetung had set this as the target for China: by the year 2000 to reach the highest levels in technology and science existing in the world. How could this be achieved?

As the summer of 1964 slipped into autumn I became disquieted by what was happening among the writers. There had been a renewal of creativity and debate on writing since 1961 and the Second Hundred Flowers; but now again broadside attacks on literary men who sapped the Party spirit in literature were occurring. A debate about the portrayal of 'middle characters', that is, people neither heroic prototypes nor villains, ended in the criticism of its proponent, a writer named Shao. 'Comrade Chou Yang never makes an ideological mistake,' I was told. Apparently Chou Yang had expounded the correct attitude. 'He understands Mao Tsetung Thought in literature thoroughly.' But Chou Yang's criticism of other writers in 1964 lacked the severity he had displayed in 1957 against Hu Feng, Ting Ling and other non-conformists. And he himself would be attacked and reviled, in an extreme manner, and for ten years, from 1966.

There was controversy about certain films, books and plays which had been published or performed. In June 1964 a reform of the Peking opera was proclaimed. Peking opera must reflect present day scenes and aspirations, the workers, soldiers, peasants, wrote the *People's Daily*; an end to feudal themes, stories of princes and scholars and beautiful ladies. Yet in 1964 there had been new and popular operas of the old type, but incorporating some modern ideas, such as *The Yang Family Women Warriors*. Its theme was the equality of women. There were successful revivals of *The White-Haired Girl*, an opera first performed in Yenan in the 1940s. There were also one or two 'new type' operas, and I was one of the first to see *Spark Among the Reeds*, which I liked very much. 'We do need new stories, new themes, new plays and new operas,' I said to Kung Peng. 'Of course I love the old plays and dramas, and they should continue, but we should have both.'

At the time, *Spark Among the Reeds* had nothing to do with Chiang Ching, Mao's wife. Her name was not mentioned in connection with the script, the music or anything to do with the opera. Neither was *The Red Regiment of Women*, later to become one of her favourite shows, connected with her. It had first been shown in 1962,* and had won a prize then Only after 1966 would these new operas be ascribed to Chiang Ching. Undoubtedly, however, in 1964 she did emerge from retirement, and was given a position in the Ministry of Culture, and immediately attempted to take over one of the opera groups in Peking.

In 1965 quotations from a speech she had made, asserting that 'All opera heroes ... must be positive figures', appeared. This meant that no vacillation, doubt, no ordinary human emotion, could be allowed the 'hero' or the 'heroine' of the new operas. Only 'positive characters', in literature as well, were recognized. 'Middle characters' were anathema.

Attacks began against a film I had greatly liked, called *Early Spring in February*. It was based on a love story written by a young communist who had died in 1931, Jou Shih. The script and the film had received the ardent support of Hsia Yen, himself an able and prolific playwright (he managed to write fifteen plays within the short space of two years), who was Vice-Minister of Culture, and whom I had met in Cairo in 1962. Another film, which Hsia Yen had scripted, *Lin's Family Shop*, based on a story by no less a person than Mao Tun, the Minister of Culture, was also being attacked. Yet, to see these and other remarkable films, there were queues of young people a kilometre long in front of the cinemas.

'This is a moving, beautifully done film,' I said of *Early Spring in February* to Hsing Chiang, my companion. Kung Peng had specially asked her friend, Hsing Chiang, who had been her schoolmate in Shanghai and who spoke Spanish as well as English, to look after me. Hsing Chiang was to prove, through the difficult years of the Cultural Revolution, reliable, staunch, patient, loyal; trying hard to help me avoid the worst mistakes caused by my hasty temper. Now she looked at me quietly and said, 'Not everyone holds the same opinion about this film.' It was soon denounced as a poisonous weed; and by 1965 both Mao Tun and Hsia Yen were being criticized, and became invisible ... I would not see Hsia Yen again until 1978.

* As a film.

Mao Tsetung Thought. Everyone is enjoined to study the four volumes of his *Selected Works*; to understand Mao Tsetung Thought, which helps scientists in their science, writers to write, and economists to plan ... Gradually the emphasis becomes more and more adulatory.

I have been looking for a history of the Communist Party in China; the one which appeared in 1959* has been withdrawn: 'Certain events were incorrect.' There is no book on recent history in China. There will be no history book available for many years. 'The correct assessment of events', I am told, delays such a book. Only when 'we have absolutely fixed every person and event in history' will a history book be written. 'How Confucianist!' I exclaim. The Chinese Revolution, like the Russian Revolution, rubs out the faces and names of those who were heroes for a while and later assessed as traitors or deviationists. 'Correct appraisal' will therefore take a very long time.

'In fact,' says a certain Comrade Ku, who is jovial, and much more talkative than most, 'one never knows whether a communist is a good communist and a good comrade until he is dead.'

I say, 'History goes on being reassessed again and again.' No one pays attention.

This lack of historical knowledge will cost dear; it will be a major cause for the destructiveness of the adolescent (and ignorant) Red Guards during the Cultural Revolution. For they do *not* know what happened, and are gullible, and easily cheated.

Anna-Louise Strong and I are asked whether we would like to try our hand at translating Chairman Mao's poems. 'They are untranslatable,' says Anna-Louise firmly. I try, but give up in three days. I have, however, translated my favourite Sung dynasty poetess, Li Tsingchao, and the translations are printed under a pseudonym in *Chinese Literature*. This will lead to a suspicion that I have tried to infuse unsuspecting readers with 'feudal and bourgeois' ideas ... but Hsing Chiang saves me by telling everyone that I translated these poems 'a very long time ago', when I was less enlightened.

There is the army. Its presence. A constant and growing eulogy of the army. Under Lin Piao, the army is undergoing a great ideological reform; and the whole country is enjoined to model itself on the P.L.A.

* By Ho Kanchih; in this book there is little mention of Lin Piao.

In 1965, officers' uniforms are abolished. Marshals and generals dress as privates do (but there are differences – officers wear leather shoes).

The army is everywhere; in every institution and factory, and especially in the schools. Not generals or officers, but simple, green-clad, plimsolled soldiers, candid and courteous, polite and earnest and hardworking. They are there to learn, to be trained, so they say: there is no army takeover, simply their presence, to enhance enthusiasm, as they preach Mao Tsetung Thought. They willingly do the dirty work; clean floors and sweep courtyards with great cheerfulness. For this is Mao Tsetung Thought, *to serve the people*; everywhere abnegation, modesty. Children's books are full of an array of army heroes, who give their lives in self-sacrifice to save others ... Schoolchildren spend a portion of their summer holidays in sports camps, where they also do military drill. The photographs fill the West with horror: children with guns! Yet China is threatened in 1965, 'contained' and constrained and hemmed in; she is apparently without a friend (although the delegations to Peking swell in size, and Mao says, 'We have friends all over the world'). In 1965 the threat from America appears to grow more menacing; and articles appear in American papers about war with China. McNamara clarions: 'China is *the* enemy'. The war in Vietnam is expanding swiftly – perhaps that is why the army is already in situ everywhere.

I lay sleepless, interrogating the ceiling. By now I had read and reread Mao; all that was available of him. Through the decades he had striven to build a Communist Party which would constantly rejuvenate itself, purify itself, through 'rectification' movements, criticism and self-criticism, not punishing dissent by physical extermination, but allowing it within limits. 'The minority is often right,' Mao had said. He had been in the minority for some years of his Party life. He had suffered greatly from the Stalinist-like purges and methods of former Party leaders. He realized that orderly dissent was necessary, was essential for the Party to function, because there was a fundamental contradiction to solve.

In a socialist state, with a single party in absolute power, it is within that party that the seeds of degeneration, corruption, of a return to the past are to be found, nowhere else. But if a revolution is to be kept going, and this means maintaining enthusiasm and devotion, sacrifice, then the system must allow the people to denounce corruption and squandering among Party members. It must, in fact, train 'rebels' to revolt against Party cadres who betray and misuse the ethic of socialism. But how could this be done, when any criticism of a Party cadre was handled as counter-revolutionary, as an attack on the whole Party? Mao met this problem head-on in many of his speeches. Again and again he tried to differentiate between 'attacks against the Party' and 'denunciation of individual wrong-doing'. The whole point of the Hundred Flowers was the fact that limited dissent must be encouraged. And now the socialist education movement was bolstering, reinforcing, strengthening grassroots organizations of ordinary poor peasants so that they would have more say in the communes and be less bullied by Party cadres. But would it work?

At present, the material ingredients which make a revolution were absent from the Chinese scene. There had been peace for many years; food, though not abundant, was sufficient; there was security for the vast majority of the people. But there was undoubtedly deliquescence within the Party; the fighting guerrillas of the pre-Liberation days were getting old. Since 1949 there had been a large intake of untried, unseasoned and possibly opportunistic members: seventeen million members by 1964, four times more than in 1950. The Party was swamped by people with no experience of the Revolution in its fighting years. How could the untrained young, not knowing Party history, not toughened by bitter experience, distinguish between what was true socialism and what was not within a Party dedicated to bringing about socialism.

I did not dare ask this question aloud. I was sure that the middle cadres would resent it, because their shuttered minds were not ready for such speculation. Only Chou Enlai, Chen Yi and Kung Peng would under-stand. 'If and when I see Chou Enlai, I shall hint towards it ... He must have this problem much on his mind.' Had he not said that there was 'degeneration' in some Party organizations?

Lenin had said that politics was 'concentrated economics.' Finally it was a problem of economics; *how* to achieve, in the shortest possible time, material prosperity. In 1960 Mao had already said to Lord Montgomery: 'We know about fighting, we know a bit about running villages ... but we don't know anything about building a new socialist economy ... we'll have to learn the hard way ... '

Mao had written, 'Let us hope that the price we shall have to pay for learning how to build socialism will not be as heavy as the one we have to pay to win the Revolution ... '

The price to pay was to be the Cultural Revolution.

In 1965, two fundamentally opposed concepts confronted each other in China. The first was that the superstructure of ideas, behaviour, consciousness, the relations governing economic production and productivity, could not change before the material environment, the productive forces, had changed. This *almost* conceded that only the introduction of industrialization, of forcible and accelerated technology, would change man, that man can only become other through change in environment, not through volition, will.

The other concept was that consciousness, awareness of the problems and a change in the relations of production, could be achieved before the material basis was changed, and indeed acted to propel material change forward. In other words, first change the whole apparatus of thinking, and this would produce material change; just as Galileo, Newton, Einstein changed the world by seeing the universe in a different way ...

But in both arguments the instrument whereby policies were implemented was declared to be the Communist Party. 'Our cadres should have a high political consciousness,' my friend Chienta said to me in all seriousness. But what did he mean? Can one be highly aware when one's knowledge of reality is restricted?

A British diplomat, seeing the eagerness for knowledge, the developing scientific institutes, said to me, 'In ten or twenty years, if China continues as she does today, she will have a large pool of literate, scientifically minded, studious people, ready for a real breakthrough in technology and in science ... '

'Seek truth from facts'; 'Less talk, more work' – small, haphazard phrases coming from seasoned scientists. But to a Chinese-attuned ear they have a political backing.

I read somewhere that 'the young do not want to join the Party ... it's too exacting ... the pay is very low ... ' The average age of the Party cadre at grassroots level, in 1965, is forty.

Philosophers I talk with say, 'There must be a campaign to obliterate the gap between theory and practice.' Which means: Less empty talk. Economists, say, 'We have to use our heads ... even the highest ones can make mistakes ... ' Which means perhaps Mao? They also say, 'Since the Leap our productivity has not gone up; even on state farms there is too much of the sickle and the spade.' Which means the whole point of agricultural mechanization has suffered a defeat. Mechanization requires investment, capital accumulation. How can it be brought about quickly?

Meanwhile, there are the millions of young, every year, coming up on the labour market, coming up ... Family planning is mooted strongly that year, and I go to Yunnan and Szechuan to find out how it is performed.

'We have 250 per cent more women attending our clinic this year than last year,' says the doctor in charge in Kunming, capital of Yunnan province.

'And how many did you have last year?'

'Ten.'

So that means thirty-five women this year, out of nineteen million inhabitants.

I go to my favourite Peihai Park to drink tea under the willows. At the next table three soldiers sit, and one reads aloud the poems of Mao Tsetung. One of his eyes is of a lighter colour than the other. He is twenty, a poor peasant's son; he learnt to read in the mass literacy drive carried out during the Great Leap Forward of 1958. 'Fifty million people like me gained sight then,' says he, meaning they learnt to read. 'I want to be a writer. I want to write poetry.' He spends all his pay on books. He asks me whether I can help him to get a translation of Rousseau, and 'some poetry of the French Revolution ... it was a great revolution, like our own ... I want to read about it, and about the Paris Commune. I want to know the poets of those magnificent years.'

Third Uncle is sleek and well in 1964. He has a new house and in the sitting room are some pieces of good furniture, and of course his tea cupboard. In Chengtu the Spring Flower Festival has been restored; everyone has gone to it. The Taoist temple has reopened. Round it all the markets flourish. I visit the temple, to pay respects to the venerable anarchist, agnostic Lao Tze, riding his black buffalo in search of Verity, Reality ...

On October 15th, Hsing Chiang says to me quietly, 'Khrushchev has fallen.' She has just heard it on the radio.

The next day China explodes her first atom bomb.

Joy. Third Uncle is happy. My cousins are happy. A Mongol second cousin of mine by marriage, who has a wonderful voice, sings extracts from *Boris Godunov*, and the windows vibrate, the glass quivers. He indeed has a marvellous voice; but he will be in jail for three years at the Cultural Revolution, wrongfully accused ... I would only know of it in 1977.

China has destroyed the blackmail of atomic supremacy. Khrushchev has been shown up. 'I am proud to be an Asian,' says Tunku Abdul

Rahman of Malaysia, voicing what every Asian, irrespective of politics, feels over China's bomb. All of us feel that Chairman Mao was right. This explosion, somehow, justifies many things for us (even, perhaps, the unjustifiable). 'Now our spine has straightened, we walk tall,' says anticommunist Francis Pan to me in Hongkong.

Before my departure in 1964, Kung Peng gives me a wonderful farewell dinner; I meet many people from the Ministry of Foreign Affairs, among them the remarkable scholar and diplomat, Wang Pingnan, whom I know already from the Laos Conference of 1961. Ambassador to Poland, he carries on with patience the long negotiations with the Americans in Warsaw, keeping hold of the tenuous Ariadne's thread through the labyrinth of hostility and hatred. There are also at the dinner Huang Hua, young and fiery, going to be ambassador in Cairo; and so many others.

The dinner is so delightful, so civilized, that I feel quite ridiculous with qualms and questions. I feel cocooned, safe … China is a Great Mother, a wise one … the people will find their way. I am reassured and when my body leaves China, my heart remains, as usual; this is a condition of my being now. I know that I serve best outside. 'China will need knowledge, science from abroad … a different viewpoint … ' This has been conveyed to me, as to others. Cultural cross-fertilization is essential for China's future. Chou Enlai believes in cross-fertilization. After all, the glorious Tang were so magnificent because they opened wide the doors of China … and their emperors were part Uighur, and Uighurs are the ancestors of the Turks – 'That is why the first Tang emperors were called Big Noses,' says Rewi Alley, who knows everything about China, to me.

My first lecture tour to the United States began in January 1965. During the next fourteen years, lecturing on China would become an adventitious part of my activities. I would travel a great deal: all over Europe, to America and to Canada, to Mexico and to Australia, to Japan, to Africa and to India. I would lecture in the most unlikely places, to the most conservative audiences: to the Paris Military Academy several times, to the Indian Military College in New Delhi, to assemblies of priests and to the disciples of Gandhi in Gujarat. I would appear on television many times in America, attend symposia and seminars on China, travelling through the United States on four major and two minor lecture tours.

On this initial tour of 1965, my first stop was Honolulu, with a *lei* welcome with hula dancers. There was a happy reunion with some of my old dormitory mates from Yenching University, where we had all been students together from 1933 to 1935. They sang 'Love is a Many-Splendoured Thing' at me, and I tried to look surprised and delighted. My lecture there was not a success; Honolulu was too far from everything that happened, too remote from the Vietnam war, a thousand light years away from Asia and her problems. Its obvious beauty was exasperating because it just wallowed in it.

I was introduced to the social distinctions between one-digit and two-digit millionaires. At an imposing dinner, the statuesque twenty-four-year-old wife of a seventy-year-old two-digit millionaire burst into howls and sobs in the middle of the steak course.

We flew to San Francisco. The power, the greatness, the technological might of America captured us. I had come prepared to despise a little, to resent certainly; but I forget all about this as Vincent's enchantment seized me. For Vincent, the engineer, the revelation was America's man-made beauty. The elevated highways flinging themselves horizonwards, the bridge crossing the sea at San Francisco, the skyscrapers, the dams, the airports; all that spelt human power, the potential of conquest of the universe. 'They'll walk the stars,' said he. For me, it was America's natural beauty, its space and immensity, but also an anxious emptiness. How empty, truly empty, America seemed to my eyes, accustomed to the crowds of Asia.

We toured a great deal of America by car, driving ourselves, stopping anywhere, discovering its tiny townlets and its enormous cities. I lectured to the Mormons in Salt Lake City, at the Synagogue in Los Angeles, and at countless women's organizations and clubs, and today I regret not a minute of the time spent. It was necessary, and it was also for me a time of learning.

We stayed with Felix Greene at Palo Alto; Felix was busy lecturing up and down America, against the Vietnam war. I too would pronounce on this war; and I said how pernicious it would be for America. But who would listen then? 'The computers have told us that if you hit an Asian hard enough he gives in' was one of the memorable sayings of 1965; 'Our bombing will shorten the war ... ' from a merciful old lady. At times it was slightly unpleasant; but on the whole I was agreeably astonished by the politeness, the courtesy, the splendid self-control of my audiences; for what I said was at times very unpalatable and blistering – and Americans were emotional then about their role in promoting democracy in Asia. Cold logic is never taken willingly; it is too much like unsweetened medicine.

In Georgia, Alabama and Tennessee, Vincent's colour caused a problem.

I did not see the glossy chocolate satin of his skin as anything but beautiful; understandably, not everyone had the same reaction. At a certain Junior League the well-bred sponsors fell back one step, then took a firm grip on their nether limbs and came forward to shake hands. Having ascertained that Vincent was Indian and not Afro-American, they were totally charming. In a restaurant, a pall of silence settled upon the noisy men at the bar as we walked in. We waited twenty minutes before a waitress came up. 'Where you folk from?' 'India.' The audible sigh of relief! In yet another small town we were denounced by the foul-mouthed local tycoon; but at night three Afro-Americans, waiters, came to our room to wring our hands. Six years later, by 1971, there was already a noticeable change. And these incidents were compensated by the general kindness, the real goodness, which we found everywhere.

All the time we were reading in the newspapers about muggings and killings and rape and violence; yet all seemed so calm, so tranquil. Vincent paid no heed until we reached Los Angeles and we went for a stroll after dinner. It was only 9.30 at night but suddenly Vincent stopped: 'Do you realize that we are the only people *walking* on this main street?' We were; and behind us, a police car was trailing us ... We turned back to the hotel.

The waste of America. Too much food on every plate – I was totally unable to consume so much food. Garbage, things thrown away, mountains of useless motor cars ... the waste. And gradually, a bleak and inward energy drain: for everywhere, after a while, we were assaulted by sameness. A conformism numbing in its unspoken, absolute authority. The people were so dissimilar in bone structure and hair colouring and eyes; but they all strove so hard to be like each other, and so earnestly did they diversify their garments to conform to the idea of being individual. The same coffee in all the cafeterias, hotels, and restaurants, dispensed by interchangeable waitresses. Identical air hostesses, all making the same mistake in English as they announced a takeoff: 'We shall be departing *momentarily*.' The same glazed eyes and tightened jaws of men sitting in cars, driving to the cities at dawn in one immense commuting flow. The same lack of books and bookshops; and me hunting hopelessly for books on drugstore shelves, behind the sanitary toilet articles.

But also: the splendid Greyhound buses, webbing America; with their marvellous, tranquil drivers. The slums of the big cities; silent nightmares all alike, suddenly erupting into shrieks and running. The entire absence of chic at every and any level among the women. American compunction, self-interrogation, hankering for righteousness and a lost paradise.

Television with Mr Gerald Ford was a delightful experience. A sincere man, easy to talk to, and modest; he did not pretend to know anything about Asia, and was surprised to hear that the Vietnamese were not Chinese. A meeting with Ambassador Goldberg, on the eve of a March 1965 meeting in Moscow designed to drum China out of the 'socialist camp': 'What will China do now?' 'She doesn't give a damn.' A meeting with Senator Fulbright, highly recommended to me by Felix Greene. I found him insubstantial; striving hard to be all things to all visitors. A good man, withal.

My most intelligent audience was at the Naval Officers' World Affairs Seminar at Bremerton. I left with the distinct impression that not all among the naval officers agreed with the Vietnam war, or Kennedy's advisers; that in fact they saw the geopolitical map of the world far more clearly than the White House pundits of that time – the Bundys and that bright, brittle, sophisticated crowd from the Eastern seaboard universities.

Astonishing to my Asian-conditioned experience was the genuine fairness and the comparative accuracy of the American press. My way of looking at truth was wary; as something extremely prone to slip away, to twist out of the grasp. Lao Tze's search for verity had proved both arduous and wayward, and in the end, possibly, he did not know whether he was not dreaming of himself searching for verity. Americans were mightily in love with truth. But it of course also escaped them; and when I tried to communicate my surprise and gratification at discovering fragments of veracity adhering to a rock of lies, they were nonplussed. But even the small town newspapers reported, scrupulously and fairly, what I said. Fabulous.

Yungmei had married an American. In November 1964 I had received a letter from her telling me that she was marrying Sidney. 'Sidney who?' I cabled back. But had no answer. Fortunately she had given me an address in New York, and we discovered Sidney Glazier, film producer, and Yungmei's husband. I thought, looking at him, that she had chosen the right man for her season of uncertainty; but of course it would not last. Sidney was impulsive, enthusiastic, protective, captivated by Yungmei's apparent frailty (actually she is Chinese-tough). However, because of Sidney and his American openness and his Jewish articulate boldness with words, it was possible for Yungmei to emerge from the murk of reticence about her adoption and to discuss it openly at last.

People marry through need; divorce also through need, often

vicariously, because they have not resolved their own lack of purpose. In Yungmei's case, I think the only good thing I did was to try to keep relations with her, her child, and Sidney as normal and amicable as possible. I saw no reason to do ugly, vulgar things to another human being. And Sidney was to prove the most generous of ex-husbands, and the best of fathers.

For Yungmei now would have a child, Karen. And Karen is so very much like me in some ways that it is almost unbelievable. But I do not know whether she has had enough obstacles, difficulties, worries, in her growing up to make her strive for anything ... only through fighting does one really grow into something. I have a fear that she may have been over-protected, too much 'thought for', too occupied with many things. And has no time or loneliness left to think with, to really grow into giving as well as taking.

In April we left America for Europe. Our eyes were now accustomed to large roaming; and kept hitting houses and crossroads. All the streets were too short and the cars diminutive. England was toyland.

In London I inaugurated, along with at least ten other people, including Vanessa Redgrave, the Society for Anglo-Chinese Understanding (SACU). I was invited to talk at the Oxford Union on the subject of the Vietnam war, my opponent being Patrick Gordon Walker. The President of the Oxford Union that year was Tariq Ali, a young Pakistani of Trotskyite views and wealthy landlord background. The debate was lively. I lost by eleven votes to Gordon Walker. 'Well, we've won,' said he. 'Not on the battlefield,' I replied with asperity.

In June I flew to Tanzania while Vincent went to see his family in India. My Egyptian friends, Mustafa and Leila El-Issawi, had invited me to Dar Es Salaam, where Mustafa was the U.A.R. Ambassador. I had known them in Singapore, and we had become very good friends. Mustafa told me that 'someone in the Singapore government' had warned Nasser that I was Jewish. 'But we have our own intelligence and we know it is not true,' said Mustafa. I told him that the Kuomingtan had first spread that rumour, and the Special Branch in Singapore had merely picked it up and placed it in my dossier.

Tanzania was sisal plantations, mostly run by Greeks, and a dust bowl beginning in its centre owing to overcutting of the forests; and the most magnificent landscapes, mountains and rivers I had seen so far. Zanzibar island, just off the coast, exhibited relics of the Chinese expeditions of the

Ming dynasty. I called on the Chinese Ambassador, who told me about the projected railway to be built by China between Tanzania and Zambia. I called on the American Ambassador, and he introduced me to one of the leaders of the Angola resistance, fighting against Portugal, and his American wife.

On to Kenya, where Malcolm was now High Commissioner. Jomo Kenyatta brandished a fly whisk and was amiably tipsy from early morning on. I wanted to ask him about the custom of clitoridectomy, which I considered horrendous, especially when it was, as in Sudan, pharaonic, that is, practised with ablation of all the external genitalia. But Jomo Kenyatta was in favour of clitoridectomy. And only in 1979 would the subject of women thus mutilated be taken up in a major way. Thirty million women, for whom love-making is deliberately made agony.

I went to the flamingo lake to see a hundred thousand pink flamingoes take wing from the bronze water, transforming the world into a whirl of pink feather.

My cousin, Armand Denis, lived in Kenya, and I went to see him. Armand was one of the world's first ecologists; he had fought since childhood against the massacre of animals. 'I only shoot with a camera,' said he. He and his American wife, Michaela, had made many films for the B.B.C. In 1962 he had come to Malaya, and deplored Asia's swift change. 'It's plastic, jazz and politics.' He became infuriated by the conditions at the zoo in Johore Bahru, where we found a black panther with a badly mutilated paw (caught in a trap). In our passion for our fellow beasts Armand and I were much alike. Armand had once taken a cheetah to a cinema in Paris. Unfortunately some dogs appeared on the screen, and the cheetah went berserk with excitement.

Armand's house in Nairobi was upon the crest of a hill; it dominated a sea-like plain through which Masai tribes travelled, their dust cloud floating in silence. The Masai were dying out; they stalked in a great muteness; perched like long-legged storks in contemplation of the empty days ahead.

I was going from Nairobi to Algiers, where an Afro-Asian meeting of heads of state of the Third World was to be held. President Sukarno had called it the meeting of the 'emergent nations'. Chou Enlai, who had made a successful tour of fourteen African countries in 1963–4, deploying great diplomatic skill, was also going to attend. It was meant to be the successor of the epochal Bandung meeting of 1955.

One afternoon Malcolm said to me, 'The Algiers meeting is off.' It had fallen apart because Ben Bella had been deposed and Houari Boumedienne had taken his place in Algeria. Some of the Kenyan ministers seemed to think it a great blow; others criticized China because Chou Enlai insisted that this was an internal Algerian affair which should not influence the venue. However, the meeting was postponed, and finally it was not held at all.

So I went back to Cairo instead, where Vincent now joined me. Kung Peng arrived from Algiers; she was staying at the Chinese Embassy, and we went to see her. Kung Peng was happy to meet Vincent, and said she hoped he would come to China. But Vincent's Indian passport was not valid for China. The Indian government would not allow its citizens to go there.

Kung Peng and I talked politics, policies and methods; I felt that China was far too candid about the Third World. 'I agree that at times we think people have read the documents we send to them ... but they haven't,' said she. I said that China gave great lashings of aid to the Third World, 'and perhaps it's a bit too much'. The discovery of the lack of seriousness, the fecklessness, of many 'heads of state' was a shock to Kung Peng. She told me that the Indian delegation had lobbied on behalf of the Soviet Union attending the Algiers conference, insisting that it was an Asian country and should be included among Afro-Asian states.

With Vincent I went to see the Palestinian refugee camps at Gaza. The train sailed through the swelling desert and the heat felled us. Gaza, by the sea, was bleak and torrid; from it rose the smell of misery, the nauseous and heart-wrenching odour of hopelessness. We were walked by the Egyptian guides through the camps, squeezed through alleyways between overcrowded shacks, stopping to listen to endless, woeful tales. 'Now you must write a *book* about all you have heard today,' said the guide impressively. I felt utterly miserable because I knew I could not write anything about this accumulation of pain, this monstrous debasement.

The Commander-in-Chief of the United Nations forces quartered for peacekeeping purposes by the Gaza strip was a jerky, punctilious Indian officer, immensely bored. He blamed Nasser for everything. 'Egypt should take in all the refugees ... they're the same race,' said he. I pointed out the fallacy of what he said, but he would not listen. The immense horror of the suffering multitudes he looked after, that perpetual lament which rose from all four quarters of Gaza, infuriated him. He longed for leave.

From Cairo back to Malaya, to Kuala Lumpur, to see Frank Sullivan and Tunku Abdul Rahman. Tunku received me amiably, and we had coffee. He made mild fun of Lee Kuanyew. It was obvious that now, having got rid of Singapore, he felt considerably better. We stayed at the British High Commission with Anthony and Dorothea Head; Dorothea was painting my portrait. We discussed the failed merger between Singapore and Malaya. Arrests continued in Singapore. The multi-millionaire Tan Laksai, who had founded Nanyang University, had been deprived of his citizenship. Somehow I felt that the British were not unhappy with the new arrangement. Perhaps they had planned it all along.

In September I received a message from Kung Peng. Would I come up to Peking for a few days? I went.

Autumn was heart-stopping in its beauty that year; long golden shadows lay across the Western Hills; the sky was high and flawless and the air gentle; Kung Peng and I took walks in the hills and watched the magpies flit through the ancestral silver pines. I roamed the bookshops; Kung Peng gave me Lin Piao's pamphlet, *Long Live the Victory of the People's War*, and it was obvious that this was a document which was at the time required reading for all Party cadres, and also for the people; because the title on the cover was in red. I procured for myself, however, two more pamphlets: one was by Lo Juiching, at the time Vice-Chairman of the National Defence Council and Chief of Staff of the Army. The other was by the very popular and prestigious Marshal Ho Lung, whose exploits had almost become a legend. Both were Long Marchers; seasoned and greatly admired Party members. But the titles of the pamphlets were respectively in blue and in green; which meant that they were not as official as Lin Piao's. I read all three together. Of course there were differences in viewpoint as to the role and function of the P.L.A. in all of them; but at the time it did not strike me that they heralded the shaking changes to follow, nor that both Lo Juiching and Ho Lung were to be, so soon, so mercilessly attacked.

For in that autumn the rupture in the Party between Mao Tsetung and Liu Shaochi was coming to a head; but no one among the middle cadres (as I verified through the years) was aware of it. 'We knew there was a big debate, but *never* thought it would be Liu Shaochi ... why, right up until spring 1966 his book was recommended study for us, along with Chairman Mao's books ... '

Neither were they aware that both Ho Lung and Lo Juiching would be in dire trouble very shortly; and a good part of the trouble would be due to the pamphlets expressing their opinions, which were not Lin Piao's opinions.

While waiting for Premier Chou Enlai to see me – for obviously this is why Kung Peng had asked me to come – I had a long interview with the prominent economist, Yung Lungkwei. He was a Director of the Economics Department of the State Planning Commission; a very striking man, most clear-minded. I wrote up a part of what he told me for an article in the Hongkong *Far Eastern Economic Review*. And I derived a strong impression of both the fundamental solidity of the system which had been laid out, and also of its errors and omissions and weaknesses. With all debts cleared, said Yung, China was poised for a material takeoff; of course it was also necessary to overhaul and streamline her industrial framework (because most of the machines had been procured from Russia, and now they would come from the West, I thought). 'We want what is most advanced ... as Chairman Mao says, we don't want to crawl behind others ... ' Yung also refuted the idea of having a wealthy, advanced urban and luxurious China sitting on top of a feudal, backward, exploited rural China. 'We are not going the way of India,' said he.

Then I saw Chou Enlai. It was the seventh time. The interview was again, as in 1956, in his own apartment, in the Chungnanhai. Kung Peng came with me. The small patch of garden in front of his apartment was a blaze of dahlias, for his wife, Teng Yingchao, loved flowers. She had cultivated roses in the hard terrain of Yenan during the war; and in later years she would come to see me with an armful of her home-grown peonies.

There was still the same old sofa; the books, the saggy and worn armchairs; the curtain separating bedroom from living room. Under a chair, discreetly, a pair of well-worn slippers ...Chou Enlai had hastily changed into shoes for my coming.

I wish I could reproduce what we talked about. But then, are words themselves so important? I might misconstrue or be misconstrued, were I to report his words exactly. He changed my bone marrow. He was, truly, not only my teacher, but my guide for life.

And this is where mere words betray, discolour, do not reflect the intensity of silence, the apprehension of a spirit waiting in muteness, receiving in muteness so much more than banal words.

What did he talk about? Everything, and nothing. Of Vietnam: the possibilities of escalation, the probabilities or not of involving China in conflict with America. I felt Chou did not think this likely, but: 'We are fully prepared and they know it. We are even prepared to be attacked from four sides at once ... India, Japan, the U.S.S.R., and the United States ... we have planned for all contingencies.' He said, 'If we are invaded or attacked, the war will have no boundaries ... but until then we shall not indulge in any provocation ... '

And then, more important to him, and also to me, for in the end all external policy was conditioned, shaped, by internal affairs, we talked of the situation in China. Looking back now, with hindsight, with so much more wisdom and knowledge than in those early, groping years of mine, it seems to me that what Chou Enlai was trying to do was to warn me. Warn me of the impending turmoil. Warn me to keep calm and cool-headed. To go on thinking on my own.

For in that September Mao Tsetung was in Shanghai, and riding towards the break with Liu Shaochi. And Chou Enlai knew what it would mean; though he did not know, at the time, what shape the rupture would take. And so he talked about China's achievements; of the necessity of social change inherent to economic change; and of the Long March, which had been China's 'from the kingdom of misery to today's sufficiency ... ' But so much remained to be done. Another and a longer march ...

Chou Enlai knew that I had now embarked on lecture tours in America. We discussed America, not at length, but pithily enough. I had, I said, the feeling that the Vietnam war would still be long. He felt that 'one day, as in Korea, the American people will have had enough of it, and there will be a débâcle ... ' Now I realize that Chou Enlai, in that autumn of 1965, was aware that a crisis would take place in America's foreign policy.

But 1965 was an unpropitious year for cool reason in America. With McNamara clamouring that China was *the* enemy, with McGeorge Bundy refusing to shake my hand because I was a 'Red', with even Margaret Mead refusing to talk to me because I was a 'communist' — how could I do anything? Nevertheless, through all possible means and all possible people, Chou hoped to project China as she really was: Edgar Snow had again come to China in 1964, and had had an interview with Mao. It was becoming increasingly hard to keep China out of the United Nations, Chou remarked. In that year of 1965 China would obtain exactly half the votes in favour of admitting her.

Now, more than ever, I was a Chou Enlai addict. I would try my best to follow his thinking. But a statesman confronted with the immensity of China, the enormous weight of her poverty, the hostility of a world in arms against her, and the multitudinous complexity of her internal

413

problems, perforce had to adopt a sinuous line, a course not always clearly charted. Chou had to use everything and everyone, including his friends; he had to be ruthless, devious, charming, flexible, impassive, glib, unsparing to himself and to all he knew in the pursuit of a single goal: China, China's future, the happiness of the Chinese people.

I did not always understand this. But I would see him keep China going under the most desperate circumstances. I would see him appreciating the rarity and worth of talent and trying to shield it. Never would he intrude himself, his own person, his likes or dislikes, his own interest in survival, in all this. I have never known anyone so brave, so single-minded. And all my life I will be a follower of Chou Enlai.

When I left Peking, Wang Wanchun came to see me off. 'Write to me,' said he happily.

This was the last time I would see Wanchun. For in 1966, the next year, when I sought him out, I was not allowed to see him. He was 'busy'. Wanchun died during the Cultural Revolution, in that hot and ugly summer of 1967, and I feel burdened and harrowed because he had written to me in the spring, 'You must write to me, write to me'. And like a fool, I did. I should *not* have listened to him. I feel that my letter helped to end his life, because precisely in that spring and summer, posters were put up against me in Shanghai, accusing me of being 'an American agent'. Wanchun was probably accused of 'passing information to outsiders' and 'having illicit relations with a foreigner'. I was also linked with Pearl Buck; both of us accused of writing malicious things against China (and me pornography).

But, many years later, when I was told of his death, I was told that it was because 'he did not trust in the future ... he was accused of adultery[!] and he could not stand it ... he threw himself out of a window'.

Threw or was thrown? During the McCarthy period in America people also 'threw' themselves out of windows. But I do not see Wanchun leaping into the street, because he had such a sense of humour. And now I shall never know.

Part Two
Phoenix Harvest
(1966-1979)

Seventeen

The Lowering Sky -
The Cultural Revolution: 1966

In January 1966 I went to Peking for ten days, because I had been invited to a seminar to be held on China at Chicago University. At least five such seminars were taking place in mid-western cities of the United States that year. I wanted to glean the latest thinking in Peking.

I filled a notebook with interviews on China's policies, on economics, and became thoroughly confused. I was not able to see Chou Enlai. Little did I then know that the most intense confrontation was occurring at the top, between Mao Tsetung and Liu Shaochi; no leaders were therefore available for interviews, and no interview could provide a definitive statement. I fell back on two sentences which I could relate to Premier Chou: 'The United States sooner or later will have to reappraise its foreign policy, because there is no direct conflict of interest between us', and 'The period before us is one of crises, great upheavals and great changes and reversals. The U.S. will have to readjust its views on its own role in the world ... ' Not very much to go on.

Kung Peng, and Tang Mingchao, who had been educated in America,* were interested by the new hesitations in America, eager to know the result of the symposia. 'It takes a long rope to catch a whale ... ' said Tang Mingchao. 'America's press seems to have much power ... it is really a separate force,' said Kung Peng. And added, 'A tree does not grow upon bare rock.'

Mao in his last interview with Edgar Snow† had been noncommittal. I had no opportunity to find out about the intense Party struggle that was going on; the pall of secrecy was clamped upon all hints. Hualan, not high enough in the cadre hierarchy to know, could only say that there would be another rectification movement 'in art and literature and also in education'. The Party establishment still envisaged the Cultural Revolu-

---

* Later in the Secretariat at the United Nations.
† See Edgar Snow's article in the *New Republic*, February 27th, 1965: 'Interview with Mao Tsetung'.

tion as merely another political campaign, of the style so customary in China.

Hualan's sister had returned from another stint in the rural areas, of 'socialist education' and the 'four cleans' in the countryside. The skin of her face was rough and her finger joints thickened with rheumatism. 'My job was to try to break down feudal and capitalist ideas ... I've had very little time to paint ... ' Many hundreds of thousands of cadres, intellectuals and students had 'gone down' in teams for this work. She was looking forward to teaching and painting again, 'But at the moment we are having a great many political study classes on Mao Tsetung Thought.' She added, 'We are taking the army as a model.' Hualan was full of enthusiasm. 'It is very important: we are fighting revisionism in all its forms.' The ballet, *The White-Haired Girl*, had been performed. It dated back to 1944 in Yenan, when it had been created (the music leaned heavily on Tchaikovsky). 'Our workers–peasants–soldiers don't like Western ballet, they don't understand it. They want ballet, opera, with which they can identify, such as this one.' A young man who was to dance the role of the Prince in *Swan Lake* came from a poor peasant family; he had rejected the role; he felt he was 'throwing away the face' of his family by dancing as a prince ... 'Only after the dancers have been to the villages can they put real emotion into the scenes of our new ballets and operas,' said Hualan.

There was hushed talk among the writers of the criticism of a theatre piece by the Vice-Mayor of Peking, Wu Han. In November 1965 a literary critic from Shanghai, Yao Wenyuan, already known for his acerbic condemnations of rightists in 1957, had written a long and scathing attack against Peking Vice-Mayor Wu Han's theatre play *Hai Jui is Dismissed from Office*. Hai Jui, an honest Ming dynasty (1368 to 1644) official, had upbraided the Emperor for not listening to the people. Now it was rumoured that his 'historical play', first shown in 1960, was a plea for the rehabilitation of Minister of Defence Peng Tehuai, who in August 1959 had openly criticized the Leap.

At dinner with some friends, the distinguished chief editor of the People's Literature Printing Press, Yen Wenching, asked me what I thought of *Hai Jui*, I replied truthfully that I had not seen the play. Historical subjects, articles about personages who had died many centuries ago, were vehicles for expressing present-day situations, events and people. This had always been done in China, and it continued to be done. But now not only Vice-Mayor Wu Han, but many other historians were being attacked and criticized as 'promoting a bourgeois line in history'.

A foreign resident in China told me that Teng To, chief editor of the monthly *Frontline* (the magazine of Peking's Party Committee), was undergoing criticism. He had written: 'Everyone must have some leisure and only eight hours of work.' 'The idea of leisure time and the idea of revolution don't go together,' said this man. Young workers in the factories had been infected by the habit of looking at the clock.

The January air was not only freezing but turgid with unvoiced apprehensions and abstruse theoretical argument. I interviewed three philosophers, who were to give me the latest 'thinking'. (I had not reckoned that the word 'thinking' would involve me in the high spheres of theoretical abstraction.) The three talked of the necessity of a cultural revolution. Only a change of thinking in the people could propel advance: a transformation of ideas and habits and behaviour *before* a change in the material conditions of living could occur. But could mankind really overleap itself in thought, overleap the environment in which it dwelt? Certainly, they replied. Had not men dreamt of flying machines before the aeroplane was invented? All progress comes from concepts, and concept strode ahead of any tangible material stimulus. The philosophers added that the theory of productive forces as the motor of progress was 'revisionist' and capitalistic, it negated the cultural revolution 'which is a fact of history'.

I was even more confused. How would I relate this to the American seminar? I seized upon my favourite topic: 'Language affects thinking; our knowledge of things *must* always be inexact and approximate since it depends on words.' I did not agree with Stalin, who pronounced language devoid of any class nature. The very shape of the Chinese ideogram was based on feudal concepts, and it had a lot to do with Chinese continued propensity to think in terms of tradition, hierarchy, precedence, with our continued literal-mindedness. 'The comrades are talking to you of Chairman Mao's Thought,' said Hsing Chiang with some asperity, reminding me that I was waffling. I thanked the philosophers and I went out and bought some very beautiful snuff bottles of agate and jade. They were cheap at the time, and looking at them eased my confusion.

The Chicago University Center for Continuing Education was an imposing pile; but access to it was through some dismal negro slums. Dirty snow piled up with the garbage in heaps, leaning against derelict clapboard bungalows. Afro-Americans walked very lightly clad. How could they endure the freezing streets in such insufficient garments?

The seminar lasted from February 8th to 12th. I was delighted to meet Harrison Salisbury of the *New York Times*; an immediate empathy developed into a valuable friendship. The organizers had provided all shades of opinion. There was Joan Robinson, an English Marxist economist; Jan Myrdal, a Swedish one; and the China experts John Lewis and Franz Schurmann. A few hawks too, like Mark Gayn and Morton Halperin. I told Schurmann (with whom I sat, for through a typical oversight my name had been listed under S instead of under H) how much I had enjoyed his book *Ideology and Organization in Communist China*. I was asked to write a piece for the *Bulletin of Atomic Scientists* by its editor, Ruth Adams. I do not think I contributed much to the seminar; but I learnt a great deal: that forces both within and outside the American administration were urging a new policy on China; that west coast businessmen and even mid-western city businessmen were overwhelmingly *for* trade relations with China.

Lectures; television appearances; many meetings ... Joy to be in New York with Sidney and Yungmei and my grand-daughter Karen, born in November 1965. Exhilarating to meet the supple minds of erudite and self-effacing American scholars, with their immediacy of contact and total lack of jargon. Some of the more renowned 'experts', however, struck me as over-estimated. But was it not the same everywhere? Word inflation, rather than lucid thought, carried a man upwards ... By June 1966, as a result of the intense battling of American scholars an editorial in the *New York Times* asserted that a revision of policy towards China was due.

Spyros Skouros, head of Twentieth Century-Fox, asked us to dinner. By that time it was clear that Paramount was having difficulties making *The Mountain is Young* into a film, despite several attempts. In 1959 Paramount had sent a team to Singapore. It was led by Ed Dmytrik as potential director of the picture, accompanied by his wife and by script-writer Bob Authur. Dmytrik had taken preventive antibiotics before leaving California, and the result of his overcaution was intestinally disastrous. His wife suffered from cultural shock, because the festival of Thaipusam coincided with their arrival in Singapore, and it is a rather gruesome affair. The sight of people jabbing themselves through both cheeks or through arms and legs with stilettos (no blood gushed), walking on blazing charcoal fires, or weighed down with *kavadis*, huge confections of flowers and tinsel propped upon metal spikes embedded in their ribs and back, was a little too much for her.

From Singapore the three proceeded to Nepal and to another culture shock. The festival of the goddess Durga, she who is frenzied for blood, was being celebrated, and the Gurkhas were sacrificing rows of bulls. This was a solemn diplomatic event, and the ambassadors in Kathmandu all attended. So did the Paramount team. The bulls were lined up, and a Gurkha approached, balancing his heavy, razor-honed blade. He took a running leap and with one blow struck off the bull's head. The Gurkhas shouted with appreciation as gallons of blood leapt in the air, and Mrs Dmytrik fainted. The Paramount team left Nepal the next day. I don't know whether Spyros knew the story. 'We would have made a great film of your book,' said he. And possibly he was right.

On to Paris, to see André Malraux, the famous author of *Man's Fate*, and Minister of Culture in de Gaulle's government.

André Malraux received me in his superb and airy office. We talked for nearly two hours; or rather he talked and I said a few words. Henri Hell, literary critic and literary editor, afterwards told me that Malraux was enchanted with our meeting. Malraux did invite me to return, and said he wanted to give me lunch at Versailles, and have me speak to the Quai d'Orsay people. He said, 'You have brought humanity and understanding to the Chinese scene through your books.' He was modest about his own splendid contributions. He described Mao, whom he had seen in 1964, and said he was vigorous and well, and 'among the few who have a *vision d'ensemble* of the world'. He contrasted Stalin and Mao. Stalin inspired the reverence of fear, while Mao compelled the respect of authority. Malraux had told Mao, 'Stalin hated you and would have killed you.' Mao, smoking away, had calmly replied, 'Yes, that is true.'

Malraux also spoke of President Kennedy, whom he had seen in 1962. 'He gave me a long rigmarole about preserving India from Chinese aggression,' said he. 'I warned Kennedy of the danger when a gap between the American dream and the reality of Asia would become manifest. America will not be able to stomach a defeat; it will cost her a generation span to recover.' He predicted defeat in Vietnam.

Malraux diverged, grimaced, gestured, but oh, what compelling brilliance! I listened, entranced. 'It's better than the Peking National Day fireworks.' Malraux did not like Liu Shaochi, nor for that matter Chou Enlai. Only Mao 'transcended his own present, as all great men must do'. But he deplored the crass ignorance of the Chinese interpreters and others who took him around. 'They did not know their own history ... did not know I had been in China in the early 1920s ... I showed them the photograph in their own museum in Kuangchow, where I am with Chinese revolutionaries. "Who is this?" I asked, pointing to myself in the photo. And they did not know.'

To London, where *The Crippled Tree* and *A Mortal Flower* were doing very well. I was finishing the third volume, *Birdless Summer*. I lectured; met many people; and we drove to Wales to call on Bertrand Russell. He was a small-boned and vivid young old man wrapped in frantic honesty and surmounted by a great shock of beautiful silver hair.

'Why did not China give a good example to the world by forswearing the atom bomb and disarming unilaterally,' he asked.

'The world is not run on good intentions alone,' I replied.

'When I think of a nuclear holocaust, I cannot sleep,' said Russell, and his light, eager voice was quavery with anguish and distress.

On to India, to call on Indira Gandhi, by the simple process of telephoning her aide in the Secretariat, my dear friend Natwar Singh, whom I had met in China in 1956. Indira looked striking; the cares of office had not yet heavied her grace. 'I haven't changed,' she said, smiling. We talked calmly about the frontier problem and about the famine in India that year, and India's great resources and her enormous potential. 'Enmity with China is not our aim,' she said. She was, however, disturbed by the 'untoward' propaganda from Peking in favour of Pakistan (when the 1965 war between India and Pakistan had taken place). 'India needs absence of tension,' said she. And Pakistan was a perpetual tension for India. 'It is a problem we'll have to solve.'

In May 1966 I went back to China. She was entirely *other* that May. Again that unpleasant throat clamp as the raucous loudspeakers assaulted my ear-drums for hours ... how was it possible to remain sane with the perpetual noise, the blaring and the shouting and the screaming and the singing? All the posters had changed. Now furious-fisted young people squashed diminutive snakes and bull-headed figures (imperialists and revisionists). A thousand portly, rosy-faced Maos everywhere. The customs officials remained calm and courteous, relaxed, impervious to the cacophony.

At the railway station no lunch was available; the waitresses were hold-ing a political meeting. I saw them practising a dance in front of a large panel painted to represent Mao. Their hands lifted imaginary hearts from their breasts towards his smile. I listened to the loudspeakers but there were too many of them and the sound waves interfered with each other so that the result was a hopeless quack.

In Hongkong the Kuomintang newspapers had predicted a rupture between Mao Tsetung and Liu Shaochi. There had been rumours of an assassination plot against Mao. Here there was much talk of a 'black line' which had for the past seventeen years infected, infested, deviated, twisted, distorted culture and education and the arts and literature in order to promote 'restoration of capitalism'. I groaned inwardly. 'That's it. The intelligentsia is going to catch it once again.' But I continued, of course, to smile and to hold myself tightly in control. And to hope my Family would not suffer too much – and that I would not break down.

In Kuangchow the well-cut suits of 1965 had disappeared. Every one of the cadres greeting me wore unpressed shirts and baggy pants and plastic sandals. There was no brilliantine upon the hair of the men, and the women cadres all had straight short hair. No more perms.

In Peking, however, the admirable Hsing Chiang continued to wear a crisp neat blouse and skirt; until one day in July when Kung Peng would say quietly to her, 'Your clothes look a bit bourgeois.' A friendly warning.

Nowhere in China, in the next few months, was there any hint that Liu Shaochi was the target of the upheaval. In fact I would see him twice. He remained visible, making speeches, receiving guests, and the Hsinhua news agency would report on the mass rallies he held for Vietnam in July. And yet, in 1970, Edgar Snow would be told by Mao that in January 1965 Mao had already decided that Liu Shaochi must go ... ★

'We shall be going to Manchuria, as you asked,' said Hsing Chiang. We would be back in June in Peking.

Manchuria. Limitless flat plains, length to abolish the horizon; space and a clean sky that ran its blueness in echoless silence. The kind of land that makes one want to be on horseback, the sound of hooves to pound the silence into music.

I saw factories, and communes, in Shenyang and Changchun and Fushun and Anshan and Harbin; the Anshan steel works; the Fushun open-cast mines (where, in 1947, nineteen years previously, Pao my husband had died). So many notes, so many people telling me of their lives. And in every factory the *tatzepao*, the wall posters, pasted upon all the walls, swinging like banners, strung across from machine to machine, almost swamping every workshop. All of them uttered dire threats against 'black liners' and 'freaks and monsters'.

On May 8th an editorial against the 'black anti-Party line' had come out. 'All those who oppose Mao Tsetung Thought must be toppled, no matter how high or how famous,' shrieked the posters. 'Down with seventeen years of black anti-Party line' blared the radios. Occasionally I discerned names ... names of experts, engineers, factory managers, not

★ See Edgar Snow, *The Long Revolution* (Hutchinson, 1973).

prominent political figures; names of educators in the universities. But obviously the Party was still firmly in control, 'directing and leading' the Cultural Revolution. And so the search for 'freaks and monsters' and for 'bull-headed devils and snake spirits' was among the middle ranks, the technical experts and professors and engineers. Not a single top leader in the Party, at the time, was mentioned. The highest in rank were Party secretaries at city level and some university chancellors.

The higher Party cadres receive me and entertain me lavishly. I eat bear paws, an expensive delicacy. I am given a marvellous ginseng root worth thousands of *yuan*, which I shall give to Wanchun when I return to Peking.

After a few days of reading accusatory editorials and slogans and listening to the radio my brain goes into a stupor. I am numbed; even by imprecations. I smile and nod and because there is too much repetition I begin to speak like the people round me, and so my trip is a success as I am outstandingly docile. I read now with practised, jaded eye the posters above the machinery: 'Sung Chiming is enforcing a revisionist line in the screws and bolts third workshop!'; 'Wang Ahmeng has countered Mao Tsetung Thought for many years by saying: Too much political verbiage, not enough scientific work'. I do not know Sung and Wang; I only hope that things won't be too hard for them.

At the Shenyang machine tool plant I meet a worker who is a specialist at cutting tools through sheer application of Mao Tsetung Thought to knife-cutting edges. In almost every factory I am told how much harm the Russians have done, and of the enormous amount of meat, rare metals, oranges, textiles and shoes paid out for equipment.

At Anshan, the great steel works and China's pride, I am shown innovations attributed to Mao Tsetung Thought. In one workshop the Party man in charge introduces me to a pretty young woman worker who writes poetry. She has written decadent, bourgeois love poetry because in school her teacher was following the decadent revisionist black line and corrupting her with feudal poems. But since the intense political studies started in January she has remoulded herself and written some excellent proletarian poetry for workers–peasants–soldiers. The pretty worker begins to recite one of her old poems so that I may judge her wickedness. Then she recites a new one. 'I would like to have some of your poems,' I say, hoping she will also give me the old one she has recited. But alas, the Party cadre has seen through my bland cunning. 'Not these, not these,' he says as she riffles through her loose-leaf notebook. I get, at last, three rather tedious slogany scribbles. 'These are the latest,' says the Party cadre, beaming. He is kind, but I turn back to look at the girl and she too is watching me, and picking meditatively at her thumb. I now wonder what will happen to my dearest friend Yeh, who has printed in *Chinese Literature*, his English monthly, some of my translations of decadent feudal song-poems of the Sung dynasty (A.D. 960–1279).

In March, Lin Piao, designated as Mao's 'close comrade-in-arms', has issued a directive to 'put politics in command'. And production has gone up by so much and so much per cent everywhere, owing to the 'heightening of revolutionary consciousness' among the workers. Production increase is no longer ascribed to the heroic, the fantastic, the real work of the marvellous, incredibly patient and stoic people of China, but solely to the study of Mao Tsetung Thought ... Cadres frown when I say that pump stations, canals, fertilizer factories, increase production ... And that here in Manchuria electrification of communes started in 1958 with the Leap Forward ...

In one commune I am shown earth mounds terraced for cultivation. This brigade has distinguished itself learning from China's model, Tachai, proclaimed by Mao in 1964 as *the* example for all China. Tachai is sited in the cratered, fissured, gullied loess region of Shansi province. There are not twenty square metres of uniform flat land in these canyons of silt. Tachai terraced its promontories and filled its gullies by hand labour. But here in Manchuria the plains are flat ... whence, then, these earth mounds? Eleven years later I shall learn the hilarious and pitiful story: the mounds I saw were artificial; they had been raised up and fields laddered upon them to resemble Tachai. That is how 'In all things learn from Tachai' had been interpreted by the literal-minded cadres.

But the official taking me around in 1966 tells me that these terraced fields are the product of the young educated middle school students sent out to labour in the countryside. 'They built these fields with one hand while their other hand was occupied by the precious book of Chairman Mao,' he says. I write it all down.

There are no foreign travellers in Manchuria in that early June. In the hotel's empty dining room I sit alone at a small table covered by a white cloth. I am surrounded by white cloth screens, and they make me feel that I am dying, that I am in a hospital, and the nurses have hastily wheeled screens round my last agony. Opposite the hotel is the main city square, and a gigantic statue of Mao is being erected, seven (or is it more?) metres high. Mao is clad in a Russian-style overcoat and points the way forward with an infallible concrete hand. The square is illuminated at night because work on the statue continues throughout the twenty-four hours.

On the radio there are thunderous fulminations and denunciations of writers I have met and liked. I get stomach cramps.

In Harbin I meet seven 'outstanding activists' of the Cultural Revolution, and only years later shall I realize how important is this meeting. Two of the seven will become prominent leaders within the next decade. One of them is Li Suwen, thirty-two years old, at present a salesgirl in a food store; later she will become member of the Central Committee, a minister, almost a vice-premier ... The other is Wen Chuming, twenty-nine, and she is a primary school teacher but she will become the vice-chairman of the revolutionary committee of Liaoning province.

Li Suwen is vibrant with energy. She talks uninterruptedly for over three hours. She describes her own life, her thinking, her emotions. She is unstoppable. I take notes, take notes ...

'What is the meaning of life, of my life? Then I read about Dr Norman Bethune, and I read Chairman Mao's works, many times, and a window opened in my heart. Unselfishness was the key! Selfishness is revisionism, is capitalism, is imperialism!'

Li Suwen sold soya sauce and vinegar and vegetables according to Mao Tsetung Thought; going to the houses of clients with the provisions. She started cleaning their houses and washing the nappies of the babies and comforting the children, and everyone praised her. There was not a shred of reticence in Comrade Li Suwen as she recited word for word the compliments heaped upon her. 'I also innovated a system of planting vegetables for Shenyang city ... this saved three hundred trainloads of vegetables for next winter ... We are the beacon of revolution because we have Mao Tsetung Thought ... we many have a few intellectuals against us, but they will disappear ...'

My hand is numb and my brain a pulp, so I interrupt. Perhaps someone else will speak? Li Suwen subsides unwillingly. But everyone is quite upset that I should dare to interrupt her.

Even Hsing Chiang, later, tells me off. 'You should not interrupt ... it is arrogant.'

I get angry. 'I think she was arrogant, taking up everyone's time, talking about herself.'

'But Li Suwen is a delegate to the National People's Congress; and a film will be made about her; we must all learn from her.'

Obviously she is a model in that gallery of new heroes for this new age.

In 1977, Li Suwen, who meanwhile has become an official in Peking and has tried to take over the Ministry of Finance from that seasoned Long Marcher and veteran, Li Hsiennien, is identified with Mao's wife and her group. She is demoted and sent back to Manchuria. 'Let her continue to sell vinegar, soya sauce and vegetables,' says Marshal Yeh Chienying benignly. Marshal Yeh's role in arresting the Gang of Four and thus saving China from total disintegration, will never be told.

I liked the second woman activist, Wen Chuming. Short, snub-nosed, she too rose, 'ascending like a missile,'* and then fell; but I persist in thinking that neither she nor Li Suwen were wicked; simply women made use of and then carried away by promises of power. I think the perception of power, how it conditions minds and is instrumental in decision-making, occurs at all levels. In that frightful struggle for power which was to develop during the Cultural Revolution these two women were only cogs.

Mid-June, and I am back in Peking. Peking is noisy, too noisy. There are processions of lorries and trucks full of workers; long files of middle school students marching, girls in front, boys at the back, holding red flags and singing. In front of each procession are carried large portraits of Mao Tsetung.

One morning, very early, I stand on the balcony of my room and I see such a group march past, and I go down quickly and follow. The marchers go up the street which is lined with mimosa trees and halt in front of the Party headquarters of the Peking Municipality, a tall building covered in white glazed tiles, vaguely like a hospital. A small knot of people representing the Peking Party Committee stands at the gate to receive the students. There are speeches and the young pledge their loyalty to the Party and to Mao Tsetung Thought. Throughout the day they come, from various schools, and thus 'report' to the Peking Party Committee. But the Peking Party Committee has itself undergone drastic change since May. Peng Chen, the Mayor of Peking has been dismissed: 'His subordinates prevented him from entering his office and he is at home.' And Teng To, who has 'viciously attacked Chairman Mao' through a series of witty, satirical articles which had wide circulation and were reprinted in many provincial newspapers. According to Peking gossip, Teng had a large private collection of priceless classical paintings and antiques illicitly obtained from museums ... Peng Chen owned a sumptuous villa

---

* In China the swift ascent of such people during the Cultural Revolution was known as 'taking a helicopter', or being 'propelled to the top like a missile'.

in the Western Hills where he held large parties. Peking loves gossip and fabricates it all the time, most of it unfounded.

But an African friend, resident in China, tells me that Peng Chen defended the Vice-Mayor Wu Han and his play *Hai Jui*. Peng Chen even said, 'All men are equal before the law.'

On June 1st an editorial, 'Sweep away all monsters' calls for action against 'the black line'. On June 3rd the reorganization of the Peking Party Committee is announced as a 'victory for Mao Tsetung Thought ... ' The old Committee was 'shot through with a black anti-Party, anti-socialist line'. On June 22nd Lin Piao calls for all factories to become 'great schools of Mao Tsetung Thought'.

There is an immense stir among the young. On June 13th some middle school asks for the abolition of 'bourgeois and élitist' examinations. This is granted by the Municipality on June 18th. About half the students are from worker and peasant origin, and examinations still favour the sons and daughters of the intelligentsia and the old bourgeoisie. For how can generations of brain sharpening, a background consummately intellectual, stores of books and erudite conversation in the family not produce young students more articulate, and therefore more successful at examinations? While peasants' and workers' sons and daughters, are still crowded in small houses, do not have a table of their own to write on; often no room of their own, and certainly no store of books to browse among. Very soon the students will divide themselves by class origin: the five good, the five bad.

What is noticeable is the effervescent enthusiasm of the young. Mao has sent a circular on May 16th, 1966, following another stormy Party conference held in Peking. It directs all university teachers and students to 'thoroughly criticize all reactionary bourgeois ideas in academic circles ... and the representatives of the bourgeoisie who have wormed their way into the Party, the government, the army and cultural circles ... ' The young are ecstatic.

'A wave of happiness swept through us,' says the son of a friend, Jenyi, who later became a Red Guard, fought for Chiang Ching, and then began to detest her (this happened to so many millions). 'It was at first like a festival, a big fun fair of criticism ... we felt we were no longer being treated like stupid children. We could criticize the officials and pour out our hearts.' The same tumult of spirit, the same straining impatience for total freedom came upon Jenyi and his generation as it had come ten years before in the Hundred Flowers.

'Chou Enlai had said in 1957: Unless the Party mends its bureaucratic ways we shall lose our youth.' Jenyi knew this; and being intelligent he had followed and understood Mao's preoccupation with the problem of 'revolutionary successors', of Party renewal; with his perturbation at the fact that the average age of Party cadres at grassroots level was forty ...

In the socialist education movement, Jenyi and other youths from his class had gone to the villages. 'The idea was that the Party should recruit from among us worthy young people, tempered by this contact with China's actual condition, the reality of the rural areas.' Nearly all the third and fourth year students from the major universities had been deployed in villages during the autumn of 1965, 'and this sensitized us to the problem of Party renewal and Party purification. We saw corruption and authoritarianism and high handedness ... we saw how the people put up with bad Party cadres. We also saw many good things, of course, but we began to question, to wonder ... ' Now they were enjoined to act, to purify the Party through their own exertions. 'The whole world was ours to change,' said Jenyi exuberantly.

Jenyi went through every step of the Cultural Revolution, and in the end he was jailed by Chiang Ching's group, which he had supported. But he found himself through this bitter ordeal. 'Now I know what being a communist means,' he says. He is one of the many millions of young people (seldom mentioned in the West) who have truly understood their own country and its problems. In people such as Jenyi resides hope for the future.

The Cultural Revolution was made under the auspices of 'vast democracy' and the 'dictatorship of the proletariat'. It was meant to involve 'the masses' ousting high Party bureaucrats who betrayed the revolutionary cause. But the Chinese Communist Party certainly meant to guide and to supervise the movement at every step. Although posters covered the university walls in May 1966, denouncing political deviations, no real political target, no tangible bureaucrat of high calibre guilty of misdeeds, was being produced. It was obvious that the first people to suffer would be the academic staff; they were at hand, and many of them were of course of 'bourgeois background'.

But the campaign turned very swiftly into an immense wrestling match for supremacy, a major struggle to capture the young. Young people under eighteen years of age must have formed at least half the population of China in 1966.

The protagonists were, on the one hand, the Party establishment; on the other, the new constellation dubbed the 'Left', whose main figures at the time were Lin Piao and Chiang Ching. Their alliance enabled Chiang Ching's rise to power.

It was Lin Piao, and not Mao, who catapulted Mao's wife, Chiang Ching, into prominence. It happened at a twenty-day symposium on art and literature, held in Shanghai in February 1966, after the final split between Liu Shaochi and Mao Tsetung. Lin Piao nominated Chiang Ching to direct all 'art and culture' in the army. 'She is most competent … thoroughly understands how to apply Mao Tsetung Thought to art,' he said. This gave Chiang Ching a very formidable platform, the army. Immediately thereafter, the Ministers of Culture, of Propaganda and of Education were attacked through the pen of the vociferous Shanghai critic Yao Wenyuan while 'activists', such as those I had seen in Manchuria, were being selected by army cadres, in factories, shops, administrative offices, institutes and schools. The Red Guards from a particular middle school attached to Tsinghua University in Peking were organized by the army.*

The offensive began May 25th, when a poster appeared in Peking University condemning the Chancellor, Lu Ping (who was also the Party First Secretary). This wall poster was allegedly composed by a woman, Nieh Yuantzu, together with several other minor staff lecturers. It was praised by Mao himself, who called it 'worthy of the Paris Commune of the 1870s'.

The idea of giving the Chinese people the right to total criticism and re-vocation of Party officials (or 'vast democracy') was borrowed from what had taken place in France, at the birth of the Paris Commune of 1870. And until 1969, echoes of the Paris Commune would haunt the Cultural Revolution. Undoubtedly it had fascinated Mao Tsetung. Mao had always been a populist, full of trust in 'the masses', always ready to 'turn Heaven upside down' in favour of the people.

But the Party machinery continued to function, and when Nieh's poster was publicized, Party work teams were sent into the universities to 'guide' the movement. The result of this guidance was the processions of young people I had seen marching to pledge loyalty before the white glazed building of the Peking Municipality.

The work teams were supposed to counter 'anarchism'. 'Who opposes the work teams opposes the Centre and the Party.' This saying was only imposing another kind of submission; it did not allow the young to express

---

* Or rather that part of the Chinese army directly, or through allies, under Lin Piao's command.

their own ideas. It was entirely at variance with trusting the people and letting them decide what was right or wrong.

The work teams, to protect high Party cadres, found 'freaks and demons' among academic staff. They not only allowed but also in many cases themselves inflicted humiliating physical punishment on chosen unfortunates. Unlucky professors, lecturers, even heads of universities, artists and writers, were thus sacrificed ... It is customary to ascribe all the violence of the Cultural Revolution to Lin Piao, Chiang Ching and her acolytes, but at the beginning brutality was used by the work teams sent by the Party; and this meant Lin Shaochi.

The writer Ouyang Shan, whom I interviewed in 1978, told me that his ill-treatment had come from the work teams. He was chairman of the Kuangtung provincial federation of literary and art circles. 'It was done in order to disgust people very quickly with the Cultural Revolution' said Ouyang Shan to me. 'The Party was desirous of winding it up, to declare all demons and pests "exterminated" [of course not physically] and to get on with progress in China ... but they had to find some demons here and there.' Ouyang Shan was one of the temporary 'demons'.

The brutalities inflicted upon hapless individuals during June and the first part of July were nothing compared to what happened when the Lin Piao–Chiang Ching alliance won the struggle in August. Neither did they succeed in stemming the Cultural Revolution. But the work teams did manage to confine the movement within the walls of the universities, offices and factories. It would not erupt on the streets until August 18th.

At the beginning of May, thousands of ordinary people had been allowed into the universities, to wander round the campuses, as curious onlookers, and to read the wall posters. 'We saw the teachers sweeping the grounds, cleaning the water closets and the kitchens. Some wore dunce's caps and others were abused as freaks and monsters.'

But in June when I returned and asked to go to Peking University to see Third Brother, I was not allowed. The students were engaged in political study, I was told, and were not to be disturbed by visitors. And the gates of the universities were closed. In Sian and other cities students were not allowed to return home ...

The work teams now turned the students against those who had distinguished themselves, like Nieh Yuantzu, by 'rebellion'. Suddenly the activists of the Cultural Revolution found themselves held incommunicado, dragged to public criticism meetings, while the students were incited to 'struggle' against them. Wen Chuming in Manchuria told me that she

431

had a dunce's cap put on her head and her clothes were bespattered with filth ... she had challenged the Party and was therefore 'counter-revolutionary'.

I had prepared for Kung Peng a memorandum outlining some of the conversations at the seminar on China in Chicago, and also those I had with Malraux and Indira Gandhi.

But I did not see Kung Peng on my return from Manchuria, and when I asked whether she had seen my letter, Hsing Chiang with an uncomfortable expression told me that she had had to destroy it.

'I put it down the toilet.'

'Why?'

'I cannot tell you.'

Some weeks later in August, seeing Kung Peng again, I realized how dangerous my chatty letter had been. The Ministry of Foreign Affairs was being attacked. Kung Peng and her husband would be paraded with dunce's caps, and Chiao in the following year would be badly beaten, so badly that he was ill for a long time. The Lin Piao–Chiang Ching group was dead against America and anything to do with America or the West.

I wondered about Chou Enlai. During these baffling first months, Chou Enlai managed to keep his head and to keep China going. The government functioned as usual, despite the dislocations which occurred. The choice Chou had made, siding with Mao and for the Cultural Revolution, of course impressed and influenced me. Obviously, if Chou was for it, it *must* be all right.

I did not understand completely at the time that Chou Enlai, whose concern was China and the Chinese people, was for the motivation of the Cultural Revolution, the bold concept of mass democracy which animated it; but not for the rising constellation of potential power-holders. He acted in the subtle, long-term, masterly way which was his: the only way to prevent a total rupture in the Party, and hence a breakdown within the country itself. I confused, as so many did, the cause with the individuals who, for a while, represented this cause.

I noticed the disappearance of all musical instruments – Chinese and Western violins, pipes, guitars – from the music shop on Peking's main street; only bamboo clappers, cymbals and drums in the window. The philatelic shop which sold and exchanged stamps from all over the world was closed, its doors padlocked. Collecting stamps was a bourgeois pastime. The flower shops were suddenly flowerless ...

Chou Yang's fall was announced. I was surprised. Chou Yang, the 'tsar of literature', was, for me, impeccable and even too orthodox a person, ardently preaching Mao Tsetung Thought, severe on writers who deviated. The opera star Chou Hsinfang was denounced; and Ho Luting, who had composed the famous guerrilla song of the Sino-Japanese war, and had organized the Chungking symphony orchestra ...

I went to see Yeh, still accessible. We remained reticent on current events, on the people we knew. Around us our friends were pilloried or defamed ... I could not say to Yeh, 'I hope you will be spared.' We talked of poetry, of Hakka proverbs and Szechuan metaphors. I asked Yeh whether he thought this was going to be a big mass movement and he looked at me incredulously, and laughed until he was out of breath.

'I always think of the rolling pin action of the masses, kneading the helpless dough of the person,' I said. And how terrifying, to be alone in the midst of a crowd which had turned against one ... 'This is what bourgeois authorities dread most ... to lose their dignity,' the newspaper had written.

'I suppose one must get used to everything,' said Yeh. 'But we have our responsibility to history. *We must endure.* I expect we shall have to fight through this like a guerrilla war.'

A guerrilla war? Attacks here and there; skirmishes; lightning raids on such and such a cultural institution, and casualties, of course. Would it remain a guerrilla war, or go on and expand? We were at the end of June ...

When I left Yeh that night, he and his wife Yuan Yin walked with me across their courtyard to the gate. The moon was pensive in the pewter sky. The easily tired grass of summer looked like brittle silver. We stopped by the peach tree. In the previous autumn Yeh had celebrated my birthday under his peach tree, and with peaches. Alas, the peach tree would not survive the next few years. It was uprooted when the Red Guards came looking for 'concealed documents' in Yeh's house and dug up his courtyard.

Across the courtyard, greeting us, came the old eunuch who lived in two rooms in the opposite building. He was one of the last survivors of the imperial dynasty. He mentioned that his son was taking part in the Cultural Revolution. For of course the eunuch was married. A peasant boy, he had been bought by another eunuch when he was seventeen, since according to Confucius the most unfilial thing was to leave no son behind one. All eunuchs therefore 'married', and adopted sons. And now the eunuch was eighty-six and his wife was eighty-one. She was a comfortable, gentle woman, and she said, 'I've missed nothing in life, I have had food and bracelets and ornaments in my hair, a husband and a son and a house. What more is needed for happiness?'

'The eunuch used to make virility wine with herbs he grows in our common garden,' said Yeh. 'He gave me a bottle.' It had had no particular effect. And then, as if we knew it would be a long time before we would meet again, we talked of Auden and Isherwood, whom Yeh had met in England. He had loved his years in England; though I told him England had changed very much. 'Memories remain fixed, while the person or event that gave rise to them has already changed,' said Yeh quoting Proust.

'I would like to attend the Afro-Asian Writers' Emergency Meeting.' It was being held at the end of June in Peking; an excellent opportunity to meet writers suddenly turned invisible. There were 180 participants from fifty-three countries listed to attend, and I went as an 'observer'. The purpose of the meeting was to prove that China was the reliable base for world revolution; to condemn both U.S. imperialism and U.S.S.R. imperialism, to indicate support for all liberation movements and especially for the heroic struggle in Vietnam.

A car was obtained for me since I could not possibly walk to the Great Hall of the People, where the meeting was held. Lowly pedestrians would not be admitted. My chauffeur was extremely surly, and never on time. I was not surprised when, in 1969, I was told that he had become a member of the notorious 'May 16' storm troopers, organized by Lin Piao and Chiang Ching.

The distinguished archaeologist, writer and poet, President of the Academy of Sciences, Kuo Mojo led the Chinese participants at the Emergency Meeting: a galaxy of eminent writers, among them some I knew well. But the foreign delegations, with the exception of the Japanese and a few excellent Third World writers, were a padding of nondescript people who could never be called 'writers' by any stretch of the imagination. I missed Lao Sheh; he was in hospital, with asthma. My friend Hsieh Pinhsin, Heart of Ice, was also unwell. But Pa Chin, the grand old man of Chinese literature, had come from Shanghai to attend the meeting. He was China's most financially independent writer; and it was said that at one time he had remarked that the officials of the Ministry of Culture treated writers like monkeys who had to go through hoops. But he was honoured and had never been harassed, and Mao Tsetung had gone to Shanghai to see him in 1957. As for Lao Sheh, he was showered with honours.

I shared a car with Pa Chin once or twice, and we exchanged small talk. I lunched with the playwright Tu Hsuan, whom I liked very much. The woman writer, Yang Mo, I had already met and travelled with, and Han Peiping and Liu Paiyu and Li Chi, the poet Chu Tzechi and Yang Shuo the essayist (who would die during the Cultural Revolution) were all there, and of course sprightly Tsao Yu, full of wit and gleam. And there was also Ching Chingmai, acclaimed for a recent novel, *The Song of Ouyang Hai*. This novel was held to fulfil all the canons of socialist art. It was, in fact, well written and lively. Last but not least, in fact the brightest star of this galaxy, was Hsu Kuangping, the widow of the great Lu Hsun, whose spirit and writings were for ever being invoked as truly revolutionary; whose statues and sayings dominated parks and cultural institutes.

A swinging speech by the Foreign Minister, Chen Yi, on June 27th started us off. Chen Yi looked full of spirit. His speech was long, and one section which made me sit up was when he spoke of the 'great proletarian Cultural Revolution'. It was slander to say that it was 'directed against all intellectuals', said he. Its aim was to destroy the social base of imperialism and modern revisionism, prevent a 'usurpation of power' by revisionists ... Neither the U.S. nor the U.S.S.R. dared to launch a cultural revolution in their countries, said Chen Yi. He put a lot of vigour into his speech, and we clapped.

At the many meetings which took place during the week, most of the speeches were praise of Mao Tsetung Thought, praise of Mao, recitation of his poems, vows of hatred to imperialism and modern revisionism. Some speeches were more distinguished than others. Kuo Mojo gave a humorous talk. Certain people abroad, said he, were concerned because, in April 1966, he had been reported as declaring that his previous work was merely fit for burning. There was no need for anxiety; he planned to write much more, which would serve the people better. Some delegates managed to instil a deep tremolo in their voices and others burst into tears while speaking. All these words, words, words, where are they now?

Almost every evening there was some kind of entertainment by the art troupes of the People's Liberation Army (since all other art troupes were in abeyance, being scrutinized for political deviation): the poems of Mao, set to music, music and songs in praise of Chairman Mao.

The foreign participants did not know me. One thought I was an interpreter and called upon me for services. Another asked me to meet him in his room. 'I need a woman,' said he. 'But not a grandmother,' I replied.

I asked the writer Ching Chingmai to lunch. *The Song of Ouyang Hai* concerned a young hero of the P.L.A. who had sacrificed his life to save his comrades. Ching was a middle school graduate and had tried to become an actor. He had written some plays. Then he went down to the communes, to manual labour, 'and there I encountered great heroes, among the common people'. He spoke of the splendour and the sacrifices of the Chinese people. Thus he had learnt of Ouyang Hai, who had given his life to save some people in danger. 'I could not forget him.' He stayed with Ouyang Hai's army company, interviewing all his friends and comrades, 'and thus I wrote the book'.

I was certain that this book would never be condemned, since Mao himself had received Ching Chingmai, and praised his work. But I was wrong. His hero had (in the first edition) seemed equally inspired by both Mao Tsetung and Liu Shaochi's writings! This was natural in 1964 and even in 1965, when the works of both men were being recommended together to Party members. Even in June 1966, while Ching and I sat on the terrace and talked, the work teams sent by the Party to guide the Cultural Revolution among university students enjoined the recalcitrant to read Liu's book, *On Perfecting Oneself*.

Ching Chingmai would try to save himself. In November 1966, he was present at a large gathering, exalting Chiang Ching, and he spoke in praise of her. But in 1969, when I asked about him, I was told he was 'counter-revolutionary'. What kind of counter-revolutionary? Right or ultra-left counter-revolutionary? He was 'ultra-left', a May 16er.

In 1979 Ching Chingmai surfaced again. Like so many of the young and not so young who, for a while, believed in Chiang Ching and served her, he was denounced and jailed when sacrificial victims were needed; he spent years in jail, was released after Chiang Ching was arrested, and has begun to write again.

I had a very interesting meeting with Hsu Kuangping, Lu Hsun's wife, and the star of our writer's gathering. She told me heinous things about the four writers who had opposed her husband and 'the Thought of Chairman Mao'. Of the four, one was Chou Yang. Hsu Kuangping told me things against Chou Yang, and this was to make me quite prejudiced against him, a prejudice which I have since tried to correct by interviewing him twice,*

* In 1978.

in order to get to the bottom of his quarrel with Lu Hsun, and why Hsu Kuangping said these things about him. She also told me that her book and a film on Lu Hsun had been suppressed and she herself held in obscurity between 1961 and 1965. She also accused Chou Yang of 'falsifying' what Lu Hsun wrote. None of us knew then that this quarrel between Chou Yang and Lu Hsun, going back to the 1930s, was to become one of the main weapons wielded by Chiang Ching and her allies to cast down the officials of the culture and propaganda departments and ministries and seize control of the whole apparatus of culture, education and propaganda.

In 1978 Chou Yang, released after eleven years, would give me his side of the story. He had never led a 'black line' against Mao in the 1930s, since Mao's line was unknown in Shanghai in those years; the Shanghai league of left wing writers was totally cut off from any directives from the Party. 'I found a progressive magazine which urged us to a United Front. The magazine was Russian,[*] and I found it at the back of an obscure bookshop in the French Concession. Since there was no way of knowing what Party policy was at the time, I thought it best to adopt this line, and in fact it was approved of later.' In this way the slogan 'Literature for national defence' came about, which later was so violently attacked as 'capitulation to Chiang Kaishek'.

'Lu Hsun did not agree,' said Chou Yang. 'He was ill, and perhaps irritable. He brooked little contradiction. We went to see him, to try to argue with him.' Obviously, this had been a personal skirmish, and Chou Yang agreed that Lu Hsun had been right. 'But it was a problem of understanding, not of wilful and deliberate betrayal of the correct political line. Anyway, after 1937, I went personally to Yenan, and there I faithfully adhered to Mao Tsetung's line in art and literature.' But this old quarrel had been resurrected, said Chou Yang, and used by the Gang of Four, who turned it into a 'counter-revolutionary plot'. 'This would enable Chiang Ching to get rid of all of us older writers, and to take over the Ministry of Culture and the Ministry of Propaganda, and also Education.'

I know how writers can hate, revile, excoriate each other; how much virulence there is in their personal resentments. But I still cannot understand Hsu Kuangping's detestation of Chou Yang. 'Chou Yang was always very nice to Hsu Kuangping ... He procured a nice house for her in which she could live and work,' said Heart of Ice to me some years later. But that Chou Yang had been harsh, intransigent with wayward

[*] Chou Yang is a translator of Tolstoy and Gorki.

writers, he would himself acknowledge, and make a thorough self-criticism upon his return in 1977. I would ask him, when I saw him in 1978, 'Mr Chou Yang, I have been told many things against you, that is why I wanted to have your own views ... now what about Ting Ling?'

The woman writer Ting Ling had been one of those who had been pursued with great venom by Chou Yang; she had been accused, along with others, of organizing a 'clique' and trying to seize control of the Writers' Federation. And in 1978 Ting Ling, about whom I had inquired several times (notably from Yang Mo in 1961), was still an accountant in a commune in the far north of Manchuria.

Chou Yang said that there were still 'some problems to be solved' about Ting Ling. But now she too is back, after twenty-three years, and exonerated. And Chou Yang, rehabilitated, has probably learnt tolerance and gentleness towards his fellow writers, however ideologically errant they may have been.

With the works of Mao in hand, Hsing Chiang and I went to the Coal Hill Park and squatted in the summer grass, seeking coolness under the glazed pavilion roofs. We talked. The word club came up.

'It's a bad word now,' said Hsing Chiang.

'Why?'

'All clubs are bad ... the Petofi Club ... intellectuals always think of organizing clubs.'

I change the subject and talk of my projected book, *Phoenix Harvest*.

'Phoenix is not a good word. It's the name given to a landlord's wife.'

'It's only a bird.'

'Not a good bird.'

Obviously, I must now make a list of bad words, not-to-be-used words.

The Emergency Meeting is coming to a close and there are major receptions. The heads of delegations are received by the top leaders while we wait in a large hall. They return, and in files Liu Shaochi, the Head of State. Madame Soong Chingling, as lovely as ever, and Teng Hsiaoping, and many others. A photograph is taken.

There is another reception on July 10th. The Great Hall of the People is brightly lit. A final communiqué of the writers' meeting has supported Vietnam and condemned the United States. In the next twelve days, there will be mass rallies all over China—Liu Shaochi presiding over one held in

Peking—condemning American imperialism and pledging total support to Vietnam, 'whatever the sacrifices we must make.'

On the rostrum of the Great Hall that day sat the American Sol Adler, who lives in Peking, and Rewi Alley, and Anna-Louise Strong, and Kinkazu Saionji of Japan and Djawoto of Indonesia. I am also happy to see there Lao Sheh, recovered, and Mao Tun, the Minister of Culture. Their presence comforts me. Perhaps things are getting back to normal. Chen Yi speaks of the insane adventurism of the United States in Vietnam and the shameful demeanour of the lords of the Kremlin. The wife of old Marshal Chu Teh, Kang Keching, who heads the Women's Federation, and the representative of the youth organization, Wang Chaohua, also speak.

Then another reception: in comes Chou Enlai, and with him are Kang Sheng and Chen Pota and Tao Chu. And there is a stir in my heart, because Chou is with the people who are identified with the 'Left', with Lin Piao and Mao. It was Kang Sheng who denounced Mayor Peng Chen, now dismissed. And as for Chen Pota, he is now editor of *Red Flag* and very powerful. He and Chiang Ching have gone together to speak to the university students; Chen Pota also went to Szechuan in the spring to 'stimulate' activists there against the established officials.

Chou Enlai is with them. And somehow because of Chou's presence, because I trust him, I think the others *must* be good people. I forget that Chou is consummately a statesman, that he will do anything, anything that is necessary for China.

Yet I do not like Chen Pota's face. But he is a close friend of Lin Piao and Chiang Ching. And people say that he is Mao's personal secretary; has been for many years ...

Chou Enlai makes an able speech. Later he catches sight of me. 'Oh, you've also come here,' he says. I cannot tell whether he thinks it a good idea or not. Somehow I get the feeling he disapproves.

Some of the foreign translators living at the Friendship Hostel are having a bad time. One of them, a Frenchman, son of a prominent Party member (pro-China) says his father owns a dog. It is impossible, his Chinese comrades say, for a true Marxist-Leninist to own a dog: he is vilifying his father. 'But he does have a dog,' replies the unhappy young Frenchman, who refuses to make a self-criticism, though enjoined to do so.

All the mirrors in the rooms are covered over with portraits of Chairman Mao. The waiters and servants are so busy holding meetings, that no one cleans the rooms any longer.

439

One night I hear great sobs. Someone rushes into an empty hotel room, and locks himself in. Somebody else comes after him. 'Open, open, don't take it like that ... it's only criticism ... open ...' There are muffled sounds, the door opens. Silence.

The Pei family have arrived, and I take them to dinner. Mr Pei and his wife are friends of mine from way back in the 1940s. They have lived a good many years in Europe, where Mr Pei worked as a scientist. Now he has decided to return to settle in China. 'I am getting old. I want to lay my bones in China. Perhaps I can do something to help.' His wife Lucy and his daughter Millie come back with him. Millie is sixteen, she glistens with youth, she has the fragrance of youth, she is like a peach, like a beautiful fruit, and her total ignorance of her beauty is compelling. She is also witty and bubbles with gaiety. The Peis have just ended a trip round China at government expense; to acquaint them with the achievements of socialism. They are enchanted. Now they will have a comfortable flat in an enclave for overseas Chinese in Peking; and Millie will attend the university. They are very happy. They know nothing about what is happening around them.

I walk back to my hotel with a poet. He does not seem unduly perturbed. 'I am not a high official,' says he; nor a Party member. We recite poetry. Poetry is a preservative and a disinfectant: it helps us to fend off the miasma of slogans and dread. A good many friends, Yeh, my late cousin Pengju, and in Hongkong Lee Tsungying, who runs *Eastern Horizon* magazine, have or had the same habit of reciting poetry to themselves. 'High hills and the moon dwindles, low tide and the rocks appear ...'

Something is going on which I cannot grasp, however queasy it makes me. If only there were less words in the air ... my gut feelings dissipate like smoke wisps before the immense wind of words, and the ersatz emotions they evoke replace true instinct. Almost I persuade myself that I must confess and be redeemed through a public denunciation of myself. But confess what? Chinese poetry holds out its melody and guards my spirit against relinquishment. 'China. China. She has opened the garden of love to me, and I must stay my heart with care of her until the end of time.'

Eighteen

Thunder and Lightning: 1966-1967

ON JULY 12TH, 1966 the universities exploded, as the tension between the work teams and the 'activists' – middle school and university students already formed into Red Guards, but not yet publicized – reached a crisis stage. Led by the lecturer Nieh Yuantzu, some forty youths denounced the 'terrorism' of the teams. During the following seven days there was total confusion in the universities.

Precisely during that week, the Afro-Asian writers left Peking, and so did I. Accompanied by writers and officials of the culture and propaganda organizations, we proceeded by train to Tientsin and on to Tangshan, to a remarkable brigade called Shashihyu (meaning sand and stone gully), formerly a haunt of beggar families. The rocky waste had been transformed into a fertile valley, nestling among hillocks now planted with thousands of fruit trees. Here soil had been brought in baskets by the inhabitants to make fields, the stones having been quarried away by hand. It had taken ten years. Two Pakistani diplomats were to write a major thesis on Shashihyu, which was published in the United States. Undoubtedly this was part of the magnificent work of China's millions, and it could not be denied that unless the Communist Party had organized these millions, and infused them with hope, this small huddle of beggar-land would not have flourished.

I lunched with a peasant family; the peasant had five children, a good house and a thriving vegetable plot, but no pig. In fact there were very few pigs at Shashihyu, 'but we plan a piggery for next year'. We returned in a bus cavalcade to Tangshan, the industrial and coal city which I knew well, for Papa had brought me here when I was a child. Tangshan supplied coal to the railway. In 1976 it would be razed in a frightful earthquake, in which nearly 400,000 people died.

There were banquets and long speeches and then a shadow play, the folk tradition of the district. By that time it was midnight and most of the 'writers' simply went to bed. I felt sorry for the folk artists who had waited to show us their subtle and intricate art, which in Indonesia and Malaya is called *wayang kulit*. Figurines cut out of animal skin and painted are manipulated behind a screen, a lamp throwing their shadows on the cloth. I had become a devotee of *wayang kulit* in Malaya.

We went south, to Changsha, and there with the fatigue, the speeches, the banqueting, the heat and above all the unease, the tirades and the threats on the loudspeakers, I had an attack of hysteria. Round me at table some 'writers' had been passing odious remarks about the Chinese, while the Chinese strove to be so tremendously hospitable; and this contributed to my nausea. All I remember of this shameful exposure of mine is a foul odour, a sweat, a clamminess, a wrenching of spirit; the sweat of fear and the babble of terror from my mouth, and Hsing Chiang listening stolidly, patiently, and with love putting me to bed ... and the Chinese cadres so kind, so self-controlled, so heroic in their fortitude, for they were under stress, every one of them, while I was safe – I would not be hit, and paraded and pummelled and reviled ...

We went to Wuhan. The Kiang Nan Hotel was reserved for the Afro-Asian writers' delegation. The heads of delegations were given beautiful suites. As an observer, tacked on at the last minute, I shared with Hsing Chiang the smallest and most stifling room in the hotel, with the sun shining in from morning to late afternoon. It was forty-one degrees Centigrade in the shade, and the air was immobile lead. Hsing Chiang again displayed masterly calm: not a word from her. She gave me the cooler bed. We sweated, we dripped from night to morning and morning to night. I wore no nightgown and went naked in the room, and Hsing Chiang was a little shocked, but did not say anything. There was not even a fan and when we asked for one we were told none was available as they had all gone to 'important writers'.

But the Chinese writers and I had delightful cups of tea together. Cheerful Yen Wenching, tall handsome Liu Paiyu, and Li Chi, so clever and good, made special time for me (though officially they devoted themselves to the others). All three were not only good writers but also veterans of wars, of guerrilla campaigns. Yen Wenching described how he had walked all the way from Yenan to Manchuria behind a mule carrying a heavy load of weapons, and the mule had sores which stank to high heaven. Liu Paiyu had been a hero in the guerrilla war, and so had Li Chi. All three were also members of the Ministry of Culture and Federation of Writers. They remained calm, unperturbed. Their very presence somehow assured one that all was well. Yet they must have been under great strain, since the attack that July was headed straight at the Ministry of Culture, at the Federation of Writers, at the Department of Propaganda; it was certain that they would also become targets of the campaign. But what splendid unruffled urbanity, what lightness of demeanour and measure of speech – what a lesson in self-control and courtesy they gave me, when they knew themselves threatened! They fulfilled scrupulously their duty, making their guests feel important and pampered. And some of their foreign 'colleagues' took themselves very seriously. What thoughts coursed through the minds of Yen, Liu and Li in the hot restless nights when they had put their charges to bed? I do not know. Yen Wenching was to suffer almost seven years of duress, Liu Paiyu and Li Chi eleven years ...

All three of them are alive. I have seen them again and talked with them about that time in Wuhan in July 1966. 'Did you know what to expect when you went back to Peking?'

'No. We thought it would be hard, but not that hard, not that long.'

July 16th. A suffocating day in Wuhan. Forty-two degrees Centigrade. We are taken to the monstrous Yangtze River here over a mile from bank to bank, which rolls its glowing ochre mud to the sea. Motor launches decorated with flags are taking to the water, and there seems to be a hierarchy of launches. But all of us are on one launch, and as we clamber on board a beaming Kuo Mojo appears, surrounded by young girls and boys, swimmers, who erupt from the cabins and form squadrons soon to leap into the stream.

Four hundred thousand people cover the shores; squares of swimmers in red and blue and green suits mass along the banks with banners on poles strapped to their shoulders, and music, music, music is relayed through loudspeakers. The swimmers plunge in, squadron by squadron.

Our launch, flag-bedecked, rolls upon waves of song. There is a small breeze; and suddenly 60,000 more swimmers precipitate themselves into the water from both sides with an immense and gleeful crescendo of acclaim.

'Chairman Mao, Chairman Mao!'

'Chairman Mao is swimming in the Yangtse River ... he is swimming,' a young interpreter, face streaming with tears is shouting. The news goes through our launch and all of us rush to the railings to see Mao. Helplessly, I take snaps, but our launch is not in front, and I can only hope that perhaps *his* head will bob up in my picture, among the many heads in the water. Our writers begin to shout and sing and wave, and some Africans begin to dance. Later they will assert that they have seen Chairman Mao. The more emotional delegates kiss each other and shout 'Long live the Revolution'. I have not quite perceived Mao's head above the water but perhaps I have, and Yen Wenching says, 'Yes, he was there.' Then I know it is so.

The next day, July 17th, we are convened to meet Chairman Mao.

It is in a large building, part residential, part hotel by the West Lake of Wuhan. We are taken there in the usual cavalcade of buses. The heads of the delegations ride in imposing cars.

We assemble in the marble-clad, air-conditioned reception hall. All is white and grey, suave stone and white curtains against the windows; an impeccable cleanliness; and the hush that surrounds greatness ... We are moved into ranks, according to that protocol which I shall never grasp. The first row is the heads of the delegations. Observers occupy the end of not the very last row, but the one before last.

And then Mao comes into the room. He looks as usual bland, benign, with that tremendous persona, that extraordinary flat calm which flattens everything in his presence. He has an extra dimension and I think: he is man-multitude, man-ocean. He brings with him something beyond time, as the ageless rock engulfs the centuries, because it just is. And I am glad that I am not in the front row, which has to grin and cheer and clap and shake hands with Mao. Three rows behind, the effluvia reach me, and I recover from the hebetude into which noise and words, too many words, have plunged me.

Mao shakes hands. We are in a state of expectancy. For usually Mao talks, jokes, with everyone, sometimes makes a little speech. But today, not a word. We continue clapping. And then he is nudged into the centre of the first row and is photographed with us. Then he waves an urbane, casual hand at us and goes away.

He has not said a word.

It is July 17th.

We smile, smile, smile. My face hurts from smiling. We file out. Mao has not spoken to us. But everyone professes himself highly gratified, honoured. Mao has received us. We get back into the buses.

The next day, July 18th, Mao flies to Peking, and the Cultural Revolution whose fires were being dampened, erupts, an uncontrollable volcano, all over China.

The first eighteen days of July have seen muted implosions, muted in the conflict between the two forces contending for supremacy. As radio telescopes detect only after light years the fury of a nebula, only now can we see what unleashed wrath was being prepared.

During the week July 12th to 18th, 'activists' appealed above the heads of the work teams to Mao. 'They are authoritarian ... they refuse to discuss problems ... they do not let us out of the university, they shut the gates and tell us to study political texts ... yet Chairman Mao has asked us to make revolution throughout the land ... ' The activists received the support of *Red Flag* and its editor, Chen Pota. Chen Pota and Chiang Ching had visited Peking University at the end of June, and officially seen Nieh Yuantzu. It is now said – on that fabulous Peking rumour-grapevine – that Chen Pota had drafted Nieh's poster, so much praised by Mao.

On July 18th Mao arrived in Peking. On the 19th and 20th Chou Enlai and Chiang Ching visited the universities together. In these visits, Chiang Ching appeared all sweetness and conciliation, eager to soothe, to unite, to reconcile; for already the students were divided into quarrelling factions. With Chou Enlai, she asked the students not to use the saying: 'Father a reactionary, son is a rotten egg. Father is a hero, son is a true revolutionary.'*

Chiang Ching was not the only top leader's wife visiting the universities. Wang Kuangmei – Liu Shaochi's wife – had been doing so since June, speaking to the students. The majority of the young were still indecisive; they did not know whom to follow.

On July 24th and 25th, the work teams were withdrawn not only from the universities but from all other units as well, after a severe admonition by Mao Tsetung.

Liu Shaochi continued to appear. He was Head of State, and Ho Chih Minh had written to him from Hanoi, appealing for China's support in the Vietnam war. Rallies were organized. Were these rallies, at which Liu appeared prominently, intended to redirect the Cultural Revolution? Were they designed to get the army prepared for confrontation with the United States on behalf of Vietnam? This is a hypothesis for which I have no definite answer. It was put to me by a very good friend of China, and it is not absurd speculation. But it remains speculation.

To make the situation even more confused, peasant delegations, workers' trade union delegations, mixed with the students in a display of massive popular support at the rallies against the war in Vietnam.

* The evidence for Chiang Ching's moderate stance at the time lies not only in the speeches she made, as reported, but also in a book, *Madame Mao*, published by the Union Research Institute, Hongkong (1968). The Institute benefits from the learned advice of the Jesuit eminence, Father Ladany, and cannot therefore be considered biased in favour of the Cultural Revolution.

Anna-Louise Strong, who became an honorary Red Guard on September 12th, tells the story of the birth of the Red Guards in her 'Letter from China' Number 50, sent to many Americans.

> They began as a movement of left-wing students to protect themselves against reactionary school authorities. The first organization is that of the middle school attached to Tsinghua University. It began at the end of May, but was 'under cover' until the new Peking Municipal party committee sent a work team to the school ... The Red Guards came out in the open on June 6.

'Who prepared them?' I asked Anna-Louise.

'I think it was Lin Piao's army units,' she replied.

By July 15th, the garrison troops in Peking had been replaced by battalions loyal to Lin Piao. From my hotel balcony I saw their olive green trucks parked in quiet alleyways and courtyards around the Forbidden City. I had not seen so many army trucks before. Later they would be used to convey the Red Guards in their millions to parade before Mao Tsetung.

All was geared to a showdown, but Mao would not proceed without another meeting of the Central Committee. He would strive once again to unite his old comrades, to win them for what he felt was most imperative: a great 'rectification' of top leaders in the Party, a change of consciousness among the masses, creating a mass movement which would be anti-revisionist, purifying the Party and renewing it with youth and revolutionary ardour ...

I was back in Peking on August 1st. At the airport I would see a great many high officials, members of the Central Committee, arriving. They came from the provinces. The Party was holding an enlarged Eleventh Plenary Session, which began that day. But the Central Committee members were outweighed, as the communiqué made clear, by members of the 'Directorate of the Cultural Revolution', a group now nineteen strong with Chen Pota and Chiang Ching in command and with 'representatives of revolutionary workers and students', that is, the Red Guards. The 'Directorate' would soon become an extremely powerful group, replacing both the Central Committee and its Executive Secretariat.

Between July 17th, when I saw Mao, and August 1st when I returned to Peking, I tried to go to Tibet. I had received permission from Chou Enlai through Kung Peng, and since the way to Lhasa was through Chengtu, I would see Third Uncle.

I had vainly attempted, in Wuhan, to visit my protégé Ying Hsiung, a young man from Malaya who worked for my clinic in Johore Bahru and who went to China to escape being jailed. He now taught English in a middle school in Wuhan. I used to drop in to see him, but in 1966 this was not allowed. 'The school is busy with political study.' I could only leave a message for him.

But first, because it was suggested to me as the thing to do, I went from Wuhan to Chairman Mao's birthplace, Shaoshan. Shaoshan was crowded with endless files of pilgrims, including many Uighurs from Sinkiang. A large building was being put up; a museum to house relics of Mao's life. In the farmhouse, sacerdotal and full of reverence, the guides indicated a rough comb for animals which had been used by Mao. I dared to finger it, an amulet of luck. I ventured to say, at one moment, that Mao Tsetung did not get on with his father, and the heavens almost fell upon me. 'This is slander ... Chairman Mao's family has been full of virtue from generation to generation ... at most, his father was *occasionally* irritable ... ' There could be no flaw in any of Mao's relatives; no reprehensible distant cousin in the whole Mao clan ... and to hint at Mao's own revelations, made to Edgar Snow, was sacrilege ... which I committed. Afterwards I was asked to write my valuable views. Of course they were to be in praise of Mao.

There is, in the district of Shaoshan, a mountain called Phoenix Mountain, where legend says the birds of the air assembled to pay homage to the great sages of antiquity, Yao and Shun. My effusion was interlarded with references to phoenixes. Using the word phoenix was a small act of defiance; since in Peking at the time the word phoenix was such a bad word.

In that atmosphere of religious exaltation, any small reproof took on phantasmagoric proportions. Thus already the titles of my books, *The Crippled Tree, A Mortal Flower*, had been denounced as 'derogatory to China'. How could China be likened to a crippled tree? I explained it really meant that the withered tree revives with the spring. As for 'mortal flower', it meant that flowers die but new flowers take their place. Agility of mind is essential in a universe of slogans. There was, among some bureaucrats, a virulent criticism of these two books, but dear Hsing Chiang carried them around with her courageously. She would turn to the photograph of Mao inside *A Mortal Flower*, to show that my heart was red-sun inclined. But here too there was a hitch. The photograph taken by Edgar Snow, showed a young Mao in Yenan, wearing patched trousers. Was there not, in the patches, an intention to deride Mao? Hsing Chiang said forcefully that it only showed how modest, frugal, heart-linked with the common people was Mao. Another mental world, a universe of symbols ... I became so careful that I began to mutter to myself. As film after film I had liked, book after book I had read, thought good and radical and not badly written, would become 'poisonous weeds' and part of the 'counter-revolutionary conspiracy' against Mao Tsetung Thought, I began to wonder whether I should not accuse myself of counter-revo-lutionary intent? My intestines failed me, as usual. Hsing Chiang strove to protect me. I must be *careful* in my language. 'Luckily you dress very simply.' She was under immense strain all the time. She knew that, as soon as I had gone, she would go into the rectification machine and be exam-ined, scrutinized, criticized. And then there were her sons in school; she worried about them. 'The young don't listen to anything any more ...'

We flew to Chengtu and there were large posters on all the avenues; posters of sturdy young men and women spearing bullheaded freaks and serpent monsters. Not as much noise as in Peking. The university was now out of bounds to me: 'Busy with political study'.

The hotel in Chengtu was totally empty. I was the only 'outsider'. In the street there were occasional processions, factory workers with posters banging drums. But a soldier was at the hotel gates and when I neared them, three men erupted from the gatekeeper's lodge. We went to the theatre, and it was all changed; no more 'feudal' plays (so beloved by me!) but a repertoire of songs, of music and dancing, consisting of two or three people at a time eulogizing Mao or impaling 'freaks and monsters' with furious gestures. And much shrieking. It was so bad that Hsing Chiang made due criticism to the director, who nodded briskly. 'It's too exag-gerated,' said she. Now was this deliberate sabotage, to make the Cultural Revolution activists ridiculous to the ever-humorous, quick-witted people of Szechuan? I learnt about the two – or multiple – faces and interpreta-tions of every so-called fact in that year.

We settled down to wait for the aeroplane to Tibet. I asked timidly to see Third Uncle. The cadres I had met on previous visits were no longer there. One of the new comrades in charge had a face which spelt 'vigilant', like a Chinese opera mask. To this category of cadres promotion comes with their zeal at discovering freaks, monsters, and hidden secret agents …

It was suggested that I go again to Tayee, where I had been in 1964, to the landlord Liu Wentsai's mansion. But this time there were no exhibits of socialist education; and the clay figures of the previous years had been rearranged, given expressions not of weariness, misery and despair, but of fierceness, fury, revolt. 'It was wrong to depict the people in these passive moods … it was revisionist,' I was told; (the artists who designed the first batch of figures must have been undergoing criticism …) Now every little baby, in its mother's arms, looked with rage at landlord Liu Wentsai.

I went to see Third Uncle and Third Aunt. A cadre and Hsing Chiang came with me. It would not be possible to be alone that day, but again heroic Hsing Chiang exerted herself mightily, and in the next days I saw them alone. The neighbourhood atmosphere had changed—it was hostile. And always in the common courtyard there would be one or other member of the street committee watching us. Of course we did not get angry or even make a remark. We simply ignored the surveillance. I knew better than to become irate and bring trouble upon Third Uncle and Third Aunt. This would be unfilial. I realize now that, perhaps after I had left, Third Uncle's rooms might have been searched, in case I had left guns, gold, or secret counter-revolutionary documents with him.

Third Uncle sat in a frightening calm, his body all gathered together, coiled upon the fear at its core. Fear that he did not voice, of course. Third Aunt sat by him, her face smooth. They endured. We sipped tea. We talked of the weather and of my going to Tibet. This was an 'exceptional honour', said Third Uncle. 'Of course we *know* you will praise the socialist achievements in Tibet,' he said, 'and also the Great Proletarian Cultural Revolution.' Having seen him the previous time almost break down at the thought of his body going into a common cemetery, in a common coffin, I knew he must be agonizing within his soul. For he never pretended to be brave; he had too much sensitiveness and imagination to pretend.

I asked after Sixth Brother, his son. 'Your Sixth Brother is very busy. He is in his organization. It is the Cultural Revolution. *Of course* we rejoice that such a great event has come; we heartily support it,' said Third Uncle. I asked to see Sixth Brother, but he was too busy. 'Political study?' 'Yes.' Third Uncle's hands played on the table, with his black fan. Never had his voice been so thready. It was extremely painful to hear him inhale, need air, between each sentence. And yet he would not falter or break down.

I unpacked the things I had brought for them. I saw by Third Uncle's face that they were not welcome. He was afraid to receive anything new, from outside, foreign. There was warm underwear, but it was of various colours, and that was bad. I gave him money. He took it without a word, holding the crisp new hundred-dollar notes in his hands, then he folded them and put them back in the envelope and left them on the table.

Every morning, for the next seven days, we went to the airport, Hsing Chiang and I, to wait for the aeroplane to Lhasa. The Ilyushin revved and whirred and strolled a bit up and down the tarmac. The very nice Szechuanese cadre in charge of security at the airport sat with us. Comrade Hu was a soldier of the P.L.A. and had been four years in Tibet. 'Many of our Szechuan people have gone there to open farms and build roads,' said he. Hu liked the Tibetans. 'They are very sincere, they like to sing and dance. They have their own wisdom.' Hu did not have a Han superiority complex. 'I wouldn't have minded staying there for ever.'

The aeroplane to Lhasa did not leave that day, or the next, or the next ... Every day Comrade Hu sat companionably with us and we played rummy waiting for the meteorological report. By ten in the morning Comrade Hu would say cheerfully, 'Time for lunch'. By noon, it would be too late to fly. 'Tomorrow perhaps.' The pilot would get out of the cockpit and come to us with a broad, happy smile saying, 'The storm over the mountains has not abated.' We would go back to the hotel and in the afternoon I would go to see Third Uncle and Third Aunt. 'Perhaps you will leave tomorrow,' Third Uncle would say. He was less distressed now than on the first day. And so we sat and looked at each other with our great love masked by a careless grin, and Third Aunt would grip my hand and we would walk a little in the courtyard, up and down, and she never stumbled though her bound feet were so small.

The teahouses of Chengtu were closed that year. The streets were curiously full of silent people, just walking. Unlike Peking, there seemed to be few processions – until sudddnly one day there was an immense rally, and great crowds assembled in the stadium, and through the streets poured serried ranks of workers with flags and drums and cymbals.

I suggested to Third Uncle and Third Aunt that I should take a photograph of them. Anything to prolong our time together. Third Uncle acquiesced. Third Aunt asked the relative who stayed with them, and who was the old concubine of Third Granduncle,★ to call the barber. The barber came and he cut Third Uncle's hair before the photographer came. The old concubine knew her place as a half servant and went on faithfully

★ See *The Crippled Tree*.

serving Third Aunt, but Third Aunt always refused to be photographed with her, so she could not appear in the picture that was taken.

Third Aunt attended classes in political study run by the street committee. 'She is most diligent in her attendance,' the street committee man said. Third Uncle could only walk with great difficulty, so was excused attendance. After almost a week of daily visits the street committee man was reassured about me and left us alone, loudly shooing away schoolchildren and women and men crowding round to catch a glimpse of the 'outsider'.

Third Uncle now did some calligraphy, which indicated that he felt better.

> A myriad families plunged into sorrow;
> Men perish amid brambles and weeds.
> Could their grief and laments but shake the earth.
> Thoughts roam wide, stretch over the wilderness.
> In the silence I hear the rumble of thunder.

I went to an exhibition and was briefed on Tibet by a supercilious cadre, who told me incredible and inaccurate stories. He spoke of Princess Wen Cheng of the Tang dynasty who had married the Tibetan King. He said that union between Tibet and China had then taken place. He was wrong; the fusion came five centuries later at the time of Kublai Khan, grandson of Genghis Khan and Emperor of China.* I said flippantly that the King of Bhutan had recently married an American girl, but that did not make Bhutan part of America. (Alas for my rashness of tongue! The cadre turned a raging pea-green and poor Hsing Chiang again rushed to shield me.)

By the seventh day I knew that, even if I waited another month, I would not be able to go to Tibet. That immovable storm over the Himalayas would not budge, the weather reports would continue to be bad. Although Chou Enlai had given me permission, no one at local level would take the responsibility of conveying me to Tibet – it might one day, turn out to have been a mistake, a 'pandering to foreigners', a 'letting out of state secrets'. Who knows?

I said goodbye to Third Uncle and Third Aunt. 'Please tell Sixth Brother I hope to see him next year.' Third Uncle nodded. His eyes were upon me, and oh, the unspoken grief in them. This was the last time I would see Third Uncle. He would die in 1968. Third Aunt is still alive, and I go to see her every year.

* The founder of the Yuan dynasty (A.D. 1271-1368).

451

The tiger heat of August in Peking drove all the bound-foot grandmothers out of doors; they sat on small stools, and fanned, and watched the rare passers-by in the small dusty *hutungs* where the children played. Hsing Chiang went home. 'I must put my affairs in order.' I merely walked around, but it was too hot, and everything was a blur.

Hualan sat in her living room hacking off the heels of her new shoes, shoes I gave her in May, from Hongkong. They were walking shoes, but they had a slight heel.

'It will spoil the shoes, Hualan.'

'Well, my dear, I still think the heels are too high ... it's a sign of bourgeois behaviour, high heels.' There was about her the same intense inner preoccupation which I had noticed in others. Suddenly she said, 'My dear, those dresses you've given me ... can you take them back?'

'But I don't want them back.'

'We may be searched.'

I stared at her.

'House searches,' she said. 'In the movement.'

'All right, I'll take them back.' But I left her a black silk dress.

She frowned at it. 'I'll have to cut off the hem.' The hem had some gold embroidery. 'I'll have to burn some of the other clothes.'

Her sister's oil paintings had been taken off the walls. Only portraits of Chairman Mao were pinned up. I went with her into her bedroom. Her brother was prizing away, one by one, the figurines of bright stone decorating her black lacquer chest. They represented women in flowing robes and with fans, a beribboned scholar, all very feudal, and suddenly nostalgically beautiful. On the veranda all the flower pots had disappeared.

Hualan walked out into the street with me. We walked slowly. Two children were playing at the street corner. One, an urchin of six or seven, shouted 'Foreign devil!' at Hualan and me.

'I haven't heard that for a long time,' I said.

'I haven't heard it for sixteen years,' said Hualan, 'but the kids now learn it from their grandmothers.'

She was wrong. It was not only from the grandmothers.

The year 1966 was the centenary of the birth of the great Sun Yatsen, who made the 1911 Revolution which ended Imperial China, and installed a Republic, and started the convulsions of China's entry into the modern age.

I went to interview Madame Soong Chingling, Sun Yatsen's widow. She lived in a large mansion which had belonged to the Manchu imperial family. She was eternally youthful and glowing, with that lustre of skin and hair, that lovely voice, and always the will of steel beneath the dazzling soft beauty. Her house was air-conditioned, but she complained of arthritis in the knees, due to the air-conditioning. She had fractured a wrist, which made writing difficult for her. 'This is the mansion where Puyi, the last Emperor, was born,' she told me. There was a large portrait in oils of her husband on the wall. The carpets were cool and sea-green, the living room austere.

'You still have not returned to live in China?' she said. Did the gracious lady ever forget anything?

'I think I can be of service even abroad,' I replied.

She then launched into the interview. 'What Dr Sun Yatsen had begun is now being accomplished. We must study the historical context when we want to judge a man. Dr Sun was not a communist but at the end of his life he was very near to the Party. Things were very difficult in those early years. I remember the last time Dr Sun returned from Japan to China. We stayed in the garret of a French newspaperman's house in the French concession in Shanghai; we disguised ourselves when we went out, and we never went out in the daytime.

'I love the American people. I consider America my second home. I have no doubt the American people will do something about the war in Vietnam before too many of their boys are killed.'

I asked what she thought of the Cultural Revolution.

'It is of vital importance; for nothing is inevitable about a new order; it must be fought for, it must be defended; a restoration of the past is always possible; it must not find a rank-and-file mentality ready to accept it ... *We must arm ourselves against ourselves*, bring in *consciously* the new order ... '

In that autumn some Red Guards would deface a shrine erected to Sun Yatsen in his native province. Sun had made a 'bourgeois' revolution, they said, and all 'bourgeois' relics, monuments, shrines of the past had to vanish. Chou Enlai promptly put an end to this vandalism, and ceremonies to commemorate Sun Yatsen were publicly held in November in Peking and other cities.

Madame Ho Hsiangning sat on her bed, dressed in black silk, her daughter by her side. She was five months away from ninety in that July of 1966.

She remembered entertaining me at dinner in 1956. Age had shrunk her, the bones were minuscule, but her spirit soared and her face was fine ivory. She still painted, muscular and sinewy tigers of beauty and power, rampaging in luminous forests. She had a strong brush stroke, and used high colour, in the Japanese manner of the Ganku school. 'I doubt that I shall reach a hundred, though I would like to see the changes wrought by this mighty Cultural Revolution of ours.' She discussed her death without a tremor, her sprightly eyes picking out every detail of my face and dress. 'This body of mine has gone through nearly a century of history; perhaps it is enough.' She spoke of her youth, studying painting together with her husband Liao Chungkai in Japan. 'But he was too busy with the Revolution to continue painting. We loved painting together, it was such happiness.' And she showed me with a youthful gesture, as if a young girl again, a composition: 'My husband painted that figure waiting under the tree.' She had painted the tree.

In 1904, as a student in Tokyo, she heard Sun Yatsen lecture and went up to offer him her services; and joined his association. Liao Chungkai became Sun Yatsen's devoted helper, and he would be murdered in August 1925, by order of Chiang Kaishek.

'Sixty years ago, Sun Yatsen made a revolution; today it is Chairman Mao Tsetung ... ' She had taught her son Liao Chengchih, and her daughter Liao Menghsin to do manual labour. 'Revolution is our family tradition.' She hoped her grandchildren would continue China's long revolution. I said she would live to be at least 120 and she laughed cheerfully and gave me replicas of two of her paintings.

Many people explained the Cultural Revolution to me; each in his own way. Rewi Alley and Ma Haiteh in unemphatic speculation; Israel Epstein, reputed a Marxist theoretician, in high-flown style.

I filled a great many pages of my notebooks with observations, theory, data ... But truth is never merely an accumulation of facts. Facts do not correspond to events, the outcome of a situation does not depend entirely on what one has put into it. Always there is the perverse, intangible unknown, unexpected, the gone awry ... The logic of verity is its illogic. I sculpt out of the unresolved a purposeful recital; imprint upon the shapeless a continuity, merely by writing it down. But reality always escapes; no computer fetters it into order. It remains the unbound mystery which animates all things and men.

As I stared at the ceiling in my usual thinking-horizontal, it seemed to

454

me that the Cultural Revolution corresponded to that streak of anti-bureaucratism so forceful in Mao when he was young. How he detested bureaucrats! Yet by 1966, the revolutionaries of the Long March had all turned, willy nilly, into greying bureaucrats. How else could a country be run, except by an organization, an Establishment wielding power? But something in Mao, wistful and perhaps childish, always hungered for revolt; the revolt against tutelage, paternalism, against obvious authority, and now, in his old age, Mao was revolting against this bureaucratic greyness and its attempts to systematize everything.

Bureaucracy. Twenty-eight ranks for cadres, four lower non-cadre ranks for service personnel, eight grades for engineers, five grades of technicians, four grades of assistant technicians, eight grades of workers. In this staircase universe, every rank stuck to itself, frequented only its equals, dared not 'intrude' upon higher ranks save through monstrously slow paperwork. And yet there was very little economic difference. The difference was in 'power wielding'; whose word counted. No lower rank dared take responsibility for any decision, so that the final three upper ranks were weighed down with decisions about the paltry trivia of regulations. So often, referring cases of abuse or malpractice to the Establishment (mostly complaints from overseas Chinese), I found that nothing could be done at lower level; even a simple bureaucratic muddle would have to go right up to Chou Enlai.

Paradoxically, this general shirking of responsibility was accompanied by the 'feudal practice of arbitrary dictation'* and against these fiats nothing could be done. This too Mao was trying to uproot. But there was more to the Cultural Revolution. Now that the Soviet Party had become 'revisionist'; was once again a Tsarist state, the duty of upholding revolutionary example had fallen upon China. She was now fortress, vanguard, solid base of all liberation ... Suddenly China became the base of world revolution. It was not easy to see the present events in the context of this grandiose vision.

Dostoevsky makes one of his characters say 'Starting from unlimited freedom, I end with limitless despotism.' Mao, in an attempt to accelerate political emancipation among his people, 'took off the lid' (as everyone was saying in July and August 1966); attempted to break the clamped control of the Establishment upon the masses. 'Mass democracy' was the herald call of the Cultural Revolution. One editorial would even suggest a universal vote. It was this exalting vision of freedom, release from all

* Mao's words.

control, which had captivated the young, but which would also victimize them in the end.

From August 1st to 10th, the Eleventh Plenary Session of the Party Central Committee (enlarged) was held in Peking. Out of it came the decisions on the Cultural Revolution; a framework of official approval, called the Sixteen Regulations of the Cultural Revolution. This document declared open hunting upon 'those within the Party *who are in authority* and taking the capitalist road'. On August 5th, in the middle of the proceedings, Mao Tsetung himself had written a wall poster, condemning the 'fifty days of white terror' of the work teams.* And Lin Piao, in a major speech at the Plenary Session, asked for a general purge of all those in the Party 'who oppose Mao Tsetung Thought'.

The executive of the Central Committee in the hands of Liu Shaochi, and its secretariat under Teng Hsiaoping, were now totally paralysed. They were replaced by the nineteen-member Directorate in charge of the Cultural Revolution, headed by Chen Pota and Chiang Ching.

On August 18th, a one-million-strong rally of Red Guards from seven cities was received by Mao.

Almost one-third of middle school and university students in Peking would become Red Guards. Within ten days the movement spread to all cities. Although the Sixteen Regulations specifically forbade violence and 'physical struggle', this was the hallmark of the next two months. By the end of September fear reigned in many cities, where gangs of youths, invading every street where there were 'bourgeois' or intellectuals living, committed brutalities upon unfortunates. Yet contradictory reports came out: 'Remarkably little violence,' said some; 'A reign of gratuitous terror –horrifying,' said others. In every city and quarter it was different: from harassment to murder, from endless interrogation to beating to death.

By October, in Peking alone, 86,000 'counter-revolutionaries' had been discovered. In Shanghai 400,000 'bourgeois and capitalists' were removed from their houses.

An overseas Chinese girl, Alice, told me in 1975, 'I was looking through my window, and I saw them come for me. I was paralysed ... I could do nothing but open the door for them. For six weeks they stayed with me in relays, group after group, questioning me; night and day and day and night ... I slept no more than two or three hours a night because they woke me up to question me. They went through all my books, my letters

* June 1st to July 20th.

... why had I so many Western friends? Why did I not confess that I was a spy, had come back to China not to serve China, but to spy for America? I had to translate every word of all my letters from my friends abroad ... Finally they let me go, but for six months I had to clean the school lavatories, sweep the courtyards ... then I went into a study period for six months. I was kept in the school, not allowed to go home, and then I went to a May 7 cadre school for a year.'*

Utterly strange to relate, this same Alice, on her return, would be changed, so changed as to believe in Chiang Ching and her group, and adhere to her although it was because of the Chiang Ching-organized Red Guards that she had suffered this harassment!

Another witness: 'Ho and I worked in the same office in the Foreign Language Press. We even shared the same lamp. The Red Guards from the Foreign Language Institute and the aviation school (they were among the worst of the lot) came to get him. They took turns beating him in the courtyard. He kept on shouting "Long live Chairman Mao". Then they took him away in a truck to the Western Hills where they kept their prisoners. I never saw him again. I don't know why they singled him out. Sometimes it was all so capricious.' He adds: 'None of us moved.'

From Uncle and Aunt Ting, who lived in one of Papa's houses: 'Band after band of Red Guards came down our street. Many of them were from other cities. They obtained from the street committees and the public security bureau the names and addresses of "bourgeois families" living in the quarter. But sometimes a person with a grudge invented a story. Our daughter had bought a bag in Shanghai. It was prettier than the Peking ones, and a neighbour coveted it. She told the Red Guards that we had foreign goods, and they turned up everything in our house, dug up the floors and the garden, chipped the plaster off the walls to uncover gold pieces or documents. They took away books, pictures, vases, anything "old" or "foreign", and also a table and a cupboard.'

Uncle Ting's house was searched, and by night he and his family left the city. They lived in a ramshackle hut in the suburbs; but they returned in 1968. Many other families of 'bourgeois origin' were compelled to go away, and their houses were occupied by workers. Papa's houses were all thus occupied. But then I had already given them up formally, writing official letters to that effect in 1965 and again in 1966. However, they were returned to me in 1972. But I never went near them until 1978, when the matter of 'compensating' me for them came up.

As for the Peis, of course a team of Red Guards came to investigate

* For May 7 cadre schools, see footnote p. 487.

them. They found that their clothes were all wrong. They did not understand why the Peis had lived abroad; why they had decided to return to China. Mr Pei was arrested and detained for three months for having 'illicit relations with foreign countries'. His wife and daughter were held incommunicado for weeks, at home. Two youths kept constant guard in their flat; even to go to the toilet they had a girl Red Guard with them.

'I nearly went through the window,' said Mrs Pei when at last she talked to me, in 1975. 'I begged them to let me die. What did they want, what did they want? Why were we treated in this way when we loved China, and wanted to come back to live here? But they did not believe us; they said we had returned to spy.'

In the end the Peis would remain in China, and be honoured, and given jobs. 'But it has taken ten years out of our lives,' says Mrs Pei.

'You may not think it can be true, but it also took ten years out of my life,' I say to her, and we both laugh.

Mr Pei, who is a perennial optimist, fared well in jail. He was not isolated, and he made many friends. After three months he was released. 'Of course due to Premier Chou Enlai,' he says.

My friends the Yangs also went to jail. 'Almost everyone I knew and respected was in jail with me. The jailers were very pleased to have important people to look after,' says Yang Hsienyi. He met there several former ministers, and also some petty thieves. 'Now the ministers are back in important positions, and they say, "Old chap, anything you have to say, come and tell us." As for the petty thieves, they will never steal anything from me.'

There were so many absurd and ugly things being done, like the trials in Shanghai of cadres supposed to have committed adultery, who were beaten on the buttocks by self-appointed youthful judges. The Red Guards changed the names of streets and of shops, until the Post Office complained that they could no longer deliver letters, 'since every street and every shop has the same name'. There were good and bad Red Guards. The good ones – among them the children of my friends – helped the peasants with the harvest, and protected people and state property. But the worst not only burnt books and destroyed historic monuments; they also killed and tortured. Chou Enlai could not shield all, protect everything, everyone, everywhere. Although he tried. He protected, at least, the top scientists and artists, and many museums and monuments. But sometimes he was too late. The harm was done.

There were the parades. My revered friend, Dr Lin Chiaochih, an eminent gynaecologist trained in America, and a great-grandmother, was paraded as a 'bourgeois authority' with a dunce's cap on her head. She told me so herself, laughingly, in 1969. And immediately after the parade (which lasted seven hours) she went straight back to the hospital and started operating on her cases for the day.

Thousands of 'bourgeois authorities', doctors and scientists, diplomats and professors, went on working, despite the harassment, the humiliations, despite being made to stand many hours in uncomfortable positions, wearing dunces' caps and labels round their necks, and having their hair pulled and their faces slapped.

'The Red Guards who beat my husband were *directed* by Lin Piao and Chiang Ching,' says Lao Sheh's wife, the painter Hu Tsietsing, to me.

Directed violence, as distinct from spontaneous brutality, would become more obvious after November 1966, when the Directorate conducted its first attempt at seizing power in all the cities, ousting all the old cadres.

But in that August the targets were the Ministry of Culture, of Propaganda, and the educational institutions. Thus not only Lao Sheh, but many other writers were 'all being beaten while in front of them burnt a huge bonfire, a great pile of theatre props, of costumes used for the Chinese opera and the stage, and musical instruments. Lao Sheh could not understand ... that he, so honoured for seventeen years, should suddenly be so treated.'* When his corpse was found in the Lake of Peace, he had clutched to his heart the writings of Chairman Mao, as if he had searched in them for an answer to what had befallen him.

I have now been to see so many of the survivors, one by one, interviewing them as soon as they could or would talk (for even the Westernized Peis would not say a word until 1975). They all say the same thing. 'At first it seemed awful ... we wondered if we could bear it ... but as the days went by, and *all* of us, all the people we knew, all the old veterans, anyone of some stature or merit, were reviled or harassed, or beaten or jailed, suddenly it became nothing ... we were all in it together—a new fraternity. It became shameful not to be harassed, to be left free.'

And so many, almost two out of three of these writers, artists, literary critics, musicians, singers, actors I talk with add this: 'We had faith. We knew it could not last.'

'Because we trusted the Party—and the Chinese people.'

In October of 1966 I flew to a Toronto University teach-in on China.

* From an eye-witness, the writer Yang Mo.

David Crooke came from Peking on purpose to deliver a speech, and Felix Greene came from England. But the whole exercise was fairly futile; all communication was actually broken. And the next year David Crooke and his wife, both staunchly communist, were to be jailed in Peking for some three years, on totally fabricated charges.

I did not write to Kung Peng about Toronto. Her husband Chiao was being treated in a most cruel way, condemned to sell newspapers on the streets. 'Please let me sell them on the back alleys,' he pleaded. 'On the main streets I might meet foreigners, and they know my face … '

I attended at that year's end a meeting of the World Family Planning Organization, in New York, and on this occasion met McGeorge Bundy and Margaret Mead, who refused to shake hands with me.

I went to India and Ceylon, and there I met again Theja Gunawardhana. An Asian economic seminar had been held in Peking at the time of our Afro-Asian writers' meeting. Theja Gunawardhana, an economist, had attended. At first she was suspicious of me, but later we became friends and I went to see her in Colombo. She seemed to have 'inside news', because two of her sons were studying in China.

Theja spoke darkly to me of plots and conspiracies. 'I have written a letter to Lin Piao,' she said firmly. Her sons were very critical of the foreigners (Americans and British) living in China, and of their role. 'Do you know that it is an American, Sidney Rittenberg, who is almost in total control of all China's radio broadcasting?' said she in outraged tones. I have since often wondered, when in the following year some of the foreigners resident in China were arrested, whether Theja had not been influenced through her sons by the spy mania prevalent in China then. Theja was a fiery and fascinating woman, but very idealistic and intransigent … She was also — total contradiction — a devout Roman Catholic as well as a Marxist revolutionary.

I was back in Hongkong in December. My friend Tsungying had returned from a trip to Kuangchow. His eyes shone more than usual, and he exhibited signs of thyroid trouble. His family in China was under great duress. In 1957 his brother and sister-in-law had been dubbed rightists, and now what would happen to them? Noble Tsungying, not a word of complaint from him for twenty years. He told me the Red Guards he had seen 'talk philosophy better than I do'. He praised their discipline, eulogized their sense of responsibility. Nothing about his own worry, his fears. And so, lulled by ignorance, I felt more reassured.

But another Chinese journalist, on his return from yet another excursion, went over to the Americans. He described corpses hanging from the trees in the parks of Kuangchow, talked of the beating to death of Nan Hanchen, Director of the Bank of China, an economist, in charge of China's economic relations abroad. Nan Hanchen, a devoted patriot, was now described as a 'counter-revolutionary'.

When I went to the American Consulate in Hongkong for my visa, because I was scheduled to do yet another lecture tour in 1967, the visa officer said to me, 'In view of what's happening in China, will you perhaps just say that you've changed your mind? Then we'll dispense with all this waiver business ... we'll just clear you.'

But I could not. 'I have not changed my mind,' I said.

He sighed. 'I thought you'd say that. Well, we'll just have to go through the usual business.'

By that time, so I learnt from a friendly State Department official, it took five hours to go through the files on me. I felt flattered. So much paper work for nothing.

Nineteen

The Storm: 1967-1968

IN JANUARY 1967 Shanghai was captured by the 'Left'* in an assault upon the Party offices by a million Red Guards and workers. The leaders were Wang Hungwen, a worker at the Seventeenth Textile Mill, and the writers Chang Chunchiao and Yao Wenyuan, the collaborators of Mao's wife. These three men and Chiang Ching would form the notorious Shanghai Group, later dubbed by Mao himself, in 1974, the 'Gang of Four'. The Mayor, Vice-Mayor and Party officials of Shanghai were hauled to criticism meetings, paraded through the city, accused of 'towering crimes' and of restoring capitalism. The Lin Piao-Chiang Ching alliance pressed on. A public exhibition was held in Peking. Peng Chen, the ex-Mayor, Chou Yang, Yang Shangkuen, head of the Party school,

---

* As the Lin Piao-Chiang Ching alliance was called. It is now called 'ultra-left' and 'counter-revolutionary'.

and Lo Juiching, former Chief of Staff, were shown, with large placards round their necks, to a crowd of five thousand – among them some Westerners resident in China. All over China such displays took place, designed to strike terror among older cadres in high positions. The writer Chao Shouli was taken from village to village through the north-west he had described so well in his books. He died of the ordeal.

Now the 'Left' proceeded to seize power in all the cities of China. They hoped, in the vacuum of authority, to establish themselves, but this was not easy. The veteran cadres fought back; so did workers' and peasants' unions who detested the bullying Red Guards. The latter, split into many factors, were fighting each other.

In the havoc lay purpose. Lin Piao wanted to consolidate his hold. The attacks against Lo Juiching, Chu Teh, and other Long Marchers of the army such as Ho Lung, were planned. Power could only be seized by placing Lin Piao's own men in their key positions. Lo Juiching was Chief of Staff, General Secretary of the Military Council, and the former head of the Public Security Bureau. He was apprehended in September 1966. In the ensuing 'investigation sessions' he was pushed – so it is alleged – through a window, and his leg was broken. He received no medical care for this injury. He was carried to his public humiliation in January 1967, in a large basket, and had to crawl on the floor, dragging his broken leg behind him. At the place of his public trial he was supplied with a chair, because there were 'outsiders' present.

Ho Lung was Vice-Chairman of the Military Council, in charge of the executive. He was an egregious man, a popular commander. He had been with Lo Juiching and Chou Enlai at the Nanchang uprising on August 1st, 1927 as had Chu Teh and Chen Yi (and Lin Piao himself, though in a subaltern position). And this memorable episode, which was the beginning of the Red Army, had forged strong bonds of friendship among these men. In fact, some Western 'experts' said Lin Piao was a 'protégé' of Chou Enlai!

The 'Left' had to break up this solid nucleus. For many months, Mao Tsetung would not agree to Ho Lung being 'investigated'. Chou Enlai would personally protect him, giving him asylum in his own house. But after months of shielding Ho Lung, Chou had to relinquish him. Mao had finally allowed an 'investigation'. Ho Lung was treated most savagely. He was diabetic, and was refused medical care. He was beaten regularly, being first wrapped in a blanket so that the welts would not show. He was allowed only three *fen* a day for food. Ho Lung believed in Mao to the end of his life. 'If Chairman Mao only knew what is happening to me.' But his petitions went unheard. They were not relayed to Mao. All this was not known—it could not be known—since Ho Lung was held in top security conditions until his death in 1969.* Mao cannot have known what was happening, for he sent a message to Ho Lung—but Ho was already dying when he received Mao's message.

In 1973, Chou held a ceremony in Ho Lung's memory, attended by more than 2,000 people. Not a word appeared about it in the press. In 1974, I would see the small casket containing Ho Lung's ashes in the building where the ashes of Party members are kept—but Ho Lung's photograph was so small that I nearly missed it. 'He died of natural causes. He was seventy-six years old,' said the keeper.

Besides these two men, the Lin Piao–Chiang Ching group would endeavour to discredit or to paralyse Chu Teh, Yeh Chienying, and Nieh Jungchen, who was in charge of the atomic power programme. Chu Teh was ignobly reviled, but such was his prestige that no one dared to drag him to jail. Yeh Chienying was so respected and popular in the army that it was impossible to mount a campaign against him—but his son, son-in-law, daughter and other members of his family were imprisoned for five to seven years. Yeh Chienying's son-in-law was none other than Liu Shikun, one of China's greatest pianists. China's other renowned pianist, Ying Shengtsung (Felix Greene made a beautiful film about him in 1960), went over to serve Chiang Ching. I would read an article by Ying in the newspaper, describing how he had been saved by her from his 'bourgeois upbringing' and ideas. This article was to serve artists as a 'model' of conversion to her and her group.

Marshal Yeh Chienying kept silent during all those years. He had saved Mao's life during the Long March, hence it was difficult to shake Mao's faith in him. But he would never mention to anyone, and does not seem to have even hinted to Mao, of the treatment that his family was enduring. His long patience was not due to fear or passivity. All China knows what she owes to old Marshal Yeh Chienying, who waited until the time had come to act.

On the civilian side, getting rid of Liu Shaochi and Teng Hsiaoping did not solve the problem of toppling the Establishment. There was one formidable obstacle, and that was of course Chou Enlai. Chou's strength lay not only in his total indispensability, but in the fact that after Mao he was the only man in China whom all the people knew by name and loved, the old as well as the young. 'No one will believe anything against Chou,

* The family of Ho Lung did not speak about his martyrdom until 1977.

not even the Old Man,'* Chen Pota is alleged to have remarked one day. Chen Pota had been entrusted by Lin Piao and Chiang Ching with the formidable task of 'getting rid of Chou'. Chou was to be denounced, at first indirectly, by innuendo, as the 'great protector' of top officials and 'capitalist roaders' in the Party, 'the mandarin who shields the imperial dynasty', to revert to the feudal phraseology with which even present-day political articles in China are so copiously riddled.

Throughout the months since that fateful August of 1966 Chou had striven to minimize disruption. He had forbidden the interference of the Red Guards with communes and with factories. 'Workers and peasants make revolution at their place of work ... revolution must stimulate production, not destroy it.' But in November, he seems to have lost out on this point to the Directorate. Chou had shielded not only Marshal Ho Lung but so many other useful and valuable people: he had recommended 'moderation' in attacks against the cadres and gone against physical violence. He had succeeded in protecting many scientists, especially in the atomic and nuclear installations, so that a clause in the Sixteen Regulations specially mentioned them.

One way to topple a man, according to the traditional Chinese art of war is to 'remove those by his side'. Attacks against Li Fuchun and Chen Yun, the economists and planners, and above all against Chen Yi, Foreign Minister, all of them Chou Enlai's helpers, advisers, friends, colleagues, were designed to weaken Chou. 'Let Chou do all his own work, let him have no rest, no sleep, harass him until he dies of strain ... ' This was the intention of the Directorate. And indeed, by August 1967, Chou would exhibit cardiac stress.

Chen Yi was attacked from February 1967 onwards, repeatedly, for many months; not only Chou stood by him but of all the ministries, the Foreign Ministry proved the toughest, refusing to yield hostages, and ninety members of the diplomatic service put up a poster in defence of Chen Yi. The ebullient Chen Yi fought every inch of the way, got angry with the Red Guards, called them 'ignorant children', shouted back at them when he was shouted at. In between sessions of 'criticism' (and physical abuse of him and his wife, the beautiful Chang Tsien) Chen Yi would go home, wash his face, change his clothes and attend a diplomatic reception or receive a foreign embassy with unruffled countenance and humour. For they all went on working, these extraordinary men; Li Hsiennien, the Finance Minister, coming back from hours of being grilled, would preside over a meeting of the Finance Committee. As for Chou

* Mao.

464

Enlai, he was everywhere, did everything—attending Red Guard rallies and lecturing them, presiding over high-level meetings on industry, electric power, finance, transport, flying here and there to the provinces to put a stop to armed conflicts, managing all China, and trying to keep food flowing into the cities.

'Chou is more dangerous than Liu and Teng.' Long before Mao had emerged as leader in 1935, Chou had already established the Communist Party organizations. He was both an intellectual and a military commander, he had created the key network of insurrection in Shanghai in the 1920s, and he was the head of the State Council, the huge government machinery which made China function. He had conciliated Chiang Kaishek in a 'United Front' in 1937, and he was the architect of Peking's foreign policy.

I am still amazed by the strength of mind, the foresight, the superb bravery of Chou Enlai in these crucial years. How he manoeuvred! How he was able to tell truths within untruths! It was supreme statesmanship, the art of arts. He played not for himself, but to save China. But how did he do it? Some parts of the immense task he undertook with such boldness and prudence are unfathomed. If ever there is a book worth a lifetime of effort, it is a book about Chou Enlai, and what he did from 1966 until the time when he died of cancer, ten years later, in January 1976.

Perhaps because of this consummate, single-minded, ability to see further than others, to utilize skilfully even reverses, and press on to his goal, Chou Enlai was for many years attacked, reviled, vilified, by Western writers, as a 'turncoat'. He was said to 'change sides', to be a 'coward' (when he was utterly brave) and to have no integrity. He was, they said, a man for all seasons, always ready to bow to the prevailing wind.*

Yet when he died, all the world mourned him.

It must have been, for Chou, a difficult decision to make, in 1965, to side with the alleged 'Left' against the Establishment which he, too, had created. But it was a decision guided by something more profound than simple loyalty to Mao or blind faith. I think it was a total realization of all the elements, contradictions, conflicts in China at the time.

He was always the great 'readjuster', the man who, when a situation appeared frozen and desperate, managed somehow to unfreeze it; to find that scarcely perceptible detail which would provide a new start; Chou Enlai, siding apparently with Lin Piao and Chiang Ching, made it

---

* Simon Leys wrote that people in China 'hated and resented Chou Enlai ... ' He could not have been more wrong.

extremely difficult to remove him ... What he would do, in the end, would be to shield and protect Mao Tsetung from his 'friends' and from his wife.

Throughout 1966, Chou Enlai had spent himself as only he could do, scarcely sleeping, always available, doing everything, including offering to polish the shoes of foreign guests at the hotels when the waiters declared they would no longer clean shoes, answer bells or serve meals. He kept the government departments working while all the administrative and technical staff running China, from coal mines to banks, from steel plants to foreign affairs, were systematically paralysed by the removal of all the senior experienced personnel, to be criticized, humiliated, beaten or jailed. Out of 70,000 people employed in the State Council under Chou, by 1970 only 10,000 or less remained. 'I have no one left to help me except Li Hsiennien,' Chou said to Edgar Snow.

The strategy of 'outwardly knock down Liu Shaochi and Teng Hsiaoping, actually destroy Chou Enlai' was started by Chen Pota in October 1966. 'Everyone can be criticized, except Chairman Mao, Lin Piao and Chiang Ching,' said he. And this meant, of course, 'Criticize Chou Enlai'.

The first poster against Chou Enlai went up on January 15th, 1967. It was, however, taken down the next day, by order of Mao Tsetung.

The Party now fought back. In February, at a high level meeting presided over by Chou Enlai, Marshal Yeh Chienying and other veterans of the Long March protested at the shambles being created. 'Too many of the old cadres are ill-treated, and without any reason at all. Most of the accusations against them are unfounded and unproved. This is illegal.' 'Will your fifteen-year-olds run the army?' shouted Marshal Yeh, who is said to have struck the table with such force that he fractured a bone in his hand.

'The affairs of the country cannot be carried out. Is the Party still necessary or do you wish to do away with it? At present it can no longer function, and the stability of the army is also imperilled ... are we old cadres still needed, or do we all have to die to satisfy you?' said the veterans of the Long March.

By then almost all the ministers in charge of production were being denounced or hauled away to kangaroo courts held by Red Guards. The Coal Minister would die of a heart attack under the verbal abuse he endured.

'You are using the mass movement as an excuse to attain your own ambitions,' said Long Marcher Tan Chenlin, a Vice-Premier.

'Every day you say: Let the masses liberate themselves. But it is not the masses you want to liberate. You want to topple the Party,' said Yeh Chienying. 'How will you run the country then?'

To which it is said that Chen Pota, who was present, talked about 'vast democracy' and 'the masses running themselves ... all power to the masses', and the Paris Commune.

Now the Paris Commune idea had received a major setback from Mao himself. When Chang and Yao, the Shanghai allies of Chiang Ching, both in the Directorate, proposed to set up a Shanghai commune, Mao refused. 'Such an organization is too loose and too weak ... it leads to anarchy.' A Shanghai commune was not set up, nor a Peking commune despite his wife's appeal to the Red Guards: 'We don't need any State Council or ministers ... there should be a Peking commune.'

But the idea of a 'vast democracy' to be run by the 'masses' suited the 'Left' too well to be abandoned. Chen Pota called a mass meeting of twenty thousand, and denounced 'the evil wind of February' which sought to 'reverse the Cultural Revolution'. Meeting after meeting would be held, for over a year, against 'the pernicious black wind of February'. It was in these circumstances that Chiang Ching would play a major role. 'Tan Chenlin is a renegade,' she would shout (he had called her 'a new empress') and this launched the 'masses' against Tan.* 'Ho Lung is a traitor,' she screamed, without any evidence. He had called her 'a second rate actress' in Yenan, thirty years previously.

The Directorate now tried to operate power seizures on the model of Shanghai in several provinces; but most of the revolutionary committees formed were unstable. The army had received from Mao a general mandate: 'Support the Left', but this proved extremely dilatory. When was a left a true left or a false left? The local commanders would interpret 'left' any way they wished. Lin Piao's commanders camouflaged their own consolidation of power under Red Guard and mass demonstrations. This led to a strife of so much complexity and such baffling confusion that no one knew, at any time, who was 'left' or who was 'right', or who supported whom, or how it had all come about. Chou Enlai, as usual called in to arbitrate, to expostulate, to stop Red Guard internecine fighting, would have to contradict himself twice on what was 'left'.

But by April it was clear that the Red Guard movement was spent, split into a thousand factions, and that restoration of order was in the hands of the army. The work of appealing to the young to unite, to stop fighting, to operate alliances, and to return to studies, fell upon Chou Enlai.

* He is of course rehabilitated, alive and well.

Many youngsters, disgusted with the violence, gave up. But it was not easy for a few hundred thousand of them,★ having tasted the frenzy of destruction, having tasted power in raw, brutal form, to return to normality. 'What, go back to study? Then what is the Cultural Revolution for?' they demanded.

And until September 1967, some groups were kept on a war footing, deliberately, as 'storm troopers', by the Directorate. Among them was the notorious 'May 16' group.

The May 16ers originated in a faction from Peking's two major universities, Tsinghua and Peking Universities, favoured by the Directorate. Recruits would accompany Chiang Ching in her jaunts through China and lead the chorus of praise at her speeches. 'Whoever attacks Comrade Chiang Ching attacks the Party, attacks Chairman Mao ... Defend Chiang Ching to the death!'

Chen Pota and other members of the Directorate organized the May 16 storm troopers into battalions, assigning them a special task, which was to topple Chou Enlai.

'We were told to discover incriminating material against the greatest mandarin of them all,' said one Red Guard, who subsequently turned against Chiang Ching. 'The Directorate would provide us with the documents, or we would look for them. These were Chou Enlai's speeches, talks, interviews. We pored over each word. Each action of Chou's was scrutinized by us. In June 1961 Chou had said, in a talk on literature, "There is an evil phenomenon extant among us ... a lack of democracy... many people do not dare to think, to speak, to act ... " Was this bourgeois liberalism? We decided it was. He had also said, "Chairman Mao has corrected his own writings ... great artists correct their own works ... great men acknowledge their errors and mistakes ... " Could this be finding fault with the invincible Thought of Chairman Mao? We coupled stray sentences here and there, from many of his talks, took them out of context and convinced ourselves that Chou Enlai must be toppled.'

Many of the recruits of the May 16ers were found among students of the Foreign Language School; the Aviation School of Peking produced another group called the June 16ers. These were devoted to Lin Piao and controlled by Lin Piao's son, Lin Likuo, who was a commander in the air force.

In the general disruption of order the cities' jails were opened and criminals released. 'We considered they had suffered from the bourgeois line of the capitalist roaders in the Party,' said a young Red Guard from

★ There were around 30 to 40 million Red Guards.

Szechuan who, ten years later, excoriated Chiang Ching and Lin Piao. 'They did terrible things ... if some of us learnt to torture people and to rape, it was they who incited us to do it.'

Despite the havoc, Chou's unceasing efforts to restore unity, to get the young back to school, seemed to have partly succeeded by May 1967. Mao was quoted as saying he wanted to unite 'the left and the centre', meaning the new constellation of power and the old cadres, whom he had proclaimed 'in the vast majority good or relatively good'. Thus the much abused Chen Yi, and Tan Chenlin, and Chu Teh, and Yeh Chienying took their place with him on Tienanmen gate on May 1st. This was, in a way, a defeat for the Lin Piao–Chiang Ching alliance. And it enhanced Chou's stature. He told the Red Guards bluntly to moderate their attacks, even on Liu Shaochi and Teng Hsiaoping; and directives for 'severe punishment' for murder, arson, plunder were posted up. Nevertheless the Directorate pressed on.

In June and July 1967 Chiang Ching, who was then at the height of her popularity, made many speeches, some of them highly emotional, to the Red Guards throughout China.

Chiang Ching had been catapulted into prominence by Lin Piao's nomination of her to direct culture in the army. Her close friendship with Yeh Chun, Lin Piao's wife, was also a feature of the alliance. They were called 'two roses on a single stem' because wherever one went there was the other, directing the applause and shouting the slogans: 'Learn from Comrade Chiang Ching', 'Swear to die to protect Comrade Chiang Ching, the standard bearer of the Cultural Revolution!'

But Chiang Ching's emergence as a political star came in November 1966, at a rally of some twenty thousand writers, painters and musicians held in Peking in the Great Hall of the People. All the speakers present, among them Chen Pota, Kang Sheng, Ching Chingmai, Kuo Mojo praised her in varying degrees. So did Chou Enlai, after a fashion. 'The achievements of the Cultural Revolution in literature and art mentioned just now ... are inseparable from the guidance given by Comrade Chiang Ching,' said he. Everyone clapped. But was it eulogy?

Chiang Ching addressed the delirious audience. Besides the official version of her speech, there is a non-official version, only obtainable many years later, in which she reviled some old cadres by name, referred to attacks against herself, and started weeping. 'Some people try to harm me, gather black material against me,' she said. These outbursts would become increasingly frequent, and at the end, she would turn in fury upon people, in a manner which strongly suggests mental derangement.

But this was 1966, and no one at the time thought her mad. However, something obsessed her. What was it?

I have sifted all the material, talking to dozens of people who encountered her through the decades, to those upon whom she wreaked her fury as well as to those devoted to her. I believe she dreaded that some episodes in her past should be made known to the general public. For even then she aimed for nothing less than supreme power, the leadership of the Party, at Mao's demise. She would say to her biographer, Roxane Witke, 'Sex and love are only for a time, but power is decisive, and is most satisfying.'*

Why was Chiang Ching so frightened? Because of sex and love.

In Shanghai, as an actress, Chiang Ching had had liaisons. Even before that – here rumour, gossip, and truth cannot be disentangled – it is said that as a poor young girl she was sold, as concubine, to a wealthy landlord who turned out to be a relative of Kang Sheng, that rigid Party member, head of the Public Security Bureau in the Red base of Yenan, and one of the 'Twenty-eight Bolsheviks' picked by Stalin to direct the Communist Party of China.†

In avant garde circles of Shanghai of the 1930s, there was more freedom in sexual matters than anywhere else in China. Sexual freedom was considered by Chiang Kaishek 'communist immorality', and lurid tales of young girls inveigled into promiscuity by communists were printed every Saturday in the newspaper which my husband Pao gave me to read, while I was in Chungking. Pao thought it would infuse in me horror of communism. He was infusing me with horror of sex.

But sexual freedom did not exist in the Communist rural bases, where, on the contrary, the peasant guerrilla army, 'an army of virgin soldiers' as Snow would describe them, had brought the purity and strict morality of China's villages with them.

'The Shanghai leftist intellectuals thought free love progressive, a defiance of old feudal mores ... but they got a shock when they went to Yenan,' Rewi Alley said to me.

In Yenan, Mao fell in love with Chiang Ching and she promptly moved into his cave and became pregnant. Mao then sought to divorce his wife

---

* *Comrade Chiang Ch'ing* (Little, Brown and Company, New York, 1977): a biography reposing chiefly on Chiang Ching's own testimony about herself. The words above are recounted slightly differently by Miss Witke; I have the Chinese version, from a witness present at the interviews between Miss Witke and Chiang Ching in 1972.

† See *The Morning Deluge*.

Ho Tzuchen and to marry Chiang Ching. There was opposition in the Party; and many 'facts' – and also unfacts – must have circulated about her at the time, gossip going from cave to cave. Chiang Ching was called all sorts of names, from 'a worn slipper' (which means a prostitute) to 'a dirty woman'.

Chiang Ching did nothing to make things easier. 'She was not wicked then,' says S., an actress who knew Chiang Ching and stayed with her for a while in the same cave. 'But she was impossibly vain; she would always have to be different, would not join with other women to talk, or go for a walk ... she wore a great cape and rode a white horse ... always she would try to attract attention ... '

Chiang Ching would never forgive those who derided her. She brooded on this, it festered and poisoned her. Twice, in 1950–1 and again in the early 1960s, she tried to work in films in China, but each time she came up against opposition.

Hsia Yen* was to tell me so himself. 'I was in charge of film editing. She was mean-spirited. She always wanted to dominate. I could not entrust her with any responsible job because she was excessive in every-thing; excessive criticism or excessive laudation ... I rejected her point of view about some scripts for films and she never forgave me ... Hence I was singled out for physical abuse.' Hsia Yen was beaten, his leg broken, and he was refused medical care.

Hsia Yen is not the only one who ascribes his ill-treatment to Chiang Ching's insatiable vindictiveness. Chou Yang had arguments with her in Shanghai; he was to be treated most cruelly. 'She was revengeful to an extreme degree ... and she had delusions ... she suffered from persecution mania and she was terrified that the Chinese people would know of her past.' Chiang Ching knew – as every woman in China knows – that the Chinese masses are still extremely 'feudal' in matters of sex. How could she become a top leader if tales of her youthful levity circulated among the people, in a land where sexual freedom is still today considered the equi-valent to promiscuity and prostitution?

A tale (which some Shanghai officials aver is true) is told of an operation mounted in Shanghai in October and November 1967 to remove from libraries, newspaper archives and private houses all films, photographs, newspaper clippings, letters, which contained any reference to Chiang Ching's previous life and career. This removal was made possible through the collaboration of Chiang Ching's Shanghai supporters, Chang

* The Vice-Minister of Culture at the time. He has been rehabilitated and has resumed his functions.

Chunchiao and Yao Wenyuan, the Red Guards, and Lin Piao's son, Lin Likuo.

The Red Guards of the Aviation Ministry (directed by Lin Likuo) were detailed to conduct searches among the people whom Chiang Ching had known in her youth. They were arrested, their houses ransacked; they were interrogated and also their friends and distant relatives were searched. Almost all those who had known her as the actress Lan Ping* were incarcerated for various 'crimes'. The prominent and very popular actress Pei Yang was accused of being an American spy. Film directors, scriptwriters, even an old servant of Lan Ping, went to jail. A few of them died there.

All the material recuperated was handed over to Chiang Ching. However, her feeling of insecurity was not allayed, and in November 1966 she seems to have begun that incoherent public babble, interspersed with weeping fits, which would increase through the years and become at last uncontrollable.

As a doctor, I feel immensely sorry for her. I understand the terror in her heart, because I suffered in a similar way. I understand that she had begun to hate the good and virtuous women, the stolid and uncomplaining guerrilla women who had frowned upon her conduct. And I understand too how these women, who had suffered and endured so much, even losing their children during the Long March, must have viewed this newcomer, with her Shanghai manners, and her arrogance, and especially her use of sexual attractiveness.

Mao's wife, Ho Tzuchen, whom he had married in the early 1930s, had borne him children; three of them were lost during the Long March. Ho Tzuchen was one of that small band of women – there were about thirty of them – who survived the Long March; everyone respected their heroism, and called them 'elder sisters'. This was a term of love and respect, and they lived up to it. But it is certain that they did not see with a joyful eye Mao divorce his courageous wife and marry Chiang Ching.

In later years, therefore, Chiang Ching sought revenge on *all* the Long Marchers. 'Whenever she saw one of the elder sisters she used to sneer,' her doctor recalled, when I interviewed him (of course many years later; he would not have opened his mouth when she was in power).

'What was she really like?' When people could safely talk, after 1976, I would go round asking those who had known her. One of the film directors of the 1930s whom she sought to kill with ill-treatment (he had apparently refused her a major role she had coveted in a picture) was back

* The name Chiang Ching gave herself in her young acting days in Shanghai.

after eleven years in jail. His health was shattered but his spirit was intact, and he was now rebuilding the film industry. 'She was beautiful and vivacious, but if there was a mirror anywhere, she looked at herself in it. She was always somehow acting a role, she lived in a make-believe world of her own, she was *inventing* her life as she lived it.' 'If she came to dinner,' says an artist who knew her then, 'one found oneself quarrelling with one's wife when she had left.' 'Her thirst for revenge was insatiable,' recalls another. 'This was her great weakness. She could not bear not to dominate. She would never be crossed, and anyone who did not agree with her was her enemy. She was small-minded, imagining slights where none were intended.'

Of course, it may be said that all this is criticism 'after the event'. But there is no doubt in my mind that Chiang Ching was suffering from paranoia. However, this kind of paranoia also induces devotion and fascination, a kind of *folie à deux*, and undoubtedly Chiang Ching also had charm, a certain charisma and vivacity. She would attract powerfully young girls in search of an idol, and frustrated women who saw in her a 'revenge against the tyranny of men'. She certainly convinced her biographer, Roxane Witke, that she was 'outstanding'.*

I would encounter Chiang Ching too; I would very gradually begin to realize that she was dangerous for China. But it takes years to check fully all that is said, especially in feudal Asian countries, where the gap between fact and fiction, truth and lies, is so very small.

The second assault on the Establishment began in summer 1967. One hundred thousand Red Guards quartered in front of the Chungnanhai, where the leaders of China lived. Here they set up loudspeakers, blaring night and day; Liu Shaochi must be delivered into their hands. Among them were the May 16 squads, whose tents were pitched nearest to the South Gate, because they were sure that Chou Enlai would come out to speak to them.† 'He will come out with Liu Shaochi, and you can kidnap him,' the young were told. Then perhaps they would do to him what they had done to other chosen victims, take him to one of the chalets in the Western hills, built for writers to retire to, but now in the hands of Red Guards. Among those lovely hills, some terrible things were done. Chou refused to yield Liu Shaochi; and after almost three weeks of great noise, the Red Guards withdrew.

* As said to the author by Miss Witke in New York on April 19th, 1973.
† Chou Enlai, being Premier, would use the South or main gate.

In July and August the Foreign Ministry was attacked. Red Guards swarmed in, encouraged by the presence of a 'revolutionary' diplomat, Yao Tengshan, the newest recruit of the 'Left'.

Yao had been Chargé d'Affaires in Indonesia, and in April 1967 the Chinese Embassy in Djakarta was involved in a scuffle with Indonesian troops. Yao was declared persona non grata. He came back as a hero and was photographed linking arms with Mao and Chiang Ching. He declared that the foreign policy which Chou Enlai and Chen Yi had practised was 'revisionist'. Bands of May 16ers pillaged the ministry, took files and documents away, while Chen Yi was brought to lengthy meetings to be reviled, and hit. Chou was besieged in his office by Red Guards for twenty-eight hours on end; he could not eat or drink or rest. He spoke with band after band of them, and such was his unflagging courage that they withdrew. 'Then we loved and respected Chou Enlai for his bravery. He made us ashamed of ourselves ... and we began to suspect Chiang Ching,' says one of the ex-Red Guards whom I would meet.

Meanwhile Yao Tengshan took over the ransacked Foreign Ministry. For almost two weeks he ruled, sending cables to all the ambassadors to return to Peking, announcing that 'the whole world has now entered the era of Mao Tsetung'. Many diplomats returned, but Huang Hua in Cairo stuck fast, an act of great courage which would cost him three and a half years of labour in a commune. Meanwhile, xenophobia was used by Yao, assaults on foreign diplomats multiplied, culminating in the burning of the British Chancery office on August 22nd. The embassies of Third World countries were not spared.

This was August 1967. Three weeks later, in September, everything changed.

Mao Tsetung had been on a tour of the provinces in July and August, returning to Peking in early September. It is probable that in this tour he met many of the regional army commanders and realized that they were not at all happy at the disruption and chaos caused by the seizure of power by the Red Guards. These seasoned fighters saw beyond the ostensible 'vast democracy of the masses'. They realized that it was a move to oust them. Earlier that year the Directorate had launched a forceful propaganda: 'Seize the capitalist roaders in the army'. It meant that the Lin Piao–Chiang Ching alliance was now out for the only power that is, in the end, decisive: the gun.* The commanders were besieged by frenzied

* 'Power grows out of the barrel of a gun.' Mao.

Red Guards, their reputations ruined by spurious accusations, while Lin Piao would place his men in control of more army units.

In July, a commander of the Wuhan garrison, Chen Tsaitao, refused to abide by the orders of the Directorate and detained two of its representatives when they came to Wuhan to tell him to support the 'Left' Red Guard organization. Chou Enlai flew to Wuhan to solve the problem, and the most curious scenario took place. Chen Tsaitao made a self-criticism, and agreed to come to Peking. But he pointedly said that he did not know that the Directorate 'had replaced the Party or the Party Secretariat'. Nothing happened to him, and Lin Piao backed down, called a meeting of regional commanders, and made conciliatory noises. Chen Tsaitao today is not only a member of the Central Committee but has been admitted to the Politburo.★

Chiang Ching always swore that she had had nothing to do with the fury of August. She could prove that the Directorate had indeed telephoned the Red Guard leaders, forbidding them to burn down the British Chancery on August 22nd. But it could also be said that on July 22nd she had told the Red Guards not to give up their badges and their weapons, contradicting Mao's orders that they return to their place of study and cease from violence. She had then used a phrase which would prove a nefarious influence—so it is now said—in the subsequent general strife which erupted throughout the provinces and the cities: 'ATTACK BY REASON, DEFEND BY FORCE'. This was the green light for continued violence, at a time when the Red Guards were attacking army garrisons and raiding arsenals. Even trains to Vietnam were looted for weaponry.

But there are, of course, many ways of explaining events; and the defenders of the Gang of Four contend that this phrase had nothing to do with the violence which already existed.

Mao severely condemned the July and August violence as 'ultra-left', and the slogan against the army as counter-revolutionary. He said the young had shown themselves petty bourgeois radicals, not true revolutionaries; and now they must learn to integrate with workers and peasants.

'On a retreat, the general lightens his chariot,' says the Chinese art of war; which means that subalterns must be cast aside and sacrificed, to save the leaders. Chen Pota, Lin Piao and Chiang Ching condemned the May 16 groups, and four or five members of the Directorate were arrested as the main instigators of that crazy summer, as was Yao Tengshan. From that time on, the Directorate, based on the Lin Piao–Chiang Ching alliance, began to crumble.

★ As of May 1979.

On September 6th, Chou Enlai made a speech, with clearly marked points. There must now be unity; the young must return to their schools, production must go on; the army must remain stable. He refused to revenge himself. Let the young, said he, learn by experience ... Chiang Ching was also called upon to make a speech. She was obviously disconcerted; but she had to denounce the May 16 groups as 'counter-revolutionary' and castigate those who attacked the army. 'Who dares to slander our beloved Premier Chou Enlai?' she would exclaim. Then she disappeared for three months; 'wearied by her labours,' said Chou Enlai blandly.

Among the Westerners living in Peking, strange things had taken place. A 'Norman Bethune' group of foreign residents, who wanted to participate in the Cultural Revolution, had been formed. They turned their suddenly discovered revolutionary ardour upon tried men, noble men, who had worked for decades in China, such as Rewi Alley and Ma Haiteh. They accused Rewi of being a 'traitor', of having 'clandestine' relations with the Kuomintang. Rewi was 'investigated' and it was found that he had written favourably on Marshal Ho Lung, and there was even a photograph of him with Ho Lung. Rewi was no longer visited by friends, except Ma Haiteh, and another doctor, Hans Miller, who stuck to him through every conceivable distress. The foreigners held a 'struggle meeting', Chinese-style, against Rewi. Later some of his books were to be destroyed.

The viciousness – there is no other word for it – exhibited by these Westerners, including Americans, is a frightening instance of mass psychosis. 'You should have seen them,' said Rewi to me years later, laughing gently. 'They were trying to do exactly like the silly kids. Their eyes popped out and they spouted fire and they thought they were the tops in revolution-making.'

In September 1967 some of these 300 per centers* were jailed. However, innocent foreigners who had not run amok were also jailed. The general accusation was 'espionage'.

The May 16 groups, abandoned by their sponsors, and dubbed 'counter-revolutionary', were now hunted down. They scattered through the provinces and some reached Hongkong. But their leaders were told to 'lie low – wait for another opportunity'.

* The name was given by Neale Hunter, an Australian writer, to the foreigners in China who demonstrated this excessive revolutionary ardour.

In January 1967 I went back to the United States for another lecture tour.

I was extremely nervous, and suffered from fits of depression because of the Cultural Revolution, and exhaustion. In Hongkong the *Takungpao* and its able director, Mr Fei Yiming, were having a hard time. The Hongkong 'troubles' and riots would occur in that spring. Fei would be called 'Red fat cat' by foreign correspondents, and at the same time was threatened as a 'capitalist roader' by young activists sent from Kuangchow to 'strengthen' and 'revolutionize' the pro-communist press in Hongkong. *Takungpao* was identified with Chou Enlai, with moderation — attacks against Chou Enlai were then being launched in China, and the Hongkong 'troubles' were part of this campaign to discredit Chou's foreign policy.

America was also seething with violence that year. We went to Harlem. The angry ooze of the air, the song-talk of those clarinet and tuba African voices with their soar and growl of syllables ... At the time the Black Panthers were still about, and Anna-Louise Strong had pinned great faith upon them. But they would be systematically shot down by 'law and order' forces, at three or four in the morning, and they disappeared by dint of assassination, and drugs, and their own betrayals. Their leaders, Huey Newton and Eldridge Cleaver — the latter I was to interview in Algeria in 1971 — and Stokeley Carmichael (who was on television with me on a Susskind show), went into religion, or respectability, or perhaps even some money. Malcolm X had been killed, and Martin Luther King even though not a Black Panther, would also be murdered.

America was, I felt then, burdened with a splendid and treacherous technology, which substituted whirrs and clicks for her existence's heartbeats, and bright dancing riffles of programmed action for her soul's humanity. The Vietnam war was now focussing both that monstrous beauty of power which had overawed Vincent and me, and its helplessness, its terror content. The trust in machines to win at every turn was ebbing, and Americans were at grips with their own conscience; very few, in 1967, still felt that the Vietnam war was a good thing. But the voices promising victory continued loud and shrill.

It was in that year, talking in San Diego College on family planning in China to an almost empty sports stadium (the student committee in charge of arrangements had resigned, and forgotten my lecture) that, from among the six people who attended the lecture walked towards me a woman, tall, auburn-haired and with beautiful grey-green eyes. 'I'm Shirley MacLaine,' said she.

This was the beginning of yet another precious friendship. Shirley

MacLaine has never let her film-star success devour her other selves; her capacity for initiative and innovation remained whole, as did her refusal to set limits to her integrity. To have come in a storm, to a lecture on family planning in China – I've never quite got over thinking how much independence it took. China was not exactly a Hollywood topic at the time.

Felix Greene had been abused by the Hsinhua news agency in a report about his activities in Vietnam (he was immensely busy speaking in America against the Vietnam war). 'I'll just drop China for a bit,' said he. Mutely I wished I too could 'drop China' like that. I could not. I would be a prisoner of the Cultural Revolution for ten long years. I remembered Malraux saying of it: 'We shall see an experiment, which will both dazzle and fragment the soul of man.' It certainly almost broke me.

I had hoped to go back to China that summer of 1967. Meanwhile, Vincent and I took a tour through France, its blessed, civilized beauty; there is no country like it in the world for making one aware of life's graces. We were accompanied by Cécile Verdurand, the representative of my French publishers. She brought her wit and robust sense, laughter and talk, and gaiety, and I would discover that intelligent, vivacious, indispensable being: the Frenchwoman. I would have many French women friends from then onwards, and find with them an immediacy of understanding of great value to me.

By April 1967 I had finished *Birdless Summer*, and also a small book called *China in the Year 2001*, requested by Pitman's, the publishers in England. I sent some proof copies of the latter book to Kung Peng.

A telegram came through Hongkong. Kung Peng advised me to make changes in the book. To begin with, the preface was all wrong. Secondly, there were quotations from Liu Shaochi and from Marshal Lo Juiching in my book. They *must* come out. I looked at the preface. It certainly was all wrong, but I could not recover the original, which I had done hastily, scribbling it because I had no typewriter available. And I had not reread it before sending it to the printer! My carelessness was due to fatigue, a dazed exhaustion, and worry over events in China played no small part in this physical depression. But other major snags were the quotes from Liu and Lo. The Liu quote was, to my mind, inoffensive; it could easily be left out because it was not important. As for Lo Juiching, I had been impressed by the clarity of his pamphlet of 1965. I knew Lo was in trouble, but was that any reason for not quoting him? However, perhaps there were many things I did not know. Kung Peng would never have advised me to do this unless it was important; for she had never previously insisted on any change. And so I took the quotes out, a matter of some ten lines, which did not make much difference to the book. Or so I thought, until I realized that the effect would be to leave Lin Piao the sole expounder of the *military* point of view of Mao.

Kung Peng was doing this for my sake. She must have known that I was being attacked in China, something I would only learn a few months later: in those wall posters in Shanghai, condemning Pearl Buck and myself as agents of American imperialism.

Another message came from Kung Peng. It was not advisable for me to come to China that year. Neither would it be advisable in 1968.

Those two years were to be among the most draining of my life. I felt desiccated, cut off from China, for how long I did not know. Suppose I could never return ... what about Third Uncle and Third Aunt and Third, Fourth and Sixth Brothers and their wives and their children? What about all my friends?

I cannot help it if I react as a Chinese, thinking of the Family, thinking of how to protect them. Thinking: 'Never do anything to imperil another human life.' Words and notions and convictions come and go; but a human life is not to be endangered lightly.

I watched with pangs other people go to China: French and British and other 'friends of China'. But Edgar Snow and I met with refusal. Ed could not understand why. He armed himself with fortitude. However, I would often break down and weep. I would wake up in the morning with streaming eyes, and Vincent would take me in his arms, his arms my shelter against all storms, and rock me like a child, and utter cooing sounds. I regressed into a total baby. I had terrible tantrums for nothing.

'It will pass, it will pass,' said Vincent, cradling me.

Ed told me how, in his last visit at the end of 1964, he had asked to interview Liu Shaochi. 'Chou Enlai did not appear too keen. He was protecting me, I think. "Now why do you want to see Liu Shaochi?" he asked me. And then he arranged that I should be at a general reception where all the leaders of China were present. There were Mao and Liu, and Liu's wife, Wang Kuangmei, sitting side by side with Mao's wife, Chiang Ching; and they all looked serene, and no one would have guessed anything was amiss. And then Chou, with that wonderful impish smile of his, said, "Well now you've seen everybody, haven't you?" ' Ed shook his head. 'I've made a lot of mistakes,' he said.

'But everyone does, Ed; and I don't think the Chinese themselves know what is going to happen ... there will be many more mistakes, but they won't be our mistakes.'

I think that when history goes as fast as it does in China, with so many sudden capsizings and reversals, the word 'mistake' is inappropriate.

In July and August 1967, everything seemed to go crazy in China. 'You're going to have a nervous breakdown. I'm taking you to India,' said Vincent, and started packing our suitcases. Vincent always does the packing. Whenever we have moved house, or country, Vincent had done the packing. Usually, when packing starts, I shirk by becoming ill.

But then came a message from Prince Sihanouk's secretary, Charles Meyer. Would I come to Phnom Penh? A short time before that message Charles had written to me, 'What is going on in China? It is unbelievable ... xenophobia ... barbarism ... this is not the China of Chou Enlai.'

Prince Norodom Sihanouk was, understandably, angry. Some of the China Friendship Associations abroad, on orders from Peking, had behaved outrageously. They had been ordered to remove the portraits of the heads of state hanging beside the portrait of Mao; and the Cambodia–China Friendship Association had duly taken down Sihanouk's picture. In Nepal as well the King's effigy had been removed.

Sihanouk was also worried about the fate of Chou Enlai. In his last trip to China with his wife, Princess Monique, in 1964, he had been very happy. With Chou he had gone to Szechuan, and through the Yangste Gorges in a brand new steamer, sketching and painting and making music all the way. He had composed a song about friendship with China, a song which Chou Enlai had learnt by heart, and hummed to himself.

Now we felt that Chou Enlai was in peril, and that the era of the warlords would return, for Lin Piao did not command the loyalty of all the military units of China. 'All this is very bad for China, and for Asia,' said the forthright Prince.

'Your wisdom, Monseigneur, will overcome this transient episode,' I said feebly, smiling hard to mask my desolation.

I wrote to Chou Enlai. I forget the exact words, but it was to tell him that I was devoted to him. I thought: If he is destroyed I shall have to give up going back to China.

Three weeks in India with Vincent's family dulled but did not cure my distress. Vincent's father was particularly kind, asking pertinent, shrewd questions about the Cultural Revolution, but not probing where it hurt.

In September all was changed. The downfall of several rabid 'revolutionaries', members of the Directorate in charge of the Cultural Revolution, indicated a major turnabout. And then, a little later, I learnt that my friends the Yangs were jailed ... what had they done?

In January 1968 the film director Fred Zinnemann and I met at lunch at the Algonquin in New York. Fred had in hand a major project, a picture based on André Malraux's book, *Man's Fate*. Three writers had tried, without success, to write a film script. 'They all sounded like the "Internationale",' said Fred. Then his wife, Renée, had suggested me. I agreed to write the script. Work was an opiate, tranquillizer, since I could not go to China that year.

Fred and his crew and I went to Hongkong, to Malaya (where I was happy to see Tunku Abdul Rahman again) and to Singapore, for locations. But most of the work was done in London. Fred was entrancing to work with: relentless as a diamond drill. No slipshod word got past him. We fought all the way through the script, we fought on the colour of clothes, on everything. He had a splendid staff, and I enjoyed every moment. I think that writing the script saved my sanity. Fred Zinnemann even went to Calcutta's railway station to get the 'feel' of misery, of hopelessness.

In late March I attended a symposium on China at North Carolina University, together with Edgar Snow and other distinguished American experts on China, including Alexander Eckstein. The symposium was marked by a major event: President Johnson's television speech in which he announced that he would not seek re-election. The implication was an admission that America's Far Eastern policies would need a major overhaul.

In May 1968 we went for a few days to Paris, just long enough to catch a glimpse of the student leader, Cohn Bendit, and his supporters marching, marching along the Boulevard St Michel. The walls of Paris blossomed with words, and here too there was hope, exaltation of purpose ... but also the acrid smell of tear gas and panic. Some timorous wealthy families were running away to Switzerland, taking with them refrigerators and television sets, all the encumbrances of non-living. The spectre of the Cultural Revolution in China haunted certain minds.

But in May 1968 in China the P.L.A. had been empowered to shoot down those who refused to relinquish their weapons, who raided and killed and burned. From May to July, grim and bloody battles were fought; battles which took place primarily between factions of Red Guards, with the army trying to intervene to keep the peace, and suffering casualties. Some commanders, however, did not exhibit much tender care for the young. The mopping up operations they undertook, while they heartened the population, were certainly tough upon errant Red Guards.

The university sector of Peking was transformed into a battlefield wherein two Red Guard factions, barricading themselves in, launched assaults on 'enemies' with everything at hand, including roof tiles, bricks, mortars and machine guns. After about a hundred days of this murderous game* and repeated calls to the Red Guard leaders, Mao Tsetung ordered teams of Peking factory workers backed by army regiments to clean up the battle areas. He then saw the faction leaders and spoke to them for some hours. 'You have resisted the workers ... you have killed and wounded workers,' said he.

Now the 'integration of youth with workers and peasants' proceeded. From September onwards millions of young people would depart for villages and state farms and army resettlement farms, in order to learn how to serve the people.

'Nothing has changed.' In January 1968 twenty factions of discontented Red Guards had published an essay, 'Whither China', concluding that the pendulum had swung back. 'The old Party committee and the old military district have now become the revolutionary committee,' they wrote; but 'nothing has changed; all is exactly as before.'

'Back to normalcy?' In Hongkong and abroad the China watchers and the newspapers surmised and speculated. In autumn 1968 Liu Shaochi was expelled from the Party as a 'traitor, renegade and scab'. And preparations to hold a Party Congress, and to fashion a new constitution, were well advanced. All over China there was haste to set up the new organs of power, revolutionary committees, to be composed of 'the masses', Party cadres, and army men. The preponderance in positions of leadership of army men was noteworthy. Since the Party organization had been badly weakened, only the army could maintain control.

I felt slightly relieved, especially when, in early 1969, I received an indirect message from Kung Peng. In October 1968, I had been invited to McGill University in Montreal to deliver three lectures on the Cultural Revolution. I realize now that some of the statements I made were excessive, in fact, 'ultra-left', and 'petty-bourgeois radical'. Chou Enlai would surely have said so had he heard them. He did when he read them. But I suffered from euphoria; for now all seemed to go gradually back to normal; Chou Enlai was strong, and even non-communist newspapers wrote optimistically of China. True, there were bad things; but it was impossible

---

* See *The Hundred Days War* by William Hinton, Monthly Review Press, New York, 1974.

at the time (and would be impossible for some years, in fact until the end of 1976) to obtain definite, hard-core information on what had happened, although I did my best. And so many people, respected scholars, wrote books praising the phenomenon of the Cultural Revolution ... I too wanted to believe that at last the enormous problems confronting China were going to find a solution.

By May 1969 I had five hundred pages of draft for *The Morning Deluge*, the first part of my book on Mao Tsetung and the Chinese Revolution. I had become absorbed, fascinated by the personality of Mao, his vision and the impact he had had on China and on the history of the world in consequence. I was determined to understand him, to understand what had happened.

It was impossible for me, during those Cultural Revolution years, to get away from this obsession. As my writer friends in China were stuck, unable to write, so was I blocked, unable to write of love, or romance, or to imagine anything light and pleasant – all that dredged up was China, China, and the Revolution in China. I had to write it down *to get rid of it*. Everything else somehow appeared mediocre, second rate, narrow squint of half-life compared to the tremendous convulsions which agitated the world of China.

Only after 1976, when Chiang Ching and her gang fell, did I feel liberated. And now I think that if I had been able to detach myself, to abandon China mentally, to write of romance while my writer friends were cleaning lavatories and being abused, I would despise myself very much today.

Before I left for Peking in the summer of 1969 I met again Charles Meyer and his wife Sika. They were on holiday in Switzerland. I spent two delightful days with them at Zermatt.

Charles had greatly changed. He fulminated, vociferated, against Sihanouk. 'He is awful,' said Charles. 'He does terrible things. He must be got rid of ... we shall be getting rid of him ... he cannot last another year ... just wait and see ... ' Charles seemed very sure that Sihanouk would be overthrown. What has got into him? I wondered.

I received my visa in Paris, from the chubby, gifted Ambassador, Huang Chen, a Long Marcher and an artist of talent.* 'Your friends are waiting for you in Peking,' said he. In the hot July of France, he opened his grey tunic and fanned his undershirt, in the best guerrilla manner, oblivious

* Now Minister of Culture.

of decorum. But he had so much personality, so much glamour, that he could carry off anything, and the French loved him.

Twenty

The Nourishing Tree of Truth: 1969

IN KUANGCHOW NONE of the thorny xenophobia apparent in 1966 remained; no one shouted 'foreign devil'. The rice was short and very green in the fields; it was the typhoon-proof kind; and the sugar cane grew tall.

Everyone had Mao badges pinned on them; some the size of small saucers. The Love the Masses Hotel was no longer available; and Ram City Hotel was now renamed The East is Red. Every shop's name was also The East is Red.

But the apparent peace was not more than glance-deep; the peace of China is that of the Pacific Ocean which brews its own cyclones. When I went for a walk, Miss H. of the Friendship Association stuck close to me. I was whisked away from a street corner where I stopped to read the posted notice calling for an immediate surrender of all weaponry and intimating death penalties to people who committed murder, raided arsenals, or set fire to state property. 'Struggle-criticism-transformation is still going on,' said Miss H., who suggested it was far too hot to walk. Why not ride in the car instead? At night, I heard gunshots and the whistle of bullets.

All the cadres I met told me how beneficial the Cultural Revolution had been for them. They admitted they had been 'shocked and shaken', but prided themselves on the manual labour they had performed. They certainly looked healthy, if dark-skinned. One of them told me how many kilogrammes of grain he could now carry: 'almost as much as a commune member.'

This would be the theme – unending, continuous, repetitious – of all the people I met that year. University professors, medical consultants from hospitals, engineers and experts, Party cadres and non-Party cadres – they all said almost the same thing. I do not think that the eighty-nine professors, doctors, lecturers whom I would meet that year (there was a singular absence of writers – I was unable to meet even one) lied to me, I think it is true that they reckoned that their experience, however unpleasant, had 'cleansed' them. 'We did believe at the time, that we had indeed been arrogant and élitist ... and we were ready to reform ourselves.' This is what they say now. And I say to them, 'Of the dozens of your confessions which I took down, I have not published a single one. Other "outsiders", honoured guests, foreign friends, have written some very large books on what you said to them at the time. I have refrained. And now many of those who simply took down your words as truth feel angry; some feel cheated. But I know you have not lied. The human capacity for self-persuasion is infinite. The human soul is an assembly of contradictions. And therefore both your versions, the one of those years, and the one you give today, are correct.'

There had been great turmoil in the factories of Kuangtung province. 'Workers were fighting each other ... but Chairman Mao said: No division in the working class, so we promoted a grand alliance in September 1967', said the workers I interviewed. But not all the factories were working, and in those I saw, about one-third of the machinery was idle. When I pointed to the empty benches, I was told that the workers were 'resting', or that 'we have fulfilled our quotas for the month', which meant that the workers had not turned up, or that raw material for processing had run out, or that the machines needed repairing.

'Many activists from the working class have come up through the Cultural Revolution. It is important to rejuvenate the Party'. This meant that young workers were becoming Party members by the million. In fact, the Party would double its numbers from 1965 to 1975.

I was not impressed by the young workers. They dawdled and smoked in small groups in the workshops; they played basketball in the court-yards; they loafed on the streets. Only the older workers seemed to work – and how they worked! As if they had to make up for the sloth of the young.

A cut-down in the plethora of 'administrators' had occurred; everywhere their numbers had been reduced; and the remaining ones were supposed to do manual labour at least part of the week. This was the superficial pattern exhibited all over China's factories in 1969. However, there was a new kind of overstaffing. In a commune, I found that three hundred young Red Guards from middle school were assigned to look after two thousand apple trees – which makes less than seven trees per person. Did they have other chores? No, the apple orchard only ... They told me that they were educated youths of the working class who had decided to remain peasants all their lives. But they were only ten kilometres from the city, they all had bicycles, and they earned full salaries as commune members. 'The working class must lead in everything,' they said again and again; which meant that they probably were members of the commune revolutionary committee, and did very little labour. They were an added load on the back of the peasantry.

Primary schools had reopened nearly all over China, including Yunnan province, which had been badly battered by the Cultural Revolution. The middle schools were in the process of reopening, but the universities were still in 'struggle–criticism–transformation'. This in Chinese is tow,pee,gay, and pretty soon it became for me a verb to be conjugated: 'Have you been *tobegayed* yet?' 'They are *tobegaying*.'*

I saw a number of primary schools in seven provinces. In many instances the teachers were not willing to teach; they had been too humiliated. The admission age was raised to seven, and as a result everywhere in the lanes of the nine cities I visited that year there were children, children, playing under the eyes of bound-footed old grandmothers, waiting for the schools to admit them.

Soldiers were in charge in every school. In March 1967 Mao had given a directive that 'the army should give political and military training in the universities, middle schools and the higher classes of primary schools.' Often the army man was a retired veteran; he turned the school into a small military camp. The classes were called platoons, and they marched in step, they sang and they studied the little red book, which was everywhere. We all had it. We carried it as a talisman, waving it at each other in greeting; and as if they had just been interrupted in a fascinating, absorbed reading of it, some cadres kept a finger in its pages at all times.

One night, returning very late along an airport road, I watched a middle school being assembled; it was going down to the countryside where there was a drought, in order to help the peasants to water their fields. The soldiers ran along the huddled youngsters shouting orders. Then, to the regular sound of whistles, they marched off. The youngsters would form long chains, passing pails of water from hand to hand, for a kilometre or perhaps two or three, to reach those parched fields away from the canal or the river.

I thought that was good.

* A joke shared with the American-Chinese doctor, Ma Haiteh.

486

On the aeroplane to Peking the hostesses entertain us with songs about Mao. At the airport there is Hsing Chiang, resilient and neat; she does not adopt the scruffy, unkempt style (unpressed shirt, worn-out and patched trousers) some cadres do to show how 'revolutionary' they are. I admire Hsing Chiang because she is always plainly *herself*. She tells me that she too has been 'shocked and splashed', the butt of criticism and attacks.

I see Kung Peng the next afternoon. Oh, how awful she looks! So thin, so thin, almost skeletal, pale and ravaged, and her walk is unsteady. She has constant headaches, but she smiles that wonderful smile of hers, and I remember her great beauty; it comes back when she smiles.

'Yes, I've changed, but do not worry,' she says. 'Believe me, it was all most necessary.'

I do not reply, because I feel shocked. Calvary was also necessary, I suppose ... shall man only be redeemed through agony?

Kung Peng will not tell me what she has endured. But others do, bits here and there ... how she had to kneel for hours, submit to abuse ... how she has been for a year in a May 7 cadre school (which some people are calling 'cattle sheds' because Mao has said it),* and laboured planting rice ... how Chou Enlai, who meanwhile has been deprived of almost all his ministers and their staff, and his own staff, recalled her, for he has no one to help him.

With her came Hsiung, once Chargé d'Affaires in England. He had been attacked, during that mad summer of 1967, by some British 300 per centers. For both in China and abroad Western 'friends of China' — fortunately a minority — also went berserk. 'The situation is excellent,' they kept on repeating, having read it in *Peking Review*. They wore enormous Mao badges, and in London they wrote posters against Hsiung as a 'revisionist' (or was it 'capitalist roader'?). The person who indulged most in these antics, however, is still going to China and is an 'expert' much valued in some circles. Hsiung brushed aside the whole matter. 'A communist must be able to endure any hardship ... He must never exact personal revenge. He must ignore the small things ... what are these trials compared to humanity's sufferings through the ages?' I have great affection for Hsiung. Under a cold exterior, he has a warm heart and a good brain.

The Temple of Heaven was being cleaned by schoolchildren; Peking's railway station too. Large posters announced that old monuments must be respected. Vandalized shrines and parks were being repaired and

* Labour camps for cadres, to reform them through work and study.

protected by Red Guards. 'We are taking youth in hand.' The most common sight that summer was the busloads of youngsters of about seventeen or eighteen, with red flags and drums, being taken away to the countryside. With them were cadres and of course army men. Two hundred thousand youths would leave Peking that year for state farms, communes and the new army resettlement farms sited in thinly populated regions such as Sinkiang and North Manchuria.

'We are still unmasking hidden class enemies,' says Hsing Chiang, 'counter-revolutionaries.' But now the term, from being so constantly used, has lost all meaning. I ask about Pa Chin, the writer. 'He's been labelled counter-revolutionary.' So has Lao Sheh ... so has ... oh, so many of the writers I know.

There are two kinds of 'counter.' The ones who are 'straight counter' and the others, who 'wave the red flag to knock down the red flag', a tortuous phrase which means that they are the ultra-left, and have been, in the name of Mao and the Revolution, killing people and raiding arsenals for weapons. 'Chairman Mao ordered a thorough investigation into the May 16 groups.' But members of May 16 contingents have run away, to Szechuan, and also to Hongkong. The hunt against them is conducted by the very same people who brought them into being. As a result, people who are *not* May 16ers are being arrested by genuine but unknown May 16ers! My Mongol cousin by marriage, he of the splendid voice – a voice which shook the window panes of the room where we sat in 1964 – becomes a victim of this deadly masquerade, and will spend three years in jail, where he will catch tuberculosis. He will be rescued in 1972 by Chou Enlai. But it will be 1977 before he will tell me what has happened to him. I meet the son of my dear friend Yeh in front of the Western District supermarket.

'How are your father and mother?'

'They are well.'

'Give them my regards.'

I stride quickly away. I do not want him to be interrogated: 'Why were you talking to this outsider? Who is she?' Neither do I go to see Yeh and Yuan Yin, his wife, although I love them well.

Yeh would thank me for my discretion when in 1971 I make bold to go to his house. But it was not before the end of 1976, when the Gang of Four were brought down, that Yeh would tell me of his ordeal, and with so much laughter and mimicry of his tormentors that we all roared and had an excellent evening.

Yeh was not 'counter-revolutionary' but he was a 'bourgeois', had 'followed the black line', so he was 'struggled against' in his own office by young Red Guards and his own subalterns. He had to stand in the corridor leading to his office for hours, clean toilets and run errands, and always be available for 'criticism sessions'.

Yet since no one else in the office was competent enough to edit the English language magazine, *Chinese Literature*, the better translators being under duress, Yeh still had to do the work on his small typewriter: translating, editing, putting the magazine together, in between bouts of being abused, having to clean the toilets, and performing other menial tasks. For almost five years, Yeh smiled, and endured, and put out the magazine, competently, on time.

'They would find fault with everything, but finally they would print it.'

'Did they beat you?'

Yeh laughs, looks at his wife, and I guess he has not told her everything. 'Only a few slaps here and there,' says he, 'and of course pulling my hair. They loved pulling people's hair.'

'Every night I went to the bus stop to wait for him,' says Yuan Yin. 'I never knew whether, one night, he would not be on any bus. Sometimes he would only manage the last bus, after midnight.'

But as soon as he was home Yeh would shake his shoulders, laugh a little and say, 'Just another day.' After some food he would settle down and write. His major novel, written in those nights, was published in China in 1979.

'You know,' Yeh says to me, 'I did not hate these childish people. I pitied them. They were so helpless. While they shouted at me, sometimes I could not stop laughing, and it made them angry.' We laugh, we are hilarious, but in our hearts is sadness. Not for us, but for the young who have become a lost generation.

Treading softly, I trod into the panorama of China in 1969; fearful of bringing trouble and sorrow to my friends and to my Family. I could not go to Szechuan that year. It was 'inconvenient'. I guessed that sporadic fighting or at least some turmoil must still be going on.

A film on the Ninth Congress of April 1969, when Lin Piao was officially designated Mao's heir, is shown. I see Chen Yi among the delegates. Mao insisted that he be there; Chen Yi is so thin, so thin ... already he is suffering from the cancer which will kill him. Chou Enlai too is thin; his face is undecipherable. I will learn (rumour?) that when the new constitution which proclaims Lin Piao as Mao's heir was taken for general discussion at all levels, Chou Enlai recommended, 'Do not discuss it too much; let it pass ... ' Why did he give this advice (if it is true that he did)? I think that Chou wanted an end to the chaos and dislocation harming China. Perhaps he felt he could work out something with Lin Piao. The key to Chou's immortality is that he was able to work even with the devil, and extract some good out of him ... He never lost sight of the main goal: China and the Chinese people.

The Directorate under Chiang Ching and Chen Pota, which had seemingly become the supreme command in 1967, has evanesced, it is no longer mentioned. It never recovered from the blow Mao gave it in September 1967 when five of its eighteen or nineteen members were arrested as 'ultra-leftists'. And now there is a new Central Committee and a new Politburo. The Central Committee is heavily loaded with peasants and workers, and also army men. Three of the four of the future Gang of Four, Chiang Ching, Chang and Yao, are on the Central Committee and in the Politburo. And so is Yeh Chun, Lin Piao's wife. But Mao has also brought back the old Long Marchers, Chu Teh, and Yeh Chienying and Li Hsiennien, and in the Military Affairs' Commission, three old stalwarts to 'balance' Lin Piao and his forceful commander in the south, Huang Yungsheng. Lin Piao's ascendancy, the fact that his men are everywhere, is obvious. But rumour notices that Yeh Chun and Chiang Ching are not as friendly as they used to be.

The *People's Daily* carries a portrait of Mao on its front page every day, and a quotation from the little red book. As a result, it is quite impossible to throw away or to tear up a newspaper without being disrespectful. All stamps carry his head too. I affix a stamp askew and am told off by the post office comrade. 'The stamp is crooked,' she says. Her mind, trained to symbolism, may see in this a deliberate insult to Mao. And perhaps Freud would agree with her. Actually I am so dizzy with the constant propaganda that I become absent-minded and my eyes do not focus well. In the hotel post office an army man sits. He will examine every letter posted at the end of the day. To make his work easier, I only write postcards.

I visit the six Peking factories specially mentioned for their excellent revolutionary behaviour. Many of their workers, both men and women, are delegates or members of revolutionary committees in the capital. Some have become members of the Central Committee. One of these factories is the Hsinhua News Agency Printing Press. I spend some hours there; the workers talk very well; they give me a full account of how, on July 27th, 1968, they invested Tsinghua University to stop the Red Guard factions entrenched there from battering each other to death. 'Some workers were killed, although they carried no weapons ... There were corpses in the dormitories.'

For their success, they have received a mango from Chairman Mao (who had been given mangoes by the Pakistan government). The mango is enthroned upon a table in preserving liquid, in a beribboned glass tank. I would visit several other factories in China honoured with a mango.

Everywhere Liu Shaochi was excoriated for 'seventeen years of a black revisionist line'. But surely not everything had been badly done in the seventeen years from 1949 to 1966? How otherwise justify the Revolution and its achievements? 'But the bourgeois line was dominant' is the reply. It was not so. But it is impossible to argue without being accused of 'defending the capitalist roaders'.

'The renegade and scab Liu Shaochi pushed material incentives in all our factories.' There is great reprobation of material incentives, but in the twenty-five factories I visit that year, I find that the question of salaries and wages is *not* settled; that remuneration 'to each according to his work', with better workers receiving more, is still being made. 'The wage scale here varies from 40 to 107 dollars,' say the Hsinhua Printing Press workers. They add, 'But what we must fight for is not money, but power. The working class must lead in everything.' This last phrase is the title of an article written by Yao Wenyuan. It has become a major study pamphlet for the whole Party. After 1976 the pamphlet will be denounced as part of the conspiracy of the Gang of Four to seize power, by organizing in factories and among workers nuclei of their own supporters.

Dinner with Kung Peng and her husband Chiao, and Hsiung, his wife and daughter. The daughter, who is sixteen, is a very charming girl. She has been a year at a state farm in Heilungkiang province. Her middle school had volunteered to 'go down' to serve the people, and she and a few other girls, refused because of their youth, had written petitions in blood, obtained by nicking their little fingers. They were allowed to go. This practice is traditional; petitions to authority written in blood indicate their seriousness. The young girl entertains us with stories of her resettlement farm. She describes a bear hunt. 'In Europe and America, do people my age do manual labour?' she asks.

'We have to sacrifice ourselves for the next generation.' Chiao looks worn out, gaunt, his jaw juts, his hands shake. He was so badly beaten that he vomited blood (he has an old tuberculous lesion). Everyone praises his fortitude, and courage.

'The young are showing an excellent spirit,' says Kung Peng. Her son and her daughter are labouring in communes. None of the children of higher ranking officials that year are in universities or high schools. Only after 1972 would some of them be able to return to study.

When I left, I felt that I had been in an after-hurricane stillness, in that exhalation of air emptied at last of fury. The survivors had calmly contemplated the hurricane's work, and now there was the rebuilding to do.

When I went to Hualan's house, the whole street turned out to watch me ring her bell. This had not happened before.

Hualan's nephew and niece were in communes. Her nephew guarded walnut trees in a production team. Had he belonged to the village, which of course was a clan village (as 95 per cent of China's villages are), he would not have had this job. 'Because he is not a clan member he can refuse to give the walnuts to the peasants who ask for them.' Otherwise, he could not have refused anyone, not even a child.

'Six to eight educated youths is all a production team can bear. More are not wanted. They have to share the workpoints, and the peasants don't like it.' All youngsters received from the government some 30 *yuan* to start them off; but many of them were unable to make enough workpoints through labour to feed themselves.

Hualan seemed distracted; her eyes unfocussed, her fingers brown with smoking. There were many things she would not tell me. 'I cannot ... I cannot.' We went for walks because her neighbour, who lived in the same courtyard, a man in his forties', had taken it upon himself to come into the living room and stand there watching us and listening. I would not have minded it, had it not been that, owing to the heat, he was in his underpants. 'It's mutual supervision,' said Hualan calmly, and of course we showed no concern. We simply ignored his standing two feet away from me. On one occasion when we went for a walk, since he was in his underwear, he could not follow. He gave up trying after that.

'If I told you everything and you let slip something, I would be in much trouble,' said Hualan.

'I never betray ... I'm like a clam.'

But Hualan was not reassured.

Hualan's brother was in charge of aeroplane engines at the airport. He had been *tobegayed* so much, dragged to so many meetings, that for a while he exhibited signs of mental imbalance. But he went on with his work, for aeroplanes had to be kept flying. For some years I would supply him with needed medicine. Thus he endured; and now he is well, completely normal, and talks with gusto and triumph of the painful years, as if they had been his private conquest, a victory. 'Now I shall never be afraid of anything, or anyone,' says he. And so many, so many people, young, and middle-aged, and old, will say the same thing to me in the years to come.

But other relatives of Hualan have died; two of them, husband and wife, committing suicide. They were called traitors; accused of 'collusion with the outside', beaten ... It is quite a miracle that Hualan was not ill-treated because of me. 'But I was asked about you and I said, "She loves China, as I do". And Premier Chou Enlai protected me because of my father. So I was only criticized.' And her mother was never persecuted at all. The old lady became gently senile. She never left the house, and blissfully did not know what was happening.

I walked the small lanes of Peking, with their many odours and their blind grey look and that seeping wonderful silver dust, and the all-seeing eyes behind their walls. I tried not to look inquisitive. But in every street, immediately, children ran to announce my coming to the street committee, and people came to stare at me. Spy mania. I walked purposefully, looking straight ahead.

I did manage to see my sister-in-law Jui. Her hands shook. Soon her hair would start to drop. Third Brother, her husband, had been sent to a 'branch' of Peking University in Hanchung district, on the borders of Shensi, Szechuan and Kansu provinces.

Every university had established branches, or teaching points, in rural areas. This was a very good idea; but they were also accessory relegation sites, where the staff were to 'study' and to reform themselves. In Hanchung, Third Brother, for the space of three years, was employed as a cook's helper. With good grace he fetched and carried water in pails from the distant well. He stoked up the fire, he kept it going with a primitive wind blower; he set the tables (a canteen for three hundred), cleaned and swept the mess hall, washed the crockery. He also had to revise some physics textbooks. But the students of Hanchung would not study. 'To study is too dangerous ... you get into trouble if you are learned,' they said, having seen what had happened to the intelligentsia.

Third Brother is himself a good cook. Like my father, he has a light, deft hand with dishes.

'Please, please,' said Jui and her children – my three nieces and my nephew, all back from the communes – 'Please, Auntie, please bring our father back to us.'

But I knew that it was impossible to bring him back immediately. I must be circumspect. I must sense the time when it would be possible for him to return. Jui had always been incapable of understanding politics. 'I will do something as soon as possible,' I said. Finally it was out of my hands, but Third Brother was back by 1970 ...

The eminent physicist, Chou Peiyuan, trained in America, received me in his house. He was co-operating gracefully with the workers and the army Mao Tsetung Thought team which had taken over Peking University in July 1968. Bloody war between Red Guard factions, as in Tsinghua University, had happened there. He agreed with a great deal of what the Cultural Revolution had done, but he stood adamant on fundamental research. 'We must go on with it,' said he. This was a point which Chou Enlai had also constantly supported, as he supported so many progressive and at the time unpopular issues (including mixed marriages, which still today provoke reactions from many cadres of the Party).

But the so-called 'Left', that is, Lin Piao and later the Gang of Four, were opposed to fundamental research, dubbing it 'metaphysical, abstract', which in the Marxist vocabulary is heinous condemnation. In 1958 the Leap had also derided research scientists 'who count the dots on the wing of a fly instead of doing something useful for the country'. It was extremely difficult to explain, especially because the Chinese language is so poor in *abstract* terms, that research unrelated to any obvious, immediate need was important; that the greatest discoveries had been due to hazard, accidents of man's inquisitiveness; that the process of experimentation with no immediate gain in view, only to satisfy a thirst for inquiry, could not be denied.

Peking University was preparing its new intake for 1970. According to Chou Peiyuan, it would be mostly from the worker–peasant–soldier background; selected not by examinations but by merit, the approval of the masses.

This seemed a good idea, promoting progress at grassroots level. But alas, like so many other excellent ideas of the Cultural Revolution it went awry in performance. Doing away with past injustice, that is, the favouring of the offspring of the intelligentsia and higher cadres through examinations, only created another injustice of a different kind, because of China's peculiar, all-encompassing, feudalism. Pretty soon, only the sons and daughters of *new* cadres – those who had taken the place of the old officials now relegated to inactivity or to the May 7 cadre schools – would be admitted to the universities; because 'the masses', whose 'approval' was paramount, would not dare to disapprove the selection of the children of new cadres.

> When there's any problem, pass the matter
> up and up to your superior,
> In any circumstance, see how the wind blows,
> And never, never, stick your neck out.

The old adage, the old doggerel, still held in China. I don't know where I got it from; but it's in my notes of that year.

I went to see Rewi Alley. He had a tail.

A security policeman, nice and young, was with him all day and every day, wherever he went. And at night he slept in Rewi's apartment.

'Oh, Rewi.' We three sat in the living room. The security chap sat some distance away, discreet and courteous.

Rewi told me that he had been accused of all sorts of things. 'Not by the Chinese, Suyin, but by my so-called friends.' The 300 percenters. Had this been done by the Chinese, it would be understandable. But what insanity befell the Westerners who thus ill-treated one of the greatest, staunchest and most useful men in China?

'Not one of my friends except Ma Haiteh and Hans Miller comes to see me now,' said Rewi, quickly wiping away a tear on his sleeve. He was shunned. He had not been allowed for some months to go to the hospital to have his skin looked at (he suffered from skin lesions), until Chou Enlai heard of the ignoble ill-treatment meted to Rewi and ordered that he go to the hospital.

'Rewi, come and have dinner with me at the Peking Hotel.'

I could not think of anything else I could do for him; except to be with him – and his tail of course – in a public restaurant.

After dinner we walked arm in arm. He missed not being able to travel. Usually he spent August at the seaside in Peitaiho. But that year – and until 1972 – he would not be allowed to go to Peitaiho.

'There's been a good deal of suffering … there always is in a revolution … now the emphasis must be on discipline. It's difficult to get people to work with each other again after they've shouted and hurled accusations at each other, and made up stories about each other.'

Rewi would not tell me until some years later that his two adopted sons had been badly mistreated. One of them was cruelly beaten: he endured eighty separate beating sessions. Rewi tried hard not to cry. 'Well, one thing can be said: Where there's life there's hope.' Survival. All China believes in survival ...

Of course, Rewi made me promise not to say a word about his tail. 'It won't do any good, lass. Only sensationalism for the Western press ... Chinese problems have to be settled in China by the Chinese themselves.'

The Cultural Revolution had also done a great deal of good, said Rewi, The school and the hospital had definitely been brought to the country-side now. There was an outburst of 'minds beginning to function'. People discussed and there was a feeling that 'government was now down among the grassroots'. There was enthusiasm and energy and audacity.

I concurred. I had felt it. Whatever the misuse of 'mass democracy', there was a stir, vibration palpable among ordinary people, beyond the pretences and the propaganda. Something alive. 'It is not possible to create such an upheaval, an explosion of *all* accepted ways, and not finally to shake up, to wake up, a good many people, out of passivity,' said Rewi.

'Do go to see Anna-Louise. She's a bit upset,' he added as we parted.

'Can you tell me what really happened during the Cultural Revolution?' said Anna-Louise to me.

She was not the only person to ask me what was happening. Until 1975 there would be people living in China who would ask me to explain events to them. I am not surprised. Americans in America do not necessarily know how their country's actions are viewed abroad, what is the impact of what they are doing. Witness the Vietnam war. And I believe the German people when they say that they were not informed about the death camps for the Jews. It is entirely possible that many knew nothing about it. 'Beans sizzling in the frying pan do not see the fire that makes them jump,' says a Chinese proverb.

Anna-Louise was upset; not only because Sidney Rittenberg, an American resident in China who had taken her up and down China with him to meet 'revolutionary Red Guards' and to promote Chiang Ching and her acolytes, was now in jail, but also because Nieh Yuantzu, the lecturer who had started the Cultural Revolution in Peking University, was now under arrest for corruption, appropriation of state funds and inciting violence. How could Anna-Louise explain this sudden reversal of roles and reputations to American readers of her 'Letter from China'?

In the desert: at Tunhuang with, *left*, Chang Jingerh, *centre left*, Chang Ying, and two students of archaeology

With Premier Chou Enlai in 1972

With Teng Yingchao, Chou Enlai's wife, in 1972

With Vice-Premier Teng Hsiaoping and Madame Teng Yingchao, 1977

Meeting Defence Minister Yeh Chienying in 1977; *in the centre*, Chairman Hua Kuofeng

Appearing on television in Peking in 1978

Something else troubled her. Her brother had not been allowed to come to China to visit her. 'I don't understand. I'm not all that young ... I haven't seen my brother for years. If only I could see Mao and explain it to him.' Anna-Louise's faith, her reputation, were based on the interviews and meetings she had had with Mao so freely for so many years.

But Anna-Louise was a great American. She straightened her shoulders, and there were no tears in her eyes, only in her voice. 'Well, no use moaning. I suppose that's that, we've all got to make some sacrifices for a good cause.'

I stayed a long time with her, many hours, and she told me a great deal about her life, which I shall not relate.

'I'll go crazy if I see one more Mao religious service,' said Richard Hung to me.

Richard Hung was an overseas Chinese who had given up everything, a wealthy family, a brilliant career, to return to China. He had laboured in the communes for two years during the socialist education movement. To keep fit he jogged a mile or two in the early morning, and thus had come upon a dawn ceremony – a courtyard full of people swinging their bodies in ecstasy in front of a large portrait of Mao Tsetung.

This was the morning invocation, asking Chairman Mao for directives: rocking of the body, chanting, dancing with 'offer hearts', gestures, calling upon Mao, in a litany of praise ('great, great, great') for his orders for the day. Then there was the opening of the little red book, and the quotation on the page fallen upon was *the* answer. Every night, they assembled again to 'report to Chairman Mao' on their day, their work, their thoughts.

'It's like the Holy Rollers and consulting the Bible for answers and the Moral Rearmament People who speak to God,' said Richard. He did not think he could put up with it any longer.However, being Chinese, he had a long fuse, and waited, patient and enduring. And by the end of 1971, no more such 'services' were being held.

By some feat of magic, I have acquired an interdicted item, Lin Piao's own little red book, quotations of the Crown Prince's imperishable 'thoughts'. It is only circulated among higher cadres; but somehow I have purloined one. It is not very interesting or revealing, and I wonder why it is a state secret. I open it. 'In all things obey orders. I obey Chairman Mao, whether I understand him or not.'

I return it to the person I stole it from, who never noticed its absence, or its return.

There are two 'voices' in the newspaper. Sometimes a burst of articles and editorials: 'Down with foreign slave study ... criticize foreign slavishness,' and a recrudescence of criticism of unfortunates such as Chou Yang, and scholars and professors; and then another voice: 'There must be reasonable rules and regulations in running industries', 'Too much anarchism is bad for the revolution.' The strongest plea of all in 1969 is for the return of intellectuals and old cadres to responsible positions. Already in September 1967 Mao had emphasized that the majority of intellectuals 'can be re-educated ... and should be welcomed ... ' but the last phrase, 'should be welcomed', has been strangely left out in the *People's Daily*. Why? Also Mao's view that 90 per cent of the cadres are good is left out ... Why?

Articles about the squandering and the outrageous privileges arbitrarily seized by the 'revolutionaries' have appeared. There are cases of their taking their families and friends on great jaunts, at government expense, to Shanghai to have a good time. Some have occupied not only the mansions of former national-capitalists, but also state buildings and schools ... it will take years before they are dislodged.

Ma Haiteh tells me that everything in the rural areas is in a state of flux; all relations between the production team, brigade and commune are being reassessed; the book-keeping method of reckoning workpoints, and remunerations. But old marriage habits and funeral habits have returned. 'Once control is loosened, the past returns damn quick.' There is already usury, and bartering of brides. And by 1975 I shall find that infanticide of female children has returned in some areas.

'The old officials may have had defects, but they were competent,' says Ma. 'Everyone is hoping that they will soon return ... but how will they work, cheek by jowl, with their persecutors, the new cadres? The latter will certainly glue themselves to their new desks, their easy chairs ... after all, it is a matter of the rice bowl.' The result will be an even larger inflation of the ranks of administrative cadres.

The Peis, my overseas Chinese friends who came back at the wrong time, have a very nice flat. But Mr Pei and his daughter Millie have no work to do (Mr Pei, is however, paid a salary by the government). Hsing Chiang, always kind, exerts herself and within a year something is found for Millie. Her father gets a job in 1971.

The Peis praise the 8341 army division, the one which guards the top leaders in Peking. In 1968, the 8341 began to 'clean up' the ultra-left and the May 16 storm troopers. 'A very nice young soldier came to us and asked us what were our grievances. We told him, and he wrote it all down. He was a country lad, and so pure! He even had the windows fixed for us, and he came regularly, to ask what we needed.' The Peis were gradually soothed; their anxiety left them. But when I said that Millie should keep a diary of these extraordinary days, the three looked at me as if I were mad. 'You could hide it,' I suggested. 'There is no way one can hide anything,' said Millie.

In Tientsin, in a dozen factories the Cultural Revolution has promoted women – many women workers, women in the revolutionary committees: 20 to 28 per cent. There is great praise of Chiang Ching, who has called for at least 30 per cent of women in administrative roles. My heart warms to her.

But when I go back to Tientsin in late 1974, my impression will be somewhat different from that of 1969. I shall then realize that Tientsin is one of the 'bases' of the Gang of Four, and especially of Madame Mao, and that women are being used to hoist her to power.

At the Tientsin watch factory the workers say that 'to hold power there must be rigorous self-discipline, frugality, sacrifice ... ' Where the scheme fails is that the young workers do not exhibit any discipline. I find dozens of them loafing about in the park with their girl friends; one is boasting loudly, 'The foreman comrade tells me: You're late. So what? I say. And I just walk out.' In one milk powder factory, my guides and I are clad in sterile white gowns and boots, but a young worker walks in without changing and spits on the floor, and no one says a word.

The Tientsin Third Wool Mill used to belong to the Sun family, capitalists who left China in 1953. It is the mill where Liu Shaochi perpetrated his 'treachery'. Old workers tell me about it; they witnessed the scene. In 1950 Liu toured the mill and encouraged the owner, saying, 'You have opened factories for the good of the workers ... capitalism is good ... exploitation is not a bad thing ... I hope you exploit a bit more ... '

I can scarcely believe this, but letters from Liu to Sun, encouraging him to go on producing, are exhibited. In Liu's defence, it could be said that at the time it was Party policy to go slow, to allow, under strict control, capitalism, in order to keep industry going. After all, in that same year, 1950, Mao had approved the 'rich peasant' policy. But this is not the point.

The workers are indignant that Liu was so deferential, so obsequious to the capitalist owner. Perhaps Liu as a Marxist theoretician felt that China could not leap from her semi-feudal state to socialism without a transition period of controlled capitalism. But I agree with Mao, and disagree with Liu. Once launched into capitalism, no one could govern China's future, and there would be no relief, only redoubled misery and horror, for China's majority population: the peasantry. China had to go crashing forward, stumbling and experimenting and suffering, but not giving up her attempt to accelerate historical progress. China could not give up her socialist revolution, or the inspiration of a better world of equality and justice, for then all the downtrodden people in the world would be compromised.

'We found a traitor here,' say the workers of a tool plant. 'He entered the Communist Party in 1945 and joined the Kuomintang in 1946.' The Tientsin bicycle factory has discovered so many 'Kuomintang agents' among its top echelons that it is baffling how it could have been so successful. Tientsin bicycles are in large demand all over north China.

A play is shown in Tientsin; a young girl, paralysed for eighteen years, is now able to walk after acupuncture treatment by the P.L.A. doctors. 'For seventeen years the bourgeois line in medicine did nothing for me.' This is the punch line: nothing was done in China about health until the Cultural Revolution! It is patently untrue. I know that great epidemics have been quelled; that venereal disease has been eradicated, that schistosomiasis has been tackled (Mao even wrote a poem praising the work done on schistosomiasis in 1956). On the contrary, after 1974, and owing to the dislocation in control, medical statistics show that malaria has returned, that tuberculosis figures are climbing, that schistosomiasis is also beginning again to spread extensively.

Acupuncture is certainly in fashion, used intensively by army medical personnel. In Tientsin, Shanghai, Harbin, I visit deaf and dumb schools. All claim that 'cure' or at least improvement for deafness is due to acupuncture treatment. The man in charge of the Tientsin school is thirty, and deaf; his tongue was stuck down with non-use, and the army doctor 'cut the bond which held down my tongue'. He speaks in the loud, uninflected voice of the deaf.

The school has its workshops; the deaf make musical instruments. 'We also give open-air concerts, singing and dancing recitals; people like it.' The deaf and dumb sing and dance for me and I am moved to tears, for they are joyful, glowing with the quiet pride of achievement. 'We are no longer handicapped. Thanks to Chairman Mao, we are equal to those who have ears.'

The harvests are excellent (they have been superb for three years). Wang Fongchun, member of the Tientsin Municipality Revolutionary Committee, delegate to the Ninth Congress, is head of the Siyuying commune, and he tells me a curious story. 'We were in the hands of a woman named Chang. She was backed by Liu Shaochi and Chou Yang. [Why Chou Yang? He explains: Chou Yang came to do his manual labour here during the socialist education movement of 1964.] Then Comrade Chen Pota came here. He discovered that the Chang woman was a black marketeer. He could tell she was no good merely by shaking her hand. She had a soft hand, the skin velvety. "Not the hand of a true worker," warned Comrade Chen Pota. We discovered a cache of money in her house.'

Truth? Lies? There is everywhere a frothy oedema of language, over-bidding, adjectival, inflated. I was so perplexed by this story that I wrote it up for *Eastern Horizon*, but only at the end of 1970. And Tsungying told me that it was not *wise* to print the story, because Chen Pota was now in trouble.

I think at times of the woman Chang and her soft, moist, velvety handshake. She must now be back, recognized as a true comrade, while Chen Pota (and perhaps also Wang Fongchun) are down?

Walking in a universe of slogans – 'The general situation is excellent ... We are purifying the class ranks ... It is a great victory for Mao Tsetung Thought' – I become impervious to the babble of tremendous conviction. Words do create a world, especially when not all the words are nonsense. Undoubtedly, good things have been done. But the mind suddenly becomes a sieve, only letting through what will please it.

In all the factories posters for discipline and quality blossom. 'Red Alert Guards', vigilante corps, appear, to see to it that work is properly done, that workers adhere to discipline: 'Too many machines broken ... Too many young workers not observing rules ... '

At Hopei University there were fifty-two professors and 121 lecturers, most of them 'from the old society'. Here moral decapitation has had great effect. 'The students go into the countryside to be re-educated by the peasantry, uproot their ideas of becoming wealthy and famous through education ... ' Seventeen professors and lecturers, plus the revolutionary committee (consisting of the Mao Tsetung Thought propaganda team of workers and army men) receive me. The team assures me that the policy towards intellectuals is not harshness, but 'to relieve them of their heavy load of anxiety and unease by liberating their minds of old ideas'. One by one the professors speak, uncovering their 'burden of guilt', accusing themselves of bourgeois thought, promising from henceforth zealous attention to the will of the masses.

'We inculcated in our young students ideas of fame and wealth; they had pictures of Madame Curie, Einstein and Pushkin on their walls.'

I murmur that Curie, Einstein and Pushkin were not particularly wealthy.

'I repressed young students from worker and peasant stock: From your handwriting I can tell you are stupid, I said.' This from one eminent consultant.

I indeed know that there was favouritism in the universities, that examinations did weigh the scales heavily against workers and peasants. For the intelligentsia, and the offspring of high cadres, had favoured backgrounds; books at home, leisure to study. Very often a worker or peasant youth did not even have a table of his own to write on, and certainly no room or even a bed of his own. 'We sometimes deliberately created handicaps for the workers' and peasants' children.' The intake of the latter in universities, which had risen to 70 per cent in 1960, had fallen back to 38 per cent by 1963.

A grudge of the young lecturers comes out: 'An old professor could never be moved ... there was no place for the young. No one dared to contradict an old teacher ... there was never any argument or debate.'

Now the handicaps which fettered worker-peasant-soldier offspring must be rectified. Special preparatory classes will be set up in every university to prepare 'the next intake', so that they will be able to follow the courses.

I visit Manchuria again. In Shenyang, the capital city of Liaoning province, the walls of factories are pock-marked with traces of bullets. Gaunt roofless structures reach upward, as after a bombing. There is litter, and cinders; burnt down plants. Here many 'foreign' things (which also means industrial) have suffered attempted destruction; and the army has been busy rounding up malefactors.

The revolutionary committee of a large plant has discovered 'Kuomintang spies and agents' among the managerial staff. Since most of the managers and chief technicians in Manchuria date back to pre-Liberation days, this is not surprising. 'Some of them are patriots. They could have run away but they did not,' I venture to say. 'We have evidence. They were spies' is the reply.

Throughout my Manchurian travels I was not left alone, except at night in my bedroom. Even if I went to the toilet, in some factories and communes, a girl worker would come along with me, and watch me.

Everywhere girls of twenty-two or twenty-three seem to be 'in charge'. 'Old people are all bourgeois,' they say (I am old too). Is this also a revolt against parental authority? Would psychologists one day analyse the Cultural Revolution as a catharsis, liberation from a phenomenal Oedipus complex? Crudely it is also a mighty scramble for jobs now available to the young, jobs which the old and middle-aged held to so tenaciously. The young now fill them, who otherwise would be drafted down to labour in villages. I am told that a delegate from Manchuria to the Ninth Congress was a girl nineteen years old. It becomes clear to me that Manchuria is a bastion of the 'Left'. I hear the name of Mao Yuanhsing, Mao's nephew. Trained in Harbin as an engineer and become a Red Guard faction leader, he is now vice-chairman of the Revolutionary Committee of Liaoning Province. Everyone expected him to become a member of the Standing Committee of the Central Committee at the Ninth Congress, but his uncle Mao Tsetung always has refused him. (He will refuse again to back his nephew at the Tenth Congress in 1973.)

But Mao Yuanhsing is 'very close to the centre'. This phrase means that he is often in Peking, allegedly to see Mao. Everyone knows, however, in the grapevine Chinese way, that it is his aunt, Chiang Ching, whom he goes to see. He has been her 'son by affection' since 1963. But he returns to Manchuria, haloed with the name of Mao, and what he says is believed to represent Mao Tsetung Thought.

Now I understand why my meeting with 'activists' in 1966 was so significant. They represented the Lin Piao–Chiang Ching alliance.

Wen Chuming, the ex-school teacher I saw in 1966, is now high on the city's revolutionary committee. She accompanies me, a signal honour. She tells me of her suffering at the hands of the work teams of Liu Shaochi, who paraded her with a big dunce's cap and held 'struggle meetings' against her. 'But my own students lay down in front of the truck and would not let it pass.' She was jailed: 'they threw excrement on me; they would not let me wash ... '

The story is almost the same on both sides.

Commander Liu Tetsai, the army representative in this area, is a short, bullet-headed man. He tells me of the rounding up of Red Guards 'misled' into committing 'crimes'.

I am lodged in a palatial mansion surrounded by a beautiful park. Behind us are the hills with the graves of the Manchu dynasty emperors ensconced among their folds. The bright morning sun woke me and I went running in the park, but immediately, from nowhere and everywhere, people join me and start running.

The steel plant of Anshan has been badly mauled. Large machinery sprawls in despair on the ground, surrounded by squatting workers trying to repair it. In one of the workshops grey-haired people work at lathes: previous administrators: 'All our cadres are doing manual labour to extricate their minds from the capitalist roader line.'

The facility of articulate expression among the workers (how they talked! I filled seven notebooks) was remarkable. They possessed relentless loquacity. This is a feature noticeable among many adherents of Chiang Ching and her group, both male and female.

At the Institute of Engineering a worker's son told me how corrupted he had become. 'I wanted to be a top engineer and to have a bright future. My parents wanted me to become an official.' Now he only thought of serving the people. But he was a Red Guard delegate and would certainly become a cadre. Eight hundred thousand youths had gone down to the countryside in this province alone, to 're-educate themselves with peasants in manual labour.'

At the Shenyang Medical College, almost everyone was still being re-educated. In teams, they went down to rural areas; searching for Chinese herbal remedies, they experimented upon themselves in acupuncture. 'We were arrogant ... we had no feeling for the sick.' Now, through inflicting pain upon their own bodies, they understood how careful they must be. Having watched some heartless colleagues in many countries, I thought it a very good idea.

I interviewed a dozen impressively articulate Red Guard delegates. They had travelled to the border to comfort the militia who had fought in the Russian border invasion in January. I went to the hospital to see a wounded P.L.A. soldier, seventeen years old, shot in the abdomen. 'The Russians fired on us ... the tops of trees were broken by their artillery. My platoon commander brought me back ... ' He was reading a book in bed.

Educated city youths now transferred to the army resettlement camps on the borders were being trained as militia. 'They will form a solid rearguard of people for our army on the borders.'

One of the Red Guards I met was a young girl of eighteen. 'Although I am of peasant stock, my ideas had changed in the city. "Three years of manual labour and you'll be back in the city," was Liu Shaochi's promise to us, as if the villages were to remain doomed places, purgatory for ever! But we shall never advance if we don't have educated teachers, doctors, book-keepers, technicians for agricultural mechanization. Consolidation of our system must come from below.' This girl and another Red Guard present, a boy named Kao, would accompany Yao Wenyuan on a trip to Albania.

I go to the Tsienchangpu brigade, a two-day motor car trip, stopping at Penghsi, an industrial city, for a night.

Tsao Yulan, twenty-three, a delegate from the brigade to the Ninth Congress, comes to Penghsi to welcome me. Again I wonder: How many delegates 'from below', young boys and girls, were at the Ninth Congress? And was it by their votes that the Central Committee members were chosen? How did they know whom to vote for?

Accompanying me is a tall, handsome P.L.A. commander. He tells me that the delegations from the communes and factories went to Peking under army care ... everything is becoming clear. The youths have been selected by the army, and here it means Lin Piao.

Tsienchangpu was a backward area, very unproductive 'because Liu Shaochi's black line prevailed here'. The brigade used only to grow ginseng on the mountain slopes (I can see the paler patches where it was planted). 'We did not grow any grain. Every year the state had to supply us with grain.' Ginseng makes money, far more money than grain. 'Now we grow grain.' However, I shall not spoil the landscape with unsavoury remarks.

The brigade consists of Koreans and Han people. Manchuria has many such mixed population communes. In 1968 the army came to the brigade and started to run classes in Mao Tsetung Thought. Of course there was 'a startling change'. Now every child is at school; teams of girls work in the fields; the brigade not only grows maize and sorghum to feed itself, but it also makes more money than before.

It is undoubtedly a well-off brigade. Nestled in a beautiful valley, the houses are of brick, and neat. But the valley floor which grows maize is filled with stones from the usual erupting, uncontrolled stream. The stones have to be sieved out by hand.

The most beautiful girl I have ever seen in my life lives in Tsienchangpu brigade. Her name is Sun Chinglan, Golden Orchid, and she was in 1969 a barefoot doctor. She was seventeen years old. I inspected Sun's clinic, neat and well kept. She really knew a good deal of medicine, for I questioned her thoroughly. 'You've passed my examination,' I said. Everyone clapped. Thanks to Golden Orchid, almost 80 per cent of the village women had been taught contraception. The tall and handsome P.L.A. commander who accompanied me was obviously head over heels in love with Golden Orchid. I think that is why he had come with me.

There is no doubt that the Cultural Revolution, in its juggernaut churning and stumbling, brought to a lot of people something different, deep and stirring and seminal. Never mind if it was also directed, mobilized, conducted; it was fraught with future potential. These people talked about themselves in ways I had not heard before. For the first time, millions were openly questioning motivations. I tried to envision the scope of this immense psychological upheaval, what it would do to the Chinese people, in the decades to come.

I slept on a *kang* that night with six other girls, a tight squeeze. About two in the morning a black frost came down, and someone knocked on the door and shouted, 'Tsao Yulan, get up! We must light the fires in the fields.' But Tsao Yulan grunted and turned over, going to sleep again. However, two other girls rose and went out. They did not return until five. The next morning, walking in the valley bottom, I would find the charred cinders of sorghum stalks; smoke from fires prevented the black frost from settling down upon the crops.

Commander Liu Tetsai arrived from Shenyang. He was a hero here, for he had chosen this brigade as a model, and worked as an unknown, sieving the valley stones and encouraging the peasants to grow sorghum and maize, in 1968. He was certainly the idol of Tsao Yulan and another girl with the ecstatic face of a saint, who grasped the little red book to her heart and vowed never to marry, for 'I want to devote myself to spreading Mao Tsetung Thought'. It was she who had tried to wake Yulan to light fires, and she had spent all night in the fields. I would see the Saint in Peking for the October 1st celebration. The village girls were uncomfortable in the city. They had never seen a lift, or a modern toilet, and Peking streets made them dizzy. 'So many cars,' they cried.

Harbin is one of China's most European cities, and a beautiful one. White Russian refugees from the Russian Revolution, refugee Jews from Nazi Germany, flocked here and prospered. It is next door to the limitless

Siberian span of earth. It has culture and art; the Harbin Ballet School and Music Institute are well-known. Its population is two million. It has 520,000 youngsters in school. There are 820 factories and 400,000 workers.

The Harbin Medical College has become since 1949 a fully-fledged medical school with 52 consultants, 170 research workers, an 800-bed teaching hospital, and 700 other beds in various hospitals. It has trained 7,000 doctors from 1949 to 1966 (five-year courses). In front of me sit some of its top medical men and research scientists. Such enormous dignity and reticence is theirs as they go through the usual phraseology. Perhaps some, like Sha Tin, the Szechuan writer, and Yen Wenching, my friend, were comforted by the fact that all of them were paraded and reviled together; they met and recognized each other in prisons, in the May 7 schools, at the struggle and criticism meetings.

Sha Tin had made his audience shake with mirth when, every time he bowed his head to acknowledge his 'crimes', the dunce's cap fell off, and proceedings had to be interrupted while one of the Red Guard 'judges' had to walk down from his seat, and readjust the cap. 'The crowd took his side and said: Enough!' There was also the great comic artist who, when the Red Guards came to fetch him, was waiting for them, a very tall dunce's cap upon his head. 'I made it myself, to spare you the trouble,' he told the stern young people affably.

Solemnly, the academic staff recited their sins. 'We practised the three getaways: from labour, from the masses, from the Revolution.' I think of Galileo, who also confessed, but only told a lie in order to be more free to serve the truth. I remember how Pao used to go on, hour after hour, shouting and ranting at me, in real 'struggle session' fashion, to make me acknowledge something which was quite preposterous but which, in the end, by dint of repetition, almost convinced me of its truth. Pao had died here in Manchuria in cold October, in the open-cast coal mine of Fushun, and his last letter to me said that he had served the wrong cause, the wrong man ... *

'We shall now select by merit, not examination. We are reducing medical studies to two years.'

I jump. 'Two years is not enough to become a doctor.'

The even flow of words has stopped; the local cadres look unhappy. But not the doctors. They gleam gently.

The army man in charge of the hospital says sourly, 'Two years is enough if we have Mao Tsetung Thought.'

* See *Birdless Summer*.

'We are cutting out all pre-medical study,' explains the professor of internal medicine.

We go to look at pathology specimens, exchanging inanities.

In the Harbin 43rd Middle School one of the teachers is obviously teaching; she has not seen us because the door was half open and I merely pushed it. But when she sees us she hastily puts the text book in her desk, slaps the desk shut and starts waving the little red book and so do all the students. Teaching does still go on. Parents *must* be talking to teachers, begging them to teach their children ... I shall capture such scenes in other schools, but one has to be able to suddenly open a door to a classroom not scheduled as part of the visitor's round. Perhaps this explains why, despite the fact that schools did not work properly for many years, there are some startling exceptions. How else is it understandable that a mathematics contest in 1977 could produce at least two score pupils of outstanding merit, right after the downfall of the Gang of Four? That a child of twelve, therefore born in 1966, the year the Cultural Revolution began, could play Mozart and Beethoven and Bach and Chopin, all of them proscribed 'foreign bourgeois musicians' in 1978, and win a prize? There must have been a soundproof room available to him somewhere ... and a good teacher.

Long live fraud on behalf of education.

Six hundred thousand young people from all over China will come to the province of Heilungkiang this year. Border settlements are to be set up; the province has very few people, and now there is oil. The harvest has been spectacular, all the storage bins are full, and everyone in the city of Harbin must take in 500 catties of grain to store until new bins are provided. On the radio it is announced that all medicines and pharmaceutical products will be reduced in price by 37 per cent, all over the country.

Phenomenal innovations are announced, all proclaimed to be the result of the Cultural Revolution. But I know that a good many were started before the Cultural Revolution ... all of them are claimed to be due to workers' ingenuity, but I know that most of them are due to scientists. I shall not say a word. Scientists must be protected by anonymity.

I meet Pan Fushen. He is the military commander of Heilungkiang province and heads the provincial revolutionary committee. He is the inventor of the May 7 cadre schools, and a national figure because he is one of the very few Party army high officials who has 'led the masses' against his own administration, or, in other words, joined the new power constellation.

In 1957 Pan Fushen had been labelled a 'rightist'. However, the label was withdrawn in 1960.

Pan is a small, wiry man, wrapped in a swirling black cape. He eats very little at dinner because he has ulcers. He says that he had not understood the proletarian Cultural Revolution during the first fifty days but then he read more of Mao and 'grasped' his thinking. On August 18th, while Mao was reviewing the Red Guards in Peking, the Liu representatives in Harbin were reviewing their own squads, organized to 'protect the Party' against the Red Guards.

'The battle was most acute,' says Pan (even tanks were used on the streets of Harbin). Pan joined the 'rebel revolutionaries', and they won. The first revolutionary committee to be set up in China was here in Harbin. Shanghai was to follow.

In autumn 1967 Pan started, at Willow River (Liuho) district, the first May 7 cadre school; so called because on May 7th, 1967, Chairman Mao had suggested such schools for the retooling of cadres. Now each organization ran its own May 7 school. The Foreign Ministry had theirs (Kung Peng had been in it for eighteen months), and so had the Ministry of Culture. Fourth Sister Ping would be in her organization's May 7 school for two years.

Pan talked of the border aggression by the U.S.S.R. 'The Soviet new tsars have stopped all our fishing in the Heilungkiang River; they have 130 gunboats on patrol.' Despite his amiability, a pall of silence falls upon us. I don't know why; I begin to ramble, and drink strong *maotai*. At last, whirling his cape, Pan Fushen goes.

Hsing Chiang, who has arranged the meeting at my request, is a bit aggrieved. 'You talked small talk only.' I want to tell Hsing Chiang that I am too subjective; I respond too obviously to the aroma a person engenders, an odour of the mind.

I never wrote up Pan Fushen, though it would have been interesting, for the *New York Times*; for which I did several Op Eds★ in those years.

Now Pan Fushen is down. He fell when Lin Piao fell. Some praise my foresight. But it was merely paralysis, part of that block which stopped

★ Op Ed: article on the editorial page of the *New York Times*.

me from writing anything except about Mao and the revolution for almost ten years.

'I could see you did not get on with Pan Fushen,' said Hsing Chiang to me recently.

'It was his black cape,' I said. 'That cape reminded me so much of Chiang Kaishek. That's what put me off.'

On to Sian, to Tachai, to Nanking, to Wusih, to Soochow, to Hangchow ... to so many places. In Tachai I meet the eminent peasant Chen Yungkwei himself, a member of the Central Committee; who tells me about his great struggles against the Liu group. In Nanking I visit fertilizer factories and chemical plants and communes, and also the new great bridge crossing the Yangtse River. Workers on the bridge, in a lengthy interview, tell me that the engineers tried to stop them from completing it in record time ... One of the workers has become an alternate on the Central Committee. I ask for his autograph, but he can scarcely sign his name. I meet so many other enthusiasts of the Cultural Revolution, young and old, among them Lai Keke, who is a veteran cadre. It seems some of them, by joining the 'Left' can escape all harassment.

In Soochow my guide is a happy young Red Guard who tells me, chortling, how his faction, after assaulting another faction with lances and spears 'got some machine guns, and then we had quite a show.'

Back to Peking for the October 1st celebration.

The atmosphere of the banquet is extraordinary. Usually it is solemn and sticky, with its careful hierarchy of officials and diplomats and high and not-so-high honoured guests. In this society there can be much sour envy and heartburn if one is placed lower than one expects to be at one of the 400-odd tables which fill the Great Hall; and one's distance from the main table, where the leaders sit, is the subject of much speculation by assembled diplomats.

But this year the Great Hall is crowded. There are twice as many tables as usual. At them sit peasants and workers, delegates from all the new revolutionary committees; and army men.

Previously, apart from the music and the set speeches, there was little noise; only the ritual clinking of glasses in toasts, the small murmur of polite conversation. Sometimes a whole table would spend the evening in glum silence. But this year the noise is continuous. The banquet is a rowdy clamourous assembly, with people shouting 'Long live Chairman Mao', drinking and eating and laughing and roaring their happiness.

The hotels are full of people 'from below', and the hotel managers complain that they go to sleep on top of the bedspreads in all their clothes and without taking off their shoes.

The people 'from below' who have come to Peking fill the streets. They buy everything in the shops. 'We never dreamt we would ever see Peking in our whole lifetime,' they say.

The parade on Tienanmen Square is a happy festival. I am squeezed out of place by a parcel of eager young girls, representatives from districts in Honan province. They want to catch sight of Chairman Mao, who is up there at the balcony of the gate. 'Can you see him? Can you?' They crane, and almost clamber on top of me for a glimpse.

The populace is gaudy and raucous and screaming its joy, untouched by bureaucracy, and their idol is Mao. The militia does not walk in step, the floats are haphazard; and the marchers will not move on as required, but remain turned towards Mao, acclaiming him ... Total disarray results.

Today, knowing how badly this candid devotion was misused, I still feel the lap of that ocean of humanity surging, rising towards the balcony where Mao stood, and my heart is moved and I want to shout, 'I won't let you down!' to the people, the long-suffering ones.

Mao was a far, round face, a white moon in the distance. He was flanked by Lin Piao and Chou Enlai, Chen Pota and Kang Sheng. Chou Enlai waved the little red book at the crowd, but in between waves he paused. Someone handed me a pair of binoculars. How tired he looked ...

Shanghai is the power base of the new constellation: Chiang Ching, Chang, Yao and the ex-worker Wang Hungwen. All four of them travel regularly between Shanghai and Peking, but Chiang Ching has no state appointment (Mao has refused to give her one).

The Number Seventeen Textile Mill of Shanghai, where Wang Hungwen worked, is organizing 'activists' for the Communist Youth League, future cadre material. This means that Wang Hungwen may take over the now moribund Youth League; that millions of youngsters will come under his control.

Madame Wang Hsiuchen is a famous woman in Shanghai. She will be written up at length in the newspapers and in *Peking Review*, and interviewed by many foreigners in the years to come. She is one of the top members of the Shanghai Revolutionary Committee; and also a Central

Committee member. She is as prolix and unquenchable as Li Suwen in Manchuria (Wang Hsiuchen also comes originally from Manchuria.)

She tell me the story of the conquest of Shanghai, called 'the January Storm'. I shall find it ably written up by many foreigners; a valuable story, full of 'facts'. Today the interpretation of these 'facts' is very different from what it was then. It was then a 'model revolutionary act'. It is now a 'base counter-revolutionary plot'.

But I find in my notes something very extraordinary (I record like an automaton, and am occasionally surprised by my own scribble). Wang Hsiuchen says that an 'underground' Shanghai organization helped Wang Hungwen to mobilize the workers for the capture of the city in January 1967. She then mentions Chen Ahta, who she says is a factory worker, as one of the leaders of this 'underground'.

Chen Ahta becomes a Central Committee member. He will have a major role to play, with Wang Hungwen, in the formation of the Shanghai militia, and of groups of activists which will be sent out to many provinces between 1974 and 1976 to take over government offices, public security bureaus, factories. When the Four are toppled, Chen Ahta will be denounced as head of a mafia, a gangster; and Wang Hungwen who has meantime become Vice-Chairman of the Party will be accused of having revived Secret Society methods, having formed 'brotherhood' links, distributed Party cards to gangsters.

But the word 'underground' may have another meaning. Chou Enlai, while in Chungking, organized and trained clandestine Communist cells throughout the whole of south-west China, under Chiang Kaishek's nose. I shall meet a good many members of these units, working in government offices in Szechuan and Yunnan provinces. Liu Shaochi similarly organized clandestine cells in 'white terror' areas. Wang Hsiuchen evidently wishes me to understand the term 'underground' as clandestine Communist Party cells in Shanghai. But after Liberation, there was no further need for an underground. Why then does she talk of it as if it had been recently organized?

Wang Hsiuchen also tells me how the former Shanghai Party Secretary Chen Peihsien, tried to crush the workers, and 'committed towering crimes'. In 1977 I would meet a small-boned smiling man at the house of one of my doctor friends in Peking. It turned out to be Chen Peihsien. 'I heard much evil about you in Shanghai in 1969 from Wang Hsiuchen,' I said, and he laughed uproariously.

The Huashan hospital was started in 1907 by American missionaries. It has a particularly well-developed department of surgical neurology, and ten brain specialists. Of course the doctors castigate their previous attitudes. One-third of the staff are away, in faraway places like Sinkiang and Tibet, to train barefoot doctors and to give medical care. When they return another third will go. They assert that formerly only Shanghai's capitalists and their wives had access to the hospital. They say that peasants were asked fabulous sums for operations, ranging from 100 to 300 *yuan*. I nearly explode. It is not true. And then I understand. This is such an exaggerated charade that I catch on. So I nod gravely when one of the doctors produces a well-worn, old remedy for mycosis of the toenails and tells me that it is a new innovation due to the Cultural Revolution ... we play a perfect dead-pan comedy and our audience does not know it.

In the wards the treatment of burns has been carried out to a high degree of perfection. The doctors have finished *tobegaying* and can go on working, and they do magnificent things. If Paris was worth a mass, being able to go on working is perhaps worth a 'confession'.

I go to a photographic exhibition, 'not for foreigners'. There are many photographs, episodes of the seizure of power in Shanghai; and a picture, six foot high, of Wang Hungwen. I notice other photographs, militia men with rifles, and below them the words: 'Battalions of the ATTACK BY REASON, DEFEND BY FORCE.'

But in Shanghai, in front of these photographs, I am told that these battalions are 'an arm of security' and for peacekeeping operations; that they started on August 4th, 1967, and that they protect state property. In 1972, and again in 1975, I shall try to find out what has happened to these battalions, but at no time shall I be told that they are held responsible for violence committed.

Passing through the street, I catch sight, here and there, of barbed wire atop walls. Probably temporary prisons. Each organization, factory, university has its own detention area.

I travel down through the green lush countryside of Chekiang province, to visit the May 7 cadre school of Shanghai Municipality. It is about fifty kilometres from the city, near an arm of brackish sea, on flat plain. But there are no swamps. I see neat houses of earth and wood. No barbed wire, but a palisade. No obvious guards. (None are necessary – where would the cadres run to?)

The cadres, 2,000 of them are here voluntarily, to remould themselves through study and labour. The first group built the houses, and now the cadres are erecting larger buildings, for meetings. The school is not far from some villages, and the peasants come and go freely, and walk into and out of school. I see ex-officials collecting vegetables for lunch from vegetable plots, others pushing manure carts. I visit the pig pens. Never have I seen such splendid-looking, healthy pigs. I congratulate the official who looks after them.

'You've got the best pigs I've seen in China.'

'Yes, the villagers all come round to see how we do it,' he says. 'I thought at one time of becoming an ambassador. Now I am content to look after pigs.'

We both laugh. Perhaps he is now an ambassador.

At first food had to be sent from the city to feed the two thousand here; much of it is now grown on the spot. There is a library and the inevitable loudspeakers. Once a month the officials return home to visit their families, that is, all those who are not labelled 'counter-revolutionary.' They receive their pay; but I know that some, the 'criminals', are given very reduced pay. Of course *tobegaying* is going on – discussions, criticism, self-criticism, probably struggle sessions, when some leading cadre is hauled out in front of everyone else. But I do not get to see the criminals.

Everyone assures me that they do not feel humiliated; that on the contrary, it is an 'honour' to remodel oneself; that manual labour is not degrading. 'We are the front-line soldiers of the Revolution,' they say. Any and every cadre will have to go to May 7 schools. It is not punishment.

What will happen, I ask, when all the fields have been laid and the houses built? Surely there will not be much manual labour left to do? Everyone laughs.

'In our May 7 school we had an excellent library,' says a friend whom I shall see some years later. 'I never had so much time to read as when I was being retooled.'

'Our place was not so good,' says Yen Wenching. 'The Red Guards and army men in charge never gave us any peace. One day I heard I was dispensed from labour. I was happy, thinking it was a favour – until I heard my name called to be struggled against at a meeting. That was bad. They made me stand in a jetplane posture* for hours ... they pulled my hair, jerking my head.' Yen and another writer thought up the bright idea of shaving their heads clean, so that there was no hair to pull at struggle sessions. 'But it did not help. They pulled on our ears instead, and it was more painful.'

* Half-bent, arms extended backwards.

There were also very bad May 7 schools, where the cadres were bullied and badly fed, and beaten and humiliated, and denied letters and books.

Back in Peking, it is late October. Soon I shall leave. But meanwhile, I wait to see Chiang Ching. I have asked to see her.

Kuo Mojo, delightful as ever, has a talk with me. He speaks of his ten years in Japan from 1927 to 1937. 'As one progresses one understands one's errors,' says he. 'I have followed Chairman Mao; as a fly stuck on a horse is carried by the horse, so am I carried by the greatness of Chairman Mao.' Kuo Mojo has written in 1967 a poem in eulogy of Chiang Ching. Is this sycophancy? I do not think so. The old man is, at all times, sincere; it is not his fault if the object of his admiration becomes unworthy.

Kuo Mojo tells me that of all the Chinese writers who participated in the Afro-Asian writers' meeting of 1966, only three are reckoned 'not bad.' He does not tell me who they are. But he says that Hsu Kuangping, Lu Hsun's wife (who died in 1968, probably of a heart attack), was 'spotless'. That leaves only two more blameless writers, out of all those assembled that July. I am depressed. It means that so many of the people I like are now 'bad': Liu Paiyu, Li Chi, not to mention Pa Chin, Tu Hsuan, Yen Wenching ... so many.

At Tsinghua University I am greeted by Comrade Hsieh Chingyi. She is the daughter of Hsieh Fuchih, now head of the Peking Revolutionary Committee (and of Public Security). A personable, clever young woman, she is a great devotee of Chiang Ching. Of course, like all the women who follow Madame Mao, she is most articulate. The revolutionary committee of Tsinghua University was formed in January 1969; and she will control it for seven years, until October 1976.

The eminent professor, Tsien Weichang, is exhibited to me. He makes the usual confession. I shall not publish a word, although I take it all down. He will repeat his exposé to Edgar Snow the following year.

Tsien is a professor of fundamental science and physics. He wanted Tsinghua to become a 'cradle for competent engineers'. He believed in technical expertise ... he took in students on marks, not on political acumen. Already in 1957 he was labelled a rightist ... 'I was very obstinate ... the Red Guards did not change me ... only when the workers' teams entered, in July 1968, did I begin to change. The workers said to me: But what about us? Where do we fit in in your scheme of excellence? Then I was moved,' says Tsien. And I believe him.

Hsieh Chingyi is knowledgeable and well organized. She tells me of the special kindergarten and nursery schools in Peking and other cities for the children of higher officials. In 1963 an educational conference sponsored by Liu Shaochi and Teng Hsiaoping had backed a system of élite schools; 1,472 primary schools and 235 secondary schools in Peking Municipality were to be selected for the 'special training' of brighter children. 'Of course this was to prepare the return to capitalism,' says she.

But strangely, it was in one of those special schools, where the children of higher officials were most numerous – the 4th Middle School attached to Tsinghua University – that the first Red Guards had been formed.

On November 7th, in the evening, I was taken to the Great Hall of the People to see Chiang Ching. I was told, 'You must not publish a word.' I could not take notes.

At first Chiang Ching would have nothing to do with me, accounting me an American agent. The first accusation had come, in 1962, from a neurotically suspicious Japanese writer, who had gone to Peking to denounce me. The Chinese had smiled and said that they did not think this was correct. However, the item had probably got into my files, as the 'information' that I was Jewish had got into Kuomintang files about me. Chou Enlai had persuaded Chiang Ching to see me. 'Premier Chou went to a great deal of trouble for you,' I was told.

Chou Enlai, Kang Sheng, and Chiang Ching sat in three armchairs. Chiang Ching was in soldier's uniform, padded ungainly, but above the uncouth garments her face was beautifully made up, with excellent cosmetics. Her black hair was waved, and glistened. It was a good-looking face in 1969, when she was fifty-seven years old.

'You asked to see Comrade Chiang Ching,' said Chou Enlai. He looked at ease, relaxed. I was happy to see him. It was he I wanted to talk to. But he did not say a word while Chiang Ching and I carried on a bafflingly unsatisfactory conversation through the next ninety minutes.

I began by saying how I had seen the revolutionary new operas and appreciated their relevance and importance; which was true. I had started seeing them in 1963. I thought they might be made accessible to a public abroad as a vehicle to express the aims of New China. I mentioned in particular *Shachiapang*, once called *A Spark Among the Reeds*. And this was my first mistake.

Chiang Ching frowned slightly. The reason (which I only discovered years later) was that *Shachiapang* had existed long before she had come on the political scene. She began to speak about two other operas, *Taking Tiger Mountain by Strategy*, and *On the Docks*. These two she considered much superior to others. 'I have seen Western operas. I do not think the West can appreciate our operas. They sing anything, like: "Do you want some tea, Yes I'll have some tea, It is very good tea". Our Chinese opera concentrates on expressing only positive emotions, important ones ... '

She went on giving her notions of 'purifying the opera'. I listened to her voice. She had a very beautiful, distinct voice in 1969; the voice of an actress, with carrying power. By 1971, when I saw her again, something had happened to her voice; something tight and desperate lived in it.

We talked about *The Red Regiment of Women*. I had seen the film in 1962. It had nothing to do with her at the time. Now a ballet would be made of it. The original film was never shown again.

Suddenly she told me about Mayor Peng Chen, how he had opposed her new operas, put obstacles in the way of performances ...

I plodded on. I strove to catch hold of something coherent to say, but every ten minutes or so there was an interruption. Chiang Ching would rise and go off to the toilet. During her absences no one spoke; we sat, fixed in the aspic of wordlessness, awaiting her return. I wondered what was wrong with her bladder. Or was it her bladder?

She asked me abruptly if I knew anything about Chinese opera. 'Nothing, I just like it,' I replied. I tried to speak about Aszucena opera, but this was my second error; Chiang Ching cut me off. She had a particular aversion to provincial opera, especially that from Szechuan, possibly because Szechuan opera is redolent with anti-bureaucratic satire. The possibility of introducing, within what looks like a serious play, ironic remarks about top leaders, and jokes about them which the audience will understand immediately, is almost infinite.

'What do you really believe in?' she asked me suddenly.

'I shall strive to learn from you,' I replied politely.

She was mollified. 'I am only a small student of our great leader Chairman Mao,' she said. And off we were again on *Taking Tiger Mountain by Strategy*. Obviously she wanted *Tiger Mountain* to be shown abroad. She told me that there were singing and gestures in it which had never been attempted before. 'Everytime she talked of *Tiger Mountain*, you would talk of *Shachiapang*,' Hsing Chiang reminded me in 1977, after Chiang Ching's downfall. I was not aware I had been so mulish.

We went on to music, and I committed my third *faux pas*. I said something about the scales of Western and Chinese music being so different that it was not possible to mix the piano and violin with Chinese instruments. She frowned heavily. For this was precisely the innovation she was contemplating.

We came back to denouncing Peng Chen and other officials. Every time she pronounced a name, she glanced at Chou Enlai, who remained quite unperturbed.

Then Chiang Ching said suddenly, 'I've had cancer, did you know?'

Had I been a trained courtier, I would have recognized the opening. I would have asked about her health, and she would have given me a blow by blow account of her life. But a perverse streak in me refused this abasement. I murmured something about hoping she was now cured. 'All she wanted was to tell you the story of her life. She was looking for someone to write her up. But you turned her down,' said Hsing Chiang later.

We floundered on. 'Can anything good be produced and created in corrupt Western society?' asked Chiang Ching. I said that there was a great deal of vulgarity, but from time to time there were good things. I mentioned, for instance, the film Z, which I had seen in Paris that spring. I thought it should be shown in China, as an instance of what the West could do to criticize itself. And of course, there was a vast number of books printed, 'many thousands a year'. And new ballets. I mentioned Béjart.

Chou Enlai was impassive. 'Oh,' I thought, 'I'm letting him down. I don't know how to handle this ... I'm doing everything wrong.'

Chiang Ching left. I rose and watched her go down the corridor, waddling in that grossly inappropriate padded uniform.

Once Chiang Ching had gone my tongue-tied stupidity vanished. I turned to Chou Enlai. I had wanted to thank him, for almost two years.

'I thank you,' I said, 'for having been so patient with me, teaching me, all through the years ... I have been a slow and stupid person ... you told me once I was slow ... '

'Was I really so rude?' said Chou, his face suddenly bright and young and amused. There was someone else there. Kang Sheng.

I had never met Kang Sheng before. He was so quiet that he could be forgotten. But he was quietly dangerous. After all, he had brought Peng Chen down; he was at all the Red Guard rallies. He had never been criticized. I asked him to tell me the meaning of the 'continuing revolution'.

He did so. He talked a long time. Then he asked me why I did not go to Latin America. Apparently he was under the impression either that I was very popular in Latin America, or that revolution was imminent there.

I thought Latin America unripe for revolution because it did not have enough people. Distances, geography, size, economic resources, culture, religion, demography all play their part in whether a revolution is possible or not. 'Besides I cannot speak Spanish.'

A faint shadow of disapproval crossed his aristocratic face. 'You can learn it.' I promised to try.

It was now almost one o'clock, and certainly Chou Enlai had work to do; he always worked until five in the morning, or even later. I left.

So this was Chiang Ching, or rather one fragment of her. Poor woman, she must have suffered ... that is why she was so bizarre, so dislocated. I was filled with compassion for her, even though her waspishness when she talked about Peng Chen grated. She was under stress and that bladder of hers: perhaps a medical case, with no final cure ...

Twenty-one

The Death of Kung Peng: 1970

IN MID OCTOBER, 1969, while I was still in China, a message came for me from Samdech Norodom Sihanouk,* inviting me to preside over an Asian film festival in Phnom Penh at the end of November. An invitation from Chino Roces, the owner of the *Manila Times*, to lecture in the Philippines came at the same time.

I told Kung Peng what Charles Meyer had said in Zermatt that spring: that there would be a coup against Sihanouk, that he would be 'got rid of', and 'before the summer of 1970'. Kung Peng assured me that this was idle talk. No such news or rumour had filtered through to the Chinese from diplomatic sources. And yet, in March 1970 – Meyer was correct almost to the month – there was a coup in Phnom Penh, and Sihanouk was driven into exile.

Meyer was to write me a jubilant letter when Sihanouk was deposed by the Lon Nol regime. He seemed to have great confidence in Lon Nol, but Lon Nol did not give him a job. Charles Meyer and his wife Sika returned to France, and Charles has since become an eminent Sinologist.

As president of the Asian film festival I was most royally treated. We

* *Samdech:* head of state.

had a magnificent apartment in the Palace; an enormous Rolls-Royce to take us to the hall where the films were viewed. I was kept extremely busy, but could not fail to notice that there was an economic crisis in Cambodia, and that Sihanouk was hard-pressed. He had given 'sanctuary' to Vietnamese troops on the border, and this was resented by Lon Nol and others in his government. 'I don't know how long I can keep my country at peace and free from invasion,' said Sihanouk.

The *Manila Times* was an independent newspaper (it has since been liquidated by President Marcos). Chino Roces, its tiny, compact, energetic owner, had the courage to make an opening to China at a time when it was almost a crime in his country.

Our suite was the best at the best hotel in Manila. A burly bodyguard, bristling with pistols, lay across the corridor at night. When we went out, bodyguards squeezed in on either side of me in the car. It is very difficult to view the landscape through two hundred pounds of brawny bodyguard knobbly with weaponry. Chino Roces had a walkie-talkie set with him, to report exactly where we were, in case of kidnapping. One afternoon I became weary of so much care and crept out while Vincent was having his noonday siesta, to wander by myself. Chino was most upset.

The Philippines are a world of seven thousand islands, and there is such great inequality and social injustice that revolution seems always just round the corner. But this is Asia, and the tropics. A revolution was almost impossible here precisely because there were seven thousand islands, absolutely disconnected, and hundreds of ethnic groups and dozens of languages.

I met some of the revolutionaries from the Philippino Communist Party who had recently surrendered to Marcos. The trouble was that they could not employ—as in China—that large web of villages to sustain a guerrilla war, and any enterprise on the Chinese model was doomed. 'Too few people,' I said to them. There was much resemblance between the Philippines and Latin America.

Some of the women wore rivulets of diamonds round their necks and one asked me, clasping her three-strand blue diamond necklace, 'Will the communists take this from me?' Just outside the walled-in enclaves where the rich dwelt was great hunger and squalor, and the stifling malodorous stink which is misery and its unwashed anger, and uncollected garbage. Contrasts so appalling that even Vincent, nurtured in India where inequalities tear one's eyes out, was shattered by the scene in Manila.

I gave a few lectures; met many people, mostly wealthy families living in fairylike palaces in the enclave of Makati.

President Marcos and his wife Imelda received me with pleasant informality. Marcos was resourceful, suave, steeped in knowledge of his own people; he would be able to stifle revolt against his rule for a considerable length of time. And in 1974 Imelda Marcos would go to Peking, and there be royally entertained by Chiang Ching.

Marcos was no stooge; he had brains and decision. He knew that precarious economics makes for uncertain political power, and he was not embarrassed by scruples. Much time and effort would be spent by the Third World nations before the hold of the industrialized and affluent nations on their resources and markets could be shaken off. 'They talk of freedom all the time; but they deny us the basic freedom from want that we need,' he remarked. And any one of us, Asians and Africans, would agree with him there.

While we talked, Marcos was awaiting a telephone call from Washington. He had asked for another loan. 'Seventeen million dollars only, just chicken feed for them,' said one of his aides to me.

Kung Peng and I had had long talks, and leisurely ones, in Peking. We had discussed America, Europe, all the more since we had not done so for many years.

Since 1968, there had been an increasing number of signals from the United States; such as allowing Americans to visit China without removing their passports, and allowing them to purchase one hundred dollars' worth of Chinese goods.

But there was hostility in China against reciprocation. Ed Snow kept on writing to Kung Peng, asking to come to China. But Ed had told me that there was no answer. I told Kung Peng and she said, frowning slightly with worry, 'In his articles he emphasizes too much Chairman Mao being old and soon to see God.' I guessed that 'some people' were opposed to a dialogue with America, and making much ado about Ed's quotation of what Mao had told him.* I said that articles abroad could not be written in the style of *Peking Review*, that Ed's report about Mao's age only occupied 5 per cent of the article, that there was a problem of subtitles; the author often had no control over titles and subtitles. I wrote to Ed and told him where the snag lay; by then I had become somewhat expert in creating the unlocking phrase which led to a common meeting of the

* See *The New Republic*, February 27th, 1965, pp. 17–23.

minds. My own articles and speeches were not approved in China at the time. They had, in fact, not been approved for many years by the 'ultras'. An acquaintance in France, connected with the Marxist-Leninist Party of France, had told me that they had been warned against having anything to do with me.

But still, I managed. Life had never been a smooth tarred road, but a brusque and capricious river, and one learns about canoeing in wayward water.

Before I left China it had been conveyed to me that if General de Gaulle was interested, he would be welcome in China ... would I sound him out? By 1969 de Gaulle had retired from official life; but he remained the only Western statesman popular and understood in the Third World. I said that I would try.

When I arrived in Hongkong I found that an 'edict' had been issued in Peking, forbidding all Chinese newsmen, or anyone having to do with the pro-Peking newspapers in Hongkong, to meet, talk, or entertain any relations whatsoever, with Americans.

Who had issued this edict? Kung Peng had not told me about it. The dichotomy in Chinese policies, the fact that at the time there was not one but several 'centres' issuing contradictory orders was now clear. I was almost being encouraged to go to the United States by Kung Peng, but all my Hongkong friends, Mr Fei, Lee Tsungying, were not allowed to talk to any American.

There were other absurdities: *Eastern Horizon*, the magazine considered entirely pro-Peking abroad, was forbidden entry in China, and accumulated dustily in the Kuangchow post office, labelled: 'Yellow revisionist material'. Yellow in Chinese means pornographic.

I ignored the edict, and that winter sought out Harrison Salisbury of the *New York Times*. Harrison had vainly searched for someone from China to talk to in Hongkong. We met in Paris, and spoke of possibilities, and probabilities, and Harrison's judgment proved most sound. He had acumen, a steady mind, a genuine concern for good relations between China and the United States, and I trusted him.

Ed Snow and I also met several times. Ed wrote to Kung Peng, explaining his use of Mao's phrase, 'I shall soon see God'. And in 1970 he and his wife Lois received their visas and went to China. Ed would see Mao there, and Mao would say to him that 'some ultra-leftists' would not even allow him to see his good friend Edgar Snow. Who were they? And how could they impede even Mao Tsetung?

In Paris I set out to find what could be done about inviting General de

Gaulle to China. I had met Couve de Murville, and Bettencourt, and other French Foreign Ministry officials in previous years. They had come to parties I had given in honour of the Chinese Ambassador, Huang Chen. But no French official could or would understand why the invitation had not come through official channels. No one was inclined to believe me. I bumped against the glazed and courteous blankness of French officialdom. Finally I went to see my friend Jacques Rueff, at his office in the French Academy. He had on his bureau a beautiful Dali timepiece. I thought, 'What I am saying must be as improbable as a limp watch.' But Jacques Rueff listened attentively. However, he too was cautious; the weeks went by, and when finally he wrote to de Gaulle, it was too late. De Gaulle died on the very day Rueff's letter should have reached him.

Fred Zinnemann was not happy. He had planned to start filming Malraux's *Man's Fate* on December 10th, and had asked me to be present, but I could not since I was then in Phnom Penh and on the way to Manila. The very morning shooting was due to start, all cameras poised, came the dictum from the new bosses of Metro-Goldwyn-Mayer: the production was cut out. Not only *Man's Fate*, but about a dozen other films were thus liquidated in a retrenchment crisis. What a curious and subjective way to run business! How easily and swiftly some prominent president of some company or other would be kicked out, and replaced! There was something totally unreal, unsolid, in the whole edifice of those vast conglomerates, such caprice in this huge money power! Fred went skiing to recover his equanimity. I told him I would refuse to have my name associated with anyone else but him, for I had so greatly enjoyed working with Fred. He had saved my sanity, taking my mind off the Cultural Revolution when it was almost at its worst (although worse was to come some years later).

In March 1970, Anna-Louise Strong had died in Peking. To describe the spirit of that extraordinary woman needs a book on its own. She had her quirks: the whole of Peking knew that under her bed she kept a collection of Mickey Spillane and other detective fiction. She had also accumulated a considerable collection of old embroidered robes, which she wore at parties. She died without seeing her brother, and now I knew that he was refused entry to China as part of the total ban on all Americans issued by the 'Left' in 1969 and broken only in 1970 by Mao himself when Edgar Snow was allowed again into China.

Anna-Louise remained, all her life, totally innocent of the intricacies, the feudal deviousness, the tortuous course of Chinese politics. She was unable to cope with them because she was too straight, used to the notion of a world running from cause to effect, readable, explainable ... whereas the feudal world of China is not at all like that. It is a world of hidden passion and groundless illogic, an implausible world where truth is only one's own story. It is not moulded in the realm of the discipline of the machine. Here time is vague; promises are ways of putting off problems until a movement of the heart solves them ... Situations are not determined by computer analyses (or statistics) but another kind of understanding, which still consults entrails and moods and watches signs in Heaven (or on the face of leaders). And the power contest would increasingly become of the order of feudal palace coups ... Anna-Louise's 'Letters from China' remain a great testimonial to the rational mind. Much of what she wrote was true; for the Chinese Revolution was a stupendous effort at reason and logic. But all the time feudalism came creeping back, polluting its nobility.

In April 1970, Vincent and I went to Australia for my first lecture tour in that continent. This coincided with the launching of China's first satellite, which went round and round the planet singing: The East is Red.

Australia was further discovery of the globe we live on; immensely empty land, a hollow land, baffling because upon its strangeness grow excrescences of little Europe – and yet Australia is geographically in Asia.

Despite adverse newspaper articles, large crowds came to my lectures, and the tour was unexpectedly successful. Afterwards there were witch-hunting questions asked in Australia's parliament: Why had television and radio given me so much time and exposure? As a result, funds for a certain popular programme were drastically cut, a punishment to the producer for having given me time.

Founded on this lecture tour success, the Friendship Association between Australia and China was started, or so its sponsors were kind enough to tell me.

Summer again, and time to go to China.

'Why don't you go to China too?' said Ambassador Huang Chen to Vincent.

'Me?'

'Yes, why not?'

Vincent was delighted. We rushed to New Delhi, to find out whether he could adjust his passport; it was, of course, invalid for China, as all Indian passports had been since 1962. But the fury of 1962 had subsided;

even if automatically the hackneyed newspaper phrase 'China's brutal aggression' recurred. Vincent found New Delhi's Ministry of External Affairs sympathetic, even happy at the idea of this 'overture', for it had political significance in their eyes. Tikki Kaul came to dinner with us and we had talks on the possibility of improved relations; on the Dalai Lama, on Tibet, and many other issues.

Vincent thus unwittingly made history (or *The Guinness Book of Records*). He became the first Indian non-diplomat and ex-army officer to go to China since 1959. At no time, in many subsequent visits, would he encounter hostility, either in India or in China.

I went off first to Peking. Vincent was to come three weeks later, as he had family matters to attend to. I was looking forward to seeing Kung Peng, telling her of my excitement at discovering Australia and the crowds and the passionate interest.* I had just been invited by *Asahi Shimbun*, the prestigious Japanese newspaper, to make a lecture tour of Japan in the autumn. All this was concrete evidence that policies were shifting beyond the clouds of deception of certain newsmen intent on stereotypes.

July: the aeroplane landed at Peking airport, and I could see Hsing Chiang, in a white blouse and blue skirt, waiting for me. I carried a heavy bag full of books. The Chinese post office, in its cultural zeal to censor and to eschew, had been confiscating the books I had sent to friends, just as in Malaya and Singapore Special Branch had impounded them. Even my first editions of Dr Sun Yatsen's biographies, sent to his widow, Madame Soong Chingling, disappeared during the Cultural Revolution. And now I brought books with me to give away.

Hsing Chiang hugged me, and then said, 'Kung Peng is very sick, I must tell you.' Her face was grave. My arm went up, in an unconscious gesture, with the heavy bag of books upon it. It must have hurt me, though I did not feel it at the time.

Chiao, Kung Peng's husband, met me that evening. We both wept, looking at each other. He told me what had happened. It was in May, warmth seeping through the coverlets of cold, grit and wind, when Kung Peng had received my first letter from Australia, and she was happy at the thought that I would come soon. And then she went to the bathroom, and suddenly fell, unable to move. She was rushed to hospital, but was not diagnosed for ten hours because the doctor in charge was not there (was he still *tobegaying*?). The specialist then returned; Kung Peng had a ruptured aneurysm of the internal artery in the brain.

All was done that could be done, said Chiao. But more was to come.

---

* See articles by Han Suyin in *Eastern Horizon* (1970) on the Australian lecture tour.

Kung Peng ruptured another blood vessel in the skull, and so became decerebrate, mindless; her upper brain totally destroyed. Since May she had been in a deep coma, kept alive, as decerebrates are, with a machine to pump her lungs, and others to feed her. The body was kept alive, but that fine mind of hers was gone for ever.

I was allowed to see Kung Peng in hospital: her face above the bed coverlets, waxen; all the tubes going into her. Of course I could do nothing, and I cried and cried like a lost child.

My colitis returned; I went around with stomach cramps and attacks of giddiness, which made me stumble. My arm began to swell and to throb. At first I paid no heed. I could think only of the body I had seen, that it was no longer Kung Peng, just a body, just cells, organs without a brain. The hospital kept her 'alive'. She was already dead.

Vincent arrived in Peking. He would go on a trip to factories and communes with a marvellous man, Mr Li, an interpreter, who became a great friend. Mr Li and some other young men I met were the fine product of the Cultural Revolution, the Red Guards who had refused to commit horrors, who risked their lives to protect people. No one talks about them, but they are there. And the future hinges upon these young people, who do not make any headlines, but who are the true successors, achievers of tomorrow.

As an engineer, knowledgeable about Indian conditions, Vincent could compare what was being done in Chinese factories in the only way Chinese industry can be compared, that is, with Indian factories. From the very start Vincent argued and inquired, and the workers responded well to him (not so well some of the more rigid cadres who were not accustomed to plain speaking). Lies were uncovered in a surprisingly short time by someone as experienced as Vincent, and he did not forbear to say that they were lies. But he also had a marvellously keen eye for the extraordinary and wonderful things that had been accomplished. Never an unconditional admirer, his judgment was all the more valuable. 'I did not believe you when you spoke of what was being done ... but now I've seen it ... it's great. You have a great country and a wonderful people.' And so he went on to Shanghai and Loyang and Chengchow, while I lingered in Peking because of Kung Peng. I was sleepless and my arm was now red and swollen. Hsing Chiang took me to the hospital and 'inflammation' was diagnosed by a young doctor. I was given diathermy, which made the swelling worse. Then another doctor (an older one) examined me and he looked grave. I had by then forgotten that when I arrived I had been carrying on my arm a bag full of books and that my arm had suddenly jerked upwards with the news of Kung Peng's illness. I could only say, 'It just began to swell.' The doctor took an X-ray; he suspected a swift-growing sarcoma.

Meanwhile, a most important engagement had been arranged for me. I had chosen two scripts of model operas and tried to put them into more decent English than the extant translations. The problem was that good translators and editors, such as my friend Yeh and the Yangs, were either in jail or being criticized, or made to 'stand aside'* while youngsters filled their jobs. Their motto was 'translation must be word for word'. The translations became ludicrous. For instance, the Chinese metaphor for integrity is 'A well-formed bamboo in the chest'. This was translated exactly as it stood in Chinese!

Now a meeting with over twenty actors and actresses from the opera groups under Chiang Ching was arranged for me, and heading them was Yu Hueiyung, the youngish man from the music academy of Shanghai, an *er-hu*† composer and player. Yu would become Minister of Culture in 1975, but he was already influential, and had earned the hatred of a good many older musicians by his brutal treatment of them. The music and script of two operas, *Taking Tiger Mountain by Strategy* and *On the Docks*, were due to him. I must confess that I found the music of both very good, despite the fact that in China today Yu, being a Gang of Four man, is denied any talent.

Yu Hueiyung was suave, deploying great charm as he handed me complimentary bound copies of the new operas. Because I could not take notes, owing to my arm, Hsing Chiang did so for me, and the notes remain probably the most complete exposé of Chiang Ching's activities in recruiting opera singers and actors, and putting on the model operas, that anyone has ever had.

The meeting began with an appraisal of my 'translations'. Yu turned me over to two young women with desiccated, fanatical faces. They were typical of the many I would see, pressed into the service of Chiang Ching. All of them had that ecstatic look.

The two ladies, Red Guards from the Foreign Language School, were selected as 'correctors', probably because of their political ferocity. For two hours I listened while they criticized my version, not omitting a comma. Hsing Chiang was irate. 'They exaggerated ... you sat so modestly and humbly, merely listening ... you were very patient.' I had

---

* This means they were suspended, under inquiry, but not actually dismissed. They still received their salaries.
† *Er-hu:* a Chinese violin.

indeed taken liberties in free interpretation; some of the 'positive' lyrics were painfully slogany, and I had altered them.

After that, one by one, the opera singers and actors told me how Chiang Ching had rescued them, saved them from playing only princesses and beautiful ladies, and what their tribulations had been at the hands of 'capitalist roaders' such as Peng Chen, the ex-Mayor of Peking, and Chou Yang.

They were candid. I am sure they believed that something new and important was being created. And I did agree (and still do) that besides the old classic operas, the plays on the past, there must be contemporary pieces on contemporary themes. In fact, one of the remarks I had made to Chiang Ching, and which perhaps did not please her entirely, was that one must not remain stuck in only anti-Japanese wartime stories. The way the Japanese visitors in Peking put up with being ridiculed in opera after opera was quite remarkable. The first two model operas, *Shachiapang*, and *The Red Lantern*, turned the Japanese into ludicrous figures.

A few years later some of the artists I saw that day would become very corrupt. They were loaded with honours, and promoted to high posts. Chiang Ching's favourites became an élite of their own, who never played for ordinary people.

After some three and a half hours of sitting with the opera stars, my arm became extremely painful; it stabbed and throbbed ... I told Mr Hsiung, who sat with me, and he cut the meeting short and rushed me to the cancer hospital. I had told him that one of the two doctors who had examined me suspected a fast-growing cancer.

And there at the cancer hospital was my old, old friend George Wu, who had been a scholarship student in Belgium at the same time as myself, in 1936–8.* George, a Chinese from Mauritius, had also studied in London, and then returned to Shanghai where he had set up China's first radium treatment institute (with radium from Belgium). At Liberation in 1949 George Wu did not leave China. He continued to work there, first in Shanghai and later in Peking. He had been extremely happy and well-treated throughout the years. Even during the first years of the Cultural Revolution, although harassed and criticized, and shoved aside, he had not been 'sent down' to the countryside to labour, or to a May 7 school, simply because he was far too valuable as China's major cancer specialist. He looked after all the Chinese leaders and was also consulted by Chiang Ching, since she had suffered from cancer of the uterus, which had been treated in the Soviet Union between 1954 and 1958.

* See *A Mortal Flower*.

I remembered George well from our Belgian student days and also from Joseph Hers's angry letter to me in 1959: 'George Wu has become as blind as you have ... he thinks China is getting on famously.' Hers could not understand that George Wu was, above all, a fervent patriot; that like me it was not Paradise we sought, but just China, our root land.

George looked cheerful (he always did, even when criticized as 'unreliable bourgeois'). He had perhaps a little less hair on his head – but he moved swiftly, and his hands were skilful as he palpated my swelling.

Then Hsing Chiang remembered how I had jerked up my arm, and the strap of the heavy bag of books must have bruised the muscle. I was put in hospital to rest. The swelling did not go down. A doctor came and pushed a thick needle in it and aspirated. Nothing came out. I came out of hospital. I could not write because my arm hurt so much. Nevertheless, I went on a small round of visits to factories; and I called on Rewi and Ma Haiteh, and dropped in quietly to see George Wu.

Then Premier Chou Enlai asked Vincent and myself to see him. He began by chiding me gently for getting so worried about my arm. 'It's Kung Peng who is seriously ill, not you,' said he, and fine lines of pain came into his face, for he cared deeply for all who worked with him. 'We must remain calm, be assured that the best is being done for Kung Peng.' I blinked back tears. There was nothing to be done; never would Kung Peng know anything any more. She was a living corpse. He knew it too. Kung Peng's sister, Pusheng, was there, and gripped my hand. 'Turn your sorrow into strength.' She too was under great strain, because her husband, an eminent diplomat, had been labelled a counter-revolutionary and a renegade; but then almost everyone I knew was 'counter-revolutionary' in those years.

Chou Enlai spoke to Vincent about the border dispute between India and China. He named the Himalayan passes involved in it. He knew each one, their height above sea-level, where along the ridges the demarcations came between the two countries. The point he made was clear; there was not, there could never be, enmity between the two nations. There must come a time when reason would prevail. Of course, in all situations left over from the colonial epoch, there must be give and take. The problem was a complex one, but relations could be improved even if the boundary question remained unsettled for a time.

Vincent said that we would soon be going to India after passing through Japan, and we would probably be seeing Mrs Gandhi in Delhi ... at least, we would try to see her.

Chou Enlai then inquired about my projected trip to Japan, and whether I had gathered sufficient information during my stay in China. He commented on Australia and the Philippines. 'All these countries would like better relations with us,' said Chou. I did not allude to Cambodia but Chou remembered: 'You told us about Prince Sihanouk being ousted before it happened.'

Of course I also called on Samdech Norodom Sihanouk and Princess Monique, his wife. In Peking Sihanouk resided at what had once been the French Embassy. Chou had made sure that he would truly have all the comforts of his palace in Phnom Penh. It was in exile that Sihanouk's grandeur, his fundamental steadiness of mind, became clear to me. He took personal disaster with great calm. All I could do was to say that I was certain that he would return soon to Cambodia. 'Five years, Monseigneur, five years and you will be back.' Monique smiled her very beautiful smile, and said, 'Do you really think so?' and was heartened.*

We walked about in the steamy heat of July, a heat I cannot remember because I kept on thinking of Kung Peng. But Vincent noticed many things, for to him China was new.

'Look at all the big black cars full of military men,' said he. Then the aspect of the street came into focus. On the avenues, in front of the big supermarkets were big black cars, but also jeeps, and khaki army vehicles, not for a state of a siege but conveying men in uniform, and their families, to the shops.

Because there was no longer a distinctive uniform for officers, at first glance these men might all be simple soldiers – but not to Vincent or to me. Vincent could smell authority; and of course I could see it – in the leather shoes (rather than the plimsolls of the lower ranks), in the cut of the pockets, and the texture of the cloth jacket. But above all in that essential, smooth extra layer of fat on cheek and neck and the paunch waddle of authority. For in China, traditionally, health, wealth and happiness are transmuted into extra calories.

'It's becoming a military state,' said Vincent crisply.

I protested. 'No, it's just that a lot of the military are now doing their shopping in the big cities.'

In 1964 it was high Party officials and their families who had requisitioned public motor cars for their private use; but now it was high army commanders. The crowds appeared indifferent, jostling amiably on the crowded pavements. But they saw, they registered; they paused, quietly stared, and then walked away.

* Sihanouk returned in 1975. This was sheer coincidence, not crystal-gazing.

'Something will be done about it. Somehow, in China, someone always finally does something,' I said.

It was late August 1970. And it was precisely at that time that the downfall of Lin Piao began.

In Japan, *Asahi Shimbun* treated me with impeccable courtesy. We were magnificently entertained, lived in marvellous suites, enjoyed superb Japanese dishes. Vincent became a favourite with the Japanese newsmen. He delighted them with his open-hearted, unfeigned enjoyment of Japan.

I think that for many Japanese Vincent's appearance brought to mind those dark-faced killers of demons of their legends. A black face in their theatre, as in Chinese opera, indicates courage; and a legendary Chinese judge, whose righteousness could not be moved by bribes, was always represented with a black face. Vincent resembled the Tang dynasty statues of heroes and warriors, and also the Buddhist traveller from India, Damo, who in Japan is revered and in fact has become a toy found everywhere. Vincent totally won Japanese hearts when he fell for Japanese wrestling, *sumo*, which he did in a major way, exclaiming his delight at the skill and speed of the elephantine wrestlers. Had I listened to Vincent, we would have done nothing except watch these enormous barrelly men pummel each other among ritual courtesies.

With us on our travels through Japan was Prince Kinkazu Saionji, heir of a noble house, with the face of a samurai warrior, the manners of an English aristocrat, and a convinced Marxist. With Saionji, there was an aura of dash and adventure about our lecture tour; his spirit was still that of his ancestors, utterly fearless, even if it appeared prosaically political in our lack-lustre days.

The lectures were very well attended; thousands of questions were asked. I would meet businessmen and scholars, among them Mr Kakuei Tanaka, later to become the Japanese Prime Minister, and Mr Ohira, today's Prime Minister. They came to inform themselves about China. The *Asahi Shimbun* director, a most able gentleman whose suits were superbly Savile Row, reflected, however, a contrary opinion. He told me that normal diplomatic relations between Japan and China would not be established 'for another ten years at least'. 'I am sorry to disagree with you, but I think they will start much sooner,' I had to reply. This was October 1970, and in 1972 Japan would indeed establish diplomatic relations with China, and Premier Tanaka would go to Peking.

It was at the Tokyo Foreign Correspondents' Club, where I delivered a lecture, that I first heard the rumour that Teng Hsiaoping might be rehabilitated. He and Liu Shaochi had together been dubbed by Lin Piao and Chiang Ching 'chief capitalist roaders', but Mao had always made a distinction between them. Everyone knew that Teng had requested hard labour for himself in a commune sited near Inner Mongolia. In 1970 Mao Tsetung was calling for the urgent return of old and competent cadres.

I wrote to Chiao Kuanhua about the result of my Japanese tour, and added the stray rumour about Teng Hsiaoping. But I never received a reply.

It was in that September–October, at the second session of the Ninth Congress of the Party, that Mao began to suspect his heir, Lin Piao. Not before. I had wrongly conjectured* that Mao had begun to suspect Lin right after the first session because of the hunt for the 'ultra-left' and the May 16ers, but I was to be told categorically, in 1977, that this was not so.

At the second session, Chou Enlai, following Mao's instructions, was urging the rebuilding of the Party committees at every level, and emphasizing that the Party committee decisions should not have to be ratified by army committees set up by Lin Piao. Mao concurred, for he had never meant China to become a military dictatorship. The army, having restored order, must now back down – it was as Party member, not as military commander, that Mao had selected Lin Piao to succeed him. 'The Party must command the gun, the gun must never command the Party.'

In 1969 Mao had repeatedly demanded the return of old, competent cadres. 'I have faith in my old comrades.' He had wanted to administer a lesson to the bureaucracy, but it did not mean casting the seasoned officials into oblivion. Chou was now carrying out Mao's purpose, but under enormous difficulties; for at all times rehabilitation of a cadre might be condemned as 'reversing the verdicts of the Cultural Revolution'.

The rumour of Teng Hsiaoping's rehabilitation in Tokyo must have been based, however wispily, on a demand for Teng's return at the time.

But the rebuilding of the Party, the return of old cadres, all this was an immense threat to Lin Piao. Heir or not, his contemporaries, his own companions of the Long March among them, would not forgive him easily the monstrous treatment he had inflicted upon them, upon Chu Teh and Lo Juiching, and Ho Lung.

And there was Chou Enlai; whom Mao now called 'the manager', who

* See *Wind in the Tower*.

had kept China going, and who since 1968, with the condemnation of the 'ultra-left', could no longer be openly attacked. However, Chen Pota and a group of military men in the Central Committee did attack Chou Enlai openly, for not subscribing to the total cult of Mao, at the second session.

The meeting was held at Lushan, the cool mountain resort where, in August 1959, Peng Tehuai, then Defence Minister, had criticized the Leap, and been demoted as a 'right opportunist'. Lin Piao's ascent to Peng's post had taken place there. And now in Lushan, Chen Pota attacked Chou Enlai for questioning the 'genius' thesis. Mao was a genius, and therefore every word of his was infallible.

What they did not realize was that Mao, with the perversity of great-ness, was getting tired of his own cult. He had used it,* and would now proceed to undo it. 'Give me back my aeroplanes,' he had shouted, staring at bosoms bedecked with Mao badges made of aluminium and other metals; 'I'm tired of being out in the sun and rain,' he had said of his statues in every public square; and he suggested that visitors in the hotels 'should see more art ... not only my face'.

Yet for Lin Piao's purposes Mao had to be a god, for how otherwise could Lin Piao be his prophet and sole expounder? Mao's every word must be infallible, even quoted out of context, even truncated. How else would Lin Piao rule over the minds of China — as Mao did — after Mao's death? And now Chou had contested the 'genius' theory, the infallibility, and Mao actually backed Chou, destroying his own infallibility!

Chen Pota attacked Chou on this theoretical point, affirming that Lenin had recognized the principle of 'genius'.

Besides this abstract polemic there were also very concrete issues. One was the question of the Head of State. Liu Shaochi had become Head of State in 1959, as well as being Vice-Chairman of the Party. Mao had been Chairman of the Party, having relinquished the post of Head of State to Liu Shaochi. Now Lin Piao wanted to be Head of State, for apart from being Mao's heir, Vice-Chairman of the Party, and Minister of Defence, he had no way of controlling the State Council and hence the Establish-ment — Chou Enlai ranked above him in such matters. Only the National People's Congress and its Head of State could prevail over Chou Enlai. But Lin Piao was not desirous of calling a National People's Congress before being sure that it would ratify him; he was not at all certain of that, and the National People's Congress was the supreme body in China. He had sent 'investigation teams' all over China the previous year, and

* As he told Edgar Snow. See *The Long Revolution* (Hutchinson, 1973).

realized that he did not have total control of the members of the National People's Congress.

Lin's scheme could not be voiced directly. Hence he and Chen Pota tabled a request that Mao Tsetung should be Head of State as well as Party Chairman, 'for then all words have weight'. Lin Piao, as Mao's heir, would then automatically become Head of State in his turn.

The second major point in dispute was foreign policy. American signalling to China was getting almost frantic ('We still don't get any reply,' a chagrined State Department official would tell me). And Chou Enlai, since the Bandung conference in 1955, had been identified with the policy of an opening out to the world, including America.

Lin Piao, and later the Gang of Four, were opposed to any contact with America. The edict of 1969 forbidding all communication with Americans had certainly come from them. Lin Piao was for improving relations with the U.S.S.R., despite the attacks on China's borders in 1969.

But in that autumn of 1970, Edgar Snow was in China and on October 1st he and his wife stood by Mao Tsetung on the Tienanmen gate, showing themselves to the Chinese millions.

There could be no more pointed evidence that Mao was for responding to American signals. He had received a letter from Nixon, secretly transmitted through Bhutto of Pakistan; and he would reply, through Edgar Snow, with an invitation to Nixon.

At the session of August–September 1970, Mao Tsetung, after having watched the 'political blitzkrieg' of Chen Pota against Chou Enlai, wrote six hundred searing words, a document circulated 'inside' only after Lin Piao's death in 1971, which I would be given to read in 1972.

'We do not need a Head of State ... I have said it many times ... I do not want to be Head of State,' wrote Mao. He refuted the genius theory. He pointed out that Chen Pota 'has never agreed with me in many ways ... and now acts as if the earth would stop turning, and the mountain of Lushan would be blown flat ... but this will not happen, the earth will continue to turn, and Lushan will not be blown flat.' He then referred to Lin Piao in veiled terms. 'We both ... must still study this question (of genius); of whether one stands on the side of idealism or materialism.'

Lin Piao, in his preface to the little red book had mentioned Mao's genius, and now Mao was refuting the whole concept of himself elaborated by Lin Piao!

The quarrel over 'genius' may appear small, but to Mao, as a theoretician, it was fundamental to a whole philosophy. Hence the many articles which then appeared, refuting that 'history is made by geniuses'.

Mao was now suspicious of Lin Piao; of the whole trend of his think-ing. Within weeks he had called upon Chen Pota, and the military members of the Central Committee who had supported his move against Chou Enlai, for their self-criticism.

I think that Mao was greatly saddened when he started to move against Lin Piao: saddened because he had truly cared for and trusted the younger man; and they had had many years of friendship together. He now waited for Lin Piao to come to him, to change, to own up ... but Lin Piao did not do so.

Lin Piao's wife, Yeh Chun, said openly, 'If there is no Head of State, what guarantee of power is there for us?'

As in a tragic play of the Renaissance, Mao and Lin Piao went on appear-ing together, acclaimed together; Lin Piao went on waving the little red book and shouting 'Long live Chairman Mao'.

And on October 1st Ed Snow, blissfully unconscious of all this, ad-dressed Lin Piao who stood by Mao, and asked him for an interview. Lin Piao turned to Mao for his agreement, and Mao looked straight into the infinite distance, as if he had not heard.

What attitude did the Shanghai Four—Chiang Ching and Wang Hungwen in the Central Committee, and her two helpers in the Politburo —adopt towards the assault upon Chou by Chen Pota? Nowhere has this ever been mentioned. Yet they were still closely identified both with Lin Piao and Chen Pota. They appeared, in fact, to form a coherent, solid 'Left'.

Perhaps, after Mao's six hundred words, the Shanghai Four hastily dropped Chen Pota and Lin Piao, 'unloading the general's chariot', as they had done with the young Red Guards who had served their purposes. Possibly they also realized that Lin Piao's overvaulting ambition would not hesitate to sacrifice them when the time came.

Towards the end of my stay in Japan, Hatano, one of the able corre-spondents of *Asahi Shimbun*, who spoke excellent Chinese and whose wife taught Chinese cooking on television, came to tell me that Kung Peng had died. Her death had now been officially announced.

I remained impassive, since for me she was already dead, and I had exhausted the externals of sorrow. For me she had died the day I had seen her in the hospital bed, her face so calm and her hair so neat, and all those tubes going in and out of her. Keeping the body alive when the mind is totally gone seems to me the height of superstition, of self-indulgence.

Hatano, being Japanese, understood me. He did not react like a Westerner, concluding only from outside appearance. 'You knew,' he said. 'I knew.' It is something we share, the art of non-exposure; reticence. I had loved Kung Peng too much to exhibit grief outside China.

Twenty-two

New Tartary: 1971

IN FEBRUARY 1971 I went to Algeria, invited by some Algerian writers I had met in 1962 at Cairo, who had now become officials in Algiers.

There was a cocky headiness, very marked among the young in Algiers. They walked tall, and my remark that everyone had a good straight spine pleased the susceptible Algerians (they are a most susceptible people). 'We have fought, we have stood up to a great war. We had a million dead out of eleven million people.' I roamed as far as I could, delighting in the Kabyle villages perched on the crests of the Djurjura ranges and in the beautiful white cities of the desert, Mzab, where women are all wrapped up, leaving only one eye with which to confront the world outside their bodies.

I gave lectures and met Houari Boumedienne. He had incorruptible gravity, the demeanour which Malaya had taught me to associate with an Islamic upbringing. He spoke intelligently about his country. But he was a military man, and in Algeria, unlike China, the word 'military' was antithetical to 'intellectual', owing to the French influence. The Algerian intelligentsia were very 'French' in habit and attitude and method of reasoning, even when opposing French colonialism. They could enthuse over de Gaulle's superb style, but not Boumedienne's excellent Arabic.

Algeria was well placed for prosperity. It had petrol, a small energetic population; excellent ports. Its valleys were fertile; agriculture would thrive when and if wheat took the place of the French-created vineyards. If only it could harness and utilize the abilities of its intelligentsia. This was the problem everywhere in the Third World, including China. But French colonialism had done little to train a professional élite: doctors, engineers, technicians. Their numbers were appallingly low. Of course there were writers; but a writer's usefulness is limited in the technology-hungry Third World.

'Our tragedy is that we are much too close to France. For many of our élite, the attraction of Paris remains overwhelming,' said Boumedienne.

How would Algeria (and so many other developing countries) reconcile the need for Western technology in the utilization of its resources, with its own cultural traditions? How would it allow the élite's demand for all Western freedoms which are but a concomitant of Western wealth – when this meant losing its élite, and very fast, to the seductive West?

In April 1971 Vincent and I were married in Madras. 'It will please your father,' I said. Vincent, like all men, had forgotten the legalities. Vincent's father, although President of the Catholic Association of India, was the most tolerant of men; he was beaming with happiness at our civil cere-mony, held in his house opposite the Cathedral of St Thomas, where reposed, in the crypt, the bones of my favourite saint, Doubting Thomas the Apostle.

At India's independence in 1947, Vincent's father had fought for tolerance of all religions to be written into the Constitution. A strong clamour for making India a Hindu religious state had started; and Hindu-ism with its caste system, is one of the most intolerant and repressive of all religious creeds. Nehru was too modern-minded to agree to this, although he was of Brahmin origin; and the Constitution proclaimed that India was a secular state. But today's Indian leaders are more inward-turning. Militant Hinduism is on the march, as militant Islam is from Bangladesh to Algeria. Should the warlike, intolerant Jan Sangh Party of India – a paramilitary arm of the Hindu religion – come to power, India's 9 million Christians and 80-odd million Muslims may be exterminated by 600 million Hindus, as Buddhism was exterminated by India's great religious wars of the past.

In May 1971, Edgar Snow came to see me in Paris. Ed's interview with Mao of December 1970, during which Mao said that President Nixon would be welcome in Peking, had been published in *Life* magazine. Ed had tried the *New York Times*, but they had dawdled, and *Life* had snapped up the story.

We talked about Chou Enlai. Chou had called for Ed one night, and spoken to him for hours, not complaining, simply thinking aloud. 'He was under great stress,' said Ed, the most discreet and trustworthy of friends.

Now it was certain that America and China would get together. Ed was working hard on his book, *The Long Revolution*. He left me, complaining of backache. A doctor pottered with his kidneys. Only at the year's end would it be discovered that Ed's backache was cancer of the pancreas. I still have Ed's letter about it, received when I returned from China in December. 'I was felled by something,' he wrote. He would be operated on, and would die in February 1972, the very month that President Nixon went to China to see Mao Tsetung.

Ed's death was for me almost like the passing of my days of youth and strength. We had known each other so long, so long; meeting at last in person in London in 1942 – through Dorothy Woodman of the *New Statesman*. Both of us had, behind us, decades of involvement with China; we had shared these extraordinary and inspiring years, through letters, meetings, concern, fascination. Ed's spirit lives on; many Americans will be grateful to him. He had the courage to fight against cowardice, obscurantism; to maintain whole and clear a vision of the future. A vision shared by Mao, when he told Anna-Louise Strong, 'I place my hopes in the American people.'

To Yugoslavia and to Italy, to attend meetings of writers and meet my publishers, and then off to New Delhi, to see Indira Gandhi. Indira was kind, but evasive. She was, that year, leaning towards the Soviet Union for reasons which would become clear: the revolt of East Pakistan against West Pakistan's rule.

Mujibur Rahman of East Pakistan led the revolt, and was openly supported by India. Bhutto of West Pakistan jailed him; but subsequently released him. Bhutto sent troops to suppress the 'rebellion', and these troops committed atrocities, or so it was profusely reported. This produced immense indignation, not only in India but throughout Europe, and the propaganda was most effective because the Soviet Union helped, through all its 'progressive' sympathizers in West Europe. Refugees from East Pakistan poured into India's Bengal (East Pakistan was actually the other half of Bengal, sundered by the British at Partition in 1947). Ten million refugees were said to be coming out. 'We cannot afford them. Our own people are starving,' clamoured the well-fed ladies and gentlemen of New Delhi to me (I was lecturing at the Press Club).

In Europe the cause of 'Bangladesh',* the new name for East Pakistan, aroused disproportionate emotion (but who remembers it now?). André Malraux announced that he was setting out to fight for Bangladesh. He desisted, however, a week later.

My visit had convinced me that East Pakistan was indeed shabbily treated by West Pakistan. But the furore engendered had another motive, as had the exaggerated refugee figures. Mujibur Rahman, India's favourite, would establish the independent state of Bangladesh with the help of the Indian army in November. This action would only be undertaken, however, after a treaty of friendship and alliance between India and the U.S.S.R. had been signed in August that year; the treaty was meant to 'warn off' China and Pakistan, should either of them intervene.

Mujibur Rahman did not last; he was assassinated within two years, and relations between India and Bangladesh were strained, since the real issues — as always — were economic: the control by India of the waters of the Indus River and the monopoly of Bangladesh jute production by the jute companies established in Calcutta. Exchanging one despot for another was not the object of the people's uprising in Bangladesh. But like all Third World countries, the way to a better future would be long and dolorous.

Meanwhile, the 'treaty' between India and the U.S.S.R. would have far-reaching consequences: it would help to establish the U.S.S.R. as a power capable of interfering in the whole of South Asia.

Late June in Peking; the sky heat-pale, and in the parks the strong smell of insecticides sprayed on the trees. I had asked to tour the landmark sites of the Long March for a chapter in my book, *The Morning Deluge*. I had also asked again to visit Tibet. Regretfully, Tibet was 'not available', but the Long March sites were, and would we like to visit Sinkiang later in the summer, instead of Tibet? Vincent and I were elated. Sinkiang had been closed for many years to visitors. We would be the first to go there since 1959.

But we went first to Shanhaikuan, the seaboard town, to see the end of the Great Wall there, a tiered gate which had just been repaired; for Vincent was fascinated by the Great Wall. Then on to Manchuria, where Commander Liu Tetsai once again welcomed us, as did Li Suwen and Wen Chuming, and other members of the provincial revolutionary committee. Somehow, I had favourably impressed Chiang Ching in my

* Meaning East Bengal.

1969 interview, hence the reception. By then Chiang Ching and her group
went scouring round for intellectuals to serve them. In the universities,
already, they had recruited a few, who would thereby escape 'cattle sheds'
and long imprisonment by putting their pens at the disposal of the Four.

We went to Dairen, and sailed with the fishing fleet, and saw the harvest
of the largest and best sea-cucumbers, with five rows of knobs on their
backs. Commander Liu took us into a mountain's heart, to view the
installations against a nuclear attack: schools, a hospital, dormitories and
food stores, canteens and water tanks and toilets—everything for the
survival of a population of 200,000.

Vincent's advice was eagerly sought in the factories and plants, but not
always well received when he gave it with his usual forthrightness. 'In
India the factory inspector would not allow such unsafe working conditions,' he would say in Dairen of the glass factory, which produced
marvels, but in most primitive surroundings. I reminded him that in India
there were appalling sweat shops and factories, and that Untouchable
children worked in the most terrible conditions in the leather industry.
'I'm talking of India's public sector,' said Vincent with indisputable logic.

We were back in Peking for Army Day and its banquet. Huang
Yungsheng, the acting chief of staff and Lin Piao's right-hand man, made
the main speech. Huang had been nicknamed 'the butcher' by the young
in Kuangtung province, because of his drastic methods of restoring order
there. He was to leave, during his years of tenure in south China, quite a
network of his men behind; and even in 1978 a clear-up of 'Lin Piao
influence' was still proceeding in Kuangchow.

In that summer of 1971 an unconfirmed rumour went about that Army
Day would be changed from August 1st to September 18th. The reason
given was that Mao Tsetung, the 'True Creator' of the Red Army, had
started the peasant insurrection called 'the Autumn Harvest Uprising' in
September 1927. It was the first skirmish utilizing Mao's basic strategy of
'the countryside surrounding the cities'. And Lin Piao, in 1965, had pinned
his reputation on a pamphlet entirely backing this strategy, but extending
it to proclaim the Third World the 'countryside', which would surround
and destroy the affluent world in a maelstrom of revolution.

August 1st, however, commemorated the Communist Party's first
armed resistance and military exploit, the capture of the city of Nanchang
under the direction of Chou Enlai, and with professional forces. In this
episode, which had been a breakthrough from the policy of supine non-
resistance to Chiang Kaishek's onslaught, Chu Teh, Chen Yi, Lo Juiching,
and Ho Lung had also distinguished themselves. And Lin Piao was

attempting to efface from history all other commanders except himself and his allies. Already Chu Teh had been 'rubbed out' at the first base created by Mao in the mountains of Chingkang in 1927. After many battles against Chiang Kaishek, Chu Teh had led his remaining battalions there, to join with Mao. Now a large oil painting had taken the place of the monument previously set up in memory of this historic event. The painting showed only Mao and Lin Piao meeting there.

Ho Lung had died 'of natural causes' (some people whispered: of diabetes and starvation) in 1969. Chen Yi was dying of cancer. Lo Juiching was denounced as a counter-revolutionary ...

But apparently Mao had refused to move the date of Army Day. I listened to Huang's speech on August 1st, and was surprised because it made only one reference to Soviet 'social-imperialism' but denounced repeatedly 'American imperialism'. Usually a speech even-handedly denounced both. What did this mean?

In the newspapers an insistent debate castigating idealism, and 'the theory of many centres' continued from the previous winter. Chen Pota had disappeared from view. But praise of Lin Piao continued. And not even the keenest China-watcher in Hongkong guessed that the articles were slings and arrows directed against Lin Piao.

I received a telephone call: Comrade Chiang Ching would like us to attend a new ballet that evening. We had tea at the British Embassy, and went on to the theatre. We were ushered into a private reception room and found it full of people waiting for Chiang Ching. There was Joris Ivens, and Marcelline Loridan, and also Yao Wenyuan and Chang Chunchiao, Chiang Ching's two allies, and Wu Teh, to become later acting Mayor of Peking, and a number of other officials, interpreters and translators.

I sat by Chang; Yao was on the opposite side of the room, talking with Marcelline and Joris. Joris had come to make films, and would begin to plan and to prepare his magnificent series of ten films on China.* I thought Yao repulsive to look at; his teeth were jagged, and he had a bad skin. He wore a cap screwed to his head at all times, until suddenly, in 1975, he appeared at a formal banquet with a thick, shining head of hair: wig or graft, for he was, despite his youth (he was forty), extremely bald.

Chang, on the contrary, looked like an intellectual, with a long, intelligent face. He had wavy dark hair. Born in 1916 of a mandarin family, he

* *How the Foolish Old Man Moved the Mountain.*

had started writing in school magazines when he was fifteen; and gravitating to Shanghai had joined the League of Left-wing Writers there in the 1930s. After 1949 he had become the director of the literary department of the Party in Shanghai; and had then recruited Yao Wenyuan, who specialized in politico-literary criticism. Both joined forces in the 1950s to denounce the 'rightists' in the aftermath of the Hundred Flowers; and by exhibiting ruthless revolutionary purity Chang had become the cultural tsar of Shanghai.

In 1963, Chiang Ching, furious at the cold shouldering she received from people like the Vice-Minister Hsia Yen, and Mayor Peng Chen, in Peking, went to Shanghai and there obtained all the support she wanted from Chang and Yao. Thus would start the nucleus of the Gang of Four. Shanghai's cultural and propaganda apparatus was mobilized for theatre reform, but also to serve Chiang Ching.

Chang had ascended the hierarchy of the Party very swiftly since 1966. He was chairman of Shanghai's Revolutionary Committee, member of the Politburo, and he would accumulate other posts. He had now recruited the Seventeenth Textile Mill 'worker', Wang Hungwen, who had led the seizure of Shanghai in January 1967. There is no doubt that he was clever as well as ambitious; in fact, he was the brains behind the organization of the Four.

Chang said to me, 'I've heard of your interest in the model operas. Comrade Chiang Ching has worked very hard. She has many interesting things to teach us. We all learn from her ... her life has been entirely in the cause of revolution.' I had never had such a direct hint that I should interest myself not only in the operas but in Chiang Ching's life story. And before I had thought what I would say, I replied, 'Unfortunately I am very busy at present ... I am writing a big book on the Chinese Revolution.' This was the most brutal and, from the point of view of anyone intent on getting into the good graces of the rising constellation, the most stupid thing I could ever have done. Thus did I turn down the second, and the most outspoken hint to write up Madame Mao's life, a hint which had certainly come from her. She had planned to recruit me. I did it not because I had any feelings against her at the time but out of stark candour, stupid ignorance of 'how to get on'.

In came Chiang Ching, like a small whirlwind, buzzing in a suit; her voice loud and imperious. She sat down and stood up, sat down again, wiped her face, wiped her arms to the elbows, wiped her neck to the armpits, with the hot towels handed to her; as if she had just come from the fields and a spell of harvesting or threshing. She had, in fact, stepped down from her car. There was a blown-up exaggeration in all this physical activity which compelled one into a feeling grotesque and unreal. But Chiang Ching did have the power to transport her viewers from solid common sense into her own world of make-believe.

Behind Chiang Ching someone carried a pile of new blouses. 'I want to reform clothing ... our women are too strict in their ideas. They should wear flowery materials.' This was meant to be, like the model operas, a major innovation. I forbore to say—though I was tempted—that I had seen flowery blouses throughout north China before the Cultural Revolution. Marcelline was handed a blouse, and the other women present too. Came my turn: Chiang Ching hesitated, then went to the toilet, came back with a fresh blouse on and handed me the one she had worn. A most signal honour. 'The very blouse Comrade Chiang Ching wore, on her own body,' whispered Vincent's interpreter to him, in an awed voice. I expressed my thanks. Chiang Ching went on talking, or rather exclaiming about the opera, and actresses, and other topics; disconnected phrases. She put on and took off her glasses. I had with me a small chain to keep one's spectacles round one's neck, and I handed it to her.

'What is this for?'

I explained. But the chain did not please her.

'It's gold,' she said, looking at it suspiciously.

'No, it's gilded.'

'I don't like anything round my neck, like a necklace,' said she.

And this conjured up for me a scene three years old: that of Liu Shaochi's wife, Wang Kuangmei, being humiliated by two thousand Red Guards at Tsinghua University, and forced to wear a necklace of ping-pong balls— because she had worn a necklace on official visits to potentates abroad. Perhaps it was Chiang Ching who had remarked on Wang Kuangmei's necklace when haranguing the young Red Guards, at the time devoted to her. Hence they had singled out this detail against Wang Kuangmei.

Chiang Ching rose, looked round at us, a satisfied circular glance. Now she started comparing our heights. A young actress was there, following her with clasped hands, as in prayer.

'We have a number of tall women here,' said Chiang Ching, and addressing herself to me, 'How tall are you?'

'I don't know,' I replied.

Silence. Thick, no sound. Chiang Ching could no longer say a word. I think now that her chatter had annoyed me, but neither Vincent nor the Ivens realized what had taken place, and no interpreter translated. Chiang Ching glared, speechless; she could not find her voice. She simply waved her hand to usher us into the auditorium. We followed her. She had put on her jacket again.

The hall was packed with a select audience of actors and actresses and musicians, and soldiers in uniform, all 'cultural workers'. They clapped and clapped. Chiang Ching waved the little red book she had taken out of her pocket, and looked round, with a gleam of triumph on her face. Joris sat on her right and I was at her left. Throughout the next two hours she kept her back firmly turned to me, and addressed herself solely to Joris Ivens, or to the row behind us, where some officials sat.

The ballet started: Chiang Ching talked steadily right through it, and all the time she talked, she wiped herself, going over her neck and face and even under her armpits, as if she sweated abundantly. And she told Joris, at the top of her voice, the story of her life; or rather, those parts of it that she wanted me to hear. For it was quite obvious that she wanted *me* to hear them. She would not otherwise have talked so loudly. Behind Joris an interpreter translated into French. Joris made cooing sounds. He was always amiable, and slightly bored.

She told Joris about her family; its poverty; how people talked 'maliciously' about her, had calumniated her and continued to do so; how she had always fought to produce revolutionary films and plays. Constantly she came back to the theme: 'People lie about me; they tell tales about me ... they seek to destroy me.'

The ballet proceeded.* It was about a heroic peasant woman who finds a wounded P.L.A. soldier lying in coma and gives him her own breast milk to drink in order to save him. Of course the dancer went off stage, returning with a cup in her hands. The soldier quaffed the beverage and from a prone position started to leap about. Suddenly Chiang Ching interrupted herself to shout, 'Red shoes, not green shoes.' (The heroine was wearing green shoes.) 'Red shoes, not green shoes,' said a resigned voice. It was that of an official seated behind her.

At the end, we trooped on stage to applaud and shake hands with the dancers and to be photographed with them. Chiang Ching had Joris and Marcelline stand next to her; I found a place a little further from her. Vincent, meanwhile, had tried to speak to Yao Wenyuan, but Yao had turned away and pretended not to hear him. Then it was over. Chiang Ching left, after another circular glance at all of us. Chang and Yao went with her, and did not shake hands with me. We went back to the hotel and to bed, and suddenly we were whispering, as if there were hidden microphones in the room.

* It was *Yi Meng Song*. It was shown several times but never really caught on.

'She's odd.'

'Yes.'

'Arrogant.'

'Well ... '

I lay awake, thinking: what kind of a person had she become, and how could Mao have such a woman to live with, next to him? But these were sacrilegious thoughts which I did not share with Vincent at the time.

I went with Hsing Chiang to Papaoshan, the hill of burial for revolutionaries, to salute the ashes of Kung Peng. Most Party members were cremated; non-Party people, like my father, often chose burial. Right through north China grave mounds still pock-marked the fields; and peasants burned paper money on them at certain times of the year.

Each time I entered the modest-sized hall where, on shelves, the ashes of Party members reposed I felt moved, remembering the past, and their deeds of valour. We found Kung Peng; a photograph adorned her casket, and Hsing Chiang and I bowed, and sorrowed. Such a small box, to contain what had been so much grace and fortitude.

In 1972 I would again come to salute Kung Peng, and I would see, further along the rows, the casket of Chen Yi, the merry and honest warrior and poet. Chen Yi died in January 1972 of cancer of the caecum. I would never hear his cheerful laughter again. George Wu, the cancer specialist, also missed him greatly. 'He noticed everything. He would say to me, "How do you stick it round here? We push you around, we criticize you—yet you go on. Why?" ' 'Because, I guess, I love China,' Wu had replied. And Chen Yi had said, 'You overseas Chinese, you have much to teach us.' Chou Enlai had delivered the funeral oration for Chen Yi, and Mao Tsetung himself had attended. A friend of mine told me how Mao had stayed on after the ceremony, staring at the wreaths, just staring, until, gently, Chou Enlai had led him away.

'Every day there are several hundred people, on Sundays a thousand or more, who come here to salute Chen Yi,' said the keeper.

I went to salute Papa's grave, now repaired after the depredations of the Red Guards, and then to see Anna-Louise. She had a magnificent marble tombstone. 'Rest happy, Anna-Louise. What you wanted to bring about has come to pass. China and America will be friends, and already the world is changed.'

545

Central Asia begins at Sian, the ancient Tang dynasty capital on the elbow of the Wei River. We flew over a million square kilometres of loess, silt brought down by the Yellow River, which has built the north China plains. Deforestation and erosion have made this solid mud a macaroni tangle of knotted cliffs and gullies, harbinger of the desert it would have become within the next century, had not the present government started taming the river, rewooding its upper reaches, building dams, making the desert shrink. It will take a century or two of work, an awesome enterprise. Meanwhile, in the limitless yellow churn, were sudden plateaus bulldozed to evenness, intensely green and fertile; state farms, communes, reclaiming the canyons, terracing the cliffs, and each terrace bearing the seed of forests to come.

I like the Islamic quarter of Sian, where an ambling goat, an occasional two-humped camel, rare as a fabled beast today, could still be accosted in the 1960s. Sian is enchanting, with its willows, the roar of its noon cicadas, its temples and museums and palaces, its delicious local beer and civilized people. From here we set out on our journey to modern Tartary, Sinkiang; we shall follow — by aeroplane — the Silk Road, as did the caravans launching themselves to cross the deserts to India, to Iran, to Tyre and Sidon, to Rome and to Alexandria.

Lanchow, capital of Kansu province, is the first oasis on the desert's edge. It nestles in a coil of the Yellow River, here a monstrous stream of ochre.

Our hotel is full of boisterous Mongols; a football team from Ninghsia has arrived to play a match with the local team. In the streets squads of people shouldering spades and pickaxes march to plant ten thousand new *mus* of land; there is a new canal, its water supply pumped up from the river.

The city is cool (1,400 metres above sea-level) and we are mothered by Madam Li of the revolutionary committee. I shall go back four times to Lanchow; which fascinates me. It is now an industrial city, the centre of China's atomic industry. Kansu was the poorest of all provinces before 1949, ruined by famines and wars since the nineteenth century. Now there are four times as many people in the city as in 1949. The railway only reached Lanchow in 1952, but it has since been built, from oasis to oasis, to reach Hami, and Urumchi, and onwards to Karamai.

In Lanchow the Cultural Revolution has been grim and fearful. 'The workers in the factories shot at each other,' says Madame Li. And this year there is a drought. 'Many trees have died ... We did wrong to plant on slopes. It is difficult to water them.' Blanket directives to grow cereal anywhere and everywhere have produced friction; for Kansu province contains national minorities: Mongols and Tibetans and Huis, whose grazing land has been reduced, to grow cereal. 'We must not go on doing it,' says Madame Li. Because of the Huis (Muslims), pig breeding is not favoured. 'Sheep and goat meat are still available, but the drought has killed a lot of animals.'

I have never seen such scrawny, dejected horses and mules as in Kansu province: almost as skeletal as in Old China, whereas one of the things I love in New China is the way the peasants' horses and mules are sleek and well-fed.

Next we fly off to Hami, two hundred metres below sea-level, renowned for its delicious melons. Once known as Qomul, on the Silk Road, it was a great trading emporium. Now it is an industrial city, as is Lanchow. At Hami airport I saw a fleet of ships upon a sparkling sea, and palm trees on the horizon. A desert mirage. Vincent, more prosaic, saw fighter planes aligned, and said that Hami must be an air force base.

Hami is the threshold to the majestic Gobi Desert. The aeroplane followed the Heavenly Mountains across the Gobi Desert, dividing Sinkiang into Zungaria in the north and the Tarim basin and the Takla-makan Desert in the south.

We took the northern route, and the oases along the mountain slopes were few; the southern slopes were the true main line of the Silk Road, swinging along the basin of the Tarim, to Turfan and Korla, to Kuche and Aksu and on to Kashgar where began the Pamirs and Afghanistan. We flew over black Gobi, a landscape of the moon, the mountains of the moon, torn by a wind already at noon wild and strong, tossing our aeroplane and rearranging the sand dunes below us into crescents and circles; shifting great tides of gravel which changed colour with the hours. And the mountains sat in vast crinolines, skirts of their own substance which had slid down their slopes and mantled their bases. 'It's the alternate heat and cold ... sometimes a montain explodes,' said the pilot. 'The Gobi is a young desert and it is still being sifted and split by wind and sun.'

There had been a plague of donkeys around Hami some years past, said the pilot. 'We don't need them any.more. We have jeeps and trucks, so now they run wild.' Once they had been the mainstay of the Shansi carters who plied up and down the Silk Road. Now, below us, a procession of lorries swirled immense dust clouds, climbing the desert dunes. The leaf-vein pattern of desert streams run dry, coming down from the mountains, ended in a pulverized mass of sand.

The Heavenly Mountains rose in height and dignity, and then there was a snow cap and many more patches of emerald green: oases, valleys. Urumchi was twenty minutes away. There towered Bogdan, God's mountain, twin-crested and radiant.

Urumchi seemed in the grip of a local flood, although there had been no rain for six months. 'Underground water.' The inhabitants had been digging air-raid shelters (all China was digging shelters that year), and a spring had been broken into and had flowed into the streets. Ismail Emet, the Uighur representative, a delegate at the Ninth Congress, welcomed us. He was thirty-four years of age, a mild and handsome man with a fair skin and curly dark hair. He wore a thick corduroy jacket and trousers and he did not sweat. Throughout our stay in Sinkiang I would be amazed to find the Uighurs heavily clad, wrapped in clothes and shawls on the hottest day.

'Urumchi is sinister,' Owen Lattimore had written; to him, it was the most thief- and dog-ridden city in China. But of course it was not so when we saw it. Like all cities of China today, it was two cities, the old and the new. And the difference is far more marked in national minority areas, such as Sinkiang, or Tibet, or in Yunnan among the Pais. Both in Urumchi and Kashgar, the old towns with their small desert-style houses, thick walls of mud bricks, shuttered and cool, painted white or ochre, might have been anywhere in Islam's great domain; and narrow lanes through which skirted women hurried were timeless, Biblical. But there were also modern Urumchi and Kashgar, with drab functional buildings of grey and red brick, with schools and hospitals and supermarkets and factories. Inelegant, but with running water and electricity.

The Uighurs are of the same origin as the Turks; the word Turk came into being in the fourth century, when their tribes came down from the Altai and into Sinkiang. 'That was six centuries after the Silk Road had been established by the Hans,' Ismail reminded me. For a while, here were great kingdoms and empires; there is no more fascinating, adventurous history than that of Central Asia.

It was not before the eighth or ninth century that the Turks went westward and began to settle in today's Turkey. The Uighur language still bears a very strong resemblance to Turkish.

There are altogether thirteen national minorities in Sinkiang, Uighurs and Tajiks, Uzbeks and Kazakhs, Tartars and others; but the whole area of over $1\frac{1}{2}$ million square kilometres, only contains eight million people: $4\frac{1}{2}$ million Uighurs, half a million other nationalities, and three million Hans. Sinkiang is now known as a Uighur autonomous region.

How beautiful the Uighurs were! Truly one of the most handsome people on earth. And how they loved to dance, to sing, to play music! All their movements were graceful, and the girls with their thick plaits, in their flowered short-sleeved dresses, were enchanting.

This is where frustration came in. We had to battle – politely – with a fairly fat military man, Comrade C., who was a security maniac – and alas not the only one. He was so careful of our safety that we could not move near anyone, and would have spent our days in Sinkiang being briefed in our guest residence, or whirling about at great speed in cars which we were not allowed to leave, had we not rebelled.

I understood the concern of Comrade C. There had been bloody episodes here during the first years of the Cultural Revolution, and he was still jittery. But it was dreary to go to a factory or to a supermarket, and find that everyone who was an ordinary person had been shooed away; that we could only be approached by a handful of people duly tutored. Mr Ma, the very able and erudite Foreign Ministry official who accompanied us on this trip, and Madame Yeh also a diplomat, did their best. But the thwarting produced awkward moments.

I remember one 'arranged' occasion in a store for native handicrafts. Not one of the 'buyers' gathered there, waiting for us to arrive in order to pretend to buy, was anything but a cadre in training! They were all young, all well-dressed, and they acted their parts very badly.

We stayed outside Urumchi in a beautiful guest house, once a warlord's residence, around it a garden with willows and camphor trees and running water. Beyond was the main road to Hami, bordered with tamarisk and poplars. And along it were communes, some of mixed Uighur and Han families, some of Uighur only.

One day at the road's edge I saw a marvellous sight. Harvesting. A high-wheeled horse cart, and the Uighur women throwing the sheaves of wheat with lovely gestures onto the cart. 'Stop, stop,' I cried, and got out of the car, and Vincent and I walked into the wheat stubble, and like a great rise of birds all the Uighurs in the field, children and women (the Uighur male seems to leave this work to women and young boys), came running towards us, laughing and cheering. I still have the scene on film.

Many of the women had babies tied to them; they crowded round us. They had none of the Confucian reticence of the Hans; they *wanted* to be filmed, to be photographed! They wanted to touch us and to be near us, and this great hunger for friendliness was something unforgettable. Marco Polo, who had come along the Silk Road in the thirteenth century, had already commented: 'They are the most friendly people.' They had not changed. Gaiety and the body's grace was theirs, always. They burst into song on invisible impulse; I had seen boys dancing in the street with the sheer joy of being alive.

And so the meaning of *oasis* came to us; of life which had dominion over gaunt death, over the dread of the terrible desert. The people were like those springs of water one discovered spurting from arid rock, unquenchable in their passion for joy.

But Military C.'s car caught up with us, and the security men surged out and started shoving the people away. 'Don't push, don't push,' I shouted angrily. It would happen a good many times. I would go back to Peking and complain about this, and say that this was not the way to treat national minorities ...

I did not know then—but I would find out the next year, when I returned to the oases and the desert—that Sinkiang was indeed an area of 'major security', not only because there was still trouble, purportedly with 'Russian agents', but chiefly because Sinkiang had become the bastion of Lin Piao, one of the regions of China in his power, and no rising of any kind could be allowed.

Vincent, who had not spent a childhood as I had on alert, avoiding warlords, escaping raids and danger; who had never been bombed, nor had had any of the experiences of my exciting life, became angry; he felt it was all childish and ridiculous. But I realized that it was not clever not to see the point of view of Comrade C. There might indeed be a terrorist attempt on us, to discredit the military holding Sinkiang. It was best, therefore, to compromise. I spoke in a conciliatory way to several people, and security slackened considerably.

It was in Kashgar that I had a wonderful experience, when I was allowed to visit, publicly, the great mosque.

The mosque was being regilded. Basil Davidson had noted in the early 1950s that the mosque was in sad disrepair, owing to the ravages before Liberation.* Obviously it had suffered some recent damage, probably from the Red Guards sent out from Peking to 'make revolution' in Sinkiang. I saluted the venerable men who came to greet me at the gates of the mosque, and I bowed towards the edifice (of course I did not enter it) with the deference of a woman. And when I walked out there was an immense crowd on the square, cheering, and suddenly I was crying as the crowd broke through a cordon of unarmed Han policemen, and children and women ran towards me. I picked up a toddler and the little boy did

---

* See *Turkestan Alive* (Cape, 1957).

not cry. He looked like me. They all looked like me. They were all Eurasians!

Policemen tried to push back the crowd and the crowd went back like docile water, pliant and unbeatable like water. Mr Ma came and said it was time to go, and docile as water I re-entered the car. But Mr Ma was pleased, and so was I. After that Ismail Emet, who had been somewhat silent, somewhat subdued by Military C., blossomed. 'We are a great people, we the Uighurs,' he said.

'Of course you are.' I added, 'And I am a member of China's smallest minority. A Eurasian. There are not more than a few hundred of us about. But I have always been so terribly proud of being Eurasian.'

And so we met through words, in our dream of a world to come. For this is the desert, which lifts the ordinary into the extraordinary; or rather shows how extraordinary everyday life is, and makes words glow as stars in its velvet night sky.

Kashgar is a marvellous place; once a great city, and destined for greatness again as China develops the whole area up to the Pamirs. Here, and all along the oases from it two great cultures, the Chinese and the Greek, met. Not only trade but religion and art; Buddhism from India and the Greco-Buddhist art of Gandhara. And Nestorians, Zoroastrians, so many others. There was glamour just in the names. They sang of splendour and adventure.

I went to see the grave of Hsiang Fei, the Fragrant Concubine. She was a Uighur, her loveliness so great that its fame reached the eighteenth-century Ching Emperor, Chien Lung, who desired her, and she was brought to him. The tradition of having Uighur wives and concubines in the imperial household was an old one; in fact the Tang dynasty was more than a little Uighur.

Fragrant Concubine's voyage across the desert took two years, but the patient Emperor was ravished. So enamoured of her did he become that he built for her a palace, and a swimming pool; and because she was forever sad, thinking of her country, he built mountains and a desert in the palace gardens. Her body gave out perfume; even the waters of her bath carried the scent; whether or not it was attar of roses is not recorded. But she pined for Kashgar, rode on horseback, wore boots and a dagger in her jewelled belt, and was painted in helmet-and-armour by the court painter, Giulio Castiglione, an Italian.

Emperor Chien Lung went on a trip, and his mother had Fragrant

Concubine strangled, alleging that she possessed a dagger and planned to kill the Emperor.

Her tomb in Kashgar is an edifice in Arab style, with glowing blue-tiled domes. Inside it she and her parents lie. An annual fair lasting a week is held here. Tents and stalls are erected all round the monument; families come from afar in their big-wheeled carts drawn by donkeys and horses. The men ride on horseback and race; the young girls titter and glance at them; and there is dancing and music and much singing of love.

A hedge of cactuses and desert date trees surrounded the garden. On the flat spiked palettes of the cactuses Red Guards (who had come perhaps to destroy the grave as 'feudal', but they had been stopped) had engraved the words: 'Destroy Wang Enmao', 'Wang Enmao is a counter-revolutionary.' Wang Enmao was the commander in charge in Sinkiang before Lin Piao took over.

Kashgar was no longer the 'sinister city' described by Sir Eric Teichman. But it was still a Central Asian city; along its lanes came women looking like the Virgin Mary, wrapped in great mantles which covered their hair. The houses were pale grey and ochre, of straw and clay bricks, bricks such as had been made by the Jews in Egypt in the Pharaohs' time; the same bricks from which the first battlements of the Great Wall of China had been built.

At one time Kashgar was such a caravanserai that each nationality had its own walled enclave, but now all the walls had been taken down. The new Kashgar had bicycle and tractor and textile and wool and fertilizer and petrochemical and heavy machinery factories. The road to it was busy; it ran from Aksu and Kuche to the north and Yarkand and Khotan south-eastwards. Trucks and lorries passed frequently, with their motors exposed to cool the engines and prevent the sand clogging them. Above the road towered the great ranges of the Karakorum, and from the slopes came many streams, making fertile valleys with grassland for pasture, and fields, right on the edge of the Taklamakan Desert.

The Kashgar middle school had as many girls as boys. Uighur was being romanized, said the headmaster. Previously the Arabic script had been used; then Cyrillic had been introduced, owing to Russian influence, from 1954 to 1956; but in 1958 Premier Chou Enlai had it changed to the roman alphabet. The headmaster told me gravely that 90 per cent of the text-books were now romanized, but he read his own speech from notes in Arabic script, and when I pointed this out he said, 'I am too old to study romanization.' Outside, all posters, banners and painted slogans were in both Han and romanized Uighur. This was the gap between rhetoric and reality, official façade and everyday life. I told the headmaster that the Turkish language had been romanized some decades ago, and he nodded again. 'It is not for an old man like me.' He was forty-two.

We lodged at what had once been the Russian Consulate; a gloomy assembly of enormous rooms separated by thick velvet hangings and drapes, so many carpets on the walls and on the floor that all sound was muffled; Vincent and I spent much time seeking each other and shouting, 'Where are you?' without an echo in reply. The toilet and bathroom were furnished with giant porcelain equipment, as in every place where Russians had lodged. Were they truly so large-bodied? Or was it merely the fashion of the times?

I lost my temper at the Kashgar hospital. The army man in charge had forced all the doctors to turn out, to sit and listen while he talked and talked about the hospital and how much it had improved now after ridding itself of 'the capitalist line'. I looked at the impassive faces around me. They were tired and thin. I got down to questions. How many nurses were there? How many beds? How many patients? Then I got angry.

'You can't run a hospital like that. There are not enough nurses for the patients – the doctors' health will break down.'

'With Mao Tsetung Thought we can do *anything*,' replied the army man fatuously.

'You can do a lot but you cannot revive people who are dead ... Your doctors are overworked.'

I left in fury.

'I'll report to Peking about this. It's sabotage,' I said to Mr Ma.

'Oh, please do,' said Ma happily.

And then I realized that that was the reason I had been sent. Not to approve of everything, but to pick faults. And I remembered that Chou Enlai had often said, 'We are not always well-informed.' I was not here just for a good time; I also had a responsibility. To see clearly, and to report what I had found, but not to collide with local authority. I must keep my temper, if possible.

We went by car to the oases of Kuche and Aksu, and on to Shohotze in the Tarim basin reclamation area. 'The women of Aksu are the most beautiful in the world,' said the very nice military man from Kashgar who came with us. He had become thoroughly Uighurized after six years in the country. 'I don't think I can live anywhere else now. My spirit needs the desert'. His gestures had unstiffened; he would almost burst into song and dance. He probably yearned to marry a Uighur girl from Aksu.

All along the roads of Sinkiang are rock caves with Buddhist and Manichean frescoes; the latter with the double eagle emblem, which was a religious symbol before it became the emblem of Tsarist Russia. But alas, we could not stop to see those priceless relics of the past.

Shohotze was one centre of the reclamation area of the Tarim basin. In summer when the river's many tributaries from the Heavenly Mountains and the Karakorum are in spate, the valley, six hundred kilometres long, is bright green, and there are poplars and groves of tamarisk and scrub and reeds. Since 1950 it had been under development by the army, and it was now an enormous collection of fertile fields with many tree belts, state farms. Three hundred thousand Hans from Szechuan and other provinces, and forty thousand 'educated youths' were settled here in 1964-5. Chou Enlai and Chen Yi had come to visit the youths, many from Peking and Shanghai, and to inquire about their living conditions.

From all I had read of previous travellers, the area was indeed unrecognizable. There had been merely swamps and some skimpy huts. Now there was electric light, telephone, running water; in this depth of Central Asia an expanse of modernism, ball-bearings instead of exotic backwardness. But then all Asia wanted ball-bearings, and the word exotic was a European invention.

Here grew cotton and wheat, and sunflowers for oil, and maize, and rice to improve the alkaline soil; for the soil was laden with salt. Date trees of a tenacious kind were grown, to anchor the sand dunes, and mushrooms. There were straight avenues lined with poplars and young firs and white wax trees; and many irrigation canals. And of course there were factories. The population was organized along military lines, as the commander told us. 'The dependents of our workers', which meant the families, 'produce secondary articles needed for the factories.' He said that the educated youths 'adapt well'; they received 30 *yuan* 30 *fen* a month; a worker received 58 *yuan*.

This was one of the many 'army resettlement camps', designed to implant a population in remote uninhabited areas. From the overcrowded provinces of China, millions would be resettled here. 'Life is better here than in many regions of east China.'

I got up early in the morning. Some women were walking on the road, and they stopped and we began to talk. They came from Szechuan.

'I go back to see my family every New Year,' said one woman. Her children were in Szechuan. 'They are used to the city. My parents look after them.'

A military man came up fast behind me and our talk was over. The woman walked away, grinning cockily.

'Really, there's just too much security,' I said to Mr Ma. 'As if I did not understand that we have to plant new settlements, to shift people. I even talked about it with Chen Yi some years ago. And to pretend that *every one* of these people comes willingly – that's nonsense. There must be both stick and carrot. Incentive and pressure. I understand all this. Why not let me speak to the people?'

After that there was no more interference, and I saw a good many families. The standard of care was very high.

We visited the Karamai oilfields, encompassed by ranges in a vast horseshoe, called the mountains of Genghis Khan; they looked like an advancing horde. The oilfield was an old one, and had pipelines to several cities of Sinkiang. The army of course ran the oilfield. Keiyoumu Maiti-miyaze, a Tajik in charge of the Karamai garrison, told me that here the struggle had been 'acute', and 'the ultra-left used knives and guns and mortars ... ' The army had crushed them, in March 1967, and production had been resumed. There were wells some 4,000 metres deep; Soviet experts had said that Karamai was finished, done for, there was no more oil, but Keiyoumu said that was not true. 'We are prospecting and there may be new gushers soon.'

We went from Urumchi to Turfan by Big Wind Pass, a narrow-throated gorge through which the sinuous road wound by a river. We sweltered, and I could imagine the whinny of horses and the lugubrious scream of camels in the hot wind which sandblasted our faces. From the grey metallic sheen of the Gobi into another desert, where the air quivered like flame and the land was red, and the low-lying horizon was red too: here were the Flame Mountains of legend. Through this furnace the monk Hsuen Tsang had travelled, accompanied by the legendary Monkey,* to seek the Buddhist scriptures in India.

All security had vanished; leaving the gorge, Ismail and I now loitered by the river bank, dipping our hands in the stream as an act of worship to the sparkling water.

Down the road came a horseman, beautiful in his saddle, saluting gravely

---

* See *Monkey*, translated by Arthur Waley (Allen and Unwin, 1942).

and behind him also on horseback a woman with a wimple on her head, as in fourteenth-century Europe.

From some ten minutes away, dancing in the heat, Turfan appeared like a green haze on the horizon, a mirage to cool the eye; and first there were its lifelines, the long ridges of *kereze* underground wells like mole burrows, bringing it water in tunnels, an irrigation technique practised in Iran and here for more than five hundred years.

The oasis of Turfan is 160 metres below sea-level; February is the sowing season and the sand wind blows burning air two days out of five. It has been described as hell by so many travellers that perhaps it is hell, but the people of Turfan call it the Vale of Paradise. Or at least so did Joshe Turudi, the head of the revolutionary committee of Turfan, who came to greet us.

Turudi was six foot two, weighed two hundred pounds and had green eyes and curly hair. From Spain to Afghanistan he would have been at home; he even looked like a Roman centurion in search of spoil. He spoke both Chinese and Uighur, and he was exhilarated by water. The way he said the word was blessing, wonder of moisture, and the glamour of Turfan in the days of caravans came to us in that single word.

There are no industries in Turfan; it is still the oasis, and the houses are mostly baked clay and reed and straw, which can be sculpted into delicate patterns. Along the ridges of higher ground, are the barns for drying the grapes, a lacework of walls like sieves to let the air through. Turfan produced the wonderful seedless grapes renowned throughout the world, from Peking to Victorian England.* The mosque of Turfan was green-tiled and small; it had been derelict when Basil Davidson came here in 1956. It was now repaired, and on Friday capped men congregated in the narrow lane leading to it, obviously waiting to pray.

How green was Turfan, green and restful to the eye after the grey desert and the red desert! And here were tales of demons and ghosts, goblins of the sands and the scalding winds. We almost forgot (although it was forty-two degrees Centigrade in the shade) our aching skins rubbed raw by sand gusts. The guest house garden was pleasant and shaded, but there was a Shanghai housekeeper in charge of it. She was thin and depressed and she kept saying, without a pause, 'Oh how hot it is how hot it is please do not move too much here is a fan or you will be too hot.' All through the time we spent in Turfan she would cry unweariedly of the unbearable heat, and her voice was an uninterrupted sad scream. The heat

---

* In Christina Rossetti's poem, *The Goblin Market*, 'pellucid grapes without one seed'.

terrorized her; she could not forget it for a moment, and she had been in Turfan eighteen years. 'I came here when I was twenty ... to serve the people of Turfan.' But she could only utter her querulous and maddeningly monotonous cry, like a stranded curlew.

With her, to look after guests, was a most beautiful Uighur girl. She wore a multi-coloured dress and she did not even sweat; her skin was like a golden peach and her hair concealed an auburn glow in the coils of her heavy, sensuous plaits.

Vincent could not stand the heat at night; though he bore it well during the day. He was provided with two fans, both turned on to him as he slept. 'But it gets cool at night,' said Turudi, wondering that an Indian did not find Turfan pleasant.

In Turfan's great trough now flowed a new canal, the Tarlan canal, three hundred kilometres long; it had been dug 'by our Han brothers,' said Turudi, and the oasis had doubled in size. There was electric light and running water now. 'Turfan *is* the valley of Paradise,' insisted Turudi. But it only rained twelve millimetres in a year, and in winter the temperature went down to minus ten degrees Centigrade. All the houses had *kangs* of clay, and in winter the families huddled together upon them; the *kang* was in use all over north China.

Around us the desert smoked and boiled, and one could cook an egg in the sand of the Flame Mountains (fifty-two degrese Centigrade) when we took the forked road to the ancient city of Karakhoja; which, at one time, some Greeks who had wandered here had called Ephesus, in memory of another Ephesus. The palaces and terraces, buffeted by the terrible wind, showed their dead windows; but it had all become part of the rock and the sand and anyway we were not allowed to tarry. We had come to see the new, not the old, and once more 'security' intervened. The new was exciting; it was greenness eating into the desert; the oases extending; the first line of small young trees, their boles slender and younger than in the middle of Turfan with its old lanes: trees aligned straight as though drawn with a ruler. These were the green shelter belts and the new fields wrested from the desert would now yield cotton and wheat and maize and there would be orchards, 'enlarging Paradise'. Rice too was being tried here for the first time in history. Turfan had been a Han garrison in the Tang dynasty, but the north China soldiers ate wheat, not rice.

We went about the oasis through shaded pathways with willows and running water; we met women and girls; none wore the veil; though older women still had their heads covered with a shawl. The girls wore earrings and plaits and the beautiful embroidered Uighur caps on their heads. We ate sitting on carpets spread on the ground under shady trees: mutton and great heaps of melons and peaches and apples and grapes. At night boys and girls with guitars and clarinets and timbrels came to sing and to dance in the gardens. But at the guest house we could not escape the Shanghai woman's gentle moan: 'It is hot, it is hot.' She wore long trousers and a buttoned jacket. She did not turn up the trouser legs to the knee, as did the Han men, who fanned their bare legs and thus cooled themselves. She did not wear the light short-sleeved dresses of the Uighur women. Her face expressed only utter lassitude. Yet she valiantly continued to serve the people in Turfan.

'This was a poor and devastated oasis. Now it is rich,' said Turudi. Former travellers, like Owen Lattimore, and the two dauntless English-women, Mildred Cable and Francesca French, wrote of hopeless misery;* the misery had gone. The average income of an oasis dweller was much higher than in China proper; it averaged 2·50 *yuan* per labour day. There were 230 pumps for new irrigation, 530 *kereze* wells. Turfan now had over 120,000 people, of which the Uighurs made up 95,000, the Huis 10,000 and the Hans 16,000.

Turudi had had a terrible childhood. His mother had been killed by the water lord in front of him. All his life had been controlled by water, or the lack of it; and in the cool night, I sat with him for hours as he told me his story. 'The Revolution has been good for us; it has made us men, it has given us pride.' He also praised the Cultural Revolution. 'Without it we were being forgotten; there was too much bureaucracy.'

One afternoon we went to the Valley of Grapes. It was a most famous valley; over our head in thick clusters hung the grapes; so many of them, so many, almost theatrically too many, heavy, translucent, nacreous grapes. Below them we sat and ate, and then we danced. On both sides of the narrow valley were the cliffs, deformed, disintegrating, sitting in grey dust. They looked like demons watching us ready to pounce, to bury us in their dust. But the Uighurs made music with tambourines and the beautiful girls of the valley danced, and we had travelled back many centuries. If Paradise is relief from grief and want and care, when the caravans came here and the poets wrote love songs, then indeed Turfan was Paradise.

Up we went to the lake in the Heavenly Mountains, to spend a day with

---

* Owen Lattimore, *Nomads and Commissars* (Oxford University Press, 1962); Mildred Cable and Francesca French, *Through the Jade Gate and Central Asia* (Hodder and Stoughton, 1950).

the Kazakhs; to drink mare's milk freshly fermented in large copper pots. A woman, booted and with ample skirts, knelt to turn and stir the milk with a ladle and to spoon it out into drinking bowls. Vincent drank six bowls and earned the admiration and affection of the Kazakhs. I could not manage even one. And then there were games on horseback, races; and we went from tent to tent, talking with the families, admiring the children. The unmarried girls wore a little tuft of owl feathers in their caps. Tzeya the Tartar was the leader of this settlement, now known as the East Wind Pastoral Commune. Tzeya said how much better off they were than in the past. Here the workpoints are high. A commune member earns something like three *yuan* a day; seven to eight times as much as the average peasant in Szechuan. Everywhere in China there are differences in earnings, but among the national minorities it is policy to raise the earnings; they are uniformly higher than in the Han areas, except among the Yis and the Miaos of Kweichow and Yunnan, where they are extremely low.*

East Wind Commune is wealthy; it owns glossy stallions from Illi. All the men are elegant in corduroy; the women and girls wear layers of petticoats, boots and stockings. Abiola is the midwife of the commune, and Tunkien the teacher. Tunkien teaches on horseback, following the herds and their families; she wears brilliant pink stockings, and handles a gun with practised ease.

On the road back, single families of Kazakhs come riding down the Bogdan with their felt tents tied upon the backs of their cattle. The women carry their babies on the high saddle in front of them.

We are honoured on leave-taking. Lung Shuchin, the top military man in Sinkiang, gives us dinner. He is tall, thin and quiet. He commanded the unit which forced the crossing of the bridge over the Tatu River, under terrible fire from the Kuomintang, during the Long March.

We have been to Tartary, we have learnt much; we have met the Uighurs, and we feel as Marco Polo did, who loved them on sight.

On to Chengtu; and here at last is Sixth Brother and his wife; it is five years since I have seen them. They look well. I want to see Third Aunt, but it is hinted that she had better come to see me. We are lodged outside the

---

* These two provinces are reckoned to be 'cheap' areas, where the cost of living is low. There are fourteen 'grades' of living standard in China, and people are paid accordingly. Peking, for instance, is only Grade Ten, while Shanghai is Grade Fourteen. A Shanghai worker will automatically be paid more than a Peking worker.

city in a spacious villa; I take the hint. There is no point in forcing things. But in the end, we do go to her house: I want to make sure that she is well cared for.

Third Uncle died in 1968. Sixth Brother affirms that it was of natural causes. However, Sixth Brother does not tell me much that year. Only the next year, 1972, will he begin to tell me, in morsels, in very small fragments, how he was grilled and grilled for weeks, accused of having 'illicit connections abroad' (which meant being my cousin!), accused of having passed secrets, and of having had other evil intentions. 'But I never gave in, I always repudiated their accusations.' Finally 'they' could not do anything to him, except cut his salary and take away all his clothes and his wife's clothes, so that the two had nothing to wear except what they had on their backs, and winter was coming. And 'they' took away his watch, saying it was foreign. He had bought it in 1962, with money I had brought, in the overseas Chinese shop.

As for Third Aunt, she said nothing to me that year except that she was well. All I could do was give her some money and hope that all was indeed well. But in 1972 I heard in Peking from Jui that Third Aunt was accused of being from a landlord family, and she had been put 'under supervision of the masses'. This meant that an old worker, Comrade Wu, was supposed to watch her every move. I would make great friends with Comrade Wu and his wife, and they looked after Third Aunt with affection and care, so that finally what could have been unendurable turned out for the best. I also protested and I was assured in Szechuan that Third Aunt had never been accused of being 'landlord class'. All this took patience, and forcefulness at the right time, and also weighing judiciously what must be said and what must not, and above all not losing one's temper. And because it was my Family, I kept my temper remarkably well and did what had to be done.

It was obvious that Chengtu had suffered a good deal. There were damaged buildings, and in the factories the machinery was ill-kept. There was an unkempt look; and when I asked Sixth Brother he said, 'Some days we could not go out at all. There was fighting on the streets ... they killed people.' Who were 'they?' The May 16ers, he said.

The bookshops were almost empty. And there was no Szechuan opera, none at all.

'Why?'

'Because the cultural workers are in the countryside, learning from the workers–peasants–soldiers.'

I think of my dear friend Miss Chen, she of the crystal voice and the beautiful face. There are no plays to see, nothing, whereas in Sinkiang, there was every night some entertainment or another.

One morning (it was September 11th), Mr Ma said he had to return to Peking immediately, for there was business to attend to.

'Madame Yeh will look after you,' said he. Ma's face was sombre. Something really worried him.

'Mr Ma, are you feeling well?'

'Oh yes, yes of course.'

'Has something serious happened?'

Travelling in inland China, not allowed to read the local newspapers (the *People's Daily* arrives three days late), we are out of touch with what happens anywhere in the world, even with what is happening in Peking.

'Nothing serious,' says Mr Ma, smiling with great effort. Then he adds, 'One can never tell, about anyone ... A person can always change ... ' He leaves that evening.

Madame Yeh tells me that instead of taking an aeroplane we shall go by train to Chungking and proceed to Kweiyang, and from there we shall go to Tsunyi. Tsunyi is the famous city in Kweichow province where, in January 1935, the Red Army arrived after the staggering losses of the first lap of the Long March (due to bad military tactics). Mao Tsetung became, at Tsunyi, the leader of the Long March and thus it became an epic, a major triumph.*

We were a day in Chungking and in every shop there were slogans posted: 'Destroy the ultra-left!' 'Down with the ultra-left!', 'Catch the ultra-left, do not let them escape!'

It was September 13th when we arrived in Tsunyi. I watched the way the rice was planted; helter-skelter, unevenly as in Malaya, not in the beautiful tight symmetry of Szechuan. This was the way national minorities planted rice. On the roads were Miao women carrying baskets on their backs, supported by a belt on their forehead, as is still done in Nepal by mountain porters.

We went to the house where in January 1935 the Party held its famous meeting, a turning point in the history of the Revolution and in the career of Mao Tsetung.

We sat in the room where it had all happened. Above us hung a large oil painting; the triumphant conclusion of the Tsunyi meeting. There was Mao, rosy, impeccable in a well-pressed uniform, and by his side, of

* See *The Morning Deluge*.

course, Lin Piao. Only Lin Piao. I could not make out anyone else in the painting.

The briefing was in keeping with the painting. Lin Piao had stood staunchly by Mao while Mao exposed the errors made. No one else was mentioned. This posed a serious problem: Lin Piao had indeed been in command of the army divisions in the forefront of the March. He had captured Tsunyi, which made the meeting possible. Was this military superiority utilized to force a decision at Tsunyi? I do not think the cadres realized what they were saying; it distorted what Mao had tried to do: which was, in his customary way, to have Party sanction for the condemnation of the 'erroneous military line', and for his own accession to authority. The people who briefed us forgot that Mao had always insisted on Party dominance over the army; even if Party decision was 'helped' by the presence of favourable army commanders.

At the end of the briefing Vincent and I exploded.

'Tell me,' said Vincent, 'were there only Mao and Lin Piao at Tsunyi? Nobody else? What about Chu Teh, and Premier Chou Enlai?'

I said, 'I have read about the Tsunyi meeting; there's been quite a lot about it printed abroad ... I have consulted historians. Everyone is agreed that other people, such as Premier Chou Enlai, also played a major role at Tsunyi. It is not historically correct to mention only Vice-Chairman Lin ...'

Silence. Madame Yeh kept an impenetrable expression. The local cadres looked at each other. 'Of course others had a role ... but Vice-Chairman Lin was the one who made Tsunyi successful.'

That night, the local cadres drank a great deal with Vincent. Everybody became very cheerful.

We left Tsunyi on September 14th. I do not know whether by then the local cadres had learnt what had happened on the night of September 11th–12th to Lin Piao.

We went by car to Juiching. And thus we saw much more of the hinterland than we would have done otherwise. We discovered mountain roads; hydro-electric power stations; exciting villages where no one had ever been. We did part of the Long March through the Miao regions, and throughout I met many Long Marchers, the rank and file ones; ordinary soldiers of those days, retired. I filled notebooks with their reminiscences: what it was like to slog on foot through the passes and the mountains; to fight, to fight, to suffer from dysentery and to fight.

We arrived in Juiching, which had been the great base for the Party and army from 1929 to 1934, and had resisted four major campaigns by Chiang Kaishek. Juiching was a pretty little city; the hills round it were mantled with new trees; they had been seeded by aeroplane but the peasants of the communes, independent and wilful, cut the young trees down for fuel. No visitor had ever come here before. We entered the peasants' homes freely. And the flexible manner in which the directives from Peking were locally interpreted never ceased to amaze me. We shopped in Juiching town; small and delightful shops; and obtained lacquer pillows, which had disappeared everywhere else. I could compare with the past, and things were much better: not only electricity and running water and fields glossy with well-being, but also people. China's elasticity—its inherent suppleness, which makes it independent of the crises of the outside world, and which absorbs its own paroxysms—I rediscovered here. It is not true that the best showpieces are reserved for visits of foreigners: on the contrary, much the best has never been shown to visitors from abroad.

From Juiching we went to Changsha, and there I interviewed Mao Tsetung's old bodyguard, Chen Changfong, who for many years, including those of the Long March, had looked after him. He had written a book, *On the Long March with Chairman Mao*. I asked Chen Changfong only personal questions; about Mao's food and habits, for instance. Mao was a rice eater, and in the north, with millet and sorghum, he developed acute constipation, so that Chen had to give him rectal enemas. He kept a rubber tube with vaseline or oil ready for use. Mao also could never get accustomed to the *kang*. He used a southern type of wooden bed, much colder to sleep on.

My days in Juiching meant not only notebooks to fill, but a whole era to understand: so many deeds of bravery, casual and unrecorded; so much heroism taken for granted. Who shall write the immortal epic of China's Revolution as it ought to be written? The Long March alone is as magnificent as the *Iliad* and I longed, as I talked to the simple soldiers (I interviewed forty of them), who merely slogged and fought without any idea that they were doing something extraordinary, to write it up as it ought to be written, in verse. The number of those who had taken part in this epic was dwindling fast; I had not world enough and time left to do it. But perhaps, if I took many notes, someone would come along, young enough and dedicated enough, to do this work. My notes would be used. The world needs grandeur, honour, a record of man's nobility. A poet—Chinese or American or European or African or Arab or Indian or Japanese—would do it one day.

Suddenly there were aeroplanes; and we flew back to Peking.

It was September 22nd.

Mr Ma was at Peking airport to greet us, and as we drank tea while waiting for our luggage, he told us that unfortunately Vincent's request to go to the Great Wall could not be granted for the time being. 'Anyway, you have seen both ends of the Great Wall,' said he, smiling expansively. He also told us that the government had decided not to hold a parade on October 1st this year, as had been customary, but to let the people enjoy themselves freely, in the parks, and everywhere, for three days.

We went back to the hotel, and immediately were deluged with information. One Japanese friend, and then others came to see me. Something had happened, something very important. Either Mao or Lin Piao had had some accident ... all aeroplanes in China had been grounded for a week ...

'So that's why we went everywhere by car,' I said to Vincent.

A very important meeting of the top leaders was being held in the Western Hills, beyond the Great Wall ... all the heads of Party provincial committees and the Central Committee were assembled there.

'So that's why I couldn't go to see the Great Wall,' said Vincent to me.

Now we began to worry. What had happened? Was Mao dead? Had something happened to him? 'That would be a major catastrophe for your country,' said Vincent, and we both worried so much that it showed in our faces.

In Peking people walked about, outwardly impassive. But there was that solidity of silence which held worry. We all felt the same way, all part of the same body of unease. No one would discuss anything. No one laughed or smiled either. 'Yes,' Hualan said, 'I am as worried as you are, my dear ... I don't know ... I only hope that nothing has happened to Chairman Mao.'

Third Brother was back in Peking, but he did not know anything. The French correspondent for Agence France-Presse came to me, and in a voice that could be heard ten metres away, stated, 'Mao is dead. He has been killed.' I met another Frenchman. He had come expressly to write a book on Lin Piao; he was going round asking the Chinese to arrange an interview for him with Lin Piao. The Chinese just smiled and said, 'We shall see.'

I went to see Rewi. He had lost his tail. 'The old cadres of my organization came back and they liberated me ... I'd got quite used to my tail ...

he was nice.' He walked slowly with me down the street, and at the end, in a small voice said, 'Cheer up, lass, it isn't too bad.' Which meant that Mao had not died.

Chiao Kuanhua had two dinners and a further two meetings with me. He asked about my trip. I told him everything about Sinkiang, about Juiching, and then Chiao asked what had happened at Tsunyi. I told him that it was wrong to distort history. 'Premier Chou is the one who really turned the balance of forces at Tsunyi by throwing his influence on the side of Chairman Mao,' I said.

Dangerous words, dangerous ... because of what we had said at Tsunyi, it was somehow suspected that I had an inkling of what had happened to Lin Piao. Otherwise, who would be so bold as to question Lin Piao's outstanding role at Tsunyi?

I went back to Peking University to show Vincent my old campus. Professor Chou Peiyuan received us, and spoke of the crushing of the 'ultra-left' at the university. Professor Chou was still carrying on his battle on behalf of fundamental research. 'It will now go on. It will pick up where it left off in 1966.' Backed by Chou Enlai, the professor would produce in 1972 important articles on the need for research; and this would arouse the fury of the Four, when once again they rose in power and influence.

Yang Chengning, the Nobel Prize winner, came to Peking. He was an American citizen and had lived in America since the late 1940s and was apprehensive. 'Please don't publicize my visit,' he said to me. By that time Kissinger had come and gone, and President Nixon was coming; but people like Dr Yang, in America's scientific community, had suffered from the McCarthy pressures in the 1950s, and they were still worried. Dr Yang had shown courage in coming to China so early: for everyone knew that his brain carried a treasure for China.

Dr Yang was duly received by Chairman Mao, and even Chiang Ching and her associates received him. He would begin a trend among scientists of Chinese origin to return to China, with the assent of the United States, in order to speed up China's development.

I thought of the humdrum, anonymous courage of those who had returned much earlier, as had Third and Fourth Brother. Three years of Third Brother's good brain wasted stoking the fires of a cook in a canteen!

I thought of the parable of the labourers in the vineyard; those who come at the eleventh hour are just as useful as those who have toiled all day. But the pioneers, those who did not count the cost, who gave their all when it was dangerous to do so – they should be remembered.

September 30th: the usual banquet; and prominently, Premier Chou Enlai was there. With Chiang Ching.

I saw many old friends sitting at tables whom I had not seen for a long time, and I walked about to speak to them. I felt the Premier's eyes on me. Nothing ever escaped Chou Enlai.

I sat at one of the tables in a row near enough to the main table. Chou Enlai and Chiang Ching went from table to table, lifting their glasses and toasting each guest. When they came to me they both glared, and Chou Enlai frowned heavily.

What had I done wrong?

On September 30th the news that a Chinese jet had crashed in Outer Mongolia, and all the nine passengers aboard had been killed, came through. The Outer Mongolian government had reported the matter. It was in all the newspapers abroad.

On October 4th I saw Premier Chou Enlai. He said, 'You must have heard a good deal of gossip about our change of plans for the October 1st festival.'

'I have heard nothing, Prime Minister.'

'That's strange. You've usually got your ear fairly close to the ground in such matters.'

'I've heard nothing, Prime Minister.'

He frowned a little, and then he knew he had made his point, as I had made mine. Whatever I knew, I knew nothing.

I had submitted a list of questions, and now Chou Enlai answered them most fully. None were about the crash. How could I say, 'Please, Your Excellency, do tell me: Is it Lin Piao who has died, or Chairman Mao?'

'In the last twenty years,' said Chou Enlai, 'we have known that never for a single moment can we relax our vigilance. Always there has been struggle, *inside the Party and outside it*. It will be so again. A revolution can easily be lost, more easily than it is made. Look at what happened in the U.S.S.R.' The Vietnam war had shown the two imperialisms, Russian and American, contending and colluding in a desperate race for superiority. 'America is trying to keep what she has: she is on the defensive. Russia is on the offensive everywhere in the world.' Europe, the Middle East, Japan, were bones of contention between the two superpowers; they agreed to transient 'arrangements'. Nevertheless, the rivalry went on.

'We were always prepared for the worst ... prepared to be attacked by both the superpowers plus India and Japan ... but this will not come to pass.' Negotiations with the U.S.S.R. about the border with China were taking place. 'We do not worry if negotiations are protracted ... ten years, twenty years ... we have been negotiating with America for sixteen years; and in the end it was President Nixon who suggested that Sino-American talks be held at a higher level ... in 1970 we received a message from him. Hence he was invited to China.'

At no time did Chou give me the impression that he believed that China would be attacked by the U.S.S.R. 'China is tough meat. They prefer soft meat. There is soft meat about.'

As for Taiwan, it was an internal issue for China to solve. No one else. There was a bourgeoisie in Taiwan, as in Hongkong and in Macao, and there must be a 'transitional period' for them to integrate. 'In the early years of China, after 1949, we even supported the national bourgeoisie with subsidies when there were not enough raw materials to keep the factories working.' No cotton had been available for the textile mills of Shanghai in 1950, 'but we paid the workers, and the managers too, even when there was no work to do'.

The total value of the national bourgeoisie assets had been estimated at 2·2 billion *yuan* by 1955; on this, 5 per cent interest had been paid until 1966, not counting salaries, emoluments and compensations. 'We shall certainly proceed in the same manner for Taiwan, Hongkong and Macao,' said Chou Enlai.

A certain school of Sinologists insists that Chou Enlai 'engineered' the fall of Lin Piao, and that he was strangled by Chou Enlai at the turn of a dim corridor in a villa in Peitaiho.

High fancy must yield to plausible concreteness. No two witnesses of an event ever tell quite the same story. Hence my personal calendar for the events leading to the death of Lin Piao.

Huang Yungsheng, Lin Piao's right hand man and acting chief of staff, made his last appearance in public on September 10th. On September 11th, Mr Ma returned in haste to Peking. On September 11th, a scheduled meeting between Premier Chou and a Japanese parliamentary delegation was postponed (I met the Japanese delegates at the hotel). On the night of September 11th, rehearsals for the celebration of the National Day parade were stopped. No further rehearsals took place. It was on the night of September 11th–12th that a Chinese Trident crashed in Outer Mongolia with nine people aboard.

The presence in Peking of the American heart specialist Paul Dudley White led to rumours that Mao had had a heart attack. The cancellation of the parade seemed to confirm it. Then came other rumours: there had been an assassination attempt on Mao as he returned by train to Peking ...

All aeroplanes in China stopped flying from September 11th to September 18th.

On October 4th, Lin Piao's name was dropped from radio broadcasts. On October 8th, Mao appeared in a photograph in the *People's Daily* welcoming the Emperor of Ethiopia, Haile Sellassie. Mao looked well.

All China sighed in relief.

I went to Hualan that day, and we hugged each other.

'He is not dead, Hualan.'

She had tears in her eyes. 'All is well, yes, my dear.'

'But then, what has happened, Hualan?'

'Who knows? Maybe someone else has died ... '

By November, the world outside China conjectured that Lin Piao, his wife and some of his supporters had died in the plane crash. But percolation of information in China from top level to bottom takes time. And the secret was well kept. No one who knew about it said a word.

It was October 18th before the picture of Lin Piao was taken down from above the main Peking bookstore. *China Pictorial* had a special October issue on Mao and Lin Piao, which could not be withdrawn from circulation in Hongkong. It would be July 1972 before an official pronouncement about Lin Piao and the manner of his death would be issued by China.

In October a small quotation appeared in the *People's Daily*: 'I fear not what my enemies do to me ... but the sinister arrow fired at my back by my ally, and his smiling face after I was wounded ... '

All of us understood. Mao was grieving, wounded by Lin Piao's treachery: for Mao had believed in him, and loved and trusted him. From that time on, Mao suddenly began to grow old, and sick, and tired.

Lin Piao had indeed plotted to seize power by a military coup. He committed his plan to paper in March 1971. This document—which I saw—set down the forces at his disposal: nine of China's thirty armies. Because of the other commanders loyal to Mao, he would have to rely on the air force, of which his son was in charge, on parachute drops and raids on major cities, the capture of key points such as air fields and railway stations, radio and television centres. There could be no general military uprising; only regional insurgencies. Lin Piao listed the areas where he held sway: among them Kuangtung and Szechuan provinces, and Sinkiang.

His 'unbounded love' for Mao, the father figure, turned to hatred. He called Mao a feudal tyrant, and 'B-52,' a bomber destroying all before him. 'He trusts people of the pen more than people of the sword.'

But Mao had not been inactive or unaware. In December 1970, a major conference in north China reorganized the military garrisons, including that of Peking; this weakened the chances of a military coup in the capital.

In July, forty minutes before he was to receive Kissinger, Mao would see a high official and discuss Lin Piao. 'What shall I do? He is plotting a coup.' After the Kissinger visit, Mao went on tour, to see the regional commanders, as he had done in 1967.

Mao Tsetung's talk with the regional commanders was circulated throughout China in 1972, as an internal document. 'We must try to save Lin Piao,' said Mao. 'When I get back to Peking, I shall go to see them [the conspirators], and discuss with them ... If they don't come to me, I'll go to them. Some can be saved; others it is not possible to save ... '

Mao told of the care he had taken to pre-empt the coup: 'Throwing stones, mixing sand with mud, and digging the wall's foot'. 'Throwing stones' refers to the numerous articles castigating 'idealism' and 'many centres', which had poured out steadily in the press. Mao had also diluted the Military Commission with new commanders ('mixing sand with mud'), and changed the garrisons of major cities ('digging the wall's foot'). Mao then coined a phrase, famous because five years later it would be used against the gang to which his wife belonged: 'Practise Marxism, not revisionism. Unite and do not split. Be open and above board; do not intrigue or conspire.'

Late in October 1971 I went to the French Embassy, and the French Ambassador, Étienne Manac'h, and I drank champagne.

'To that great man, His Excellency, Prime Minister Chou Enlai,' said Étienne Manac'h. 'The hour of Chou Enlai has come, and it is a good hour for China.'

Twenty-three

The Hour of Chou Enlai: 1972-1973

I FLEW TO New York directly after leaving China, on October 25th, 1971. *The Morning Deluge*, my first book of Mao's impact on the Chinese Revolution, would be published in 1972. Harry Sions, the chief editor of Little, Brown had taken a gamble on this book, for anything favourable to Mao Tsetung challenged anchored prejudice. But he was a courageous man and an excellent editor, and he was delighted with the chapter on the Long March, although he thought some others too flattering to Mao. His death three years later much afflicted me.

I gave some lectures in America, in Belgium and France, and in London, but I have totally forgotten what I said. By now I had given so many lectures that I could talk without any preparation; but as soon as a speech was over I had rubbed it out of mind. Thus I preserved myself from being submerged by my own activity.

On May 4th, 1972 I was back in China. My friends the Yangs were out of jail. Yeh could have me at home for dinner. How wonderful it was, to see some of my old friends again! 'Chou Enlai,' they said. Of course it was Chou Enlai who had opened the jail gates for them. In the next two years many hundreds of thousands would be released ...

Gladys and Hsienyi did not talk of their jail experience for a long time. Gladys had had the worst of it, for she had been in solitary confinement. And this not through viciousness, but through respect for her higher status as a foreigner! This Englishwoman stood the ordeal nobly and came out luminous, calm, and sane, ready to serve China again (although she could have asked to leave). What strength of character! What fortitude! 'I now understand the quirks of a revolution much better,' said Gladys in her quiet upper-class voice.

But she was worried about her son. It had been a great strain for her children; parents in jail as 'counter-revolutionaries', and the children Eurasians. Her daughters were adapting remarkably well; they would marry excellent Chinese husbands of the new kind, who accept woman's equality. They would pursue university careers, and exhibit no trauma of any kind. But her son, after having been an extremely enthusiastic Red

Guard, was now bitter, cynical. He had wanted to be all-Chinese; now he wanted to be all-English. It was quite understandable. Among the Eurasians, the male children often were more vulnerable.

'Girls do seem more resilient, more able than boys to take catastrophe and tragedy. They live through them and come out enriched, matured ... perhaps because women have always had to confront so much daily unpleasantness,' said Gladys.

Hsienyi said he had known about Lin Piao's downfall probably before many other people in China. 'Each one of us had a copy of the little red book in jail. One day our jailers asked all of us to give them back.The copies were returned the next day, but the preface page written by Lin Piao had been cut out of each one. That's how we knew. He was erased, effaced. We looked at each other with big smiles. We thought we would be out very soon.'

The Yangs had returned to their flat, redecorated for them at government expense. Nothing was missing. They were paid their back salaries in full. And the next year Gladys would go to England, and her English sister would come to China to see her.

Simon and Irène Hua had also had problems. Their eldest daughter had been jailed in 1967, on her return to China from Paris.

I had seen her in Paris that year. I had made a speech defending the Cultural Revolution (and I was right to defend it; I am more convinced than ever that it had to be). But I dissuaded her from returning to China. 'Although the *principle* of the Cultural Revolution is correct, history in its faltering is never straightforward, and you may be misunderstood.' I added, 'We Eurasians are much too easy targets for anyone's attack, at any time.' But Monique was in love with China, and she was patriotic. She had been sent by the Chinese government to France as a university student; she did not understand all the complexities and contradictions of the land she loved. Not as I understood them now. She was young, as I had been in 1938. She plunged into the tempest as I had done when I was twenty-one, armed with nothing but love and enthusiasm. I had reaped a harvest of pain, she reaped three years of jail, although no ill-treatment.

One of the reasons for jailing her was 'bringing in pornographic books'. It was Sika Meyer, the Chinese wife of Charles, Sihanouk's secretary, who told me. Monique had returned via Phnom Penh; she stayed a few days with the Meyers. Sika took exception to the books Monique read. 'All those sex books ... she should not have taken them with her.' I checked. They were not pornography; merely the ordinary run of French love stories. Monique's judgment about what was acceptable or not in China had become muddled in Paris. 'I tried to warn her,' said Sika.

I could well imagine what happened. Monique, back from France, thought the Cultural Revolution in China was a festival of youth, liberty and loving kindness. Which in some ways it was, so protean a phenomenon, embracing all contradictory statements and proving them all both true and false.

Simon and Irène came to see me about Monique. They too were in trouble, but it was nothing very serious. Irène had lost her temper after many hours of being harassed and criticized by a woman cadre, and had slapped her. They were moved from their Western-type flat to a small, typical Chinese home. But their servant stuck loyally to them and continued to serve them. A privilege they were refused was to spend the summer months at the seaside, but Irène bore it with great fortitude. 'I do not mind being deprived of this privilege. My Chinese comrades never enjoyed it.' But why was their daughter in jail?

I was approached by some of Monique's French friends in Paris. 'If you make a row, she'll be in jail much longer,' I warned them. 'Illicit connections with foreigners' would be confirmed, and she would be in greater trouble. Simon wrote to Premier Chou Enlai, but there was no answer. 'Chou Enlai ignores no request, forgets no one. Perhaps he cannot move at the moment on this matter. Trust him and wait,' I said. And sure enough Monique came out of jail, and was assigned a job, and the Huas were once again given a good flat.

Chou Enlai was pulling China together after the strain, the tosses, the upheavals. 'Readjustment, consolidation, elevation' were the key words; also a condemnation of waste and extravagance.

There were the visible signs of a return to normality in each factory. The emphasis was on quality; no more shoddy work; there were rules and regulations. Technical and industrial exhibitions were held in the major cities. A swarm of Japanese businessmen hove into Peking.

The painters returned. Huang Chou, condemned to going about with an ass because he had painted the charming donkeys of Sinkiang, was 'liberated'. I saw his paintings once again, albeit only in the small shops, because it took time to reverse in people's minds the condemnations which had been issued so liberally during the first years of the Cultural Revolution.

Chou Enlai would in 1973 call for a meeting of China's best painters and ask them to create three hundred works to decorate the new hotels and other places of interest, because China was now expecting a major influx of visitors. Mao's face disappeared from the hotel rooms (with Mao's approval). 'We are going to open up many more new sites in China for visitors,' said Chang Ying, of the Foreign Ministry, who accompanied me on my travels that year. She was the wife of the very able Ambassador, Chiang Wenching; I liked them both very much.

There were many more books in the bookstores, among them the major classics, *The Dream of the Red Chamber* and *The Scholars*. The ravenous Japanese bought up all the old books they could find. There was the return of seal carving; and of seals, and a lot of beautiful handicrafts. Once again there were flower shops, and lovely silk and ivory pieces for sale, and everyone breathed easily. One thing would not return. In Peking, on both sides of the houses' street doors there always had been carved stone lions. Almost all of them had been broken as 'feudal', and now only deformed lumps of stone remained.

The parks were again full of strollers. Suddenly in 1973 my favourite park, the Peihai, was closed to the public. 'Repairs.' 'Why? I've been to it. It is not in bad shape.' 'Repairs,' said someone firmly. Only at the end of 1976 would I know that the whole public park had been taken over by Chiang Ching, to become her private garden. She rode in it, on a white horse, imitating her favourite star, Greta Garbo, in *Queen Christina*, a film of which she was very fond.

Timidly, from the provinces, came certain new operas and plays in 1972 and 1973; some of the local folk art came back in the cities. But Szechuan opera remained firmly banned in Szechuan, and in Peking and Shanghai only the 'model operas' could be seen.

There was talk of the Hundred Flowers being revived. Professor Chou Peiyuan of Peking University wrote boldly in support of fundamental research; artists painted, some writers started to write again.

The Mao badges disappeared from all chests (the little red book had gone by November 1971). Only overseas Chinese, visiting their relatives and not up to the latest fashion in politics, still wore badges or carried the book. But once with their families, they gave up what was now called 'formalism'.

Was this 'demaoization?'

Panting like greyhounds after a race, China-watchers in Hongkong and elsewhere, some of them possessed of a burning hatred for Mao and of China's socialist system, were already announcing 'demaoization' in 1972. But Mao was not Stalin. This was Mao without the crazy cult of Mao,

Mao 'demaoized' by himself, whose visions were implemented by Chou Enlai, as I would write in articles for the *New York Times* in those years.

Had Mao not suffered, after Lin Piao's death, a series of small strokes, which cut down his mobility, made him half blind, and increasingly helpless; had Chou Enlai not been struck with cancer at the end of 1972 or in early 1973, the Gang of Four would not have emerged, to destroy so much of what had been accomplished.

In 1972, none of us knew this would happen. All we knew was that universities were starting to function; that by the end of 1971 examinations had been restored in Szechuan middle schools, in Tientsin's Nankai middle school, and in higher institutes, for the next student intake. The Cultural Revolution was being assessed calmly, its losses and gains. It was not a question of returning to the pre-1966 days; it was a problem of how to 'summarize experience', as Chou Enlai said; of finding out what was valid and what did not work, always with the same object in view: to chart China's road to swift development, to speed her progress.

I travelled a great deal up and down China. I too was 'summarizing experience', trying to reach a comprehensive appraisal of events.

The outburst of intellectual energy, the scientific expansion which I had noted in 1964 and 1965, continued to have effect, despite the turmoil of the years 1966–9. For instance, in July 1966, a type of radioactive isotope gauge, automatically regulating the thickness of steel plates, strips and sheets during processing, had been produced. There had also been advance in the development of nuclear weaponry, and the production of a hydrogen bomb, and in 1970 of an earth satellite.

But these, the results of previous years of effort, having occurred during the Cultural Revolution, were claimed to be due to an outburst of ingenuity on the part of workers–peasants–soldiers inspired by Mao Tsetung Thought. Despite the harassment of many scientists and researchers during the Cultural Revolution, the majority of these dedicated men continued to work, even if less efficiently. Therefore the picture is not clear-cut; even in 1974 economists abroad could justly claim achievements and commendable performance in Chinese industry and agriculture during the Cultural Revolution; which in today's backlash is not recognized. But then the continued forward movement of a country on the march, especially such a huge country as China, seems to swallow up all these contradictions; the residue is what has been achieved.

'The gap between China and the advanced nations was narrowing

before 1966,' Teng Hsiaoping said to me when I saw him in September 1977, 'but because of the sabotage of the Four, it is now much wider.'*
Already in 1972 I had discussed the 'gap' in the economy, and in industrial development, and with Chiao Kuanhua, the Foreign Minister. 'Yes, there is a big gap,' he had said to me. 'For almost six years there's been very little studying ... and that means almost a generation of university students has been lost to us. Yet we need so many technicians, so many doctors and scientists ... all lost. There's a very big youth problem now.'

I found out in 1972 and 1973 that 'ultra-left' ideas, at the time solely ascribed to Lin Piao (since no one accused Chiang Ching), persisted, despite all exhortation. It had become a habit—pleasant, since it was part of their revolt against a millenarian parental authoritarianism—among many young people, to label older ones (forty seemed to be the watershed age). They shouted 'reactionary' or 'counter-revolutionary' whenever any mention of study, discipline, or abiding by rules (including rules of hygiene) was made. There was such a loosening of discipline that since the young now crowded the organizations, efforts to get proper work done were hindered. There was also the problem of the 'reversal of the correct verdicts of the Cultural Revolution'. What did this mean? It meant that many older cadres had been wantonly accused—without any evidence—of multiple crimes, and that anyone arguing for them was in danger of being looked upon as an 'unrepentant capitalist roader', trying to 'reverse the correct verdicts'. In this context, Chiang Ching was the prime mover: any word from her had the weight of an accusation, and no accusation could be proved or disproved; word became fact. Chou Enlai therefore moved cautiously, yet courageously, rehabilitating competent older officials and reinstating discipline.

In the new Party constitution of 1969, a grievous lacuna had occurred. In it was a clause which did not admit intellectuals to the Party, only 'workers–peasants–soldiers' of approved revolutionary demeanour. There was also a clause that renegades and spies, and power-holders who 'had followed the capitalist road' should be expelled from the Party and not allowed to rejoin. It was based on these two clauses that the return to effective work and to authority of certain high-calibre officials was proving very slow and difficult. Yet so many of them had been accused without evidence, and in these wanton accusations the 'Shanghai troika'†—as they

---

* See article by Han Suyin in *Der Spiegel*, November 1978.
† Chiang Ching, Chang and Yao. Wang Hungwen was not involved in 'cultural' affairs until 1973.

were then known—had played an outstanding role, especially Chiang Ching. She would leave no one alone. Thus the able and devoted Liao Chengchih was called by her a 'playboy' and 'untrustworthy'. As a result he had, for years, not been able to function properly; and this because so much authority in China is also a question of personal influence, of being accepted by one's colleagues, and especially one's subordinates. In the absence of any functioning legal system, wanton denunciation had the effect of a virtual judgment. It plunged the cadres into a catatonic stupor, and it sterilized effectively any attempt to counter baseless accusations.

However, in 1972, the Shanghai group appeared to unite with Chou Enlai, at least in the matter of facing the aftermath of the Lin Piao affair. It was very difficult for Chou at the time to fault them. Had they not been 'recuperated' by him from the 'ultra-left?' How difficult to start immediately criticizing them and perhaps bringing about a crisis in the badly mauled Party, in dire need of stable, constructive leadership.

Chou Enlai had, with supreme ability, succeeded in managing the post-Lin Piao interlude. There had been no uprisings, no armed strife, from the nine armies of Lin Piao; no recrudescence of disorder among the people; no increased tension with Moscow over the Lin Piao affair. The Kremlin showed itself non-provocative and prudent, although it could have claimed that it had adherents, even up to Mao's heir, in the Chinese Party.

'There is no more struggle for power now,' wrote the China expert, Robert Guillain, in France's Le Monde. He could not have been more wrong; but at the time it really looked peaceful, and I was much relieved. I wrote a letter to Harrison Salisbury, saying that now I would have no more worries. All was plain sailing, with Chou Enlai back, the great manager of China. 'Now I can go back to writing love stories.' I hoped that the Cultural Revolution would soon be wound up, and of course that rehabilitations, reassessments would take place. The Chinese Party had always made reappraisals of its own performance and policies, which is what I liked about it. Then wrongs would be righted—in fact, Chou had already begun. Rewi, Ma Haiteh and Hans Miller, the German doctor who had worked devotedly for China for fifty years, rejoiced with me. In that year, they would be able to go to the seaside in August, and Rewi would travel up and down China again, and this walking encyclopaedia would delight me with his true and sharp assessment of the accomplishments, and also the deficiencies, of the past seven years.

'There's just been too much empty talk of politics … Now there will be efficiency, production, science, technology once again,' said the scientists I met.

The year 1972 was one of triumph for Chou Enlai's foreign policy, not only because of President Nixon's visit in February, and China's entry to the United Nations in the previous October, but also because of the resurrection of Mao's old slogan, 'Let foreign things serve China', presaging a wide opening to the West; and a vast surge of sympathy, enthusiasm and admiration from all the nations of the earth.

Chou Enlai looked well, he moved with lithe elegance, he reminded me of mercury; he was seventy-three, and he bore the weight of twenty-three years of governing China upon his shoulders without, apparently, any strain.

The new Japanese Prime Minister, Kakuei Tanaka, signed an agreement in Peking; this was a breakthrough for the future. Twenty-two American editors visited China. Some of them were fascinated. 'A garden of Eden' one man called it. 'The change is miraculous,' wrote the historian John Fairbank. 'No other group of 750 million people has ever been held together ... ' The Americans, so emotionally involved with China for over a century, understood the miracle accomplished since 1949. They knew, deep in their bones, that it could not have been done without the Communist Party, without Mao and his companions, and they did not lie to themselves. 'The Maoist revolution is on the whole the best thing that has happened to China in centuries,' wrote John Fairbank.

I was no longer being reviled as a 'Red' and a 'Maoist', except by some envious 'Sinologists'. It all seemed worthwhile now: the lectures, the running about, the sacrifices too (although mine were minuscule in the Chinese scale). Chou Enlai had spoken well of the Cultural Revolution to Edgar Snow, emphasizing its gains, not for a moment letting on to the bitterness of the attacks against him. Unlike so many subjective people who think that what happens to them is all that matters in the Universe, Chou Enlai had tremendous self-abnegation; he would have cheerfully agreed to being slow-roasted alive if this was good for China. Chou's immortality began that year, when people began calling him Our Beloved Premier Chou.

I wrote a small Op Ed for the *New York Times*, stating that Chou Enlai had 'saved so many lives' during the Cultural Revolution, and that he was very popular.

In 1973 Mao's popularity went down perceptibly; a decline which was not signalled in words, but in a certain pulse, heartbeat, silence, tone of voice. People still cared for him, revered him, but they also felt strangely sorry for him. And some felt resentful. They referred to him as the Great Chairman Mao. It was respect, but not that total giving of the heart which had been his for so many years, as China's true liberator.

Unworded, as an odour which strikes the nostril, detected under all conversations, mostly by the fact of silence, was the unease and dislike of Chiang Ching, Mao's wife. Never did I hear a word against her; and it was precisely because of this wordlessness that the feeling came through, strong and unimpeded. No one wanted to converse about her. Dislike is mute as the grass, or a stone.

And because of his wife, there was in the patient, oh so patient, minds of the Chinese people an unworded question: how can Mao Tsetung have a wife like that?

Nevertheless, having from the start got her hands on the formation of mass public opinion – and there I think the Four showed themselves extremely aware of the enormous power of press, television, all communication media which are mind manipulators, whether in the East or in the West – Chiang Ching had her photographs in the newspapers, her eulogists, her adherents. The campaign for her was superbly orchestrated; it deserves a book on its own. And her particular success was to project an image which attracted to her potentially half of China's population: the women; not all, of course, but a certain kind of woman or young girl. It took me almost two years to recognize the type, not through secondhand reading, but through direct contact.

The women who picked – or were picked by – the Four were all personable; garrulously persuasive; forcibly active; and endowed with great imagination and a transporting element of disregard for fact. I had interviewed Li Suwen in Manchuria, and Wang Hsiuchen in Shanghai; and now I met a great many others, at all levels. Edgar Snow and I exchanged data. He had interviewed the woman worker Wu Kueihsien, in Sian. Wu Kueihsien would later become a Vice-Premier, yet she was barely literate. She was interviewed by Roxane Witke, who wrote an article about her.* Ed huffed: 'Silence is beautiful in a woman.'

Docile crowds (there was a ticket distribution in every factory, school, organization) clapped at the model operas. At first no one minded them; not until 1974, when we realized that nothing else was being produced! Chiang Ching in 1972–3 was a pain in the neck, but we all put up with her because of Mao, because of Chou Enlai. We did not realize the considerable foothold her Shanghai Mafia had gained in the mass media, and also in the

---

* *China Quarterly*, No. 64, December 1975.

organs of power, the revolutionary committees, through the new cadres. Between 1966 and 1976, the Communist Party had doubled in number, from seventeen million to thirty-five million, and many new cadres owed their Party membership to the Four.

But not one of the cadres, the writers, the diplomats like Huang Hua, out from the 'cattle pens' and the May 7 schools, said a word against Chiang Ching in deference to Mao. All the violence, everything that had gone wrong, was ascribed to Lin Piao, and to Liu Shaochi. And in those last years of his grace and strength, Chou Enlai too sought to win Chiang Ching, as he had won so many enemies and turned them into friends – to form a collective leadership, for the sake of unity and stability. China badly needed unity and stability.

In Hongkong there was a rumour, uncorroborated, that Mao was angry with his wife, and that she now had a separate establishment in Peking, as well as houses in Shanghai, Hainan Island, and the hot springs near Kuangchow. But despite this semi-official separation, Chiang Ching continued to preface her speeches and public appearances with the words, 'I bring you greetings from Chairman Mao.' And no one knew of the separation. She was still able to control Mao's environment (more so, as Chou became ill) and the people he saw. By the end of 1974, his nephew, Mao Yuanhsing, and two young nurses chosen by Chiang Ching, became, with her, the only people who had unlimited access to him.

Chang Chunchiao had started a major strategy. He began to recruit, in 1972–3, in all the universities, able 'pens' to write for the Four. By 1974 they had organized, in Peking's two universities, some forty to fifty top intellectuals.* Chang also acquired a collection of writers in Shanghai Futan University (which used to be the famous Jesuit University Aurore). Scholars found themselves serving – sometimes unknown to themselves – the purposes of the Gang of Four. Finally, the Gang began making advances even to older cadres, and to veterans: 'Only serve us, and we'll look after you.'

A Japanese ballet company had come to Peking, and danced *The White-Haired Girl*, and also *The Red Regiment of Women*. Some of the dancers had trained in China during the Cultural Revolution and had learnt the new ballets. They were excellent performers, and would go on to win international prizes. But the Japanese choreographer had made some changes in

* They wrote under pseudonyms, the favourite one being Liang Hsiao, which phonetically meant 'the two universities'.

The White-Haired Girl, expanding the love scenes between the heroine and her rescuer, who was also her childhood friend.

Chiang Ching had already begun to 'improve' ballets and operas, cutting out anything faintly related to ordinary human emotions. Thus in the opera *Shachiapang*, a scene showed the heroine, captured by the Kuomintang, asking herself, 'What shall I do?' when hard pressed to betray the Communist cause or to see her mother killed in front of her eyes. Chiang Ching cut out the words. 'A communist never doubts,' said she. Never must a 'positive character' falter, or be anything but thoroughly positive. I would see *Shachiapang* at least eight times through the years. I noticed the stultification of the script and mentioned it.

'Why cut this out? It added some humanity to the character.'

'But it was not good politics,' was the reply.

Another opera, *Azalea Mountain*, I first saw in Szechuan in 1972. When I viewed it again in Pêking, all the humour had gone. The lines where the peasant guerrillas, discovering that the Party comrade they had come to rescue was a girl and not a man, the byplay when she gives orders and they feel affronted – all this was now erased. It was replaced by much vigorous hand-shaking and fist-waving.

It was the same with *The White-Haired Girl*. I had seen it three times before 1966; and in the years under Chiang Ching I watched the beautiful work, which had contained love and passion, become shorn of all emotion except wrath. The rape scene, which was the point of the whole story, was cut out. All that remained was 'revolutionary fury', and people shaking hands repeatedly with piston-like movements of their arms, and then marching off, up a ramp, to the sounds of the 'International'.

The Japanese choreographer's changes were, artistically, an improvement, but I noticed the stern faces around me. Then Chou Enlai spoke about it to me. He told me that the sentiment of the ballet had been transformed; that the 'greatest emotion' was meant to be that of the old father towards his daughter, and not that of the two young lovers. Chou did not speak for himself; he cared about people, their lives and loves. But he expressed the objection – probably Chiang Ching's – to the changes. I had noticed the absence of Chiang Ching at the première of the ballet, although she had been expected to attend.

Chiang Ching would never authorize any change, even the slightest, in what she had laid down. All over China, no artist was allowed a gesture, a word, a tone, not even a button, or the colour of the shoes, or a patch on a coat, which was different from the 'model' laid down by her. 'Everything had to be exactly the same,' said my friend the Szechuan opera singer, Miss Chen Shoufang in 1977. Because the tones of our mono-syllabic words alter the meaning, and each province has its own tones, a great deal of silliness occurred. For instance, the phrase 'I have waited a long time' in Peking tonality would mean 'I've got some good wine' in another province. The misinterpretation was worst in Kuangchow, Cantonese dialect being totally different.

I replied respectfully to Chou Enlai that I felt the Japanese had the right to modify the ballet when they danced it ... such modifications are constantly made in the West ... every ballet troupe interprets a piece its own way ... Chou Enlai, straightening in his chair, looked relieved, and immediately spoke of other matters.

I had been captured, entranced by the desert in 1971. Now I wanted to visit Tunhuang, the famous Buddhist painted caves on the Silk Road,★ and in 1972 went with Chang Ying. Hsing Chiang was at the time doing her manual labour in a May 7 school. Sending a senior person like Chang Ying with me was Chou's way of saying, 'Don't believe everything you see; keep your eyes open', just as Mr Ma and Madame Yeh had kept their eyes and ears open in Sinkiang the previous year.

Chang Ying and I talked freely of many things, including the problems of youth and employment. The State Council was recruiting young people from among the Red Guards who had not committed crimes or brutali-ties (the majority had been very well-behaved). Some of them had even been to jail, or to 'study and labour' camps, for having resisted the 'ultra-left', protested against the brutality towards old cadres and refused to undertake beatings and destruction.

'But we have some bad young people,' said Chang Ying, 'and we have to ask ourselves: How did it happen? What went wrong with our edu-cation? At one time we thought that automatically, any child born "under the red flag" must somehow be better than us, we the old people who come from the old society ... but then we discovered that it was not so.'

'Too much pampering.'

The most worrying thing was 'the gap'. Successors in the fields of science and technology were not there. 'How to train them well, yet not create an élite and lose the revolution? That has been the problem all along.'

The deep stir and turmoil of the Cultural Revolution had spread, however, and enlarged the hunger for many things which China was still

★ The earliest known painted caves dated from A.D. 366.

too poor to afford. There were rising expectations – but a diminished sense of the necessity of study and knowledge among the young. The 'ultra-left' ideas, that to study was 'revisionist' and landed one in trouble, were strong among them, and there was also discontent, because so many felt cheated by all that had happened.

My way to Tunhuang was circuitous. I meandered, visiting communes; seeing everywhere the 'five small' of alternative technology: small fertilizer plants, small iron and steel making plants, small electric plants, methane gas installations, processing factories. In that year, each production team was confirmed in its private plots, in its storage bins, in its manpower. There were fairs and free markets, but the harvests would not be excellent. Drought.

We went by car from Lanchow, following the Silk Road's string of oases, Tienchu and Wu Wei, and Shandan, where Rewi Alley had laboured so many years founding the Gung Ho co-operatives.* Shandan – in the eighth century A.D. – had been famous for its city walls, its trees and palaces and running fountains, described by Arab travellers. A great commercial centre, it produced cinnabar, and it had a big Nestorian church.

On to Changye and to Chiu Chuan, the Fountain of Wine, which had been a Han garrison outpost in 115 B.C. I would meet on the way Oriats (or Buriats), Tibetans and Mongols, and in the Muslim quarter of the Fountain of Wine we ate delicious dates. They had been the staple food of the oases in the Chou dynasty.† Here also was the jade called Light in Darkness, worked for many centuries; cups of it had been given to barbaric chieftains, and the jade was said to 'show', to change colour, if poison was used. Poems had been written in Persia about its glow. Now a co-operative with seventy-five workers turned out, by hand, 4,500 cups a year; for each there were twenty-two separate grindings.

In the morning I rose to look at the snow-capped Tsilien Mountains which gave birth to the jade, green and black and white. 'This is the false Gobi Desert, layers of black gravel but with good earth under it,' said the head of the revolutionary committee of the district, a Mongol with a face like burnished copper. We were 1,500 metres above sea-level, and the Yumen oilfields were quite near, and there was a pipeline from them; the new city of the Fountain of Wine had a petrol refinery. There were only

* See *Yo Banfa*, by Rewi Alley (New Zealand–China Association, Auckland, 1976).
† 770–221 B.C.

70,000 people in the whole district, but 900 million trees had been planted in the last twenty years. 'We could open more fields if we had more people.' There was no family planning here at all.

From the old town stemmed the worn battlements of former Great Walls, almost melted into the sand. I went to see the western end of the Great Wall, the Gate of Prosperity, repainted and restored, terminus of the Wall's 5,000-kilometre journey from the sea. On the road were some carts pulled by camels, but they had rubber tyres.

On to Tunhuang, 400 kilometres away. The wind scorched our faces, the scalding sand blistered the skin. To Kara, where there was a spring which had allowed the Han garrison to survive in 300 B.C. And then we crossed the Pass of Jade. 'The breath of spring does not reach beyond the Pass of Jade' was a line in an ancient poem. The famed General Tso Tsungtang had consolidated Sinkiang against the encroaching Russians* and then had rebuilt the Silk Road, making it five metres wide and planting trees along both its sides, on his march. He had written his reply to this poem, many centuries later:

I have planted three thousand *li*† of willows
And brought the breath of spring beyond the Pass of Jade.

On the hills were the sites of ancient beacons, for warning of invasion by barbarians from the West. Each site had been guarded by a village oasis. At Ansi there were communes, producing wheat and linseed oil, and here too a great number of children. A doctor in Peking had told me, 'When we went into that region to introduce family planning the inhabitants threw us out. "Don't come back or we'll kill you," they shouted.' The doctors had withdrawn. Here, as in Szechuan, every child born received a full ration of grain and oil. 'All our families have more than four children,' said Ma, the Muslim head of Ansi, with great pride. 'In the past, all our children died. Now they live.'

We reached Tunhuang one late afternoon, in a desert splendidly pink with sunset. I turned to watch the desert road marked by its interminable march of disfigured stupas, as if along the wind-blown track would come a slow-paced caravan of camels and donkeys and mules; and the voices singing their gladness as they approached the Buddhist caves and their spring of live water, their promises of the spirit's and the body's ease.

---

* The campaign of 1873–9.
† 1 *li* is 0·5 of a kilometre.

My host was the incomparable professor Tsang Shuhung, who was also a painter, Paris-educated, as was his wife. Both had been in Tunhuang for thirty years. Professor Tsang's whole life was caring for the cave paintings, deciphering the writings in the caves and restoring and preventing the ravages of time. He spoke agreeably of history; he was most learned. The great tidal waves of peoples in this land ocean of Central Asia fascinated me. He told marvellous tales: of the kings of the Huns, who were red-haired and blue-eyed warriors and who used human skulls as drinking cups.

For the next week we went from cave to cave, visiting over a hundred of them. And in the dimness we shone our flashlights, to gaze upon the incandescent swirl and whorl and cascade of ecstatic elongated bodies; rapt faces, a firmament of longing, outburst of man's desire for the sublimity of God. Dug in the friable cliffs, which crumbled even as I looked at them, they were splendour and passion and a total absence of stiffness; and although from Tunhuang I went on to other Buddhist caves, to Yunkang, and then to Lungmen, there was something incomparable in Tunhuang, the great shock of universality.

Every night we sat and talked in the charming guest house with its lovely roofs. By day we went from cave to cave, or strolled by the brook which flowed near by, under sycamore and camphor trees. Professor Tsang would point out the herbs along the pathways, among them liquorice, or suddenly pounce upon a mushroom, for they grew wild, and we often had fresh mushrooms for dinner.

Enchanted hours: the name of Alexander, the tale of the Roman garrison that lost its way and obtained asylum from the Chinese emperor, somewhere near Tunhuang ... I went to see the village called Five Beacons, where the last Romans had quartered; but the inhabitants looked Chinese, except that some heads were curly (and that might be Tibetan blood). Five Beacons fed me with wonderful dates and grapes. There were sand grouse and small eagles in the desert and the oases. 'The desert is not dead. It lives a most intense life,' said Tsang.

Only in 1977 would I know that my coming had been Professor Tsang's deliverance. He was still being criticized and made to 'stand aside' because the local authorities dragged their feet over his case for fear of being accused of 'reversing verdicts'. Then they heard I was coming, and Tsang was hastily rehabilitated. A good dentist came to fix his teeth, which ached. And after my visit he could not be criticized again. In 1978, aged seventy-six, Tsang painted a picture of Mount Everest, which is now being exhibited in the national gallery in Peking.

Tsang was worried about the decrepit state of some of the cave paintings not because of destruction by the 'ultra-left', but because of poor quality of the rock in which the caves had been dug. Much work propping up the cliffs had been done since 1949, but there had been many decades of neglect before that, and also of theft, both by visiting Europeans and by local warlords. The sand wind chipped away at the rock, and some caves had fallen. 'But we shall save Tunhuang, for it is one of the great miracles of art,' said stubborn Professor Tsang.

To him China was a universality; it had been a welcoming land for many centuries, asylum for the persecuted from the West. Heretics of the Christian religion, such as the Nestorians and Manicheans, had found refuge here. The Tang emperors sent their travellers abroad to discover and to describe for them the customs of other nations, and their resources, and to make maps. They had built roads for commerce, and there were people from Honan province in Arabia, and a Jewish community in Kaifeng city. Paper was sent from China through Samarkand to Alexandria. 'In the Sui dynasty, the Emperor Yang Ti came here to see twenty ambassadors of as many nations. He gave them silk and gold, and a banquet lasting fifteen days, with eighteen thousand musicians,' said Tsang. But the Ming dynasty in the fifteenth century had been inward looking and Tunhuang had started to decay, and gradually with the rise of the West no more silk went by the Silk Road. The Manchu Ch'ing dynasty had tried to revive Tunhuang. But then had come wars and the colonial powers in China.

Skirting oases with tamarisks, we visited the pleasant town of Tunhuang. The calligraphic curves of the jujubes with their delightful fragrances and small, close flowers were about us. And three kilometres by jeep across the sand from Five Beacons village was the Crescent Moon Lake which Ian Morrison, my dead love, had spoken to me about. Tsang and I sat by the azure lake's dwindling curve—for it was getting smaller, it was shrinking—and we walked on the dunes to hear the song of the sand. Alas, the lovely Ming temple which had been erected on a small island in the middle of the lake was no more. Ian had shown me a photograph of it. It had been destroyed during the Cultural Revolution. Nothing was left of it but a few hacked balustrade pillars. The island was planted with rye and buckwheat, and a donkey went round and round the well, which had once been the temple well, turning a winch in endless pacing.

In all this area no rice was eaten, only bread made from flour. People resented maize, saying it gave them a bitter stomach. Because no snow fell, the winter wheat was covered with sand and mule and donkey and horse manure.

Everywhere the walls of the small towns had been destroyed, which was a great pity, for the sand now swept in unhindered, and wolves had roamed around the streets, until killed off.

Yumen town was well laid out; with water and electric light; tarred roads and a population of 50,000... But it was 2,400 metres above sea-level and Chang Ying, who had mitral stenosis, became blue in the face. I inquired about babies; and was proudly told that last year 835 babies had been born among the 4,000 families 'with breeding possibilities'. This was a record low!

We left Yumen, and in the faultless blue sky was a dark blot of hawks; and suddenly a bar of white wing as an eagle circled above us. We caught stupid, pretty sand grouse. Their little heads shook and their golden eyes trembled, and I was sorry for them, but the drivers were happy, thinking how tasty they would be.

Back in Lanchow, I met another Long Marcher, Comrade Chang. He described the battle he had fought at a pass so narrow that the sky was but a thread of white above, and the Long Marchers were attacked by Tibetan cavalrymen. Comrade Chang was doing a survey of the Yellow River's upper reaches. 'We must tame it,' he said. 'All this area will be electrified one day.'

Kansu province had been unpeopled by war and plague in the past. The present birth rate was 42·4 per thousand among national minorities, and 29 per thousand among the Han; obviously Kansu was not doing much family planning.

We went to bow to the Yellow River – or rather to look at its new pumps. 'Look how much clearer the water is now,' said Madame Li, pointing to the thick ochre slush delightedly.

I returned from the desert rejuvenated, my vitality increased. This would also happen to me when I went to Tibet in 1975.

Vincent arrived, and at Peking airport we met Chou Enlai who had come to greet Prince Sihanouk, back from a trip to North Korea.

Chou stepped down from a small black car, a fairly decrepit one, not a Zis, but one of those Shanghai-made models. He carried his own brief-case, and almost ran, followed by one bodyguard. He crossed the tarmac and then he saw us. He grinned and shook hands. And he asked Vincent, 'How was Singapore?' Then he was in the waiting room, as we were, ignoring the 'top sofa' and the protocol and sitting with us.

Vincent had taken an aeroplane which stopped in Singapore; he thought of looking up my adopted daughter, Huei Ying and my old friends the Lokes. But the unwritten ban still held: he was surrounded by police with machine guns at the ready, and hustled back into the next aeroplane after a few hours' detention.

Chou had heard of it. Vincent said, 'Singapore is just the same as ever.' Chou laughed. He looked radiant.

I watched him striding up to the aeroplane, his right arm a little crooked from that old accident in Yenan. It was an Indian doctor* who had set his elbow, but it remained flexed. I thought, 'He is getting thinner.' That night, at dinner, Rewi also said, 'Chou is getting almost transparent. He works too hard. How can we stop him from working?' But he was as zestful as a young man of twenty. And all of us loved him and felt safe with him; and untiringly told stories about him, as people do about someone they love. And perhaps Chou knew it, and was buoyed up with the love and trust not only of the old, the middle-aged, but also of the young. Those who had now seen through the 'ultra-left' and its cruelties, millions of young people, now turned to Chou Enlai because he had never betrayed them. Neither did he come down hard on them, nor seek revenge. In the end, he would be the only one to help them.

Yungmei and Karen, her daughter, arrived. I had said to Yungmei, 'Why don't you come to China this year?' Now it was safe, and so they came. I took them to Szechuan, and I asked Yungmei whether she wanted to see her own mother. The government of China was ready to trace her mother for her. But Yungmei said no; which is something I do not quite understand. For in her place I could not have resisted, just through sheer curiosity, even if it had hurt me greatly. But my family, for my sake, now adopted her as my true daughter. And they have been good to her ever since.

The trip to China did Yungmei immense good. She immediately integrated, because she knew Chinese; and now she understood why I had forced the language into her. Third Aunt, seeing Karen, was delighted and would not let go of her hand — for her it was like having a great-grand-daughter. For Karen too it would be achieving a wholeness, coming to terms with the wealth of her double heritage.

On my return to that other world outside China in which I also lived, I lectured in Paris at the Military Academy (Cours Supérieur Inter-allié). I would lecture there once a year for four years. I made another lecture

* Five Indian doctors went to Yenan in 1937, to participate in the Chinese Revolution.

tour, in early 1973, in the United States. It was successful and happy. By then the greatness of Mao and his enterprises, the boldness and vision of the Revolution, including the Cultural Revolution, had gripped me. My faith in the ultimate result remained unshaken; Chou Enlai had infused me with hope and courage. I wished now for a swift normalization of relations with America; because there were still in China people hostile to Mao's and Chou Enlai's foreign policy. If America delayed, dawdled, this would be used by Chou's opponents against him.

I tried to explain this to some State Department people I met in Washington. A liaison office with David Bruce as its head, was set up in Peking, and there could not have been a better choice. But then Watergate began, and this would delay some major decisions. Another cause of hesitancy – on the part of America – would certainly be the rise of the Four, and the confusion it introduced both in domestic and foreign affairs in China.

In New York in April 1973, I went to see Huang Hua, now Ambassador to the United Nations. And we had lunch with Shirley MacLaine, who wanted to go to China, and did so shortly afterwards.

Huang Hua had been a very famous student leader at Yenching University,* and at times still made pointed hints at my 'waywardness' when we were there as students together in the 1930s. He had been devoted to Edgar Snow, whose interpreter he had been in Yenan, and had stayed by his side through Ed's agony after his operation in Switzerland. He was a seasoned, careful, hardworking diplomat, and his wife Lilian was gifted with intelligence and charm.

One afternoon, a telephone call came from Huang Hua's secretary: had I time to see a Miss Roxane Witke?

'Who is she?'

'She has just come back from China.'

I thought Huang Hua must want me to see her and so I said, 'Ask her to come to dinner with me.'

Into the flat came a tall, auburn-haired good-looking woman. Conversation was easy. Roxane Witke was a historian; she told me that in August 1972 she had gone to China, and had seen Chiang Ching, and had had long interviews with her; almost sixty hours on tape. She had obtained a visa to China when she had told Huang Hua that as an historian she wanted to gather information on the women's liberation movement in China, a most worthy task.

In Peking, she had met many women leaders including Teng Yingchao,

* See *A Mortal Flower*.

Chou Enlai's wife; she had also briefly seen Premier Chou Enlai. She said that it was Chou who had agreed, or suggested, that she see Chiang Ching. (It is not clear to me whether she had asked, or whether Chou had suggested it to her.)

The rest is related by Roxane Witke herself in her book, *Comrade Chiang Ching*. She met Chiang Ching, and instead of writing about women in China she became Chiang Ching's biographer. 'You will be my Edgar Snow,' Chiang Ching exclaimed, or so I was told.* Apparently Roxane Witke and Chiang Ching also discussed me.† I prefer to ignore what they said; however, this had probably prompted Miss Witke to come to see me.

Roxane Witke thought that Chiang Ching was 'somewhat imperious'. The court around her reminded her of the Empress Tzuhsi. 'Yao Wenyuan looks just like a eunuch,' she said. We both laughed. But she was carried away by the feeling that Chiang Ching would be a most important person. She told me so. I demurred. 'No, Chiang Ching is not going to be a very important person.' 'I disagree ... I think she will be a very important and influential woman in China's history,' said Miss Witke.

We were walking back along First Avenue, and it was time to say good-bye. I had something to tell her and I said it. 'May I give you some advice? The Chinese people do not like the lady very much, so do be careful.'

Instantly I regretted warning her. Supposing she repeated to Huang Hua what I had said ... and supposing Huang Hua repeated it ... already, I shared that all-pervasive feeling of being scared of Chiang Ching.

I saw Huang Hua the next day. He was worried, he said, about Miss Witke's work. After all, she had gone to China to write on women's liberation. She should stick to the subject for which she went. 'How can she?' I said. 'She's been given all this material. Of course she'll use it. It'll be a sensation, and all America loves a sensation.'

'Regular as the swallow,' said Chang Ying, hugging me, as in May 1973 I was back in Peking. I mentioned Roxane Witke to her, because Chang Ying had been present at the interviews given to Miss Witke. Chang Ying said, 'What top leaders do is beyond our control.' She was not going to comment upon the intensely personal character Chiang Ching had given to her outpourings. But it was very clear that she disapproved. There was a precedent. Had not Mao himself spoken to Edgar Snow in Yenan, telling him all of his life? In both of us the thought that Mao's wife was trying to

* By witnesses, present at the interviews between Roxane Witke and Chiang Ching.
† Ibid.

emulate her husband was present. This could only have one meaning: she wanted to succeed him.

My son-in-law Sidney now came to China and every day recorded, on a tape, his impressions for his daughter Karen; being one of the most devoted fathers one could wish for. He had brought some of his films with him, just as Vincent had brought some records of Indian music. We duly offered the lot to the respective authorities, to transmit to Madame Mao. But we were met by stony silence; not even an acknowledgment.

Somehow the matter of a book on Chiang Ching became known among the Chinese public; but the story was distorted. Not Witke, but I, said the 'small lane news', had written a book entitled *Empress of the Red Fortress*, criticizing Chiang Ching. By 1975 this 'news' would be all over China, all the universities; passed from mouth to mouth among the young. 'Of course it is Han Suyin who has written a book ... a friend of mine has seen it in Hongkong ... ' The number of copies sold was even mentioned: thirty-five thousand at the first printing. It had now been translated into several languages and was a best-seller. As usual, the last person to hear the 'news' was me. It would be September 1975 before a very bold friend would inform me. My relatives, Hualan, everyone had heard it, and for a while had been uneasy. Yeh and his wife, Yen Wenching, and Heart of Ice and her husband; all the writers had heard it. But all of them said, 'Han Suyin would not do such a thing.' They knew I could not, and would not put them all in great danger through such utter foolishness. And so they did not avoid me, which was very courageous of them.

Fourth Sister, back from two and a half years in a May 7 school and with a sick husband, was a trifle worried at first, but she checked up, and was assured I had not perpetrated such a book. She did not, however, tell me of the rumour, so great was her fear of the Dragon Lady, or 'Three Drops of Water' – Chiang Ching's current nicknames in 1973–4, and until she was called China's calamity, in 1976.

The rumour was based on wishful thinking. Many young people, frustrated and resentful, let down by Chiang Ching, were hoping for such a denunciation. Only in December 1976 was it possible for me to deny the rumour, and through the same 'small lane news' the denial went right through China within a week.

Other 'rumours' at the end of 1973 were that Mao was furious with his wife because she had not had the approval of the Politburo before she had launched her biography upon the world, and that Chiang Ching lived at Tiaoyutai, a residence for official guests, and not with Mao.

In 1975, other items about Chiang Ching, began to circulate; ugly stories, about her treatment of Mao's son, Anching, who went mad, and the persecution of Li Ming, his daughter by his former wife.* So widespread were the rumours that the monthly magazine *Red Flag*, came out with a warning against 'small lane news' and in 1974 and 1975 the public security bureau received orders from the Politburo to investigate rumours and pursue 'fabricators' with the utmost severity. Anyone 'betraying state secrets' or 'concocting rumours' was counter-revolutionary. This would clamp most effectively what is now known as 'the Terror of the Gang of Four' upon China.

I had the surprise of seeing Teng Hsiaoping in late 1972. I forget which occasion it was; and my notes do not give the exact date. There was a party; Party officials were there, and among them the recognizably short, squat figure topped by the big head of Teng. And he had a tail. The security man with him was young and tall (they all seemed young and tall). At the end of the party, Teng and his tail walked out, not through the door used by other officials, but through the equivalent of a back door. But there he was. And then the news became semi-official. Teng Hsiaoping was back. Mao wanted him back. 'Talent is hard to find,' Mao said. By April 1973 Teng was able to move about. And he no longer had a tail.

I did not see Chou Enlai in 1973. But his wife, Teng Yingchao, honoured me by receiving me, surrounded by about twenty people from the Foreign Ministry and the Friendship Association, and talking to me for two hours about women's liberation, family planning and many other topics.

She was called Big Sister Teng. Everyone loved her. There was a warmth in the voice and a smile when people talked of her, and in China, where silence is eloquent, the overt fondness for Teng Yingchao was meant to show up the way no one ever pronounced the name of Chiang Ching.

On March 8th, Women's Day, a reception took place for the Western experts living in Peking and in other Chinese cities. Chou Enlai was host; he gave a talk none of them would ever forget. As so often happens in China with a 'breakthrough' speech, there was no official report of it. But the people present would write to their friends abroad, would speak about it.

Chou Enlai said that 'bad elements', such as Lin Piao and others, had taken advantage of the dislocation in the first years of the Cultural

---

* Ho Tzechen, who has now reappeared (1980) and become a member of the National People's Congress. Chiang Ching's own daughter, her only child, Li Na, is a schizophrenic.

Revolution, and done many evil things; one of these was the jailing of Westerners on false charges, or even no charges at all. On behalf of the government, he apologized to the Westerners who had thus suffered, and promised them redress. Chou then walked to several tables, shaking hands and hugging people, among them an American woman who had indeed suffered a great deal, yet who continued to work in China, of her own free will. 'What happens to me is quite secondary ... it is what happens to China which matters,' she said. 'If Chou had asked me to go to jail I would have done it, so long as it advanced the Revolution,' said Simon Hua. 'Then I understood much better how complicated the Revolution was, and we wanted to stay in China more than ever,' said David Crooke, an Englishman who had been jailed on spurious charges for almost four years.

Thus Chou Enlai suddenly transformed their doubts and questionings and their torments into something quite different. Just as the Long March, with its losses and sufferings and agony had been metamorphosed into an epic of human endurance and a triumph, so the wretchedness, the puzzling punishments, acquired meaning and nobility. They were not senseless ordeals, time wasted, never to return; they became part of this creation, the creation of a new and better world. And this was fulfilment.

Chou Enlai went further. He said there was chauvinism and racialism in the treatment of foreigners in China. 'What is wrong with a Chinese and a foreigner getting married?' said he. Mao Tsetung had castigated his own people for their tenacious conservatism and cliquism. 'This attitude won't enable China to make her proper contribution to mankind,' said Chou Enlai.

Throughout 1973 there were echoes of Chou's speech. Elation, enthusiasm, optimism. But so far the speech has not yet been published. The forces of conservatism are indeed strong in China. In 1977 it would take a great deal of pushing to get permission for a Chinese and a foreigner to marry; finally it would be Teng Hsiaoping, following Chou Enlai, who would declare marriages between foreigners and Chinese perfectly acceptable.

'Young girls still seek a matchmaker to introduce a young man to them,' said Gladys Yang.

Gladys knew a girl who had been 'noticed' by a young man, but he could not approach her until properly introduced; a matchmaker was found, who arranged a meeting place at the Summer Palace park. The girl with her brother, would be in a queue for a boat, to glide among the lake's lotuses and the boy and matchmaker would meet her there. But already a queue a mile long of young people, probably quite a few in the throes of introduction was waiting, and it would take three and a half hours to get a boat; the venue was then changed to another park. However, an untoward hailstorm drove them home. The Great Wall was finally selected, with milling crowds, all going there to relax in the beautiful May weather. But by the time this third rendezvous had been arranged, the young man's leave in Peking was up, and it was his last day in the city. He had to get on his bicycle, after scarcely time to say a few words, and leave in order to catch a train. The girl, however, followed him on her bicycle, and it was at the station, saying goodbye, that they fell in love.

We talked about courtship among the young. 'They make their own rules,' said Gladys. A girl had refused to go on after one meeting with a personable boy. 'He did not talk to me of his ideas and ideals, only of love. How do I know what he is, when he only talks to please me?' 'A lot of young people are very serious-minded. A girl feels humiliated if she thinks she's talked down to.'

There were vague reports of cases of rape of little girls; of the acquisition of young mistresses by old cadres. One of the high cadres who thus took a girl of sixteen as his mistress was Mao's nephew in Manchuria. Educated young girls in the rural areas had been raped by peasants in the communes. Hundreds of letters from parents began to pour in to the State Council, asking for their sons' and daughters' return. All the children of higher cadres had been sent to the rural areas, so that none were at university. Chou Enlai's own nephew had been sent down, and had now been away five years. He wrote to his uncle asking to return, but Chou said no, he could not favour his own family. Mao received in May a letter from a distraught mother, whose son had been away; now her daughter had married and gone away, and she was alone. The law said one child must remain to look after the old parents. But the mother had to send money to her son, as he was unable to live on peasant workpoints. Orders to re-examine each case were given; but it would take a long time. There would have been millions of cases to re-examine.

The revolutionary committees were also being reappraised. Stuffed with youths scarcely out of middle school, inexperienced and at times unscrupulous, corruption had set in in some of them. Nieh Yuantzu and other revolutionaries of 1966, now dubbed 'ultra-left', had committed serious crimes, including beating people to death. 'From time to time we hold meetings and have some of them out of jail to criticize them,' said Hualan.

Hualan did not tell me until 1976 that during the Cultural Revolution two of her relatives had committed suicide, accused of 'illicit connection with foreigners'. They had been beaten in front of her, and Hualan had cried, 'Stop please stop,' but the squad of beaters were May 16ers, and particularly vicious. Hualan's elation in seeing justice done to the criminals was understandable.

Hualan's painter sister was again teaching students, but it was difficult 'because the ideas of the ultra-left are still rampant among them'. The students brawled among themselves a great deal; they argued as to the propriety or not of drawing the human body. China's traditional painters had not used human models; and since the Cultural Revolution drawing the naked human body was condemned as 'revisionist' and 'yellow', (pornographic), although it had been done before 1966 in art academies teaching Western oil painting. One of the students, in mockery of the prudery exhibited, had drawn a pair of trousers hanging on a washing line and entitled the picture 'Genuinely Human Legs'.

'There's something wrong with our brains, something wrong with our thinking,' said Hualan, smoking furiously. I said wearily, 'Hualan, you haven't married a feudal Chinese, as I have. It's just feudalism. All the time I am reminded of Pao and the way he thought.'

Yeh only had half of his house. In the other half lived a worker's family. His books were sealed off, and he could not touch them. This had also been done to Pa Chin, and to some other writers. But the books had not been removed. It was, however, frustrating to look at one's books, unable to lay a finger upon them or open a page ... merely stare through the glass pane. But Yeh was unruffled and calm, and laughed in such a jolly fashion that no one thought him distressed. By the end of 1973, the books were released.

Yen Wenching came back from his May 7 school; he wore shorts, spoke of the problems of pig breeding. Three and a half years of labour had followed two years of detention. He had resumed his position as editor, and his house had been restored to him.

I was asked to give talks to several magazines regarding the way to present facts about China to the West. I did have a few things to say – had I not been infuriated by the inanity of some Chinese publications ever since 1956? But nothing came of it; although it was said that Premier Chou had suggested my talking to the people working on the magazines. 'They listen, but hear not, and nothing will change,' said Hualan. The deadly style of writing, the bombast, continued, but in 1978, after much prodding, and because newspapers and publications in Chinese took the lead in telling the truth at last, the magazines for circulation abroad followed suit and are now better.

As for family planning, the educated youth settled in the countryside were producing babies out of wedlock; the babies were taken back to parents in the cities to be reared. It was particularly so in Manchuria, perhaps because the winter nights are long there. In Peking and other cities, from 1973 onwards, doctors were busy performing abortions on demand; a good many of them were on young unmarried girls. Going through the lanes, on dark nights, one came upon couples in dark corners. Curiously enough, it was precisely when, during 1974-6, the ostensible ban on any expression of love reached its peak, and love became almost counter-revolutionary, with foreigners living in China expressing their horror at the sexless lives of the Chinese, that a 'boom' came in the production of babies, and that in the 'small lane news' everyone knew that prostitution was returning, though not extensively.

Stupidly, or artlessly, or both, I said this to friends in Hongkong; they did not betray me but begged me to consider that 'small lane' rumours were dangerous. I would, however, inconsiderately repeat some of this talk to European Marxists–Leninists. I encountered immediately their indignation and hostility. Of course I was a bourgeois, I could not understand theory ... any innuendo against the so-called 'radicals', at the time, put them on the defensive.

By 1973, the Shanghai Four had got themselves into all the liaison organizations with Marxist–Leninist parties abroad; Yao Wenyuan being in charge of this department. The net result was that Westerners, especially the more idealistic ones, firmly believed that the Four were thorough revolutionaries. This was reinforced by the appearance of the magazine *Study and Criticism*. Originally published in September 1973 as a magazine for internal consumption by Futan University in Shanghai (which had been Université Aurore, run by French Jesuits), it spread abroad, where it was translated into several languages, in Paris, London, Rome and America. It was, so I have been told, extremely well done, and was regarded for three years as the most revolutionary, most truly Marxist theoretical work extant.

I was earnestly advised to read it by two fairly eminent Marxist thinkers in the West, when I ventured to express to them my puzzlement and confusion. This cowed me. I know that I am not a 'thinker', nor do I pretend to be one. I never did get to read *Study and Criticism*, and now it has been utterly condemned. But through this magazine the Four did manage a most effective brainwashing of some of the intellectuals in France, Italy and other places.

In trips to Yunnan province that year I had visited Kunming's major hospital. The doctors there were recently back; they told me that several diseases, practically non-existent for the last two years, had returned. One hundred and fifty thousand people in the province had died of malignant malaria in the last three years; resistance to the disease, which had been high before 1949, had disappeared because of the long twenty-year period without any cases.

'We have been unable to investigate tuberculosis in our industrial areas for some years now ... but with B.C.G. being given to all the young people, we hope it is less prevalent than before,' said the forthright doctors. The figures for tuberculosis, however, which had come down drastically since 1954, were now again climbing; and the doctors knew it.

In Kunming University the professors were just back; and the first intake of students – after examinations – was due. But would they now be admitted? 'The standards are low ... we run preparatory courses.'

Yunnan was obviously a 'calamity' area, which means it had suffered badly from the Cultural Revolution; as had Szechuan province.* Readjustment had not yet reached these far-flung regions. It is false to think that directives in the Party were obeyed everywhere automatically, especially at that time, when the Party contained so many new recruits whose only claim to Party membership was their obedience to Lin Piao, and later to Chiang Ching and her allies.

The return of feudal practices, eschewing all 'legality', the reign of arbitrary personal whim, had now become very apparent. When would constitutionalism, true respect for the law, guaranteeing personal rights, come to China?

'Only when the Chinese people, who are not legality-minded, realize how necessary it is,' said Hualan. And she was right.

'Water too pure breeds no fish, too harsh a master has no pupils.' Mr Pei wrote this sentence down on a piece of paper and gave it to me. I still have the slip of paper and the date: May 24th, 1973. 'From Chairman Mao,' said he. Mao had lately scolded the 'radicals' with this quotation from a

* See *Wind in the Tower*. Casualties in both these provinces were high.

Sung poet. 'You find fault too much ... with everything ... every minor defect becomes for you a political crime.'

A famous painter, a poet, a scientist from the Peking planetarium sat with the Peis and me, and our euphoria was that of people who have surmounted some malady and find themselves well again. Mr Pei mimicked with the poet, one of the 'trials' which the May 16ers used to inflict.

'Now confess your crimes,' he said sternly.

The poet pretended to tremble. 'I have not committed crimes.'

'Ha, ah, you are an obdurate, unrepentant counter-revolutionary! Beat him until he confesses his crimes!'

The poet said, 'I used to suffer from constipation, but not once did it bother me during my three years of labour in the countryside.' He told the amusing story of the day when, lined up with other 'criminals', a man next to him suddenly emitted a tremendous snore. 'It was Old Wang; he had actually fallen asleep standing up during his trial.' 'You are not allowed to snore,' barked one of the 'judges'. But already the audience had broken into laughter, and no one could go on with the meeting. 'The people would certainly not condemn anyone that day, and so they let us all go.'

Thus what had been pain and anguish became buffoonery.

A Chinese proverb says, 'One leaf can conceal Mount Taishan.' The reassurance of Chou Enlai's presence, of the measures he took, the return of Teng Hsiaoping, and of other old cadres, disguised the thrust for power of the Shanghai Four and lulled us into thinking that all would be well again.

The Tenth Congress of the Party took place in August 1973. It was to wind up the Lin Piao episode. Would another successor be named by Mao? Apparently not. However, the rapid ascent of the young worker, Wang Hungwen of Shanghai, was noted; he became Vice-Chairman (one of five) of the Party. Was Mao thus once again asserting the leadership role of the working class, as well as the necessity of having 'young blood' in the Party?

All the year through, people I trusted reassured me that there was now 'unity'. Nothing could have been less true. But it was certain that Teng's return augured a 'collective leadership', for this is what Teng had advocated as Party Secretary-General, since 1956. He had also supported all moves for creating codes of law, a workable legal system. Perhaps now this would come to pass.

Looking at the Politburo composition, there seemed to be a balance between the 'centre' and 'left', just as Mao had envisaged. The Shanghai Four were in the Politburo, and in its Standing Committee were Wang Hungwen and Chang Chunchiao. This would be the chief snag some two years later, for it is the Standing Committee which handles executive affairs; and it is its Secretary—in this case Chang—who gets all the mail addressed to Politburo members. In 1977 letters addressed to other members of the Politburo, confiscated by Chang, would be found in files he had kept in his home.

The only unknown quantity in the Politburo was a man named Hua Kuofeng. Hua had been a provincial cadre from Hunan; both a soldier and an administrator, rising steadily through sheer merit and hard work from the lower ranks; and although criticized during the Cultural Revolution, he had not then been important enough to be jailed. In September 1971 he had been co-opted to Peking by Mao Tsetung and Chou Enlai because he had done much excellent work in Hunan, especially in preventing a seizure of the province by Lin Piao. He worked with Chou in the State Council; and he was so quiet that no one really bothered about him at the time.

'The tree would like to be still, but the wind does not stop blowing.' In 1973, the Shanghai Mafia began its strategy for seizing power. The first move was to get Wang Hungwen to Peking that year—or rather to commute between Peking and Shanghai—and then to be elected Vice-Chairman of the Party. Another move, in February 1973, was to have the Communist Youth League Congress held in Shanghai first; the second congress was held in Liaoning province, where Mao's nephew, Chiang Ching's aficionado, ruled. This indicated clearly the target of the Four: once again it was the young.

In July 1973, the battle in the sensitive sector of education began. The case of an 'educated', that is, middle school man of twenty-five, Chang Tiesheng, was splashed on the radio in Liaoning province. He had been so devoted to his work in a commune that, faced with studying for an examination or helping with the harvest, he chose the harvest—and turned in a blank sheet.* He wrote to the newspapers explaining that he felt examinations were a way of corrupting youth, turning away the thoughts of the young from caring for the workers-peasants-soldiers. *Red Flag* and

---

* This was later proved a fabrication. He did sit for the examination, answered the questions, but obtained too low a mark to pass. The author saw the photocopy of his examination paper in 1977.

the *People's Daily* took up the battle, criticizing the reintroduction of academic criteria for entrance to educational institutions.

This 'blank sheet' case became part of a nationwide debate on how to run universities, middle schools and primary schools; it would play havoc with education until the fall of the Four. With millions of youngsters hungering to get back to the cities and return to study, yet aware that they could never pass the examinations required, the Tiesheng affair was a godsend. 'Why admission to university on questions framed by bourgeois authorities? Why not be admitted on our proletarian revolutionary spirit alone?' Counter articles produced Mao's dictum that there must also be 'knowledge', but this was drowned in the wrath of the millions of youngsters with little schooling but vast ambitions; they would never have more schooling (and were incapable of it) but they felt, each one of them, capable of 'proletarian leadership'. 'We must not cultivate bookworms ... we evaluate the quality of teaching first of all by the political orientation,' the editorials stormed.

In December 1973 another 'incident': a twelve-year-old girl, Huang Shuai, wrote a letter criticizing her school teacher's behaviour, the way she taught, and the content of the curriculum. The press took the case up and published her letter; millions of youngsters of twelve and thirteen started attacking their teachers. So successful was the shambles thus created that by mid-1974 many schools could not function; and that is when, in Peking, in Chungking, in Wuhan and even in Lhasa, the windows of all middle schools began to be systematically broken by 'rebel' students.

Now newspaper articles appeared, praising the 'militia' of Shanghai. The formation of militia corps in every factory was advocated; it did not at first appear abnormal, since militia training had been called for since 1958. But its sinister significance as the power struggle intensified would become obvious in 1976.

Thus every active sector in China was being sucked into the struggle. There is no doubt that the Four did deploy fantastic energy and a very extraordinary knowledge of psychological warfare. And owing to the obstacles placed in the way of the return of the cadres to the cultural, journalistic and propaganda sectors, they now controlled the mass media: the press, films, radio and television, and publishing houses.

The main attack, directed against Chou Enlai, began in September 1973. It started as a campaign, or movement, against Confucius, and it was led by two old and revered scholars: Professor Yang Jungkuo, an expert on Confucius, and Professor Feng Yulan, who had studied in America and had long been known for his reverence for Old Master Kung.

Twenty-four

The Rise of the Four and the Death of Chou Enlai: 1974-1976

1974 TO 1976 was a time of perplexity and anguish for Chinese, both in China and abroad. A malaise which remained largely unvoiced. My relatives and my friends went on hoping that there would not be another political paroxysm. I continued my efforts to widen the opening between China and the rest of the world. Chou Enlai had said to me, 'There is no conflict of interest between the people of China and the peoples of the world.' I believed him. But if China was to progress, she must admit the contrary winds of other nations. If her system were good, it must be tested in practice, and not shielded from alien encounter.

I now belittled the viciousness and the danger of the Four because I was convinced that Chou Enlai would be able to maintain stability, unity and progress. The shocking exposure of Lin Piao seemed to me sobering enough. It should make all of us more careful. And surely Chiang Ching, as Mao's wife, *must* understand that 'ultra-leftism' was harmful. Had Mao not repeated in 1973 that there must be stability and progress, and that 'the cultural policy of the Hundred Flowers ... must be applied'?

I sought to bring to China members of the American Cancer Society. Cancer, with heart disease, was now the major killer in China. George Wu and his colleague, Dr Li Ping, and I spent many hours talking of cancer research, and the detection of early cases. Millions of women coming as routine cases to the hospitals were examined for uterine and cervical cancer. Cancer of the oesophagus was prevalent in the Taihang mountain area; of the liver in east China, of the naso-pharynx in the south. Chou Enlai had approved plans for a major hospital and research centre in Peking, endowed with the latest equipment. Fourteen other cancer hospitals were to be built in the provinces.

But for three years I got nowhere with my efforts on behalf of the American Cancer Society. The reason — unknown to me then — was the attitude of the Health Minister, Madame Liu Hsiangping. She was tall and so fat that we called her 'the Hippo'. Her husband was the head of the

Peking Revolutionary Committee and also head of Peking's security police. Her daughter was the personable Hsieh Chingyi, in charge of Tsinghua University, whom I had interviewed in 1969. The family was devoted to the Four.

I also tried to get Dr Isaac Berliner and his wife Martha into China. Berliner was doing pioneering research in contraceptives. They received a visa, but Liu Hsiangping refused to meet them. And though Berliner lectured in China to medical staff, nothing came of his efforts. 'Some people want a withdrawal ... to close us in again,' Ma Haiteh would tell me. That year he could not obtain leave to go to America to see his brother.

I went to Mexico and gave the first public lecture on family planning which Mexico City had ever heard. President Echeverria was worried about Mexico's population increase, but the Catholic Church remained adamantly against contraception.

The tragedy of the Third World countries is that revolutions in health and in education have been made before an industrial revolution. Europe's nineteenth-century industrialization, present affluence and technological advances occurred through the exploitation not only of her own people but of other nations, and included black slavery. And this exploitation went on unhindered for many decades. But the Third World, in its emergence from colonialism, devised modern health and education programmes while its industrial development remained centuries behind. It thus brought upon itself demographic problems on an unprecedented scale.

I attended a United Nations meeting on family planning in Bucharest, and found myself pitted against Dr Mario Peccei of the Club of Rome. His idea of a 'supreme council' of the 'eminent' (Western experts from the affluent countries) to 'organize all the world's resources' evoked anger from Third World delegates present. How could the Third World further entrust its resources to the ruling of the affluent, I said, when their waste, extravagance and spoliation of the world's resources remains the outstanding crime of our era? And while they continue to perpetuate among us poverty and political instability by denying us an equal share of the world's resources?*

Back to China. And to the roller-coaster feeling. A miasma of disquiet in the air. It is due to the Dragon Lady, Chiang Ching. Her nickname this

* The Manila conference of 1979 has proved this true once again.

year is Three Drops of Water. My insistence that she is irresponsible, mentally deranged, is unacceptable to my friends. They see in her a wilful demoniac, and the muttering dislike of 1972 is changing into an almost pathological hatred. Everything that went wrong, every cruelty, every death is now her fault. 'There isn't a family in China which has not suffered because of her,' says Hualan. I disagree, of course. She cannot be held fully guilty for everything, I say.

The anti-Confucius campaign was in full swing; it was now called 'anti-Confucius, anti-Lin Piao', *Pilin Pikung*. Mao was said to have launched it. It had become, however, an ambiguous drive.

With a spate of academic and historical articles to give it respectability, the movement had at first been turned against Chou Enlai and his policies. It attacked the return of old cadres, 'restoration of the past', 'conservatism', and 'the greatest Confucianist mandarin of them all, who is negating the Cultural Revolution'.* The return of Teng Hsiaoping provoked inspired wall posters on the 'return of capitalist roaders ... who interfere in the factories and seek to negate the Cultural Revolution'.

But in March 1974 Chou Enlai foiled the onslaught. The occasion was the visit of Kenneth Kaunda, President of Zambia. In June 1967, worried about China, Kaunda had gone to Peking; Chou had extolled the Cultural Revolution to him precisely when he was subject to its most vicious attacks. Now Chou Enlai extolled the anti-Confucius movement; said it was an 'anti-Confucius, anti-Lin Piao' campaign, necessary to clear people's minds of the feudal ideas instilled by Lin Piao. The implication that it was an attack against him thus became untenable.

Political conflicts in China have always been fought with the weapons of historical analogy and historical allusion; figures of the past are surrogates, to attack present-day persons. This is as true today as ten centuries ago. Round after round of articles appeared in 1974, tracing the history of China as a 'two-line struggle' between the progressive 'legalists' and the reactionary 'Confucianists'. But the qualities attributed to legalists and Confucianists varied according to who wrote the articles. Lin Piao became a typical Confucian, and having been condemned as ultra-left, became suddenly ultra-right. Chou Enlai's weighty words at the Tenth Congress of 1973 were quoted: 'Very often one tendency covers another'. What appears radical and revolutionary might be serving the most reactionary forces.

With consummate skill Chou Enlai and the returned officials seized upon the campaign to push the rebuilding of Party institutions, to promote

* Premier Chou Enlai.

legality, unity and economic production, since all three had been 'legalist' theses in Chinese history. At the same time, Chou insisted that the campaign was against élitism, bureaucratism and the inferior condition of women.

'When will the National People's Congress be held?' I asked Wu Chienta and Hsing Chiang. Chienta had had an awful time for almost four years. It would take another two years before he stopped looking dazed.

'We shall hold it when more unity is achieved,' replied Hsing Chiang sagely.

'That was giving you a scoop,' remarked Ma Haiteh later. For it implied that a major battle was proceeding in the highest echelon.

'That's the Cultural Revolution's contribution to our people's brains,' said Hualan. 'We, the people, would not have dreamt of questioning unity among the leaders before. Now every child in China knows that they are constantly bickering and battling among themselves; and so no one is a god anymore.'

'But cannot a paroxysm, a climax, be avoided?' I asked her.

'Perhaps ... but so far we've had a crisis every five or six years. Maybe another one will come ... '

'Your temper, your temper – it's a flame nine metres high', said Hsing Chiang, sighing. My temper was getting very dangerous. I was on edge. 'It's because the anti-Confucius movement is carried out in a very Confucian manner,' I retorted.

There were troubles in China that year, ignored by the press but whispered about in the 'small lane news'. The situation in Sinkiang was 'ugly', Lung Shuching, Lin Piao's man there, had been removed, but it was difficult to take in hand every place in Sinkiang, and there were stoppages in the factories, and even some fighting.

Trouble in the factories had actually erupted in several provinces. In Wuhan, the steel workers were on strike. The strike extended to other steel plants by 1975; then it was stopped by Teng Hsiaoping's energetic measures, only to surge again in 1976. In 1977 Teng Hsiaoping would tell me that due to the 'sabotage' of the Gang of Four a shortage of 27 million tonnes of steel between 1974 and 1976 had occurred.*

* Interview published by *Der Spiegel*. I was at the time asked by Vice-Premier Teng not to give the exact figure; it was mentioned officially four months later.

There was trouble in the silk factories of Hangchow. Wang Hungwen was there, and appointed one of his 'Mafia brothers,' Wen Senho, to supervise the factories. But high officials issued statements that the strikes were 'of no importance', which fooled people like myself.

In 1976, shortages of food and consumer goods would occur in certain cities. Taiyuan, Chengtu, Wuhan. No meat was to be had in Taiyuan for a year. In Chengtu, by 1974, there were already eighty different ration tickets for as many goods, and the goods were hard to find. Szechuan had suffered greatly from the Cultural Revolution, and continued to suffer.

I went to see my second-degree cousins, the sons of my Uncle Liu; who had died at the age of ninety-four. My cousins were all workers in factories. They were voluntarily cleaning the sewers in their district, on the Sunday I went to see them. When I left them they insisted on accompanying me through the meander of *hutungs* to the main avenue. 'There are bad people around ... they may try to rob you,' whispered Liu's second wife to me. Liu's second wife was very active in her street committee, spreading family planning knowledge, perhaps because Uncle Liu had bred altogether sixteen children, twelve by his first and four by his second wife.

People that year were inclined to whisper, as if there were microphones about. Everything was 'secret'; I must not repeat a word.

Adolescent gangs: 'They start at twelve or thirteen. Everything now happens at a younger age. Instead of copying the positive characters in the new model operas, they copy the villains ... Some of the youngsters are even cultivating moustaches, like the bandits in *Taking Tiger Mountain by Strategy*.' The gangs had 'chieftains' of fifteen. They vandalized, they broke windows ... 'A lost generation,' said Mr Pei.

Yeh's wife, Yuan Yin, was much in demand by her street committee to solve delinquency problems. In their neighbourhood two 'armies' of adolescents were acting out old tales of chivalry, battling with each other once a week, at night. The prize was the 'princess', a pretty girl who used to watch these tournaments, wearing a white veil on her head. 'She becomes the mascot of the winning side; the boys bring her presents, even steal money from their parents for her.

'The youngsters have no schools to go to; and if they go to school they are told to bully the teachers. To study is to show bourgeois tendencies.' The examples of Chang Tiesheng and Huang Shuai, promoted by the Four, had been only too effective. But parents came secretly to teachers, imploring them to give private tuition at night to their children.

Chang Tiesheng (Blank-Sheet Chang) was in 1974 promoted to regional representative at the National People's Congress to be held in January 1975. He was sent to Japan as youth representative, and in 1976 would become Vice-Minister of Culture under the Four. Huang Shuai, the thirteen-year-old, was in the same school as one of my nieces. My niece said very little about her except that she 'is often travelling'. Huang Shuai went from school to school to lecture the students; she had a car to convey her from home to school and back.

'The young are told to grow spikes all over their body and horny antlers all over their heads,' said Jui, my sister-in-law. 'Fortunately our children do not listen to this nonsense.' But many youngsters became insolent, rude and lazy, since these attitudes were now virtues. The sales-girls and boys in the shops would not serve clients, and tales of their hostility to potential buyers became common talk. But so many of these youths had jobs in the cities because they must look after their parents; they could not be moved, or fired. So they did as they pleased.

I went to see the painter Wu Tsojen and his wife. Wu Tsojen was a cheerful and talkative man. He had been criticized during the Cultural Revolution, but now he was in deep trouble because he had wanted the works of that other great painter renowned all over the world, Tsi Paishih, to be adequately preserved. Chiang Ching had railed against Tsi Paishih as a 'miser' who could not paint, as she had abused other famous painters such as Li Kejan and Pan Tienshou.

Wu Tsojen was glum. 'I am not well.' A visit to the art shops revealed that neither his paintings nor those of Li Kejan, nor anyone else of renown, were to be seen. Reproductions of their work were no longer on sale, and the salesgirls frowned heavily when I mentioned them.

Only in 1975 did I hear about the 'black' exhibition of paintings held in spring 1974 in Shanghai. Since then rumour has proved true, confirmed event.

In 1973 Chiang Ching, and the other members of the Politburo had approved a selection of the works of famous painters commissioned by Chou Enlai to decorate public buildings and hotels. Mao had expressed the wish that 'a hundred flowers blossom' and that 'my face should not be in every room'.

But in the spring of 1974, the very works which had been approved by the Four were condemned by them as 'black' and 'attempts to restore capitalism'. For instance, a painting of fish in water: if the water were not 'realistic' enough, it meant 'fish out of water', and it was an insult to the working class attaining administrative posts. If a mountain had many rocks, it was a way of wishing they would fall on the fields and ruin the harvest. And so on. Yao Wenyuan surpassed himself by calling one painting 'a revelation of the spy and enemy agent nature of the painter'. The whole episode sounds so paranoiac that it is scarcely credible. Yet dozens of painters, who suffered at the 'black' exhibition told me similar stories, in Szechuan, in Shanghai, and Peking. This raises once again the problem of the mental balance of Chiang Ching; and of the men around her.

Art academies, which had been closed in 1967, and reopened in 1971 were once more closed while the teachers and their students trudged down to 'integrate' in the villages. In the end this descent of eminent artists among the peasantry – which had first occurred in 1958 – did give rise to some excellent peasant paintings, and promoted among thousands of peasants the need and the urge to paint.*

Millie Pei, now a university student, but working in a factory for six months to compose, with the workers, a new dictionary of Chinese scientific terms, gave me the flavour of the current disquiet. 'The people feel that they are pawns. They are tired of political movements. They say: Today we are told to run in direction A, and anything else is counter-revolutionary. Tomorrow we are told that A is counter-revolutionary and we must run in direction B. We are not punished; we are simply called "the deluded masses". But who has deluded us? Why is it that yesterday's wrong is today's right?' The young were becoming cynical, and the middle-aged were playing safe. 'They don't want to suffer again for criticizing X or Y today and seeing them return to power tomorrow ... They say: Let's wait and see.'

As for studying, or becoming an expert at anything – it now took courage to do so. 'Have you heard the doggerel: "Expert, expert, that's the way to eat dirt. See not, hear not, speak not, you wear a clean shirt".' Millie told me of the waste and extravagance in the factory she worked in. 'I go around turning off taps, turning off lights, and I'm accused of being bourgeois and "material production minded" instead of "revolution minded". But what is socialism, if not an end to waste, and increased production? That's what Marx, Lenin and Chairman Mao said, but the young workers say, "Better no production than capitalism". Then how shall we live?' asked Millie.

* The Huhsien peasant paintings, exhibited in London, Paris and the United States, are examples of this collaboration between peasant and professional artist.

By 1975 there were once again 'study sessions' in all Party units. They centred on a major article by Chang Chunchiao, which became required study for all Party members. The women cadres brought their knitting with them to the meetings. 'We have time to catch up with our winter woollies.' This was passive resistance of a kind no one could take exception to; since knitting was a kind of manual labour. In Chengtu and Chungking, girls would walk on the streets, knitting away, their long hair spread on their shoulders in a way thought 'indecent' by the prim northern Chinese. They would explain that they had just washed their hair, and were walking about to dry it.

'Knit, talk food, talk sickness, and you are safe.'

Food was a good topic, unlikely to be suspect, provided shortages were not mentioned. There was the ritual phrase, 'The general situation is excellent', which meant: but the particular situation is quite awful. Everyone understood the sarcastic implication.

Sickness was the other safe topic of conversation. Comparing symptoms could lead a whole group of women, en masse, to leave the office and seek a doctor urgently. Mild epidemics of headache with blurred vision even required a small autocar, to take a group, as to a picnic, to the hospital.

The doctors were almost all back by 1974; even though there were young heads of departments, who knew very little, and older consultants in subordinate positions. But the conscience of the doctors never faltered. The admirable way in which they accepted working in an inferior position, and continued to do their best, makes them true heroes. The endless queues of waiting patients were not surprising. Older cadres, fearing renewed abuse, humiliation and disgrace, simply became ill. The doctors understood that they must remain under hospital care for 'weak heart', neurasthenia or gastric ulcers. They could not be sent to labour or be bullied, for deaths during bullying, and suicides, in the early years of the Cultural Revolution, had been very much resented.

There were professional betrayers, among them a poet; he participated in writers' meetings, then went off on his bicycle to report to 'them'. 'But why on a bicycle?' 'Because if he went in a car it would be noticed.'

My friend, Yen Wenching, back from May 7 school, had six hundred manuscripts on his editorial desk awaiting publication. He could not send one to the printers.

'Why?'

'Because publication depends on Yao Wenyuan's approval.'

'Why no literary magazines? It was announced they would reappear ... '

But Yao Wenyuan, now editor of *Red Flag*, would not allow any magazine which might print articles disagreeing with the Four.

'Are there such articles?'

'Hundreds,' replied Yen Wenching, crinkling his eyes at me.

The core of the unease was Chou Enlai's illness. Chou Enlai had been in hospital since April 1974. Some people said that already in 1973 he had been unwell. What was he suffering from? Diplomats said it was cardiac disease. George Wu, who should have known, said that he had no idea, but his face was sombre.

I gathered from George the erroneous impression that Chou would soon get better. This was, of course, not true. But George could not betray what was both a professional and a state secret. And Chou continued to work; daily, high officials came to see him at the hospital.

'Suppose something goes wrong with Chou ... what will happen to China?'

Rewi was vague. 'The Young Turks are pushing the Dragon Lady on top.'

'Maybe Teng Hsiaoping can manage them now.' Teng was in charge of the daily work Chou could no longer do.

'We all hope so,' said Rewi, looking grim.

Articles on class origin and class struggle, and talk about 'class origin goes back three generations', abounded. If acted upon it meant that my nephews and nieces would have mighty little chance of getting into a university, ever. Now there were nine instead of five 'bad categories', and the intelligentsia was 'the stinking ninth', according to the Dragon Lady.★ Articles about 'new Liu Shaochis', warnings of 'erroneous tendencies in the Party', exhortations to 'go against the tide', a phrase used by Wang Hungwen at the Tenth Congress—all this showed a new outburst of ultra-leftism. Going against the tide was a favourite cliché among the young. It meant going against all educationalists. A film, *Counterattack*, would be made, based on the 'blank-sheet' episode of Chang Tiesheng. Another film, *Spring Seedlets*, showed all the old cadres, older doctors (above forty) as rotten, incompetent and heartless. The only heroic,

---

★ Landlords, rich peasants, reactionaries, hooligans, capitalist roaders, the old national bourgeoisie, the bourgeoisie within the Party, spies and people in collusion with abroad, and the 'unreformed' intelligentsia.

devoted and successful figures were young boys and girls, young barefoot doctors of seventeen, eighteen.

Many absurd slogans were current that year. 'Better a socialist train running late than a capitalist train on time.' This was licence for everything not to run on schedule. City transport became badly disorganized (except in Shanghai) because bus drivers made it a revolutionary attitude to run buses not on time – or even not at all. But in Shanghai the workers were paid 20 per cent more than anywhere else and production was encouraged by the Four, because it was their main bastion, and no strikes or dissent were allowed. Everywhere else they instigated conflict, breakage of machinery, stoppages, to prove that Teng Hsiaoping could not run things and that people opposed him.

Already in summer 1974 the overseas Chinese were leaving in droves. Eighty thousand of them applied to leave China, and 45,000 were given permission. 'They're afraid that violence is beginning all over again. They don't want to put up with it any longer.' A friend of mine from Yenching, a doctor, could not stay. He had been, in 1956, so full of enthusiasm. In 1974 he left China. 'I can no longer bear it ... I gave up a big job in 1950 to return to serve China ... '

I went to Tientsin, and down the railway to Chengchow and to Loyang. The railway line's terminus was Shanghai. Now I understand that I was, that year, the subject of an operation designed to win me over to Chiang Ching. Almost all the places I visited were under her influence, particularly the railway stations of Tientsin, Chengchow and Paoting. The Four had a long-term plan to capture the railway, in order to move the armed militia they nurtured in Shanghai up north, if necessary, joining with forces from Manchuria under Mao's nephew, Mao Yuanhsing, and capturing Peking.

Tientsin was depressing; the railway station was surrounded by silent, sinister youths. Some wore small moustaches; others were obviously vagrants. I had another shock the next morning. Almost every shop window showed at least one dress, in a pastel colour, with ample skirt and a V neck. It was *the* Chiang Ching dress, designed by her. I knew about *the* dress because Shuan came to tell me of it. Shuan was to create new patterns for the material used in the dress. All the tailors were told they must make only this model and no other. Every woman in China was to wear *the* dress. But Shuan said it took almost five metres of material and cost at least thirty *yuan*, the monthly salary of a young worker, and more than a month's wage for a street factory worker. And breast-feeding women could not wear it, for it did not unbutton, and how and where could they take it off when they wanted to feed their babies? 'Three Drops of Water' had also decided that there would be five basic colours, according to rank: peasant, worker, cadre, woman soldier, higher leading cadre. Ambassadors' wives would wear *the* dress abroad. However, counter-revolutionaries and people of bad origin would not be allowed to wear it. They would have to stick to trousers.

Tientsin was now the Dragon Lady's city. A meeting of national women representatives had been held here. All those who attended wore *the* dress while Chiang Ching spoke to them. 'She said, "Why should not a woman have male concubines? The Empress Wu Tzetien had male concubines ... " Because of her a woman cadre now openly entertains her boyfriends at her home and the husband dare not protest. And a woman and her daughter have started a prostitution ring ... ' Thus my informant, a woman cadre.

I meet in Tientsin Pa Mulan. She is a typical Chiang Ching recruit; good-looking, energetic, and above all prolix. 'Listening to you, I wish I had a tape recorder,' I say. She explains to me women's liberation and its astounding progress, owing to the *Pilin Pikung* movement. All revolutionary committees in Tientsin have 30 per cent women members.

We go to Takang, the offshore oilfield near Tientsin. Young girls are 'in charge' of routine work at many posts in the oilfield. They are between eighteen and twenty-nine years old. The visit ends disastrously. I am shown a very modern machine, obviously either Swedish or Japanese, which just stands next to an older machine. I am told that it was made by the workers 'out of bits and pieces of discarded material'. I explode. 'It just is not true.' Great awkwardness. 'You're pouring cold water on the workers' enthusiasm,' says Hsing Chiang. 'Enthusiasm does not mean telling lies,' I reply, and Hsing Chiang utters a deep sigh, for I make life very difficult for her. She is torn in two, and Party discipline does not allow her to say anything.

The Nankai middle school was established in 1904. Chou Enlai studied there. The Assistant Dean, Chu Ta, is affable. No classes are held because the students are 'going down to help the peasants ... ' Twice Mr Chu refers to 'our beloved Premier Chou', and we look at each other in great sadness. 'His recovery is the fervent wish of all the Chinese people,' says he pointedly. Next to him sits the school heroine, the seventeen-year-old Wei, a disciple of the 'model', Huang Shuai. She wrote a wall poster against her teachers and against the Dean of Nankai. 'We went against the tide, as Vice-Chairman Wang Hungwen enjoined us to do,' says she. Students and teachers apparently spend two evenings a week criticizing Confucius.

The Tientsin railway station workers are writing the history of their railway station and its vicissitudes. An admirable project. 'Are the trains running well?' 'Better than before.' They say it was Liu Shaochi and Lin Piao who stopped the trains. And yet, in 1975, all along that railway line and others, young workers will 'go against the tide' and the trains will be hours late, and accidents will occur on several railroads.

Must I or must I not believe the stories I am told by these railway workers: how they serve the people by selling tickets at the schools and factories, how they strive to make things easier at holiday time for those who go home to see their families? Eighty per cent of the train attendants are girls. Part of women's liberation is giving jobs to girls. I think of the hostile young men outside the railway station.

Siaodjing village near Tientsin is Chiang Ching's model brigade. All the women here have learnt to read and to write, and the village practises total equality in workpoints, which is still quite rare in rural China. Poems against Confucius are written on the walls by the villagers, and poetry competitions are held.

A young girl, a 'model' in the fight against Confucius, tells me of the way she 'uprooted Confucian ideas' in her production team. She is twenty-six. 'Do you intend to get married?' 'I have not yet found a master,' she replies. 'What did you say?' I ask innocently, and she blushes scarlet. She has used the old, Confucian term, a slip of the tongue ...

Evident progress has taken place in women's liberation everywhere in China, but it is simply not true that everything started at the Cultural Revolution of 1966, and that all of it is due to Chiang Ching launching the slogan: Every revolutionary committee must have 30 per cent of women.

In Loyang the tractor factory is a mess. Screws and bolts and spare parts of every description litter the floor in untidy heaps; the engineer who takes me around does not attempt to explain. He shows me one workshop and then says, 'Our production is not too good. We have had ultra-left sabotage. But it will pick up now.' He hopes, of course, that Teng Hsiaoping will intervene and make things work.

Of all the disciplines, only archaeology has never been obstructed during the Cultural Revolution. Most important archaeological finds have taken place during those years of turmoil. I have been to Tatung, following the tracks of Buddhism, to see the Wei dynasty Yungkang caves. I now see the Lungmen caves in Loyang, and their thousands of carved Buddhas, from the gigantic to the tiny. I am told of 'the great contribution' of Empress Wu Tzetien to the sculptures and treasures of the Lungmen caves. I shall hear a great deal about Empress Wu of the Tang dynasty, and also about Empress Lu of the Han dynasty, in the next two years. Both these women apparently were progressive, legalists, anti-Confucian. Both added great lustre and prosperity to the Empire. So write the 'new historians' collected in the universities by the Four. Does this mean that we shall have a new empress in China?

In Chengchow, in Loyang, everywhere there are wall posters, writings on walls and bridges and atop telegraph poles; in black paint which cannot be rubbed off. Some welcome the army; some call for the start of a workers' militia to patrol the streets; some demand that there be street protection units; some accuse capitalist roaders, 'people like Liu Shaochi', in authority; some say, 'We are not going back to the cattle pens ... ', 'There must be better arrangements for education . . .' 'There are false revolutionaries; all they want is power ... ', 'Down with the ultra-left who wave the red flag to knock down the red flag'. There are also many torn posters. My driver goes very fast through the streets.

The fields around Chengchow are almost eighteen metres below the Yellow River level, and the dykes are constantly added to. The roads are used as threshing floors, and there is a jam of peasant carts. My driver says, 'What is life like in the West? Here we have security, but it is so terribly monotonous ... ' Monotonous! When so much is happening! In Loyang the army called to quell riots and round up hooligans and stop the armed attacks on banks ...

On family planning, the statistics I am given in 1974 and 1975 are more than suspect, because of 'Hippo', the Health Minister. I cannot use them, except one or two specific examples. The son of a friend, who is now a factory worker, tells me that in his plant the leading cadres all have six to ten children. The workers, urged to have no more than three, have put up a poster: 'In family planning, modestly follow the example of our factory leadership.'

In another city I feel around me a tightening surveillance, as in 1969. Someone thinks there are things I must not know. My friends are more than usually reticent. One person will tell me how he has been warned only to talk to me of 'positive aspects'.

In Peking, Hualan is not reticent. 'People who have beaten and tortured others are now being admitted to the Party ... the Party's filling up with them. With membership of the Party they can do anything ... so who dares to complain?' Especially not to someone who might say something outside, and be quoted in the newspapers. Every person I have met will be questioned if I am quoted repeating, for instance, Hualan's phrase.

I can well conceive the following scenario: I am fêted, shown around, and given interviews; although I am somewhat disappointing because I publish so little of what I am told, unlike a good many authoritative visitors who have managed entire books based solely on interviews, interpreters and three solid weeks of conducted tours.

Meanwhile, my friends and Family members are being told what to say to me, and perhaps someone will be incarcerated because I have been indiscreet. I feel my skin crawl with apprehension at the thought. And this could happen now, because Chou Enlai is ill, and Kung Peng is no longer there, and I have no protection ... I don't know Teng Hsiaoping; as for Chiao Kuanhua, he is always very busy.

Now I am seriously perturbed. Does Three Drops really mean to become Party Chairman, or Empress? Perhaps Roxane Witke was right and I was wrong. I am convinced in my bone marrow that Chiang Ching's access to supreme power will be very bad for China. I think: 'She's like Caligula, the crazy Roman Emperor. Let her mess with culture or whatever for a while, and sooner or later the people will get rid of her. But not, oh not Party Chairman.'

I go to see Claire Hollingworth, correspondent for the *Daily Telegraph*, whom I met at the Hsinchiao Hotel. I tried to help her with her very unsatisfactory interpreter. 'He's totally inert,' she said. 'He's always tired and going off to sleep.' This inertia was a defensive reaction, perhaps also one of hostility. So many youths are now hostile. I spoke to Chiao Kuanhua about it but Chiao was unhelpful. 'She is a difficult woman,' said he.

Now I plan to ask Claire to write about *the* dress. The best way to attack Chiang Ching is by ridicule; showing her up as a foolish bizarre woman. Anything else, especially as so much is gossip and conjecture,* will only enhance that dread of her which unhinges us all.

Besides the dress, I tell Claire how much people are frightened; how the formerly renowned film star, Pei Yang, has been declared 'an American spy'. I do not tell her of the accusation suspended above my head – or rather, above my Family's head. I know that it can be used at any time against me, but Claire, being English, will think me melodramatic and disbelieve me if I tell her. Claire says that she cannot write the story because she cannot quote me. But she will try to pass it 'through a French newspaper'.

The French paper apparently refused the story, deeming it of little value. Claire, as correspondent in Peking, could not be identified with an article

---

* Until 1977, when I made sure of facts, through witnesses and documents in the handwriting of the Four.

against Madame Mao without being thrown out. 'You must understand my position ... I have family and friends here; it's a sword over my head,' I said. 'Are you quite serious?' asked Claire. Perhaps I sounded histrionic to her. So I said, 'Never mind.' And we talked of Chou Enlai.

But already our two meetings were suspect. As we walked back to the hotel (for I never talked in Claire's room, of course, only outside), a young girl passed us and said to me, 'Talking to a foreigner – what are you talking about?' and walked on. And Chiao let me know that the less I had to do with Claire the better.

The waitresses of the Peking Hotel blossomed into pleated skirts.

I asked Little Chou, my favourite waitress, 'How much did it cost?'

'A lot. And I've four children.'

Rewi said, 'The Dragon Lady makes life difficult for everybody.'

The latest rumour was about the jailing of a geography lecturer who had a photograph of Armstrong walking on the moon. A friend had sent it to him from America. Someone had reported the fact to Chiang Ching, and she had said, 'Investigate'. And so he had been jailed.

I lost my temper. 'Everything is always her fault ... why pick on her every time? Surely bad things have been done by other people ... ' I could not believe all the rumours; there were simply too many, too many. It was indeed pathological. All the hatred. all the resentment, were directed at her. 'She's not normal, she's mentally disturbed,' I said. But Hualan would not listen. 'She's the most wicked woman in the world ... we hate her, hate her ... we wish we could boil her alive ... '

In September Mrs Imelda Marcos came to China for eight days, and suddenly a lot of women were having their hair done to look like Imelda.

Chiang Ching took Mrs Marcos to the model Siaodjing brigade. 'You had the same trip as Imelda Marcos,' said Hsing Chiang to me. A great compliment. It is now claimed that Chiang Ching inspired Chairman Mao to instigate the rectification in art and literature in Yenan in 1942 (she married him in 1938).* 'Whoever is against the revolution in art and literature is against the Party' is the theme of an article. Criticism of Chiang Ching is tantamount to criticism of the revolution in art and literature, and that means being anti-Party, therefore counter-revolutionary. It's very neat.

On television I see Chairman Mao receiving Mrs Marcos, who looks exquisite. I am shattered because Mao is old, so old. His lower jaw hangs

* See *The Morning Deluge*.

and his hands shake. I write to Chiao Kuanhua, whom I continue to trust, telling him that Mao appears very ill. I do not get a reply.

Chiao Kuanhua has married again. We, his friends, are happy for him. Chang Handje is very beautiful. She has divorced her husband to marry Chiao. Some people have to wait years for a divorce, but for Chiao it has gone very quickly. For the first time there is criticism of Chiao (who until now has been something of a hero among the people). The son of Chang Handje goes abroad to study, but Chiao's own son and daughter by Kung Peng do not get any privileges. They have done labour in the communes.

I have seen Chang Handje at a sports meeting; she sat behind Wang Hungwen, whose English interpreter she appears to have been.

Chang Handje does not receive me. No more dinners with Chiao, only formal cups of tea and a talk in the official residence.

Prince Sihanouk and Princess Monique give me a wonderful lunch for my birthday, September 12th. The Prince has cooked it himself. In 1973, at great risk, the Prince and his wife went back to Cambodia through the Ho Chih Minh Trail, and spent some weeks with the Khmer Rouge guerrillas in the jungle. Sihanouk even reached Angkor, and was photographed among the monuments. In 1974 it is obvious that the Vietnam war – and its corollary, the Cambodian war – will be wound up. 'My position is now very strong,' said Sihanouk. 'The Americans are defeated. Victory is ours.'

Kissinger, in Peking to see Mao and Chou Enlai, has asked them, so says rumour, to intercede with Sihanouk. The latter should be 'reasonable', and parley with Lon Nol, rather than let the Khmer Rouge take over in a final and decisive military victory. But Sihanouk tells me now that the Americans are 'duping' the Chinese. 'Vous avez été dupés,' he says. He refuses to talk with Lon Nol. Boumedienne of Algeria has also written, asking him to be 'flexible'. But Sihanouk will only talk with Washington 'if they get rid of Lon Nol'.

Kissinger's attitude to Sihanouk is abusive and irrational. The two men simply detest each other. But Sihanouk was willing that I should talk to the head of the American Liaison Office, David Bruce, in Peking; which I now proceeded to do.

Meeting David Bruce and his wife was a joyful experience, illuminating that gloomy year when I felt crushed by the emergence of Chiang Ching as political superstar. We talked at the house of a friendly ambassador. Bruce was very shrewd. He spoke about 'woman power ... something not to be neglected'. He shared the general view that Chiang Ching might come to reign, and the less said about her the better. He had just read an article on Empress Wu Tzetien and another one on women leaders in revolutionary struggles.

Bruce told some funny stories to put me at ease, then said seriously, 'Don't let anyone get their hands on your oil.' About Chou's ill health he said, 'A great impediment at the moment ... it makes steady negotiations difficult. Neither is Chairman Mao capable of sustained effort.' 'But American hesitation will weaken Chou further,' I said. Bruce's handsome face showed he understood what I meant.

On Cambodia Bruce was emphatic. The coup against Sihanouk had not been instigated by the Americans. 'We only came afterwards, to prevent a takeover by some of Sihanouk's friends ... he should know that.' Sihanouk's attitude made it impossible for America to get rid of Lon Nol. 'We can't be seen grovelling too much ... '

I went to see Étienne Manac'h, the French Ambassador, a friend of great wisdom and vision. De Gaulle had started Nixon thinking of relations with China, and Manac'h had greatly helped. 'Kissinger at one point suggested getting the Russians to approach the Chinese. He had his priorities wrong,' said Manac'h, who thought Kissinger 'slightly hyperactive'. 'As for détente, there is less and less of it, but the Western world is not yet ready to face the fact.' He could not help at all with the Lon Nol problem. 'Both sides are rigid ... a dénouement must come, which may not be the best solution.'

September 30th, and the usual evening banquet for the celebration of October 1st, National Day.

I was seated next to the famous pianist, Yin Shentsung, one of the two best in China. The other is Liu Shekun, but Liu was then in jail because he was the son-in-law of Marshal Yeh Chienying. It was a way of pressuring the old Marshal.

Yin was trained by Russian masters, and used to play Chopin and Liszt. He is now a devotee of Chiang Ching, and has lavished praise on her in many articles. 'You will enjoy talking with Comrade Yin,' says the head of protocol, seating me. Yin was an intellectual who had 'reformed,' gone over to the Four.

I congratulate Yin on his playing of *Symphony of the Yellow River*. It was composed in Yenan in 1944, but now is claimed as a 'fruit' of the Cultural Revolution, and of Chiang Ching's influence. At every one of the first two rows of tables I can see two or three actors, film stars or musicians; all Chiang Ching's people.

Suddenly the national anthem sounds and hands are clapping. We rise, the leaders file in, and at their head is Chou Enlai. He has come. He is there, he is back. He is very thin, but he is there.

Chiang Ching comes in. Dramatic, in *the* dress, black, a big black skirt. Yin Shentsung turns to me amiably. 'Comrade Chiang Ching is *very* healthy now.' He is full of goodwill. 'Pay attention. She is the rising power', is what he means to convey to me.

Only the night before, I have had a conversation with an overseas Chinese girl who appears to have gone over to Chiang Ching. 'Who do you think will be Party Chairman after Mao?' 'Of course, Comrade Chiang Ching,' she said. And I said, 'Oh heavens!' and left her.

So I reply to Yin Shentsung, 'Yes, she *is* fatter.'

After that, we know where we stand.

Now two young girls, opera stars, both dressed in *the* dress, go from table to table toasting the guests. This has never been done before. And I think of the bitter doggerel I heard in Szechuan:

> It is better to dance a model ballet
> Than to have fought the Long March.
> It is better to sing a model opera
> Than to have a body full of bullet holes.

The resentment against these young upstarts, basking in the sunshine effulgence of 'the Empress' ... I share it.

Chou Enlai stands up to speak. And we all stand and clap, clap, clap. We cannot stop applauding him and there is love and sorrow and rejoicing in our clapping. We go on and on until our hands are sore. At some tables, the artists of Chiang Ching do not clap. But Yin does. And I am crying, the tears running down my cheeks. When we stop, Chou speaks. His voice is still strong. It is not what he says, but the feeling in it which is utterly poignant. 'Unity,' he cries, 'unity. We *must* unite.' He repeats it again and again. He is making a last appeal, so that another crisis may be averted. I turn to Yin when he has finished. 'Premier Chou is one of the greatest men in the world.' Yin nods but does not say yes or no.

In Hongkong I ring up Leo Goodstadt, editor of the *Far Eastern Economic*

Review, and tell him that my hopes are with Teng Hsiaoping. I see Lee Tsungying and tell him that I feel dubious about Chiang Ching. I repeat some of the things I have heard. He says, 'Wait and see. Wait and see.' He is a little frightened. So is Percy Chen, to whom I talk. 'Mum's the word,' he says. But they do not betray me.

'We could not say anything, even to each other,' says Tsungying, years later. And it is true. Already friends do not trust each other, and parents cannot trust their children. Children are urged to report on their parents; a nightmare feeling of fear and suspicion is being created.

I am asked by Mr Fei of the *Takungpao* newspaper to make a speech on women's liberation in China. I make the speech, but I do it without once mentioning Chiang Ching or her 'standard bearer' role in women's liberation. Not once does her name pass my lips.

In January 1975, the Third National People's Congress is held, and it is a triumph for Chou Enlai, for stability and unity and progress.

Of the Shanghai Group, only one, Chang Chunchiao, obtains a post, as head of the general political department in the army. Chiang Ching is nowhere. In the allotment of vice-premierships, too, the 'Young Turks' are in a minority. Teng Hsiaoping comes top of the list of Vice-Premiers. He is also Chief of Staff of the Army.

Since November 1974 there have been rumours that Chang Chunchiao is becoming more pragmatic, that he is joining the older cadres. After all, he is sixty in 1975.

Chou announces the programme for the modernization of China. It is not a new departure. Ever since 1956, this has been the goal. To announce it now means that the situation is stabilized. 'Everything will be all right,' says Tsungying. And Mr Fei, who is a delegate for the Hongkong Chinese at the Congress, tells me that unity is restored; that Wang Hungwen behaved with the utmost courtesy to 'old and venerated Long Marchers' such as Chu Teh.

The new man, Hua Kuofeng, also becomes a Vice-Premier. He is known as a very hardworking, very thorough man, and he has no clique, is not identified with anyone. He has no backing but his own merit. He is entrusted with public security, and no one objects.

Why were the Four, so fierce and so assured in October 1974, flaunting their power, defeated at the Congress of January 1975?

There are, of course, two versions. The one favoured by certain sinologists and Western newsmen lumps Mao with the Four, and explains that he was put in a minority when he tried to give them power at the Congress.

This version – like the one about Chou strangling Lin Piao – is not only fanciful, it is laughable. But it will become part of the sedulous myth that Mao and the Four had one identity until the end. Anyone who studies Mao's personality and vision would not hold this view for a moment. And all I have seen, heard, checked and double checked convinces me that it was not so. On the contrary, since 1973, Mao Tsetung had decided that although it was necessary to have an equilibrium in order not to fall back into a mandarin bureaucracy, at the same time, he would not give power to any junta which utilized his wife.

I saw in 1977 and 1978 documents which, because they are in the handwriting of the Four, I cannot doubt. Wang Hungwen went several times to Mao with reports against Chou Enlai in the autumn of 1974, accusing Chou of 'plotting and conspiring'. 'He is not sick at all, he is merely conspiring,' said Chiang Ching to her husband. Mao would not listen to Wang Hungwen. Chiang Ching then sent a personal messenger (who happened to be Mao's own niece, a young woman, Wang Haijung) to her husband. The reason for a messenger was that, since 1974, Mao had refused to see her. She asked her husband, through Haijung, to give her 'responsible work', to promote Chang Chunchiao to the position of Premier and allow him to form a new cabinet; to nominate Wang Hungwen as Chairman of the Standing Committee to the National People's Congress.

Mao refused all of these requests. 'You are far too ambitious', he told his wife. He would repeat an injunction which already in 1974 he had made publicly: 'You four ... you stick together, forming a gang, like in the bad old days of the Mafia in Shanghai. Do not form a gang of four ... no good will come of it.'

There are other instances of Mao objecting to his wife's actions. 'She does not represent me ... ' he would say. But how could he stop her from beginning her public speeches with the phrase, 'I bring you greetings from Chairman Mao', which of course meant every word was Mao's own word?

Mao's power had never been supreme; as what I have written so far amply proves. And now he was increasingly limited by his deteriorating physical and mental condition; by his nephew; by his entourage – two young nurses devoted to his wife, who would whip a document from his hands, saying, 'You mustn't read!' After all, the nurses had been picked as 'reliable' by the Minister of Health, Liu Hsiangping.

The Four played a subdued role for a while, before the convening of the Congress. Chang wrote a penitent letter to Mao: 'Henceforth we shall certainly stop making a gang of four.'

This letter was at the origin of the rumours that there was a change in Chang, the wily, ruthless and supremely clever 'brain' of the Four; that he was becoming 'moderate'.

I was back in China in September 1975, and everyone seemed much happier. 'Teng really gets things going,' said Rewi, smiling broadly. Teng was becoming very popular because food was more plentiful, factories were working, and Teng had drawn up plans for industrialization; three documents, on science, technology and economics. More competent cadres were coming back, and working. And old Marshal Yeh Chienying, whom everyone liked so much, was now Defence Minister. Teng's clashes with the Four in the Politburo meetings, his Szechuan wit and virulence, were endlessly relayed on the people's grapevine. Everyone chuckled when he said of Chiang Ching's cultural attempts, 'A single flower blooms'. And he would say, 'Certain of our comrades slap their cheek until it swells and say: See how fat and healthy I am.' Little Bottle★ was becoming a popular hero.

Yet there were ominous signs. Orders for machinery from Western countries had gone down badly in late 1974; production too had lagged, owing to the strikes. I had seen the strikes in textile factories in October 1974. Long rows of peasant horse carts, filled to the brim with raw cotton, standing outside the factories waiting. Hundreds of them outside the gates, and the factories were closed. No one took the cotton in. What would the peasants do if no one was there to pay them for the cotton they had grown?

But by the summer of 1975 the Hangchow silk factories, which had been under a 'small brother' of Wang Hungwen, were working again. Teng had used the army to restore order, and this, although perhaps not quite the way he should have done it, was effective. Abroad the overseas Chinese said that the living standard had been going down and that Teng was trying to bring it up again.

The Party had been studying a new article by Chang Chunchiao, which

★ A nickname for Teng Hsiaoping.

had Mao's backing—or so it was said—on 'the bourgeoisie in the Party.' It was persuasive, and appeared to me to be a salutary reminder that the danger of a new class, a new mandarinate, was always present. But this danger did not come from the old cadres; it was, rather, the new cadres, the young, promoted by the Four, who exhibited an amazingly swift tendency to become corrupt.

Again a September 30th banquet. I am in the front row of tables. But now I know (I have been told) what is the matter with Chou Enlai, and that he will not recover.

A man in a wheel-chair is pushed in, and some people rise to clap, to crowd around him and shake his hand. It is Lo Juiching, so badly treated in 1966–7. I see Teng Yingchao sitting at a table; she goes up to Lo and shakes both his hands. So I go up to salute her, and to ask her to give Premier Chou my wishes for his health.

The leaders come in, Teng Hsiaoping at their head. There are none of the actors and actresses of Chiang Ching at the tables, as in the previous year. At my table a Western woman leans towards the host, an eminent member of the Friendship Association, and says that she wants to write a biography of that remarkable woman, Madame Mao. She does not know that the wife of the official she is addressing committed suicide and that rumour holds Madame Mao responsible for this death. The official simply nods, and changes the conversation.

Teng's speech was pithy and direct. Unity and stability. And hard work to reach the goal. A speech remarkably free of slogans. But that was Teng all over. He was so forthright that he laid himself open to attack ...

Wang Hungwen was not there. Teng had just stripped the Hangchow factories of his Mafia friends.

The next evening Madame Soong Chingling invited me to dinner with Rewi Alley and Ma Haiteh. She said, 'Did you see the two sides glare at each other like porcelain dogs?'

When a high member of the Party is ill, to see that all is well done, to procure for him the best of care, a special committee is appointed to supervise the medical staff treating the case.

Why was it that in Chou Enlai's case, the man who headed the committee of supervision was Wang Hungwen?

I went to see George Wu. We both wept bitterly in that October of

1975, thinking of Chou Enlai dying in hospital. His agony would be long and painful.

'Have you seen him, George?'

'Yes, but,' his face screwed up with pain, 'I have been declared untrustworthy by the Minister of Health ... and that bloody woman is in charge.'

All Chou's enemies were in charge of the case ... And why was it that the treatment recommended by the best cancer specialist in China was not followed?

'Premier Chou was hounded to the day of his death ... they would allow him no rest ... even while we were giving him a blood transfusion, Chiang Ching would ring up and *order* that the transfusion be stopped while she talked nonsense to him, calling it "matters of state".' And George Wu weeps uncontrollably as he tells me this in 1977.

Heart of Ice and her husband, Wu Wentsao, came to see me, and I went to see them. Both of them suffered a great deal, but Heart of Ice never complained. We talked of writing, and of love, of friendship, and of betrayal. Heart of Ice said Chou Yang was now freed, though not yet employed. I told her how much Lu Hsun's widow, Hsu Kuangping, seemed to detest him.

'But she was wrong,' said Heart of Ice. Hsu Kuangping was turned against Chou Yang. Actually he was always good to her. But so many people got turned against each other then.

We talked of writing love stories (she used to write such wonderful ones). 'It's now taboo,' she said, smiling a little. I remembered Hsu Kuangping telling me how, opening a book long after Lu Hsun had died, she had found in it a love poem, dedicated to her.

'Perhaps we must now do this, leave love poems in books to be found by our loved ones,' said Heart of Ice, looking at Wu Wentsao and both smiled, a little shy, startled to find their love so fresh. When they left they walked hand in hand down the hotel corridor.

They are only in their late seventies, and therefore very young.

Norodom Sihanouk was preparing to return to Phnom Penh. I lunched with him and Princess Monique, and with Phoumi Vong Vichit, the Premier of Laos and his wife, on October 1st. Sihanouk looked forward to having a role to play in his country, even if 'the Khmer Rouge are pitiless ... '

Half the population of Cambodia, three million people, had become refugees in the city of Phnom Penh, which originally held less than 400,000 people. Their evacuation was now taking place. 'It is quite impossible to feed all these people in the city,' said Sihanouk. Some members of his own family had been given spades and told to dig. 'There will be a drastic clean-up. It's not going to be pretty.' In Laos, said Phoumi Vong Vichit, six traitors had been sent out of the country. 'The people were angry. They wanted to execute them.' Sihanouk talked of executions in his country. 'They're drastic,' he repeated, laughing a little nervously. He gave me a tree leaf from the Ho Chih Minh Trail, which I keep preciously.

Before leaving Peking, Sihanouk together with the Khmer Rouge Minister, Khiu Samphan, would see Mao.

'What do you plan to do?' Mao asked.

'We plan to work together,' replied Khiu.

'Good,' Mao said, 'you must be united.'

But instead of using Sihanouk, the Khmer Rouge would hold him and Princess Monique virtual prisoners for three long years. The Chinese were not at all happy about this. 'They're "ultra-left",' they would mutter. The Khmer Rouge was one of the few governments to send congratulations to Peking on the fall of Teng Hsiaoping in April 1976.

In September 1978, I would try to see Sihanouk in Phnom Penh. I wrote to Ieng Sary, the Foreign Minister. Ieng Sary wrote back that I would be welcome in Cambodia, but I could not see Sihanouk. 'In that case I shall not go,' I said to the Ambassador, and wrote back, refusing.

Three months later, in December, the Vietnamese invasion of Cambodia took place. Sihanouk, his wife and their two sons were evacuated, on the very last day before Phnom Penh was occupied by the Vietnamese, by a special aeroplane from China.

I went to Tibet that year, passing through Szechuan, since the aeroplane for Tibet started at Chengtu.*

Szechuan was not doing well. Many thousands of people were going down the river, leaving for other places. There were plays and articles against 'spontaneous capitalism in the countryside'. But Sixth Brother said it was not so much capitalism as ultra-leftism which plagued Szechuan. The private plots had been abolished and the peasants did not like it. He and his wife were once more involved in 'study sessions', and likely to be investigated again.

* See *Lhasa, the Open City*.

Third Aunt had everything she needed, and with money one could go into the countryside and buy eggs and meat, both rare in Chengtu. Sixth Brother got on his bicycle at weekends, and searched for food for his mother.

I would tell Chiao Kuanhua of this and other things I had noticed. 'Production seems to be falling.' But he assured me that it had never been better.

I ended my second book on Mao and the Chinese Revolution, *Wind in the Tower*, in the spring of 1975, and on a hopeful note. My euphoria was due to the holding of the Third National People's Congress. Perhaps I should have waited, since there was to be so much change immediately, and all conjectures and conclusions were proved invalid.

My Chinese friends do not blame me for being over-sanguine. They too were caught in the dramatic, the unexpected, the unforeseen. 'In a revolution, people's characters change most swiftly,' they say. 'We learn the heights and depths of human behaviour; and the meaning of loyalty and treachery, in our own hearts.'

On January 8th, 1976, Chou Enlai passed away.

I was asked on European television and radio networks about Chou; and who I thought would succeed him. 'Teng Hsiaoping,' I replied. 'Everyone in China hopes it will be Teng Hsiaoping. He's hot-tempered and blunt but he's popular … '

I would have forgotten my own answer but that my television appearance was reported to China; and that Chang Ying would remind me of it a year later. 'That is what you said … ' She smiled. 'It was quite right.' It was not courage, but only the fact that suddenly I was on the point of exploding, of exploding as were the people of China, against the Four, and particularly against Chiang Ching. Again I have no explanation; for until then I had tried, despite my dislike, to be fair to her; bending backwards to defend her … But now Chou Enlai was dead. And somehow this released in me what turned to hatred of his enemies.

Even today I weep for him. For no one else, not even Ian Morrison, nor even my father, have I mourned so long.

624

Twenty-five

The Fall of the Four: 1976

WHEN CHOU ENLAI died, I received telephone calls from overseas Chinese in America and in Canada. 'What is going to happen now? We are afraid.' Millions of Chinese were worried. And some even entertained the sacrilegious thought: '*Perhaps* Chairman Mao should have passed away before Premier Chou Enlai ... then we could have dealt with the White-Boned Devil before she ruined China.' Chiang Ching was now called the Devil, the Plague, the Witch. We all knew that Mao was too old, too feeble, to deal with her; and anyway the bond between man and wife yields not to logic and reason. 'Why does he not get rid of her?' overseas Chinese asked.

We all cared for Mao deeply; and so we kept silent about his wife, although his name and our love for him were besmirched, tainted by her and her companions. And now the hatred proliferated. It extended even into the villages; where in 1974, and again in 1976, private plots were seized, seasoned cadres persecuted, and the production teams were not paid for their sales to the state.

Overseas Chinese abroad kept stoically silent, refused to talk to foreigners, poured out to me their bitterness about the renewed ill-treatment of their relatives ... one of them condemned to fifteen years of labour for owning records of Western music ...

And yet, in those years since 1973, Chiang Ching had bought films in America, for her private viewing. My son-in-law, Sidney, had helped some Chinese diplomats to purchase these films, happy in the thought that they would encourage 'cultural exchanges'. But the films were for Chiang Ching's own delectation. I had protested to the Foreign Minister, Chiao Kuanhua, about these purchases in 1974. 'If films are bought, the public should see them.' 'Of course, of course,' Chiao had soothed me. But 'of course' nothing was done.

Chou was dead. There was only Teng Hsiaoping to withstand the Four. He quarrelled violently with them at Politburo meetings; he settled strikes with a firm hand – sometimes too firm. 'He shoots all his arrows in one skirmish,' said my friends. 'That's because he is from Szechuan, full of red pepper.' The Four sneered at him: 'How can you trust a man who has to hitch up his trousers under his shoulder blades?' referring thus to his small size. But the people liked him all the better; he had put up major programmes for industry and technology, which the Four condemned as 'poisonous weeds', 'a return of the productive forces revisionist theory', 'the stinking capitalist wind'.

Chou's death elated Yao Wenyuan, who gave a banquet the day after (within a week, I had had the news through the overseas network). But the people mourned greatly. A deep and true sorrow.

Only in autumn 1977 would a film made of Chou's last drive, to his incinerator, be shown in Peking. The Four had tried to confiscate every copy, but courageous newsmen hid parts of the film in their own houses.

A small white ambulance was waiting at the hospital gate. Chou's coffin was taken out; a small simple black coffin, so small. It was placed in the vehicle, which drove off. And suddenly the doctors and nurses who stood there began to wail, and one nurse even sobbed and jumped up and down like a child bereft. It was not faked. And there was no ceremony of any kind.

The little ambulance went on through the wide avenues of Peking, followed by a few cars: Chou's wife, the ministers he worked with, old comrades. No guard of honour. No music. Nothing. It was dusk and all along the avenue, mile upon mile, stood the people. Silent people. The whole city seemed to have turned out to see Chou pass. And in that enormous silence, only the small roar of the ambulance motor was heard.

The million and a half who lined the way had waited many hours for this last glimpse of their beloved Premier. Some had waited since the morning and others had come from work. No outer sign, no lament. Just this terrible silence. And as the ambulance went by, the men took off their caps; the women simply stood. There were no close-ups of faces, and the film was too dark. But the immobility was heavy with meaning as was that immense silence in the cold air. It was twelve degrees below zero that evening.

How is it that the Four missed the warning of these unmoving faces?

Chou's body was reduced to ashes, and after the memorial ceremony they were strewn over the rivers and the mountains of China.

Because Chou thus became non-substance, refusing a tangible grave, a monument, embalming, he would remain with us always. From this dust scattered in the air all of us caught spirit and defiance.

The people went home, and in silence grew their anger. Chou became part of themselves, of their ancestors, their family. He who had never had a child was most blessed now; for he became everyone's father, uncle, grandfather. Most blessed in his posterity, all China's children now adopted him. And so the Four lost the people, all of them, even the young and the very young.

In the press — controlled by Yao Wenyuan — within forty-eight hours of Chou's death appeared an article, 'The revolution of education in Tsinghua University occupies all our thoughts.'

Thousands of angry letters were sent to the *People's Daily*. 'We are plunged in sorrow because of the death of our beloved Premier ... and you dare to put an article on education in Tsinghua ... what kind of people are you?' Many cancelled their subscription.

The attacks against Teng, 'the unrepentant capitalist roader', and the 'right deviationist wind' he blew, assumed a new intensity.

From January 15th to February 3rd, 1976, meetings of the Central Committee and the Politburo were held to debate the appointment of Chou's successor. It should have been Teng. But such was the opposition of the Four — even Mao Yuanhsin came down from Manchuria to see his uncle and talk ill of Teng — that the end was inconclusive. Mao refused to nominate Chang Chunchiao as Premier, and this is not conjecture, but fact. On February 7th, Hua Kuofeng became acting Premier. Thus the Four, and Teng, were bypassed. A compromise solution.

Hua Kuofeng, the new man from the provinces, had no clique and no powerful patron. But Mao had called him in 1970 from Hunan, to deal with Lin Piao; and he had worked with Chou Enlai since 1971. He had a reputation for hard work and probity. Mao said, 'Hua is noble-minded, not pompous, and good-mannered.' A man who kept his temper, his head, his tongue. He had befriended old Marshal Yeh Chienying, Minister of Defence, when the latter was virtually under house arrest; supplied him with coal and daily necessities.*

'It's us or them ... heads will have to roll ... we haven't killed enough,' said Chang Chunchiao meaning: killed enough of the old cadres. 'First bring Teng down, then deal with Hua.'

In April was the Feast of the Dead, *Tsingming*, meaning clear and light. On that day we sweep our ancestors' graves and commune with them; renewing our spirit and strengthening our lives with their memory; for the dead are companionable, benign and powerful if we honour them.

---

* This is celebrated in a painting exhibited in Shanghai in 1978, and seen by the author.

And man lives not alone; he blossoms within the fulfilled past and the engendering of posterity.

Already by mid-March, in every factory, school, organization, preparations to mourn Chou Enlai had begun. Women came to work with white flowers in their hair. They were asked, 'Why do you mourn?'

'For a relative.'

One cannot arrest two million mourners.

The Four were uneasy. Everywhere incidents: in Kuangchow a young girl suddenly shouting, 'Down with Chiang Ching!' In the night, posters against them: 'Down with the Shanghai Gang!'*

The spark came when in the newspapers in Shanghai, Nanking and Wuhan, Yao Wenyuan foolishly caused slanderous articles to be printed against Chou Enlai. Although not naming Chou, they were clearly enough against him; even taking up alleged 'events' in his private life.

The result was immense indignation. In Nanking, in Wuhan, even in Shanghai, bastion of the Four, thousands of letters of protest came to the newspapers. 'Why do you print such filth? We do not believe a word of it.'

Far more was to happen. Nanking city started it. Around thirty thousand people, among them students and young workers, marched upon the newspaper offices in Nanking, shouting and waving banners for Chou Enlai. This also happened in some other cities, although the demonstrations were quickly squashed.

The Nanking garrison was supposed to be under the command of Chang Chunchiao. It is perhaps one of the more feudal features of the Chinese administration—inherited from the past, for the Kuomintang also practised it—that one man should accumulate many diverse functions, which give him leverage and influence in many quarters. Chang was not only political commissar of the army, he was also the overall head of the Nanking army group.

The military forces in Nanking were ordered to crush the 'counter-revolutionaries'. There were thousands of arrests. But no news of this event filtered into the newspapers, although even the train carriages were covered with posters against the Four. By word of mouth, by telephone, or simply by that extraordinary almost biological osmosis which happens in all popular uprisings, people in Chengtu, in Kuangchow, in Kunming, in Peking, knew of the Nanking demonstration almost immediately.

'I heard the news the day after. I went to my room and I was so excited

* They were called the Shanghai Gang or Mafia by the people until it was known, through the circulation of the letters of Chang himself, that Mao had called them the Gang of Four.

and so enraged with the Four that I started tearing up newspapers and muttering, "Let them die let them die" ... I wanted to run on to the streets and shout it to everybody,' said a young girl, an interpreter I met in Szechuan. She had been criticized for trying to keep up her English.

'How did you learn of what happened?'

'A friend of a person I know was on the train from Nanking to Wuhan ... a friend of mine in Wuhan heard it. She told my aunt, who told me ... '

The great anger of the people rose, irresistible as lava from a volcano in eruption. In Peking, on April 1st, the children and the adolescents had begun to make white paper flowers, cutting out the petals with scissors, minutely and with love, twisting them skilfully with thin thread or wire. Boys worked on wreaths, with green paper for leaves, and silver foil. All the shops had under the counter supplies of paper, sold by the single sheet. In the textile mill and the post offices and the banks, groups huddled, making wreaths. At night, youths and workers would sit together, composing wall posters; others sat alone, writing poems. There would be thousands of poems, thousands of posters.

My nephews and nieces, and Hualan's nephews, and the children of my friends, and Millie Pei—all the young I know were in this immense people's conspiracy. 'Of course no one organized us. We organized ourselves. All of us wanted to do it. We would have choked with anger if we had not done it.' My niece said, 'In school, we made paper flowers during recreation time. The teachers also made them; and when we had made them, we wrote: To Grandpa Chou, your grandchild who loves you. And then we went to Tienanmen Square, each class walking in orderly manner. We stuck our small flowers on the twigs of the trees.'

When four hundred thousand children between seven and fourteen make four hundred thousand white flowers, pretty soon the trees look as if a snowfall has settled on them. The primary school children now came, school by school marching solemnly up to the square, and no one could stop them. They put their wreaths at the foot of the Monument to the Revolutionary Heroes. They stuck their white flowers on the trees.

Millie said, 'In our university, we were told that we must not leave the campus. The gates were locked. But at four in the morning we went over the wall, hoisting ourselves up on each other's shoulders. Those who had to stay behind handed us their poems. We did this on the nights of April 3rd and 4th.'

By April 2nd, the crowds walking about Tienanmen Square were unusually large. By the 3rd the wreaths were beginning to pile up; and now processions of workers marched into the square, to bring more. On the 4th, the wreaths on the Monument to the Revolutionary Heroes in the centre of Tienanmen Square were piled so high that there was no place left for more. The inscription on the monument was in Chou Enlai's calligraphy.

When the workers saw that no more wreaths could be placed on the monument, they brought their tools and erected scaffoldings; they nailed their wreaths to them. They brought ladders, and hung the wreaths on the lamp-posts round the square. When these were covered, they went further up the avenue; attaching their offerings with stout wire, so that they could not be easily taken away.

The security police came into action. They removed the wreaths. But this became almost impossible, especially in the daytime, when hundreds of thousands milled in the square, copying the poems and the posters or reading them aloud for others to write down. People began to sing. 'We went,' say my cousins, 'but we wore mufflers. We knew that the Four had their militia in the square.' The militia now came in lorries to remove the wreaths, the poems and the posters.

On the morning of the 5th, young men and young women stood on platforms and spoke to the crowds, haranguing them with loudspeakers. Groups went about shouting, 'Long live Chou Enlai', 'Down with the pseudo-Marxists'.

It had all been very orderly up to the 5th. But now incidents began. The militia and security police scuffled with and arrested demonstrators; agents of the Four insulted Chou, and were beaten up by the crowd. Later it was alleged that 'counter-revolutionaries' had burnt cars and a jeep, and also a building (a wooden telephone booth). Little damage was done, but many hundreds were arrested on the 5th, and as night came the square was cleared.

The whole incident was written up in great detail by the Hsinhua news agency. And what is quite extraordinary about the write-up is that despite the 'indignation' expressed by the reporters in their article, the delight they felt came through; they even quoted almost in full a poem against the Four:

> When I weep, the wolves howl with joy.
> I shall shed my blood on the altar of dead heroes.
> Lift my head; and my sword shall leap from its scabbard ...
> The Chinese people are no longer ignorant!
> Down with false Marxist-Leninists!

Yao Wenyuan was not fooled by the 'indignation'. 'Why did you have to write up this counter-revolutionary incident in such detail?' he raged at the newsmen. He could no longer cover up, minimize, the Tienanmen demonstration after this report.

Thousands of poems — now assembled in two volumes* — were very clearly against the Four. Posters read: 'We don't want an empress!', 'No Indira Gandhi in China'.

During the next three months the hunt for 'counter-revolutionaries' went on. 'They came to our dormitories, asking each one what we had done on those nights ... they offered rewards to those who would speak up,' said Millie. In the schools, the children were interrogated about their parents. 'It is revolutionary to unmask the bourgeoisie ... even if it is your father ... '

But this 'incident', which was an enormous people's manifestation against the Four, initiated their downfall. Their bluff had been called, and they could only exercise repression. Forty-two youths, it is said, were executed out of hand on the night of the 5th for 'counter-revolutionary activity'. Several hundred were incarcerated. Five thousand were still being investigated when, in October 1976, the Four were arrested.

On Wednesday April 7th, two resolutions of the Central Committee were published. One cited Mao's 'proposal' to strip Teng Hsiaoping of all his posts, but to allow him to keep his Party membership, 'to see how he will behave in the future'. The Tienanmen incident was declared 'counter-revolutionary'. The other resolution was to nominate Hua Kuofeng to be First Vice-Chairman of the Party and appoint him Premier of the State Council.

This was a cruel defeat for the Four, the third in two years. They had shouldered Teng out of the way temporarily, but they had not succeeded in getting 'the seals of power' from Mao: Mao might be misinformed; he was almost isolated by his nephew and his two nurses; Hua Kuofeng and Teng Hsiaoping were denied access to him 'by order of the doctors'; Mao was becoming blind, and unable to walk — but even in his deteriorating state, he would not give power to his wife. It is clear to me that the old man fought, to the last, to keep her from succeeding him.

On April 8th, the Four arranged a counter-demonstration, both in Peking and in Shanghai. Two hundred thousand people were mustered in Peking to celebrate the victory against the 'unrepentant capitalist roader',

---

* These two volumes are only a beginning. Every city in China is collecting its poems written for Chou Enlai.

Teng Hsiaoping. Among those who marched, was my old friend, the Foreign Minister, Chiao Kuanhua.

'Once again they have had their way ... but in the end, every old door charm shall be replaced by new peachwood,' wrote Chang, quoting an old poem. He had fully expected to become Premier, but he had again been bypassed.

A kind of hysteria now seized the Four. 'All the old cadres naturally become bourgeois,' they declared, as a 'Marxist' truth. This warned of a widespread witch-hunt designed to topple, at all levels, the old and middle-aged cadres, replacing them with youths who swore loyalty to the Four. After all, demography was on their side.

Young gangsters called 'revolutionary rebels' assaulted cadres, stopped workers in almost every plant in China from working, becoming 'slaves of the capitalist road'. In Chengtu, 1,800 youths 'with horns and spikes', specially trained in Shanghai, seized the public security bureaus. They distributed Party cards to anyone who swore fealty to the Four. Out of the thousands of idle youths wandering in the streets (the schools had stopped in summer 1976), they recruited some twelve thousand new Party members in the city. These proceeded to wreck every organization. The structure of the Establishment again broke down.

Yet the people had now realized that the 'wind of capitalism', blowing since 1974, was not due to Teng Hsiaoping, but to the disorder created by the Four, because the only way to survive was by black marketeering, hoarding and bribing; and even printing false money; and Secret Societies, prostitution, everything came back ...

'It takes ten years to build something, and ten days to destroy it,' the Szechuan cadres would say to me. Beggars and vagrants reappeared; and even opium addicts and drug users among the young, Sixth Brother would tell me in 1977.

Writers and opera stars of Szechuan disguised themselves, and fled the cities; they went down the great River, as did many thousands of ordinary people, running away from Szechuan. And thus followed a pattern centuries old.

In a hospital in Chungking, a surgeon was called out in the middle of an operation, to be criticized. 'But I cannot leave the patient,' he protested. Nevertheless, he was dragged out to be shouted at. Another surgeon took his place.

A scientist was also attacked. 'When the earth satellite went up in the sky, the red flag came down to earth ... Down with science, which destroys revolution!' shouted the young who assaulted him. His laboratory instruments were smashed.

The earthquake which started on July 28th in Tangshan had bred waves of counter-shock in Szechuan. The technician in charge of the seismic instruments was told to 'make revolution' and to leave his post. He refused, and was beaten.

In Shanghai a group of 'historians' under Chang Chunchiao rewrote history. Renowned Long Marchers were effaced; or existed only as saboteurs and deviationists, striving against Mao's line. The Revolution had been made by Mao under the inspiration of Chiang Ching.

In Hangchow, again a total stoppage in the factories. Worse, pillage began. The hotels were ransacked. In one factory where the older workers insisted on continuing to work, a woman worker had her hand smashed with a hammer.*

A musician who refused to kneel to the 'Minister of Culture' appointed by the Four, Yu Hueiyung, to beg forgiveness for his crimes was shut in a small room without light for nine months. He came out in October 1976; I would see him in Shanghai. His eyes were still affected.

Some of the young workers jailed after the Tienanmen incident were obliged to feed themselves by kneeling on the floor and lapping the food from bowls, with their hands tied behind their backs. 'Never was there such barbarism ... it was pure fascism,' said many of those who suffered under the Four. 'It was worse than the Kuomintang.'

Breakdown, sabotage, chaos, disorder ... yet some places were preserved, such as Shanghai; Shanghai had to be shown as *the* model. The factories flourished there, whereas destruction blossomed elsewhere. And this was done to prove that Teng Hsiaoping, and now Hua Kuofeng, could not manage things at all.

I was supposed to return to China in May 1976. But now, with Teng demoted – and it was he who had signed the permission for me to go to Tibet in 1975 – and the Four ostensibly triumphant, I realized that I could not do so without exposing myself to being pressured, or coerced, into serving Chiang Ching.

Because Chiang Ching was a woman, Mao's wife, and because as a doctor, she was for me a medical case, a warped being, I had taken a long time to hate her. I had not understood how dangerous a mean, mediocre

* Interviewed by the author, January 1977.

mind can be when power is available to it. I said to Vincent and to Cécile Verdurand, and I wrote to a couple of overseas Chinese I could trust, 'If that woman comes to power, I may have to fight against China.'

But this would put my Family in terrible danger. Could I bring disaster upon them and their children, my nephews and nieces?

I went to the Chinese Embassy. The diplomats had their misgivings, but I could not expect them to share their worries with me. I said that, being extremely busy, I would not be able to go to China that year, possibly not before the end of the year, instead of returning, as usual, in May or June.

And that is why, in 1976, I did not go to China until December. I waited. 'There'll be something ... I can't believe we'll let the Plague run China,' I said to Vincent.

Wind in the Tower was published; I was to be attacked by critics (among them some prestigious sinologists) for not denouncing Teng Hsiaoping. The next year I would be attacked by other critics for having written some favourable comments on Chiang Ching.

In July and August the frightful earthquake occurred which devastated Tangshan, and caused seven hundred thousand deaths. My niece, daughter of Fourth Sister, went with her nursing team to dig people out, and she stayed awake fifty-three hours on end. 'The earth was all changed. It was as if mud had boiled up in waves,' she said. Hua Kuofeng gathered cadres, sent medical rescue teams, and went personally to tour the earthquake area. The wounded were evacuated to many cities; twelve thousand were taken to Wuhan. Kaimei, a Malayan Chinese doctor in the Wuhan Children's Hospital, worked round the clock for three days, caring for the wounded children.'

The Four did not go to the earthquake area. Chiang Ching did not even inquire about it. She was 'resting' at the seaside. Evidence that madness becomes a collective phenomenon, Yao Wenyuan wrote an exultant poem about the earthquake: 'Such natural spasms portend new and wondrous change.' Not a word for the immense desolation, the dead and the wounded, the losses.

The press controlled by him went further. 'Earthquake relief work must not be used as an excuse to stop the criticism of Teng Hsiaoping. Some people want to use relief work to brush aside the mighty surge of revolution ... ' That was actually an attack on Hua Kuofeng.

On September 9th, at ten minutes past midnight, Mao Tsetung died.

The sorrow, the grief at Mao's passing were genuine, deepened by apprehension that China was falling to pieces, that a new era of warlords would come, and civil war. The earthquake and the Yellow River floods — the latter went unreported — were, millions believed, portents of the disasters to come.

Hua Kuofeng is a quiet man with a mild, deliberate manner. He had not been inactive, although never involved — as Teng was — in head-on conflict with the Four.

Since April, as Premier, he accompanied foreign heads of state to see Mao. He thus managed to meet Mao, and to talk to him alone. Wang Hungwen, who had been present on such occasions several times before, was fortunately absent.

Hua Kuofeng obtained from Mao on April 30th a written and dated message: 'With you in charge, I am at ease.' And a directive in Mao's hand: 'Act according to past precedent.'

In June, Hua took another step. Mao would no longer be receiving heads of state; the last occasion would be a meeting in May with Lee Kuanyew of Singapore. Mao was by then unable to hold his head straight. It was cruel to keep on exhibiting him in his condition. Immediately, the Four attacked Hua in a 'historical' article, comparing him to a plotting prime minister who had conspired to isolate the emperor.

In the month from September 9th to October 6th which followed Mao's death, the fever for the final power contest was at its height. The Four were now preparing for a 'show of force'. The workers' militia, which Wang Hungwen had controlled for some years, would be used; as it had been used at Tienanmen in April to arrest the demonstrators. There were three million militiamen available in Shanghai. Each factory had its militia. The issue of modern weaponry to the militia began on September 20th. The Four ordered that all documents sent to the Politburo must come to them. Since Chang was Secretary of its Standing Committee, this went unchallenged.

In Paoting, an army corps was told to hold itself ready (the commander was reckoned a sympathizer of the Four). Mao Yuanhsin, by then, Deputy Commissar of the 8341 Division which guarded the leaders in Peking, mustered troops in Manchuria. Back and forth, between Shenyang, Shanghai and Peking, went the Four and their allies, preparing a military seizure of power.

An intensive propaganda drive started, centering on what Mao was alleged to have said to Chiang Ching before expiring: ACT ACCORDING TO THE PRINCIPLES LAID DOWN. Which principles? The principles of the continuing revolution, which they personified. The Four thus claimed to be the heirs of Mao's Thought. Two days before the memorial service to Mao Tsetung on September 18th, this phrase was launched in editorials. At the same time, Yao 'stimulated' letters from all over China demanding that Chiang Ching become Party Chairman. Several hundred such letters were collected ... pitifully few, by Chinese standards.

But the Four were already outplayed. Hua could show Mao's April 30th handwritten directive: ACT ACCORDING TO PAST PRECEDENT. Also the fact that Hua was nominated First Vice-Chairman meant that he would automatically become acting Chairman of the Party until a new Chairman could be elected by the Central Committee. And as for the distinction between, 'Act according to past precedent' and 'Act according to principles laid down', 'three words in the last formula are incorrect,' wrote Hua. Thus the claim of the Four to be Mao's heirs was denied.

The Four prepared: the coup was to take place on October 13th or 14th.

On October 11th, Monday morning, about 8 o'clock, I was rung up from London by the B.B.C. Did I know, asked the B.B.C. that Chiang Ching had been arrested over the weekend?

'Is it official?'

'No, just a rumour.'

'Then no comment.'

I could not believe it. It seemed too good to be true.

All my friends in China had the same reaction. 'We could not believe it. Then we went into the streets, walked about, watching to see if other people knew ... ' In front of the wine and liquor shops they saw queues; queues which grew by the minute. 'Then we knew it was true.'

'I went out, and there were people buying wine, so I too bought wine ... On the street there were people selling autumn crabs: "Three male and a female crab, to go with your wine," they sang. Then I knew that the Four had been arrested. We all bought crabs, and boiled them. We felt that the Four should be boiled alive.' This from my good friend, the eminent painter Huang Yungyu.

And Sixth Brother in Chengtu said, 'I could not believe it ... but then a friend came and whispered in my ear, and we went into the streets and people were so happy ... everyone was shaking hands and laughing.'

'Within two days the hospitals were emptying ... ambulant patients wanted to return to their families, to celebrate ... ' From one of my doctor friends.

China was exuberant. There were monster parades, millions pouring into the streets to celebrate, to beat drums and to dance. 'In Wuhan the steel workers spontaneously went back to work within twenty-four hours. The buses began to run again,' wrote Gladys Yang to me.

'You do realize that this was prepared a year, eighteen months ago? Since April 1975, when Mao said quietly one day to some old veterans in the Politburo, "This problem must be settled ... if not this year, next year," ' said Ma Haiteh, when I saw him that winter. 'It was Chairman Hua's decision and old Marshal Yeh Chienying. They saved China from disaster by arresting the Four.'

Yeh Chienying, Minister of Defence, was a man of such integrity and discipline that he would not even intervene to save his own daughter or son from jail. For years he had kept quiet, enduring injustice. He saw no one in private. Often he went fishing, all alone.

How the arrests were arranged will probably be revealed one day. But if Hua Kuofeng had not given the order, they could not have been made. And therefore, in my mind, Hua and Yeh cannot be separated in this affair.

In early October, the commander of troops in Paoting—reckoned a sympathizer of the Four—was told by Wang Hungwen to march on to Peking. The commander telephoned the Ministry of Defence in Peking. Then he countermanded the march. The Manchurian forces were told by Mao Yuanhsin to march to Peking 'for a change of garrison'. At a certain point, the commander sat down and telephoned. Then he marched back to Manchuria.

'It is time.' Yeh Chienying made the gesture of opening his hand and closing it, as one gathers a handful of grass. Hua Kuofeng issued the order. The 8341 Division now moved. They arrested the three men, Chang, Wang and Yao, while they were preparing to go to a Politburo meeting on the night of October 6th. They arrested Chiang Ching in her house.

'But I am Chairman Mao's widow, you don't dare to arrest me,' she screamed.

'You must still come with us,' said the officer in charge.

Hualan told me later, when I was in Peking, that Chiang Ching's last words before going into captivity were: 'Well, I've had my revenge on my enemies ... '

'She gets one *yuan* fifty a day for food, twice as much as I get,' said Hualan, who loathes Chiang Ching, and holds her responsible for the deaths in her family. 'I think it's too much. We should let her starve on three cents a day, as she did Ho Lung.'

'The Four were duly warned,' said my old friend Yeh. A week after Mao died, the newspapers began printing mild-toned articles, quoting Mao's phrase, used in 1971, when he told the regional commanders of Lin Piao's treachery, 'Unite and don't split, be open and above board, do not intrigue or conspire'. This due 'warning' was not heeded by the Four. But the Chinese people felt satisfied. The Plague had been handled in a masterly way, 'nobly and with good manners'. A decent month of mourning was allowed the widow; there were repeated injunctions not to 'intrigue'; and the arrests had been swift and clean. No messy conflict. The allies of the Four were also warned: Give yourselves up, or ... The militia, duly informed, turned in their weapons and started rejoicing with the rest of the population. The art of war is a minimum, not a maximum of bloodshed.

'Never has a new reign begun without some conflict, but this time it has been managed, and this is the most happy augury,' said Lin Lin, my friend. He had suffered enormously for years. He quoted at length from Chinese history, 'Now we are in for a great period, a period of order and harmony, of reconciliation and stability ... we must not have another Gang of Four. Never again.'

On October 20th I applied to go to China. At the Embassy everyone was smiling; all gloom dispelled.

But I had a nagging, remaining worry. Chiao Kuanhua. What had possessed him to demonstrate against Teng in April? Perhaps he was forced to, and this temporary lapse would certainly be forgiven. Every new reign begins with amnesties, 'great forgiveness'.

I arrived in China and discovered things were not well with Chiao Kuanhua. 'He became a Gang of Four man. But it was the fault of his wife, Chang Handje.' In the midst of the bliss of seeing all my old friends, of listening to their stories, rejoicing with them, sorrowing over the dead, was this ugliness: Chiao's betrayal of Chou Enlai. 'If Kung Peng had been alive this would not have happened,' said Hsing Chiang. And we both were very sad, for now, when we went to Papaoshan to bow to Kung Peng, we would know that perhaps her husband would not be by her side.

Chiao's many friends were grieved. 'How could he do this?' Chou Enlai had been Chiao's protector, mentor, teacher; had elevated him from being a journalist to become Foreign Minister. How could he join Chou's enemies?

'Chang Handje.' She was beautiful. Beauty's snare, weakening a man's resolve. She was ambitious. Some averred that the marriage had been arranged by Chiang Ching.

On April 7th, 1976, the day before the great demonstration against Teng, Chiang Ching had made a threatening speech to all the heads of the ministries and departments of the State Council. 'Some of you have not yet made clear your attitude,' she said. 'We must know where you stand.' And Chiao, 'came clear' the next day, shouting 'Down with Teng' and marching, while many other ministers went sick or simply stayed at home.

Chiao would have been forgiven this, I think; so many, so many cadres, had had to outwardly acquiesce, to shout obediently, to wave banners. But he did more. In October, at the United Nations, Chiao made a speech. In his original draft he had used the Gang of Four sentence: ACT ACCORDING TO PRINCIPLES LAID DOWN. And Hua Kuofeng, reading the draft before Chiao's departure for New York, picked out the sentence. 'This is erroneous ... three words in it are incorrect,' wrote Hua in the margin of the draft.

Since summer's dreadful earthquake, people in China had been cursing 'the Three Witches'. Big Witch, Chiang Ching, Middle Witch, the Health Minister Liu Hsiangping, (Hippo); and Small Witch, Chang Handje, the Foreign Minister's wife ...

Perhaps it was fear of suffering all over again, as he had suffered in 1966-7. He was on the lists found in the houses of the Four, marked to become Vice-Premier when Chang Chunchiao became Premier. The Four had lists of those who had to be killed, and those to be promoted. And, in the great renewal of China, I hope he will be forgiven, and will have a place where his talents can be used.

Chiao is not under arrest, merely retired at home.

December in Peking was all talk, talk of Chiang Ching. A wild relief, catharsis, hundreds of stories, some of them exceedingly filthy, about her. 'A prostitute ... a dirty woman ... a worn slipper ... ' Even my sisters-in-law Jui and Shuan, so proper, giggle a little at the semi-dirty stories which they hear. Everyone is letting off steam, exhaling jubilant hatred. Third Brother attends the criticism meetings against Peking University tyrants; George Wu attends the meetings against 'the Hippo', ex-minister of Health. They are getting their own back, after years of torment.

In the newspapers, too, there are emotional, sometimes childish tales of the crimes of the Gang of Four. 'They should be tried publicly,' says a Western woman, appalled at the Chinese outburst. These verbal explosions greatly shock Westerners, who think in legal terms. They do not realize that in China 'legality' has never existed. Not in the Western sense.

I do not share in this shattering hatred. I tell Hsing Chiang, 'I know it's relief, and so many have horribly suffered and *must* now talk. But it is not good to do this. Not for Chairman Mao. After all, she was his wife.' But I understand and condone the need for feudal incantation, for exorcism through words of 'the Plague Demons', and especially 'the Woman Plague'. Chiang Ching is the epitome of all evil in China now. But she was also the product of China's evil; of its male oppression, of the thwarted and distorted attitudes to sex and to love in Old China; and she herself, being feudal, acted in turn like a tyrant and an oppressor. I still see her as such: her malady became monstrous evil because of her power. I no longer hate her now, but I hope that she has not hurt too much the cause of women's liberation in China. For now, how easy to fall back into the old pattern: 'See what dreadful things happen when a woman is entrusted with power: In Chinese history always women rulers have been a disaster!' This could have been the reaction of public opinion, leading to a strong backlash against the so painfully acquired new status of women in China.

Fortunately this has not happened. The past cannot return entirely, although there has been regression in the last decade, such as renewed arranged marriages, bartering of brides, dowries, families ruining themselves to acquire an enviable daughter-in-law ... Today the average man in China must give his intended a watch, a sewing machine and a bicycle before she will look at him.

The National Federation of Women has started again to work. 'The main problems are the alleviation of housework, and family planning,' their leaders say. The women survivors of the Long March, Teng Ying-chao, Kang Keching, have picked up where, ten years ago, everything stopped.

Nevertheless, there is bound to be a certain reaction against women, due to the excesses of Chiang Ching. Wife beating, which had been almost abolished, has resurfaced, and was discussed at the National People's Congress meetings in 1979; of course, with the emphasis on the protection of women as equal citizens.

Twenty-six

Phoenix China: 1976-1979

SINCE THAT FREEZING December of 1976 after the toppling of the Four when I returned to friends and relatives eager and willing to tell me all that had happened to them, I have not ceased going up and down the land. I have ridden on the new inland railways, visiting out of the way places. I have tape-recorded and interviewed four score of writers, painters, opera stars, musicians, both in provincial towns and in major cities. I have captured their words and their emotions before second thought, prudence, or politics, streamlined them into something more coherent, less revealing. Thus I made mine the happiness and the relief, to which the arrest of the Four gave rise.

For China will never be the same. Everything in its past, recent and ancient, has been exploded and laid bare. In this volcanic eruption, the people have found their own power. They have flexed their muscles and their minds in an exhibition of massive effervescence, and even if there still are persistent attempts to make everything 'as it was before', the present awareness of the millions makes it impossible to return entirely to despotic obscurantism.

The millions of China no longer believe in words, slogans. Words have proved empty, myths have collapsed. 'No more lies.' Everything that is said has to be proved, in action. 'We shall have to rethink and to reword every issue and every problem ... the language itself must totally change,' I say to my friends. All the questions the people ask must be answered, sooner or later. There can be no more evasion, shirking under pretence of 'state secrecy'. 'The people are no longer ignorant' is the cry of China's workers and peasants, of the young and the old. For the greatest achievement of the thirty years has been literacy at village level; bringing the ability to communicate and to *think*. And the paradox of the Cultural Revolution is that it has destroyed submission, docility, the cowed muteness which accepted that 'leaders' are perforce wiser than ordinary men. So many leaders have proved unworthy: so many acclaimed figures have ended in ignominy. As a result, every child in China knows and feels that he has as much right to his own view as the topmost man in the government ... for independence of mind, like liberty, must be an experience before it becomes a principle and a habit.

The Cultural Revolution, and the tyranny to which it gave birth, have revealed the Chinese people to themselves. We examine our own twisted feudalist minds and realize that the Four, under cover of revolutionary phrases, were the concentrated essence of what inhabits each one of us still. Everyone says it now.

'We can no longer blame colonialism, the outside world, imperialism, the Kuomintang for what has happened,' say Party members to me. 'We must interrogate our own souls. The fault is there, in ourselves.'

And this clarity of self-knowledge, this widespread self-awareness, means a great deal to China's future. 'Our revolution begins now,' I say to the Yangs. 'Self-knowledge is the threshold we have crossed into the future; now we shall have to think and act in a modern way.'

The feeling that everything must be overhauled – the Party itself, by the Party, interrogating itself on *everything* – is all-pervasive. It gives to the air around us a headiness, and lifts all talk out of conventional courtesy. I am happy and hopeful. If there is one thing that the Chinese Communist Party has shown, through its almost sixty years of life, it is an ability to reappraise, to overhaul itself, its policies and methods. This will now be carried even further. Within the highest councils of Marxist-Leninist philosophers, the topmost cadre schools, a thorough study of the total theory, of all the works from Marx to Mao, will probably have to be undertaken. Already Marxist scholars have begun. After all, the very essence of Mao's innovative talent was not blind obedience, not dogmatism, but the link between 'practice' and 'theory'. Mao departed from the Soviet model in the 1930s because the physical condition of China made it invalid. The scientific search for truth must never lose sight of reality. Theory cannot remain mere phantasm of the mind. It has to work.

The success of the Chinese Revolution was founded upon Mao's unorthodoxy; and today's new Chinese Revolution requires new thinking which discards outmoded postulates.

China: phoenix reborn from its ashes; but the fire has seared us all, and some of us most grievously. A few old scholars and artists are very bitter, because of the wasted years. Bitter also people like Sixth Brother. He was courageous, full of self-control; he never let on to me – until now – what he has really suffered. 'Ten years ago I was full of energy, at the height of my power. I wanted to learn and to innovate. But now my brain is not so good, and I feel tired ... my memory cannot retain new things. I could have done so much. Now I feel diminished.'

But the bitterness cannot last. Diminished or not, the tired old men who come out of jail, out of May 7 schools, who are no longer 'shunted aside', men in their sixties and their seventies, are our greatest treasure, our most precious people. They have the knowledge. They must teach, must bridge the generation gap. And the very fact that they are so desperately needed heals them, gives them a new lease of life. 'I feel reborn,' says an eighty-two-year-old painter to me. 'I shall now work until I die.' 'The secret of eternal youth is to be needed to our last dying breath,' says George Wu, who is over sixty. All fear but one thing: that their bodies might fail them before they have been able to transmit knowledge to the 'successors'. Teng Hsiaoping tells me, 'I am seventy-five ... but I am looking forward to working for another twenty years.' In every sector of learning there is a dearth of young specialists – and so our generation, the sixty to eighty-year-olds, are mobilizing themselves.

Some of the young say, 'We feel a big black hole inside our spirit. The heart has gone out of us; it is not easy to patch up this vacancy.' But the most common phrase heard at public meetings and symposia which I attend is the following: 'I am still troubled ... "they" might return ... and therefore I shall not come out with all I think.'

Defeatism, cynicism, fear of a return of tyranny – these are unavoidable. We, the old ones, exhort and encourage and try to reassure. It is up to us to save the 'lost generation'. There will not be another Gang of Four!

I say, 'Unless you get off the fence, and manifest your thinking, it will start again. Weakness and vacillation will certainly play into the hands of small despots waiting in the shadows to pounce.'

My friends say to me, 'You have manifested yourself. You have very clearly taken sides.'

The doubtful and the hesitant are many, but courageous people, young and middle-aged and old, who come out with their opinions, are also in great numbers. Among them is the great painter Huang Yungyu, in his late forties. He endured vicious treatment but went on working, refusing to give in. 'The Four throve on our fear. Stand up to tyrants and bullies, and they recoil. Had they come to power, I would have gone into the mountains and started a guerrilla war.'

Everywhere the old and middle-aged are tremendously busy, training the young. And although there are hopeless cases, young men and women permanently crippled in mind, who do not want to work or to study and will never be recuperated, we discover, to our joy, that there are also millions of youths whom the Cultural Revolution has matured, made wise, thoughtful beyond their years. We call them the 'thinking generation'. They use their brains without fear; they no longer think in the feudal way. They reason from cause to effect, they work, and work hard. We discover much talent, intelligence, reasoning power, eagerness for knowledge. 'In ten years we may have made up our losses, if all goes well,' some of the educational experts say to me. But if one asks these youths what they believe in, they grin and say, 'We wait and see.' I think this is healthy scepticism. It is up to us to create material and spiritual improvement, so that they can believe the system works. The thinking generation must be made to participate at all levels in decision-making processes; this will create enthusiasm, responsibility. Otherwise frustration will set in.

The present Chinese leaders know that in order to succeed, the people must be with them. For this they must ensure stability and peace, food in abundance and consumer goods.* But above all they must give constitutional guarantees of rights and liberties for the individual. This is where the new breakthrough has come. 'Twenty years ago you said to Kung Peng: Democracy in twenty years,' Fourth Sister reminds me. 'Now we speak of democracy all the time.'

Industrialization, modernization, is. necessarily accompanied by social changes. It is not enough simply to buy machines, put up factories, embark on crash programmes for the construction of steel and oil plants. The whole texture of thought and action, the approach to knowledge — everything must change. And the Party leaders say this openly, officially. Change is now inevitable (or so we devoutly hope).

'Essential for success in China's four modernizations is democracy.' Mao's major speech of 1962 on democracy is reprinted. This means, of course, 'socialist democracy'.

These words: democracy, law, constitutional rights, are heard in all the meetings held since 1977. They are the main themes of the assemblies of the National People's Congress, which, far from being a 'rubber-stamp body' (as Western reports used to call it), is now forceful and exceedingly vocal as the highest body of authority in the land. At the Congress, the Party members are in the minority. 'They used to sit right in front, as if leading the meetings ... now they sit scattered, with non-Party dele-

* Already in Szechuan in 1978 no more rationing was needed; meat was abundant, and cheap.

gates.'* The most astounding and severe criticisms of 'privileged high cadres', of corruption and high-handedness among Party officials, have been heard at the Congress. Guarantees that the total illegality which became in the Cultural Revolution the rule of the Four should not recur are the most urgent demand. 'Stalin used legal methods to commit illegalities,' I remark to a friend who is a member of the Congress. 'A legal system alone cannot guarantee legality, justice. In Russia courts of law condemned people to death. The courts cannot become the instrument of a political Party.'

In China, where courts of law have been in abeyance (as bourgeois manifestations) during the last few years, 'mass movements' have taken the place of law. Every organization, unit, assembled its employees, its staff (called 'the masses'), and conducted its own 'judgments'. 'This judgment by the masses ... the Four made the masses carry out their foregone conclusions; revile people they had already decided to label as counter-revolutionaries. To utilize so-called public opinion so outrageously ... probably no other country has ever done this on such a large scale,' say my friends.

For the intelligentsia, the worst of these mass meetings (which condemned them to doing menial work such as cleaning toilets) was the humiliation, not death. Comparatively speaking, very few people died. Mao's injunction against the death sentence remained effective throughout; though of course deaths did occur.

Now all such 'mass movements' are strictly forbidden. I remember interviewing the Minister of Justice in 1956, and being told about the project for framing laws, a civil code, a penal code, a juridical code.† The then Chairman of the National People's Congress, the old and revered Tung Piwu, a founder of the Communist Party of China in 1921, had said that 'mass movements must give place to a regular system of laws and courts of law.' But this was not done until over twenty years later, when at last his words are being put into practice, with the solid backing of the new Party Chairman, Hua Kuofeng, and the government.

'We have no tradition of democracy,' says Hsia Yen to me. He was the Vice-Minister of Culture who suffered so much because he had clashed with Chiang Ching over films that she had denounced. 'We had legalists and codes of law in imperial times, but a distinction was made between some men and others. The mandarin was not punished as was the common man, and the Emperor was above the law. It has always depended upon the "upright, superior man", the mandarin, to fulfil his duty towards

* The N.P.C. has about 4,000 members.   † See pp. 142-3.

lesser beings, to see that "justice" was administered, but the idea of equality before a common law has been foreign to us.'

Now everything has changed. 'All men are equal before the law,' repeats Peng Chen, the ex-Mayor of Peking, who has been rehabilitated. And Marshal Yeh Chienying, whose words carry enormous weight in China, says it even more explicitly: 'All citizens are equal before the law, which is not subject to the will of any leader.' This is momentous. It means, in the final analysis, an almost independent judiciary. It certainly means that high-ranking bureaucrats are amenable to law at last.

There will be long hard battles to wage. Almost daily now, in the newspapers, ardent 'thinking' young men dedicated to truth launch attacks against the arrogance, high-handedness and the privileges of high cadres; against their corruption. They place themselves above any law; and consider that their authority must be absolute. They request — and obtain — perks in every way: houses and cars, and university entrance without examinations for their offspring. Anything like people's rights and liberties are considered by them as dangerous to their positions, their status.

'As long as there is no democracy, we shall continue to have palace intrigues and palace coups,' warns Hsia Yen. Around any high bureaucrat congregate sycophants, flatterers ... they build for him a cohort of power, a clique, echelon by echelon; it is very hard to get rid of such cliques.

But the people's demand for legal guarantees does not go unheeded. Encouraged by Teng Hsiaoping and Hua Kuofeng, and bolstered by popular opinion, lawmakers proceed to frame a series of codes of law, a system of justice which has not existed before in China. At the same time, the government orders hundreds of thousands of people to be rehabilitated. The Tienanmen incident after Chou Enlai's death becomes a landmark in the history of China, a glorious anniversary, on a par with China's famous May 4th, 1919 movement;* it becomes the capture of the Bastille in the French Revolution; it is the Boston Tea Party of the American Revolution.

The new leadership and the lawmakers and the Congress go further. By January 1st, 1980, there will be the introduction of the secret ballot at village and district assembly level. This is of momentous significance. It means that the grassroot peasant organizations (and peasants still form 85 per cent of the population) will freely elect their heads of villages and representatives, and that these need not be Party members. In factories, too, the workers will secretly elect their representatives and their administrators from among competent, qualified staff, without 'Party leadership' committees interfering. Neither will the production and management of

* See *A Mortal Flower.*

factories be subject to constant political surveillance. The most resented practice, which grew especially during the Cultural Revolution, was the 'Party leadership' committees having to be referred to at every point, for every activity. Nothing could be done without permission. Any initiative had to pass through them, and since they were ignorant of new techniques, and their power and authority resided in negativism, they would condemn any new idea as 'adventurism' or 'bourgeois'. 'It got to the point where one couldn't fart without asking Party leadership permission,' said an exasperated foreman to me. 'The Party leadership committees even gave themselves the right to refuse permission to marry to young couples,' said a girl worker, who had defied the 'leadership', had married, and not only been ostracized but treated almost as a criminal.

There have been other changes, including a thorough revision of the class origin concept. The intelligentsia are now stated to be part of the working class. There is no distinction between mental and manual labour. Both are equally valid, and 'intellectuals work very hard.' They are no longer the 'stinking ninth class', the butt of every political campaign. I do not know what this big dent in dogma will ultimately lead to.

In the villages the peasants have put up petitions pleading for the progeny of their former landlords to be treated as ordinary peasants and commune members. 'The old landlords who oppressed us are dead. To maintain "class origin" distinction is to shift the sins of dead parents on to their innocent sons and daughters, who are hardworking people, as we are.'

Of course there is a reason for this. Villages in China are clan villages. Quite often the landlord was also a 'relative'. Thus to maintain 'class origin' created turmoil, discontent, during the Cultural Revolution. 'The people have an innate sense of justice, moderation. We must trust them,' say the Congress delegates.

In 1979 the people are greatly pleased by Chairman Hua's report on the national economy because he gives figures, not percentages; economic indicators, and with so much frankness, without hiding a single unpleasant fact. Immediately the people respond with approval and enthusiasm. I think back to Chou Enlai, who always wanted figures, not percentages, but was not authorized to quote anything in his reports but percentages on so many occasions.

Change, but also continuity. Not all these breakthroughs are new thoughts. Some were conceived, but laid aside, way back in the 1950s and 1960s. I find myself going back to my old notebooks, finding glimpses, suggestions, of what is now being attempted.

'China must follow her own road.' Of course it will be 'socialism', but adapted to China. Capitalist development is not possible, even though some methods borrowed from capitalist expertise will surely be tried. But because of the vast and informed population of China, we cannot do what India can still do: use 120 million Untouchables in a semi-feudal countryside to feed the prosperity of the cities. In China the peasantry still determines the rise and fall of dynasties, socialist or not. 'We cannot have trouble in the rural areas. Immediately the whole economy is affected,' says a vice-minister to me. 'The discontent of youth in the cities is only a minor matter. But no system in China can be stable without a contented peasantry. We must raise the living standards and the purchasing power of the peasantry swiftly. We must decentralize industry, bring it to the villages. We must continue to have informed, literate peasants.' Giving priority to the peasantry (which Mao also insisted on) means that no 'crash industrialization' programme, concentrating all investment in heavy industry, is possible. Such over-sanguine projects (mooted at first in 1977 and 1978) have had to yield to more reasonable, even if slower-paced, development plans, with more investment in rural areas.

Industrialization is idealized by the Third World. But it has never provided the means of coping with unemployment. On the contrary, it produces further unemployment. Europe, in its industrial heyday of the nineteenth century, exported its surplus labour to America, to Australia, to Canada. Periodic and numerous wars in Europe took care of extra numbers; even created, temporarily, labour shortages. But China cannot solve in the same manner the problem of twenty million young who come on to the labour market every year. 'We have no limitless, unpopulated Siberia to send people to, as did the Tsars for nearly two hundred years,' say my friends. 'We shall have to find a way to solve our own population problems within the limits of our own land.' There must be, first of all, intensive, nationwide family planning, which I have considered of prime importance for over twenty years. At last, all over China, I get accurate figures; particularly in Szechuan province, which contains 10 per cent of China's peoples, and where family planning is now undertaken very seriously. Five *yuan* a month will be given to the one-child family. Its bestowal will cease if the family acquires a second child. In Pihsien, my native town, the birth rate has dropped to 6 per 1,000 in 1978. Even so, China's population will pass the billion mark very soon, and by the year 2000 we may have 240 million couples able to procreate. Obviously we cannot merely industrialize. We must find work, productive work, and food, for all these young millions, and satisfy their rising expectations. We must, therefore, find our own road to cope with these problems.

Bureaucracy—one of the Cultural Revolution's targets—has not diminished but increased. Besides the old cadres returning, there are the new cadres who have been promoted during the last ten years. Two bureaucracies, uneasily co-existing. The Party has grown from 17 million in 1966 to 35 million in 1976. How many of the new members are hidden partisans of the Four? How many are obscurantists who would like to get rid of all the old cadres? To bolster themselves, they quote Mao, in and out of context.

Anyone who has read Mao thoroughly realizes that he was a populist; that he tried hard to give the people of China more voice in their own affairs; that he tried to curb bureaucracy; that he retained the eight non-communist parties of China when some Party chiefs wanted to abolish them. These parties only represent altogether 1 per cent of the population, but, said Mao, 'They are a long-term necessity'. No other socialist country, no other head of a communist party, has kept alive and functioning—even on a minor scale—potential rivals.

Mao remains China's great liberator. Without him, the present-day rebirth could not have happened. And even if the Cultural Revolution was monstrously deviated and twisted, and brought hardship and suffering, yet it left no one in China untouched, unstirred, or unthinking. History's verdict on it is not yet; it may be kinder than expected.

Even if Mao himself, in his last years, was incapable of living up to his vision, he still remains the man whose great dreams and words wrought wonders. China cannot do without him. There will not be, because there cannot be, a 'demaoization'. Mao's place in Chinese history is unequalled.

In January 1977 old Marshal Yeh Chienying receives me. My father liked him very much; he looked after the engineers so well who were restoring the coal mines at Tatung. Yeh Chienying, with Hua Kuofeng, laid the plans for the arrest of the Four.

Marshal Yeh is eighty years old, but he is certainly not doddery, and there is instant liking between us. He talks to me as a friend, plunging right into the heart of the matter without any circumlocution. 'What do you think of the Vietnamese incursions? They've been shooting at us since late 1975. It's the Polar Bear,* no doubt, instigating it. We shan't say anything yet. We'll give them a chance.'

He tells me that Albania now disagrees with China's new stance. 'But

* The U.S.S.R.

649

we shall ignore them. We had to tell them we had no spare rice for them this year.' For more than two decades China has given rice, and many other things, to Albania.

Marshal Yeh speaks of the Gang of Four. But not of what his relatives suffered. By his side is his faithful secretary, who stuck to him when he was under house arrest. He says, 'We shall certainly give work to Teng Hsiaoping.' It is January; Teng will be back in July. Marshal Yeh knows, as I do, that people in China walk about the streets with little bottles full of red ink, which they hang on trees. Teng Hsiaoping's nickname is Little Bottle, and the red ink means that people think he is a true revolutionary.

'We shall be neither soft-handed nor soft-headed,' says Yeh mildly, and this means that the Four and their close allies have no chance at all. The people apprehended or punished must be important malefactors, not the small fry. Extensive random purges, self-defeating, would shatter the demoralized Party at all levels.

'We want, we need stability and unity,' says Teng Hsiaoping to me when I see him in September 1977. 'It is good that the Party Chairman is a younger man. I do not want to be Chairman or Premier. I am seventy-five and all I want to do is to be useful. We need a young Chairman, long continuity in the Party.'

I am also received by Chairman Hua. It is true that he is a man most calm, of few words, not at all like the ebullient Teng. He has great poise, and I think back to what I have been told about him: 'Noble-minded, not mean; good-mannered, and very cool-headed'.

Thus am I integrated in China's rebirth, accepted at last as I am, and everything I have done has acquired meaning, is a minute stitch in that great tapestry of living and doing wrought by the many millions of China. I am linked with them now, more than ever. But at the same time, at last, totally liberated.

Twenty-seven

The End and the Beginning

CHINA IS THIRTY years old and I am over sixty. In these thirty years I have lived through her an abundance and a multiplicity of lives, emotions and passions. I have pursued my beautiful chimera with Chinese obstinacy; yet I have not ignored or cast away other gifts of living, other lands and peoples. I have friends all over the world. And if I do not write about them, that is not forgetfulness, only lack of space in this book.

Neither do I forget how much Europe and America, Australia and India, South East Asia and so many other lands gave me, enlarging my horizons, until the whole world became my home, until my roots extended and broadened to encompass the round earth. A harvest of knowledge is beyond price, and I keep on learning.

But this book is about the fixed star of my self-completion, the one I had to follow despite all hazards. In doing so, I was only following in the footsteps of my Chinese and my Belgian heritage, continuing the story which was begun at the turn of the century.

My father. I have a photograph of him when he was nineteen, leaving Szechuan province to go to Europe in 1903 to study engineering. He was to return in order to build railways in his province. But when he came back in 1913 China was torn by internal wars, and until 1949 my father coped with war and destruction, and kept the railways running, patching them up, making do.

My mother. That stubborn woman I hated with such utter love; and how beneficial and stimulating this hate proved, pushing me to do all the things she did not want me to do! And now I like her, know what she gave to me, although my mind is not built as hers was. She braved all the prejudices of her day, her staid Belgian family, to fall in love with a Chinese. She came to China with him, and gave birth to eight children, and lived in the stations along the railway lines of China. Their decades together were of sorrow and pain and insecurity, of war and running away and making do; and seeing their children despised for being Eurasians. Only I had the courage (or the foolishness) to scream against the general contempt for Eurasians, 'But we are the future.' I stuck to my 'foolishness', and in this extravagance I was like her when she chose Papa, deliberately becoming pregnant to force her marriage.

But it is from Papa, from being born in China, from all my childhood and growing up there that I have this inescapable passion and obsession with China. In this I have been, all unknown to myself, a Chinese intellectual of my generation and of my time. All my reactions, everything I have done, has always been conditioned by this inner prompting of the heart, of which I am only now fully aware.

I think of three childhood scenes perhaps responsible for my obsession, since they constantly recur to me. One is of our rickshaw coolie, and his back. He pulled me and my sisters, this man, in those terrible days of Old China when men were used as beasts. He was beautiful. I think I was six years old; and my first erotic experience was seeing his back, naked in the hot summer, glistening with sweat. He was so beautiful that even today my heart is seized by the remembrance of his back, and I smell it again.

The second is of the dead babies wrapped in newspapers which I saw on my way to school in the blizzards of winter. Their purple-black faces like rotting fruit sometimes protruded from the frozen package.

The third was going to the Catholic church with Mama, hacking our way through the beggars clawing and whining, and the white stones for eyes of the blind beggar children.

These, and not intellectual conviction, explain my commitment. It is almost biological; only later would come reinforcing knowledge and understanding. But I had to live by what was imprinted in my cells, remaining averse to and suspicious of high-flown abstractions, but totally engaged to that smell and savour and warmth, that feel of the tide, blood beat, which is for me the people of China. With others, exultant ideologies may have priority, but it has never been so with me. I shoulder and make do with systems, with ideologies. I am not committed to any. Only one thing concerns me: in the great sweep of history, will this or that system have been another step forward for the Chinese people? They are the only 'side' I am on.

I often pass in Peking the hospital where as a typist not quite fifteen years old I earned money in order to go to university, to study and to become a doctor. On to Yenching University, and then a scholarship to Brussels, to study medicine. But the Japanese invaded China, and this old biological stir took over: I could *not* stay in peace in Europe, studying, when there was war in China. I gave up scholarship, studies and a boy friend. I returned to China. I was twenty-one.

I married on a misunderstanding: that Pao and I would serve China together. Then I discovered what 'feudalism' meant. I lived it. For seven years I endured the illogicality, the madness of a feudal mind and its self-torturing angers and its reasoning by symbolism. For seven years Pao tried to 'remould' me. Thought remoulding was practised by the Kuomintang. His was by physical beating; striving to teach me proper humility and virtue because I had not been a virgin at marriage.

He scarred me for ever, deep down in my woman being. I never completely recovered, but today how grateful I am to him, how grateful! For his training so well enabled me to understand China in all her many ambiguities and contradictory facets. It enabled me to understand Chiang

Ching, Mao's wife; and her paranoia and her pursuit of revenge. It also increased my conviction and hope that one day, one day, the Chinese people would grasp their own destiny ...

London during the war, and again medicine. And then again the stir, the crazy hankering, making me leave for Hongkong. And there came to me, at last, love, Ian Morrison. He will be with me always. I knew then the great marvel and enchantment of love; it cured me, almost. And after that life was kind, and even fame came, but it never meant a great deal to me. When it came to choosing what I would do, I would always choose the loyalty of my emotions. Not fame or money or opportunity.

And so I had to go back to China once again, only to find that there was no place for me at the time. I waited. Twenty years. And lived divided in a divided world, whose divisions I would never accept. The metaphysical distortion does not inhabit my spirit. For me good and evil are two faces of the same coin, not mutually exclusive but intimately bound.

Twenty years, and today comes my harvest, so abundant that I shall not have enough of the next twenty years to use it up. Before me a whole new generation, a China reborn. My books will one day help them greatly to know how to believe without faith; how to keep faith with oneself and serve Man's cause with a clean heart. I want to help others to write their stories; the young will need to know them. Stories of courage and loyalty and unshaken devotion. Because I have refused to see the world in white/black, good/evil terms, all worlds are mine. I have built bridges which many people will cross from one civilization and culture and mode of thinking to another. Bridges of goodwill.

Sometimes I am told that I have sacrificed 'popularity and success' by 'giving up' writing love stories and novels, writing all too serious books. But I could not do otherwise, from 1966 until today, during the Cultural Revolution. I would despise myself today had I not *also* been blocked, even though no visible compulsion existed, by something stronger than compulsion. Just as in 1938 I gave up my precious studies to return to China, so during the Cultural Revolution I could not face entertaining readers in the West while my colleagues and friends were undergoing great stress, were unable to write. I was as much a prisoner as they were of the Cultural Revolution. And perhaps, in the end, the result will be a great burst of creativity ...

Now it is over. I am liberated, as they are. They are writing, creating, in a frenzy, making up for the lost years. I have garnered such a harvest of love and care that twenty years will not be enough to set it down. Not for me the thin gossamer of shadows, but love, with its many faces, and

653

the infinite diversity of the human heart in love. Not only the love of another human being. Not only that urgency between the legs so often described. All this and more. The real substance and the reality of love.

I have not missed love.

Patient and observant and watchful and silent and joyous and enduring, for twenty-three years now with me. Vincent.

Vincent, who has let me work out my magnificent obsession and hunt my dream. Who has endured days and weeks and months when I saw him not, heard him not, even though he was with me. Because I thought of China. And yet all the time he was there; comforting me, his arms warm around me, cradling me. Giving all of himself to my fabulous other passion. Not because he was resigned, but because he loved me. All of me. Without trying to change me in any way. Can many women boast of having been loved like that?

Vincent. Essential as earth itself; forgotten at times as earth, lifegiving and bounteous, is forgotten ... yet never lost.

Vincent, bringing me another world: the world of India. And all the amazement and wondrous new ways of looking at everything and all things that are India.

India. China. Together half the world's peoples.

'Vincent, how could you stand it all these years?' He looks at me; his eyebrow goes up (the left one). He fits into no niche, evades all description. He does not correspond to any of that dreary catalogue of stereotypes which men live by. Vincent just is.

Vincent loves me. It is his universe and the explanation of the universe for him. He is so sure of his love that he never questions it or worries about its existence. Love is like the sun. The sun shines. Even at night the sun is there. One has only to wait until the night is over. He waits without waiting, in the tranquillity of night.

'I would have been bored with any other woman. With you, I never know what is going to happen next. How can I ever bless God for letting you be with me?' says Vincent.

'Let us go back to the Himalayas, where we began,' I say. 'Now I really can write a love story. Because China is in the hands of her own people, at last.'

I want to write about love: the love of Heart of Ice for her husband; when they held hands gently going down the dim hotel corridor in Peking together. I want to write about my friend Yeh and his wife, and her long waits in the dark nights by the bus stop ... seven years, every day, waiting, not knowing whether he would or would not be on the last bus ... I want to write about so many, so many loves; about what it is like to grow young with love when one is old.

'Autumn is the best time,' says Vincent. 'We shall go to the Himalayas in autumn. Autumn is the time of the golden sun and the innocent sky.'

In another twenty years, perhaps, I shall say to Vincent, 'Do you remember when sunlight fell on the slight twigs and our ears heard the beating of a bird's wing?'

I hear it now, the beating of great wings. Perhaps it is the phoenix of my heart; but perhaps it is only the friendly sparrow flying on to my balcony, to pick at the breadcrumbs I scatter.

When calm and lovely death shall come for me, it will add to my treasure trove of love. I shall be one of a goodly company. How can I forget what the dead gave me? Chou Enlai and Chen Yi and Kung Peng ... how strong is their whisper in my spirit: 'None of us live for ourselves alone. That is the way of the beast; the way of Man is to live for others, for posterity.'

And this is what I too have tried to do.